*f*P

FROM
PLATO
TO
NATO

THE IDEA OF THE WEST
AND ITS OPPONENTS

DAVID GRESS

THE FREE PRESS
New York London Toronto
Sydney Singapore

*f*P

THE FREE PRESS
A Division of Simon & Schuster Inc.
1230 Avenue of the Americas
New York, NY 10020

Designed by Carla Bolte

Manufactured in the United States of America

10   9   8   7   6   5   4   3   2   1

Library of Congress Cataloging-in-Publication Data

Gress, David, 1953–
    From Plato to NATO : the idea of the West and its opponents /
David Gress.
        p.   cm.
    Includes bibliographical references and index.
    ISBN 0-684-82789-1
    1. Civilization, Western—Historiography.   2. Civilization,
Western—Philosophy.   3. Liberalism—Philosophy.   4. Political
science—Europe—Philosophy—History.   5. Philosophy, Ancient—
Influence.   I. Title.
CB425.G745   1998
909′.09812—dc21   98-18523
                                                                      CIP

ISBN 0-684-82789-1

TO MY CHILDREN

JONATHAN, THOMAS, CATHARINA

I saw how out of Eastern lands

A stream of light was flowing

And from the West in turn I saw

A surge of power growing

—Friedrich Rückert, 1814

Comrade, look not on the west:

'Twill have your heart out of your breast;

'Twill take your thoughts and sink them far,

Leagues beyond the sunset bar

—A. E. Housman, ca. 1898

Ure æghwhylc sceal ende gebidan

worolde lifes; wyrce se the mote

domes ær deathe

[Each of us must abide the end of this world's life,

let him who is able achieve fame before death]

—*Beowulf,* ca. 800

Contents

Preface

Friedrich Nietzsche said that "every act of writing is an act of impudence." After writing this book I am sharply aware of the multiple truth of that statement. For one thing, I chose an impossibly ambitious subject, namely, the logic of world history and the changing identities of Western civilization. If Arnold Toynbee could not do justice to the first of these topics in twelve thick volumes, who was I to try to address both in twelve chapters? It is true that the book grew somewhat in the writing, but it remains, despite what some may consider its generous bulk, selective and, some may well think, skimpy.

For another thing, this is a work of interpretation and judgment. I have borrowed mercilessly from the thousands of scholar-years that have gone into each of the major issues covered. Where I have borrowed a quote, the source is given in the notes, but I have only selectively annotated ideas or issues. This is partly because to do so fully would have made the notes longer than the text, and partly because many of the notions that I discuss, criticize, or endorse are so much part of my mental inventory that it would be invidious to blame my understanding on one or two people who would thus be, unfairly, singled out at the expense of others who may be truer authors of my views.

A reasonable policy of acknowledgment, in such a situation, might be not to exaggerate the impudence by naming names, beyond those whose actual words I have quoted and who are named in the notes. But such a policy would, in this case, be not so much a matter of holding others harmless as unfair to those whose help was essential, in practical as well as intellectual terms, in keeping this project alive through an unusually rocky history. It was born at one institution, lived its infancy at another, matured in the gap between that and a third, and achieved its final shape at a fourth. Of these four institutions, three were in different countries and continents, and all placed justifiable calls on my time that preempted work on a project that belonged, in full, to none of them. The fact is that this book is the work of what, with apologies to the Romany people, our era calls a "gypsy scholar," that is, of an itinerant worker in an era of cultural as well as institutional downsizing. Undoubtedly, these dislocations and discontinuities revealed aspects of the world to me that benefited the work; just as clearly, and more obviously, they introduced delays and inconveniences.

It was in the late 1970s that I first realized that the key to what we call the West lies in what this book names the sceptical Enlightenment, that is, a liberalism that does not reject history, religion, or human nature, but seeks the conditions of possibility of liberty and prosperity within those givens and not in abstract rights or visions of justice. Years of preoccupation with more immediate issues of policy and contemporary history put that realization on the back burner. The first plan for this book, in 1990, hardly included this line of thought, which came to prominence only as I was writing and it became obvious that the history of Western identity pointed crucially and repeatedly to this open liberalism as the key to its logic and to the logic of its opponents.

Let me now, with apologies to those whom I have not named, thank the following for starting and keeping the ball rolling and bringing me back to it when the outlook seemed dimmest. No one, of course, is responsible for my exploitation or abuse of his or her opinions. My editor at The Free Press, Adam Bellow, first suggested a book on the idea of the West in 1989, and had he not insisted that the book existed in my mind if I would only put my mind to it, it would have remained forever imaginary, as marginal jottings on restaurant notepaper. Especially in the last phases of writing, I have often recalled his encouraging statement that "it's only a book, after all!" I cannot thank him enough for making me, at last, do it.

Exhortations would not have been enough, however, without other forms of help. To the John M. Olin Foundation and its research director, Dr. James E. Piereson, go, therefore, my deepest thanks for research support for this project in 1994–96. Olin, to its credit, keeps many irons in the fire, and in a world where many foundations have chosen, after the Cold War, to go domestic and short term, it deserves praise for keeping a wider view and a broader interest. Next, I want to express my gratitude to the Earhart Foundation and its director of programs, Antony Sullivan, for their support and for maintaining a commitment to questions of religion, world history, and world politics. I thank the master and fellows of Gonville and Caius College, Cambridge, for admitting me as a visitor in 1993–95, and for conversation and ideas, some of which have made their way into the book. At the college of

Michael Oakeshott, I learned to thank his shade, and among those very much alive at Caius and elsewhere in Cambridge, I thank Derek Beales, Tim Blanning, John Casey, Patricia Crone, Brendan Simms, Quentin Skinner, and Joachim Whaley for talk about the West and its enemies. A conversation with Ernest Gellner a few months before his death put me right on his understanding of human social evolution, to which I owe a good part of my general schema. Outside Cambridge but still in England I am grateful for various kinds of inspiration to Noel Malcolm and Norman Stone. It was my good fortune in America to see Malcolm Cowling almost every day for a year or so after he retired from Cambridge—a series of encounters that not only prolonged my Cambridge stay by proxy but introduced me to one of the most vital thinkers on the relations of liberal thought and religion. Finally, I do not want to leave Cambridge without paying tribute to a scholar and gentleman who learned of this project, thought it vague and overambitious, but nevertheless on three memorable evenings gave freely of his abundance of knowledge and wisdom about the conditions of liberty and human flourishing—the late Edward Shils.

To the Foreign Policy Research Institute of Philadelphia, which took me in as senior fellow in 1995, I am grateful for this, and for introducing me to an amazing level of intellectual intensity and a solidity of human capital that would be remarkable in an institution ten times its size and wealth. The Institute's president, Harvey Sicherman, and vice president, Alan Luxenberg, made the project theirs in ways that were profoundly heartening and, I dare say, necessary. In particular, the weekends for teachers conducted under the Institute's History Academy forced me to think through some of the topics as if I actually had to explain them to others. In New York, let me also thank Hilton Kramer, who, though he may now regret it, was the first to suggest that I do a book about culture, and Roger Kimball, who has let me offer occasional small servings from the big pot of the West in *The New Criterion*. Likewise in the United States, I benefited from the conversation, provocation, and insights into things I would not otherwise have thought about of Dennis L. Bark, Mikhail Bernstam, Robert P. George, Stanley Hoffmann, Samuel P. Huntington, Tony Judt, Paul Kurth, Ronald Radosh, and Gail Verdi. Whether these experiences have left any worthwhile traces in the text is for readers to judge. Walter McDougall, as colleague at FPRI and editor of *Orbis*, allowed me to try out some ideas in the journal. At the Danish Institute of International Affairs (DUPI), my other intellectual home, I thank Niels-Jørgen Nehring, Bertel Heurlin, and Svend Aage Christensen not only for accommodating the last, hectic, and disruptive stages of the project, but also for reintroducing me to those big issues of international politics at the threshold of the third millennium which will necessarily be the proving ground for Western survival and Western identity. Uffe Østergård of DUPI and the University of Aarhus read and commented on the final chapter and revealed to me my functionalist inclinations. Also in Denmark, for a twenty-year conversation on liberalism that I hope will still be alive after he reads this book, I thank Tøger Seidenfaden.

My family has endured with fortitude and good cheer both the bigger disruptions of our multiple moves and the more immediate disruptions of writing at all hours. No more than any author can I find words to thank my wife, Jessica, for being indispensably and completely there for our children and her preoccupied husband despite her own stressful and time-consuming cares. Books are great crimes against family life, and I am glad this one is over; to Jonathan, Thomas, and Catharina, my children and dedicatees, who have asked plaintively "why can't daddy play with us after work like other daddies?" my answer is, because he foolishly agreed to write a book, but now it's done.

David Gress
March 1998

Introduction

L iberty grew because it served the interests of power. This apparent paradox was the core of Western identity. It was obscured by the conventional account of that identity, the account that I have dubbed the "Grand Narrative." This account rightly saw liberty as fundamental to the West, but mistakenly defined liberty as an abstract, philosophical principle, which it then traced through a series of great books and great ideas divorced from passions and politics back to classical Greece. In that account, liberty existed from Plato to NATO as an ideal that was only ever partially realized and that had always to be asserted against an unruly reality. The key historical insight underlying this book is that liberty, and Western identity in general, are not primarily to be understood in the abstract, but as a set of practices and institutions that evolved, not from Greece, but from the synthesis of classical, Christian, and Germanic culture that took shape from the fifth to the eighth centuries A.D. These practices and institutions, which made up the Western forms of the market, the state, the church, and what I call Christian ethnicity, were not possible before the synthesis, which is therefore the true origin of Western identity. That the Greeks invented political liberty remains true; but to define the West exclusively as its legacy is misleading.

The Grand Narrative was misleading for other reasons. First, because it was moralistic. It established a false dichotomy between some high principles, which existed outside history, and a flawed reality, characterized by inequality, prejudice, exploitation, and war. This dichotomy placed a burden of justification on the West and its most important political form, democracy, whose defenders were compelled always to explain how the reality differed from the ideal, and to see that difference as a problem to be addressed by political will—the will of the enlightened few. But the fact that political institutions did not satisfy all ideals was neither surprising nor unique to the West.

1

What was unique to the West was how the prejudices, passions, and cruelties that we correctly see as the stuff of history engendered the niches of liberty that founded both prosperity and democracy. Western liberty was not something marvelously distinct from historical reality, but the initially unintended side effect of the drive for power. Rulers competing for power found that the niches of liberty of local communities made their societies stronger and more prosperous, hence more fit to compete. The passion for God, gold, and glory that launched the Christian holy wars of the crusades and sent the conquistador Hernán Cortés to Mexico yielded cruelty and war, but also spawned Western liberty out of the womb of ambition. In that perspective, what needs explaining is not liberty as a great idea sailing alongside history from the Greeks to modernity, but liberty as the tool and by-product of power in the geopolitical conditions of Europe, a by-product that ultimately overshadowed its source, establishing the local and partial rights to property, security, and influence on government that enabled economic development and led to popular sovereignty and modern liberal democracy.

The Grand Narrative's second error was its universalism. It saw liberty and democracy, conceived by the Greeks and revived by modernity, not only as results of Western history and thus part of Western identity, but as universally valid. This universalism went with a third error, which I call the illusion of newness. The Grand Narrative imagined modern democracy as an invention of the Enlightenment and of the American and French Revolutions, an invention that owed less to Western history than to its own ambitions to shape the future. No one expressed that ambition better than Jean-Jacques Rousseau when he said, "it makes no sense for the will to put bonds on its own future actions."[1] True democracy lay ahead, not here and now. It thus became a future-oriented search for justice, whereas democracy was in fact an old practice in the niches of liberty, and one impossible to explain apart from the Christian ethnicity of the Old Western synthesis. Democracy and its political philosophy of liberalism were not creations of the eighteenth century, but practices constantly being invented, oppressed, and revived throughout Western history, and impossible to understand or appreciate apart from that history. The modern (or postmodern) West therefore was no abstract universalism based on some imaginary set of multiculturally applicable political ethics, but no more and no less than the institutional and cultural result of over a thousand years of the joint practice of power and liberty.

This book is not a history of liberty or of economic development in the West, for good histories exist, from which I have drawn or extrapolated the insights summarized above.[2] It explains, rather, why the conventional

Grand Narrative and its ideology of centrist liberalism were always inadequate as accounts of Western identity and its history. For some decades in
the mid-twentieth century, they served a political purpose as a lowest common denominator in American—and to a lesser extent European—higher
education and public opinion of an idea of the West as progressive, secular,
democratic, and moderately capitalist. Centrist liberalism rested on a humanitarian belief in social, moral, and economic progress growing out of
the use of reason to define and solve problems, and assumed further that
no problems, whether political, personal, or ethical, were ultimately insolu-
ble. The canon of great books was selected to ground and confirm this
bland but pleasant teaching.

The high point of centrist liberalism in America was the first two
decades after World War II. In 1960, a well-known sociologist announced
that the West had reached the "end of ideology."[3] Yet in this era of consensus and prosperity began the attack on centrist liberalism. This attack came
in two waves. In the 1960s, radicals promoted and supported by the very
affluence they condemned charged the so-called Establishment with cynicism, exploitation, and immorality. The economically more difficult circumstances of the 1970s muted this attack but did not end it; rather, the
radicals consolidated their hold on intellectual life while adapting to the
competitive and capitalist values of American society and political culture.
The second wave of attack came out of the atmosphere of crisis and limits
of the 1970s, and took a harsher and gloomier view of the world and of
its target, the liberal West. In particular, the attacks of the second wave
discarded the one central feature of the West that all sides had shared in
the 1960s, namely, the faith in reason. In the 1960s, the radicals accused
their opponents of not using their reason correctly. In the 1980s, in the era
of postmodernism and relativism, they accused rationalism itself of being
at the source of the crimes of the West: racism, sexism, environmental degradation, and inhumanity.

Beginning in the later 1980s, a series of books and events brought into
focus this second wave of attacks on the idea of the West. These attacks presented no new arguments. They, and the reactions to them, did, however, reveal a fundamental confusion about what was being attacked or defended. To
explain and resolve that confusion is one of the aims of this book.

In 1986, students at Stanford University demonstrated against the core
curriculum in Western civilization under the slogan "Hey hey, ho ho, Western
culture's gotta go!" Because this episode took place on the occasion of a visit to
the campus by the well-known black politician and presidential candidate

Jesse Jackson, it received global attention and was alternately praised or vilified either as an overdue demand for revision of a curriculum that supposedly justified white male privilege or as a barbarous onslaught on cultural literacy. The demonstrators objected not only to the core curriculum, but to having to learn about a civilization they considered racist, sexist, and monocultural.

A year after this opening salvo in the 1980s curriculum wars—themselves a pale rerun of the 1960s—anti-Western activists everywhere were hugely cheered by the first volume of a work that promised to subvert the traditional idea of the West. This was *Black Athena* by Martin Bernal, subtitled *The Afroasiatic Roots of Classical Civilization.*[4] Bernal was a left-wing China scholar, a veteran of campus protests against the Vietnam War, who had devoted a number of years to studying the Bronze Age of Greece, Egypt, and the Near East, so that he could rewrite its history to serve the agenda of contemporary black activism. Bernal argued that white scholars had constructed a self-congratulatory image of the ancient Greeks as white Europeans, as a uniquely creative people whose originality proved that Westerners were innately creative and who, thanks to this construct, could be appropriated as models and ancestors of a superior, racist West. In fact, Bernal maintained, Greek civilization was indeed unique, but its uniqueness was not due to any native excellence, nor were the Greeks white Europeans. Rather, Greek civilization was borrowed from, and owed its essence to, nonwhite people: Egyptians and Near Easterners. If the West continued to look to Greece for its origins, he implied, it would find that these origins were African and Asiatic.

The quincentenary of Christopher Columbus's first voyage to the West Indies in 1992 evoked a small torrent of revisionist works striving to prove that Columbus was a mercenary imperialist, that he brought the greed, colonialism, and violence of Europe to the peaceful and ecologically balanced societies of the New World. Kirkpatrick Sale, who like Bernal was a veteran of 1960s leftism, denounced the effects of Columbus as a blasphemy against the moral and ecological order of innocent native cultures and of mother earth, as the "conquest of Paradise."[5] Official America, and particularly American schools, which had unself-consciously celebrated earlier anniversaries of Columbus as landmarks in the history of human achievement, turned agonized somersaults to avoid any appearance of residual triumphalism and spent considerable effort teaching the schoolchildren and the public of 1992 that Columbus was no hero, that the Europeans were the least acceptable of the three equal cultures of early America—the others being the Indian and the African—and that the lesson of Columbus for today was diversity and multiculturalism.

These subversions of what their authors clearly still considered a hegemonic idea of the West took place in a broader context of cultural criticism and self-doubt in American society. In 1987, the same year as Bernal, the political philosopher Allan Bloom published "a meditation on the state of our souls," which he called *The Closing of the American Mind*.[6] Starting in the 1960s, Bloom said, "the culture leeches, professional and amateur, began their great spiritual bleeding" of a hitherto vigorous and self-confident democratic political culture. By the 1980s, American universities, where the elite went for its education, were dominated by relativism and cynicism—a relativism that, in the name of openness and diversity, refused to grant value to American history or society, and a cynicism that saw America and the West as cultures of greed and exploitation.

Bloom proposed to restore more than the lowest common denominator of centrist liberalism. He suggested that Western civilization was deeper, more ambiguous, and more tragic than the optimists of the "end of ideology" had acknowledged. In a paradoxical sense, Bloom accepted the radical point that the centrist liberal idea of the West was hopelessly inadequate. But where the radicals saw themselves as brave opponents of a hegemonic capitalist liberalism, he saw them as merely the final stage, the degenerate product, of that same capitalist liberalism. To him, the centrist liberal West and its radical opponents were allies under the skin, engaged in the same trivialization of a great tradition. From his perspective, left and right both saw the liberal consensus as hegemonic, differing only in whether that hegemony was good or bad.

Also in 1987, from a radically different angle, came the historian Paul Kennedy's warning, in *Rise and Decline of the Great Powers*, that the United States, like imperial Spain, France, Germany, and Britain before it, was doomed to decline.[7] A sign of a great power on the verge of decline was its government's taking on international commitments beyond its means or maintaining a large military establishment, or its leadership demonstrating arrogance or insensitivity. Although Kennedy devoted only a few pages to contemporary affairs, many liberal and left-wing readers seized on those pages as indictments of what they saw as Ronald Reagan's needlessly provocative foreign policy, his high-handed interventions against left-wing regimes, his neglect of social problems at home, and his unapologetic American triumphalism. Such readers were delighted to learn from a distinguished historian that regimes indulging in such "imperial overstretch" inevitably would bankrupt themselves. Pointing to the large budget deficits of the Reagan administration, they waited eagerly for the inevitable collapse.[8]

Two years after Bernal, Bloom, and Kennedy, the declinists met what at first sight seemed a decisive refutation in Francis Fukuyama's essay on "The End of History," later expanded into a book-length analysis of the modern Western personality and its universal fate.[9] Fukuyama did not even stop to consider Bloom's warning that relativism was sapping the foundations of American democracy and literacy. Rather, he argued that democratic liberalism, exemplified above all in the United States, was the political philosophy and practice most in accord with the needs and feelings of contemporary humanity across the globe. Therefore, democratic liberalism would inevitably become the worldwide standard of society and government. So far from being an age that had abandoned Western rationalism and meritocracy in favor of relativism and cynicism, Fukuyama said, our age was one of growing consensus about the objective validity of the Western ideals and methods of science, democracy, and capitalism.

The attacks on the Western canon, the fight over relativism, and the opposed diagnoses of decline or triumph indicated that something was at stake below the surface of debate on short-term policies in education, international affairs, or race relations. Clearly there was a battle over the West and its identity. And although Sale, Bernal, and the Stanford students liked to believe that they were facing a powerful opponent in the shape of the traditional, liberal idea of the West, their attacks were so popular and met with such wide understanding in public opinion that it was evident that the Grand Narrative, the story many readers of this book may recollect, had collapsed or become a shell of itself.[10] The attacks also demonstrated, however, that nothing had been put in its place.

By the 1980s, academics and politicians had largely dismissed its canon of great books and ideas as apologies for privilege and assimilationism. In response to Bernal, Sale, and the other radicals, the liberals did not look to Bloom for moral rearmament and for renewed faith in their idea of the West. Rather, they vilified Bloom as an elitist enemy of justice and of the essential new pedagogy of diversity. In short, they became more liberal, assuring their critics that they, too, deplored the sins of the West. In the 1990s, a revised version of the liberal idea of the West came into circulation that repudiated its canon of great books and its scientific rationalism in favor of a global, democratic humanism, antiseptically purged of its historical baggage and presented as the only morally adequate political philosophy for a diverse, open, multiculturalist society. Proponents of this revised, superficially optimistic version combined a revised liberalism with a Fukuyama-like belief in its universalist virtues, but without Fukuyama's robust and unapologetic faith that liberal democracy was deservedly superior. The result was an idea of the West from which all the incorrect, hard edges—of science, meritocracy, sexism, and racism—had been filed away. The result was a West fit for the new universalism, a West without the West, as it were.

This book argues that the chanting students, the Bernals, and the Sales were right to attack the liberal idea of the West, but for the wrong reasons. The Grand Narrative's idea of the West fell to history because it forgot history. It was, as the critics maintained, inadequate, but not because it was exclusive, chauvinistic, or politically incorrect. It was inadequate because it defined the West as modernity and its core, liberty, as an abstract principle derived from the Greeks and transported, outside time, to its modern resurrection in the Enlightenment and in twentieth-century liberal American democracy. By contrast, this book presents an idea of the West as the institutional and political fruit of various critical conflicts and interactions: of Greece with Rome, of both with Christianity, and of all three with the ideal of heroic freedom imported by the Germanic settlers of the former Roman Empire. These interactions did not take place in the elevated atmosphere of great books and great ideas. They were full of destructive as well as creative passion and, often, of cruelty. The marriage of Germanic and Christian ideas of liberty with the Roman idea of imperial order yielded democracy and capitalism, but they also yielded holy wars, black slavery in the New World, religious inquisitions, and economic exploitation.

The most persistent opponents of the idea of the West were therefore not the radical critics of the 1960s to the 1990s, but the authors of the Grand Narrative who, for the best of motives, constructed the ahistorical West of progress and morality that, torn from its moorings in religion and in the actual practice of imperfect liberties, proved defenseless when called on its faults. By presenting the West as a moral enterprise, the Grand Narrative made itself fatally vulnerable to moralist assault.

This is not to say that the critics will welcome an idea of the West that roots its manifestations—emphatically including democracy and capitalism—in what I call the Old West or the medieval synthesis, the blend of Christianity with Germanic and classical culture. Returning the New West to its historic identity is to defy both the multiculturalists and the centrist liberals in their 1990s incarnation as global universalists. But then that is the point, implicit in the beginning and explicit toward the end of this book, that the West is not the world. It is the West; and whatever its contribution to the future interplay of civilizations that may emerge in the third millennium from the worldwide sweep of modernization, that contribution will be made, if at all, from within its historically conditioned identity, and not from some illusory vantage point of universal humanism.

The method adopted is to move through the stages of Western evolution, as conventionally defined, from Greece to the twentieth century, taking the Grand Narrative as the starting point and showing its shortcomings. By contrasting this catalog of opinions with the actual cultural characteristics of the regions of the West at various times, we obtain what I take to be a fuller and more accurate delineation of Western identity. What also emerges, I hope, is an account of the central belief system of the New West, democratic liberalism, which refutes its three weaknesses: the illusion of newness, economism, and its ambivalence about whether liberty is absence of coercion or empowerment. These three weaknesses appear the moment that liberalism is defined as a purely secular and individualistic doctrine. Such a definition opens the door to those in the 1960s and after who argued, repeating older arguments, that economic liberty was a fraud, because its reality was the bourgeois pathology of greed and wealth maximization and that the natural and inevitable end of liberalism was therefore nihilism.

Does the West, appropriately redefined, have a future? And if it does, what sort of future? One of the most significant political and philosophical distinctions at the end of the twentieth century was between those who thought such questions silly and those who took them seriously. Those who thought it silly to doubt the future of the West were the optimists, the new universalists. According to them, the West not only had a future, it *was* the future. They pointed out that, in the 1980s and 1990s, the vast majority of the world's people had demonstrated by their actions and their stated desires that they wanted market capitalism, liberal democracy, and human rights. The most dramatic illustration of this was the fall of communism in central and Eastern Europe, including the former Soviet Union. But the Western optimists could easily adduce other illustrations. In many Latin American countries, for example, new or reinvigorated political movements for democracy, human rights, and economic freedom had transformed the political landscape since the 1980s. Likewise, the most numerous people on Earth, the Chinese, while still laboring, for the most part, under a bureaucratic, corrupt, and mafialike communist regime, were discovering and unleashing economic and productive energies that, so the optimists claimed, would in a space of twenty years or so lead inevitably to a democratic regime respectful of human rights.

Since democratic capitalism, human rights, and personal freedom were Western in origin, the optimists held, their worldwide spread would yield a Westernized world, or at the very least, one favorable to Western survival and Western interests. The optimists differed on how long this would take. Some saw a Westernized, democratic world as a likely reality in the space of a few decades; others predicted a longer transition, of perhaps a century or two. But the final outcome was, they thought, certain, and it was also certain that it was an outcome that the overwhelming majority of people, of whatever race, creed, or country, eagerly desired. One last question remained for the optimists: once the people of the world had achieved a world broadly democratic, capitalist, and libertarian, would history—meaning large-scale conflict over fundamental questions of ideology, geopolitics, and control, leading to revolutions, changes of regime, and political upheaval—come to an end, or would the many communities of the human race discover new reasons for conflict?

Some optimists justified their vision by anthropology and biology. Human beings, they said, were naturally disposed to want, and whenever possible, to establish democracy and capitalism. Another way of putting this was to say that human beings achieved their true and full potential only in democratic and capitalist regimes. Since, in the optimist vision, men must naturally want to live as full and free a life as possible, it was inevitable that, once democracy and capitalism became possible, they therefore also became desirable and their ultimate and universal victory inevitable.

Others were content to note that certain people had, in a particular time and place, namely, early modern Europe, discovered or invented the principles of democratic order and economic growth. Whether a preference for these principles was hardwired into the human biochemical behavior system or whether they were simply fortunate accidents was not the point. The point was that once they were discovered, the results they produced proved effective and popular among many people and groups, including those who had not themselves made the discovery. The power of example, of liberty and prosperity, was enough to explain why democracy and capitalism must expand and flourish whenever and wherever possible. It was also enough to explain why contrary systems of order and production, such as communism, must fail. In the long run, such contrary systems could neither mobilize support nor deploy resources efficiently enough to stop the people they controlled from open or secret revolt in favor of democracy and capitalism.

Whether democracy and capitalism were natural or merely fortuitous, therefore, their success, once they had appeared, was certain. And since both were the core of the West, it was an easy leap to argue that the worldwide spread of democracy and capitalism also meant the worldwide spread of the West. Did the West have a future? Silly question!

Much in this optimistic and universalist account of the late twentieth century and its extrapolation into the future was attractive and flattering, not least to Western vanity. Some of it was perhaps even true. Certainly, democratic and capitalist societies were, on average, richer and freer than others, by any reasonable measure. Late-twentieth-century scholars were also confirming what Immanuel Kant had argued during the eighteenth-century Enlightenment, namely, that free and prosperous societies—Kant spoke of "republics"—were likely to prefer peace to war in international relations, that therefore a world consisting largely of democratic and capitalist societies would be a more peaceful world. Governments in free societies, moreover, were also less likely, and less able, than others to use force or fraud against their citizens. The best method to minimize domestic oppression and interstate war was therefore the same method prescribed if you wanted to reduce overall poverty—to expand the zones of democracy and capitalism. The optimists held that democracy, capitalism, and Westernization were three aspects of the same trend, which was irresistible.

On the other side of the divide were those who did not find the question of the future of the West silly at all. This other camp contained various groups, some of whose agendas were radically incompatible. Unlike the optimists, they did not present a coherent story, but rather made political, historical, philosophical, or cultural arguments that undermined the optimists' position that the West not only had a future, it was the future. Four groups, or types, of argument seemed especially pertinent.

The first group, represented by the former prime minister Lee Kuan Yew of Singapore, made two points. First, that economic growth did not require democracy. Western liberal democracy, these people said, had become an obstacle to rational economic policies because of its many competing interest groups, its licentiousness, its pandering to opinion and prejudice, its false populism. Second, that economic growth, though it began in the West, was no longer, at the end of the twentieth century, a Western prerogative. Lee and his followers went further. The West, they said, had lost its productive, competitive, and intellectual edge. It was no longer as inventive or as fast-growing as before. The sources of economic growth and therefore of stability and prosperity in the future were to be found in China and Southeast Asia. The future of the world might be capitalist, but it would not be Western. The West, in the long term, was more likely to become an economic and cultural backwater, its shrinking numbers of semiliterate hedonists dependent on the skills, productivity, and competence of others. At bottom, Lee's argument was that the West had no future as a world-dominating culture because it had become incompetent.

Lee and his followers claimed that "Asian values" of family cohesion, thrift, and foresight were better suited to achieve prosperity and social stability in the coming century than the individualism of the West, which had indeed achieved prosperity, but at the cost of social stability. The economic crisis that struck Japan, Korea, and Southeast Asia in 1997 seemed at first blush to question that claim. The Asian crisis was not in the least mysterious; it was the inevitable consequence of financial mismanagement and of people thinking they could disobey the fundamental laws of economics. "The cosy relationship between governments, banks and firms insulated business from market forces, encouraging excessive borrowing and a wasteful use of resources," a leading analyst accurately observed. The crisis, therefore, did not discredit Lee's Asian values. Rather, it revealed "cronyism and corruption," thanks to which East Asian savings were "invested often for political or personal favour rather than maximum rates of return." It was the denial of market forces and of accountability, not "Asian values," that provoked the meltdown.[11]

The idea of Asian values was in any case vacuous. Those values, as Lee expressed them, were no different from the basic values of early Western capitalism and boiled down, in essence, to the economic commonplace that there is no free lunch, to St. Paul's dictum from the New Testament that he who does not work shall not eat, and to the basic rule of capitalism which said that accountability was the foundation of a market economy and a guarantee that distortions would be self-correcting. What remained of Lee's argument was therefore the point that prosperity and social stability were not, as some Western analysts held, opposites, but rather complementary, and that behavior that sought one at the expense of the other was self-defeating. According to the Asians, the West since the 1960s had forgotten economic fundamentals in the search for self-realization and autonomy; conversely, one could say that Asian leaders and managers in the 1990s had sought social stability, and affluence for themselves, at the expense of autonomy—of the kind of autonomy expressed, for example, in Western pluralism, where both politics and the economy were subject to the checks and balances that curbed the sort of secretive, insider dealing that caused the Asian crisis.

If the Asian crisis did nothing else, it at least disposed of the fallacious Asian values argument and refocused attention on how prosperity, social stability, and liberty were not contradictory, but flourished only in symbiosis—a point which is one of the basic claims of this book.

The second type of argument was what one could call the realist case, made by two quite different sets of people: Western social scientists and Third World intellectuals. Among the Western social scientists making this case were the American political scientist Samuel P. Huntington, the British anthropologist Ernest Gellner, and the Syrian-born German political scientist Bassam Tibi; among the Third World intellectuals, the sociologist Ali Mazrui. They agreed that democracy and capitalism were Western inventions but did not agree that their global spread implied global Westernization. The opposite would occur, they predicted. As non-Western societies adapted market institutions and practices, they would become less, not more, patient with Western cultural and economic hegemony. Even democracy was not by any means a guarantee of Westernization, rather the opposite. As the broad masses in non-Western cultures achieved political influence, they would want their leaders to use that influence not to Westernize but to combat Westernization and to assert their own cultural, political, religious, and social identities.

This argument contested the core of the optimist case, which was that democracy and capitalism were inherently and inescapably Western, so that societies that admitted them were necessarily choosing to become more like the West. Democracy and capitalism, according to the optimists, were not simply procedures of decision and efficient production. They carried within them the code of Western civilization, and no society could adopt them without also importing that code and permitting it to transcribe itself into the receiving society. This portion of the optimist case had an impressive history in Western scholarship, since an early version of it had been formulated by Max Weber, one of the founders of modern social science itself. The case rested on a prior assumption about human social behavior, namely, that you could not separate institutions and procedures from character, values, and ideals. A society in which certain institutions, such as those of democracy and capitalism, predominated would also be a society that encouraged and rewarded a certain kind of person. So influential was this argument that many scholars and thinkers had come to assume it to be intuitively obvious. Therefore, the realist countercase of the 1990s appeared to many shocking and implausible.

The realists made two arguments, of which only one cut to the core of the basic thesis. This more powerful argument said that you could and should distinguish between procedures and institutions on the one hand, and political culture, social norms, and ideals on the other. Capitalist methods and democratic voting procedures did not automatically reprogram the psyche or change a society so that its influential leaders, thinkers, and shapers became like Westerners.

But in the 1990s, most realists merely questioned that democracy and capitalism meant inevitable Westernization. This lesser case simply said that, yes, democracy and capitalism were spreading, but that this was leading to less, not more, Western influence. This was not something the West could do anything about. The realists did not claim that the West had become incompetent. What the West would or could do was beside the point. The realist case was, rather, that fundamental laws of social and cultural change, confirmed time and again in human history, indicated that the best future of the West was not as the single culture, but as one among several, and not necessarily the most powerful. And there was nothing anyone in the West could, or ought to, do about this.

The scholars and polemicists in these two groups shared a coherent and mostly positive view of the West as the civilization that invented modern democracy and economic growth and that had therefore, on balance, made substantial net contributions to human happiness and freedom. Their main gripe against the optimists was that they were too simpleminded in extrapolating from past Western success to a Western-dominated future for the whole world.

The third and fourth groups of anti-optimists argued less from the outside than from the inside. They were not so much concerned with what Westerners could or should achieve, with whether their global power was getting stronger or weaker. They were participants, rather, in the internal Western debates on identity, survival, justification, and legitimacy. The third group believed the West was declining for internal reasons and would therefore not become the universal civilization foreseen by the optimists, whereas the fourth group believed the West was not worthy to become universal and should not have a future.

The third group, the straightforward pessimists, saw Western decline as inevitable and rooted in the West's own institutions and culture. The pessimists represented a long and respectable tradition in Western cultural debate. In fact, all civilizations on occasion produced philosophers who described or foresaw inevitable decline. The West was not unique in that respect. Western cultural pessimism was unusual in its prevalence and in its reappearance in virtually all periods of Western history. In the later twentieth century, prophets or, as they themselves believed, analysts of decline blamed a number of features, some of them opposites of each other. Thus, some, on the liberal side of the spectrum, saw the West as doomed by creeping superstition, whereas some conservatives saw radical scepticism and free thought as threats to the culture. Some accused individualism, others mass society, and some both at the same time. Some thought the West was wasting resources on defense, others that it was neglecting its own defense. While they found many reasons for pessimism, the members of this third group all shared a sense that the decline of the West was a tragedy—for some, an inevitable tragedy, for others, one that could have been avoided. But, in either case, a tragedy.

The fourth group, found mainly on the left of the political spectrum, was different in this respect. These people did not want the West to have a future, or at least not until it had radically transformed itself according to a particular agenda. Never before the twentieth century had any civilization produced within itself as powerful, as varied, or as wide-ranging a tradition of radical self-criticism as that of the West. Some of these critics were what many of them claimed to be: critics pointing out hypocrisy, inconsistency, and injustice, and appealing from present practice to ideals and promises, to what Abraham Lincoln called "the better angels of our nature." In other words, they expected the West to live up to their standards and were willing to grant that it could do so. But others were more or less overtly hoping for the end, in some cases the violent end, of their own civilization. The West, according to the more outspoken members of this fourth group, was, of all civilizations, uniquely rapacious, racist, sexist, exploitative, environmentally destructive, and hostile to all human dignity. It was unredeemable. Only if the West went down to destruction could the rest of the human race hope to survive. The historian Arthur Herman referred to the "sadistically redemptive" outlook of those who, in this tradition, denied the West a right to a future.[12]

The optimist case that the West both had a future and was the future was contradicted by the mere fact that many people, some of them influential scholars, politicians, and thinkers, disagreed. One found more obvious evidence that the future of the West was in doubt in the political and cultural history of the 1990s. At the beginning of that decade, most influential thinkers, including many of the doubters, agreed that the West, the civilization of democracy and capitalism, had won an overwhelming victory and that the political and economic future of the human race promised more peace and prosperity for more people than had been the case before the fall of the Soviet Union. But as the 1990s progressed, the pessimists returned in force. During the Cold War, the pessimist case, classically put by James

Burnham in *Suicide of the West*, written in 1963, was essentially a simple one: the West could not outcompete the Soviet Union because it was too fragmented, too decadent, too soft, and not willing to assume the long burden of struggle against a determined and radically hostile enemy. The reason for this weakness, Burnham argued, was liberalism itself, which he presented as a teaching that believed in progress and universal common purposes, and that therefore had no answer to those who refused to accept those premises. Liberalism, he claimed, was the ideology of Western suicide, for it taught the West to accept its own destruction as reasonable and even desirable. All the older and deeper traditions of pessimism were temporarily overshadowed by this more urgent variant. In 1991, this case became moot. The Soviet Union unilaterally ended the contest; the West won by default. The result was not that the optimists gained sole control, but that older varieties of pessimism reemerged. As for the anti-Western Westerners, those who thought the West did not deserve to survive, they had been active all along, but also found themselves, perhaps to their own surprise, with new freedom and new arguments after the Cold War.

One paradox of the 1990s in the West was, then, that the wind went out of the sails of Western self-confidence just as that self-confidence had received its possibly greatest boost ever. Some people, the optimists, were unaffected. But the paradox, as it affected those many other people who found themselves assailed by new or revived doubts about the legitimacy, viability, or justification of the West, was not impossible to understand. One reason for it was that many people were not sure whether the victorious forces of democracy and capitalism were really as solid or as full of promise as they seemed. Another was that some people thought they were solid enough, but wondered if they were as beneficial as the optimists claimed. A third reason for the paradox, and the main reason for this book, was that the confusion about the West's future rested on a prior confusion about the West itself.

This confusion explains why both those who believed in and those who doubted the West's future came in so many guises. It was not that they were unusually imaginative or creative; rather, the West they were praising, deploring, criticizing, attacking, or merely investigating was ambiguous and protean. A feature identified by one analyst as the core of the West, say, capitalism, might seem to another as the mere by-product of its real core, say, Christianity. Likewise, two people might agree on the definition but disagree about its implications; what one considered a great good might seem to another to have produced disaster. For example, some identified the West with the impulse to discovery, which led to science and to Christopher Columbus.

The optimists might consider both results beneficial: science uncovered the laws of nature and revealed the universe; Columbus connected the New World to the Old and thereby made possible the modern world economy and the United States of America, the most powerful liberal democracy. On the other hand, people like Kirkpatrick Sale considered both science and Columbus as nearly unmitigated disasters of human history. Science, they held, was not about truth but about power; it gave immense power to greedy, sinister people who used it to oppress others. As for Columbus, many people in the 1990s thought he belonged with the worst archvillains of human history, not only because he came from an evil, corrupt, and rapacious European culture, but because he and the other European explorers unwittingly introduced Old World microbes to the New World that killed nine-tenths of its indigenous population.

The purpose of this book is not to attack or defend either the proposition that the West is the future of the world or any one of the declinist, pessimist, or radically hostile propositions. It is rather to step back from that debate to ask what the participants were arguing about. It is to explain how and why different people defined the West differently, and to argue that the standard history of Western civilization from Plato to NATO was inadequate. My title, therefore, is ironic. The standard history began with the Greeks and ended with the political West as organized for mutual security in the Atlantic Alliance, in NATO. This history, described in chapter 1, was not so much wrong as superficial. The West was never a single entity that one could define neatly as beginning in Greece, slowly growing during the Roman Empire and the Middle Ages, and reaching its fruition in the later centuries of the second millennium A.D., all the while maintaining an essential identity. Rather, throughout this history, various Wests coexisted, defined in terms of different principles, regions, beliefs, and ambitions. The West was not a single story, but several stories, most of which neither began with Plato nor ended with NATO. The two most important versions of the West were the Old West, identified as the synthesis of classical, Christian, and Germanic cultures, and the New West, the synthesis of reason, liberty, and progress; or science, democracy, and capitalism; or technology, human rights, and the pursuit of happiness. As indicated above, I believe that the opposition between these two that is at the basis of the liberal Grand Narrative of the West as the march to freedom is mistaken: the New West goes off its rails if it divorces itself from its Old origins. The optimist vision of the West as triumphant democracy and capitalism utterly ignored the Old West and was therefore superficial and therefore unable to bear the weight of universal significance that the optimists gave it.

Above all, my pedagogical purpose is to add chronological and philosophical depth to both the optimist and the nonoptimist visions. Those who followed the arguments for or against the future of the West in the 1990s might easily be misled into believing that history had become irrelevant to the question. The end of the Cold War, like it or not, demonstrated that democracy and capitalism were successful. The only remaining questions, some said, were whether they would continue to be successful, whether they would bring the benefits their proponents promised, and whether the result would be a Westernized world or something else.

On the contrary, I believe that the history of the West, or better, the history of the various ideas of the West and their interaction, became relevant again in the 1990s after having been less relevant during the course of what people, misleadingly, called the Cold War of 1947–91. Misleadingly, because the actual Cold War of U.S.-Soviet confrontation, when the two sides were barely talking, and a Soviet attack on the United States and NATO was genuinely possible, covered only a small part of that period, certainly 1947–55, possibly 1958–63, and, somewhat less plausibly, 1981–86. The simplistic and misleading usage, however, became dominant as soon as the Soviet Union dissolved and will therefore, unavoidably, be followed here.

History became relevant again because, during that period known as the Cold War, the Western democracies shared a dominant common interest in deterring Soviet military attack. This interest was neither false nor exaggerated. But it did create an artificial and ahistorical community of danger that emphasized strategy, defense, and the immediate political balance of power between East and West. Within that community, politicians, citizens, and analysts naturally focused on the structure of institutions and events that bound "the NATO West" together and on how that structure was faring in its strategic, diplomatic, and political struggle with the Soviet Union. Some of these politicians, citizens, and analysts were dissenters; they did not believe in a Soviet threat, and some thought the United States a greater danger to peace than the communists. But even these critics developed their arguments and established their beliefs within the framework of the Cold War, within that structure of institutions and events that came together in 1945–48 and that could, or so people thought, be adequately explained and understood in terms of a simple Grand Narrative of Western civilization culminating in the Atlantic Alliance.

When the Soviet Union ended in 1991, the logic of this structure of institutions and events also ended. Two new, or hitherto overshadowed, factors brought long-term history, including the history of Western institutions, ideas, and realities, back to the agenda. The first was the new landscape of world politics, no longer dominated by a single major conflict, but by a variety of relationships and dynamics, some tense, others loose. The second was the self-doubt within the West and in particular within the United States. Unfortunately, many people in the 1990s continued to discuss both world politics and domestic American problems with little or no reference to any history going back more than a few years. Indeed, at times it seemed that the close time horizon of Cold War debate had been replaced by an even closer horizon. At least, during the Cold War, those who discussed politics, survival, and the future agreed to look back to the 1940s. After the Cold War, many people seemed to think that the world began anew in 1989–91 and that no earlier history, even that of the Cold War, was relevant to understanding the present or predicting the future. This was the opposite of the truth. No discussion of the West, whether in an optimistic, a pessimistic, or a radically hostile vein, could properly take place after 1991 without a long-term perspective.

Thus, one of the sources of confusion in the discussions of the West after 1991 was that many people continued to talk as though the historical perspective was unnecessary. The optimists looked forward to democracy and capitalism spreading worldwide without much thought about how these two principles related to the history of Western civilization and how this complex relationship might fare in the post-Soviet world. The various pessimists and enemies of the West continued, often, to talk as though the West was adequately defined as a political system consisting of the United States, NATO, and very little else. It is to combat this chronological myopia that I offer these reflections.

Although this book does not defend optimists, pessimists, realists, or anti-Westerners, its author does have an opinion about the prospects of the West. Democracy and capitalism were indeed in harmony with human nature, as late-twentieth-century evolutionary psychology and sociology were describing it. But that did not mean either that they would easily spread across the world, or that their spread meant universal Westernization. Three points will illustrate these uncertainties.

The first is that human nature is flawed. Just because the natural and social sciences of the late twentieth century gradually gave us a better fix on what arrangements were good for people, what made them flourish, this did not mean that people or institutions would quickly, or ever, conform to this knowledge. For one thing, many people disagreed that science was discovering the truth about human nature. No government, certainly no Western government, would find it easy to transform this new knowledge of human nature into laws and prescriptions for behavior, even assuming that politicians wanted to do so. Second, most people remained happily ignorant of these supposed discoveries. Third, even if they were familiar with them or intuited their truth, people did not always do what they knew to be right or in their interests properly understood. The "human nature" of the late-twentieth-century evolutionary psychologists, anthropologists, and neurologists was somewhat like the economists' "rational actor." If people had perfect and complete information, and if their reason was not subject to their desires, they would act in perfect conformity to their best interests, which would also be the best interests of their community. But, to repeat, people were not perfect. Finally, laws, procedures, institutions, practices—all the arrangements that made up a society or a culture—were inevitably a mix of prejudice, interests, and occasionally a smattering of insight into what was good for people. Such arrangements, however seemingly irrational, had tremendous inertia. Societies did not change overnight. Just because democracy and capitalism, in some form or other, corresponded to some ideal and scientifically established human nature was no evidence that these practices would, in the short or medium term, spread or become universal.

Even if they did, the result would not be a Western world. This second point about the future of the West is that democracy and capitalism, by the end of the twentieth century, no longer implied Westernization. So far, the realists were right. Singapore, China, and Southeast Asia provided cases of capitalist or protocapitalist societies that showed little if any inclination to Westernize their cultures. In Iran in 1979 and elsewhere in the Islamic world, popular movements claiming power on the democratic principle of majority rule also did not wish, when in power, to Westernize their cultures, economies, or social structures. On the contrary, capitalist development and popular political movements made it more, not less, possible for the elites of non-Western societies to emphasize, rejuvenate, and reassert their own identities using all the means of late-twentieth-century technology, from cassette tapes to the Internet.

This point had a broader implication. Democracy and capitalism grew slowly in the West from the fourteenth to the nineteenth centuries, transforming the West out of all recognition. One could argue that democracy and capitalism, along with other aspects of modernity such as science and individualism, were likely to transform the non-Western world in the third millennium A.D., just as they had transformed the West in the second half of the second millennium. But the end result of this transformation would not be a

Western world but a world in which all peoples would be shaping their societies and cultures using the tools of modernity without thereby being Western. The West was simply the first of several cultures to have undergone the revolutions of modernity; this leading position should not be taken to imply that those revolutions would produce identical outcomes in other cultures. That modernity began in the West was no accident. The West created the conditions of global modernization. It did not and would not determine its results.

Moreover, and this is my third point about the future of the West, what was this West whose future we are discussing, this West that would either become global or not? Was it even possible for the optimists to define a simple West whose habits, institutions, culture, and social arrangements were becoming global? Such a definition was possible only by ignoring history and in particular by ignoring those who defined the West in ways incompatible with the short-term narrative of Western identity prevalent both during and after the Cold War. In the broader perspective of the various ideas of the West that coexisted before the Grand, or standard, Narrative took over, it was logically impossible to Westernize the world, because there was no single model of the West to impose. One model, that of liberal democracy and capitalism, would, for example, exclude another model, that of Christian theocracy. So even if democracy and capitalism spread quickly worldwide, and even if non-Westerners refrained from using democracy and capitalism to reassert their own identities, this would not mean that the world was Western. At most it would mean that much of the world had adopted a partial and fragmentary model of the West, one that excluded other and historically better grounded ones.

No, the future of the West was not as the single culture of a homogeneous world of democratic capitalist societies. Rather, it was as one of several cultures reforged in the crucible of modernity, of democracy, capitalism, science, and individualism, expressed, for example, in the demand for human rights. The interesting question about the future of the West was not when or how it was going to achieve global hegemony, because that question was moot, but what the West would look like in the third millennium, in the new era of global coexistence of several distinct but modern civilizations. The fate of the West in that coexistence would depend in large part on how well Westerners, and others, understood their past and the history of their own identity. And the essential preliminary to gaining that understanding was to look at the versions of Western civilization that had crystallized in Western history itself over the preceding two millennia.

Noting the variety of definitions of the West, some scholars denied that the phrase had any coherent meaning or connotation at all. Never mind whether the West was good, evil, in decline, or headed for a glorious future. These options were irrelevant, for their subject, the West, did not exist. The West, such critics argued, was whatever the person using the phrase wanted it to be at any given moment. The historian Norman Davies went further. He listed twelve variants of Western civilization, of which the most important were the Roman Empire, Christendom, the French West of the Enlightenment, the imperialist West, the German-controlled West based in central Europe, the White Anglo-Saxon Protestant or WASP West, the American-led Cold War West that included Japan and Saudi Arabia, and finally a European West based on the European Union. The WASP West was particularly significant, because during and after World War II, this definition of the West was responsible for the Grand Narrative, which Davies called "the Allied scheme of history." This version permeated education, public opinion, and political doctrines in much of Western Europe and the United States from the 1940s to the 1980s. Proponents of this scheme, Davies claimed, asserted a "unique, secular brand of Western civilization" in which "the Atlantic community," or NATO, was "the pinnacle of human progress," having emerged from Anglo-Saxon democracy, liberal capitalism, and the Anglo-American alliance for democracy of World War II. The "Allied scheme" was based on denouncing Germany as an enemy, on an indulgent view of the Soviet Union, which had been a wartime ally of the democracies and therefore was never considered as morally deficient as Hitler's Germany, and, third, on accepting the division of Europe into East and West as the natural consequence of age-old cultural, geopolitical, and economic differences. The Allied scheme suffered a body blow when American universities eviscerated or abolished their Western civilization courses, but its ghost lived on into the 1990s. The American news media's obsession, more than fifty years after World War II, with the "Nazi gold" held by Swiss banks made little sense compared with other atrocities that one might investigate—except for the enduring force of the Allied scheme, whose proponents demonized Germany and downplayed other regimes of terror, whether closer or more remote in time and space.

Because some politicians and ideologues had coined and used a range of ideas of the West, Davies concluded "that Western civilization is essentially an amalgam of intellectual constructs which were designed to further the interest of their authors." He condemned "the really vicious quality" of the idea of the West, because books based on that idea and its variants "present idealized, and hence essentially false, pictures of past reality . . . judging from some of the textbooks, one gets the distinct impression that everyone in the

'West' was a genius."[13] Certainly, many of the older-style textbooks on Western civilization were selective. Whether they stated or implied that the West consisted only of geniuses and included no fools or knaves would require a full, and boring, textual analysis. Davies's real gravamen against the idea of the West was in any case not that it was selective, but that it was selective in a particular respect, namely, in positing an artificial and damaging dividing line in Europe and in excluding eastern Europe from something called the West. Davies was not wrong in making this charge, although he overstated his case by claiming that ideas of the West, named in his list of twelve variants, were purely ideological constructs without any value as genuine attempts to conceptualize and understand important features of history. He insisted that the Slavs and other eastern European peoples were as fully a part of European history as the British and the French, who played a greater role in the traditional Western civilization courses. Of course they were; but arguing for a more comprehensive view of European history was not the same thing as proving that there was no such thing as Western identity. The question of Western identity or identities and its relation to the Slavic peoples was important; it was, among other things, a question of where the West stopped, geographically, as well as a question about the status of such elements of Western identity as medieval scholastic philosophy, the Renaissance, the Reformation, and the Enlightenment. Davies wrote about the political, social, religious, economic, and cultural history of Europe, but that should not delegitimate accounts of the West, just as histories of the Arab peoples or of the Chinese should not delegitimate accounts of Islamic or of Chinese civilization.

If one wanted to warn against distortions of history, there were in any case other, arguably more urgent perils facing Americans and Europeans of the late 1990s than the danger of an overvalued West. Citizens of that era were not likely to encounter simplistic narratives featuring only the great and the good and touting Western superiority. They were more likely to read statements confirming widespread prejudices against the West. In a review of a book about the slave trade to the New World, for example, a learned historian wrote that "no group has made such widespread use of enforced labour over such a long span of time and such a vast geographical area as the peoples of Europe." He offered no evidence for this statement, which was easily contradicted in a letter by a less-well-known and less learned but also less prejudiced historian. But the learned historian was by no means untypical; he was merely conforming to the opinions of his peers. He began his article with a disappointingly safe and false statement rather than one that would have been provocative but true. That the job of a historian was not to conform but to learn and to resist the prejudices of the age was a principle of intellectual hygiene that many leading Westerners decided to neglect in the second half of the twentieth century. Thus, in this case, the one civilization that voluntarily abolished both the slave trade and slavery—the West—was offhandedly denounced as uniquely evil. Such reflexive rhetoric served the cause not of enlightenment but of that particular and damaging kind of obscurantism favored by the literate classes.[14]

The purpose of this book is not to "present idealized, and hence essentially false, pictures of past reality." It is not a political and social history of Europe or of America, nor is it yet another history of Western civilization of the type that Davies castigated. It is an investigation of the most important meanings of the West counterposed to the Grand Narrative, which corresponds to what Davies called the "WASP West" and its "Allied scheme of history." The WASP West cut eastern Europe off from the West and ignored religion and any history that did not fit into the simple Plato-to-NATO scheme of constant improvement. These were its two cardinal sins. Proponents of other variants of the West similarly ignored those features that did not enter into their definition of the essence of the West, the true West. This book argues that all the Wests emphasize some part of a broad story, that no story can ever be truly complete, and that the history of civilization is only one kind of history; as Davies trenchantly argued, there is also the political, religious, economic, and social history of particular regions, nations, people, faiths, territories, groups, and individuals.

Three themes run through the book. The first is that the standard story is partial and incomplete. It was created to serve the needs of mass higher education after the world wars and had, therefore, to be simple in outline but rich in content. Above all, the story had to be consistent, linear, progressive, with a start date in ancient Greece and an end date in 1950s America. But, midcentury American liberalism, for all its qualities as a political doctrine, was not the only legitimate or possible representation of the idea of the West. And to argue, as the story did, that the idea of the West found its fulfillment in that doctrine was dangerously wrong.

Dangerous for two reasons. First, because citizens whose notion of the West depended on the traditional story had little with which to resist those who challenged the story with the intention of destroying its influence. Thus, we saw American elites abandoning the liberal story in droves, starting in the 1960s, until by the 1990s the story, if it was told at all, was told mainly as a joke or as a butt of criticism and attack. And dangerous, second, because the narrow understanding of the West implicit in the traditional story made it difficult if not impossible to resist those critics who said that the West was not merely oppressive, white-male-chauvinist, and evil, but that it was morally empty and spiritually vacant.

A second theme is that the standard story was deaf to religion and theology as cultural forces in their own right, and not merely as contributors of ideas to a Grand Narrative. Thus, the standard story could use parts of what came to be called the Judeo-Christian tradition: dignity of the individual, value of each life, and the hopes and struggles for human rights and moral equality that flowed from that tradition. But it could not so easily use others: the belief that the next life was as important as, if not more important than, this and that worldly success was therefore not to be sought; the value of contemplation over action; doctrinal orthodoxy; intolerance; religious wars; anti-Semitism. Because it was deaf to religion, the standard story presented both classical religion and Christianity as peripheral, derivative, and largely irrelevant, except as providers of ideas whose true role was to function as stepping-stones in the great secular drama of Western ascendancy from Plato to NATO.

The third theme running through the book is that the standard story was flawed because it took only what it wanted from history and built a linear narrative from it: from the Greeks it took democracy and philosophy; from the Romans, law; from the Renaissance and Enlightenment, individual autonomy; from the revolutionary era, liberal democracy, from the modern era science and technology. But the Grand Liberal Narrative was possible only if you ignored great chunks of Greek, Roman, medieval, and early modern European civilization. The Greeks, Romans, and early Christians were not protoliberals.

Inherent in the oldest recoverable meanings of the word *West* were the idea of movement toward or beyond the (western) horizon and the idea of sunset, evening, the fall of night. The English word *west*, unchanged since Saxon times, and its identical cognates in German and Scandinavian was an adverb of direction, as in "to go west." It derived from the Proto-Germanic *westra*, and it, in turn, from an Indo-European word, *wes-tero*, which was the comparative form of an adverb, *wes-*, meaning "down, away." West thus originally meant "farther down, farther away," then, by extension, "something farther down and farther away; the direction of something farther down and farther away." From the Indo-European root *wes-* also derived, or so linguists held, a word *wesperos, "evening," which became in classical Greek *hesperos* or *hespera*, which meant both "evening" and "west." This joint meaning provided rich echoes in classical mythology. For example, the Hesperides, the daughters of evening, lived on the western ocean, where they kept a tree of golden apples given by the goddess of Earth as a wedding present to Hera, the bride of Zeus, father of gods and men. One of the twelve labors of Hercules was to slay the dragon that guarded the tree and take the apples. The magical apple tree in the West appeared also in Celtic mythology, on the island of Emain Ablach, the home of the sea god Manannán mac Lir.

To the ancient Egyptians, to go west was to die, for beyond the sunset lay the kingdom of the dead. The evening sun, Atum, entered that kingdom and moved through it beneath the earth, to be reborn as the morning sun, Chepre, in the east. The two categories, death and rebirth, belonged to different kinds of time. The death that brought all beings, including the sun, to the "beautiful West" led out of time as change into time as permanent result—*jet*—a space in which the deceased continued their life without change, in eternal duration.[15] The Celts also had stories about otherworldly realms beyond the West, such as the story of the journey of the hero Bran to Emain Ablach, or the *Voyage of St. Brendan*, one of the most popular tales throughout Europe in the Middle Ages. *Tír na n-Óg*, the land of youth, was sometimes placed beyond the sunset and could be reached only at the end of a particular kind of voyage, an *immram*, which was both a voyage in space and a voyage within oneself. At its end, one saw

> *Beanntaichean àrda is àillidh leacainnean*
> *Sluagh ann an còmhnuidh is còire cleachdainnean*
> *'S aotrom mo cheum a' leum g'am faicinn*
> *Is fanaidh mi tacan le deòin.*

> [High mountains with lovely slopes
> Folk abiding there whose nature is to be kind
> Light is my step when I go leaping to see them
> And I will remain a while there willingly.[16]]

Early in European culture, certainly by Roman times, people began associating a different idea with the geographical direction west, and with the sunset, namely, the idea of youth and vigor, the idea that lands to the west were fresher, younger, and more vigorous than those to the east. This idea was related to such myths as those of the apples of the Hesperides or of Emain Ablach, to *Tír na n-Óg*, and to the story of Bran's voyage to magical realms of pleasure and wonder, but in the classical world it became an idea about the immediate, not the magical, world. This notion was understandable because in the Mediterranean basin it happened to be the case, as it was also in China, that the lands at the eastern end had the older and more established culture, whereas those to the west were more recent, ruder, and less developed. The idea of the West as the direction of youth, innocence, and vigor contradicted the idea of the West as the country of sunset, which could be interpreted metaphorically as decline.

The most famous of all stories associating the West with youth and rebirth was that of King Arthur in the isle of Avalon. According to Geoffrey of Monmouth, a Welshman descended from Bretons, who in the twelfth century re-told many of the old Celtic tales about Arthur, the king was fatally wounded at the battle of Camlan, to which he had been treacherously lured by his evil son and dark counterpart, Mordred. His wound doomed him to death in the mundane world, but by divine grace he was transported to Avalon, "the island of apple-trees" in the West, where nine women with magical powers—counterparts of the Hesperides—healed the king and allowed him to remain alive in Avalon in a sort of half-state between heaven and earth, ready to return in the final battle of good and evil.[17]

This idea of the West as the region of vigor and youth came into its own in the age of exploration. The other two ideas—of the West as the region of sunset and decline, and as the goal of travel and yearning, whether mundane or supernatural—returned to feed the romantic imagination of the nineteenth century and the cultural pessimism of the twentieth. All these ideas suggested a richer heritage that was in some ways as alien to the technocratic, liberal West as any non-Western civilization. As a prolegomenon to recovering some of this heritage, and particularly its Old Western manifestation, this book offers a rediscovery of a different past than that of the simple story of great ideas from Plato to NATO.

From the foregoing it will be clear that both the institutions and the resonances of myth that entered into Western identity were much deeper and broader than what was captured either in the Grand Narrative or in the critical antinarratives. For the same reason, the defense of the West mounted by some of the optimists and by neoconservatives in the 1980s—the defense, for example, of William Bennett in his *Book of Virtues*—was, however well meant, unable to restore the cultural balance. The problem with such defenses, and with the neo-optimist case that ignored the attacks, was that they took the liberal narrative for granted and neglected the multiple and alternative traditions of the West. Thus, they did not answer the critics on solid ground, but on the shifting ground of contemporary cultural debate. But if, as I argue, the Grand Narrative was itself flawed and was itself the basic obstacle to understanding Western identity, these defenses conceded both too much and too little—they conceded the value of much of the critics' case but did not abandon the Grand Narrative. The defenses were partial. I want to show a broader picture of Western identity to give both defenders and attackers a better target.

Optimists, pessimists, realists, and enemies of the West all had their favorite moments in history, when the particular feature or features they considered as the essence of the West made their appearance. Those who admired or praised the West looked for what I call Magic Moments, those who despised it or foresaw its decline looked for Original Sins. All such groups were engaged in establishing or inventing some particular idea of the West to suit their interests. In the late twentieth century, the searches both for Magic Moments and Original Sins took place against the background of the Grand Narrative. What did this narrative look like?

CHAPTER ONE

The Grand Narrative and Its Fate

Happy he who has come to understand the causes of things
—Virgil

The first step to recovering the history of Western identity from the wreckage of the Grand Narrative is to understand that the narrative was not some revealed truth about Western civilization temporarily granted to American educators during the hegemony of the classical—assimilationist, meritocratic, and humanistic—version of American liberalism in culture and education, and then taken away again as that hegemony succumbed to political and cultural attack in the 1960s and following decades. In hindsight, we can see that the hegemony of this centrist liberalism was rather brief: it gathered steam in the wake of Progressivism and World War I, rose to its first eminence in the Depression decade of the 1930s, became near-universal during and after World War II, and seemed to stand uncontested until 1965—until the moment when the Vietnam War began to divide the American elites, and the leaders of the adversary culture launched their long and magnificently successful march through the institutions.[1] The centrist liberal hegemony in culture and education lasted some thirty years, a generation, in other words. In terms of political history, it reached critical mass under one Democratic president, Franklin Roosevelt, and began to crumble under another, Lyndon Johnson. But even such an account overstates its power, for how could it give way so quickly from the mid-1960s on if it was not already seriously undermined from within? The adversary culture did not appear from nowhere in 1965, but had been there all along as a steadily more vociferous undercurrent in politics and in the elite colleges, media, and cultural institutions.

Nevertheless, the point here is not to trace the fatal flaws of American liberalism that led to its post–1965 split and permitted a bureaucratic, egalitarian, and multiculturalist version to replace the meritocratic and assimilationist version of earlier decades. Rather, the point is that the Grand Narrative, as a convincing and comprehensive story of Western identity and of America as the legitimate culmination of that identity, was not an independent discovery of scholars, but a political and pedagogical construct of the same spirit that drove centrist liberalism to its brief moment of power. It was liberalism's historical and cultural account of itself, its roots, history, and legitimacy.

The Grand Narrative dominated elite higher education, and therefore elite culture, in America from the 1920s to the 1960s. It provided the cultural and historical basis of a liberal consensus about the merits and potential of the West that was unapologetically rationalist, progressive, and confident of the benefits of science and industry—a consensus that sought excellence in education, common ground in politics, and assimilation and harmony in social relations. And because the Grand Narrative was a construct of American liberalism, therefore, when American liberals stopped believing in excellence, reason, science, and assimilation, they also lost confidence in the Grand Narrative that underpinned those beliefs.

The second step is to understand why the Grand Narrative was invented when it was, and by whom. The typical version of the Grand Narrative was the undergraduate course in Western civilization as taught in elite colleges during the decades of centrist liberal hegemony. One common answer to why the story of the West was told in this way has been to say that these were the decades when higher education became a mass phenomenon—some said an entitlement—in the United States, and that educators realized that the many new beneficiaries of higher education needed some common ground, some common core of information and knowledge on which to build their citizenship in a mass democracy. That is true, but it is only part of the reason. Other industrial and capitalist democracies developed mass higher education during the twentieth century, but none felt the need to center that education on a common or general curriculum the way that American educators did.[2] There was nothing in the notion of mass higher education in itself that required a college-level core curriculum. Rather, it was the peculiar circumstances of America, as they appeared to leading educators in the early years of the twentieth century, that indicated not only that mass higher education was on its way, but that it should rest on a common core curriculum.

One critical difference between America and other Western countries was that America, at least until mass immigration ceased in 1924, was receiving relatively large numbers of immigrants at a time when the elites believed strongly in assimilation. Assimilation was therefore the main motive of those who constructed the Grand Narrative in the early years of the twentieth century. At that time, America was receiving more immigrants, relative to the size of the population, than ever before or since. And unlike the situation after the 1960s, the American elites considered it their duty to assimilate new arrivals to the dominant Anglo-Saxon political and economic culture and its accompanying social norms.

Assimilation took two forms. For those who were already adult when they arrived, assimilation was American life itself; the need to survive in the brutal economy of the day was, all by itself, a force sufficient to shave off whatever ethnic or cultural peculiarities the newcomers might bring with them, if those peculiarities hindered them in becoming efficient producers. For those who were children, a broader and more conscious strategy suggested itself. They were more malleable and had a longer future in America. It was especially important to see to it that the schools and colleges made them into genuine Americans, more American than their parents. "It was an atmosphere," recalled a grandson of Hungarian immigrants, "in which the Anglo-American culture, the world of Jefferson, Washington, Franklin, Jackson, Lincoln, Teddy Roosevelt, Hawthorne, Thomas Edison, Mark Twain and the Wright Brothers, was honored. We were all expected to learn it, absorb it, and become as much a part of it as any young Anglo graduate of Choate and Yale."[3]

The catalyst that precipitated the Grand Narrative in its developed form was World War I. America helped win the war, but the American elite now found itself faced with another challenge of assimilation. This was the assimilation not just of immigrant children, but of young adults, who were not necessarily immigrants but who had not the least idea of the political principles of American government or the democratic heritage of Western civilization.

When America entered the war in 1917, the U.S. government asked educators at elite colleges to prepare for a mass influx of returning servicemen, and to prepare "War and Peace courses" to teach them what they had been fighting for and why. The returning doughboys were to be sent to college, there to learn the basics of Western civilization. Such teaching would perform two functions increasingly seen as essential in a modern society, and especially in America, the most modern and progressive of all societies. It was supposed to turn illiterate boys from the slums and backwoods of America into competent citizens, by means of Plato, John Locke, and Thomas Jefferson. The power of the great idea and the great book was to be deployed to counteract the barbarization of war and to turn former soldiers into prospective philosopher-kings.

One place where the call to devise courses on War and Peace had particular resonance was Columbia College in New York, which became the alma mater of one of the two main forms that the Grand Narrative took in American culture of the twentieth century. In 1919, teachers at the college presented the first version of what they called the Contemporary Civilization course. This course covered the history of Western political and social ideas with particular reference to America and American identity over two semesters. It remained, in 1998, a required course for all Columbia undergraduates; Columbia, indeed, was one of few colleges in the 1990s that still prescribed an extensive core curriculum, rather than allowing students to design their own. When it was first taught in 1919, the Columbia Contemporary Civilization course was one of the most important spinoffs of what became known as the general education movement of the 1910s to the 1930s, and which transformed American higher education. This was done not just by introducing the standard Western civilization course, but by introducing the idea that everyone ought, ideally, to receive some college education, and that this education should not be vocational, but "general," that is, it should consist of nonspecialized teaching about great ideas and great books. Thus was born the modern, twentieth-century, and, as it turned out, short-lived idea of liberal higher education.

One of the young men of Columbia who helped devise the Contemporary Civilization course and who went on to become a leading exponent of the Grand Narrative was John Herman Randall, who in 1919 was majoring as an undergraduate in history under Charles A. Beard and James H. Robinson, two leading American historians of their generation. Beard was about to leave Columbia to found the New School for Social Research, in lower Manhattan, partly because his book *The Economic Interpretation of the Constitution*, published in 1913, had offended more traditional historians by its argument that the American Founding Fathers had economic and political interests, just like other powerful groups in history, and that one could not understand the whys and wherefores of the American Revolution without taking those interests into account. Young Randall did not follow Beard to the New School but remained at Columbia for the next fifty years. His classic texts *The Making of the Modern Mind*, first published in 1924, and *The*

Career of Philosophy from the 1960s represented the Columbia version of the Grand Narrative in elegant and comprehensive form. These books were detailed expositions of the philosophical systems that shaped the modern West and of the intellectual and cultural conditions of their emergence. Brilliantly learned and well written, Randall's books shared the Grand Narrative's basic characteristic—that it was a history of great ideas and of how superior ideas replaced inferior ones until the "modern mind" was fully shaped.

The second fundamental version of the Grand Narrative was that associated with the University of Chicago and its "Great Books" program. This idealistic endeavor had a different genesis from that of the Columbia Contemporary Civilization course, although the two formed a powerful and complementary duet of cultural assimilation and liberal humanism in their heyday. The two versions overlapped in the person of Mortimer Adler, who took the Contemporary Civilization course at Columbia before doing his Ph.D. at Chicago and joining the law faculty in 1928. The Chicago operation was largely the brainchild of Robert Maynard Hutchins, one of the most brilliant and certainly the most precocious American educator of his time. Hutchins, who was born only a month before Randall in 1899, was dean of the Yale Law School at twenty-eight and president of the University of Chicago at thirty. At Chicago, Hutchins met Adler and recruited him to help in an ambitious reorganization of the university's entire spectrum of undergraduate study. The Hutchins-Adler team produced the "Chicago Plan" for undergraduate study, which emphasized broad reading and comprehensive examinations rather than specific courses leading to specific tests of knowledge. The axis of the Chicago Plan was the study of Great Books. Undaunted by the timidity of later ages, Hutchins and Adler had no problem deciding what books were Great; and in true American technocratic fashion they went so far as to publish, for the general market, special editions of the chosen works, fifty-two in number, under the title *Great Books of the Western World*.

Hutchins and Adler had complete faith in the civilizing effect of study and reflection on the great ideas of the past. Born intellectuals both, they saw reading and knowledge as direct sources of virtue and citizenship and could not understand why anyone at a university would want to pursue any other activities than those of the mind. As president of Chicago, Hutchins downgraded athletics, while Adler had been refused his diploma at Columbia for refusing to take part in obligatory physical education. From the 1940s on, both were associated with the *Encyclopaedia Britannica*, which despite its name had become an American operation and which, in its American incarnation, became one of the most successful operations in mass-marketing knowledge and information of all time.

Hutchins left Chicago in 1951, after which the university abandoned the Chicago Plan, although it continued to publish the Great Books. He spent the latter decades of his life at the University of California at Santa Barbara, where he tried to create a community of freewheeling scholars discussing the fundamental issues facing the contemporary world—peace and war, individual freedom, ecology, and, toward the end, the rights of minorities and women. This well-meaning but utterly ineffectual effort symbolized a basic flaw of the Grand Narrative, at least in its Great Books version: the fact that it consisted exclusively of great ideas divorced from their historical, ideological, and institutional context.

A third form of the Grand Narrative that differed from the Columbia and Chicago versions in being directed not at students, but at interested citizens, and in being based not on a naive faith in the power of study to produce virtue, but on the idea that the history of culture should include all of history, was that of Will Durant. This version was never represented in a college curriculum or a Great Books list, and it was the product of one man—later of two people—rather than of distinguished academics. It had also a longer history, since it began before World War I. For these reasons, Durant's contribution was not precisely comparable to the Contemporary Civilization course or the Chicago Plan, though it arguably had a greater effect.

It began humbly among the uneducated workmen of New York City. Even before World War I, churches, workmen's associations, and other volunteer groups had begun, on their own, and mostly in the big cities, to offer night classes on history, philosophy, and culture to ordinary working people, most of whom had, at best, a grade school education. Some of these groups were politically radical, and the purpose of their schools and evening classes was to raise up generations of citizens prepared for dramatic social change and fired by visions of justice. One of these schools was the Ferrer School of New York City. At that time, radicals believed that one of the greatest sources of social and economic inequality was that the poor and the oppressed lacked education. If you could teach the poor, the ordinary working people, you were handing them the tools of their own liberation and the key to the revolution that was to come. Therefore, in early-twentieth-century radicalism and socialism, education in the classics and in the great books and ideas of the West was not seen as limiting or as imposing the hegemony of dead white males, but on the contrary, as opening possibility and laying the essential foundations of social change. For in the radical world-view, the new world to come would necessarily be an enlightened, educated world, one in which to know Plato, Locke, and Jefferson was not the privilege of the few but the right of the many.

In 1911 the Ferrer School welcomed a new teacher, a twenty-six-year-old former journalist, college instructor, and lapsed Catholic seminarian named Will Durant. He had leaped from Catholicism to the equally demanding faith of radical political ideology, and like his radical friends he believed strongly in education as the key to mass liberation. But Durant's future turned out to be quite different from that of his radical friends in 1911. At Ferrer, he discovered that he had a fantastic knack for presenting the history of ideas, societies, and manners in a way that gripped his audience, removed them from their humdrum and exhausting daily lives, and gave breadth of vision and a taste of a wider world. Durant soon ran up against his own limitations of knowledge. Having in the meantime found a patron, he took two years off to tour Europe and take graduate courses at Columbia, in biology and philosophy as well as in political and cultural history. Since this was the early twentieth century, these topics were limited to their Western aspects; history then was the history of the West.

In 1914, Durant returned to the streets of New York, specifically to the Presbyterian Church then located at Fourteenth Street and Second Avenue. Fortified by his travels and studies, he began to give here the lectures that he later published as *The Story of Philosophy*. This book became an instant bestseller and could have kept Durant and his wife, Ariel, comfortably off for life had they so wished. But Durant had now realized just how much he enjoyed learning and teaching. His ambition grew: he was going to tell the working men and women of New York City the story of their civilization, and he was going to write this story down so it could be read and enjoyed anywhere. Thus he began the long program of study and teaching that, in 1935, bore fruit in the first volume of *The Story of Civilization*. The project continued to grow, as the Durants ploughed through time from Egypt and Persia via Greece, Rome, the Middle Ages, to the Renaissance and the Reformation. By the late 1950s, Durant, now in his seventies, was tackling what he called the Age of Reason, and began including his wife's name on the title page. Undaunted by age, the Durants continued their task until the age of the French Revolution and Napoleon, published in 1975 when Will was ninety and Ariel seventy-seven. They both died six years later, within a fortnight of each other.

The Story of Civilization was the apotheosis of the Grand Narrative. Vastly superior to the textbook versions, immensely learned, vividly written, and informed throughout by an obvious delight in storytelling that never, or rarely, turned into condescension to the reader, the twelve-volume, nine-thousand-page, four-and-a-half-million-word saga covered all of life, as defined by Western civilization. Philosophy, climate, poetry, diet, music, disease, politics, sexual practices, architecture, passions, class distinctions, and the endless variations of custom, taste, and belief—these were the interwoven themes of Durant's version. It was a nearly perfect achievement, within its, admittedly broad, limitations. First of all, Durant defined civilization as Western civilization and its history as one tending to more freedom, greater equality, and broader rights, which was the ideological core of the Grand Narrative. Second, he had his favorites, and religious or mystical people, times, and places were not among them. He was polite and, within his secular limits, understanding, but his tolerance to the reader was not always matched by tolerance to his characters. After a few thousand pages, even the most curious reader might begin to weary of the sheer liberal urbanity of the man, his unshakable sense that he knew best, and that the reason he knew best was that he had read and understood everyone of any importance, and many of no importance. Above all, Durant's story was a story with a goal and a moral, and a story that demoted all those characters, events, or situations that did not square easily with the goal and the moral. The goal was an idealized, progressive, individualistic America, and the moral was that the West was good, but was most truly itself when engaged on the long march to that worthy goal.

The Grand Narrative rose to its culmination and began its fall while the Durants were writing. The first volume appeared in the era of Franklin Roosevelt and the Depression, when optimistic progressives such as Durant still believed that one key to progress was education in the great books and great ideas. The last volume appeared the year that Saigon fell to the communists and American helicopters lifted a few lucky escapees from the roof of the American Embassy, symbolizing the ignominious retreat of American power. The Vietnam War that thus ended had been, in America, the single most significant triggering event of the radical movement of the 1960s, which, among much else, had on its agenda to attack and delegitimize the liberal story of the West and Western identity itself.

Shortly before the attack on the Grand Narrative began, a University of Chicago historian produced a book that, if one judged by its title, might easily be taken for a triumphalist restatement of the narrative on the eve of its fall. This was William McNeill's *The Rise of the West*, subtitled "A History of the Human Community," which first appeared in 1963. Writing about it in 1988, McNeill admitted that "in retrospect it seems obvious that *The Rise of the West* should be seen as an expression of the postwar imperial mood in the United States."[4] McNeill had attended Chicago early in the reign of Hutchins and Adler, but explaining great books or teaching working-class Americans about the roots of Western culture was not among his self-imposed tasks. His book was rather an attempt to understand cultural change as a never-ending process of interaction between societies, each equipped with its own package of skills, interests, and material conditions. In McNeill's world view, history was the result of such interaction and of cultures learning—consciously or not, willingly or not—from each other.

Most people who heard the title, however, assumed that because the book concluded that the West was in fact dominant in the twentieth century, therefore the book was a celebration of that fact, which it was not. To critics of the narrative, *The Rise of the West* was merely another politically objectionable expression of the Western triumphalism they saw in the Grand Narrative, and that they were determined to destroy.

As radical students in the 1960s, Martin Bernal and Kirkpatrick Sale—to name just two—encountered the Grand Narrative, saw the Vietnam War, and drew the conclusion that the one was part of the enabling apparatus of the other. American imperialism, hunger in the Third World, racial injustice at home, and the capitalist rapacity that exploited poor people as well as the natural environment became for them icons of evil that had to be brought down, and, as writers and academics, they determined that their own contribution to that effort should take the form of undermining and deconstructing what they saw as the misleading, biased, and ideologically unsound story of the West represented by the Grand Narrative. By the 1990s, Bernal, Sale, and their many allies had succeeded in their task. The Grand Narrative existed in most places only as a shell. Courses in Western civilization still existed—for example, the Columbia Contemporary Civilization course—but the content and in particular the presentation had changed. The West was no longer the culmination of the great books and great ideas of the past, but, at best, a morally dubious enterprise whose only chance of redemption was to adopt the multiculturalist, feminist, and environmentalist agenda of the new, post–1960s American liberalism.

The irony of this attack, and of its success, was that the deconstructionists were right in one thing: the Grand Narrative was misleading. History, including the history of Western identity and Western civilization, was not adequately described as a sequence of great ideas and great books. The narrative, whether in its assimilationist Columbia version, its intellectualist Chicago version, or its more populist Durant version, was, as this book will show, built on a series of distortions, beginning with the distortion that all the great ideas began in Greece and that the Greeks were the first Westerners. But the distortions were not the ones Bernal and Sale fixed on. They disliked the narrative because, to them, it justified a West they saw as evil and inadequate. But this criticism was itself at least as ideological and biased as its target. It did not remove the moralism; it merely stood the moralism on its head, and one of the basic flaws of the narrative was precisely its moralism, the fact that it presented the story of the West as a pedagogical adventure with a happy ending. The radicals reversed the logic and presented their own pedagogical adventure, which had a tragic ending but also promised redemption, if people would only adopt the radical agenda.

But the problem with the narrative was never that it defended unjust social and political arrangements, but that it was bad history, and it was bad history because it rested on three fundamental fallacies: that the history of culture was the history of its great ideas, that the West was a moral story with a happy ending, and that this story could be adequately defined as an axis of continuity that began with the Greeks, jumped lightly over the Romans, Christians, and Dark Age Germanic tribes, to land, finally, in modern America and modern liberalism.

The third step to recovering the history of Western identity is therefore to disentangle the actual stages of that history from the distortions of both moralisms: that of the Grand Narrative and that of its radical deconstructors. The fact that the deconstructors won is not in itself a reason to return to the Grand Narrative, for they did not correct its errors; they added more serious errors of their own, for example, the error that the history of the West was a history of injustice and iniquity. Such a vision was even more ideological and fallacious than a vision based on great ideas, for at least the Grand Narrative tried to understand those ideas sympathetically, whereas the deconstructors had only contempt for the target of their attacks. Disentangling the history of Western identity thus involves defending against both old and new errors with the help of the serious and disinterested scholarship that, by the late twentieth century, made a comprehensive vision of that history possible. If that comprehensive vision turns out to have moral implications, these should emerge from social and historical reality and not from preconceived ideas. The distinction is basic: the narrative and its enemies both imposed their standards on the past; a recovered history of Western identity observes the past and may—or may not—find lessons there about the moral implications of the particular, Western forms of human endeavor and human activity.

To take that third step is the purpose of the rest of this book. But first, what did a typical version of the Grand Narrative look like? If one could establish a synthesis of its three versions, what story would that synthesis tell us?

The liberal Grand Narrative presented the West as a coherent entity emerging triumphantly through history in a series of stages, each contributing an essential element to the whole. Western civilization, according to this story, was a synthesis of democracy, capitalism, science, human rights, religious pluralism, individual autonomy, and the power of unfettered human reason to solve human problems. The most important stages, or Magic Moments, of Western evolution were ancient Greece, Rome, the synthesis of classical civilization and Christianity, the European Renaissance and the voyages of discovery, the rise of modern science, and, in the last two centuries, the rise of modern liberal democracy, the spread of prosperity, and, with the end of the Cold War, the prospect of global peace and stability. Cumulatively, these Magic Moments shaped the spiritual, geographical, political, and moral entity defined by the narrative as the modern West.

This confident and optimistic story was, as we have seen, created as a tool of mass higher education and in the face of serious challenges to Western identity. For much of the twentieth century, it held the stage as the foundation of elite education in America, and to a lesser extent in Europe. Throughout that period, it was under attack for being arrogant, unhistorical, misleading, or simply wrong. From the late 1960s on, the critics began gaining the upper hand in American education and culture, so that by the 1990s the optimistic story had been fundamentally recast in a number of variants: stories of guilt, doubt, decline, and apology.

Both the optimistic narrative and the critical, or postmodern, antinarratives shared crucial assumptions. The most important of these concerned the origins of the West. Although both operated with a series of stages, Magic Moments in the positive version and Original Sins in the negative, both also argued that the key elements of the West could be traced back to ancient Greece. While it was true that the modern Western versions of democracy, science, philosophy, history, art, and civic values appeared only in recent centuries, their remote origins were nevertheless to be found in Greece. The Greeks were the first Westerners, because they first had the ideas and formulated the aesthetic and philosophical ideals that by a recognizable line of descent became what the narratives called modern Western civilization. Not only were they the first Westerners, they were also, in some versions of the narrative, models of perfection. Not only did they first discover and formulate the ideal canon of Western values; they did so with incomparable clarity and to a standard never since attained.

The Grand Narrative was both a version of history and a description of the ideal modern Western identity. In its basic form, the Grand Narrative followed an axis that spanned five millennia, from ancient Egypt and Mesopotamia to mid-twentieth-century America. It was a history of reason, democracy, and economic growth. Its authors assumed that progress was real, objectively definable, and universally desirable. Being free was better than being enslaved, being rich was better than being poor, being healthy better than being sick, being enlightened better than being superstitious, being at peace better than being at war. Progress meant moving from subjection, poverty, disease, superstition, and violence to democracy, prosperity, health, science, and peace both domestic and international. The Grand Narrative was the story of how a lucky part of the human race found the key to such progress, and how they used that key to achieve it. This basic faith in progress was both a strength and a weakness. By tracing the remote origins of contemporary institutions and doctrines, the Grand Narrative provided, at its best, a sweeping, eagle's-eye view of the long haul of history that could be, and often was, inspiring to students and citizens alike. On the other hand, by looking at the past mainly, if not exclusively, to find the origins of the superior present, the authors of the Grand Narrative unhistorically ignored those areas of past cultures not compatible with the modern liberal West. The Grand Narrative assumed what it set out to explain: that the West existed, and that it was good.

Its crucial turning points and heroes defined the Magic Moments of the West.[5] History, the narrative stated, began in the ancient Near East and in Egypt about five thousand years ago. The ancient Mesopotamians and Egyptians lived in monarchies of various kinds, in which one man or woman was supreme and the rest subjects. The ruler might be a god himself, or he might simply be close to the gods; in either case, he was raised above the rest of humanity. Both the early high cultures, Egypt and Mesopotamia, arose along great rivers and depended for survival on being able to predict and control the seasonal variations in water flow. Without accurate knowledge and without the technology of irrigation, organized society was impossible. Centralized, autocratic power was necessary to codify this knowledge and maintain the technology. The ability to mobilize vast human armies to ensure water for crops was both the precondition and the result of civilization in Mesopotamia. In Egypt, where the Nile river rose every year and automatically inundated the fertile land along its banks, the state did not need armies of ditchdiggers; it did need men who could keep track of the seasons and predict how much the Nile would rise. In both these early civilizations, crops and hence survival depended on responding in an organized manner to a collective event, the rise of a river.

In the early first millennium B.C., the focus moved west from Mesopotamia and north from Egypt to Israel and Greece. The Israelites were not unusual among the peoples of the ancient Near East in their general culture or language, which was closely related to those spoken throughout the area. The Israelites, or Hebrews, were unusual in their religion, because unlike the other Near Easterners they claimed that their god was the only god, that he had made the world and everything in it, but was separate from the world, that he had made a special covenant with them, and that, as part of this covenant, he had given them a full set of laws and rules on how to live and how to worship him. The Israelites thus contributed monotheism to the West. This contribution was important not as religion or theology, but because monotheism made a radical distinction between the divine and the human. This distinction had two consequences. It emphasized the moral value of individual human acts and thus helped to create the idea of an individual conscience and individual responsibility. Second, it directed human attention to understanding nature, both human and nonhuman, and this impulse, together with Greek rationalism and modern European principles of freedom and toleration, made possible science and democracy.

In the Grand Narrative, the ancient empires and Israel were not early stages of the West, but its prehistory. Greek civilization, according to the Grand Narrative, was unprecedented and richer than any other—before the modern West, that is. Ancient Greece, and particularly the city of Athens in the fifth century B.C., was the Magic Moment of Magic Moments. Western literature, democracy, and philosophy all began there, as did the organized study of how the present emerged from the past, that is, the writing of history.

The favorite Greek in the Grand Narrative was the philosopher Socrates, who appeared in it as the inventor of moral individualism, that is, of the idea that it was the duty of the individual to make his own discovery of right action, of what duty prescribed. Morality was not something in the air, but something that had to be understood to be valuable and effective. Second, Socrates appeared as the first victim of populist resistance to bold ideas, the first martyr for truth and freedom of expression. In the year 399 B.C., he was tried and executed for blasphemy. Because the Grand Narrative was not especially sympathetic to religion and tended to see religion as a secondary force in social development, its authors downplayed the actual wording of the charge against Socrates and reinterpreted it as an attack on his philosophical ideas, particularly his moral individualism. This attack was cloaked in religious language, because that was the only language available in Athenian law. Socrates was thus removed from his historical setting and turned into a larger-than-life figure outside history, an early liberal, in fact. We shall see that this Americanization of the Greeks was an absurd distortion, but also that it had a long history, going back to the cult of the Greeks as the most perfect, natural human beings, a cult launched by the German romantics and idealists in the late eighteenth century to replace Christianity.

The following centuries of ancient history—the long story of the slow decline of the Greek democracies, the rise of the Macedonian Empire under Alexander, and the subsequent rise of Rome to hegemony in the Mediterranean—were not much emphasized in the narrative. The liberal story of a West that evolved by logical stages from prehistory to modern democracy found little of use in an era dominated by great empires and by a culture condemned as derivative. The rise of Rome was significant for two reasons: Rome made peace in the Mediterranean, which facilitated social and cultural communication, allowing Greek civilization and, later, Christianity, to spread westward. The other Roman contribution was law. Roman law was one of the roots of later Western systems of law, even though the narrative had little sympathy for the autocratic and cruel features of Roman political life that Roman law expressed.

From the first to the fourth centuries A.D., Christianity slowly grew in the western Roman Empire until, after A.D. 312, it became the official religion of the empire. Over the following centuries, classical civilization and Christianity formed a synthesis that determined the shape of the West. The narrative took an instrumental view of this synthesis. The marriage of classical culture and Christianity was, in this view, a Magic Moment not because it produced the civilization of the European Middle Ages, because that civilization was not yet liberal and democratic. Rather, the marriage was, in the liberal story, providential in a secular sense, because modern democracy, and in particular the modern doctrine of universal human rights, had their roots in the classical political philosophy of freedom as the obligation to participate in civic life, in the Roman respect for law and duty, and in Christianity seen as an ethical teaching about social justice and the moral equality of all human beings. Modern democracy, in the liberal version, was the fully developed West, the true West.

The Western synthesis of Rome and Christianity, in the liberal story, was a necessary condition of the West, whereas to conservative Christians it was the West itself. Although Christianity was more vigorous in America in the twentieth century than in Europe, it was the liberal Grand Narrative that was most often taught in American colleges and honored in public discourse. This was not surprising, because the Old West of the Christian story was hierarchical and undemocratic and denigrated the pursuit of material prosperity and economic growth that was a fundamental part of American ideology. Americans identified politically and economically with the liberal Grand Narrative and the new West that it proclaimed, but most of them remained committed to a religion that questioned that narrative. This contradiction was not always noticed in the heyday of the liberal Grand Narrative, because most of the Christian churches in America had made their accommodation with the liberal story. But after left-wing critics, starting in the 1960s, had delegitimated or revised the liberal Grand Narrative, this deeper contradiction between America's identity as the modern West and the Christian religion of most Americans, which, in principle if not in practice, questioned the legitimacy of the modern West's claim to be the true West, came to the surface.

The synthesis was actually a process that took several centuries, starting with St. Paul, the apostle to the Gentiles who was also a Roman citizen and enjoyed the safety of Roman order in his travels and writings, in the mid-first century A.D. For over two hundred years after his day, Christians lived, peacefully for the most part, among other inhabitants of the Roman Empire. Until the late third century, they generally avoided notice by pagan writers or authorities. Technically, Christianity was a treasonable and therefore illegal religion, punishable by death, but in practice persecutions were, until the 290s, few and far between. In the late third century, Diocletian and his co-emperors were restoring order after more than half a century of invasions, civil wars, and economic disruption. The empire shed its last vestiges of republican customs and became a military dictatorship in which the survival of the state was the paramount law. Christians, meanwhile, had become more numerous. Both their numbers and their beliefs were a threat to the new order. Diocletian therefore determined to extirpate them. The persecution failed. Its final result was Constantine's conversion, which, in purely political terms, was the greatest example in history of the precept "if you can't beat 'em, join 'em."

The Grand Narrative skated lightly over the following centuries, which to modern liberal eyes had the dual disadvantage of being both seriously Christian and in cultural decline. The next Magic Moment, which in the Grand Narrative, American version, was second only to the founding synthesis of Rome and Christianity, was the voyage of Christopher Columbus in 1492 and what the Grand Narrative called his discovery of America. This came at the high point of the Renaissance, considered by many of its own leading thinkers and by the Grand Narrative as the reawakening of Europe after a millennium of ignorance and superstition. At the time, few noticed Columbus. The year 1492 was notorious in Europe not because he sailed from Cadiz, but for another Spanish event, the fall of Grenada, which marked the end of the *reconquista*, the Christian counteroffensive against the Islamic invaders of Spain who arrived in 711.

From Columbus to the twentieth century, the Grand Narrative allowed dozens, if not scores, of Magic Moments. The general heading of the period was progress: political, economic, social, and technological. Politically, progress meant the rise and spread of democratic ideas, and later of democratic government. The beginnings of capitalism and sustained economic growth leading, eventually, to widespread prosperity in the West defined economic progress. Criteria of social progress were, for example, growing literacy, the decline in casual violence, the rise of a well-mannered and polite society, growing respect for members of other social classes than one's own, the rise in public status of women. Finally, machines and procedures to make work, and life in general, less painful and more productive were for long the prime examples of technological progress.

Another theme of the period, according to the Grand Narrative, was universality. The good things of the West were not just for those who invented them, but for everyone. The voyages of discovery concretely expressed the West's universalist impulse. It wanted to go everywhere, learn everything, and put everything to practical use. Its success was evidence that it had found the right way to do things, to study the world and exploit its riches. And universalism was the apparently logical child of success. What worked for the West must work for everyone, and what was good for the West was good for everyone.

The Grand Narrative of the last half of the second millennium A.D. was, in all its variants, based on a simple scheme, which ran something like this: in the Renaissance, people freed themselves of superstition and released their minds and their imaginations. One result of this new freedom was courage: the courage of Columbus in 1492, or of Martin Luther in 1517 when he broke with the Catholic Church in the name of personal faith. The new freedom produced two further results: one was the rediscovery of classical civilization and all its riches, which thus became the inheritance of the modern West. The second was the idea of a human nature that was generally the same in all times and places, regardless, for example, of religion or culture. This second idea meant that one could construct valid theories of history, culture, morality, and politics. And in politics, the idea of a common human nature led eventually, by a series of inevitable steps, to the notion, the desire, and the justification of democracy. Democracy, finally, was the end point of the Grand Narrative.

Five Magic Moments among many—one for every century—encapsulated the Grand Narrative of the modern West's emergence and growth as a story of progress, freedom, and their universal meaning from Columbus to mid-twentieth-century America: the defeat of the Spanish Armada in 1588, the Glorious Revolution of 1688–89, the American Revolution of 1776–87, the Emancipation Proclamation of 1862, and the Atlantic Charter of 1941.

In 1588, Philip II of Spain sent a fleet to invade England. Spain was the core state of Catholicism, the strongest power in Europe, the metropolis of a global empire. Every year, a fleet from America brought silver from the mines of Mexico to the king's treasury. England was a poor, small, Protestant country of some three million people on the edge of Europe. Faced with the threat of invasion, the English, like other groups in similar crises, discovered a sense of national identity. They rallied round their queen, Elizabeth, and by dint of skill and courage defeated the invasion fleet with inferior forces. The victory resounded throughout Europe. Spanish prestige suffered a blow from which it never recovered. The theme, in this version of the story, was freedom, understood in its modern sense as pointing toward democracy and economic liberalism. The message of the Armada was that freedom, which led to prosperity and democracy, was saved in the English Channel in the summer of 1588. This was not exactly wrong; English freedom was indeed saved. But that freedom, at the time, was mainly a religious and not a political idea, or that the Spanish cause was as just, in its terms, as the English, were complications that did not fit the narrative and so were largely ignored.

In the Glorious Revolution of 1688–89, William, Prince of Orange, related to the Stuart kings of England and Scotland by blood and marriage, invaded England to protect the Protestant state religion and constitutional government. The Grand Narrative saw the Glorious Revolution as a triumph of civil rights and popular control of arbitrary government. The next two Magic Moments took place in America. The American Revolution proclaimed the doctrine of equal and universal rights and established a government and society based on that doctrine. The Constitution of 1787 determined that the government would be divided, so as to avoid concentrations of power, and would be federal, with only such power granted to the central government as was necessary for it to carry out its functions of assuring general security. The individual states remained sovereign in most areas. Those that wished could, for example, retain the institution of slavery. Slavery, and other indentured servitude, was inconsistent with the egalitarian and meritocratic ideology of the revolution, and this inconsistency ultimately led to the Civil War and Emancipation. Thus, by the later nineteenth century, the modern West was being born in the United States, which was of all nations the most advanced toward the liberal democratic capitalism idealized in the Grand Narrative.

The Atlantic Charter of 1941 was a fitting Magic Moment with which to end a Plato to NATO sequence, because this statement of principles by the American and British heads of government in the midst of World War II was among the most important political and philosophical foundations of NATO, the Atlantic Alliance. In August 1941, the American president, Franklin Roosevelt, and the British prime minister, Winston Churchill, met on a U.S. Navy ship in Placentia Bay off Newfoundland, where they issued a joint policy declaration that became known as the Atlantic Charter. It listed three paramount postwar goals: self-determination, collective security, and open markets. All three were in the mainstream of the Grand Narrative; they defined the identity of the modern West as a set of political and economic norms and arrangements. In the charter, they were stated as goals that ought to be, and were, shared by all right-thinking people, and, moreover, as goals that would and could be realized, not merely as wishful thinking about the world.

The Atlantic Charter differed, then, from earlier Magic Moments in that its authors were consciously defining Western civilization, stating their commitment to it, and proclaiming that the purpose of their war effort was to secure that civilization and extend its benefits. This was not surprising. By the 1940s, the Grand Narrative was a central part of elite education in the United States and Britain. Both Roosevelt and Churchill had learned early versions of it in their respective elite schools of Groton and Harrow. Nor was their presentation of its values in the charter by any means deliberately hypocritical or fraudulent. The postwar transatlantic civilization of peace, prosperity, and technology that grew out of the allied victory served, for several decades, as ample practical confirmation, in most people's eyes, of the justice and vigor of the Grand Narrative's image of what the West was and should be.

That, in a nutshell, was the outline of the liberal story of the West and its identity. While Durant's great book sold many copies and found many admirers, it was not the version of the Grand Narrative encountered by most students. No undergraduate had time for such monstrous learning. The problems of the Grand Narrative in its more common form were, on the practical level, a function of its necessary place in a crowded curriculum. It had to cover the great books and ideas in, usually, two semesters. That meant few stories and lots of condensed ideas. Most versions, therefore, were abstract and impersonal, about ideas rather than the people who had them. Another problem was that as a story with a goal, namely, the modern liberal West, its authors chose and interpreted its material in terms of how the material served that goal, and not in terms of the past itself. The episodes of the Grand Narrative appeared because the narrative needed them to build its image of the West, and not in their own concrete reality. A third problem was that choosing material for how it contributed to a final goal meant that you had to ignore the sheer confusion, complexity, and con-tradictions of the past, the fact that people then mostly did not know or care that their actions might someday be seen as creating the West. The Grand Narrative tore bits and pieces out of the past and set them up as a sequence, whereas these bits and pieces could not be properly understood out of their concrete context of people, passions, and places, some of them, in modern Western terms, ugly and immoral. History is strong drink, and the Grand Narrative turned it into soda pop.

The fate of the Grand Narrative was part of the fate of modern American liberalism, which began as optimistic individualism and faith in the power of great ideas to lift the masses from squalor and ignorance to enlightenment and ended in fragmented self-doubt and the hectic search for new legitimacy in multiculturalism and the other post–1960s doctrines of moral and politi-cal correctness. It was only superficially ironic that the opening shots in what became known as the American culture wars should have shattered the bas-tions of the Grand Narrative in higher education, because those bastions were indeed the outerworks of American liberalism as it saw itself through the middle third of the twentieth century.

The Grand Narrative therefore did not tell the story of the West, but was itself part of that story, part of Western identity in one of its later incarna-tions. Any story of the West, or of any other culture, is bound to be partial. The significance of the Grand Narrative was that its partial vision was both tied to its time and place and very influential, thanks to its half-century of intellectual and pedagogical dominance. It was when one compared the Grand Narrative to the actual story of Western identity that its historical limitations appeared.

The fourth step to recovering the history of Western identity is, then, to disentangle it from the moralizing distortions of both the Grand Narrative and its detractors. But once that is done, as it will be in the following chapters, there remains a final, fifth step. Once we have separated the history of the West from the arguments about it and about the liberal story, we have yet to ask what the future holds. Has Western identity been buried so deep, first by the ideology of centrist liberalism, then by that of egalitarian, bureaucratic, and multiculturalist neoliberalism, that its recovery is a quixotic task—one that can, perhaps, be carried out in a book like this, but that has no cultural or political relevance to any world in which readers may find themselves? Must we remain content with the fragmented, balkanized West of the culture wars—a West torn between defenders and attackers, praised and damned with equal fervor and equal disregard for history?

I believe not. Recovering a Western identity free of the twin moralisms of the old and the new liberalism frees us, the observers of history, to understand the true stakes of Western survival in the third millennium far better than we can if we allow ourselves to remain within the cages of stories that force us either to approve or disapprove. The recovered history of the West will turn out to be a story of creativity and destruction, of joy and tragedy, of loss as well as gain. But understanding that story permits us to draw the only genuinely moral lessons of history, which are the lessons of how societies, cultures, and personalities change, and how civilizations grow, not as icons of perfection or evil, but as social and individual realities.

The history of the West will emerge in this book as the story of two great syntheses, the synthesis of ancient, Christian, and Germanic cultures in the era known as late antiquity, and the synthesis of liberty, reason, and development—or democracy, science, and capitalism—that defined modernity. The central argument of this book is that these two syntheses were not mutually exclusive but part of a continuous story; that the second, modern synthesis grew out of the first and could not have happened without it.

The survival of what I call the New West—the modern triad of democracy, science, and capitalism—is thus not assured by the hectic apostles of market capitalism and democratic procedures that, in the 1990s, provided what seemed to be a sound defense of the West but was in fact only a shrill invocation of its surface manifestations. The survival of the New West as a player in the global game and sustainer of our own identities will rest on a higher synthesis—a recovery of what binds the two historical syntheses together. It is the recovery of the Old West within the New, and the renaissance promised by that recovery, to which this book, in its final chapter, calls its readers.

CHAPTER TWO

The Battle over Hellas

Me thinks we should not so soon yield our consents captive to
the authority of Antiquity, unless we saw more reason; all our
understandings are not to be built by the square of Greece
and Italy.

—Samuel Daniel

It appears then that upon the majority of mankind the classics
can hardly be said to exert the transforming influence which is
claimed for them.

—A. E. Housman

Greek civilization, according to the Grand Narrative, was unprecedented and richer than any other—before the modern West, that
is. Ancient Greece, and particularly the city of Athens in the fifth
century B.C., was the Magic Moment of Magic Moments. Western literature,
democracy, and philosophy all began there, as did the organized study of
how the present emerged from the past that we call history.[1]
    The ancestors of the Greeks arrived in what was to become Greece long
before classical civilization began. In the later second millennium B.C., they
produced a Bronze Age culture, literate and artistic, centered on ten palaces,
of which Mycenae was the most famous. This culture was part of the eastern
Mediterranean and Near Eastern world of its time; Mycenae enjoyed social,
artistic, and military ties, both friendly and hostile, to Egypt and the contem-

porary cultures of Anatolia. But the Mycenaean palace-based culture disappeared completely around 1200 B.C., leaving no legacy, and for reasons that were of little concern to the Grand Narrative and over which scholars were still arguing in the 1990s. Perhaps new populations invading from the north, using new weapons and fighting tactics, were to blame.[2] Whatever the reasons, the inhabitants of Greece fell, or were thrust, into a dark age of subsistence farming and illiteracy that lasted four centuries. Their great palaces were ruined, their gold and their art was lost, their writing became incomprehensible. When a new culture based on cities rather than palaces reappeared with its crafts, commerce, and art centuries later, in what was now the Iron Age, it was a new beginning, unrelated to the past, created by people who had to claw their own way up the gradient of civilization.

Perhaps the most startling of the several phenomenal paradoxes of Greek civilization was that its greatest literary works, the *Iliad* and the *Odyssey*, were also its earliest. These two epic poems, about sixteen thousand and twelve thousand lines long, were composed in a culture without writing, by two, or perhaps only one, poet, whom the Greeks knew as Homer. Literacy began to reappear in Greece around 700 B.C.; the poems appear to be somewhat older. Homer, to give them, or him, the conventional name, thus composed, memorized, and passed on the epics to posterity without writing, perhaps without even knowing what writing was.[3]

The second, almost more astonishing, feature of the *Iliad* and the *Odyssey* is their dramatic sophistication, their quality as stories held together over thousands of lines by major, unifying themes. Other nonliterate cultures had epics; none rivaled the Homeric poems in either skill or sheer size. The archaeological record shows dark age Greece to have been a poor, rural culture without the trappings normally found in cultures that have generated epic poetry. The impression is therefore of works of unsurpassed structural and dramatic complexity appearing literally out of nowhere, and in no time. The language of the poems is also quite extraordinary. Its grammar and phrasing is elaborate, so elaborate that it must have been a language used only for poetry; no one was likely to have spoken it. Homer's vocabulary is enormous, more than twice as large as that of any later Greek poet.

The stories of the poems are stories of the Trojan War, evidently known to all in dark age and classical Greece and imagined by Greeks to have taken place in the remote past, many generations before their own time, whatever that time happened to be. Thanks to Homer, the Trojan War became a founding myth of the literate West as well.[4]

The Trojan War happened because a prince of Troy, Paris, abducted

Helen, the most beautiful woman in the world, from her husband, Menelaus, whose brother Agamemnon was the high king of all the Greeks. To avenge the rape, Agamemnon assembled a vast fleet that included all the Greek heroes: Achilles, Diomedes, Odysseus, Ajax, and many others. For ten years they laid siege to Troy. Many heroes on both sides fell, including the two greatest, Achilles on the Greek side and Hector of Troy, brother to Paris. Finally, the Greeks took the city and restored Helen to her husband.

If the *Iliad* is about war and the pride and emotions of heroes at war, the *Odyssey* is about individual endurance and a struggle to return home, to restore family life after war and separation. The first word of the *Iliad* is "anger," the anger of Achilles that is the axis of the tale. The first word of the *Odyssey* is "man," and the man is Odysseus, the long-suffering and clever hero, who needs his wits and his strength of mind in adversity as much as his fighting skills, if he is to survive hostile gods and monsters and men both stupid and hostile and resume his place as king, husband, and father in Ithaca.

The Homeric epics were instantly recognized as the common patrimony of all Greek speakers. They were learned by heart by professional reciters and were eventually written down. Quotes and allusions to them appear throughout Greek literature, which tells us not only how universally known they were, but that, apart from trivial variations, their text in classical times was the same as that recorded in the medieval manuscripts on which modern printed texts are based.

Having established that the Greeks invented Western literature, the Grand Narrative also asserted that the Greeks invented science and philosophy. These two were in origin the same, being based on wonder about the natural world and the desire to understand it. Two Magic Moments were relevant in the origins of rational thought. On May 28, 585 B.C., a total solar eclipse was visible from the Greek towns of Ionia, the Aegean coastlands of Asia Minor, which at that time was the heartland of archaic Greek civilization. The event caused a sensation because it had been predicted some time before by Thales the Milesian, to whom the Grand Narrative, following Aristotle, gave the honor of being the first natural philosopher, or scientist. Thales believed that water was the primal substance of the universe, from which everything else had emerged. He inaugurated the tradition of Ionian speculation about nature, in the course of which various thinkers proposed various theories about the universe, all of them based on matter and natural causes rather than on conscious, divine intervention. By the mid-fifth century the most advanced Ionian thinkers were going beyond theories of matter to what the modern West would recognize as genuine philosophy, that is, speculation about knowledge itself and about abstract concepts.

The second Magic Moment in the origins of rational thought was the day in 399 B.C. when the Athenians executed Socrates the philosopher for denying the gods and corrupting the young. Unlike the early Ionians, Socrates was less interested in the nature and origins of the universe than in those of human beings, of vice and virtue, ignorance and knowledge. As reported by his pupil Plato, Socrates invented, or developed, a method of talking to people that was designed to make them question their assumptions about what they knew and how they knew it. Most of the concepts, questions, and methods of Western philosophy found their first airing in the dialogues of Socrates. Why should we do good rather than evil? What is the good? What is justice? What is truth? What is beauty? What is meaning? What would a perfect society look like? The answers Socrates proposed, or indicated, were less important than the questions, which no one had asked before. Socrates and his followers sought truth from reason and from the human capacity to reason, and not in the stories and examples of myth and legend.

Fifth-century B.C. Greece, and especially Athens, was the site of other Magic Moments; to no small extent the whole age was one long Magic Moment, and so it was often seen by the Grand Narrative. Literature, founded by Homer, came to fruition in the tragedies of Aeschylus, Sophocles, and Euripides. Representational art, which lay at the core of modern Western identity from the Renaissance to the twentieth century, reached heights never since rivaled in the sculptures of the Parthenon at Athens or the temple of Apollo at Olympia. Philosophy matured in Socrates and culminated, in the fourth century, in Plato and Aristotle. As if all that were not enough, the Greeks also invented democracy and the study of history, and the two were related, just as philosophy and the scientific outlook on nature were related.

The father of history, according to the Grand Narrative, was Herodotus of Halicarnassus, who set out to study and explain the causes of the greatest event of his day, the wars of the Greeks and Persians in the early fifth century B.C., which ended with the astonishing defeat of the vast Persian Empire at the hands of the quarrelsome and outnumbered Greeks. How could this have happened? Because the Greeks, though few, were free, and free men fought better than the slaves of an absolute monarch. Herodotus's explanation of why this was so became a classic text of Western political identity according to the Grand Narrative, just as the Homeric poems became the classic text of Western literature.

Demaratus was a king of Sparta who fell victim to an intrigue at home and therefore went into exile at the Persian court. There were quite a few like him, disappointed men who hoped to ride Persian coattails back to power in their homelands as governors of occupied Greece under Persian control. The Persian wars did not pit Persians against Greeks, but a multi-ethnic Persian army, including many Greeks, against other Greeks, namely, those who did not want to submit. In 480 B.C., the Persian king, Xerxes, led his great army across the Hellespont to Europe. Safely arrived on the European side, the king held muster of his host. Herodotus listed its contingents in a spectacular panorama of empire: Indians, Scythians, Egyptians, Libyans, Medes, Arabs, Assyrians, Ethiopians, and a dozen lesser-known tribes and nations participated in the invasion force. With a sense of drama worthy of Homer, Herodotus did not follow this list of hundreds of thousands of men, in all their ethnic diversity, marching to the command of one man, with a list of the opposing Greek forces. Against the seemingly invincible array on the Persian side stood an idea, and the idea was decisive.

After inspecting his vast army, Xerxes, we are told, asked Demaratus if the Greeks would dare to resist. "I believe that not even if all the Greeks and the rest of the people living in the West were gathered together, would they be able to withstand me in battle, not being united." Alluding to the opulence of the display—Herodotus made a point of noting the rich dress and equipment of the contingents—Demaratus replied that Greece (unlike Persia) was by nature a poor country, and that *arete* (courage, virtue) was the result of the harsh discipline of poverty, wisdom, and strict laws. The Greeks could not afford to take life for granted; it was a struggle, and this struggle taught the Greeks that virtue was necessary. "Using courage and virtue, Greece defends herself against both poverty and subjection." This passage is one of few in ancient Greek literature where the name of the country itself, *Hellas*, is personified.

Xerxes ridiculed this notion. In another dramatic masterstroke, Herodotus let the Persian king and not the Greek exile bring up the next key idea—freedom and its political significance. "If your political life is as you tell me," Xerxes answered, meaning: if you are brave, wise, and law-abiding, and if these qualities make you able to defeat poverty and aggression, then you, as a former king of the exceptionally poor and law-abiding city of Sparta, should be able to defeat twenty men single-handedly, which is absurd. Furthermore, the great king went on, returning to his theme of Greek disunity, the Greeks would not be able to resist, "being all equally free and not commanded by one man." To Xerxes, "free" meant "disorganized." The great king used the words "political" and "free," but Herotodus meant this to be ironic, for Xerxes obviously did not share the Greek understanding of these phrases. The Greeks, being poor, had not the luxury of constructing a rich empire, but rather had to learn virtuous ways to survive. And because these habits of virtue and courage were learned and not inborn, they were, Demaratus implied, the more effective. Demaratus then explained that "though they may be free, they are not free in all things. For above them is a master, the law, which they fear far more than your subjects fear you." And this master commanded them never to flee but "remaining in the ranks, either to win or die."

The word for law was *nomos*, which could mean a regulation or statute. Demaratus, however, was not saying that the Greek cities all had laws forbidding cowardice in battle. He was using the word in its broader sense of fundamental social custom, the political bond that created society and that all members had to learn. To break the bond was to put oneself outside the political community. Nomos was both social and political in a way typically Greek but alien to the modern Western distinction between politics, the sphere of decision, on the one hand, and society, where people found and lived out their values, on the other. To the Greeks, the social was the political, and vice versa.

In constructing this marvelous scene and having it hinge in part on the irony that Xerxes, the despot, spoke of "political life" and "freedom" without knowing what they meant, Herodotus set up the inevitable result of the drama, the defeat of the powerful and opulent Persian army, whose discipline was the result of external coercion and obedience, by the poor and outnumbered Greeks, who fought because they knew they had to and not because they were ordered. The Greek law, or norm, of remaining in the ranks to win or die was stronger than the command of a despot. The Greeks owned themselves freely, and this principle was the foundation also of Athenian democracy, which prevailed for most of the fifth and fourth centuries. It rested on two principles, the right of the male citizens to express their opinions on public matters and their duty to participate in shaping the collective decisions and policies of the city.

The Grand Narrative's idea of Greek democracy as the source of Western democratic virtues and ideals derived from many sources; probably the most famous was a passage from Thucydides, the other father of history, who wrote the story of the Peloponnesian War (431–404 B.C.), in which the two most powerful Greek cities, Athens and Sparta, fought for hegemony. Athens lost and with it ended the golden age of classical civilization. The passage in question was the so-called Funeral Oration of Pericles, the leading Athenian citizen of his time. It was supposedly held at the end of the first year's campaign to honor the Athenian dead. In the speech, Thucydides had Pericles say that he would honor the dead by describing the constitution of their city. "Our forefathers, who have always inhabited this land, by their *arete* (courage and virtue) handed it down in liberty from generation to generation." As in Herotodus, the essential quality of the free man was *arete*, that most characteristic and untranslatable of Greek terms, which connoted skill, strength, personal courage, and the pursuit of excellence in all activities.

Pericles then praised his audience, the present generation, for having worthily received and extended the power of the land handed down to them in liberty by their forefathers. What was the secret of their strength? How had Athens become strong, and what kept her so? The answer was the constitution. "For we live by a constitution that does not seek to rival the laws of our neighbors, since we are rather an example to others than their emulators. And because this constitution is settled on the many rather than on the few it is named *demokratia*," which literally meant "rule by the people." Democracy gave every man a stake in the success of the city and called forth his *arete* in its defense. Because each knew that he was coresponsible for the fate of all, including his own, each would want to do his best. Democracy made men eager to learn so that they could properly take their part in ruling the city and taking the great decisions necessary to protect its power. Not to participate was a betrayal of duty, a kind of treason. "We alone call the man who does not participate not a private man, but a useless one." To hammer home the pervasive theme that democracy made men strong and committed, not weak and dependent, Pericles insisted that "we love beauty without affectation and pursue wisdom without becoming effete." "All in all," he concluded, "our city is the model of instruction for Greece . . . we need no Homer to sing our praises."

Herodotus taught that the Greeks were free because they were poor and few, relative to their enemies. They had to fend for themselves in the most economical fashion and so quickly learned from necessity that the virtue of each was the condition of survival of all. But not all poor societies were free. It was *arete*, virtue in the Greek sense that connoted both acting for the common good and technical skill, that gave Greeks the energy, or, to use a phrase from the 1990s, the social capital to maintain their political freedom and to put it into practice in Athens and some other places in the form of direct democracy.[5] For over two thousand years after Herodotus, political philosophers assumed that democracy or popular government could arise only in small societies without great disparities of wealth, because democracy, until the late eighteenth century, was

defined as direct participation by all citizens, that is, all free adult males, in decisions, and because men were most likely to seek *arete* and display it in conditions where their joint responsibility for security and welfare was obvious, and
where each therefore willingly submitted to the laws that he had personally
helped to pass. Without *arete* popular government was not viable, for in the absence of a recognized ruling class or a despot, chaos would ensue if each pursued his own good and not that of the city.

Not all Greeks or even all Athenians agreed that democracy was a good
thing. Many thought that Xerxes had a point when he equated freedom with
chaos and lack of discipline. In the Peloponnesian War, democratic Athens
lost to militaristic Sparta, and in 338 B.C., all of Greece fell to Philip of
Macedon and his son, Alexander the Great. Alexander defeated and conquered the Persian Empire and launched the Hellenistic age, which lasted
until the Roman Empire, in the first century B.C., swallowed up all the cities
and countries around the Mediterranean. The Grand Narrative found few
Magic Moments in the Hellenistic period, which stood as a sort of afternoon
culture, living off the literature and philosophy of the classical era and
spreading knowledge of Greek civilization eastward into Asia and westward
to Rome, but without great originality of its own.

Such, in outline, was the typical story of the Greeks as told by the Grand
Narrative. It chose episodes and aspects that cumulatively built up an image
of the Greeks as the origins of the West, as the people who invented the fundamental political and intellectual components of the liberal Western identity: democracy, philosophy, curiosity about nature and ethics, civic virtue,
and the critical study of history as the study of how the past created the
present. The narrative did not make these aspects up, but by choosing them
rather than others and by suggesting continuity from ancient Greece to
the modern West, it presupposed what a proper historical investigation
would first have to show, that the West began in ancient Greece. And before
such an investigation could begin, it would have to determine what was
meant by the West. The narrative rarely came to grips with that question,
which was one reason that it remained, at best, misleading and deceptive. It
suggested that it was the liberal West of post–Enlightenment values, of economic development, political equality, human rights, science, and technology that was evolving through history, starting with the Greeks. In fact there
was no such one-directional evolution. Nor did the narrative allow for fundamental changes in Western identity. Finally, the idea that the West began in
Greece misrepresented not only the history of Western identity, but that of
Greek civilization.

The Grand Narrative's West, the New West, did not begin in Greece, and the Greeks were not the first Westerners. Where, then, did this core notion of the narrative come from?

The modern Western cult of Greece began in the Enlightenment, but its basic idea, that the ancient Greeks were models of thought and action, was as old as Greece itself. The most fervent proponents of Greek perfection, however, were not the Greeks themselves but the Romans, who throughout their history believed themselves culturally inferior to Greece. This inferiority was not assuaged when Rome conquered Greece in the second century B.C.; on the contrary, it got worse. In 200 B.C., the Romans began that conquest by declaring that they would protect Greece, and especially Athens, against Macedonian aggression. The Roman conquest of Greece thus began as an act of cultural homage that need not have been hypocritical, for Romans felt no need to justify other conquests. Four years later, in 196, the Roman general Flamininus took a break from campaigning in Greece and appeared at the Isthmian Games, where he spoke fervently for Greek freedom, using the language of Herodotus. His point was that the responsibility for helping the Greeks to maintain their freedom against despots who would enslave them had now fallen to Rome, as a solemn and demanding duty. In the late first century B.C., the poet Horace summarized the Roman sense of what Greece meant when he wrote of the Roman conquest that "captive Greece captured her savage victor and brought civilization to rustic Latium."

For the next three centuries, the cult and imitation of Greek language, style, and philosophy—philhellenism—dominated education and literature for the elite of the Roman Empire. Wealthy Romans wrote and thought in Greek, much as the political elite of early modern Europe wrote and thought in French, and just as nobles and rich men of the seventeenth and eighteenth centuries took the grand tour of France and Italy, so did rich and powerful Romans go on what amounted to cultural pilgrimages to Greece. But the cultural traffic was not entirely one way. Greek thought and ideas dominated Rome but were also transformed by the encounter. Stoicism, for example, which said that only the virtuous man can be truly happy, spread throughout the Roman upper classes and turned out to be the ideal philosophy for the ruling class of a multinational, continent-spanning empire. It was a Stoic who first invented the term *cosmopolitan*.

Philhellenism reached a high point in the writings of Plutarch, who lived around A.D. 100. This humane and kindly man was the ideal exponent of the gentle and optimistic hope of his age for "a partnership between Greece, the educator, and Rome, the great power, and of the compatibility of the two loyalties."[6] His most famous works, the *Parallel Lives* of leading Greek and Roman public figures, became instant classics and, when translated in the Renaissance into Western languages, inspired thinkers and writers from Shakespeare to Emerson and statesmen from Cromwell to Washington. The point of the *Lives* was to reveal character and its role in public affairs. But he wrote much else, including treatises of popular philosophy and ethics on such subjects as "Friends and Flatterers," "The Control of Anger," "Rules for Politicians," and "Advice on Marriage." In some ways he was the Will Durant of his era, in his range and appeal; a good writer with a comforting, somewhat paternal style that made the reader feel safe and well guided and not condescended to, immensely learned, with strong yet not obtrusive views on ethics and politics, and in harmony with his age, which he trusted was proceeding steadily toward greater virtue and understanding.

After the empire fell apart in the fifth and sixth centuries A.D., Greek learning and culture were lost in the West, even though the West's new religion, Christianity, had come originally from the Greek-speaking East. The last philhellenist was Isidore of Seville in Spain, a seventh-century encyclopedist who still read Greek and who, in his Latin work known as the *Etymologies*, saved countless bits of pagan lore for posterity. A few works of Plato and Aristotle also survived in Latin versions or commentaries. Apart from these examples, known to the few who were literate, Greece and Greek culture were almost entirely unknown during those centuries, when the Western synthesis of classical and Christian culture took place.

The monks who were in charge of what education was available knew little or no Greek and had little desire to know more. Greek learning and literature were pagan, and should therefore be treated with caution. It was enough to have Plato's mystical works, which could be said to point forward to Christian truth, and Aristotle's treatises on logic. Furthermore, the Christian Greeks of the present time—that is, of the sixth century and later—were, from the Western perspective, disturbingly inclined to heresy. Whether pagan or Christian, therefore, Greek civilization faded from Western knowledge at the very time that the West achieved its identity.

Starting in the thirteenth century, Western thinkers rediscovered a broader range of ancient Greek thought when complete Latin versions of Plato and Aristotle became available, some translated directly from Greek and others, including some of the most important works, translated from Arabic versions and commentaries. But this renaissance was restricted, overwhelmingly, to Latin editions and to philosophy. Greek historians, poets, artists, and writers other than Plato and Aristotle remained known only to a few, and later medieval Europe knew nothing like the philhellenism of the Roman Empire. Its first tentative return was the work of a few Renaissance scholars who, breaking, at some risk, with Christian orthodoxy, reconstituted the cult of Greece as the source of true wisdom, philosophy, political insight, historical method, and scientific speculation. This renewed interest in Greece was restricted to a few circles, notably that of Marsilio Ficino in Florence. Apart from him and his friends, most of the European scholars, poets, and theologians of the Renaissance and Reformation eras who looked to the ancient world for inspiration looked to Rome and to Latin, not to Athens and to Greek.

Many scholars in the next three centuries learned Greek and began recovering the complete range of ancient Greek literature, philosophy, history, theology, and medical writings. The scholars of that era, the era of the Christian and monarchical West of the old regimes of Europe, saw the Greeks as remarkable and interesting, but never as exemplars or ancestors. They were, after all, pagan, and one of the basic points about Greek philosophy, history, and literature, as far as the antiquarian scholars of the old regime were concerned, was that they were alien and distant, superseded by Christianity. It was this distance that made the work of recovery both difficult and valuable.

The study of ancient Greece flourished in the English Renaissance, both before and after the Reformation, but then gave way to the rising tide of Puritanism and doctrinal debate within Anglicanism that led to the English Civil War. From the early seventeenth to the late eighteenth century the colleges of Oxford and Cambridge, with a few shining exceptions, were largely forgotten backwaters where a few lucky and lazy men lived indolent and well-fed lives without any thought of the original, medieval obligations of prayer, learning, and worship that used to be the counterpart of privilege.

From the Reformation onward the college had been an anomaly. Its original purpose was devotional. The Reformation took away that purpose but permitted the college to survive, mainly as a training center for Protestant clergy. This did not fill the gap left when the medieval order dissolved. Hence the purposeless drifting of the eighteenth century. When classical scholarship arrived on the scene, renovated and rejuvenated by the Germans, it filled the need left by the religious void. Nineteenth-century fellows were still like monks; they remained celibate and had to conform to Anglican doctrine. Now they had, again, a real source of worship and meaning in their lives: ancient Greece as interpreted by the new scholarship became an ersatz religion. Greece was adopted by the modern West as, in part, a replacement for Christianity. This was not the actual Greece of two thousand five hundred years ago, however, but the Greece re-created by adoring scholars, mostly in Germany and England, starting around 1770.

The modern cult of Greece started in Germany, when the religious and political foundations of the old regime began to crumble. The two men most responsible for starting it were Johann Joachim Winckelmann and Johann Wolfgang von Goethe, the former the founder of modern art history and the second the universal genius of German literature and romantic philosophy, the "last concentration of the Western spirit."[7]

Goethe believed that Christianity was declining and wanted to create a new religion for a free, natural humanity. The ancient Greeks, as the most natural of all people, became the key to this new religion. Where the antiquarians had spent much effort in showing that pagan religion anticipated or paralleled Christianity, Goethe and his followers rejected such efforts as irrelevant or demeaning to the Greeks. For Goethe, the point about the Greeks was precisely that they were not Christian, but something other, different, and better, and that it was necessary to find and describe this true character of the Greeks to see how they, in fact, were both the origins of civilization and the model for a new civilization of the West beyond Christianity. It was a short step from this view to what a British scholar early in the twentieth century called "the tyranny of Greece over Germany," and to the almost religious piety with which many classicists over the years regarded the object of their studies. The source of this worship, however, was not Goethe but Winckelmann.

Johann Joachim Winckelmann was born in 1717 as the son of a poor cobbler in the country town of Stendal in the Mark Brandenburg, north of Berlin. Through his own efforts he became a Greek scholar and an admirer of ancient art. This was not easy in rural Germany of the mid-eighteenth century. Since the Thirty Years' War of 1618–48, much of Germany had been an impoverished cultural wasteland. Greek texts were hard to find, tutors even scarcer, and libraries with books by classical authors or studies of the ancient world were virtually nonexistent. The teaching of classics that came into being partly as a result of Winckelmann's work hardly existed. Nevertheless, in the 1760s, after years of humble existence as a private tutor, he got himself to Italy, where his encounter with actual relics of Greek art had, to him, the force of a divine encounter. Reflecting on his first view of the so-called *Apollo of Belvedere*, a work of Leochares, Winckelmann reported: "In that first instant, I was, as it were, torn away and removed to a holy grove, and I thought I was seeing the god himself, as he appeared to mortals."[8] He defined the purpose of his aesthetic task as "pursuing the thought of beauty . . . to awaken a poetic beauty for myself."

Winckelmann was the opposite of a naive aesthete, although such phrases taken out of context may give that impression. He had struggled hard and overcome great challenges to see for himself the visible evidence of the world he had glimpsed in Greek poetry and myth back home in Brandenburg. He had decided earlier that what the Greeks had written had already been thoroughly understood and interpreted by others; there was nothing left for him to accomplish in philological or literary erudition. That left their physical legacy in works of art. "For art is not exhausted," he wrote. He arrived in Rome expecting to be overwhelmed, and expecting also to learn the universal nature of art from the ancients.

The works he saw in Rome were, with very few exceptions, not originals. The *Apollo of Belvedere*, for example, was a second-century B.C. copy of Leochares' lost sculpture of about 350 B.C.. The elites of Rome, like those of Germany after Winckelmann, worshipped Greece and ordered copies of the masterpieces of Phidias, Praxiteles, Lysippus, Leochares, and others. There was thus plenty of Greek art in Rome, much of it discovered and collected in the three centuries before Winckelmann, though almost all of it was in Hellenistic or Roman copies made after the time of Alexander the Great (336–323 B.C.). Scholars, and Winckelmann above all, learned to distinguish good copies from bad and to discern the canons of genuine Greek art by which they could judge how close the copies were. Most important, Winckelmann unerringly analyzed what to him and his followers was the timeless essence of Greek art, and its importance for his own age.

Winckelmann's appreciation of Greek art rested on two doctrines that had a vast influence on later art history. The first was that art could not be naively understood by an act of intuitive appropriation. Such an act must be followed by intellectual analysis and explanation. If you could not rise through your emotions to the "elevated point of view" and explain what the work of art represented, how it accomplished its effect, and what it conveyed both about its subject and the culture that it came from, you had not understood it.[9]

The second doctrine was the teaching that Greek art was uniquely capable of expressing nature, which primarily meant human emotions and human beauty, "the highest final goal and focal point of art." All artists aimed at beauty: "the greatest artists of the Greeks, who necessarily saw themselves as new creators, although they worked less for the mind than for the senses, tried to overcome the hard reality of their raw material and, if possible, to infuse it with spirit." Because beauty was their goal, they represented each subject, human or beast, male or female, mortal or divine, according to the law of that subject's highest potentiality. Unlike Christian religious art, which was always symbolic, whatever its degree of representational realism, Greek art sought the most beautiful presentation of the thing itself, and not of something beyond that thing.

Winckelmann also had an explanation for why the Greeks were able to accomplish this translation of beauty into bronze and stone: their political freedom. This was equivalent to Herodotus's idea that the Greeks defeated the Persians in 480 B.C. because they were free, and because Greek freedom was the key to Greek courage and realism about life. Winckelmann drew a connection between political freedom in Greece and Greek realism, which he interpreted as truthfulness to nature. The Greeks, he said, put nature above reflection. This did not make them savage brutes; on the contrary. Preferring immediate nature to thought, in Greek civilization, was to seek truth, in particular the truth of emotions expressed by the human body. The sculptor Lysippus, for example, "on his path . . . went toward perfection in art: this path is to seek the source itself and return to the beginning, in order to find truth pure and unmixed. The source and beginning in art is nature herself." The idea that nature held truth, and that seeking nature raised you up rather than thrust you down, as Christian doctrine might suggest, likewise appealed to Goethe and was a central ingredient of the cult of Greece.

Winckelmann's worship of Greece found a ready audience among the crop of young, gifted, intense poets and philosophers that emerged in the 1780s and 1790s, possibly the most talented and astonishing literary generation in all of Western history, including Goethe's younger friend Friedrich Schiller, the philosophers Georg Wilhelm Friedrich Hegel and Johann Gottlieb Fichte, the visionary poet Friedrich Hölderlin, and the two founders of tragic romanticism, Heinrich von Kleist and Friedrich von Hardenberg, known as Novalis. By a historical accident, the French invasion of the 1790s touched a Germany that was politically weak and disorganized but culturally at its peak. The response of this formidable generation, immersed for twenty years already in the worship of ancient Greece, was bound to have profound repercussions.

Goethe, developing his own philosophy of nature, agreed that the Greeks were the most natural, the most truly human of people, and that Greek culture was the archetype of all human cultural endeavor. Because of his vast influence as national poet and wise man of Germany, Goethe was, as the classicist Hugh Lloyd-Jones put it, "more than any other individual . . . responsible for the immense energy devoted to classical studies by Germany during the nineteenth century."[10] This "immense energy" began in what Lloyd-Jones called the "second Renaissance" that began in Germany not long after Winckelmann's death and was due, in large part, to his writings.[11] The first Renaissance of the fifteenth century drew on ancient Rome and on Latin; the second on the Greeks. It was not until this second Renaissance that classical scholarship, and especially Greek scholarship, replaced philosophy as the queen of the humanities and reigned supreme for a century.

Goethe himself was never a classical scholar, but a poet and an esoteric philosopher with a cosmic range of interests and sympathies who found inspiration and confirmation of his own deepest beliefs in Greek art and poetry. In his own writings, Goethe sought always to define and convey the natural, "original essence" (*Urwesen*) or "original form" (*Urform*) of any aspect of life, whether physical or emotional. In the Greeks he saw a people for whom this "original essence" of things was always present and immediate, so that their art, poetry, and philosophy represented the human body, emotions, feelings, actions, and aspirations with total fidelity to their essential nature. And, as he said, creating art and poetry faithful in this exalted way to nature, using the necessary creative laws of nature and not "arbitrary, made-up, artificial" rules, to recognize and follow nature's rules in this manner, was "to be God."[12]

When Goethe spoke of following nature's laws, he was not speaking of Newton's or Kepler's laws of motion, gravity, and the behavior of material objects, the kind of natural law most modern Westerners think of as the basis of science. In Goethe's thought, nature was alive, capable of transforming the observer and of being transformed by him. Nature and the self were not distinct but interactive, and their interaction was God, or at least partook of the divine essence. The foundation and beginning of all such deep knowledge of nature was the kind of informed admiration that Winckelmann applied to the *Apollo of Belvedere* when he deliberately moved from awe through his "exalted point of view" to a state where he both grasped the essence of the work and was transformed by it in an act intellectual, emotional, and mystical.

Winckelmann and Goethe expressed in their philosophy of beauty, art, and nature one of the points where the esoteric West and its traditions of secret knowledge and inner transformation met and influenced the exoteric West of public identity. Together, they laid the foundation of over a century's cult of Greece.

The tyranny of Greece over Germany that began in the 1770s had its counterpart in a Roman tyranny over France, which became politically significant during the French Revolution that began in 1789 but began far earlier. The playwright Pierre Corneille, starting in the 1630s, taught the French aristocracy to compare itself to the virtuous, modest, pious, and patriotic heroes and heroines of early Rome. During the reign of Louis XIV in the second half of the seventeenth century classicism, defined as a cult of Roman ideals and imagery, dominated aristocratic French culture and that of the vast court at Versailles. Louis liked to portray himself as a Roman emperor who had stilled the passions and enmities of civil war and who brought glory to his country by winning foreign victories. Classicism of this kind faded from view after Louis's death in 1715, and when the revolution brought back a cult of Rome, it was with a radically changed emphasis. The revolutionaries sought models in the intense patriotism and virtuous frugality of early Rome, as represented by later historians. The Rome that dominated the political imaginations of a Marat or a Maximilien Robespierre was not the opulent, world-spanning empire of the Caesars, but the small, mobilized, and threatened city-state of the early republic. Two traditions of early Rome seemed directly relevant and inspiring to the revolutionaries: the tradition of how the Romans won their liberty and expelled their oppressive king, and the tradition of how the resulting republic again and again defended itself victoriously against overwhelming odds, thanks to its virtue, that is, the devotion and courage of its citizens. This ethos of sacrifice and of the mutual bond of patriotic solidarity that the revolutionaries saw in early Rome was to them a model for how their own national community should forget all divisions and stand together to win its own freedom and defend it against enemies both foreign and domestic. In 1792, when a Parisian mob lynched hundreds of priests and other religious prisoners in the so-called September Massacres to cries of *vive la Patrie*, Robespierre justified the killings by quoting Cicero: "The Republic killed them in order not to fall by their hands."[13] The radical Saint-Just demanded in 1793 that "revolutionaries must be Romans!" meaning that they must learn to act with the same ruthless will to preserve the state and the same disregard of personal feelings as the legendary figures of Roman history who sacrificed their own sons if required by the public good.

When Napoleon Bonaparte dissolved the revolutionary government and took power for himself in 1799, he called himself "consul," the title of the prime magistrate of the Roman Republic. When he had himself crowned emperor of the French in 1804, he downplayed the role of pope and Church and stressed the Roman imagery of the event, insisting, just as had Augustus in 27 B.C., that he was emperor by popular will and acclamation, and that his mission was to bring law, clarity, and order to a Europe riven by strife and conflict. Painting his progress in Roman colors permitted Napoleon to assert that, like Augustus, he was not ending the republic but simply continuing it in the only way possible.

The French cult of Rome provoked reactions in those countries that felt the brunt of French expansion in the revolutionary and Napoleonic wars from 1792 to 1814. In both Britain and Germany, the Roman models invoked by Robespierre and Napoleon to justify their policies enhanced the prestige of Greece, already growing thanks to the writings of Winckelmann and Goethe. In Britain, people compared their struggle against Napoleon to the Greek struggle against the Persians and insisted that the final British victory against great odds was due, as was the Greek victory, to the superior morale and commitment of a free people. The reasons people turned to Greece in Germany were somewhat different. Unlike Britain, Germany had been defeated and overrun by the French. Germany in the 1790s, when the wars began, was not, like Britain, a cohesive national state with a single center of government. The Germans were divided among hundreds of states, provinces, and principalities, and between two religions, Catholic and Protestant. The French conquests thus produced not a national resistance movement but rather fragmentation, ignominious squabbling, and unseemly opportunism. Those German princes who escaped French occupation were only too eager to exploit the condition of their less fortunate colleagues.

The situation in Germany in 1807, after the first wave of French attacks, reminded scholars such as the young Barthold Niebuhr of Greece in the face of the Macedonian invasion of 338 B.C. and of the Roman onslaughts of the second century. This was not surprising. For two decades, German literary culture had been thoroughly Hellenized. "The Germans," wrote the linguist and political philosopher Wilhelm von Humboldt, "possess the undeniable merit of being the first to have justly and profoundly understood Greek civilization."[14] Because the Germans had so well understood Greece—because, as Humboldt claimed, they had a unique affinity for Greece—it was not a big jump to saying that, in effect, the Germans *were* the Greeks; they represented, as it were, the Greeks to modern Europe. Goethe had defined the Greeks as the perfect incarnations of natural humanity; if the Germans were the Greeks of today, that must mean that they, too, were perfect incarnations of natural humanity. This was precisely the conclusion drawn by Fichte in his *Addresses to the German Nation* of 1807, in which he sought to revive the spirits of his Prussian countrymen, downcast by Napoleon's victories, by telling them that they had a universal mission to save humanity that far exceeded the deceptive glitter of the French Revolution or Napoleon. The German mission was to bring moral enlightenment through universal education. Only the Germans could carry out this mission, for the Germans were the universal, the absolute, the most natural of all nations.

In his youth, Fichte had constructed the archetypal romantic philosophy, which saw the self-conscious individual as the center and sum of all reality. The poet Hölderlin became passionately committed to this idea, which he interpreted to mean that the vision of the enlightened poet was the means by which the individual could become free and aware. Hölderlin combined this poetic and metaphysical individualism with a passionate love of Greece; indeed, he was perhaps the purest exponent of the cult of Greece. To Hölderlin, Greek antiquity, especially the archaic age, was the golden dawn of the human race, when all things were knowable and the poetic imagination possessed unlimited creative power. The Greeks, so he claimed, were uniquely able to combine clarity and passion, what a later German thinker, Friedrich Nietzsche, was to name the Apollonian and the Dionysiac elements. According to Hölderlin, the Greeks, beginning with Homer, never had to struggle to express passion, for it was native to them; therefore, their energies were free to combine passion with "Western clarity." Since the Germans lacked this gift, it was their duty to study the Greeks, for only by doing so would they complete their own true nature.

The romantic individualism of Goethe, Fichte, and especially Hölderlin stimulated an extraordinarily intense, almost religious philhellenism. In his verse, Hölderlin invoked the power of Greece to save humanity, while at the same time lamenting the distance that now separated modern man from antiquity, when the gods walked the earth and spoke to poets:

Blessed Greece! Home of all the immortals,
Is it true, then, what we heard in our youth?
Hall of feasting! Its floor is the ocean! Its tables the mountains!
Built truly from of old for one purpose only!

But where are the thrones and the temples, and where are the beakers
of nectar,
Where, to pleasure the gods, is the joy of song?
Where, where do they glisten, those words that strike from a distance?
Delphi sleeps—none hears the echo of fate . . .
Ah friend! We come too late. The gods may yet live,
But far over our heads, high above us, in another world.[15]

Unlike Fichte, Hölderlin remained a fervent supporter of the French Revolution, which he interpreted in the spirit of Jean-Jacques Rousseau as the
promise of universal liberation. The revolution heralded a "second antiquity," a renaissance of natural man. Hölderlin proclaimed in his verse that
the gates of creation had been opened again, that man would one day walk
again the path of Greece.

Unfortunately, Hölderlin went insane before he convinced the world of
his message. In one of his last and greatest poems he suggested that the time
of renewal was very close, that the final crisis was imminent:

Close at hand and hard to grasp is the god.
But where danger is, there also grows that
Which can save us.
In darkness live the eagles, and fearlessly
The sons of the Alps march over the chasm
On lightly-built bridges.
And, as they are circled round about
By the summits of time, and the dearest ones
Live close by, resting on
The far-separated peaks,
Give us then water without blame,
O give us wings, give us the power
To cross over and to return, faithful in spirit.[16]

Hölderlin's gentle tolerance extended to the radical revolutionaries in France,
who modeled their revolution and their empire not so much on the Greeks
as on the Romans. To him, this French cult of Rome was additional evidence
that a second dawn of antiquity was breaking. Most of his compatriots took a
different view, putting themselves in the place of the defeated Greeks suffering under a Roman yoke.

With the exception of Hölderlin, German thinkers and poets saw themselves as Greek victims of Roman imperialism. This parallelism strengthened

the tyranny of Greece over Germany and ultimately gave further impetus to scholarship on Greece. But unlike the scholarship of Britain, the German interest in Greece was to discover the causes of Greek political decline to prevent a similar fate from overtaking Germany. In particular, historians explored the reasons for the Greek failure to organize nationally against foreign enemies. This focus often led to a contempt for the Athenian democracy, since ancient Greek writers themselves, notably Plato, had suggested that democracy was a hindrance to effective governance in war and therefore to victory. The lessons drawn were obvious: national cohesion, martial vigor, athletic training, and indoctrination of youth, or keep your powder dry and never trust the French.

The Germans' favorite Greek historian was Thucydides. While it was true that Thucydides had Pericles of Athens argue that democracy made men brave, determined, and patriotic, his brilliant record of the Peloponnesian War between Sparta and Athens (431–404 B.C.) was also an insidious indictment of how democracy could go wrong. That indictment was followed by the mainstream of German classicists, culminating in the pro-Spartan bias of Julius Beloch in the 1890s and Helmut Berve in the 1930s. Beloch, normally a precise historian who never believed anything a source told him unless he could confirm it, took the general view that regular wars were necessary if a society was to remain vigorous. That Athens lost the war against Sparta proved that the Athenians had become soft: too much democracy had sapped their martial spirit. Berve, a quiet and studious man who would not have lasted long in boot camp, based his history of Greece on the premise that it was the Spartans and their militarism, not Athenian democracy, that was most truly Greek and thus contained the finest lessons for posterity. That posterity, in Berve's own time, was the National Socialist regime of Germany, which he praised as the true successor to Sparta and the veritable embodiment of Greece.

According to Thucydides, Athens lost the war because the citizens, after Pericles' death, listened to demagogues who promised riches and easy victories. Democracy, he implied, degenerated into policy by popular whim unless controlled by an authoritative leader, such as Pericles. By contrast, Herodotus was more popular in Britain, because his history of the Persian War (490–479 B.C.) was also a paean to liberty. Herodotus, as we saw, held that the reason a few Greek city-states could defeat the massed hordes of an empire was that the citizens of Greece were fighting for freedom and as free men, whereas the soldiers of the Persian Empire were fighting under compulsion and as slaves. This was what many Greeks thought at the time of the

Persian Wars. The playwright Aeschylus wrote *The Persians* in 472; it was unique among Greek tragedies in its contemporary setting. Its theme is the hubris of the Persians, leading to their surprise defeat by the outnumbered Greeks, who go into battle with this war-cry:

> O sons of the Greeks, go
> Free your country, free your children, your women
> The shrines of your ancestral gods
> And the tombs of your forefathers. You are fighting for everything now.

The analogy to Britain's stand against Napoleon was too clear to miss.[17]

The Germans had little use for Herodotus. He was an optimist, and they considered themselves rational pessimists, at least in politics. Democracy was a dangerous gamble, especially if you lived in the middle of a continent, as they did, with borders open to enemies on all sides. If German classicists took anything from Herodotus, it was not his account of freedom, but his account of how poverty and strict laws made a people martial, heroic, and able to defeat superior forces. That Herodotus directly linked poverty and laws to civic virtue and liberty was not emphasized by those academics who came to dominate the study and teaching of classics in the later nineteenth century. Rather, as the century proceeded, the cult of Greece as the cult of natural man became, by degrees, the cult of physical courage and energy as the true legacy of Greece, as displayed, for example, by the last stand of Leonidas and the three hundred Spartans in the pass of Thermopylae. To Herodotus, this sacrifice saved Greek freedom by giving the Athenians time to evacuate their city and assemble their fleet. To men like Beloch and Berve, it was not so much Greek freedom as the Greek nation that Leonidas and his men saved. Gradually, the idea of the nation as a collective entity, morally superior to the individual, replaced Goethe's and Hölderlin's natural man as the focus of German philhellenism.

An important stage on the road from Goethe to these martial pessimists occurred in 1872, when the young Friedrich Nietzsche, twenty-eight years old and recently appointed professor of classics at the University of Basel in Switzerland, published his first major work, *The Birth of Tragedy from the Spirit of Music*. Although he was still, at the time, writing as a professor, Nietzsche's purpose in *The Birth of Tragedy* was not scholarly. It was, in the words of Michael Tanner, to try to answer the question, "How can existence be made bearable, once we grasp what it is really like?"[18] In *The Birth of*

Tragedy, Nietzsche attacked the optimistic rationalism associated with the Athenian democracy of the later fifth century B.C. and with the progressive political doctrines—liberalism, socialism—of his own day. Optimistic rationalism was a lie about reality and therefore more unbearable and certainly more unacceptable than the truth. But the truth was also unbearable and had to be presented and partly concealed in art to be heard. "Human kind," as T. S. Eliot, in some ways a good Nietzschean, was to write much later, "cannot bear very much reality."[19] In a later note, Nietzsche wrote that "my first book was devoted to the relation of art to truth. The *Birth of Tragedy* believes in art against the background of another belief: that it is not possible to live with truth, and that the 'will to truth' is already a symptom of decadence."[20]

Nietzsche's diagnosis of culture is fundamental to any substantive discussion of the crisis of the modern West. First, he meant it literally that "it is not possible to live with truth." This being so, any attempt to get at the truth about existence was necessarily dishonest because no one really wanted to find it. Nietzsche's chief example was Christianity, which purported to tell the truth about life, but in reality undermined health and confidence. The search for truth was also pathological because a healthy society would not concern itself with something that would weaken it. Therefore, only late societies in the grip of decline, such as Nietzsche considered his own time, would place a supreme value on finding "the truth." Finally, the "will to truth" often concealed agendas of power, because those who could define the terms of truth in a society were by definition its rulers.[21]

Nietzsche saw Greek civilization as shaped fundamentally by the contrast between the two gods Apollo and Dionysus—the god of clarity, art, and culture on the one hand, and the god of ecstasy, abandon, and primal nature on the other. The Apollonian experience was contemplative, calm, tranquil. It sought to create and enjoy a "world of beautiful appearance as a release from [the struggle of] becoming." The epics of Homer and the wisdom of Socrates, and the aesthetic emotions they evoked in the reader, reflected this Apollonian principle.

The Apollonian impulse was balanced, in Greek culture, by the Dionysiac. The Apollonian tendency tried to overcome the struggle and pain of becoming in an aesthetic resolution; the Dionysiac expressed the pain of becoming "actively, with subjective feeling, as the raging lust of the creator, who also knows the fury of the destroyer." Apollonian desire wanted, like Winckelmann, to preserve forever moments of beauty; Dionysiac desire knew and wanted change and the constant ebb and flow of creation and destruction.

Nietzsche found the Dionysiac element in the ecstatic and orgiastic experience of tragic drama as performed in the annual festivals that were held in honor of the god Dionysus. "Tragic art, rich in both forms of experience, is defined [in my book] as the reconciliation of Apollo and Dionysus: by the grace of Dionysus we see the deep significance of the [beautiful] vision, but that vision is also denied, and denied with *pleasure . . . Dionysiac bliss reaches its apex in the destruction of even the most beautiful vision.*"[22] In short, the one could not exist without the other; Greek culture was not, as George Grote held, fundamentally rational and therefore a fitting inspiration for Victorian Britain; it was a necessary mixture of the rational and the ecstatic, for only such a mixture allowed the human being to endure the truth of life. At the festivals of Dionysus, the citizens of Athens entered a world beyond the clarity of day, in which the art of the tragedies performed on the stage allowed them to glimpse the truth in the only way tolerable. Thus, Greek civilization in its balance of Apolline and Dionysiac elements permitted, in Eliot's words,

> both a new world
> And the old made explicit, understood
> In the completion of its partial ecstasy,
> The resolution of its partial horror.[23]

These lines aptly summarized Nietzsche's sense of the world and the function of art, especially Greek art, in making it tolerable. All culture and art aimed at beauty, but, as Rilke wrote not long after Nietzsche,

> Beauty is nothing
> But the beginning of terror, which we are still just able to endure
> And we are so awed by it because it serenely disdains to annihilate us.[24]

This beauty, inspiring awe and fear in the beholder, was, to Nietzsche, the necessary core of art.

The Birth of Tragedy provoked outrage among classicists, many of whom thought he had insulted the Greeks horribly. Nietzsche was just as eager as any member of Humboldt's generation to see the Greeks as the pinnacle of perfection and the models of the West; it was just that his particular Magic Moment was the Festivals of Dionysus, when Apollonian and Dionysiac came together to provide cathartic relief. To Nietzsche, Greek culture was "the highest affirmation of the world and of existence ever achieved on earth." The Greeks "tried to interpret the final secrets of the fate of the soul . . . through their Dionysiac experiences." He condemned Winckelmann and

Goethe for their naive "immodesty" in claiming to have understood the Greeks; only he, Nietzsche, had arrived at such profound understanding. To do so, one had first to "overcome all Christianity through a super-Christianity, because Christian teaching was the opposite of the Dionysiac." Only then could one "reconquer southern [that is, Mediterranean] health and the hidden, southern powers of the spirit and become . . . truly Greek, for Greece was the first great linkage and synthesis of everything Oriental and thereby also the beginning of the European soul."[25]

In the hundred years since Winckelmann, classical scholarship had moved from worship to science. *The Birth of Tragedy* may have thus been pathbreaking as philosophy, but it was reactionary as history. It retained a Magic Moment view of the Greeks at a time when philologists, historians of law and custom, and archaeologists had been busy for decades collecting, analyzing, and publishing the actual evidence surviving from the ancient world, and what they were discovering did not always resemble what Winckelmann and Humboldt had so admired.

Nietzsche's most important antagonist in the controversy was a man who, although four years younger than he, was already on his way to becoming the greatest classical scholar of his generation, possibly of all time: Ulrich von Wilamowitz-Moellendorf. Wilamowitz, who had attended the same school as Nietzsche, was a Prussian aristocrat with an aristocrat's contempt for bourgeois values and customs. His abilities as a teacher and scholar were legendary, as was his Prussian work ethic; he published fifty-two books in addition to hundreds of articles.[26] And the books were not pamphlets or think-pieces; some of them were multivolume works and reflected intense and time-consuming philological scholarship, all of it done in the days before research assistants. Not that assistants would have been any use to Wilamowitz; his writings all rested on his own, unique and comprehensive knowledge of ancient Greek literature.

In 1872, the young Wilamowitz produced his one and only venture into polemics, an attack on *The Birth of Tragedy* consisting of two biting and sarcastic pamphlets that accused Nietzsche of falsifying history and presenting an image of the Greeks that owed little to Greece and almost everything to what Wilamowitz considered Nietzsche's pathological compulsion to derive his own "irreligious religion" from that of the Greeks. Nietzsche in the end had a greater impact on the world than Wilamowitz, and it was Nietzsche's followers who got to write the story of nineteenth-century philosophy, and they portrayed Wilamowitz as an insensitive bigot.

Wilamowitz spanned the gap between the world of midcentury scholarship and that of Oswald Spengler. He despised the search for Magic Moments and devoted his life to showing that the Greeks were much like anyone else. The way to understand them was not to construct false images for worship, but to know them as broadly as possible. The Greeks, in his view, were not semidivine, neither were they incomprehensibly alien. Yet, contrary to his wishes, Wilamowitz's work helped open the crevasse between the Greeks and the West and thereby to justify relativism, Spenglerian gloom, and the twentieth-century battle over the West. How this could be is clear from his last work on Greek religion, which he all but completed on his deathbed in the fall of 1931.

That final book, which Wilamowitz—old, ill, and suffering from the death of his son in combat in 1914—conceived as summing up his own faith as well as that of the Greeks, was a paradoxical mixture of scholarship and reverence. Wilamowitz had stated a few years earlier that his own religion was that of Plato, a firm faith in a supernatural reality of the good, the beautiful, and love. Platonic religion was without clergy or churches; Wilamowitz was as anticlerical as George Grote. Since he himself despised religious practice, he felt free to ignore the vast majority of recorded manifestations of Greek religiosity. His subject was not what most Greeks believed; rather, he described how the divine and heroic myths that formed the matter of epic and tragic poetry evolved, and how Plato and later philosophers went beyond these myths to create an even more perfect faith. The only way to understand this "faith of the Greeks," according to Wilamowitz, was to recreate it in oneself, "to believe as they believed."[27] But by turning himself into a virtual Greek to demonstrate what ancient Greek faith was, Wilamowitz produced an odd, if also magnificent, book about some people who, in Western terms, were quite evidently alien.

The tyranny of Greece over Europe and America reached its apogee in the years before World War I.[28] Thanks in large part to Winckelmann and Goethe, the young of the elite studied Greek and Latin, modeled themselves on what they conceived to be the passions and ambitions of ancient statesmen, philosophers, and poets, and built their houses and often their very lifestyles on what they thought would have appealed to a Plato, an Aristotle, or a Cicero. Most of them would have agreed that the modern, late-Victorian West was indeed the heir and pupil of antiquity. World War I put an end to liberal optimism, but it did not discredit the idea that the West descended from the Greeks. On the contrary, it was during World War I that American educators first came up with the idea of teaching a Grand Narrative of the West, starting with the Greeks, as the foundation of mass higher education. Ironically, it was just before World War I that the first serious blow was launched against the idea of the West as the child of Greece.

Shortly before World War I, an obscure mathematician named Oswald Spengler, who had failed to get the academic teaching position he hoped for, completed the first version of the book that, after World War I, was to revolutionize thinking about the West. This book, *The Decline of the West*, was not written as a comment on the suicidal war of 1914–18 but as a wide-ranging diagnosis of Western civilization as it appeared in its heyday before that war began. It was Spengler's point that the very triumphs of liberal culture, economic development, and technical skill were in reality evidence that the West had ceased to be creative and was entering a long afternoon phase of sterility and American domination. Spengler was writing at the precise moment, immediately before World War I, when Western elites were starting to recognize themselves as Western and not just as "civilization" *tout court*, and were beginning to devise the Grand Narrative to explain and justify their sense of being Western.

Spengler rejected the cult of Greece that Goethe and Winckelmann started and that Nietzsche had continued. To him, the Greeks and Romans were not Western, but part of a different culture with its own cycle. Ancient civilization, like the modern West, had its phases of growth and decay, and, again like the West, antiquity ended in an era of sterility and stagnation. Spengler dated the first beginnings of decline in ancient civilization to the Peloponnesian War, a turning point taken up slightly later by an English scholar, Arnold Toynbee, who, in the 1920s and 1930s, wrote an interpretation of world history destined for even greater success than that of Spengler.

To illustrate how the Greeks were not really our ancestors, Spengler pointed to the matter of writing. Writing was the base of Western civilization, he said. At no point in its history, which he dated from the tenth century A.D., was the West wholly illiterate. Writing, in the form of letters, records of inventory, poetry, biography, reports, constitutions, political statements, even down to the fundamental text of the West, the Bible, was indispensable. To a Westerner, culture was inconceivable without writing. And yet, the Greeks, supposedly our ancestors, were illiterate for much of their early history. Writing, the alphabet, did not appear in Greece until centuries after their culture began. The foundation epics of Western literature, the *Iliad* and the *Odyssey*, were composed orally and existed for perhaps a century before the art of writing came to Greece. How, Spengler asked, could a culture in which writing was indispensable be the direct descendant or pupil of one whose most important literary document resulted from an illiterate culture?

And what about another Greek achievement often touted as ancestral to the West—the writing of history? Spengler did not deny that the Greek historians, Herodotus, Thucydides, Polybius, and the others, were brilliant writers. But what they wrote was not nearly as much like modern Western historical writing as people thought. Victorian historiography, the great, multivolume works on the nations, religions, customs, and practices of peoples and cultures, depended on accurate chronology, on precise dating, and on the careful reconstruction of cause and effect. Greek historiography, by contrast, operated with only the most primitive notions of time and chronology. The Greeks typically dated by the name of annual officials of each city or by reference to some famous event. Unlike the Romans, who dated from an absolute starting point, the foundation of Rome, the Greeks had no universally recognized dating system.

Spengler's attack on the idea that the Greeks were ancestors of the West was part of his general philosophy of history. That philosophy was truly multicultural in the constructive sense of that word, in that it denied the absolute validity of the Western scheme of history, the tripartite division of time into antiquity, Middle Ages, and modernity. That scheme was fine for the West, where it actually referred to something, but was useless for other cultures, such as Islam or China. On the Greeks, Spengler was more right than wrong. In important ways, they were not the first Westerners. Those who, like Winckelmann, Grote, and Nietzsche, looked to ancient Greece as a source of absolute standards and models of conduct valid for the West interpreted the Greek legacy in Western terms, stressing similarities and ignoring discrepancies. Of course, the West inherited a legacy from the Greeks, as it did from the ancient Near East, Rome, Judaism, early Christianity, medieval Islam, China, and other civilizations. But the West was more than the sum of these legacies, nor were the legacies necessarily representative of the civilizations that spawned them. These distinctions were particularly important when dealing with the Greeks, whose culture could easily be presented as familiar and understandable, especially if one agreed with the premise of the cult of Greece, namely, that the Greeks were the most truly natural and perfect people. In fact, it was precisely in those areas where the Greeks were supposedly most truly the ancestors of the West—in morality and politics—that the philhellenists most effectively invented similarities and obscured radical differences.

The Grand Narrative saw the Greeks as founders of democracy and, in the teaching of Socrates, Plato, and Aristotle, of the individualist morality and ethical standards of the West. These were the things that, according to Goethe, Wilamowitz, and the Grand Narrative, were their most characteristic achievements and hence their most conspicuous contribution to Western civilization. Therefore, if the West began in Greece, its politics, ethics, and religion should be recognizably Greek, and if the Greeks were not the origins of the West, then their politics, ethics, and religion should provide the evidence.

One prominent element of Western culture, certainly of the humanitarian, liberal culture of the nineteenth century, was an ethic of compassion. Though Nietzsche despised it, such an ethic was a powerful force in the minds of the impractical visionary Friedrich Hölderlin, of the banker and businessman George Grote, and of thousands of schoolmasters and their middle-class pupils across Europe and North America in the century and a half after Goethe. These people certainly believed that their ethics were directly descended from Greece. Were they?

Those who looked for examples of an ethic of compassion in Greek culture might point to the celebrated scene in book 6 of the *Iliad*, where Hector, the Trojan hero, takes leave of his wife, Andromache, and their infant son, Astyanax. It is their only encounter in the poem. Two days after their meeting, Hector is slain by Achilles, and his conversation with Andromache is full of forebodings of disaster. The scene opens with Hector hurrying through the city toward the gates and battle. He wants to see his wife one last time and has been told she has gone to the walls to watch the fighting. She has heard that the Greeks are strong on the battlefield and fears for her husband's life, but turns to run back to the palace upon hearing that Hector is still in the city. So they meet in the street, Hector rushing down toward the gates and Andromache, accompanied by a maid carrying the infant, hurrying in the opposite direction. Hector smiles at the child, but his wife is in no mood for putting a brave face on things. Weeping, she begs him to stay: "Your own fierce valor will destroy you, and you show no pity, neither for your infant son nor for unhappy me, who shall soon be your widow, for soon the Greeks, rushing forward all together, will kill you, and it would be better for me, after losing you, to sink into the earth . . . so show pity and stay here on the watch-tower, and don't make your child an orphan and your wife a widow."[29] Hector replies "woman, all these things are on my mind, too," but instead of adding some phrase to the effect that "I wish I could keep you both safe," he immediately explains that he cannot stay away from the battle "like a villain" because "I respect the men of Troy and the women of Troy in their sweeping gowns." Respecting others does not, here, mean taking care of them; it means taking care of your own glory and reputation, so you will be remembered in honor. Therefore, he goes out to fight, to kill, and ultimately to be killed, even though he knows well that Troy must fall and that Andromache will be led into slavery.[30]

Hector's pity, if pity it is, is strange by Western standards, because after painting a vivid picture of his wife enslaved by the Greek conquerors, he concludes by saying that however pitiful his wife's future will be, "I would rather that the heaped earth cover my dead body before I hear your cries as they drag you into captivity."[31] It is a pity limited by his own pride and honor, his *kudos*, which does not permit him to survive and protect his wife and son, because to do so would be to court shame and to shirk his true destiny as a warrior—even if that destiny brings immediate death. Hector feels no obligation toward his wife and child as such; the only obligation he recognizes as unconditional is that he must uphold his reputation as a warrior. And because he happens to be the bravest and fiercest of the Trojans, he is obliged, by that same iron duty, to be constantly in the forefront of battle, for the one thing he cannot do is fail to live up to his reputation.[32]

Christian or Western ethical rules of duty to others would have told Hector that his responsibilities as husband and father, especially if disaster was going to strike, outweighed his warrior's pride. The Greek ideal of pride in personal excellence, or *arete*, was not Western and it was the counterpart of the Greek sense that existence was capricious and subject to sudden upheaval. In such a precarious world, where no one could be certain of divine favor, heroic pride was a statement of individuality, of the will to win fame, at the cost of one's life if necessary. Fame and honor were the only things that the gods could never take away from a man.

There is one other famous passage in the *Iliad* where glory, shame, and pity come together, this time with a different outcome, and that is the story in book 24 of how King Priam of Troy, Hector's aged father, visits the Greek camp to beg the body of Hector from Achilles. The Greek hero had killed Hector to avenge his friend Patroclus, whom Hector had killed in book 16. In his rage, Achilles dishonored Hector's body, refusing to bury it or treat it with the respect normally due to a dead enemy. Priam risked his own death in visiting the furious Achilles, who is shown at the beginning of book 24 as being still tormented with grief for Patroclus.

Arriving at Achilles' tent, Priam grasps Achilles by the knees "and kissed his terrible, man-slaying hands, which killed many of his sons." Achilles is struck dumb with amazement at seeing Hector's father, who seizes his chance and starts his appeal with a rhetorical master-stroke. "Remember your father" are his first words to Achilles. This was the one approach Achilles could not angrily reject, because he was himself painfully aware that by following his fate to seek glory at Troy he was leaving his old father defenseless at home, "and there is no one to ward off evil and ruin" from him. Achilles knew that he was fated to fall himself at Troy, and had already decided that he must nevertheless seek glory, for that was his *moira*, his lot, but knowing this in no way assuaged his grief at his father's suffering. Priam then reminds Achilles that he has lost many sons to the Greeks, the last and best being Hector. "For his sake I come now to the ships of the Greeks to ransom him from you, and I bear lavish gifts. But you should feel shame before the gods, Achilles, and pity (*eleeson*) me, remembering your father, and I am even more to be pitied, because I have endured what no other earth-dwelling mortal has endured: I have drawn the hand of my child's killer to my lips."[33]

The thought of his father overwhelms Achilles, and he and Priam both weep. Achilles praises Priam's courage in coming to see him, "and let us put sorrows to rest in our minds." He adds a sentence that sums up the Greek religious outlook that underlay and explained the ethic of glory: "thus did the gods weave a web for wretched mortals, to make them live lives of pain and labor; they themselves are free of care."[34]

The words for feeling shame and showing pity, *aideisthai* and *eleeinai*, are the same as those used by Andromache and Hector, but where the two impulses conflicted in book 6, here, as Priam shows, they agree, and the action they command is that Achilles should release Hector's body. It would not be compatible with Achilles' reputation, his glory, if he continued to insult the body. The very shame that forbade Hector to yield to pity by staying away from battle now commands Achilles to yield to pity. But it is a restricted pity. Achilles had long before decided not to yield to the pity that urged him to stay home and give his father a safe old age. He emphatically did not yield to pity for Hector when they were fighting in book 22. Only now, when Priam can show him that he is risking divine wrath by his vindictive behavior to Hector's corpse, does Achilles see that he must show pity to avoid offending the gods and to avoid falling short of his own glory. In Greek thought, the worst human failing was ignorance because it was remediable by effort, and not making the effort was to fall short of one's duty. The rational man knew that pity in itself was pointless. It was, in fact, immoral, because to show gratuitous mercy was to act irrationally and thus to violate the highest command of Greek morality, the command to "know yourself." When Achilles "knew himself," he realized that he was risking divine wrath by venting his rage on Hector's body, and so relented.

Pity and compassion, to the Greeks, were comprehensible only if they served pride and the drive for fame. To ancient philosophers, from Plato in the fourth century B.C. to Marcus Aurelius in the second century A.D., gratuitous pity "was a defect of character unworthy of the wise and excusable only in those who have not yet grown up. It was an impulsive response based on ignorance. Plato had removed the problem of beggars from his ideal state by dumping them over the borders."[35] Plato, however, was describing an imaginary society. A more striking illustration of how Greeks and Romans felt about a situation that, in the West, would normally evoke pity was the universal practice of infanticide. Infants were objects that could be kept or discarded at will. The Roman historian Tacitus condemned the Jewish teaching that infanticide and abortion were sinful as a "sinister and revolting" doctrine.[36] Nor was this sentiment only theory; it was put into practice on an enormous scale. In 1991, archaeologists digging in the Hellenistic port city of Ashkelon found the bones "of nearly 100 little babies apparently murdered and thrown into the sewer."[37] Laws of both Athens and Rome assumed that weak or deformed infants would be routinely exposed to die.

Few things illustrate the gap separating ancient from modern morality than the question of pity—immoral folly to the Greeks, a moral obligation in the West. At the bottom of this difference was religion, the way the Greeks conceived their gods, the supernatural powers affecting their lives. Religion, in all civilizations before the modern West, was at the heart of society. Therefore, if Greek religion was radically different from that of the West, the Greeks, in an essential part of their life, were neither Western nor ancestors of the West.

The Christian God loved his human creatures and wanted them to be saved; if they were not, it was because of original sin that was in man, not God. The Greek gods, by contrast, were, at bottom, indifferent to the fate of human beings, whom they had not created. Many have seen in this difference the abyss separating not just the Christian West, but also the secular, liberal West, from classical civilization. This view opposed a Christian or liberal belief in justice and in the value of human life to a Greek idea that fate, or the gods, was capricious and that the purpose of human life was to seek glory while not offending the gods.

Human happiness was, to the gods of antiquity, "a secondary consideration."[38] But they might, unpredictably, take an interest, and when they did so, it was often to punish rather than to help. As Tacitus put it in a passage commenting on the brutality of the Roman Civil War of A.D. 68–69, "never was it more fully proved by awful disasters of the Roman people or by certain signs that the gods care not for our safety, but for our punishment" (*non esse curae deis securitatem nostram, esse ultionem*).[39] In Tacitus, the gods were like judges in a totalitarian state, who might—or might not—mete out punishment to anyone at any time. Homer's gods, and those of the tragedians, were more like cruel adolescents who delighted in the cunning ways they spread pain and confusion. By chance or genius, Shakespeare expressed the prevalent Greek view in the blinded Gloucester's lines in *King Lear*:

> As flies to wanton boys are we to th' gods;
> They kill us for their sport.[40]

Why did the gods punish men? The great Greek tragedies of Aeschylus and Sophocles addressed this very question, and the answer was, "because men commit what in the gods' eyes are crimes." The greatest crimes were violations of the divine order of nature: killing your relatives, incest, breaking oaths, betrayal.[41] But in the famous cases of legend, the perpetrator either did not know he was committing a crime or had no choice. That ignorance or lack of choice, in fact, was the essence of the tragedy. King Oedipus belonged to the first category. Little good did his ignorance do him, even less that his misfortune was an inherited curse; punishment struck him nonetheless. An example of the second was Agamemnon.

His story, as recalled in Aeschylus's tragedy *Agamemnon*, illustrates not only the Greek view of the gods but the obligations to community that overwhelm human pity and individual feeling. Agamemnon was the chief king of the Greeks in the Trojan War and the supreme commander of the army that sailed to Troy to bring back Agamemnon's sister-in-law, his brother Menelaus's beautiful wife, Helen. Why was Helen in Troy? Because the Trojan prince Paris had abducted her, having been authorized to do so by the goddess of love, Aphrodite, whom Paris had named the most beautiful goddess in his notorious judgment. Why was Paris asked to make this judgment? Because the three goddesses Hera, Athena, and Aphrodite, inflamed by the apple of discord, were having an argument to see who would be named the most beautiful by the mortal man most competent to make that judgment,

and who happened to be Paris. The sheer caprice of the gods and the incalcu-
lable, disastrous, and cataclysmic effects of that caprice on mortals were never
more clearly demonstrated than in this story.

What were the effects of Aphrodite's jealous wrangling with her divine
colleagues? The whole Trojan War, for one thing, which lasted ten years
and ended in the destruction of Troy, the death of her leading men, and
that of Achilles and many other heroes on the Greek side as well. A second
set of effects were those on Agamemnon and his house. Agamemnon was
killed promptly on his return to Greece by his wife, Clytemnestra, who had
taken as lover Aegisthus. This excessive sanction on a dawdling husband
had a simple explanation: ten years earlier, when the Greek expedition to
Troy was setting out, Agamemnon had been obliged to sacrifice their
daughter Iphigenia to obtain, from the gods, fair winds for the passage.
Killing one's own child was an unpardonable offense, and Agamemnon
duly died for it.

But was not Agamemnon *obliged* to sacrifice Iphigenia? Yes; it was made
clear to him, Aeschylus tells us, that unless he did so, the gods would not
send fair winds, the expedition could not sail, and all the Greeks and their
justified cause against the Trojans would be disgraced. Some of the gods were
angry at Agamemnon's family because of a previous insult, and killing his
own daughter was the only way he could regain their favor. But just because
Agamemnon *had* to sacrifice his daughter to fulfil a divine and social obligation—to go to Troy to avenge the rape of Helen—was absolutely irrelevant
and no excuse. He *did* kill his daughter. He *did* incur the gods' wrath. His
death was both deserved and inevitable.

All of this was embedded in an even vaster background of myth, according to which Agamemnon's whole lamentable fate was the punishment for
something his father and grandfather had done—the curse of the house of
Pelops. But that, to a modern Westerner, is neither explanation nor excuse
for the punishment he suffered. To the Greeks, on the other hand, it did not
really matter who started it all or why, or even whether that distant original
criminal was himself under some irresistible compulsion, under the force of
what the Greeks called "necessity" (*anangke*) and which they often treated as
a divine power in its own right.

What mattered, and what made the story tragic, was that Agamemnon
could not escape acting as he did, and could not, therefore, escape his punishment. He was punished for remaining true to his obligations as king and
war leader, but Aeschylus dismissed in half a line the notion that he could
have simply deserted. Because then not only would he have been less than a

man, he would have incurred some other and equally terrible punishment for shirking his duty.[42]

Hector and Agamemnon demonstrated the fundamental difference between ancient religion and the religion of the Old West, namely, Christianity. This was not merely a difference between the polytheistic background of the stories of Homer and monotheism, for the same difference separated ancient monotheists, such as Plato or the Stoic emperor Marcus Aurelius, from Christians. The difference was this: the Greeks were obliged to obey the gods and accept fate, but the gods had no responsibility in return. For the Greeks, the purpose of life was to discover and to obey the cosmic rules of behavior. If it was impossible to obey them all, or if, as in Agamemnon's case, obeying some meant disobeying others, you could be absolutely sure of divine vengeance. The relation of the Greek to his gods was one-sided. The starting point was the command of the Delphic oracle to "know yourself." Faced with the power of the gods and fate, you needed to know that the purpose of self-knowledge was to remember that you were mortal and to avoid the confidence or arrogance (*hubris*) of excessive pride in your skill or good fortune. The man who forgot himself provoked the gods and brought down their vengeance.

These cosmic rules were not made up by the gods but were part of the impersonal structure of the universe, of necessity (*anangke*), fate (*moira*), or destiny (*heimarmene*). Neither the multiple gods of Homer nor the single god of Plato or the Stoics was a creator like the Jewish or Christian god. Ancient gods were themselves part of the structure of the universe, but differed from mortals in that they were not subject to sorrow, *anangke*, or the penalties of resisting *moira*. They did, however, punish those mortals who broke the rules, and in doing so upheld the balance and the justice (*dike*) of the universe.

In the face of such implacable forces, Greeks and Romans had no sure hope of joy or peace of mind, only the knowledge that they must do their best to pursue glory, for that was their only, and very fragile, chance of satisfaction. A Greek prayer rested not on divine promises, for the gods made none, but on the hope of catching a god's favorable attention at the right moment. Few statements better express this than these lines of the poet Theognis, which combine bleak resignation and helpless anger:

> Olympian Zeus, fulfil now for me my timely wish:
> Grant that instead of evils I may also experience something good.
> I want to die if I cannot find brief respite from my evil cares,
> Or else I want to pay back my troubles in kind.[43]

We are quite a distance here from the Western idea of religion, which remained Christian even in the era of secularization. Contrary to Greek beliefs, Christianity stated that the human race had fallen from an original condition of grace; that God had taken pity on man; and that he had provided means of redemption. Judaism offered a less clear strategy, since it held redemption to be still in the future, and recommended instead a discipline of patient waiting in the hope that the just would not perish. But both faiths differed radically from the Greek and Roman view that divine wrath was unpredictable and that the gods were primarily interested in punishing *hubris*, not in providing redemption.

The Grand Narrative suggested that the Greeks were the first and best Westerners because its liberal and secular authors were not especially concerned with religion. They were, rather, the successors to the eighteenth- and nineteenth-century cult of Greece, particularly its political and progressive version, exemplified by George Grote's *History of Greece*. The progressive cult of Greece superseded, for some, Winckelmann's and Goethe's desire to replace a dying Christianity with a new, natural religion that would reinstate the Greeks as the models of a rejuvenated Western civilization.

Thus, in Germany, the cult of Greece produced an apolitical and aesthetic ambition to join the Greeks in a sphere of beauty remote from the real world. To the progressive philhellenists, on the other hand, the Greek essence of the West was democracy. In England, geopolitics, liberalism, and general good fortune maintained a golden vision of Greece as the birthplace of democracy and a model for further reform. The founder of modern liberalism, John Stuart Mill, wrote that the battle of Marathon in 490 B.C., when the Greeks defeated the first Persian invasion, was "more important as an event in English history than the battle of Hastings." Mill identified his own idea of liberty with that defended by the Greeks, in an intellectual move that prefigured the Grand Narrative's claim that a direct, intimate link bound Greece to the modern West. The idea of the Greeks as a model for reform in Victorian Britain relied on this misleading analogy between Greek and modern freedom and Greek and modern democracy. The Victorians established their system of elite education on the premise that Greece was the source of the best and truest standards of excellence as well as guides to political doctrine and ideals. For two generations, the British government and ruling elite operated on the assumption that the best preparation for managing a global political and commercial empire, and running the world's most advanced economy, was to spend six years immersed in the classical languages, an effort that, for the hardest-working, culminated in the ability to render Shakespeare and Milton into Greek tetrameters.[44]

In the less favored German political climate, people like Oswald Spengler in the early twentieth century drew different lessons from the study of Greece, both of them sombre. One lesson was that Greece was an irrelevant or even dangerous model, because Greek democracy had sapped the martial vigor of the nation in the face of its ruthless enemies, the Macedonians, and, later, the Romans. In other words, according to pessimists like the ancient historian Eduard Meyer, Herodotus and Thucydides had it exactly wrong when they claimed that freedom and democracy made a people proud, powerful, and patriotic. Another lesson was that even the supposedly sunny sides of Greek culture, such as those favored by the British Victorians, in fact concealed irrational, violent depths. Looking too closely into those depths could be dangerous.

England, as the French historian Jules Michelet famously if not quite accurately put it, was an island. Despite coming close to defeat by Napoleon in the early 1800s, the British remained undefeated, even when they stood alone as ten million against the more than hundred million people of the French-controlled Continent. They mainly survived because of their impassable twenty-two-mile-wide moat, the English Channel. But in their own estimation, they survived thanks to their invincible patriotism, which rested in turn on the supposedly deep-seated British virtues of inventiveness, self-reliance, and craftsmanship. In times of peace, those virtues manifested themselves in the commercial and technological genius of the Industrial Revolution and in political liberalism. Into this mix of material progress, social change, and incipient democracy came the rediscovery of the Greeks in British schools and public culture, of which the greatest example was the twelve-volume *History of Greece* by the liberal and anticlerical freethinker, banker, and independent scholar George Grote, which first appeared between 1846 and 1856.

As the eldest son of practical parents, Grote, born in 1797, was not permitted to attend university, which, at that time, was only for aspiring clergymen, for the frivolous, or for the idle rich. He was instead put to work in his father's bank. Only after ensuring that the family's material circumstances were safe did his father allow George's younger brother John to attend university. John went on to become professor of philosophy at Cambridge, whereas George had to wait until, at forty-nine, he was independently wealthy before he could devote himself full-time to his beloved Greeks. It was as a banker and businessman that George, in 1826, took an active part in founding the University of London, the first university in England outside Oxford and Cambridge and the first not to require its members to subscribe to Anglican doctrine.

Grote was a democrat and a freethinker. Like David Hume in the eighteenth century, he saw no reason to accept traditional Christianity, because it was impossible to ground it in reason. Religious belief and the feelings of virtue it might engender were purely irrational and ought to be replaced by justified feelings of virtue flowing from practical deeds and from rational belief in liberal political principles. Grote was a follower of Jeremy Bentham, who argued that the purpose of all action, especially political action, should be the greatest good of the greatest number. A few years after helping to found the University of London, Grote, along with Bentham and other liberal thinkers, promoted the Reform Act of 1832, which brought the Liberal party to power and marked the beginning of majority rule.

Grote published his *History of Greece* to demonstrate that Athenian democracy was both liberal and secular and constructed on principles opposed to the aristocratic and religious principles of the British old regime. He began his great work to disprove a prevalent view of the Greeks, namely, that their artistic, literary, and philosophical achievements owed nothing to Athenian democracy and that the democracy of Athens was, if anything, inimical to greatness, but wanted to show that the opposite was true, that the "expanding and stimulating Athenian democracy . . . called forth a similar creative genius in oratory, in dramatic poetry, and in philosophical speculation."[45] Grote, almost alone among leading historians, defended the Athenian democracy against both its ancient and modern detractors. His readers were left in no doubt that the message for their own time was to encourage political reform, greater economic equality, and critical attitudes to religion and authority.

The Victorian view of Greece, strongly influenced by Grote, was positive and emphatic. Victorian liberals understood from Grote that Athenian democracy was the greatest political achievement in human history before their own day. The Greeks were our ancestors; their example showed that cultural and political progress could, and ought to, go hand in hand. His less discriminating followers, however, cast ancient Athens in the image of liberal Britain, ignoring the differences and worshipping the similarities. Thus, by the early twentieth century, the Grand Narrative read Herodotus and Thucydides with modern spectacles, and understood their praise of Greek courage, will to independence, and Athenian democracy in the perspective of modern ideas of freedom and democracy.

One fundamental difference in political philosophy between Greeks and the modern West was described in 1819 by the French philosopher Benjamin Constant, in his essay *On the Liberty of the Ancients Compared to that of the Moderns.*[46] Constant wanted to show that modern liberty, as represented by the French and American Revolutions and by the liberal movement of his own day, marked a genuine advance in human civilization. A century before he wrote, the so-called Quarrel of the Ancients and Moderns had pitted those who sought truth in ancient learning against those who believed in progress, discovery, and the scientific method. The moderns won, and they produced the European and American Enlightenment. But the victory of the moderns persuaded people to stop looking to the Greeks and Romans for reliable information about science and society. More important, the moderns fatally undermined the prestige of the West's own Christian past, the Middle Ages, as a source of superior knowledge. Consequently, the Enlightenment was above all an attack on Christian political, social, and moral ideas. The resulting crisis of belief led Goethe to propose the cult of Greece as the new religion of the West. Constant was among those disturbed by this cult, which threatened to disparage or obscure the real achievements of the liberal Enlightenment and of the French and American Revolutions. He launched a new attack of moderns against ancients, not against those who were too respectful of medieval Christianity, but against those who, in their search for the timeless wisdom of Greece, ignored the real progress toward liberty and democracy of their own contemporaries.

To demonstrate that modernity was superior, Constant showed in his essay that in ancient Greece, liberty meant "the right of governing the State by taking a direct part in its administration. Rights of individuals were unknown . . . As a citizen, the individual could decide on peace and war; he was entitled to judge and to control the administration; as a subject of the State he had simply to make his conduct conform to the standard imposed by the State. The citizen is sovereign in public affairs, a slave in private matters."[47] Constant summarized the idea of freedom in Greece as "the division of power between all the citizens of a country," and modern liberty as the individual's "secure right to his personal pursuits," and, one might add, interests and beliefs.

The ancient Greeks defined freedom as the right to participate in government, not as the right to choose and pursue your own private goals. This fundamental difference was starkly illustrated in the most famous criminal case in Greek history, the trial of Socrates the philosopher in 399 B.C.

Those who saw the trial as an example of democratic excess missed the most important points about it. First, one of the two charges against Socrates was blasphemy. It was because they thought he was denying the common gods and hence the legitimacy of the city that the Athenians put Socrates on trial, not because of his moral philosophy. Second, the trial did not demonstrate that Athenian democracy had gone overboard, because, as Pericles said, "we consider a man who does not share in political life not as someone who minds his own business, but as a useless man."[48] If Socrates used his time in philosophical investigations rather than in serving the city, he was a traitor. To see the trial as an example of democratic excess was to equate Athenian and modern democracy and hence to misinterpret the Greeks. Finally, the Athenians did not intend to kill Socrates. In fact, the evidence indicates that they wanted to make an example of a man they found politically and theologically dangerous, in the hope that he would shut up and go away. His own actions made the outcome inevitable.

At the time of his trial, Socrates was seventy years old, a great age in ancient Greece, where life expectancy was around forty. Until the 1960s, every schoolchild in the West learned the story, as Socrates' pupil Plato told it in the *Apology*: Socrates faced trial for *asebeia*, impiety. This was, or could be, a capital crime because it was tantamount to treason. Impiety was treason because religion was a public function that expressed loyalty to the city. Not to believe in the gods that the city had declared to be its gods was to deny the legitimacy of the city.

The trial took place before a court of 501 citizens who volunteered to serve. It was public, and the audience included Plato himself and other young followers of Socrates. In his defense, as Plato reported it, Socrates did not apologize or explain away the charges. Yes, he was a man who went about asking questions. Yes, he took pride in confusing people and forcing them to think about their beliefs and what they thought was common sense. No, he could not honestly say that he believed in the city's gods, it was true that he drew inspiration from what he called his *daimonion*, his "godlet," but he really could not say whether the official gods existed or not. He saw his task as that of goading the citizenry into alertness and new thoughts, rather like a gadfly that stings a "great, noble horse" into sudden action.

The 501 jurors found him guilty by what, given his uncompromising tone, was a rather small margin—281 against 220. Then came the sentencing. The court had, as a mark of honor, asked him to name his own sentence, expecting him to propose exile. Instead, Socrates thanked them for their concern and proposed that, as proper recompense for his achievements, he be sentenced to dining at public expense in the Prytaneum, one of the official buildings of Athens. The right to dine free at the Prytaneum was a singular honor conferred by Athens on its most distinguished citizens, often victorious athletes. By his suggestion, Socrates was saying that he was a unique asset to Athens and that, as such, he deserved, not punishment but the highest honor the city could confer. It would be hard to imagine a response more designed to infuriate the court, which, in its own view, was making a substantial gesture of respect to its prisoner by offering him the chance to get off free after having been condemned. At this point, some of Socrates' rich young followers in the audience shouted at him to propose a substantial fine, so he said: "Now look, Plato and Crito and Critobulus and Apollodorus are shouting at me to propose a fine of 30 mines; they will guarantee payment." This was indeed a substantial amount: the normal ransom for a prisoner of war was one or two mines. But the court refused to listen to this offer, which was anyway not made by Socrates but by his rich friends. The court had heard Socrates' own opinion of his guilt, which did not put it in an accommodating mood. Sentence of death was passed by a substantial majority and carried out soon after by giving him a poison—the hemlock—to drink. The Athenians carried out their law, but lost at the bar of history.

Socrates' trial and death was one of the defining moments of Greek civilization and also of the West. The Grand Narrative inherited, or rediscovered, the image of Socrates as the martyr to philosophy, to truth seeking, to fearless inquiry, to civilization in short, and the contrary image of the prosecutors and jurors as narrow-minded bigots. In fact, these images were as bland and false as was the adulation of Greek art and poetry propounded by the less gifted followers of Winckelmann and Goethe. What really happened was more interesting than the images suggest and sheds light on the relationship of Athenian democracy and philosophy to their Western counterparts.

Socrates did not exactly set out to charm the court. What we know of his character from other sources indicates that he was not the kind of person who would consider winning this sort of case by charm. For about thirty years before the trial, he had been a fixture of Athenian life, exploring ordinary people's assumptions about their work, their knowledge, their moral and ethical certainties, their supernatural beliefs. He single-handedly created moral philosophy and was the first known example of a radical methodological and moral individualist.

This Socratic individualism had a political aspect, which played an important part in his trial. Socrates led his philosophical life during the Peloponnesian War. This war, the subject of the greatest Greek work of history, that of Thucydides, pitted Athens and her allies against the rival city of Sparta, and her allies. The stake was predominance in Greece. Athens was primarily a sea power; her allies were islands or coastal towns, and her strength lay in her navy. Sparta, by contrast, was a land power, where political control rested with those citizens who could afford the full Greek infantry, or hoplite, equipment. During the early years, Athens had the upper hand, but never decisively so, and Spartan forces often raided up to the walls of Athens. In 415, the Athenians tried to end the war by a bold stroke—sending an expedition to Syracuse in Sicily, which at that time was largely a Greek region. Annexing the rich city of Syracuse would tilt the balance definitively against Sparta. Unfortunately for Athens, the expedition failed miserably—in Thucydides' account, largely because of bad leadership, and because the expedition was undertaken in large part on a whim of the democratic mob at Athens.

The Sicilian disaster provoked a political reaction in Athens against those held responsible. For the last ten years of the war, power in Athens lay mostly with the leaders of the poorer classes, who provided the manpower for the navy. The final defeat in 404 led to a right-wing reaction that temporarily brought to power the so-called Thirty Tyrants. In this junta were several friends and former pupils of Socrates.

The Thirty Tyrants fell in 403 and democracy, in its peculiar Athenian form, was restored. But Anytus, Meletus, and others remembered Socrates' association with the Tyrants and this lay behind the charge of "corrupting the young."

Socrates, then, was the victim of a populist backlash against authoritarian government, a backlash exacerbated by many years' irritation with this questioner who upset people by not thinking and living like the majority. The bland image suggested courage and martyrdom; the truer image suggested a clash between two legitimate interests: Athenian democracy's insistence that citizens take part in government and not sabotage it either by their opinions or their actions, and the independent mind's interest in free thought and expression. But what if that expression had political consequences? Was that reason enough to execute its author? Socrates' speech was, on occasion, deliberately, rhetorically offensive to those whose received opinions he wanted to rattle. His fate showed that democratic societies, whether of the Athenian or the modern representative model, were perhaps not the safest places to offend popular sentiment.

According to I.F. Stone, the left-wing American journalist who wrote a penetrating study of *The Trial of Socrates* in the 1980s, the backlash was against a man who had done little to oppose the enemies of Athenian democracy and who taught that democracy was an inferior form of government, because the many were incapable of acquiring the sort of knowledge necessary to rule. The premise of Athenian democracy was that all citizens had not only the duty but the ability to participate in government. The duty included supporting the city's religion and opposing its enemies. Socrates, by contrast, admired Sparta, which was governed by a narrow oligarchy, and denied that citizens, whom he compared to a herd of cattle, had the ability to govern. For both Socrates and the democrats, that ability rested on virtue. They disagreed, however, about where virtue in turn came from. The democratic theorists, including Aristotle, derived virtue from character, which was found throughout society. A poor man might be more virtuous than a rich man. According to the antidemocrats such as Socrates and Plato, virtue was a superior form of knowledge, available only to the few. A conspicuous element in the city's grievance against Socrates was that the two most prominent of his pupils, Alcibiades and Critias, had between them done more harm to the city than any other two men of their time. Neither, in short, had demonstrated virtue; both had bad characters. Indeed, Xenophon reported that what attracted Critias and Alcibiades to Socrates was that he could teach them to manipulate by argument.[49]

Stone argued that the Athenians killed Socrates because his idea that the many were incapable of government had become dangerous and treasonable after the Spartan victory of 404 and the dictatorship of the Thirty Tyrants in 403. Socrates admired Sparta, and one of the Thirty had been a pupil of his. What had for long seemed eccentric but harmless opinions were now seen as supporting the powerful forces that threatened Athenian democracy in the aftermath of the unfortunate Peloponnesian War. The events of 404–403 explained why the democrats put Socrates on trial at this time and not many years before. Behind the trial lurked the fundamental opposition between Socrates and most Athenians: "He and his disciples saw the human community as a herd that had to be ruled by a king or kings, as sheep by a shepherd. The Athenians, on the other hand, believed—as Aristotle later said—that man was 'a political animal,' endowed unlike other animals with *logos*, or reason, and thus capable of distinguishing good from evil and of governing himself in a *polis*."[50]

The Grand Narrative saw Socrates as the West's founding father: the inventor of moral philosophy and of radical self-questioning. According to Stone, however, Socrates questioned many things, but never his own antidemocratic beliefs or his idea of a superior form of knowledge available only to a chosen few. Socrates' known political associations were authoritarian. Could it be, as Stone suggested, that there was a natural affinity between Socratic individualism and a sceptical, even hostile attitude to democracy? Consider that the two greatest Socratic thinkers of the modern West, Kierkegaard and Nietzsche, were intensely opposed to democracy in its broad modern sense. Both held that truth was individual and could never be found in consensus. "The mass is untruth," said Kierkegaard. Nietzsche feared that mass suffrage and popular sovereignty weakened the will of the rulers and led inevitably to social and political decadence. Both preferred absolutist monarchy to democracy. Both were, by temperament, Old Westerners dismayed by the superficial, leveling, trivializing forces of the New West.

Socratic individualism, in its most notorious representatives, was not liberal but illiberal. In other words: the hero of the Western origin legend—St. Socrates, as Stone called him—was not Western, if by Western one meant liberal and egalitarian. That middle-class culture of the nineteenth and early twentieth centuries that turned Socrates into a founding father of the West was only one, if perhaps the most important, result of the cult of Greece. But it was not the only one. How a culture defined individual freedom, or whether it did so, depended in part on how members of that culture defined human nature. How did the Greeks differ from the West in this regard?

A French thinker, Pierre Manent, provided a thought-provoking answer in a book published in 1994.[51] Manent's purpose was nothing less than to describe the modern Western or liberal personality. This modern personality rested on a paradox: on the one hand, modern liberal man believed in freedom and autonomy, and hence in democracy and human rights as the foundations of political, personal, social, and even emotional existence. The paradox was that modern man believed in these things dogmatically, as absolutes. Yet, modern political philosophy from the eighteenth to the late twentieth century tended to deny absolutes, and in particular that there was such a thing as human nature. This denial was at the root of democratic freedom, in which everyone was the shaper not merely of his own fortune, but, more important, of his own desires and goals. Democracy was the form of politics, social interaction, and personal behavior most compatible with the claim that there was no such thing as human nature.

The purpose of political society, in the words of the American Declaration of Independence, was to protect "life, liberty, and the pursuit of happiness." In democratic theory, individuals pursuing their own goods jointly produced and protected the liberty of all. The Greeks thought differently. Their view of society was less rosy, more contradictory. To them, political society was an arena of competition, where men displaying and honoring different sorts of excellence fought for preeminence, for the chance to direct the fortunes of all: excellence of birth, of wealth, of virtue, of courage. The ethic of competition that Homer described survived into the sixth, fifth, and fourth centuries B.C., into the era of Athenian democracy. So did its ethical and religious implications. According to the Greeks, the purpose of political society—what Manent called 'the city'—was not to protect individual desires, but to find and maintain the just balance between the goods and the goals sought by the incompatible desires of varying excellences. Greek thinkers did not focus on desire itself as a value, but on the purpose of the desire—was what was desired good or bad, would it serve or harm the city?

Another, related difference between Greeks and moderns, according to Manent, was that the primary political virtue in ancient Greece was what they called magnanimity, great-heartedness, or great-spiritedness. Magnanimity was ambition, skill, constancy, courage, and moderation rolled into one—the mark of the superior man. The magnanimous man sought victory without embarrassment because of the great things he would accomplish. There was another vital difference here between Greeks and modern Westerners: the magnanimous man, to the Greeks, was self-sufficient, needing no one's aid. By contrast, the primary political virtue, whether honored in the breach or in the observance, of Western democratic modernity was collaboration, which required humility, namely, the humility to recognize that achievement rested on interdependence.

The Greeks, who believed in a human nature, valued competition, magnanimity, and self-reliance, whereas democrats, who believed in individual rights, valued—or pretended to value—humility and collaboration. Thus, the individual autonomy extolled in democratic liberalism was something quite different from the magnanimity extolled by the Greeks.

The difference, according to Manent, could be traced to the long centuries of Christianity that incubated democratic modernity. Christianity proclaimed man's radical imperfection, his dependence on God and neighbor, and that nothing great or good could result from individual desire alone. Desire, conscience, and will must be instructed by faith and by humility. Following Alexis de Tocqueville, Manent claimed that the Christian teaching of original sin and of humanity's flawed nature made modern democracy possible. The democratic pursuit of individual autonomy needed the balance of humility if it was not to degenerate into anarchy or the rule of some ideology, such as, in the twentieth century, Marxism or National Socialism.

The cult of Greece was a profound fact of cultural life in the West in the nineteenth century. Three to four generations of European and American elites grew up learning that all that was best in their own civilization came from the Greeks, who held the key to poetic, philosophical, and artistic truth. They also learned that their own civilization, that of the modern West, was superior both to its own past and to all other cultures in the world, a doctrine that might seem incompatible with the doctrine of Greek excellence, but which was made compatible by the argument that Greek truth was timeless, and that the modern West, thanks to its superior methods, was better able to get at that truth than any earlier epoch.

However eager and well intentioned its practitioners, the cult of Greece obscured both the realities of ancient Greece and the independent reality of Western civilization. When, in the aftermath of World War I, American educators produced the Grand Narrative, they inherited the idea of Greek excellence as well as the contradictory idea of progress and of the superiority of the modern West. With the collapse of the Grand Narrative from the 1960s on, those who wanted to understand Western evolution and identity no longer had to labor under the burden of either error. Instead, they could ask more fruitful questions, for example: who were the Greeks? What was the West? And, given that the Greeks were not the first Westerners, what was the connection between them?

For that there was a connection no one could reasonably deny. The difficulty in describing that connection in the time of the Grand Narrative was that doing so raised further points that did not fit easily within the Grand Narrative's story of democratic, liberal, and capitalist progress. One such point was that, for the West to emerge, Greece had to die; Greek ethics, religion, and politics had to be fundamentally transformed and blended with other elements. The originality of the West was unfairly obscured by the cult of Greece and by its intellectual offspring, the Grand Narrative. But when the Grand Narrative lost prestige in the 1960s and after, this did not refocus attention on the real history of the West. Rather, the critics of the Grand

Narrative threw out the baby with the bathwater. The West, from being wholly good, became wholly bad. The critics saw no point in discussing Western origins except to condemn them, just as the authors of the Grand Narrative had not been able to distinguish the West from its alleged Greek ancestors. Finally, the reconstructed optimist narrative of the 1990s, the narrative that said that the West consisted of democracy and free markets, was a future-oriented narrative with little historical depth and no more interest in ancient history or the Greeks than either the Grand Narrative or its critics.

The Greeks, to conclude, were not the first Westerners. To believe that they were was an error of the nineteenth century, perpetuated by the Grand Narrative, that did more to obscure than to illuminate the real history of the West and its elements. Greek ethics, politics, and religion formed a whole that identified a particular civilization, the Greek, that, sometime in the early centuries of the Christian era, faded into the synthesis of Roman order and Christian religion that defined the starting conditions of the West. To see how the real West emerged it was necessary, first, to remove the distorting mirror of the cult of Greece. The next step is to look at Rome.

Yet the question of Western origins and identity remained important, if only because many of the critics as well as the neo-optimists remained, in some sense at least, Westerners, and it was a pity that they often did not know what they were talking about. And the truth about Western origins was that they were a complex synthesis of apparently incompatible elements, in which Greek identity was transformed by the impact of two forces that both the Grand Narrative and its enemies tended to disparage or ignore: Rome and Christianity.

CHAPTER THREE

The Burden of Rome

Founding the Roman nation was a huge task
—Virgil

Every stage in the rise of Rome marks a step toward the purer
distillation of Western culture and its view of life
—Bachofen

I n 46 B.C., Cleopatra, the last descendant of the Greek kings of Hellenistic Egypt, paid a triumphal visit to Rome, according to a tradition sumptuously portrayed in the 1963 Hollywood epic starring Elizabeth Taylor in the title role and Richard Burton as her Roman lover, Mark Antony. In the film, the visit to Rome marks the occasion when Cleopatra turns her affections from Julius Caesar, whose child she had borne two years earlier, to Antony. To her Roman contemporaries, Cleopatra represented the dangerous East: opulent, decadent, and corrupt. When Mark Antony became ruler of the eastern half of the Roman dominions and went to live with Cleopatra in Egypt in 41 B.C., patriotic Romans took this as evidence of the queen's sorcerous powers as well as of the lure of eastern riches. During the next decade, Cleopatra and Antony built up an eastern empire based on Egypt and claiming authority over all the regions, from Greece to Persia, once ruled by Alexander the Great and divided by his generals, among whom was her own ancestor Ptolemy. Mark Antony's partner, Octavian, who controlled Rome's western provinces, believed, as did many other Romans, that this eastern power threatened to undermine Roman rule, either by establishing a separate, eastern empire or by flooding all Roman lands with dangerous eastern superstitions and customs, fueled and supported by eastern riches and bribery. When the two former friends fell out, and Octavian defeated the eastern forces at Actium, off the western coast of Greece, in 31, poets greeted his victory as restoring balance to the Roman world and warding off the cultural, political, and moral threat of the dangerous East. Horace declared "now is the time for drinking and dancing." The West had won; the eastern threat was defeated, for the time being at least; and the conservative Roman elite could continue their westernizing of the Greeks.

The battle of Actium became one of the main symbolic instances of the great struggle of the West against the East, of liberty against despotism, honesty against corruption, frugality against opulence, simplicity against sophistication, and virtue against depravity. Herodotus's story of the poor and outnumbered Greeks defeating the rich and numerous Persians was one of the first, but it was not until Roman times that the polarity of West and East began taking on a sustained geopolitical significance that never since entirely faded from view. The battle of Actium as the hard-fought defeat of a dangerous threat was one of the main ideological building blocks of the East-West line that was Rome's geopolitical legacy to the West. It also represented, to Romans, the defense of Roman laws against the arbitrary despotism of the East. Finally, Cleopatra's wealth and power constituted the caricature of the ordered, law-bound power that Romans liked to regard as the foundation of their empire. Where she, according to the Roman poets and to the film, flaunted her riches and used her empire to gratify herself, the Roman ethic prescribed parsimony and insisted that the purpose of empire was not to indulge the whims of the powerful but, in Virgil's words, to "spare those who submit themselves and cast down the proud."

Rome did three things: she established the geopolitical boundaries of the West and thereby adumbrated one of the most fateful dividing lines in history—the East-West line. Second, she Westernized the Greeks, introducing Greek culture to a more primitive audience in the western part of the Mediterranean and preparing it for transmission to medieval and modern Europe. Third, she created and left her own myth of empire. In Germany, Britain, and the United States, the Roman myth was overshadowed, though not entirely erased, by the cult of Greece and its ideological descendant, the Grand Narrative.

Despite its origins in the romantic cult of Greece, that narrative was, as a pedagogical and political program for mass higher education, mainly an

American invention, starting with the Columbia Contemporary Civilization course of 1917 and the Chicago Great Books program of the 1920s and 1930s. German scholars and intellectuals continued to worship the ideals of Greece, but higher education was not a mass phenomenon in Germany until after World War II, and when young Germans began attending university in large numbers in the late 1950s and 1960s, they did not come to study classics, culture, or history, but contemporary social and political sciences. More significant in the first two decades after World War II was a different sort of history, pursued by conservative scholars who had exchanged an earlier nationalism, rendered unacceptable by the misdeeds of Adolf Hitler, for a pan-Western outlook that presented an idea of the West as a synthesis of classical and Christian culture, threatened by Soviet communism and defensible only by an alliance of old Europe and young America. This approach emphasized the traditions of Roman law and the legacy of the Roman and medieval Western Empires as geopolitical factors of order in central and western Europe. It meshed quite well with the French cult of Rome, derived both from the French monarchy and from the French Revolution. Together with the many Roman legal and institutional traditions of Italy, the post–1945 German and French ideas of the West defined a Continental Grand Narrative in which Roman law, learning, and order, rather than Greek democracy and philosophy, lay at the political and institutional origins of the West. This Continental story of the West found an incarnation in the European Common Market of 1957, and later, in the 1990s, in the European Union. Especially in countries with a Catholic tradition such as Italy, France, or large parts of Germany, the myth of Rome survived. For Americans on the threshold of the twenty-first century, understanding that myth was not merely a matter of cultural history, but of contemporary foreign policy as well.

The Continental narrative based Western identity on geopolitics, law, and political institutions, on facts manifested in political, economic, and social change, rather than on ideas such as democracy and morality. This pointed to Rome rather than Greece as the origin of the West. Geopolitically, it was the Romans who first consistently defined the East-West line that constituted the border of the West until and beyond the end of the Cold War in the 1990s. Roman law influenced the legal systems and concepts of most Western countries, especially in the areas of contract, inheritance, tort, and property. Third, more than any other forerunner of the West, Rome introduced the idea of empire and the fascination of great power exercised over long distances and across generations of time. All three came together in the Roman story of how Cleopatra seduced her lovers Julius Caesar and Mark Antony and nearly destroyed the unity of Roman dominion.[1]

Rooting the West in Greece meant defining Western identity in terms of ideas—democracy and philosophy—that supposedly descended directly from the Greeks. By implying that Western democracy evolved from Greek democracy, and Western morality and ethics from Greek philosophy, this approach posited an ahistorical link that distorted and obscured the actual, institutional and ideological, sources of the modern West, including its democratic and ethical beliefs. If, however, the Greeks were not the first Westerners, and if their deepest beliefs, values, and understandings of life were alien to the West, where should we then look for its beginnings? Could it be that the Roman contribution was not simply that of a humble, musclebound, and slightly stupid guardian, or mindless destroyer?

Rooting the West in Rome and defining the West as the result of Roman law and order, as the Continental narrative suggested doing, had the merit of seeking continuity in geopolitics, institutions, and social development. Thus, the Roman claim to be the origin of the West demands to be reconsidered. Doing so means surveying the legacy of Rome itself—the East-West line, preserving Greek civilization, and the idea of law and of empire—and then examining the great transition that spanned the fourth to the seventh centuries A.D., the transition known as the decline and fall of the Roman Empire. That transition, and the many and conflicting ways it was interpreted throughout Western history, made possible the synthesis that shaped the Old West.

Rome, according to a cliché of the Grand Narrative, could learn but not create. Her originality was in developing the tools of power—law, discipline, administrative and military skills—but these were not, in the liberal view, the heart of civilization. In that view, Rome's contribution was that of a transmission belt: it was only because Rome copied and protected Greek culture that the modern West could come into being. For several centuries, Rome executed that function and then, her duty done, could be dismissed by the Grand Narrative into the mists of history. However, even those who saw Rome as mainly an instrument of the Western idea on its road from Greece to the Atlantic agreed that Rome's geopolitical legacy, the East-West line, was a key element of Western identity. They also accepted that it was the Roman imperial order that enabled the Greek legacy, the true origin of the West, to survive.

The Romans established a civilization around the entire shore of the Mediterranean, connected by sea-lanes that linked a civic and commercial network of towns and regions of production. Roman armies, followed by traders, builders, and craftsmen, penetrated the hinterlands of central and western Europe. By the early centuries A.D., settlements on the Rhine and in Britain had become part of this great network. The settlements became towns with literate ruling classes. When ancient civilization disintegrated, the culture that had flowed through the network left enough skills, writings, and administrative practices behind that the West, left stranded by the eastward retreat of organized imperial administration, was eventually able to climb back up the gradient of civilization—helped by new forces, of which one, Christianity, had flowed west through channels dug by Rome.

Blinded by the cult of Greece and by anti-Roman prejudice, the liberal authors of the Grand Narrative ignored the complex interactions of Greek culture, Roman culture, and Roman power. Far from being a passive conduit of precious cultural essences from elsewhere, Rome was an active element in the cultural synthesis of late classical civilization, a synthesis that helped to shape, though it did not by itself create, the later West.

The three elements of the Roman legacy grew out of the peculiarities of Roman history and of the story that leading Romans told about themselves after their city had become powerful and the capital of an empire. The chief peculiarity was that it was a long story, one reaching back centuries, where by contrast the Greeks of the classical era looked back at most a few generations. Another peculiarity was the Roman idea of freedom, *libertas*, which marked the distinction between the kings who ruled early Rome and the republic that followed them. To a Roman, as to a Greek, the most basic freedom was freedom from slavery or, as in Herodotus, from foreign occupation. But Roman freedom included another aspect that related more directly to later Western notions. This was the idea of freedom as the right of the citizen not to be abused by the government, the freedom that implied equality before the law, and that was guaranteed by time-hallowed and solemn laws and by designated officials. Roman *libertas* in this sense had little to do with the Greek idea that the mark of the free citizen was that he participated equally in political decisions. The government of the Roman Republic was elected by a small number of rich and influential people and the republic was always an oligarchy. So in Rome, to be free meant that however insignificant the citizen, there were certain things the government could not do to him, because he was protected by laws that stood above any government.

"Rome, from the outset, was ruled by kings."[2] So began the *Annals* of Tacitus, written in the early second century A.D.. The *Annals* were not about early Rome at all, but about the early empire, from the death of Augustus in A.D. 14 to the death of Nero in A.D. 68. Tacitus chose to open his account by referring to the state of Rome eight hundred years earlier partly because, like all Roman historians, he thought in centuries. It was also to make the point that the early Romans shook off the monarchy and became—in the sense described—free, only to lose that freedom through greed and shortsighted self-indulgence. These failings led to disastrous civil wars, which persuaded the people that the only way to restore stability was to submit to a new despotism, that of the emperors.

Tacitus's opening also illustrated two strikingly odd features of Roman historical writing. The first was the length of time involved. The Greek fathers of history, Herodotus and Thucydides, wrote contemporary history, describing events that had taken place either in their own lifetimes or a generation earlier. The Roman historians whose surviving accounts told modern scholars most of what they knew about early Rome were writing at least five centuries after the events they described. Those ancient Roman historians, of whom Titus Livius, known in the English-speaking world as Livy, was the most important, had their sources. These sources were, in most cases, written several centuries after the beginnings of the city.

The second odd feature had to do with the "kings" that Tacitus mentioned. The one fundamental idea that all ancient historians of Rome passed on to the modern world was that Rome began as a monarchy, that the monarchy was overthrown, and that, ever after, the name of king was hateful to the Roman people. The defining principle of the Roman Republic, the form of government that replaced the monarchy, was *libertas*. Herodotus made great use of the word *freedom* in his account of the Persian Wars. To him, freedom meant freedom from alien rule. Roman *libertas* was something rather different. It meant, fundamentally, freedom from monarchy. But as modern scholarship easily demonstrated, the Roman Republic was not a free society in any contemporary sense. On the contrary, the Roman Republic was, throughout its history, an oligarchy in which a propertied ruling class made all the decisions, filled all the offices, and controlled the lives and fates of the populace as a whole. In Athens, democracy may have been limited to male citizens, excluding women and slaves, but within that constituency, democracy was absolute. Every man had exactly the same right to state his opinion and cast his vote, and every vote was equal. In Rome, by contrast, the system was elaborately weighted to give the votes of the wealthy few many times the effect of the poor. It was never possible in Rome, as it was in Athens, for a poor majority to vote itself benefits at the expense of the rich.

Another point about Roman *libertas* that made it hard to understand for modern liberals was that it was an aristocratic freedom, the freedom of a social and cultural elite not to bow to the authority of one man. It was a type of freedom well understood in Europe of the old regime, before the French Revolution, but not afterward, because it was incompatible with the principle of equality and equal rights of free expression and belief. In his writings on moden democracy, Alexis de Tocqueville, who was himself an aristocrat, defended this freedom while acknowledging that its time had passed. By definition, aristocratic freedom could not be for the many, for it required wealth and land, and especially a sense of aristocratic identity. Tocqueville regretted its passing, for he believed that democratic freedom, being more individualistic and egalitarian, might easily slide into conformity. His point was that democracy was vulnerable to tyranny, whereas aristocratic *libertas* was the best defense against the chance that any one man should seize unlimited power.

The two features of Roman history, its long perspective in time and its ideology of aristocratic freedom, were reflected in the traditional values of the early Roman Republic: courage, moderation, strict honesty, rigid devotion to duty, justice, and patriotism. The stories of early Rome, as told by Livy, insisted that these virtues remained unchanged for centuries; they were the essential and indispensable foundation of Roman power and greatness. In the liberal story, Roman greatness rested on these republican virtues, and the rise of the empire marked the end of true Roman greatness, although Rome continued to become more powerful. Thus, the true cause of the Fall of Rome, to modern liberals, was the tyranny of the empire and the dishonesty, hypocrisy, and corruption it generated.

The most important legend of early Rome was the story of the fall of the monarchy. According to Livy, Rome had seven kings, starting with the founder, Romulus. The first six were good kings. Each of them contributed an essential element of the state. For example, the second king, Numa Pompilius, established the religious rituals. The fourth, Ancus Marcius, built the first bridge across the Tiber, the Sublician Bridge, and founded the port town of Ostia at the river's mouth. The sixth king, Servius Tullius, was one of the most important. He built temples, public buildings, and the first wall around Rome. He also divided the people into classes according to their wealth and the city's territory into tribes. The seventh and last king, Tarquinius Superbus, or Tarquin the Proud, was a tyrant. According to one story, he "forced the people to construct sewers; and when this hardship caused many to hang themselves, he ordered their bodies to be crucified."[3]

Tarquin then began his greatest project: to enlarge and adorn the temple of Rome's highest god, Capitoline Jove. While this work was under way, a portent occurred. A huge snake slid out of a crack in a wooden pillar in the king's house in the Forum, the *Regia*. Determined to find out what this might mean, Tarquin sent two of his sons and his nephew Lucius Junius Brutus to the oracle of Delphi in Greece. The oracle told the princes, "He who shall be the first to kiss his mother shall hold the supreme power in Rome." The two princes decided to keep this secret from their youngest brother, Sextus, who had remained in Rome. Brutus, however, who also heard the oracle, pretended to stumble and fall, touching his lips to the earth, the mother of all living things.

Back in Rome, in the two hundred and forty-fourth year of the city, corresponding to 510 B.C., Sextus and his two brothers happened to be drinking with friends when the conversation turned to the virtues of women. One of the party, Collatinus, insisted that his wife, Lucretia, was the finest woman in Rome. If they were all to go to his house at that moment, he said, they would find her engaged in some virtuous task. So it proved: the party found her spinning by lamplight. Collatinus delightedly praised his wife and asked his friends to stay for supper.

Sextus, unfortunately, conceived an immediate and violent passion for Lucretia. A few nights later he returned to find her alone. He threatened her with death unless she submitted to him. She refused to give in. He then said that he would not only kill her, he would kill a slave and place his naked body next to Lucretia's. She then submitted. The next day she told Collatinus, Brutus, and her father what had happened, after which she drew a knife and stabbed herself through the heart. Drawing the knife from her body, Brutus swore revenge on Tarquin, "and never again will I let him, his children, or any other man be king in Rome!" Collatinus and her father joined the conspiracy along with another noble, Publius Valerius Publicola. The conspirators bided their time until the king was away on campaign at Ardea, a few miles from the city. They then rallied the people, who were already suffering under Tarquin's exactions.

Hearing of the coup, the king left the army, leaving his sons in command, and hastened back to Rome, but found the gates barred against him. Meanwhile, the conspirators hurried to the army and persuaded it to mutiny against the king's sons. Marching back to Rome, Brutus and Collatinus became the first consuls, or joint magistrates, of the city. Brutus exacted an oath of all the people never again to accept a king and to punish with death anyone who tried to restore the monarchy.

But Tarquin was not a man to yield power easily. He managed to win over Brutus's two sons, who agreed to help him win back the throne. A slave revealed the plot, and Brutus himself, upholding the classical value of paternal severity and exercising *patria potestas*, the father's permanent power of life and death over his offspring, killed his own sons to obey his own law and to preserve the republic.

Tarquin then rallied support from the Etruscan towns to the north of Rome. At the battle of Silva Arsia, he and his Etruscan army killed Brutus, but were themselves defeated. Tarquin then sought help from another Etruscan king, Lars Porsenna of Clusium, who in 508 B.C. occupied the Janiculum hill across the Tiber from old Rome. His forces attacked the city across the Sublician Bridge, built by king Ancus Marcius. A Roman hero, Horatius Cocles, held the bridge against the enemy until it could be thrown down. Thomas Macaulay captured his heroic effort in his *Lays of Ancient Rome*:

> Then out spake brave Horatius,
> The Captain of the Gate:
> "To every man upon this earth
> Death cometh soon or late.
> And how can man die better
> Than facing fearful odds,
> For the ashes of his fathers,
> And the temples of his Gods,
> And for the tender mother
> Who dandled him to rest,
> And for the wife who nurses
> His baby at her breast."[4]

This was Roman republican virtue as understood and taught to the young elite of Western nations from the Renaissance to the nineteenth century. Niccolò Machiavelli, the Florentine political philosopher, devoted his leisure hours to drawing lessons from the early books of Livy on how an aristocratically governed state, such as his own Florence, could maintain itself in a hostile world. The secret, Machiavelli deduced, was *virtù*, virtue, which he found in pure form in early republican Rome. This virtue, or courage to act in accordance with informed insight, was rather like the *arete* praised by Herodotus in one respect: it was the power and skill of a poor people gov-

erned by strict laws who had to defend itself against richer and more powerful enemies. From Machiavelli in the sixteenth to Macaulay in the nineteenth
century, the civic virtue of early Rome formed a staple of Western identity,
reaching a high point in the French Revolution.

Written a generation after the revolution, and in England, the *Lays* were
ballads that retold famous stories from Livy of early Rome. They were
Macaulay's idea of how early Roman poets might have told these stories, the
legends as Livy himself heard them. They did not represent Macaulay's own
values; personally, he was a Whig and a liberal like his fellow countryman
George Grote, and he had good things to say even about the radical French
revolutionaries. As he put it, "the author speaks, not in his own person, but
in the persons of ancient minstrels who know only what a Roman citizen,
born three or four hundred years before the Christian æra, may be supposed
to have known, and who are in nowise above the passions and prejudices of
their age and nation." It is easy to see how such poetry might confirm a sympathetic view of early Rome in Victorian times and an identification of ancient Romans and embattled Britons in the early years of World War II. It is
also easy to see why the *Lays* fell out of fashion in British and American
schoolrooms after the 1960s.[5]

The story of Lucretia, Brutus, and Tarquin echoed through Roman history and, in Livy's dramatic version, became one of the central sources of the
Roman ideals of chastity, pride, inflexible justice, and aristocratic freedom.
Along with the related ideals of modesty and noble simplicity they formed
one half of the myth of Rome in the later West, which survived until partly
superseded by the cult of Greece.

The classic story of noble simplicity was the legend of Lucius Quinctius
Cincinnatus. Although a patrician, a member of the highest nobility of
Rome, he tilled his own land outside the city walls. On one occasion, about
fifty years after the time of Brutus and Tarquin, the Roman army was
trapped by the hostile tribe of the Aequi and threatened with destruction.
Respected for his wisdom and stern morality, Cincinnatus was the city's last
hope. Yielding to its appeal, he left his plow and was appointed dictator.
(This was an emergency appointment used in the early republic, and granted
its recipient unlimited control of civil and military resources for up to six
months.) Within fifteen days, Cincinnatus assembled a new army and defeated the Aequi. Then he returned to Rome, laid down his dictatorship, and
went back to his plow. Americans used to be very familiar with the story of
Cincinnatus, for it was repeated, so people held, in the story of George
Washington, who, after winning the War of Independence, voluntarily laid

down his command and returned to his farm, refusing to turn his military victory into permanent rule.

Stories like those of Lucretia and Brutus or of the noble Cincinnatus fell victim to the Grand Narrative's disapproval of aristocratic values and its exaltation of those elements in the past that pointed forward to democracy, equality, and individual rights. They also fell victim to modern historical scholarship.

The first serious Roman historian of the nineteenth century was Barthold Niebuhr, son of the Niebuhr who first copied the cuneiform inscriptions at Persepolis. Niebuhr and his younger contemporary Gustav Droysen, who wrote on the Hellenistic era of the third and second centuries B.C., established the rules of conduct for ancient history that gradually permeated the field and drove cultural speculation on the meaning of ancient history for the West to the margins, or beyond them, to poets, philosophers, and amateurs. The most important of these rules were that writing history was for scholars, not poets; that scholarship was possible only by dividing the vast realm of history into smaller and smaller specialties; that ancient history in particular rested on source criticism; and that the publication of scholarly editions of original sources was and must remain the alpha and omega of the discipline.

Niebuhr determined to write a history of early Rome that reported only what critical methods could establish. He found that almost nothing reported in Livy or other Roman historians from the early centuries could be independently confirmed. His history was therefore a history of gaps, interrupted only by a few episodes and facts. So sceptical was he that he revived and endorsed an earlier idea, first mooted in the seventeenth century, that the Roman legends of Lucretia, Cincinnatus, and others began as banquet songs in the later republic and were without any value whatever as history. Niebuhr was succeeded by Theodor Mommsen, who used Roman laws and legal traditions to deduce the shape of the early Roman constitution. Both Niebuhr and Mommsen wrote before organized archaeological excavations had taken place in Rome.

By around 1900, the professional opinion was that the stories of the kings of Rome were all made up, whether as banquet songs or for other occasions. Historians at that time were inclined to study Roman history on the pattern of Greek history, where the sources were mainly contemporary with the events they described, and where it was well established that you could deduce nothing reliable about any period more than about two centuries earlier than the time of your source.

The impact of archaeology on Roman history was immense and occurred in two waves, with roughly opposite results. The first wave, conducted mainly in the first half of the twentieth century, revealed a great deal about the nature and extent of early settlement, but could say very little about the people or political events that Livy wrote about. In 1899, archaeologists in the Roman Forum uncovered a sanctuary beneath a black marble paving. Inside, they found a black stone with an inscription in archaic Latin. The first surprise was that this stone seemed to confirm an ancient Roman historian, who spoke, in the second century B.C., of a "black stone in the Assembly area." This alone was astonishing, because the historians of the time disbelieved any written source not confirmed by other evidence. Did this mean that other statements of ancient historians were more reliable than they had seemed?

The second surprise was much greater. The inscription was largely unreadable, but one word was all too clear. It was the word *recei*, a dative form of *rex*, the word for "king." This was the first tangible evidence, outside the written sources, that there had been such a thing as a king in Rome. Elaborately constructed sceptical theories crashed to the ground.

For the next half-century, historians tried to combine what they were learning from archaeology with an increasingly unjustified scepticism about the written sources. In the 1950s and 1960s, this tendency culminated in the work of a Swedish archaeologist, Einar Gjerstad, who wrote six learned volumes on early Rome accepting that Rome had kings, but insisting that the traditional dates were off by almost two centuries. His key claims were, first, that Rome did not become a single community until the sixth century B.C.; that Rome was not founded and organized by the kings, but that the kings appeared after Rome had already come together as a community; and that the republic began in an orderly manner and not because of a rape and a conspiracy, in the mid-fifth century.

Unfortunately for Gjerstad's theory, a second wave of discoveries in and around Rome undermined the sceptical chronology and suggested that the founding of Rome as an organized community lay in the seventh century B.C.. Some of these discoveries were, in their own way, as surprising as the black stone. For example, in 1977 an inscribed block of stone was found in a temple in Satricum, some twenty miles south of Rome. It could be dated with confidence to before 500 B.C. The inscription recorded a dedication to Mars, the Roman god of war, by the companions of a man named in the archaic inscription as Poplios Valesios. In classical Latin, this would be Publius Valerius. Possibly this was a common name, but common men did not have associates who offered dedications, and it was at least a remarkable coincidence that the name and date fit those of Brutus's supposedly legendary friend and ally, Publius Valerius Publicola.

The battle over Rome and its significance began in the Roman Empire itself. Eusebius, a Christian writer of the fourth century who wrote a history of the rise of Christianity from its origins to the conversion of the emperor Constantine (306–337), quoted a certain Melito, bishop of Sardis in Asia Minor in the late second century A.D., who considered it providential that Christianity began at the same time as the Roman Empire, because as the power of the Empire had grown in the East, so had Christianity spread and flourished.

As far as the modern West was concerned, the battle over Rome began during the French Revolution, whose doctrine and imagery were inspired by Roman models, or by what the revolutionaries thought were Roman models. The painter Jacques-Louis David supported the revolution from the start and provided the new regime with a stream of spectacular portrayals of early Roman virtue, for example Brutus ordering his sons' execution. When, in 1799, the republic became the consulate and then the empire of Napoleon Bonaparte, the government continued to draw on Roman imagery, only now it was imagery and models from the imperial, not the republican era.

Napoleon's ideology explained why Roman inspiration remained valued in France, but was suspect and even despised in both Britain and Germany. These two countries were the victims of French aggression, and they were also the countries where Greek scholarship and the worship of ancient Greece spread in this same period. Ever since Napoleonic times, French thinkers, even liberals and socialists, looked to Rome and accepted Rome's contribution to the West, while progressive Germans, Britons, and Americans tended to see Rome as at best a necessary evil and to choose the Greeks as models.

The liberal nineteenth century produced two classic works of ancient history. The first was George Grote's *History of Greece*. The second was Theodor Mommsen's *Roman History*, published in four thick volumes by a young man in his thirties in the incredibly short time of three years (1854–56). This book violated all three of Niebuhr's rules of historical scholarship, although Mommsen made reparation by breaking off after volume four and devoting the last four-fifths of his career to publishing sources. His history was vividly written, full of passion and partiality—partiality for the old Roman Republic as it was before it fell into the hands of demagogues, imperialists, and financial operators. Mommsen was a liberal and, though he did not import his ideology into the past, he did choose for his subject a past where a conservative liberal such as he and many of his contemporaries in the German educated elite might have felt at home. And though many wondered why he broke off after volume four and never wrote the history of the empire, the political explanation was perhaps not misleading, that he did not feel able to do justice to men, events, and results that contradicted his own beliefs and preferences for the human race. Although Mommsen disappointed his many readers by not completing the massive torso of his work, his success was assured. Nor was he quickly forgotten; in 1903 the eighty-one year old received one of the first Nobel prizes in literature, for his *Roman History*.

Even in the liberal story told by Mommsen and his followers, Rome was credited with one undoubted contribution: without it, the idea of the West could not exist in the fundamental, geographical, and cultural sense, as that of a civilization and a community distinct from, and opposed to, the East. Both the idea of the West and that of Europe received their first formulations in the Roman Empire.

One of the greatest liberal authors of the Grand Narrative and a fervent member of the cult of Greece was Ernest Barker. Barker was a classical English liberal of the great generation, born in the 1870s and 1880s, who read Grote and Mommsen in school. He believed in progress, democracy, and mass education before World War I; after it, he trusted in the League of Nations to preserve peace. When right-wing totalitarian movements took power in Germany and Italy, he trusted in modern progressive sentiments at home and alliance with the Soviet Union abroad to resist them. During World War II, he was, along with the overwhelming majority of other Western liberals, in favor of the alliance with Josef Stalin against Germany. After it, in old age, he transferred his hopes for the future to the United Nations.

More important than his political opinions was his role as a popularizer of Greek political philosophy to the enlightened liberal public of his day. His interpretations of Plato and Aristotle, and his translation of Aristotle's *Politics*, remain valuable introductions to Greek thought. In his old age, he developed an interest in the later centuries of Greek and Roman civilization and in the political thought of the Byzantine Greek culture that emerged from that of classical Greece and Rome in the eastern Mediterranean from the fourth to the seventh centuries A.D., and that lasted until the Turks captured Constantinople and occupied Greece in the 1450s.

In the 1920s, Barker wrote an essay on politics and culture in the Roman Empire for an edited volume entitled *The Legacy of Rome*, which for sixty years provided the educated Anglo-Saxon public with an informed account of how Rome appeared in the liberal story of the West. Barker's essay was a typically liberal interpretation and justification of Rome. The Roman Empire, he said, realized—Westernized—the originally Greek ideal of a single universal society, a cosmopolis, in which all free men were equal under the law. He quoted a Roman legal maxim, *omnes homines natura aequales sunt,* "all men are by nature equal." This Greek ideal was that of Stoicism, a philosophical movement that, by the first century B.C., influenced the thought and ideals of much of the Roman elite. Stoics held that human nature was essentially social. Arnaldo Momigliano said of the Stoics that they "reduced liberty to the identification of the will of Man with universal reason and consequently to impassivity."[6] This was something quite other than the classical Greek idea, formulated by Aristotle, of man as a "political animal." Aristotle meant that human nature required for its fulfilment not only life in cities, but an active life of political participation, a life of competition and magnanimous struggle.

The Stoic ideal of social life, by contrast, meant that human nature reached its fulfilment through life in ordered communities without internal struggle and competition, but with an overarching, universal purpose, that of upholding an order and a system of rule common to all humanity. The critical difference was that Aristotle saw political struggle and activity as the goal, whereas the Stoics saw patience, order, and calm as the vital principles.

According to Barker, Stoic ideals influenced the first emperor, Augustus. They certainly suited his interests, which were to convince the peoples of the empire that they should live out their lives in patience and effort and not seek political activity, for such activity was potentially destructive. In the Stoic view, the fundamental distinction in society was not that between Greeks and Romans on the one hand and barbarians on the other, but between good and bad men. The bad man was the subversive who would not support the universal order.

For over a century, Barker claimed, the peoples of the Roman world lived according to Stoic precepts. Augustus, moreover, had combined Stoicism with an emphasis on the old Roman virtues of thrift, piety, and diligence, replacing the supposedly Oriental excesses of his rivals for power, Antony and Cleopatra.

Barker overdid the role of Stoic thought in the early empire. According to Momigliano, Stoicism was a tradition among upper-class intellectuals, and was moreover, for a century after Augustus, a subversive rather than a stabilizing doctrine. However, both agreed that from the early second century onward, the Stoic elite "became fundamentally reconciled to the empire."[7] By the third century, Barker went on, the emperors were looking eastward again for sources of legitimacy. By the late third century, they were building temples to the Sun God and identifying with him as absolute monarch of the universe. According to Barker, religion, instead of being "an attribute or dependency of the State," was becoming "the basis of human organization."

Christianity was merely the latest and most successful of these new eastern cults, in Barker's account. Stoicism as a public philosophy had the advantage that the good of the universal state, its stability and security, were the goals of life. When "religion" replaced this secular faith, the goal of life was no longer to uphold the Roman Empire, but to seek personal salvation. And this was fatal to the empire as well as being somewhat distasteful to liberals such as Barker.

According to Barker, the East, "which gave religion and the Church to the West, fell under the control of the State. The West, which gave politics and the State to the East, came under the sovereignty of the Church." Augustus and the early emperors pacified the Mediterranean world, including the Near East. From the Near East in due course emerged religious doctrines that taught either total submission to an absolute monarch or personal salvation, or both. Thanks to the Roman order established by Augustus, these doctrines were able to spread and to conquer. By conquering, however, they also fatally undermined the Roman order to which they owed their success.

Barker and other progressive liberals did not try to explain why these Eastern religions were successful in replacing both the old Roman religion and Stoicism. One who tried to do so, applying Freudian insights to the study of Greek and Roman culture, was a truculent Irishman named Eric Dodds, who taught Greek at Oxford from the late 1930s to the 1960s. Dodds, whose merits as a scholar of Greek language and literature almost rivaled those of Wilamowitz, brought powerful analytic ability and immense learning to the study of the irrational side of classical civilization and the reasons for its decline. He took from Nietzsche the basic point that the Greeks were not always creatures of light and reason, from Spengler the notion of decline, and from Freud the granite conviction that it was possible to explain both the dark side of Greece and the culture of late antiquity by psychoanalyzing their inhabitants. His most famous book, a genuine best-seller of classical studies, was entitled *The Greeks and the Irrational*. One of his main pieces of evidence that irrational or Dionysiac elements were more prominent in Greece than most classicists would admit was, as for Nietzsche, tragedy, and particularly *The Bacchae* of Euripides. This play told the story of king Pentheus, who was dismembered alive by the maenads, female worshippers of Dionysus who, in divine ecstasy, thought they were killing a sacrificial deer.

In 1965, Dodds suggested that the third century A.D. was an "age of anxiety." This phrase enjoyed a wide popularity and helped to confirm a standard view that influenced the Grand Narrative and held sway among many scholars until replaced by the more upbeat and cheerful approach of Peter Brown and his followers. Since religion, according to Dodds's Freudian view, could not have any independent force but had to be due solely to social or psychological causes, he needed to find such causes to explain the spread of salvation religions, such as Christianity, in late antiquity. He found those causes in what Freud would have called a collective neurosis, produced by the economic, military, and cultural crises that began in the late second century. Dodds drew parallels between the religious paranoia, as he saw it, of late Rome and the paranoia of the twentieth century that had produced totalitarian movements and had, in Spengler's wake, fomented the general fear of decline.[8]

By the fourth century, those who wished to uphold the Roman Empire faced an impossible dilemma. Stoicism no longer commanded much allegiance. The emperors could no longer rule simply by trumpeting the virtues of the empire as a political and social arrangement. Instead, they turned to Christianity, which "offered itself as a world-religion to hold together on the ground of religious unity an empire which was doomed to dissolution if it sought to remain on the ground of political unity." But this strategy could not work either. Precisely because Christianity was a religion and not, like Stoicism, a secular faith in order and stability, its adherents did not consider imperial order as their highest goal. Loyalty to that order could never be fully reestablished. And so, inevitably, it continued to disintegrate. Barker thus concluded, following Edward Gibbon in the eighteenth century and generations of liberal progressives after him, that the fall of the Roman Empire—an issue taken up in the next chapter—was indeed closely linked, if not entirely due, to Christianity.[9]

The conventional view that Barker held and that remained widespread at the end of the twentieth century was that much of the cultural and religious history of Rome was that of a struggle between Western and Eastern elements, with the West exemplified by old Roman traditions, beliefs, and values, and the East by the doctrines of absolute monarchy and the salvation religions that, between them, brought about the decline and Fall of Rome. Liberals of Barker's stripe might reject the traditional Christian version of the story, namely, that Rome's contribution to the West was to enable Christianity to triumph. They could nevertheless deduce another moral from Roman history, namely, that Eastern doctrines and influences were always dangerous to the West. Crudely put, Rome fell because it became orientalized. Rome's true and only contribution to the idea of the West was to be found either in its early, republican phase, when the old Roman virtues of thrift, honor, and loyalty survived, or in the legal thought and administrative skills of the early imperial period.

In 1993, a leading British historian of Rome, Fergus Millar, published a major work aimed squarely at demolishing this conventional view. *The Roman Near East* set out to document that, so far from being Eastern and alien, the spiritual and material culture of the eastern Mediterreanean was the direct continuation of the Hellenistic Greek culture of the region that developed from the age of Alexander the Great in the fourth century B.C. Millar entirely reversed the standard view that the lands of the eastern Mediterranean functioned like a conduit, taking in Oriental culture from the East and distributing it westward.

The essential feature of Near Eastern society in the first four centuries A.D., Millar said, was not that Oriental cults and ideas were spreading west into the Roman world, but that Roman imperial power arrived and became the framework within which society and culture flourished. From the 160s to 363 A.D., moreover, Roman power expanded further, into northern Mesopotamia, the region known in the twentieth century as Kurdistan. To someone used to reading the history of the eastern part of the Roman Empire as a constant series of military challenges by various Eastern powers and of cultural challenges by Eastern doctrines and cults, Millar's work was indeed a surprise.

As for those Oriental cults, Millar declared that one should see them as "internal constructs which cannot be shown to have owed anything to supposed origins in the East."[10] At a stroke, the conventional picture of an uprightly Stoical Roman world being sapped by alien doctrines disappeared. In its place was a more pluralistic image of a Mediterranean world in which most religious and social movements adapted themselves to, or emerged from, a dominant Roman order. This was true of Christianity as well.

Mommsen, who had a clear eye for variation and change in and between the various regions of the Roman Empire, would doubtless have welcomed Millar's work as providing a needed balance to both the Gibbon tradition of seeing Eastern cults as a threat to Roman civilization and the Christian tradition of condemning a Roman decadence that was saved by Christianity. Liberal historical writing in Mommsen's tradition produced a stream of superlative accounts of Rome from the mid-nineteenth century on, while simultaneously intellectuals and political writers argued whether Rome was good or bad and whether its fall was good or bad.

E arly Rome established aristocratic freedom and the rule of inflexible law as the bases of a durable order. As part of their record of that order, the Roman historians embroidered their stories and constructed a history unique in the ancient world for its length and consistency. Emerging from this history, Roman generals, poets, and entrepreneurs encountered Greece, saw the contrast between the Greek past and the sorry present, and began a process of cultural importation and strategic organization. In the five centuries between 200 B.C. and A.D. 300, the Romans gradually shifted the East-West line from the Hellespont and the Aegean to the Adriatic and the middle Danube. At the same time, they adopted and internalized certain aspects of Greek culture, such as Stoicism, a canon of Greek literature and philosophy including most of the writers known to the later West and thousands of copies of masterpieces of Greek art, including most of those that entranced Winckelmann in the 1760s.

During those same centuries, the Romans also added to their early legend as rustic and upright servants of the state a second legend as empire builders and bringers of order to a troubled world. The two legends may have clashed in reality, since the empire was built to a large extent by greedy, ambitious, and ruthless men who shared few of the noble qualities of a Brutus or a Cincinnatus. In the later West, and especially in Catholic Europe, they harmonized into a myth of Rome as a promise of law, order, and piety. The cult of Greece obscured both the myth and the geopolitical shifts, removed the Greeks from the Roman embrace, and installed them as the source and model of the West in a sphere of timeless perfection.

Given its American origins and purposes, the liberal Grand Narrative adopted the cult of Greece as the first Westerners, forgetting how they came to be Western. Given its liberal slant, it downplayed the Romans, both of whose aspects caused discomfort:the aristocratic and patriarchal *libertas* of the early fathers and the slave-holding, exploitative imperialism of the later conquerors and their henchmen. The rustic innocence of early Rome found echoes in the early American republic, which faded in America as it had in Rome herself.

The collapse of the Grand Narrative after the 1960s left the cult of Greece and the notion of the Greeks as the first Westerners strangely untouched, as Martin Bernal paradoxically proved when he thought to attack Western identity by claiming African ancestry for the Greeks. Neither Bernal nor the optimists of the 1990s with their mini-narrative of the West as democracy and free markets appreciated that the Roman geopolitical shifts and use of the Greek legacy were necessary stages on the way from an alien Greece to the West. Necessary, but not sufficient, because the entire Roman design of a geopolitically Westernized Greco-Roman culture was only one half of the foundation of the West. The other half was the synthesis of that culture with Christianity.

The Grand Narrative saw the Romans as bringers of law and empire to the Mediterranean world after centuries of conflict, establishing the peace and cultural unity necessary to the later synthesis of Christian faith and Roman order that was the true beginning of the West. Where the Greeks admired and encouraged new and daring thoughts and demanded that practices, ideas, and customs be justified by reason rather than mere age, the Romans, in the Grand Narrative, abhorred innovation. Roman virtue was always the virtue of the past, of the older and better time when Rome was small and poor, and when conduct was governed by *mos maiorum*, the way of the ancestors. Whenever a Roman needed to justify a change, he portrayed it as a return to the past and a restoration of old customs that had become lost or dishonored.

S everal stories of early Rome developed the themes of *patria potestas* and filial loyalty. In 362 B.C., a young man, Titus Manlius Torquatus, was nearly beaten to death by his father but nevertheless refused to allow a prosecution. Much later, one of his own sons won a victory for Rome by killing the enemy chieftain in a duel. But his father had given orders not to break ranks. His son had disobeyed that order, so the father, while praising the deed, also condemned his son to death.

The Magic Moments of Roman civilization were not points in time but rather the idea of duty and tradition incorporated in stories such as these, or the institutions that incorporated the main Roman contributions, of which law and the empire were the most impressive. The laws of contract, property, buying and selling, liability, defamation, and inheritance were largely Roman creations, as was much of the law of procedure and evidence. Until well into the twentieth century, serious lawyers in Western countries were expected to know Latin and to be familiar with the Roman origins of important legal concepts and practices.

The Roman Empire grew out of the inveterate tendency of the Romans to discover, after conquering a tribe, region, or city, that they would not be secure in their control if they did not conquer the adjacent tribes, regions, and cities as well. This process began in central Italy in the fifth century B.C. and ended only in the first century A.D., when the Romans tried and failed to conquer the Germanic tribes east of the Rhine. This last attempt at expansion fit the tradition perfectly. It was the culmination of a sequence, logical in retrospect, that began in 386 B.C.

In that year Gallic tribes living in the Po valley, then considered part of Gaul, raided deep into Italy. They got as far as Rome itself, which they burned. This was the last time any non-Roman enemy actually captured the city before the Visigothic invasion of A.D. 410. For the next century and a half, Gallic raids continued. By the 220s, Rome was strong enough to take action against this threat at its root. In 222 B.C., the Romans occupied Milan and annexed the flat, fertile plain between the Appenines and the Alps that became the province of Cisalpine Gaul, meaning Gaul on this side of the Alps.

Following the interruption of the Second Punic War, which brought Rome close to defeat, the Romans picked up where they left off. In the second century B.C., they built roads into Cisalpine Gaul and began a process of intensive colonization and distribution of agricultural land to Roman settlers. By the late second century, the region was largely Romanized. It had also become a tempting target of raids to the Gallic tribes beyond the Alps. To secure Cisalpine Gaul, the Romans therefore had to occupy Gaul beyond the Alps. The road to Transalpine Gaul passed, oddly enough, through Spain.

The Second Punic War had shown that the Iberian peninsula was a potential threat and resource base for an enemy. It therefore had to be conquered, which happened in the mid-second century B.C. The conquest of Spain left the coastal region of Transalpine Gaul, later known as southern France, as a vacuum between Roman Spain and the province of Cisalpine Gaul. This region contained the Greek city of Massilia (later Marseilles), which was likewise unprotected against raids from interior Gaul. Roman protection of Massilia, which meant occupation of southern Transalpine Gaul, was required, and duly occurred in 122 B.C.

Now the problem shifted to Gaul proper. The northern boundary of the Roman province of southern Transalpine Gaul was not secure. As long as any part of "long-haired Gaul," the wild hinterland, was unoccupied, Gallic raiders might still sweep down on Massilia, and maybe even into the Po valley itself. At any rate, that was what Julius Caesar claimed when he chose Gaul as his area of operations after his consulate in 59 B.C. It had become the custom, as Rome expanded, to give to retiring consuls a province to manage. In most cases, consuls chose places where they could extort enough revenue to compensate them for the costs of their consulate, which were often heavy, as they included lavish games, free food for the poor of Rome, and bribes. Caesar chose a province where he could train and use an army in order, later, to seize power in Rome.

Having found a pretext to move into central Gaul in 58, Caesar did so and spent the next seven years subduing it. At the end of that period, Roman power extended to the Rhine. This advance, in accordance with the time-honored principle of Roman conquest, opened a new can of worms. Across the Rhine were Germanic tribes who were about to invade "long-haired Gaul" when Caesar beat them to it. His successor, Augustus, the first emperor, therefore decided that the Germans would also have to be conquered. The Roman frontier would have to move forward once again, from the Rhine to the Elbe. An Elbe frontier would connect more easily to the Danube, which was already the Roman frontier in eastern Europe, and would create a shorter and thus more defensible line from the North Sea to the Black Sea.

The Romans never discovered what new perils the Elbe frontier would have raised against them, because in A.D. 9 the Germanic chieftain Arminius, a Roman citizen and former Roman soldier who had returned home to command his native tribe, the Cheruscans, lured an army of three Roman legions into wooded country near modern-day Bremen and destroyed it. So traumatic was this defeat that Augustus and his successors abandoned all plans to conquer Germany. The tide that began in 386 B.C. after the Gallic sack of Rome and that had risen to cover much of western Europe had reached its high-water mark.

Analogous conquests extended Roman power to the Sahara Desert, to the Euphrates River in the Near East, to the shores of the Black Sea, to the Carpathians, to the forests of Moravia and Bavaria, and to northern Britain. But from the mid-first century to the later third century A.D., there was little movement of the borders, except when the emperor Trajan briefly occupied Mesopotamia in A.D. 115–117. When movement began again in 270, it was backward. Yet nothing very serious happened until the late fourth century, when Germanic tribes began occupying Roman territory and receiving permission to settle under their own kings and laws. During the early fifth century, such tribes tore off substantial chunks of the western empire, while leaving intact the eastern empire, meaning the provinces to the east of a line running through the Adriatic and crossing north Africa east of Tunisia. These provinces were governed not from Rome but from the new capital of Constantinople, founded in A.D. 324 on the site of the Greek city of Byzantium. They remained safe from invasion, reasonably well administered, and supplied with the amenities of Roman culture until the Islamic and the Slavonic invasions of the seventh century. The former lopped off Egypt, Palestine, Syria, and Armenia; the latter took most of the Balkans.

In the first century B.C., Caesar and Augustus between them had put an end to the republic. Twenty years of civil war from 50 to 31 B.C. showed that an empire spanning the Mediterranean could no longer be governed by laws and practices that had evolved centuries earlier to fit a small peasant society of a few square miles. The question was not whether the Roman constitution would change, but how. In typical Roman fashion, Augustus presented the new constitutional arrangement, with a single ruler at the head of the empire, as restoring, not abolishing, the republic. The old forms—the consulate, the Senate, the various offices and procedures—remained as scaffolding surrounding the new center of power. This new center, the emperor, commanded the armies, but they were at the frontiers, and in Rome he held no formal office. So it was quite easy to present the change from senatorial to imperial government as a necessary revision that did not violate continuity. The fact of the matter, which became clear under Augustus's heirs, was that one man ruled. The appearance, at first, was that this man was merely the first citizen, who happened also to have permanent and universal military command. Only by pretending to restore the republic was Augustus able to introduce the monarchy, which in his, probably justified, opinion was the only means to avoid more civil war and the end of Roman civilization.

Liberal and progressive authors of the Grand Narrative, such as Will Durant, placed the Greeks at the head of the West and saw the Romans as secondary. Secondary in time, because Rome hardly existed even as an obscure village when Greece already had Homer and his epics. Secondary in importance, because the Romans did not discover history, philosophy, tragedy, or democracy. Secondary, finally, in civility and sophistication.

A number of criteria seemed to confirm this last opinion. The Latin language, for example, was poorer, cruder, and less expressive than Greek. The subtlety, emotional and intellectual range, and heart-wrenching pathos of Greek tragedy or of Greek philosophical writing were unmatchable in Latin. Moreover, the Greek achievements were, as Thucydides said of his own history, "possessions for ever." They were, or seemed to be, humanly valuable on the modern, liberal scale. They were about spiritual discovery, philosophical and scientific insight, literary and artistic excellence, and historical understanding. The Greeks may have been often at war, but war and power were not the essence of their culture; they were rather unavoidable necessities that philosophers, historians, and tragedians could use to produce their stories and lasting insights into deep human truths.

The Romans, by contrast, appeared to be defined largely by war and power. Rome did not invent history, democracy, or literature: she invented law, discipline, and empire. Moreover, what some saw as law, discipline, and empire looked to others like oppression, force, and arrogance. Consequently, the tradition of the Grand Narrative offered two somewhat different perspectives on Rome. The first, foreshadowed by some Romans themselves, was a condescending view that saw Rome as crude and rustic, virtuous, at least in its early phases, and fundamentally well intentioned. Rome respected Greece and knew that if she could never rival Greek achievements, she could at least preserve and learn from them. This was the attitude of the poet Horace when he wrote in the first century B.C. that "captive Greece captured her savage conqueror." In the same vein, the modern narrative lauded Roman achievements as the unfortunate but necessary means by which the true and permanent elements of classical culture were protected and preserved for the West.

The other perspective was that of the modern left. The left-wing view saw Rome as a destructive conqueror whose armies put a final end to Greek independence and sucked the last drops of vitality from Greek civilization. Roman society itself was primitive, unable and unwilling (except for a small elite) to learn from Greece or respect what modern liberals called civilized values. The poet and critic A.E. Housman, who was no leftist, partly adopted this view when, in 1911, he spoke of the Romans to an English audience as "men whose religion you disbelieve, whose chief institution you abominate, whose manners you do not like to talk about."[11] By "chief institution" he meant slavery, and by "manners" he meant, for example, the popular Roman pastime of watching men kill each other in the arena. Both liberals and leftists would have agreed with the English classics teacher who in 1932 wrote of Athens that "in the days of her greatness she taught the world by the production of masterpieces. In her declining years she was content to act as interpreter of her past achievements and to pass to another and less gifted nation [Rome] the torch that had grown dim in her own hands."[12]

The left-wing version was expressed most classically in Howard Fast's novel *Spartacus* and the 1960 film of this novel by Stanley Kubrick, which starred Kirk Douglas as the rebellious gladiator who assembled a slave army of 120,000, defeated several Roman armies, looted much of Italy, and was finally destroyed in 71 B.C. by Marcus Licinius Crassus. In line with his communist sympathies, Fast portrayed Spartacus as a proletarian leader, groping for ideas of human dignity and universal justice. Crassus, by contrast, appeared as the caricature of a right-wing militarist and authoritarian; as a protofascist, in short. Roman slavery could be, and often was, brutal for its victims. In a notorious case of A.D. 61, a slave killed his master, a rich official called Pedanius. In retaliation, all four hundred of Pedanius's other slaves were executed, including women and children.[13] In both Greece and Rome, the evidence of slaves was accepted in law only if it had been extracted by torture. Spartacus, by all accounts, was a brave and humane leader. In 1917, the first German communists called themselves Spartakists, conjuring the image of the hopelessly oppressed struggling bravely against the overwhelming odds that favored the violent, the powerful, and the unjust. According to Marxist doctrine, the stages of history were marked by changes in the modes of production, from slavery through feudalism to capitalism and finally to communism. These changes were impersonal and vast, not subject to individual will. Therefore, Spartacus was, in strict Marxist terms, a fool to rebel, because Rome was a slave-holding society and nothing any individual could do would change that. You did not have to introduce Marxist theory to understand that a slave uprising in central Italy at the height of Roman power was not a viable proposition. Nevertheless, this very futility gave Spartacus a tragic grandeur that appealed to many in modern times, whether communist or liberal.

In the later twentieth century, a new generation of historians using archaeology to strengthen, rather than undermine, the written evidence moved toward a synthesis on early Rome that was more compatible with the Romans' own stories than anything since Niebuhr. The key figure in this movement of literary and archaeological revisionism was the Italian historian Arnaldo Momigliano. Apart from some early works in his twenties, he wrote no books; rather, he produced hundreds of articles, essays, and reviews, and trained a group of scholars who virtually revolutionized the study of Rome, in both the classical and Christian eras. Momigliano had a unique command of all the original sources of ancient history, whether Greek, Roman, Jewish, or Christian, and of all the writing about antiquity in the modern West. He took an intense interest in the origins of Rome and in the religious and cultural changes that shaped late antiquity, an era that scholars, starting in the 1960s, began to recognize as an era to be understood in its own right and not merely as one of decline and decadence.

Momigliano exploded many myths and contributed in his own work and that of his leading pupils, Peter Brown and Timothy Cornell, to recovering the lost realities of early and late Rome, two ages and cultures as dissimilar as any in the ancient world. In so doing, he provided a sound basis on which to judge, in the era after the fall of the Grand Narrative, the lasting contributions of Rome to the West.

The first of these contributions was the East-West distinction, fateful in history because it divided Europe into a part belonging to the later West and another that was partly Western. Some historians of Europe, such as Norman Davies, deeply regretted this distinction, which they considered artificial and damaging. In 1996, Davies, a historian of Poland, published a monumental history of Europe in which he argued that the idea of the West had, for many decades, supported a false notion in western Europe and North America of a common Western identity that did not include eastern or Slavonic Europe, which, as Davies showed, had always been the largest and most populous part of the continent. The idea, or rather ideology, of the West was an illusion, for it implied that the regions that belonged to it had a unitary and harmonious history, whereas in fact the history of Europe was anything but unitary and harmonious.[14] To historians such as Davies, the East-West line artificially divided Europe and encouraged the idea of the West, which they considered to be a somewhat arbitrary set of values shared by western Europeans and Americans.

Much of this criticism was justified. The Grand Narrative of the West was often no more than a set of values chosen for their compatibility with modern liberalism and that were in no sense confined to western Europe and North America. Yet no historian could deny that European and Western history had for over a millennium and a half turned on the East-West distinction.

Victorian liberals like George Grote traced the origin of the East-West distinction to the Persian Wars in the early fifth century B.C. Many classical scholars followed them, such as the Swedish historian Hermann Bengtsson, who stated, in his widely used textbook on Greek history written in the 1930s, that the idea of Europe was born after the Greek victory over Persia.

Writers such as these, who strongly influenced the Grand Narrative, harked back to Herodotus and his contrast between Greek freedom and Persian despotism. They saw the Persian Wars as a turning point, after which Greeks and, later, Romans, became aware that something distinguished people west of the Hellespont—the strait separating Europe from Asia Minor—from those east of it. The dividing line was, as Herodotus implied, the line between Europe and Asia. To the west of that line, civic virtue and pride in skill and achievement (all these things implied in the single Greek word *arete*), freedom, individual conscience, and patriotism. To the east, despotism, huge and opulent empires, mystery, sorcery, and massed hordes marching to the command of exalted rulers who were unaccountable to their subjects. The critical and decisive contribution of Rome was to shift this line westward, until it ran not between Greece and Asia but between Italy and Greece. That shift constructed the West as western Europe and its overseas extensions in the colonial and modern eras. It also entailed a huge irony: Greece, where the West supposedly began, was now excluded from the geographic West. This was a development with many cultural and political consequences. The fraught and contentious role of Greece in NATO and the European Union in the late twentieth century was a remote but nevertheless direct consequence of the Roman geopolitical shift of the East-West line from the Hellespont to the Adriatic.

The Greeks knew the name "Europe" in various senses. The etymology is unclear; the word may be of Semitic origin or may derive from the Greek words *eurus* and *ops*, which would yield the sense "ample, wide to look upon." In archaic Greece, Europe was the name of various local goddesses worshipped at a range of sites. These divinities had only the name in common with that more famous Europa, whose story appeared in Ovid's *Metamorphoses*. In this Greek legend, Europa was a princess of Tyre, the daughter of Agenor. Zeus, the supreme god, fell in love with her. Disguised as a bull, he appeared from the sea when she and her brothers were playing on the beach and carried her off, as portrayed most famously by Titian in his *Rape of Europa* (1562). Nietzsche once wrote about this story, "Europe is, after all, a woman, and the legend tells us that such a woman in certain circumstances lets herself be dragged off by beasts. Earlier, in the time of the Greeks, it was an ox. Nowadays—heaven preserve me from naming the beast."[15]

Zeus took Europa to Crete, where they had three children: Minos and Rhadamanthys, who became judges of the underworld, and the hero Sarpedon. When Zeus returned to his divine dwelling on Mount Olympus, Europa married the king of Crete. Meanwhile, her father sent his sons Cadmus,

Phoenix, and Cilix to find Europa. They never did, but settled in various countries where they gave rise to legends of their own.

The story of Europa and the bull was widely known in ancient Greece. Whether or not this "Europa" was in any way connected to the name of the continent, we find the name "Europe" applied to the part of the world that included Greece from the fifth century B.C. on. Herodotus used the name in two senses: to mean all lands west and north of the Hellespont, or to mean only those parts immediately adjacent to those straits. In the latter sense, "Europe" was a small area that did not include Greece proper.

Later Greek writers tended to use Europe to mean all of Greece and an undefined area to the north and west. The fourth-century B.C. orator Theopompus used "Europe" to mean all the known world north and west of the Hellespont, including Rome, whose growing power was known to informed Greeks. All of these usages defined Europe's eastern boundary as the Hellespont and the western shore of the Black Sea as far as the river Don. The cultural significance of this line remained as Herodotus had defined it: to the west, in Europe, wisdom, courage, manliness, frugality, and freedom tempered by realism; to the east, in Asia, opulence, magical arts, back-stabbing cowardice, effeminacy, and despotism.

Over a period of four centuries, the Romans transformed both the terms and the location of this distinction. They kept the idea of a line separating virtue from vice, honesty from subtle cunning, and freedom from tyranny. But they shifted this line to the west, so that the Greeks, who invented the distinction, found themselves classed among those who were vicious, cunning, and despotic. At the same time, the Romans absorbed what they most liked in Greek civilization, purging it of its suspicious eastern elements. Thus, the geopolitical shift of the East-West boundary and the Westernization of Greek culture were two sides of the same coin, namely, the construction of a proto-West combining Greek and Roman elements protected by Roman power.

This double shift, of the East-West line and of the Greek legacy, began as soon as the Romans encountered the Greeks in the third century B.C. By the early second century, Roman commanders and poets had both discovered Greece. What they found there was a cultural legacy of art, philosophy, literature, and historical writing vastly more sophisticated than their own amid a scene of contemporary decadence. Second-century Greece was but a shadow of its former self, and this suggested to the Romans that classical Greek civilization deserved to be recovered and used to enrich and inspire Rome. It also suggested that the Roman task was to preserve the best of Greece while maintaining a strict vigilance against the threat of eastern decadence.

Late republican Rome received Greek culture, but she also received many eastern cults, practices, and mystical beliefs. The threat of the east reached a political culmination when Cleopatra ensnared both Julius Caesar and Mark Antony, using their military power to maintain her Greco-Egyptian kingdom as long as possible. Cleopatra was an object lesson to conservative Romans in the perils of the East: a Greek queen, descended from one of Alexander's generals, who had surrendered to the luxury and superstitions of the East and was now preparing to corrupt good Roman commanders and impose her eastern decadence on Rome itself.

Starting in the late second century A.D., the Roman Empire was often divided between two or more emperors, sometimes peacefully, usually not. Thus, in the year 211, the two sons of the emperor Septimius Severus, Caracalla and Geta, divided the empire at the Hellespont: Caracalla got the northern and western part, Geta got Asia and Egypt. The contemporary Greek historian Herodian described this treaty and noted how the two emperors also divided the Roman Senate, with the senators from Asia joining Geta, and the "Europeans" (*europaikoi*) remaining with Caracalla.

By the third century, strategic considerations began to confirm the cultural divide sensed by the early Roman military and intellectual explorers of Greece. Thus, in the 280s, the emperor Diocletian formalized the division of the empire not at the Hellespont but along a line running through the Roman province of Illyria (twentieth-century Yugoslavia), across the Adriatic and Mediterranean, and separating the Roman provinces of Egypt and Libya. In his time, "Europe" again acquired the restricted meaning of "the region immediately north and west of the Hellespont," what we would call extreme southeastern Europe.

It was this restricted use of the name of Europe, a use linked closely to the administrative and military needs of the later empire, that gave rise to some of the earliest geopolitical uses of the word *West*. This occurred in a life of the emperor Aurelian (270–275), itself part of a peculiar document of the late fourth century called the *Historia Augusta*. When Aurelian seized power, secessionist rulers held both the extreme west and extreme east of the empire. In Gaul, a certain Tetricus called himself emperor; in the Syrian city of Palmyra, the Arab princess Zenobia had established an independent state. Aurelian defeated both her and Tetricus. The *Historia Augusta* described Aurelius's victories over his two rivals as "triumphs over Zenobia and Tetricus, that is over East and West" (*de Oriente et Occidente*), implying the lands of the sunrise and the sunset. "Europe," to this author, was neither East nor West, neither the land of sunrise nor of sunset. Perhaps it was the center of the world, what the Germanic tribes north of the empire called middle-earth, later known as *middangeard* to the Anglo-Saxons, *midgaard* to the Danes.[16]

The new East-West line, which became permanent, had far-reaching implications. In 476, Romulus Augustulus ("little Augustus"), the last emperor of the western part, was deposed; in the words of a contemporary chronicler, "the western empire of the Roman people ended." Consequently, what used to be an internal administrative dividing line became the frontier between the remaining eastern part of the empire and the Germanic kingdoms of western Europe. When, centuries later, the peoples of these kingdoms developed a sense of themselves as Western, that sense ran only to the old frontier and did not include the Greek-speaking lands, much less the Semitic or Egyptian lands, of the old eastern empire.

That old dividing line was the remote reason that twentieth-century Americans and Europeans viewed the West as extending only to the borders of Yugoslavia. That sense of the West as including western Europe and America but not central, eastern, or southeastern Europe was more than geographical; it was political, cultural, and religious as well. It predated the Soviet occupation of central Europe in 1944–45 and the Cold War that followed, and in the 1990s it was clear it had outlasted these phenomena.

The third contribution of Rome was its image as the bringer of order, empire, and civilization. The liberal Grand Narrative disparaged such achievements, and more left-wing versions denounced them as protofascist. Thanks both to the cult of Greece and to these ideological blinkers, Americans who learned the Grand Narrative did not know where to place the Romans. Critics of the Grand Narrative were even less likely to do them justice. Yet the role of Rome in the modern idea of the West was varied and complex. The Roman legacy was undeniably alive in European institutions, practices, beliefs, and language, unlike that of Greece, which had to be recovered. Unlike Greece as well, Rome was morally ambivalent. Rome represented to some a permanent memory of peace, order, and harmony and a challenge to the modern West to repeat the achievement. To others, Rome was an oppressive, brutal, and immoral society, a model not for all the best in the West, but for the worst.

The living legacy of Rome was more obvious in Europe than in America, except perhaps in Washington, D.C. Most Americans rarely felt comfortable with the full range of Roman models, including imperialism, slavery, authoritarian government, and the ethic of individual sacrifice for the common good. Roman or civil law predominated on the Continent, languages derived from Latin were spoken across southern Europe, and scores of millions of Europeans lived in regions that had been part of Rome for a thousand years or more when the empire ended. Roman names for political practices and institutions, such as consul, prefect, diocese, senate, forum, market, republic, city, or province, retained a resonance in Europe that neither did nor could exist in the new transatlantic democracy. Americans prided themselves on being innovators and free of the past; Europeans, including the revolutionaries of France, prided themselves on continuity. Even the sign of the eagle changed character after its migration. In an amazing feat of symbolic transformation, Americans succeeded in defining their eagle as a bird of freedom and defiance, rather than symbolizing military conquest and the power of an authoritarian state.

Again unlike America, Rome also survived as a political dream of continental unity and harmony. The whole history of Europe could be read as the never-ending attempt to recreate the Roman Empire on foundations stronger, more permanent, and morally better than the original. For a thousand years after the pope crowned Charlemagne emperor in A.D. 800, an empire existed in western and central Europe; its most common name was *sacrum imperium romanum*, the Holy Roman Empire. After the violent attempts at unification by Napoleon, imperial Germany, and Adolf Hitler, Europeans rallied in the 1950s for one final attempt, this time under the peaceful and commercial aegis of the Common Market, later known as the European Union. In the last years of the twentieth century, this dream of Western unity came under severe stress as European policymakers had to decide whether to admit the inhabitants of territories east of the fateful East-West line, such as Poles, Czechs, or Hungarians, not to mention Turks.

The idea of Rome survived, perhaps most powerfully of all, in the Roman Catholic Church, described by the Protestant Thomas Hobbes in the seventeenth century as "the ghost of the Roman Empire, sitting crowned upon the grave thereof." The heads of this church, the bishops of Rome, represented in the twentieth century the last remaining institution with an unbroken history from the time of the original Roman Empire. The argument over what was Roman and what was Christian in Catholicism and how those two legacies should blend was an important part of the battle for Western identity.

Rome had also survived through the centuries when Greece was unknown as a subject and model of elite education. The Latin language remained in use in the church and in learned discourse. Education beyond the lowest level of literacy in Europe was, until the nineteenth century, education in the language, history, laws, heroes, and poetry of Rome.

Morally, the fight over Rome was as old as Rome itself. Was Rome good or bad, a Magic Moment of glory or of sin? The locus classicus for the confrontation of the two visions of Rome in the medieval and modern West was perhaps the statement of St. Paul, the Christian apostle, that he was a Roman citizen; *civis romanus sum*. Paul was the prophet of a religion that preached a kingdom not of this earth and that exhorted its adherents to obey God first and Caesar, meaning the government of the Roman Empire, second. Yet that same prophet, imprisoned for subversion, secured his release by claiming his right as a Roman citizen to appeal to Caesar in Rome. Rome, therefore, furnished to her subject Paul the freedom to continue his subversive preaching and thus, on one reading, wrote her own death warrant.

Since at least the mid-nineteenth century, the Grand Narrative, in America and Britain, downplayed the hard edges of the Roman contribution. Yes, Rome brought empire, law, and order, but these things were justified, not in themselves, but because they enabled Greek culture and, later, Christianity to spread West. The modern liberal West rested, its Anglo-Saxon defenders held, more on Greece and Christianity than on Rome, whose role was that of facilitator.

The debate on Rome after World War II was therefore not a debate between defenders of the West and revisionist critics, but a debate within the West. On one side were Anglo-American liberals with their Christian-inspired, postimperial guilt; on the other, French and Italian thinkers for whom Rome was part of their history, and who saw it not as an oppressor but as the guarantor of order and peace. This rhetoric could still be heard from officials of the European Union in the 1990s.

The Continental narrative of Western identity culminated in a synthesis of Rome, Christianity, and modern social democracy. The liberal narrative preferred Greece, the Renaissance, and individualism. Both thought in terms of syntheses, and both circumvented history by jumping from selected high points of the past to a present that, by definition, was the highest point of all.

The burden of Rome was that the Romans established the geopolitical West and gave it a westernized, transformed version of Greek civilization. Rome also introduced an idea of freedom as the right to be safe from arbitrary power. The Roman role was creative, not merely derivative. On the other hand, while Roman freedom contributed something not found in Greek freedom, the Romans also destroyed an essential element of the latter—the idea of freedom as social and political equality, the right to be a participant in political affairs. In place of Greek freedom, the Romans offered universal empire and the vision of a Stoic, cosmopolitan order.

But the empire, however universal as an ideal, was limited in reality to a specific geographical space. That space was the Mediterranean basin with extensions into western Europe and the Near East. The Romans conquered that space as culturally inferior latecomers, constantly aware that while they themselves came from the West, they would not be civilized unless they controlled the East—an East that was also a threat of corruption, decadence, and superstition. Thus the Romans, especially after Actium, constructed an East-West distinction that was both geopolitical and geocultural, but that at the same time contained a basic ambiguity: to the west of the line lay Rome itself and the source of the ancient Roman virtues, but also barbarism and ignorance. To the east of the line lay Greece and its civilization, as well as Egypt, Syria, and the rival empire of Persia. Rome had therefore to decide whether her destiny lay in the rustic and primitive West or in the cultured, but also dangerous, East.

In A.D. 324, the emperor Constantine made his decision. Rome would move east, and the empire would recenter its geopolitical base on Constantinople, protected by walls and the sea but also nearer to the spheres of action, both cultural and military. Constantine's move implied that the core of the empire would slowly become Greek and eastern, and enabled this easternized and rejuvenated Rome to maintain its universalist ambitions in conflict with the rival universalism of Persia and, later, of Islam.

The move left the regions west of the line, including the city of Rome itself, on the margins of civilization. One might have expected this culturally inferior, poorer, underpopulated, and militarily vulnerable West to fade away completely, leaving little more than vague memories, as the Roman Empire survived in the only way possible, by moving east and abandoning the West. But this did not happen, and the reason was that a new force had entered the matrix of possibilities, namely, Christianity. The head of this new force was domiciled in western Rome and did not move when Constantine did. This development saved the West through its era of marginal existence, when Roman imperial power had shifted to Constantinople and abandoned the West to the barbarians. It was able to do so in part because it was free from political control, because the source of that control—the emperor—had gone east.

As Roman political power moved east, the religious power that had taken over the empire, Christianity, moved west. This paradoxical double movement defined the period known as late antiquity, the era from the third to the seventh centuries. The outcome of late antiquity was that Roman imperial power survived, but in the eastern guise that later ages called Byzantine. The geographical West remained what it was before Rome became a cosmopolitan society, a marginal, rustic zone of poverty and minimal culture. Yet it was in this marginal zone, defined by the East-West line, that the legacy of Rome joined with Christianity and the barbarians to produce the synthesis of the Old West. That synthesis, and its modern heir, the liberal and democratic New West, emerged from the history of institutions and social forces, not from modern ideologies. The following chapters examine that emergence, starting with the biggest of all the questions of Western history—the question that shaped the life work of Edward Gibbon and Oswald Spengler and cast a shadow over much of the argument about the West in the twentieth century: the question of why Rome fell, and what that fall might mean for those who came after.

CHAPTER FOUR

Christianity and the Fall of Rome

The Roman Empire fell to external attacks, not internal division,
although the latter often made the former possible
—Grotius

The Romans, by destroying all peoples, destroyed themselves
—Montesquieu

All great matters are full of ambiguity
—Tacitus

I n popular imagination, the fall of the Roman Empire usually involved images of massed barbarian hordes on the march, dramatic battles, and burning cities along with more prurient fantasies of Roman orgies and the lusty couplings of virile barbarians and dusky Mediterranean beauties. Such imaginations were politically incorrect both in terms of the Grand Narrative and even more in the neopuritanical 1980s and 1990s. More to the point, the military explanation, however favored by boys and war-game–playing adults, was implicitly denied during most of the twentieth century not only by most scholars but by the most spectacular of all popular representations of Rome's decline, the 1965 Hollywood epic *The Fall of the Roman Empire*.

This Samuel Bronston production was one of the last sword-and-toga spectaculars, released five years after *Spartacus* and six years after the greatest of them all, *Ben Hur*. It contained its share of marching armies, decadent Romans, gorgeous women, and lusty barbarians, but the message of the film was that Rome fell not because she was conquered, but because of internal moral decline, the arrogance of power, and greed. The story and the underlying message bore the distinct marks of the film's historical consultant, Will Durant, who can fairly be called Mr. Grand Narrative himself.

The film begins in A.D. 180, the last year of the emperor Marcus Aurelius. This indubitably good and noble man was a hero of the Grand Narrative, the man who, though a philosopher by temperament, gave up the chance of a quiet life to serve the state and the common good. For many years, Marcus Aurelius, the least military of men, led the Roman armies on the Danube in person, restoring the frontier after invasion and plague had devastated northern Italy. During all this time he kept a diary, notes to himself on life, death, ethics, piety, and duty. These were his *Meditations*, one of the basic documents of Stoic philosophy and the one ancient book that, in the 1990s, retained an immediate appeal to American college students. Its core teaching was "welcome all that comes to pass, even though it appears rather cruel, because it leads to . . . the health of the Universe."[1]

Marcus Aurelius, played by Alec Guinness, has a dream. It is the Stoic dream of a world community under a world government, in which all citizens work together in duty and self-sacrifice for the good of the whole. In an early scene, Marcus Aurelius views a pageant of delegations from remote provinces and beyond the empire. He hopes to unite all these disparate and diverse peoples in a cosmopolitan society. To do so is to carry out the true mission of Rome. This vision is supported by his friend the philosopher Timonides (James Mason), a made-up character, who lives in the camp out of devotion to the emperor but who has his own private dream of leaving army life and creating his own little Stoic paradise, a sort of rural commune of farmer-philosophers.

The emperor is ailing and knows he will soon die. He hopes that the young soldier Livius (Stephen Boyd), also an imaginary figure, will succeed him, because Livius understands the cosmopolitan vision but is also a just and brave commander. The purpose of the long campaign, Marcus Aurelius says, is not to defeat or subjugate the barbarians but to convince them to join his vision of a Stoic world-empire. Unfortunately, Marcus Aurelius has a son, Commodus (Christopher Plummer), who is greedy, spoiled, and petulant. According to Edward Gibbon, he was not "a tiger born with an insatiate thirst of human blood," but rather a weak and foolish young man, whose "simplicity and timidity rendered him the slave of his attendants, who gradually corrupted his mind. His cruelty, which at first obeyed the dictates of others, degenerated into habit, and at length became the ruling passion of the soul."[2] We are later told that he is not really the emperor's son, but the fruit of a temporary liaison between his mother the empress and a gladiator. Commodus has evil supporters in the camp who hope for riches and power if he succeeds his father. These plotters poison Marcus Aurelius before he has a chance to make Livius his heir.

The canard that Commodus was not really the son of Marcus Aurelius is found in the ancient sources but is almost certainly false. The film follows the written sources in portraying Commodus as a megalomaniac psychopath, who thought he was a god on Earth and one of whose last decisions was to rename Rome itself; henceforth, the city would be known as Colonia Commodiana, the settlement of Commodus. Almost all modern historians, starting with Gibbon in 1776, followed the sources in seeing Commodus as the first truly decadent emperor, several cuts worse than Caligula and Nero a century and a half earlier. The one exception was the enigmatic Sicilian historian Santo Mazzarino, who saw in provincial inscriptions evidence that Commodus was hailed as a peacemaker and friend of the people.

The Fall of the Roman Empire follows the standard view of Commodus. He succeeds to the empire, loyally supported by Livius, who does not suspect that the emperor was murdered, and immediately breaks off the campaign. Back in Rome, Commodus begins acting the tyrant, raising taxes and plundering his own provinces. Livius brings a group of captured Germanic barbarians to Rome. They are portrayed as primitive but honest, fighting Rome because they want to stay free. A corrupt and fawning Senate showers Livius with honors because it believes him to be the new emperor's friend, and allows him to settle the barbarians in Italy. Timonides becomes the teacher of this community and is set to realize his miniature Stoic utopia.

In reality, the Germanic invasions across the Danube in the 160s took the Romans by surprise because the tribes involved, the Marcomanni and the Lombards, had been among the friendliest and most docile for a century and a half, and trade, contacts, mutual relations among these tribes, their kings, their chieftains, and Rome had been intense. Roman products and works of art appear in greater numbers in those very zones from which the violent and destructive attacks came, starting in 166. The film's sentimental, United Nations image of crude but noble barbarians (i.e., the Third World) who do not understand why they have to submit to Rome (i.e., American hegemony) is a travesty of the historical record. A more realistic view is that it was precisely because they knew that the Roman Empire was rich and undefended that they attacked.³ But such a point would have contradicted the film's Stoic and humanitarian moralism.

As Commodus's tyranny gets worse, Livius, who loves Commodus's sister Lucilla, is tempted to rebel. At Commodus's command, Lucilla (played by Sophia Loren) marries the king of Armenia. Enraged by Commodus's exactions, the Armenians rise in revolt. For one last time, Livius leads a Roman army against an enemy, although in his heart he agrees with their grievance. He kills the king and returns, with Lucilla, to Rome in triumph. In this case, the film is gentler than history: the real Lucilla was indeed exiled to the east in 182, but she did not marry the king of Armenia, because she was killed on Commodus's orders.

Commodus next orders Timonides and the Germanic tribesmen killed and their village destroyed. Livius rebels and leads an army to the gates of Rome. The army, however, is bribed by Commodus to defect. Desperate, Livius enters Rome and is captured. Commodus, in a fit of arrogance, says he will fight Livius in single combat, as a gladiator. As Livius kills Commodus, we hear rich senators and generals offering bribes to the praetorian guard to win its support in seizing imperial power. As the bidding reaches insane heights, Livius and Lucilla walk off hand in hand. A voice-over reminds us that it took Rome centuries to fall, longer than the entire span of some civilizations. The voice utters the final lesson of the film, that no civilization can stand that has lost its own soul. Rome, according to Samuel Bronston and Will Durant, fell because Romans lost the Stoic devotion to duty of Marcus Aurelius. Instead, they fawned on power, losing all dignity, and, when the tyrannical power fell, they tried to buy it for themselves.

The closing scene of the bidding for empire is partly historical. Commodus was not killed in the arena, but strangled on the orders of the commander of the praetorian guard, who feared for his own life, on New Year's Eve of 192. One of the murderers was Commodus's concubine, Marcia, who according to a persistent legend was Christian. A few months later, his successor was also murdered, and it was on that occasion that a rich senator bought the empire at auction in the praetorian camp.

The Fall of the Roman Empire told an odd story, given its title. For one thing, to set the "fall" of Rome in the late second century was to anticipate the event by over two hundred years. Not until the fifth century did imperial power and administration begin to break down in the western half of the empire, and in the East they continued for centuries longer. The only reason for choosing the reign of Commodus was to make the historical point that the

Fall of Rome was not a matter of military defeat or even bad government and civil collapse, but of abandoning Stoic morality.

The barbarians, meanwhile, were portrayed only in the most perfunctory sense as enemies of Rome. It was true that the opening scenes showed Marcus Aurelius as a soldier, and Livius capturing the barbarians and their chieftain on a daring raid beyond the frontier. But these scenes merely set up the contradiction, essential to the plot, between corrupt Romans and simple but honest barbarians. The barbarians, we are told in no uncertain terms, were the true and natural citizens of Marcus Aurelius's Stoic commonwealth, for they were free and could easily learn the old Roman virtues of duty and collaboration. The pathetic senators of Rome, on the other hand, had none of the qualities required for the Stoic utopia. Durant wanted us to see Commodus and the Romans as worse than barbarian, combining shortsighted greed with sophisticated, decadent cunning.

Given the picture's date, 1965, one may suspect that Durant was sending a classic liberal message to Lyndon Johnson's America, which was beginning its massive intervention in Vietnam. Imperial power, arrogance, low cunning, greed, and violent disregard of alien cultures went together, the film warned; the only just and reasonable policy for a great, world-bestriding superpower was to offer the world's diverse peoples a Stoic commonwealth of responsible freedom in humble devotion to duty and human betterment. Because Rome abandoned this mission and chose the path of Commodus, she fell.

The Stoic philosophy of Marcus Aurelius and its vision of an earnest, civilized, multicultural world community was an ideal match for the 1960s liberal political sensibility, which instinctively rejected explanations of Rome's fall in terms of military crisis and invasion. Durant's version of Rome's fall confirmed the first part of Alexander Demandt's observation that "left-liberal authors often advance socioeconomic explanations of decline, those of the center, explanations in terms of domestic policy and misgovernment, whereas the right wing seems to prefer explanations in terms of foreign policy," in this case, Germanic invasion.[4] By the 1980s, despite liberal attempts to ignore it, the right-wing explanation began to seem increasingly plausible.

Even so, one did not have to adopt the barbarian theory to see that the Durant version was radically insufficient. For one thing, it constructed an ideal vision of Rome, incarnated in the Stoic ideal, and defined the failure of that ideal as decline and fall. The Romans, in the time of Commodus, faced a choice: to remain Roman or to fall. Such a false dichotomy elided the three or four centuries after Commodus, the centuries rediscovered and interpreted as a cultural epoch with its own identity by twentieth-century scholarship, and especially by Peter Brown, as late antiquity.[5] Only by recognizing this long span of time—longer than that of the Roman Empire from Julius Caesar to Marcus Aurelius—as the formative era of the later West could one arrive at a proper understanding of the Fall of Rome as a historical, rather than a moral, tale. Second, the most decisive new development in late antiquity was the rise of Christianity to become the religion of the Roman Empire. Of this, not a trace in Durant's version. A version of Rome's fall that left out Christianity and failed to portray late antiquity in its own terms was a caricature that obscured more than it revealed.

The Christianization of the empire and the rise of late antiquity were the preconditions of the synthesis that produced the Old West, the medieval Western world. These phenomena in turn exploited the geopolitical shift that the Roman Republic and early empire accomplished. The Romans westernized Greek culture and shifted the geopolitical boundary of East and West, thereby drawing the fateful East-West distinction and making it possible, for the first time, to speak of the West as a place, and not merely a set of ideas. But these shifts did not create the West. At the height of Roman power, as Roman elites enjoyed Greek learning and sought to combine Stoic philosophical principles with imperial authority, new movements from the East threatened the geopolitical and cultural balance of the Roman Empire.

These movements were religious. Traditional Greek and Roman religion encouraged man to know himself to avoid breaking the divine rules of cosmic justice. And cosmic justice was cool, impersonal, abstract. Even when the gods were friendly, they remained emotionally distant. It was hard to imagine a relation of personal faith with them. They might help you and even like you, but they could not save your soul.

Yet people craved personal faith. Plato proposed a monotheistic doctrine, in which a supreme divine power, defined as the good and the beautiful, was the worthy goal of love and striving for mortals. Followers of the Platonic tradition learned how to understand, believe in, and search for this ultimate deity. But even though Platonism, in its mystical aspects, could provide surety of salvation for a few, it could never become a mass religion. The broad masses of later Greek and Roman civilization therefore sought personal faith in a variety of other, more approachable and less intellectual cults.

One of the most widespread was the cult of the goddess Chance. In earlier times, the idea of chance served to explain many of the unexpected, disastrous, or gratifying turns of fate; chance in this sense was simply more evidence that gods and men were far apart, and that mortals would never reach a satisfactory understanding or justification of why things happened to them.

By Hellenistic and Roman times, from the third century B.C. onward, Greeks and Romans began to imagine Chance as a personal goddess, as though they wanted to conjure the basic problem of their lives, their exposure to unaccountable fate, by turning that very uncertainty into an explanation.

C hristianity was the final and most successful of the answers to the quest of ancient civilization for personal religion. It was also the last of the Eastern cultural invasions. The Westernization of Christianity added the missing piece to the Greco-Roman cultural design and, with the help of the Germanic tribes that conquered and settled the western Roman Empire, produced the synthesis that modern observers, whether friendly or hostile, called the West. The synthesis lasted, by a rough count, some sixteen hundred years.

The Christianization of the Roman Empire was a process that began in the first century A.D., when Paul the apostle traveled to Rome around the year 64, and when, at about the same time, the emperor Nero ordered a persecution of Christians, "detested," as Tacitus wrote some decades later, "for their abominations and popularly known by the name of Christians after one Christus who was put to death in the reign of Tiberius by the procurator, Pontius Pilate."[6] It was a process mostly completed some four centuries later, when the Roman Empire, at least in the West, disappeared.

One of the abominations, in Roman eyes, may have been the Christian view of women, which differed radically from that prevalent in pagan culture—as radically, in fact, as pagan pity differed from Christian pity. In another passage of his *Annals*, Tacitus reported that one Pomponia Graecina, a woman of the senatorial class, was accused in the reign of Nero of "depraved and alien superstition."[7] Pomponia was, most likely, a Christian and far from alone among upper-class Roman women as early as the mid-first century A.D. Throughout the first centuries of Christianization, the typical convert was a woman of above average wealth and status. This conclusion, which was that of most scholars in the 1990s, starkly contradicted the earlier standard view that Christianity spread first and fastest among the poor, the marginal, and the oppressed. For example, Arnold Toynbee defined the Christians of the Roman Empire as the key element of the "internal proletariat," all those alienated from the majority culture who were destined to supplant it, to put an end to existing civilization, and to "incubate" both a new civilization and a new world religion. For Toynbee, an "internal proletariat" was an inevitable part of a universal empire, which was the last stage of a civilization. Without an internal proletariat to incubate the ideas and the social forms of the future, the civilization in question would not die on schedule, and its successor could not be born. So in the case of ancient and Western civilization, Toynbee's theory required that the successor civilization—in this case, the West—begin in the form of the culture and beliefs of the "internal proletariat" of the parent civilization. In particular, the crucial vehicle of the successor civilization, its religion, had necessarily to be found among the "internal proletariat"; it had to be marginal, otherwise it would not be the religion of the future.

Unfortunately for Toynbee's scheme, Christianity spread first and foremost among influential and prominent people. Women, in particular, were attracted to the new religion because it raised their status, whereas Roman society put a low value on women and especially on wives. Roman poetry devalued marriage by portraying wives as difficult and irresponsible. Roman society tolerated, even recommended infanticide, and demographic analysis carried out in the 1960s suggested that most exposed infants were girls and that only one family in a hundred reared more than one daughter. A first-century B.C. Egyptian wrote to his pregnant wife that if she should bear her child before he returned from his trip, then, "if it is a boy keep it, if a girl discard it."[8] As a consequence of such attitudes, the sex ratios in the Roman Empire were extreme, on the order of 140 males for every 100 females. Christianity, by contrast, followed Judaism in prohibiting abortion, infanticide, divorce, incest, polygamy, and infidelity. Clearly, many women would consider themselves better off in a Christian environment.

Most early Christians were, for these reasons, women. Because Christianity prohibited infanticide and encouraged lifelong marriage, they were likely to marry and to have more daughters than their pagan contemporaries. But because many of these were upper-class women, they faced a shortage of acceptable men within the Christian community—especially since, under Roman law, their husbands would assume control of their property upon marriage. Therefore, many of them married pagan men, whom they converted. Secondary conversion, of husbands by Christian women, appears from the sources to have been one of the main mechanisms of Christianization.[9]

The highest accolade a Roman could bestow on his wife was one found on numerous tombstones: the letters D M L F, standing for *domo mansit, lanam fecit,* "she stayed at home, she span wool," like Lucretia in the story of Tarquin, Brutus, and the end of the monarchy. Christianity offered other avenues of activity and reward for women, some of them merely challenging, others tragic. In A.D. 203, the Roman governor of Carthage sentenced a group of Christians to death. Two of them, Perpetua and Felicitas, were young mothers. Tertullian, the bishop of Africa, recorded the sacrifices and included a statement probably composed by Perpetua herself immediately before she was killed. In it, she described how she and Felicitas comforted their fellow-prisoners and encouraged them with the sure hope of heavenly reward. Felicitas gave birth only a day or so before her death; Perpetua weaned her child in prison. She noted that she felt no pain in her breasts when she stopped nursing. On the last day, the prisoners were led into the arena; Felicitas was bleeding from the birth and her breasts were dripping milk; a sight that evoked dismay even from the crowd that was waiting to see the killings.

As Christianity became the public and official religion, the differences between women's status in the church and in society at large converged. This illustrated a rule of social structure: the greater the number of women relative to men in a society, the higher their status.[10] In early Christianity, women enjoyed a favorable sex ratio and therefore, by that rule, greater freedom. In Athens and Rome, the sex ratio favored men and a structure in which women, being relatively scarce, were sequestered and granted only minimal freedoms. As Christianization proceeded, the sex ratios of Christian and non-Christian populations converged, until in Christendom—the Old West—the sex ratio was approximately equal. Women accordingly were less socially prominent than in the early church, but substantially more than in Greek or Roman civilization.

Was it true, then, that Christianity softened and feminized a ruthless and brutal culture? Not exactly. While it was still a minority cult without official status, Christianity indeed offered a haven of different values. Once it became the only tolerated public religion, it was no longer in opposition to the culture; it was the culture. And as historians ever since Gibbon never tired of pointing out, dominant Christianity was at times more intolerant and often as brutal as the pagan society it replaced.

Yet Christianization entailed a number of changes in values and behavior, some of which outlasted Christianity's rise to political and social control of the Roman Empire. In 390, for example, there occurred in Milan the first and arguably most memorable of all the confrontations of religious and political authority—confrontations inconceivable in pagan civilization, which lacked the distinction, central to Western identity, of two distinct sources of power, legitimacy and authority.

The emperor at the time was Theodosius, who by a decree of 381 had made Christianity the only permitted religion of the empire. In the 380s, the emperor authorized several acts of violence against pagan sanctuaries and idols. He was also committed to reasserting a unified imperial authority across the whole Empire, from Britain to Syria. Traitors and rebels could expect the harshest treatment, once Theodosius caught up with them.

Thessalonica, the capital of the Illyrian provinces, was one of the largest and most prosperous cities of the empire. As in Constantinople and Rome, the populace expected mass entertainment at state expense; if they did not get it, they would riot. Since gladiator games were now outlawed, the main form of entertainment was chariot racing. Popular charioteers were popular superstars, and the people organized themselves in support of the various teams: blue, green, red, and white. One of the leading charioteers of Thessalonica tried to seduce a young boy, a slave of the garrison commander, who happened to be a Goth named Botheric. To preserve discipline, Botheric arrested the charioteer. This enraged the urban rabble, which invaded the army command and massacred Botheric and his aides. Upon hearing the news, Theodosius determined on a bloody and devious revenge. He announced to the Thessalonicans that he was sponsoring a set of races of exceptional magnificence, but at the same time dispatched a force of barbarian soldiers to the city. On the appointed day, thousands streamed into the circus. Gibbon tells what happened next:

> As soon as the assembly was complete, the soldiers, who had secretly been posted around the circus, received the signal, not of the races, but of a general massacre. The promiscuous carnage continued three hours, without discrimination of strangers or natives, of age or sex, of innocence or guilt; the most moderate accounts state the number of the slain at seven thousand . . . A foreign merchant . . . offered his own life, and all his wealth, to supply the place of *one* of his two sons; but, while the father hesitated with equal tenderness, while he was doubtful to choose, and unwilling to condemn, the soldiers determined his suspense, by plunging their daggers at the same moment into the breasts of the defenceless youths. The apology of the assassins, that they were obliged to produce the prescribed number of heads, serves only to increase, by an appearance of order and design, the horrors of the massacre, which was executed by the commands of Theodosius.

Theodosius had his headquarters at Milan. The archbishop of this city, the military capital of the empire, was Ambrose. Theodosius knew that Ambrose wanted some act of penance, but assumed that it would be a private one. The notion of a Roman emperor apologizing in public for anything was utterly inconceivable. Imagine his surprise, therefore, when he appeared at the cathedral church of Milan expecting to perform the usual prayers, only to be met by Ambrose, "who, in the tone and language of an ambassador of Heaven, declared to his sovereign, that private contrition was not sufficient to atone for a public fault, or to appease the justice of the offended Deity. Theodosius humbly represented, that if he had contracted the guilt of homicide, David, the man after God's own heart, had been guilty, not only of murder, but of adultery. 'You have imitated David in his crime, imitate then his repentance,' was the reply of the undaunted Ambrose."[11] The emperor was compelled to present himself in pauper's dress at the porch of the cathedral, there to beg, in full view of the multitude, pardon for his sins. For eight months the emperor periodically repeated this ritual abasement, until Ambrose absolved him.

Something in the Roman world was not as before if a confrontation such as that of Ambrose and Theodosius could take place with such an outcome. It was the first of many encounters of the two Western principles of legitimacy, and in a certain sense one may say that the scene at the door of the cathedral of Milan was the foundation of the Old West.

Few doubted that these three developments—the rise of Christianity, the Fall of Rome, the rise of the West—were connected. The question that preoccupied more philosophers, thinkers, historians, and polemicists in the West than any other from the sixteenth to the twentieth century was how they were related. Why did Rome fall? Because of Christianity, or in spite of it? Did Rome have to fall for the West to rise? If the West, along with Christianity, survived and grew out of Rome, did that make the West Christian? How Christian was the West, then or later?

The Grand Narrative had little to say about the Fall of Rome, the mother of all big questions in the debate on history and civilizations. In most versions, it moved quickly from the end of the Greek Golden Age, through Rome and Christianity, stopping for breath only at the Renaissance and Columbus. Rome and the Middle Ages got fairly brief treatment, and still less time was left for the period when the one was turning into the other, from the late third to the late sixth century A.D.

Reasons for this reticence are not far to seek. For one thing, the Grand Narrative was a story of progress toward a goal: mid-twentieth-century America, NATO, and the liberal consensus. The narrative was not comfortable with eras of decline. Another reason was that the Grand Narrative was firmly secular and liberal. Liberals might not necessarily share the view that Christians were responsible for the Fall of Rome, but when it came to late antiquity, the Grand Narrative took the line that Rome was civilized, the Dark Ages were not. A third reason was that the narrative had a basic problem in dealing with religion at all, whether Christian, pagan, or anything else. Religion as a force in human affairs, as motivating conversion, agitation, war, expansion, destruction, propaganda, or passion, did not fit the liberal world view.

At best, the Grand Narrative took an instrumental view of what others came to call late antiquity. The late antique synthesis received a secular seal of approval as the geopolitical foundation of the modern liberal West that only really got going in the eighteenth century. In such terms, the question of whether the West was Christian had little meaning.

The Fall of Rome was the great example of how a civilization ended. Why did it end? Did she fall or was she pushed? Was this great event good or bad, a gain or a loss, and by what measure? These questions, and the many answers offered, defined the debate on Western identity long before Oswald Spengler. The most famous answer was that of Edward Gibbon, who wrote his *History of the Decline and Fall of the Roman Empire* from 1764 to 1788. His definition of the event as "the triumph of barbarism and religion" puzzled and misled many over the next two centuries.[12] Most read it to mean that Rome fell because a barbarous religion, Christianity, had degraded ancient culture and undermined civic morality. But that was not what Gibbon had in mind. He meant that Roman culture had already become barbarous and demoralized, and that this decline both preceded and enabled Christianity. It also enabled the barbarian invasions, which Gibbon in another, less-well-known sentence called "the principal and immediate cause of the fall of the Western Empire of Rome."[13]

Gibbon was a rationalist and true son of the age of enlightenment in which he lived, but his attitude to religion, the key to his work and his interests, was by no means as clear-cut as the simple reading of his definition implied. He was not a militant agnostic or anticlerical like Voltaire, whom he knew and respected, but whose rallying cry, *"Ecrasez l'infâme!"* or "destroy the infamy [of religion]," he never could have shared. The Englishman was curious about the political and social effects of faith, and wanted to understand the cultural conditions that encouraged it. But he was not worried, as were Voltaire and the other followers of the radical Enlightenment, by religion in his own day. His interest was historical.

As a young man, Gibbon went through two crises that produced his mature, distant, almost excessively reasonable and judicious persona. The first was, in fact, a religious crisis. Gibbon, who was born in 1737, had been a frail, sickly child who spent much time visiting old country houses in the south of England with his father, where his favorite pastime was to peruse the many ancient volumes of laws, chronicles, and histories found in their libraries. This was an entirely different, more opulent, and vastly more learned world than that of poor Winckelmann in Brandenburg a few years earlier. When Gibbon was barely fifteen, his father sent him to Magdalen College at Oxford, where the boy's health improved but not his learning. In his *Autobiography*, Gibbon provided a humorous account of the indolent, port-swilling, and ignorant dons of Magdalen, which was later to become the glory of Oxford. Learning was at a low ebb there in the eighteenth century. Fellows of colleges were obliged to be celibate, a remnant of medieval monastic discipline that sat oddly with the requirement that the fellows, like all public servants in Britain, had to subscribe to Anglican doctrine. As celibacy was required of no one else in Protestant England, it was no surprise that the colleges of Oxford and Cambridge were hardly able to attract the intellectual elite.

Not only were the fellows ignorant and lazy, the very opposite of scholars, they also neglected their pastoral duties toward young Edward. By the end of his second year at university, he had devised for himself a course of reading in theology that persuaded him to convert to Catholicism, which at that time was still considered a treasonable act and could even be dangerous, as it was forbidden to practice the Catholic religion in Britain. Gibbon's father, learning of his son's conversion, shipped him off to the house of a Calvinist minister in Lausanne, Switzerland. Over the next eighteen months, Gibbon, in his own words, "suspended my religious enquiries, acquiescing with implicit belief in the tenets and mysteries which are adopted by the general consent of Catholics and Protestants." These guarded and ambiguous words—what, for example, was "implicit belief"?—seemed to say that while overtly reembracing Protestantism, Gibbon had moved to a lofty indifference toward all religion, and certainly toward faith. Ever after, he reserved his greatest scorn for the intolerant, who used religion to claim special power and consideration; the most important example being, of course, the Christians who took control of the Roman Empire in the fourth century. By contrast, he praised those who respected all faiths while giving privileges to none. This condition, he believed, characterized the second century, when "the various modes of worship, which prevailed in the Roman world, were all considered by the people, as equally true; by the philosopher, as equally false; and by the magistrate, as equally useful."[14]

The second crisis of young Gibbon's life was that he fell in love with Suzanne Curchod, the daughter of another Calvinist minister in Switzerland. In 1758, the twenty-one-year-old Gibbon was summoned home by his father and stepmother and given an annuity of £300, enough to keep him comfortably, but also told that he had to break off the engagement. In another of his famous lapidary sentences, Gibbon recorded that "I sighed as a lover, I obeyed as a son." The objection to Mademoiselle Curchod was that she had no money. She later made a very good match indeed, marrying Jacques Necker, the financial wizard who worked with incredible audacity and skill to save the finances of Louis XVI.[15] When the king dismissed him under pressure from discontented nobles who disapproved of Necker's taxes, the people of Paris responded by storming the Bastille and starting the French Revolution.

Gibbon's brief and unfortunate experiences with religion and love evidently persuaded him to confine his passions to history, where his constant concern was the fragility of reason and of a culture based on reason, threatened on all sides by ambition and greed, which could take the guise of faith. In 1764, while on a visit to Rome, Gibbon sat one afternoon overlooking the Roman Forum, "musing amid the ruins of the Capitol while the barefoot friars were singing vespers in the temple of Jupiter." It was at that moment, he wrote in his *Autobiography*, that the notion of writing the decline and fall of the city—and later of the empire—occurred to him. His life's ambition was clear, and he never looked back. In England in the early 1770s, he was able to devote himself full-time to the project. The first volume, which included two notorious chapters on the rise of Christianity, appeared in 1776, taking the story to the reign of Constantine the Great in the early fourth century, and the next two, dealing with the next century and a half, until the fall of the western empire, in 1781. The year after, when the government of Lord North fell, Gibbon lost his official sinecure, which allowed him to live in London. He returned to Lausanne, where he completed his *History* in three more volumes on the East Roman or Byzantine Empire until its fall in 1453, with an epilogue on the early Renaissance and the prospects for a renewal of learning and civilization in the modern age.

Gibbon's fundamental theme was that the human race was happiest under a government that allowed free thought, an ideal that, like the Stoics, he found realized in second-century Rome. When rulers allowed the ideal to slip, as happened in the Roman Empire after Marcus Aurelius, ambition and greed became acceptable standards of behavior. A society ruled by ambition was one in which the strong oppressed the weak, both socially and intellectually, and where the ambitious used any excuse to gain power. Such was the condition of the Roman Empire in the third century. Now religion, in Gibbon's view, provided high-sounding reasons for policies and behavior that were really motivated by baser passions, and was especially useful as a camouflage in times of turmoil. Christian fanatics thus exploited the time of troubles of the third century to rise to positions of prestige and influence. By the fourth century, Christianity was taking over the empire, but, in Gibbon's view, this only served further to undermine the shaky Roman order. "The clergy successfully preached the doctrines of patience and pusillanimity; the active virtues of society were discouraged; and the last remains of military spirit were buried in the cloister: a large portion of public and private wealth was consecrated to the specious demands of charity and devotion; and the soldiers' pay was lavished on the useless multitudes of both sexes, who could only plead the merits of abstinence and chastity."[16] Christianization, he implied, opened the frontiers to the barbarians.

One of the many ironies of the Fall of Rome debate was that some of the best scholars at the end of the twentieth century were coming round to the second opinion of Gibbon's, that Rome fell because she was conquered. This had been distinctly a minority view in the two centuries after Gibbon. In 1947, a French historian, André Piganiol, concluded his history of the fourth century with the comment, "Roman civilization did not die its own death. It was murdered."[17] These words became famous among students of late Roman history but were usually regarded as some kind of eccentricity, explicable perhaps by the fact that Piganiol was a Catholic from the south of France, and that he was writing at the end of World War II and therefore understandably inclined to take a dim view of Germans. Arnaldo Momigliano called the outburst "a *cri de cœur* of a valiant Frenchman against boches and collaborationists."[18] In fact, Piganiol was echoing and contradicting a sentence by another historian, Etienne Gautier, who had written in 1932 that "Rome died her own death, from inability to go on living and, as it were, in her bed. She was not murdered."[19]

The venerable discussion of the Fall of Rome appears to confirm that there truly is nothing new under the sun. Most of the basic explanations were already old by the mid-nineteenth century, when both the scholarly and the polemical arguments began to heat up. The interesting point therefore was not whether the theories stressed moral, economic, religious, or military factors, but why they were presented, and by whom.

Take the idea that Western civilization began as a synthesis combining westernized Greek culture, Roman order, and Christianity, and that the Roman Empire founded Western geopolitical identity by shifting the East-West line so that it ran west of Greece. This could be either a neutral description or an argument that the West was, and should be, defined in opposition to a threatening, corrupt, or immoral East. A number of such arguments saw the light of day in the years following World War II. In 1947, a German scholar, Hans Erich Stier, asserted that classical culture laid "the spiritual foundations of Western civilization" by separating from and resisting the East. Unfortunately, the East did not remain defeated but continued to subvert and infiltrate ancient culture, so that "the ancient ideals became paralyzed, as orientalization and barbarization progressed," a process leading to "anarchistic individualism and violent selfishness." It was a purified, Western Christianity, "free of eastern distortions," that "saved the West from the eastern stranglehold." Stier warned his contemporaries against succumbing to the renewed temptations of an "orientalism" in which he included both National Socialism and communism. Defining the West as a healthy, Western Christendom constantly threatened by various forms of oriental despotism was a commonplace in Europe in the early days of the Cold War, amounting, in effect, to a Christian Democratic idea of the West that combined ideological geopolitics with a spiritualized definition of culture.[20] The Christian Democratic defenders of the West explained the Fall of Rome as a providential disaster that was necessary for Western Christendom to emerge. They thus confirmed their Western identity in opposition to an eternal Eastern threat; two thousand years ago, that threat had the face of Cleopatra, in the 1950s, of Soviet communism. At the other end of the spectrum were those accounts that flatly denied that anything very dramatic happened when Rome fell. In the 1930s, an economic historian referred to the "so-called decline of ancient civilization," which was no disaster for those affected by it, but rather a "relatively harmless transitional period." If Roman civilization did not decline, but merely changed, that let both Christians and Germanic invaders off the hook.

This argument was welcome to many Germans after World War I, who felt unjustly blamed for the war and stereotyped as aggressive and belligerent. An Austrian economist, Alfons Dopsch, claimed in the 1920s that the Germanic invaders not only did not destroy Roman culture, but maintained and continued it. Late Roman society in the West was oppressed and mismanaged by wasteful landlords and corrupt officials; the Germanic invasions improved the standard of living of average people, protecting farmers and cutting taxes. In late antiquity, he concluded, it was the Germans who were the builders of culture, whereas the late Roman state was its enemy.

A vast spectrum of reasons from absolutism to zealotry was wittily catalogued by the historian Alexander Demandt, who listed 210 of them in his book *Der Fall Roms* (The Fall [or Case] of Rome—*Fall* in German means both). Some were frivolous, such as the claim that Rome fell because its inhabitants were too fond of gladiatorial games. Others were so broad as to be incapable of proof, such as that late Romans were sad, or suffered from collective psychoses. Quite a few theories, dating especially from the late nineteenth century, blamed sex, either too much of it or too much of the wrong kind. More credible bids at understanding included growing inequality, fragmented leadership, pacifism, urban collapse, and population pressure. All 210 factors could be classified into six general types of explanation: Rome fell because of religion, social and economic crisis, environmental degradation, bad government and instability, inevitable decadence, or invasion. One could boil them down further, to three basic models: Rome fell because the forces of destruction overcame the forces of order, or because all empires are fated to die, or because those in charge were not up to the task.[21]

Until the Enlightenment, the standard explanation for Rome's fall was decadence caused by excessive wealth, pride, and luxury. Ancient philosophy and political thought developed the idea that cities and empires followed an inevitable evolution that was both social and moral. First a city is well governed, its various classes are at peace, the poor do not envy the rich, and the rich do not exploit the poor. Because it is well governed, it is able to defend itself, and its virtuous citizens live well, if modestly. Then, thanks to its virtues, the city grows and prospers. It becomes rich. Wealth creates disparities, envy, greed, display, hedonism. Luxury palls; the rich become sated. Then, feeling the need to act, they develop immodest ambitions. They think nothing can stop them. They undertake adventurous gambles. The result, whether by domestic disruption or by defeat, is collapse and disaster, until the cycle begins again.

Something like this simple, moralistic scheme underlay Will Durant's Hollywood version of Rome's fall, which harked back to an explanatory model that was at least two and half millennia old, since it was found in a saying of Pythagoras: "First luxury enters into cities, then satiety, then immodest ambition, and after those things, destruction."[22] Durant, in fact, specifically evoked each of the elements of the ancient model in the film. Luxury: Commodus plundered temples and provinces to collect gold for his own pleasure in Rome. Satiety: Commodus idly invented new psychopathic pleasures, but none satisfied him. Immodest ambition: the men who killed Marcus had wild dreams of domination once they helped Commodus to power; Commodus renamed Rome "Commodus' settlement." Destruction: the one element left hanging, since Rome did not physically fall until two to three hundred years after Commodus.

The one idea common to virtually all accounts was that late antiquity was an era of transition between Greco-Roman and medieval society. The idea that ancient civilization did not become medieval in a short span of time but that the process took several centuries was the single great insight of all scholarly work on late antiquity from Gibbon onward. The question was: what changed, when did it change, and how quickly?

The late-second-century world of Marcus Aurelius was still largely that of Augustus two hundred years earlier. Stoicism, a growing movement in the time of Augustus, had become something like the official ethic of the Roman ruling class, as his own writings showed. But across the Roman Empire, the search for personal religion was becoming more intense, while the old doctrines and ideas seemed increasingly inadequate.

The century after Marcus Aurelius was one of political, economic, and military disasters. The year 193, after Commodus was killed, was the second "Year of Four Emperors." The first was in 69, after Nero, another tyrant, died. Tacitus wrote of the year after Nero that "the secret of empire was discovered, that it was possible to create emperors elsewhere than in Rome." After Commodus, and especially after the last emperor of the Severan dynasty, who died in 235, the secret came out again with a vengeance. From 235 to 284, armies repeatedly proclaimed emperors in distant provinces, marched on Rome, sometimes won, and collected huge payments, but then had to face the next rival who made the discovery that any general with an army could try for the prize. Foreign invaders exploited these internal struggles, and in the 250s and 260s, these invasions from the east and from the north reached a climax. In 269, in an ominous precedent, Gothic hordes invaded Greece. Their king told his men not to burn the libraries of Athens, because as long as the Greeks could study, they would not fight.[23]

That opportunistic generals or foreign enemies exploited a disorganized and weakened empire was hardly surprising. Much more so was the amazing recovery that began in 270. Strong emperors like Aurelian and Diocletian restored discipline, drove out the invaders, and reorganized the army. Diocletian's successor, Constantine, ruled for almost thirty years, the last thirteen as sole emperor. By the time of his death in 337, the empire had been reconstituted and by some measures was stronger than ever.

This was especially true of imperial authority, now usually divided between two or more emperors. This arrangement sometimes tempted an emperor to attack his co-emperors rather than foreign enemies, but most of the time it served its main purpose, which was to prevent endless claimants from appearing, secure army loyalty, and strengthen government and administration. The practice confirmed the geopolitical shift of the East-West line, since East and West, after 284, usually had different emperors. To some degree, the division of government in the fourth century became a division of culture as the western and eastern halves of the empire began to acquire separate identities. But the western empire ended in 476, and from the late fifth century onward, the cultural identity of the West was not that of the western half of the empire, but something else—regional, tribal, Catholic, or, somewhat later, European and Western. The eastern half of the empire, by contrast, survived until 1453.

In 212, by a decree of the emperor Caracalla, all free persons in the empire became full Roman citizens. The reforms of Diocletian and Constantine continued the leveling process. All subjects were henceforth tied more closely to their places of work and residence, at least in theory. Inhabitants were to be available for taxes, war, and other civic duties, and deterred from apostasy and rebellion. In 312, when he defeated his rival Maxentius near Rome, Constantine claimed to have dreamed that the Christian God promised him victory. In 313, he declared Christianity legal. On his deathbed, he received baptism. In 381, his successor, Theodosius, declared Christianity the only legal religion. This was the third and most far-reaching revolution of the fourth century, and it had little to do with crises or invasions and much to do with a realistic response at the top to religious change in society at large. The Christians were not a majority, at least not in the western empire, but they were a growing and influential group, and if they could be enlisted as loyal subjects rather than potentially disloyal traitors, the empire stood to gain.

The fourth-century changes strengthened the empire, but later scholars could show how some of them contributed to the slow, gradual transformation that by around 600 moved what used to be the western empire out of the Roman and into the medieval world. One social process evident in the archaeological record, though not in contemporary sources, was the growth in population and economic activity of the long frontier zones, from the North Sea to central Europe and in Syria and Arabia. The late Roman army was more numerous and at the same time more permanently settled along the borders. Around the camps, where soldiers lived family lives, raised children, and often had businesses on the side, vital new communities sprang up that were often rich missionary grounds for Christianity as well as places where the so-called barbarians encountered the civilization of the empire. Some of these frontier towns, especially in latter-day Germany, such as Cologne, Mainz, or Nuremberg, became cultural and religious centers that survived the breakdown and went on to rich futures in the Middle Ages.

The religious, administrative, social, and economic reforms that established the late Roman Empire and what became known as the Great Church, the Church of the Empire, shaped late antiquity as a cultural epoch with its own identity. If it took scholars a long time to formulate this identity, which never percolated to the Grand Narrative, this was in part because Western pedagogy and scholarship were, until well into the twentieth century, dominated by the idea of the Three Ages: antiquity, the Middle Ages, and modern times. In its crudest form, still alive and well in textbooks at century's end, antiquity was everything before A.D. 500, the Middle Ages lasted exactly one thousand years, until 1500, and were succeeded by the modern epoch, which continued ever after.

The idea of the Three Ages was invented by the humanist scholars of the fifteenth-century Renaissance to differentiate their own age from what went before. That era was defined, somewhat contemptuously, as a "middle age" of superstition and obscure struggles between popes and emperors, and was distinguished in turn from the ancient world, which was characterized, like the fifteenth-century present, by scholarship, philosophy, and reason. The Three Ages scheme was deployed first by Renaissance humanists, then by Protestants, in opposition to the previously dominant scheme of the Four World Empires, a model derived ultimately from a passage in the biblical book of Daniel (chapter 2, verses 37–44).[24]

The scheme received its decisive formulation in the most influential history textbook ever written, Christoph Cellarius's *Historia Antiqua*, or "ancient history," of 1685, which subsumed all the Four Empires, from Babylon to pagan Rome, into the category of "ancient history," the unit that still dominated Western curricula and scholarship in the late 1900s. Cellarius ended this era in 306, when Constantine became emperor, and the "history of the middle age" began.

The term *late antiquity* was devised in the 1850s by the Swiss philosopher of history, Jacob Burckhardt, to avoid the disparaging implications of such earlier phrases as "lower empire," contrasted to a higher, better, and earlier empire. But having agreed that the period from, say, 300 to 600 was a unit, scholars and polemicists disagreed about its content. Was it, as Theodor Mommsen said, "virtually all new," was it a continuation of the old, or was it, more likely, a blend, with the elements of change gradually outweighing the elements of continuity?[25]

The liberal Mommsen thought it was "all new" because he believed that the later empire, for which he coined the name "dominate," was an empire ruled by divine right and absolute authority, as opposed to that of Augustus and Marcus Aurelius, in which the emperor was the chief magistrate, ruling by popular will. More recent scholars saw elements of continuity in the imperial bureaucracy or the law codes compiled in the fifth and sixth century on the basis of laws and decrees of preceding centuries. Others, like Peter Brown, looked at how Christian beliefs gradually transformed religion, culture, and society, concluding that the ancient world was becoming "medieval" by the early fifth century.

The church became rich and increasingly independent because people, including rich people, gave it their wealth. One of the most famous illustrations was the story of the two Melanias, the elder and the younger. The elder Melania was born in 342 to one of the richest families in Rome, the senatorial clan of the Valerii. At a time when few senatorial families were yet Christian, Melania was both pious and very studious. At the age of thirty, she left Rome and went to Palestine, where she used some of her wealth to found a monastery on the Mount of Olives as a house of prayer and hostel for pilgrims. Melania spent twenty-seven years there, personally caring for pilgrims, reading, and praying. Her fame spread across the Mediterranean. When, in 399, she returned to Italy, her rich relatives "thought they were cleared from the pollution of their riches if they succeeded in gathering some of the dirt from her feet."[26]

At that time, her granddaughter Melania the Younger was a girl of about ten. She was the only heir of the Valerii, and had, in 410, houses and estates in and around Rome, near Naples, in Apulia, Spain, Africa, Britain, and Gaul. Her palace in Rome was so costly that not even the wife of Stilicho, who commanded all the armies of the western empire, could afford it. The annual income of her property amounted to 120,000 *solidi*, equivalent to 1,600 pounds of pure gold. Against the wishes of her father, Melania and her husband sold these estates and freed eight thousand of their slaves. They used the proceeds to buy "monasteries of monks and virgins and gave them as a gift to those who lived there, furnishing each place with a sufficient amount of gold. They presented their numerous and expensive silk clothes at the altars of churches and monasteries. They broke up their silver, of which they had a great deal, and made altars and ecclesiastical treasures from it, and many other offerings to God."[27] Excavations in the 1970s under Melania's Roman palace uncovered a silver treasure, probably buried in 410 when Alaric the Visigoth was laying siege to the city, and lists of the family's clients and business connections.

Such massive piety in action both demonstrated a new mentality and altered the economic balance of the empire. This sort of thing drove Enlightenment historians, such as Gibbon, to distraction: could not these people see what they were doing by depriving the Roman state of their wealth, commitment, and skills? Some went much further. Friedrich Nietzsche, who liked neither the Christians nor the Germanic barbarians, denounced both, but especially the Christians, as depraved traitors who deliberately undermined the Roman Empire, which was the "most spectacular form of organization ever established, and under the most difficult conditions . . . These holy anarchists claimed to be performing a work of 'piety' in destroying the 'world,' that is, the Roman Empire, until no stone was left standing, until even Germans and other thugs were able to take over."[28]

People in late antiquity were clearly very different from people in the age of Pericles, Augustus, or Marcus Aurelius. At what point did these differences bring about the Fall of Rome, or, for those who resisted the rhetoric of decline, the change that ended imperial power in the West?

The explanations in terms of religion and cultural crisis were related. Edward Gibbon launched the first when he blamed Christianity for undermining civic morale. This simplistic interpretation was not wholly fair to Gibbon, who thought the Romans first lost their civic morality and then succumbed to superstition and, later, invasion. The Christian explanation, nevertheless, enjoyed a large following among Catholics, liberals, and German nationalists.

Catholics disagreed about late Rome. Some, like André Piganiol, believed that the synthesis of church and empire was a providential step forward for humanity and that the resulting late antique civilization was both valuable and viable. The Christian empire was not a temporary or ramshackle construction, but a solid base of civilization, full of hope and prospects. It did not have to end, and when it did, it could not possibly be the fault of the Christians. The opposing view was presented most eloquently in 1831 by François René de Chateaubriand, one of the most prolific and multifaceted doers and thinkers of his age. Unlike Piganiol, Chateaubriand saw no hope whatever in late antiquity, a concept that did not exist in his day. Pagan Rome, he held, had become superstitious, cowardly, cruel, and effete, dominated by "institutions contrary to human truth." Christianity could not save this world, which was beyond redemption. The new religion could not properly flourish in such rotten soil, "a new faith needed new people," and these were the Christians and the Germans, who together provided the "intellectual force" and the "material force for destroying the pagan world." Chateaubriand inverted Gibbon's explanation: Rome fell because of inner decay, but where Gibbon saw Christianity as Rome's executioner, along with the barbarians, the Catholic French aristocrat saw it as intervening in the nick of time to save what could be saved from the wreckage of antiquity. His hero Constantine, "by embracing Christianity and founding the Church, by settling the barbarians within the Empire, by establishing a titled and hierarchical nobility . . . truly engendered the Middle Ages."[29]

Although they gave Christianity pride of place as the proximate reason for Rome's fall, both Gibbon and Chateaubriand, and those whom they inspired, sensed that Rome would not have fallen either to the Christians or the barbarians unless pagan civilization had already collapsed from within. This line of thinking produced what was probably the most widespread of all the explanatory models in the twentieth century: the argument from cultural or social crisis. Even those who focused on economic changes, such as growing inequality, rising taxes, or class warfare, tended to attribute these economic factors to deeper-seated cultural or social ones, factors of belief, hope, anxiety, and aspiration. The cultural and socioeconomic argument underlay reflection on the Fall of Rome from the 1920s to the 1960s and produced a large and varied stream of writings, all of which assumed that the Fall of Rome was also a decline of Roman culture from its classical roots, and that late antiquity, dominated by unreason and religion, was a deplorable interlude in a Western story that was essentially one of reason and progress.

Or at least that it ought to be such a story. Particularly in the interwar years, when reason and progress seemed to be failing in the West, many people pessimistically thought that asserting reason as the rule of the West was too ambitious. Reason was doomed to be history's permanent loser; look at the Fall of Rome, at Adolf Hitler, at hedonism and cultural decline in Britain, France, and America. In some thinkers, like T.S. Eliot, pessimism about reason turned into a defiant reassertion of religion and myth, and, some argued, into an anti-Semitic attack on Jews for contributing to Western cultural collapse.

One powerful influence behind this line of thinking about decline ancient and modern, alongside Nietzsche and Spengler, was Sigmund Freud. Freud, who was an eager reader of Nietzsche and absorbed many of his ideas, performed the amazing feat of making the irrational rational. His psychoanalytic theory of personality explained passion, violence, ecstasy, and seemingly un-reasonable behavior in apparently scientific and highly rational terms. This combination of cultural pessimism, the idea that reason is doomed, with a powerful theory in the best nineteenth-century scientific mode proved irre-sistible to many of those who, after Spengler, thought about the Fall of Rome and the likely fate of their own civilization.

To Freud, religious belief was solely the expression of a psychological con-dition. Spirituality and faith had no objective content or purpose. When he began writing on religion, a subject to which he did not turn until rather late in life, Freud defined it as a pathology. The obsessional neuroses that he had spent his first decades as a doctor in studying were, he asserted, private reli-gious systems; conversely, religions were no more, and no less, than the col-lective obsessional neuroses of the human race.

Two years after Eric Dodds published *Pagan and Christian in an Age of Anxiety*, Peter Brown began demolishing this whole approach with his own life of Saint Augustine. For Brown, religion did not need an explanation and was not a reactive neurosis, but was itself a cause of change. Brown did not have to look for causes of anxiety, and because he stopped looking for causes, the anxiety largely disappeared. Instead, his work over more than two decades created a colorful, pointillistic canvas of late antiquity as "an exotic territory, populated by wild monks and excitable virgins and dominated by the clash of religions, mentalities and lifestyles."[30] If this whole wonderful pageant came to an end, it was not because of neurotic anxiety, but for the positive reason that pious Christians and local nobles found other purposes in life than supporting the Roman state. It was notable that Brown defined the collapse as that of the "imperial government" only. This reduced the Fall of Rome to an administrative event that allowed the positive forces of Chris-tian fervor and aristocratic regionalism to flourish.[31] This was to say that the Fall of Rome was necessary for the future of the West.

The second group favoring the religious and cultural account of Rome's fall was the liberals. Their attitude, like that of the Catholics, was often contradic-tory. Rome was not a liberal society, so perhaps one should not deplore its end. On the other hand, Roman order was valuable to those living under it; life after Rome was, at least for some centuries, nastier, more brutal, and shorter for many people. Culture declined, buildings collapsed, literature was lost, superstition spread. The population of Rome itself fell from the late fifth to the seventh century from over half a million to a few tens of thousands.

The decline of culture that accompanied the end of Roman order was a problem for liberals in a more general sense. Liberalism, and the liberal story of the West, believed in reason, continuity, and progress in history. Decadence, decline, and destruction did not easily fit the story. They were uncomfortable reminders that disasters could happen despite one's best wishes and efforts. Liberal proponents of the idea of the West, especially in America and Britain, saw the Fall of Rome as a terrible warning of what could happen to their own liberal world, whether because of invasion from outside or from a religious revival within. During the Cold War, such reflections produced a defensive liberal interpretation of Rome's fall as a warning to the modern West to retain its inner strength and keep its powder dry.[32]

Of all the other twentieth-century scholars working on the late Roman Empire, it was the Russian émigré Michael Rostovtzev whose views, along with those of Dodds, were perhaps the most influential. Rostovtzev was a Russian aristocrat who escaped penniless from the communist takeover of his country in 1917. Although only twenty-five, Rostovtzev had already published important work on ancient economic and social questions. He eventually wound up in America, where he secured, in 1930, a five-thousand-dollar post at the University of Wisconsin. His subsequent fame rested on two multivolume works, a social and economic history of the Hellenistic world and one of the Roman Empire.

No scholar before or since approached Rostovtzev's absolute command of the evidence—written, carved, built, or buried—from ancient civilization. It was therefore noteworthy that he concluded his lifetime's investigation of the ancient economy by deciding that no purely economic explanation of Roman decline was tenable. Rather, Rostovtzev explained the Fall of Rome in reverse Marxist terms: as the rise of an uneducated proletariat—an underclass—that ignorantly destroyed the high culture of the Greco-Roman elites. Marxist students of antiquity, like Geoffrey de Sainte Croix, argued that Christianity was the ideological superstructure established to justify greater exploitation and inequality. Rome fell and classical culture died, in this view, because inequality grew worse until the social structure ruptured. Rostovtzev agreed that the structure fell apart, but instead of blaming elites, he blamed the "masses." They were the true exploiters, because they were parasites on the high culture, administrative skills, and largesse of the elites.

The triggering factor for the spiral of decline was the military crisis of the third century. In response, the imperial government increased taxes and obligations of service, which hit peasants and laborers the hardest. They were the least able to escape, because they had to stay on the land to survive. The ever more heavily burdened rural poor reacted by waging their own "class war"—the phrase was Rostovtzev's, one in the eye for his Bolshevik persecutors—against the towns. The late-third-century reforms merely confirmed the harsh regime in the countryside. In the fourth century, peasants and landless laborers began allying with local nobles, who shifted their own power base from the towns to the countryside. Thus, the "Oriental despotism" of the fourth-century empire alienated first its peasants, then its local magnates. The final stage occurred when the new rural coalition of peasants, soldiers, and landowners invaded the urban elites and reduced them to their own level, thereby destroying the elites' ability to reproduce the high culture.

Where Eric Dodds explained decline by the rise of religion alone, Rostovtzev provided a broader theory. The rise of superstitious cults, according to Rostovtzev, was simply one aspect of what one might call the dumbing down of classical civilization that took place starting around A.D. 200. Rostovtzev managed to include the barbarians by arguing that the real barbarians were not those beyond the borders, but the ignorant and superstitious masses that arose on the ruins of high culture; the barbarians were the Romans themselves, in their dumbed-down and parasitical state. Rostovtzev's influential theory thus contributed to postponing discussion of what the barbarians actually meant for the decline of Rome. Moreover, his social determinism reduced late antique religion to a side effect of cultural decline and the rise of mass society. Religion was something for the uneducated masses, and it was only to be expected that it would gain ground as rational, elite culture and administrative skills disappeared.

Nothing could be further from this aristocratic reverse Marxism than Santo Mazzarino's work on the end of the ancient world, summarized in his book *La fine del mondo antico*, first published in 1959. Mazzarino broke with the mold set by Freud and Marx, but not in the way that Arnaldo Momigliano and Peter Brown were to do it. Mazzarino argued that the rise of religion was neither superstitious nor a product of fear, but a vigorous and positive development; what arose in late antiquity was not uneducated masses, but a vibrant new popular culture with its own elites, standards, and desires. In short, Christianity was not merely a religious revolution, but a social revolution, which Mazzarino did not hesitate to describe as a "democratization" of late imperial culture.[33]

Where Rostovtzev saw "democratization" as a terrible decline, the Sicilian Catholic saw it as a blessed relief from a stifling and oppressive ruling class. Where Rostovtzev saw proletarian insurrection, Mazzarino saw the breaking out, all across the Mediterranean, of new freedoms, a kind of democracy of spirit and expression closer to the modern than the ancient Greek version.

And where Eric Dodds saw fear producing superstition, Mazzarino saw vigorous popular culture. He took a similarly positive view of the barbarian invasions that began in earnest in the 370s. The Germanic tribes that settled on Roman territory, and that gradually dissolved Roman social and political order in the West, were also, to Mazzarino, the providential tools of the Christian spiritual revolution.[34]

The Roman Empire, Gibbon said, fell because of the "triumph of barbarism and religion." Mazzarino would not disagree, but unlike Gibbon he saw the hand of Providence in that triumph. Mazzarino did not deny that the Fall of Rome was a tragedy, because the universalist, transnational Roman vision of order was great and noble, but he also welcomed it because it freed marginal nations and a marginal faith from the dead hand of an empty culture.

Although Rostovtzev presented the unsurpassed masterpiece of the socioeconomic explanation, the idea was much older. In his essay on the greatness and decline of Rome of 1734, Charles de Secondat de Montesquieu stated that the Roman Empire fell because it had become too big to administer effectively, because its ruling class sank into overindulgence and spent irreplaceable resources on foreign luxuries, and because exploitation and the needs of defense reduced the population. In modern terms, Montesquieu blamed the Fall of Rome on imperial overstretch and conspicuous consumption by its elites, both of which depressed healthy economic activity: a diagnosis very close to that applied by the liberal historian Paul Kennedy to America's position at the end of the twentieth century.

Imperial authority, barbarian tribes, Christian religion—these were and remained the three main factors in the drama of late antiquity. If, like Gibbon, you treasured pagan Rome, you deplored its fall and blamed "barbarism," even if by that you meant internal decay rather than foreign invasions. If, like André Piganiol and others from Catholic Europe, you treasured Christian, not pagan, Rome, you blamed the barbarians for destroying a still viable civilization. By the 1980s, some were insisting that the whole issue of downfall and blame was misplaced. "As for the argument from decline," one scholar wrote, "like the arguments from corruption and superstition, it proceeds from within a historiographical discourse which is itself highly authoritarian."[35] By the 1990s, Spengler's prime case of cultural decline had been stood on its head. The Roman Empire, we were now told, fell neither to external attack nor to internal decay, but because its leading elites wanted transformation. The empire ended itself.

Such a conclusion would truly subvert much of the use made of the Fall of Rome in the debate on the West in the last two centuries, particularly since

Spengler, whose ominous comparison of the Fall of Rome to the future of the West of his day helped to create the pessimism of the interwar years and the resulting search for comfort in tradition.

The Spenglerian account of the Fall of Rome was that it was inevitable, because civilizations were like organisms; they grew old and died. To Spengler, the Fall of Rome was an essential precondition of the West. The division of the Roman world into East and West was something that had to happen for the West to emerge as an entity in its own right, separate from ancient civilization. But those who saw the Fall of Rome in Spenglerian terms overlooked Spengler's basic point about the ancient world, namely, that its inevitable decline began not in the third, fourth, or fifth century, but in the age of Julius Caesar and Augustus. The Roman Empire itself, the imperial structure of government, administration, and command, embodied decline, for by entering the imperial epoch ancient civilization surrendered its last shreds of vitality and creativity. The events of the fourth to sixth centuries—the rise of the church, oppressive bureaucracy, barbarian invasions, and the end of the western empire—were mere details of no significance whatever in the desert of stagnation that separated ancient civilization from the rise of the "Faustian" West, which Spengler dated to around A.D. 1000.

Arnold Toynbee moved the beginning of the end of ancient civilization even further back, to the outbreak of the Peloponnesian War in 431 B.C.[36] The young Englishman explained this insight as a revelation that struck him in August 1914, when World War I was breaking out. He realized then, he later wrote, that the great war just beginning would mark a fateful change in the history of the West, the end of its creative period and the start of its Time of Troubles. In the next instant he understood, in an intuitive flash, that what he was seeing in 1914 was the equivalent of what had happened to ancient civilization in 431 B.C. The Peloponnesian War had marked the end of the Golden Age of Greece and the beginning of what Toynbee saw as a continuous Time of Troubles lasting until the Romans unified the Mediterranean world in the second and first centuries B.C. The Roman Empire was the universal empire, the final stage of ancient civilization, and the final destiny of all civilizations. Such an empire gave peace to a troubled world, but it was a stagnant and uncreative peace. The culture of a universal empire was eclectic, derivative, and ultimately fragile, as its various enemies grew in strength both inside and outside its borders and prepared the attacks that would bring it to an end. This belief became the cornerstone of Toynbee's twelve-volume *Study of History*, published from 1936 to 1961.

A century before Rostovtzev, Barthold Niebuhr argued that declining population was a reason for Rome's fall. This explanation appealed to many people, especially the French, who had been obsessed with the same problem ever since the drastic bloodletting of the revolution and the Napoleonic Wars. The historian Pierre Chaunu, a father of ten and the author, by the mid-1990s, of some one hundred books on social, economic, and cultural history, maintained that medieval population growth was a contributing factor of crisis, that this led to delayed marriage and sexual renunciation, and that these cultural factors in turn played a part in promoting the Reformation. But on ancient Rome he was out of his depth. In 1976 he asked whether "the suicide of the West can still be prevented," drawing the familiar analogy between the crisis of late antiquity and that of the contemporary West. The Romans aborted and refused to have children; so did the West; look to Rome and be warned. In a book of 1981, he developed his charge that the late Romans caused their own collapse by decadently refusing to have many children. However, archaeological evidence had, since the 1940s, demonstrated that the traditional view that the population of the late empire was declining everywhere was unsustainable. Certain provinces suffered decline, because people fled from taxes, invasion, or other troubles, but other provinces enjoyed rapid growth and social development.

The final category of explanations stated that internal crises were not enough in themselves, and that however weak the empire, it would not have expired unless someone killed it. After 476, Germanic kings ruled the entire western empire. Therefore, the Germans did it.

Two events in the fourth century symbolized the start of the serious Germanic invasions. The first was the Gothic treaty of October 3, 382, which for the first time permitted a Germanic tribe to settle within the confines of the Roman Empire under its own king and its own laws. The background was this. Starting at the end of the second century and with increasing frequency since the 250s, Germanic tribes had invaded and plundered the border provinces of the empire. By the 260s and 270s, they were making raids into northern Italy; in 269, as we saw, they plundered Athens. The Roman revival that began in the 270s stopped the incursions for a century, but in the 370s they began again, this time with more vigor and more manpower, because the Germanic world from the Baltic to the Black Sea was itself in turmoil, under pressure of other tribes and peoples farther east. Ambrose of Milan described the domino effect of the Hunnish movements beyond the Volga: "The Huns rose against the Alans, the Alans against the Goths, the Goths against the Sarmatians."

In 376, the Visigothic branch of the Goths, who had ruled a wide area from the Dniester to the Danube, were disastrously defeated by the Huns in Moldavia. Expelled from the lands where they had lived for over a century, they crossed the Danube into the empire in search of asylum. For two years, Visigothic hordes scores of thousands strong, including men, women, children, and animals, crisscrossed the northern Balkans in search of food. The Roman government tried to persuade them to leave, but they would not and in the summer of 378 the emperor Valens led an army against the Visigoths. This army, which itself included many men of barbarian background, was destroyed by the Visigoths at Adrianople on August 9, 378. The emperor was killed.

Fifth-century Romans saw in Adrianople the beginning of the end of Roman power. Most popular stories of the end of Rome until the late twentieth century shared that assessment. In particular, historians held that Adrianople, which the Visigoths won thanks to their horsemen, broke the seven-hundred-year dominance of the Roman infantry legion and marked the military beginning of the Middle Ages, dominated by armed cavalry.

The Gothic treaty of 382 was epochal. It took place after four more years of destruction, when the Roman government finally agreed, in October 382, to permit the entire Visigothic nation to settle as a people on the Roman side of the Danube, not subject to Roman taxes and with an annual grant in return for their promise to defend the Danube line against other tribes.[37] This agreement became the model for similar agreements and was the start of the dismemberment of the empire.

The second symbolic event was the scene supposedly witnessed by observers on the bank of the frozen Rhine on New Year's Eve of 406. By this time, several Germanic tribes were living on Roman territory. Yet the Rhine frontier was still intact. Roman legions kept the watch from the North Sea to the Alps. The writers and poets of Rome still divided the world along the great rivers separating Rome from the barbarians.

But on that night the barbarian trickle became a tide that never receded. In the winter night, under a bright moon sparkling on the ice of the frozen river, a great horde of men, women, children, animals, wagons, and sledges moved like a dark torrent across the Rhine and into Roman Gaul. The Vandals, one of the most feared Germanic tribes, were on the move from their homes in latter-day Poland and Hungary, driven west by the same force that drove the Visigoths, namely, the Huns. Within four years of the Vandal invasion, the Visigoths had sacked the city of Rome. Within twenty, the Vandals were conquering the Roman province of Africa.[38]

In the 1980s, the historian Alexander Demandt proposed a novel exercise. Instead of examining the Roman Empire, Roman civilization, and Christianity from all angles and perspectives to detect the wellsprings of change, what if historians were to look at the Germans? The Germans were warlike, they were freedom-loving, and their populations were growing more rapidly than their homelands could support. These factors were not unknown either to the ancients themselves or to modern historians. It was just that explanations based on them seemed too simple and naive to be true. But what if all the ancient authors were correct when they unanimously described the Germans as warlike, proud, freedom-loving, and fecund? What if this very consistency of evidence showed not that many Roman authors of widely disparate temperament and interests succumbed to the same prejudice, but that they were describing a genuine set of characteristics?

Julius Caesar, who met Germanic tribesmen in the mid-first century B.C., noted that they "spend their whole lives in hunting or in studying war." Tacitus confirmed this, adding that they were proud and irascible. This was a good thing for Rome, he thought, for it meant that the Germans were more inclined to argue among themselves than to mobilize their strength to attack the empire. "I pray," he wrote, "that these people shall ever retain, if not love of us, then at least hatred of each other. In a time of crisis for the Empire fortune can grant us no greater favor than the discord of our enemies."[39]

On one occasion in the 50s A.D., two German chieftains visited Rome. They were shown the sights of Rome and the blessings of civilization, culminating in a visit to the theater. Here, the two chieftains ascertained which were the finest seats, reserved for the emperor, and promptly sat down in them, explaining that they could not sit in less-distinguished seats, because "no one comes before Germans in might or virtue."[40]

In late antiquity, warrior values were as disparaged in all social classes in Rome as they were respected and encouraged among the Germans. This difference in the social prestige of the warrior was a fact with momentous consequences. It explained how it was possible for the Germanic tribes, who were vastly poorer and less well equipped than the Romans, to win. Adherents of socioeconomic explanations of decline denied that the barbarian invasions could be decisive, because the inhabitants of the empire were better off. Since "money is the sinew of war," as a Greek and Roman saying had it, the richer society, or so a liberal prejudice suggested, could never be defeated by the poorer. However, wealth did not necessarily translate into military strength. Niccolò Machiavelli drew from the history of early Rome, whose warrior ethos resembled that of the Germans, the lesson that "not gold . . . but good soldiers are the sinew of war; for gold is not sufficient to find good soldiers, but good soldiers are quite sufficient to find gold."[41] This accorded with his basic principle of political science, that a state lived by the *virtù*—the commitment, courage, and civic spirit—of its leaders and citizens and if that spirit declined, wealth would not prevent disaster. Applied to the Fall of Rome, this meant, according to Machiavelli, that "if one looks for the mainspring of decline of the Roman Empire, one will find that it was when they began hiring Goths [Germans] as soldiers; for from that beginning the forces of the Roman Empire began to weaken; and all the *virtù* that departed from it was given to them . . . I therefore conclude that without arms of its own no state is secure."[42]

In that observation lay a basic reason not merely for the Germanic victories, but for the victories of all poor but determined tribesmen over settled and debellicized communities, from the Amorite invasions of ancient Babylonia to the Arab conquests of the seventh and eighth centuries A.D. As these examples show, the Germanic invasions were not a unique event nor were they fortuitous. They could be explained anthropologically, in terms of the values of German tribal society. They could also be explained geopolitically, in terms of the changing balance of power between the Germanic zones of Europe and the Roman Empire. The Germans of the early centuries produced many children, and the ones who could not be fed at home were sent abroad to seek their fortune. For a time, this export of people provided a safety valve, but at some point in the third or fourth century, the demographic balance tipped. The crisis could not be solved by sending younger men away singly or in small groups, but only by migrations of whole tribes: thus began the movement that led to Adrianople, the Gothic treaty of 382, and the fall of Africa in 429.

No one asserted that the Germanic tribes were solely responsible for ending the Roman Empire in the West. But people who found it worth while to ask about the fall rather than explaining it away had come round, by the 1980s, to concluding that some of the oldest theories were right. "Taken together, the inner forces of decline reduced the late Empire to such a condition that it collapsed in the face of Germanic pressure." With the exception of the deterministic Spenglerian theory, every single one of the internal causes—religion, cultural barbarization, socioeconomic imbalances, declining yields from agriculture—could be turned on its head. The rise of Christianity, for some a disaster, was for others a liberation. Rostovtzev's class war of the ignorant against the educated was also Mazzarino's democratization. Economic imbalances in one province spurred growth in another. Overtaxation here meant more government spending elsewhere. Agricultural crises led to innovation and migration to healthier and more productive zones. Factors yielding such sets of diametrically opposed theories of decline could not be sufficient explanation in themselves. In short, they ignored the Germans.

On August 23, 476, the German troops serving the empire in Italy proclaimed their commander Odoacer, a member of the royal family of the Scirian tribe, king. They were angry because the imperial commander in Italy, Orestes, who was also the father of the western emperor, Romulus Augustulus ("little Augustus"), refused to give them a third of all land in Italy, as they demanded. Odoacer retaliated by deposing Romulus Augustulus, and that was the end of the Roman Empire in the West.

Twentieth-century historians tended to point out that all that really happened in 476 was that a Germanic ruler in Italy deposed the last western emperor. The empire itself, based in Constantinople, continued unaffected. Arnaldo Momigliano called the end of the western empire in 476 a nonevent, a "silent collapse."[43] But it was not silent to contemporaries; as one of them wrote, "the western empire of the Roman people ended." It was true that Odoacer and some of the other Germanic kings settled on Roman territory continued to regard themselves, officially, as servants of the empire. But because there was no longer an emperor in the West, the kingdoms and regions began to move more rapidly away from a Christian Roman identity to one that was Christian, tribal, and, somewhat later, European or Western. In other words, the particular time, place, and occasion that terminated the western empire was accidental. When it happened was not significant; that it happened was.

The Germanic invasions ended the Roman order and, crudely but effectively, added their own contribution to the synthesis that late antique Romans were producing, of a westernized Greco-Roman civilization and a westernized Christianity. The synthesis remained Christian, for the Germanic tribes, remarkably enough, did not want to reverse the Christianization of western Europe; they wanted to promote it. Though the invasions were decisive in ending the western empire, they did not change the character of what followed for the next sixteen hundred years, namely, the Christian West.

Ancient civilization ended in the West in the century following Odoacer and the fall of the western empire. In the 530s, the Roman noble Cassiodorus proposed to the pope that they jointly found a college of higher learning in Rome, which would preserve Christian and secular literature, philosophy, and religious writings. This was the last gasp of the ancient world, for Cassiodorus still thought there would be use for such things as literature and philosophy. Soon after, he had to leave Rome, for war had come to Italy. The emperor Justinian had decided to restore the empire to its full extent. He therefore sent an army to Italy, but it was resisted by the Ostrogoths, who controlled the Italian peninsula. The war over Italy lasted twenty years and wrought immeasurable destruction to cities, farms, fields, aqueducts, and the populace. Toward the end of the war, plague came. By the 550s, the Ostrogoths were defeated, but the prize was ruined. When Cassiodorus returned to Italy in 554, he retreated to a monastery. There, as a very old man, he wrote his last book in 580. Not a book of philosophy, ethical reflection, elevated theology, or literature, it was instead a book on spelling, because the monks had told him that they could no longer read the theological works in their own library nor could they set down their thoughts. Literacy, here in Italy, the heartland of the West, was visibly draining away. Gone were the ambitions for a college, for a learned elite, for precise and elaborate discussion of logical theorems, moral dilemmas, or the difference among epic, tragedy, and comedy. Cassiodorus went to his grave merely hoping that his own little band of monks would be able to read Scripture and recite the psalms. And they were the elite.[44]

Elsewhere in the West, the situation both for literacy and for culture generally was comparably worse. The name Dark Ages went out of fashion to describe the two or three centuries after around 550 but remained accurate as far as literate culture was concerned. Fewer people wrote books, and when they wrote, their subjects, themes, and style were simpler and cruder than anything that the ancient world had produced in over a thousand years. To call this mere change, and not decline, as late-twentieth-century historians were determined to do, was surely to deprive these terms of meaning.

The Fall of Rome was much on the minds of the survivors of World War I, many of whom saw their age as recapitulating the violence and spiritual uncertainty of the third century, the barbarian invasions of the fourth and fifth, or the demographic collapse that scholars of the time detected throughout late antiquity. As American educators formulated early versions of the Grand Narrative to provide an upbeat legitimation of the New West, pessimistic poets and philosophers in Europe lamented what they saw as the cataclysmic results of technological progress and liberal democracy and harked back to the Old Western synthesis. Some—Carl Schmitt in Germany, for example, who will reappear later—hoped to recover that synthesis by political means; for others, it could be recovered only as myth and metaphysics.

Which path you chose—recovering the synthesis or exploring the mythical—depended on temperament or, sometimes, on ideological convictions. T.S. Eliot was unusual in that, at different times in his life, he pursued both paths. Like the surrealists, he wanted to restore myth through modernist poetry. Like them, he represented a post–Spenglerian movement that defied secularism and what he saw as the collapse of values during and after World War I, and that responded not with resignation but with art. He also, at times, blamed Jews for promoting the secular and material values that blinded Westerners to the power of myth or the truth of Christianity.

Eliot's defense of the Christian West colored his later poetry and essays, from the late 1920s on. The later Eliot argued that Western civilization needed both the church and the literary tradition of antiquity. The West, in short, needed the Roman synthesis of a westernized Greek culture, represented by Virgil as the supreme classic poet of the West, and Christianity, represented by the church. It was, however, as a younger man and a fully committed member of the modernist movement that also included the surrealists that he presented the first version of his critique of secularism. The burden of this attack was that the West was dying because it had forgotten its own tradition, one of myth and the hidden traces of the sacred that could be discovered, with proper attention, even in the horrible banality of twentieth-century Western existence.

What Eliot saw was that the West was becoming a world, an outlook, and a culture that no longer wanted or needed tradition. The West by 1920 was not a civilization that had lost its traditional moorings, which one could perhaps restore or at least rediscover and describe. It was a civilization that rejected moorings of any sort. The essence of the modern West was that it had no essence, no heritage, no tradition. Tradition had become not the missing center of culture, but something that the culture increasingly regarded as its enemy.

This realization and its consequences gave every search for tradition after World War I, including that of Eliot and the surrealists, an air of counterrevolutionary subversion. For the rest of the twentieth century, those who tried to define the West as something more than the secular utopia of the Grand Narrative all shared this double consciousness. Many made honest, sincere, often highly sophisticated attempts to define the essence of the West in terms comprehensible to modernity. On the other hand, they were waging an impossible battle, because they were trying to give the culture what it did and could not want. Some ignored this contradiction and plunged ahead regardless; this was the case for the explicitly traditionalist proposals. Some understood the contradiction but objected that, willing or not, the West needed tradition because without tradition it would die.

Eliot's mythical suggestions for the West culminated in *The Waste Land*, published in 1922, the same year as James Joyce's *Ulysses*, a year defined by a literary critic as "literary modernism's grand climacteric." Eliot's friend and fellow-poet Ezra Pound, who also, and far more seriously than Eliot, got into political hot water with liberalism for his fascist activities, called *The Waste Land* "the justification of the 'movement,' of our modern experiment, since 1900."[45] Along the way, World War I happened, the Bolsheviks seized power in Russia, Spengler published *The Decline of the West*, and the world was full of echoes of the Fall of Rome. Rostovtzev, fresh from Russia, warned the West that proletarianization and class warfare might do to Europe and America what, in his view, they had done to Rome. *The Waste Land* at one level suggested that the contemporary West, like late antiquity, was

> A heap of broken images, where the sun beats
> And the dead tree gives no shelter[46]

Many members of the generation that lived through World War I saw their experiences, and the world to which they now returned, as analogous to the breakdown of the fifth to eighth centuries A.D. An older culture—sure of itself, transnational, rational, committed to order, hierarchy, and administration—collapsed, giving way to uncertainty, violence, and new forms of faith and hope. Cultural decline, the sense that one was living through an irreversible fall from civilization, law, literacy, gentility, and sophistication into a rude age of insecurity, violence, and ignorance, was arguably common to, say, fifth-century Gaul and 1920s Europe. A visitor of about 1919 to a Polish nobleman, the impoverished owner of a large estate, described this feeling in a letter. The author noted the dilapidated castle, the overgrown park, the neglected fields. In the evening, he sat with the owner in the candlelit library, talking about plays they had seen, ideas and hopes they had shared, and other debris of the prewar international civilization. Of what use now, in 1919, were these memories or the thousands of volumes of poetry, theater, novels, literary essays, and philosophy? How many people in Poland knew or cared about these things? That was what it was like for the educated elite of fifth-century Gaul, with Roman culture ebbing and new and dangerous powers growing. Such people heard what Eliot described:

> Murmur of maternal lamentation . . .
> hooded hordes swarming
> Over endless plains

In a note on this passage, Eliot quoted an outburst by the German writer

Hermann Hesse on the Russian Revolution: "[A]lready half of Europe, already half, at least, of eastern Europe is on the way to chaos."

The Waste Land was the modern West, like late antiquity, at the end of its tether. The mythical element in the poem, the message to the West that there was hidden meaning in mundane reality, which the West desperately needed to find, lay in the double meaning of the title and its echoes of Christian and Celtic legend.

A waste land could, like Rome in the sixth century, be the result of plunder, neglect, decay, or stupidity. But that which was once laid waste could again be made fertile. In choosing his title, Eliot was drawing on the mythological studies of Jessie Weston, who argued that the medieval legends of the Holy Grail contained elements of a lost cult of the mysteries and powers of nature, brought in prehistoric times by traders from the eastern Mediterranean to Britain—"a ritual which once claimed to be the accredited guardian of the deepest secrets of Life."[47] Weston believed that secret initiation rites into this cult survived into Christian times. That Weston's general thesis was since disproved made no difference, of course, to how she was read by Eliot and others who found fascinating the idea of an archaic, lost, mythical world. Its very brokenness, its character as a symbiosis of pagan, Eastern, Christian, and magical elements had a particular attraction in a time when incompatible forces were roiling the culture of the contemporary West.

The image or episode of the Waste Land was one of several myths incorporated in the legends of King Arthur and the Holy Grail, the so-called Matter of Britain, the earliest versions of which were written in northern France in the twelfth and thirteenth centuries. Chrétien of Troyes, who composed these versions, told the story of the boy Perceval, who ran off from his grieving mother to join King Arthur's court. He was too young to be a knight, so Gornemant, one of Arthur's knights, gave him a little training and then sent him away with the strange admonition, "Do not ask too many questions!" On his way home, he came one evening to a river. It was wide and deep. A boat appeared, with two men in it, one of whom was fishing in the river. The Fisherman told Perceval to ride up the steep bank of the river until he came to a house, where he would find lodging for the night. Perceval did so and was received as an honored guest. In the hall of the castle he found the Fisherman, who was wounded and could not rise to greet Perceval. Chrétien continued:

> While they were talking of this and that, a squire entered from a chamber, grasping by the middle a white lance, and passed between the fire, and those

seated on the couch. All present beheld the white lance and the white point, from which a drop of red blood ran down to the squire's hand. The youth who had arrived that night [Perceval] watched this marvel, but he refrained from asking what this meant, for he was mindful of the lesson which Gornemant gave him, warning him against too much speech, and he feared that if he asked, it would be considered rude. So he held his peace.

Then two other squires came in, right handsome, bearing in their hands candelabra of fine gold and niello work, and in each candelabrum were at least ten candles. A damsel came in with these squires, holding between her two hands a grail. She was beautiful, gracious, splendidly garbed, and as she entered with the grail in her hands, there was such a brilliant light that the candles lost their brightness, just as the stars do when the moon or the sun rises.

Several times the damsel carried the luminous grail past the company, and always Perceval held his tongue. After a long evening he was taken to his chamber. The next morning, he woke to find the castle deserted and left. The Fisher King's land was under a curse, and the curse would be lifted only if a young knight, seeing the grail, innocently and without prompting asked about it and about the Fisher King's wound. According to Chrétien, the Fisher King was wounded in battle. Other versions added more details. Wolfram von Eschenbach, who wrote the version used by Richard Wagner in his opera *Parsifal*, explained that the Fisher King had a mistress for whom he went to battle, rather than for God. A pagan knight wounded him in his genitals with a poisoned spear. The wound did not heal, and only if a knight came and asked the right question would the king be healed, and the questioner become grail king in his place.

The curse of the Waste Land and its wounded ruler, the Fisher King, were the essence of the ancient ritual of Life detected by Weston. From prehistoric times, peoples across Eurasia had identified the health of the land with that of its ruler. The way to ensure health was by a ritual of Life that granted to him who performed it successfully the power to make the land fertile. In this view, fish and fisher were "Life symbols of immemorial antiquity" deriving from the ancestral cult that, in medieval Europe, became the "romance" of the Grail and its healing power.[48] The curious fact that the healing power could be released only by an unknowing bystander was the romantic remnant of the ancient ritual requirement that the new giver of health be an innocent youth; one who, in the earliest forms of the cult, was actually sacrificed so that his vigorous blood could fertilize the land.

The wounded and infertile, perhaps self-mutilated king sadly presiding over an infertile Waste Land was a powerful image. Though Eliot used that image only once in the poem, its entire text is an emotional and syntactical Waste Land, a series of abrupt, fragmented conversations, snatches of poetry, incantations, jangles, and banal phrases of twentieth-century urban existence. The whole is set in London, but it is not only the London known to street maps; it is also an "Unreal City / Under the brown fog of a winter dawn." Unreal, because the poem juxtaposes the terminal boredom of humdrum, goalless, unmagical life with the mythical patterns that lie just beneath the surface, if we could only detect them.

The first two of five parts present the debris of war among civilians; returning soldiers, dubiously faithful wives, down-at-heel veterans in pubs, with or without their petty purposes. The third turns on a scene of loveless sex between "the typist home at teatime . . . bored and tired" and "the young man carbuncular," but this scene is witnessed by the invisible Tiresias, the legendary and long-lived seer of ancient Thebes. According to Hesiod, Tiresias had been both a man and a woman. He once surprised and wounded two copulating snakes; he was instantly turned into a woman for seven years, until he saw the snakes again "and his prior form and native appearance returned to him." Tiresias also offended the goddess Hera by claiming that women enjoyed sex more than men. The myth of the all-knowing hermaphrodite, combining male and female emotions and wisdom, anticipated Carl Jung's teaching about the anima and the animus, the female and the male aspects of the psyche. Trapped in necessary but limiting sexual identities, the citizens of the dark "unreal city" of the twentieth-century West grope toward an ecstasy that never arrives. This section of the poem ends, in the fourth part, with double allusions to the Buddha and to Saint Augustine, who represent Eastern and Western asceticism, contrasted to the sex and the commerce of the London docks.

The fifth part of *The Waste Land* is entitled "What the Thunder Said," reminding us of Zeus, the god of thunder and destroyer of men and worlds. The doom of the West seems close at hand: "We who were living are now dying / With a little patience." Water, necessary for life and a metaphor of vitality and civilization, is lacking. In the myth of the Waste Land, one of the effects of the curse is drought, and in her analysis, Weston pointed to the ancient Indian myth of how the god Indra "freed the waters" as early evidence that the ritual of life designed to keep the king healthy and the land fertile could be traced back to the earliest origins of the Indo-European tribes.

In Eliot's poem, the people lament their hopeless lives, looking for sources of new energy, but there is no water, only "red sullen faces" that "sneer and snarl." And worse: the rumblings of mindless revolution, barbarian destruction are heard. An empty chapel stands in the waste, its door swinging. Even the house of God, the Western God, is desolate. All that is left, at the end, is the resigned king, who has long since given up hope of his deliverer:

> I sat upon the shore
> Fishing . . .
> Shall I at least set my lands in order?

The Waste Land promised no redemption of civilization. It taught, rather, that resignation could be a pleasure if drenched in awareness of the Western culture of the past and of the hidden depths still discoverable today. It was not a positive program of recovery, but it was a cut above Spengler's determinism. Spengler would not have advised the Fisher King to bother to "shore fragments" against ruin.

Eliot's cultural program was, in both its guises, the semisurrealist modernism of The Waste Land and the Christian and Virgilian pedagogy of the 1930s and 1940s, an attempt to deny that Nietzsche and Spengler were right or that World War I had definitively inaugurated the end of the West. From the perspective of the 1990s the effort appeared doomed, yet splendid in its defiance. Eliot sensed this, which may have helped him find comfort in his own cyclical view of history, his view, from "Burnt Norton" (1935), the first of the Four Quartets, that

> What might have been and what has been
> Point to one end, which is always present

The young Eliot's melancholy and ironic culture game in The Waste Land implicitly allowed that time was unredeemable; an attitude that, by the way, he contradicted in one of his later essays. He suggested that the West needed myth and ritual, and described chillingly the secularized world divorced from myth. He later came to reassert the old synthesis of Greco-Roman civilization and Christianity. In no case did he analyze the synthesis, nor was he, as a poet, under any obligation to do so. The fact remained, however, that the synthesis had all along had a third element, the Germanic and warrior element, which did not always sit easily either with Rome or Christianity. Yet it was the larger synthesis of those three—the ancient philosopher, the Christian priest, and the Germanic warrior—that truly defined the Old West.

CHAPTER FIVE

Germanic Freedom and the Old Western Synthesis

The beginnings of Western culture are to be found in the new spiritual community which arose from the ruins of the Roman Empire owing to the conversion of the Northern barbarians to the Christian faith.

—Christopher Dawson

Let each man take heed to strike great blows,
  That no ill song can be made of us.
Pagans are wrong and Christians are right.
  Never shall a bad example be made of me.

—Song of Roland

The liberal Grand Narrative produced a Western identity that was modern, secular, and liberal and that rested on an imaginary direct line connecting the modern West to the ancient Greeks, an imaginary line from Plato to NATO, in which everything in between formed an orderly sequence culminating in liberal modernity. This version descended from the romantic and nineteenth-century cult of Greece and misunderstood both the Greeks and the West—creating an idealized vision of Greece seen through the lens of a West defined as the heir of that idealized Greece. It also misunderstood the intervening history, which was defined as a long preamble to modernity and not appreciated as an authentic and valid form of Western identity.

That earlier, premodern Western identity—what this book calls the Old West—was martial, religious, and traditional. Unlike the narrative and its image of the New West as the belated child of Greece, the Old West was not an imaginary construct, but the political, literary, constitutional, and cultural fruit of the synthesis of Greece—real, not imagined—Rome, Christianity, and the Germanic tribes, a synthesis that lasted for sixteen hundred years. The old Western identity did not constitute an orderly sequence from a glorious past to an even more glorious present, but a civilization in itself, that is, a set of ideals and institutions that were sometimes contradictory and sometimes harmonious, that were abused and exploited as often as they were honored and upheld. Out of this Old West came, in due course, the New West and liberalism, which then justified itself by inventing a history of the West destined to produce liberalism. The purpose of that history was to downgrade the Old West, emphasizing what was progressive, as defined by New Western values, and ignoring what was not.

Thus, while the main versions of the Grand Narrative—the Columbia and Chicago story and the Durant epic—paid some attention to Rome and to medieval Europe, they did so in awkward and often apologetic fashion, as if to say, how unfortunate and ignorant were these people; but we have to notice them because they were links in the chain that carried the legacy of Greece forward until it could fertilize and inspire the only true West, namely, the modern, democratic, egalitarian, and peace-loving West.

The fundamental reason for this approach, which was both unhistorical and unjust, was that the Grand Narrative was not primarily an exercise in scholarship but in political pedagogy. In terms of this pedagogy, modern values were correct and premodern values acceptable only insofar as they pointed toward modern ones. On this standard, the premodern West was flawed, since it was not democratic, egalitarian, secular, or peace loving, but rather seemed defined by hierarchy, faith, and war.

The post-1960s antinarratives fully shared this approach, for their grievance against the modern West was not that it was too democratic, secular, or peace loving, but that it was in reality none of these things, but rather imperialistic, fanatical, and violent. Thus, both centrist liberals and their critics agreed that the bulk of Western history, the sixteen centuries from late antiquity to the twentieth century, was in the most basic sense not legitimate, not worthy of understanding on its own terms. This was unjust because by downgrading the Old West, the New West obscured its own origins.

It is, however, in the Old West that we find the basic dramas of Western identity—the drama of power, of freedom, and of empire. Every civilization knows the drama of power, the tension of justice and force, and it was an illusion of the Grand Narrative, and even more of the neoliberal antinarratives, to pretend that this drama was over, or could be resolved by a simplistic universalism. But in the Western case, the liberal denial of the drama of power led to a startling paradox, because the very core of the New West, the idea of freedom, emerged from that drama as it was enacted in the centuries known to modern historians and modern public opinion as the Middle Ages. The New West saw itself as the civilization of liberty, which it was; but it forgot that this liberty was not only a gift from the Greeks but, in its Western form, inseparable in its origins from the drama of power and specifically from the contribution of the last of the three elements of the Old Western synthesis, the Germanic element.

In Western history, the drama of power was inseparably tied to two other fundamental and recurrent themes—empire and universalism. Power was necessary for empire, which was a constant aspiration of the greatest Old Western rulers, because they believed that a universal empire was the only right order for humankind; just as there was only one God in heaven, so there should be only one world ruler on earth. This universalism was something very different from the universalism of the New West, which asserted—in both its liberal and multicultural versions—that the only legitimate political order was a global civilization of democratic humanism divorced from all specific cultural roots. By contrast, the dreams of empire and universal dominion of Old Western rulers and thinkers were part and parcel of their identity, of the synthesis of Roman, Christian, and Germanic culture. And the great paradox of this Old Western universalism was that it never succeeded, and that the very attempts to make it succeed promoted that which undermined it—the Western idea of political and social freedom.

The drama of power is therefore the key to Western identity. It tempted the figures that, each in his time, dominated Western political history, from Charlemagne through the emperors Frederick II and Charles V to Napoleon and Adolf Hitler. But while imposing suffering on many people, none of them succeeded in establishing his universal empire, and the net result of their efforts was always a growth of freedom. To say that the drama of power is the key to Western identity is therefore to make more than the banal point that power and imperialism were important in the West, for they were important in all cultures. What created the peculiar dynamic of the West—a dynamic not recognized if the New West is kept separate from its Old West origins—was that imperialism never succeeded throughout the West or for very long at a time, and that it inevitably strengthened the forces opposed to it: the forces of pluralism, individualism, and ethnic identity.

The search for power and empire was thus, paradoxically, the precondition of liberty. Sometimes this liberty took forms unfamiliar to the New West, for example, the religious liberty of the Protestant reformers of the sixteenth century. The search for power had other consequences not easily captured by the Grand Narrative: the drive for conquest that produced both the European expansion of the sixteenth century, the slave trade, and the rise of modern science. All these elements—imperialism, expansion, science, and liberty—were marked by the red thread of individualism, which became a core feature of Western identity, but which for most of its history was not the mild-mannered and civil trait imagined by Will Durant or Robert Maynard Hutchins, but an ambiguous and dangerous force, marked by the twin poles of greed and altruism.

Freedom, conquest, and imperialism were, then, not contradictions but parts of a whole: the Old Western synthesis. But the key to the synthesis, the principle that shaped it out of the materials left by late antiquity, was the first of these, namely, freedom, with which we begin.

The liberal American story of the West took freedom as its axis and located the origins of freedom in Greece. Greek freedom, however, was different from modern freedom, and, in any event, Greek freedom ended in 338 B.C., when Philip of Macedon conquered Athens. The liberal version failed to explain how freedom could be the foundation of the West if it was largely absent between 338 B.C. and A.D. 1776, when it was resurrected by Thomas Jefferson in the American Declaration of Independence. The Continental narrative emphasized Roman law and institutions as the foundation of the West, which was historically more accurate. Neither gave an account of how modern freedom grew in the centuries separating late antiquity from the liberal era. The essential missing element in that story was the Germanic ethos of aristocratic and heroic freedom. What happened in the centuries after that ethos encountered the Roman and Christian traditions was something that no one who knew only Rome, Christianity, or the Germans could have predicted, something that only their synthesis made possible: the political, social, and economic phenomenon of modern liberty. The history of that synthesis—the history of the Old West—was a long, slow working out of its latent potential for freedom.

The birth of modern freedom, hailed by Jefferson and the French revolutionaries, was a new and astonishing transformation, but also the logical result of the Old Western synthesis. The new freedom, the keystone of the New West, did not spring full-grown from the minds of liberal thinkers, but was rooted in habits, institutions, culture, and social development. It was the great contribution of the sceptical or moderate Enlightenment—of Montesquieu, Hume, and most of the American Founders—that they saw freedom as rooted in history and institutions and not as a radical design for a revolutionary leap to a higher and morally superior form of society. Some of them also sensed that the origins of the freedom they saw as maturing in their own day were to be sought in the deep past, in the time of the Old Western synthesis.

The thinkers of the radical Enlightenment, however—Voltaire, Rousseau, and most of the French revolutionaries—shaped the original pattern of the Grand Narrative in opposite terms, as the story of liberal and secular ideals, long suppressed by force and superstition. On that reading, the New West was the defeat of the Old, the fruit of political acts designed to lead to the happy modern era of free citizens in a free and unconstrained civil society. The major obstacle, according to the radical Enlightenment, was institutional Christianity—Christendom as the political and cultural expression of the Old Western synthesis. Christendom was a geopolitical as well as a religious and social concept. It meant that the synthesis of late antiquity had laid the permanent foundations of Western civilization as one where political, social, and economic life would be governed by Christian ethics, and where the marriage of church and state would guide the conscience and the policies of all. Western civilization existed wherever the synthesis and the basic terms of the ancient bargains were upheld, that is, in Europe west of the East-West line established in Roman times, and wherever else Europeans had introduced or imposed their political and cultural systems. In the eighteenth century, that meant the Americas: north and south.

Few if any of the founders of liberalism wanted to do away with Christianity as a religion and a faith. Their grievance was against Christendom in the strong sense of that term, against the idea that the church should have political power and influence, or that any principle other than secular reason should govern free political debate. Liberalism proposed that morality and hence the judgment of policies would emerge from civil society, and that civil society was a guarantee of greater overall freedom and well-being than any set of absolute guidelines deduced from an alleged revelation that, even if one granted that such a thing could exist, was mediated by fallible and power-hungry men. Classical liberals held that the individual citizen could, as a private person, obey any revelation he pleased, but that political arguments and decisions derived from the free competition of ideas judged only by principles of reason, which were the equal right and inheritance of all.

Liberals thus denied that the Old Western synthesis and its result, Christendom, defined the West; or, if it defined the Old West, it ought not to define the New West, which was liberal and secular. They disagreed with those who maintained that the West was most itself when the synthesis was strong and the ancient bargains still shaped politics and culture.

The sceptical Enlightenment and its descendants—including this book—disagree: the very principle by which the New West and its liberal apologists defined the West—freedom—was itself part of the long and ambiguous history that the New West rejected. To explain that history, the sceptical Enlightenment constructed what one might call the Germanic model, in contrast to the Greek model of Western identity propagated by the cult of Greece. Where the Greek model asserted a continuity outside time from Plato to NATO, the Germanic model delved into time to understand and define the Old Western synthesis.

The Germanic model enjoyed considerable support in the eighteenth and nineteenth centuries; in American debate and pedagogy, it was more than a rival to the Greek model until early in the twentieth century. Rather, the two models were complementary: the Greeks were the standards of perfect humanity and the source of the greatest literature and philosophy of the West, but it was the Germanic tribes who inaugurated modern freedom and who laid the earliest foundations of the national and political pluralism of Western civilization.

But if the Germanic model was superior to the Greek, why did it disappear from public debate and so completely from the Grand Narrative that it was almost impossible to find any traces of it? For two reasons: World War I and World War II. The Grand Narrative received its decisive formulations as America was helping to defeat Germany in World War I. One could hardly expect John Herman Randall and the other scholars and intellectuals who first taught the Columbia Contemporary Civilization course in 1919 to distinguish between the Germans whom their country had just defeated in the name of democracy and the Germanic tribes who invaded the Roman Empire. The purpose of the Contemporary Civilization course was to teach returning servicemen and future cohorts of young Americans what the war had been about. According to the doctrine that inspired the course, the war had been a war in defense of liberal democracy, represented by the United States, and against tyranny and barbarism, represented by Germany.[1] America in World War I and the years after was awash in anti-German chauvinism and prejudice. Popular feeling against Germany and Germans in America around 1920 was deeper, stronger, and more radical than anti-Russian or anti-Soviet feelings after World War II.

The key claim of the Germanic model—that the Germanic invaders of Rome represented a new principle of freedom that drove all subsequent Western history—was both offensive and incomprehensible in 1918. Within only a few years, the influence of the Germanic model in American pedagogy was broken and its fundamental claim stood on its head. The model had said that the Germanic invaders brought liberty and fresh energy to a decadent, tyrannized society. The evidence of World War I appeared to be that Germans were, as the anti-German argument had always held, barbarians and destroyers. In 1914, they brought destruction across the Rhine; in the fifth century, their ancestors had likewise brought destruction across the Rhine. The freedom-loving German of the sceptical Enlightenment was, at least as far as the Grand Narrative and popular Western identity went, stone dead. The American Grand Narrative instead adopted what had originally been a German invention, the cult of Greece as the origin of the West.

Attempts to rehabilitate the Germanic model in the interwar years took an ideological tack that made sure the model could not survive World War II. Before Adolf Hitler and his regime discredited doctrines of racial hierarchy and eugenics in popular discourse, such doctrines had wide appeal, not least among liberals and progressives. Many scholars in the interwar years considered it innovative and modern to introduce theories of racial vigor, eugenics, and degeneration into their historical accounts. Thus, in Germany primarily, but also in America, the argument that Rome fell because of genetic decadence among the Romans and genetic superiority of the Germans gained considerable ground in the 1920s and 1930s. "It was because the giants of the past had given place to a bastard brood that the final catastrophe came," wrote one scholar in 1928.[2] By World War II, the Germanic model, insofar as it survived outside Germany, held that the Germanic tribes defeated Rome because of their superior blood. This ideological version of the Germanic model was, in its own way, as dogmatic as the Greek model. It purported to explain Western history as a struggle for the survival of the fittest, and not by an argument about the constitutional and political history of Europe as the outgrowth of the Germanic invasions.

The racist Germanic model went back to Otto Seeck's dysgenic account from 1895 of Rome's fall as due to the "extermination of the best people," the argument that the Roman elite committed racial and genetic suicide. The two countries where such theories were the most popular, until 1945, were Germany and the United States. Mass immigration from southern and eastern Europe from the 1870s on raised constant fears among American elites that American identity, power, and survival were at risk from contamination by alien elements. These had therefore to be selected according to qualities compatible with white Anglo-Saxon hegemony, and, when they arrived, strictly Americanized. Scholars drew analogies to Rome and warned that unless America learned from Rome to watch its borders and safeguard its white, Anglo-Saxon identity, it would go the way of Rome. David Starr Jordan, the president of Stanford University, developed Seeck's argument in a book subtitled "a study of the decay of races through the survival of the unfit." The best men of Rome died in the wars of the late republic, he argued; this led to "the rise of the mob and of the emperor, who is the mob's exponent." Since "the blood of a nation determines its history," America, learning from Rome's example, must remember that "a race of men or a herd of cattle are governed by the same laws of selection," and that just as "the Republic of Rome lasted so long as there were Romans," so "the Republic of America will last so long as its people, in blood and spirit, remain what we have learned to call Americans."[3]

The classic exponent of the dysgenic model was another American, Madison Grant, who in *The Passing of the Great Race*, written during World War I, warned that America was losing its best men in war just as the Romans had done, and that this could spell a Roman fate for America.[4] It was only in America, Grant argued, that the Nordic race dominated political and social life, but this domination was threatened by war, which devoured the bravest, and by miscegenation and democracy. In a later edition of the work, he claimed credit for having changed the climate of opinion against mass immigration, a change sanctioned by the Immigration Act of 1924, which closed the American frontiers for forty years. Grant was obsessed with his idea, derived from vulgar Darwinism and from German nationalist writers of the 1880s and later, that the "Nordic race" was uniquely creative and dynamic. Its "passing," he warned, would be the end of America. Similarly, in the ancient world, it was only "Nordic mercenaries" who "kept the Western Empire alive for three centuries after the ancient Roman stock had virtually ceased to exist." Christianity further undermined Roman vigor with its egalitarian morality, its pacifism, and its cult of weakness. Adolf Hitler fully agreed. He stated in 1942 that "the mobilization of the mob in the name of Christianity meant the end of the ancient world."[5]

The racist Germanic model produced other odd claims. Because Greece and Rome had once been strong and victorious in war, and yet Rome, in the end, succumbed to the Germans, the model's adherents had not only to explain how Rome degenerated, but why she had formerly been strong. According to the racist thesis, this was because Greeks and Romans were originally members of the same Aryan racial stock as the Germans but had allowed their stock to become contaminated by lesser races. So another American, the economic historian Tenney Frank, proposed in the 1930s that the original Romans were pure representatives of a morally and psychologically sound Indo-European race, but that too much civilization had undermined their racial instincts. They had become too enlightened for their own ethnic good. Adolf Hitler went a step further. Because only the Aryan Germans were truly creative, therefore the early Greeks and Romans, who created a great civilization, must have been Germanic by blood. They fell, however, to "blood poisoning" by lesser races and to the Jewish-inspired Christian religion, which undermined their psychological vitality.

In 1945, the record of German barbarity in World War II, driven as it was by the racist dogma of Hitler's regime, discredited the racist model of the ancient Germans even more thoroughly than World War I had discredited the Enlightenment Germanic model. But whereas the racist model rested on dogma and the presumption of a hierarchy of nations or races, universally condemned by postwar liberalism, the Enlightenment model contained substantive arguments about the nature of the West and of Western history. The defeat of racist Germany in 1945 undermined the doctrine that the Germans were genetically superior, and also the proposition that the Germans brought freedom to the West. And the two were not the same; in fact, they were opposed. The democratic freedoms in whose name America waged both world wars were, according to the Enlightenment Germanic model, descendants of the very freedoms by which the ancient Germans had revitalized the decaying body of the Roman West.

The Grand Narrative and its Greek model of the West won the day in 1918 and 1945 thanks, in part, to the simplistic equation of ancient and modern Germans. Anti-German feeling determined claims about Western history in America because people concluded that because both groups had the same name, they were morally and politically identical. By reverse transtemporal infection, German war guilt in 1918 and 1945 reached back to blacken all German history, even to the time of the Germanic invasions, passing easily over the objection that the tribesmen only doubtfully belonged to the same history as modern Germans. The same Germanic tribesmen who were virtuous, freedom-loving, and energetic bearers of new cultural vitality in 1914 were in 1918 relegated to the dungeons of history. In both world wars, German ideologues had themselves encouraged the identification by loudly proclaiming that today's Germany, whether that of the Kaiser in 1914 or that of Hitler in 1939, was the true, loyal, and legitimate heir of the ancient tribes. But did this make sense? Who were the ancient Germans, what was their relation to the modern German nation, and in what did their contribution to Western freedom consist?

The ancient Germans were all those who spoke Germanic dialects and who shared a material and religious culture as evidenced by ancient written sources, all of which are Greek or Roman, and by archaeology. Not all Germanic speakers shared the same culture, and some people who were Germanic in culture did not speak a Germanic dialect. The fit, however, was close enough. In the last few centuries B.C., the inhabitants of central and western Europe shared a material and religious culture that modern scholars named Celtic. The original Germanic tribes lived north of this area, around the Baltic Sea and in the countries later known as Scandinavia.

Beginning in the fourth or third century B.C., Germanic tribes began moving south, into Celtic territory. At first, these tribes adopted the culture of the Celts, and were identified as Celts in ancient sources until the time of Julius Caesar. The first ethnic Germans to appear in history were, probably, the Bastarnae, a tribe that established itself on the lower Danube in the late third century B.C. The Bastarnae were energetic and fecund, anticipating the traits noted of later Germanic peoples. The origins and original meaning of the word *Germans* are unknown; most likely it was a Celtic name, given by Celts to their new neighbors, and signaling thereby that these new neighbors were different.

At the end of the second century B.C., three Germanic tribes from Jutland—the Cimbri, the Teutones, and the Ambrones—allegedly driven by famines and floods from their home, moved south en masse and invaded Gaul and Italy. Though they were eventually defeated—killed, enslaved, or driven out—they left a lasting impression as resembling a terrible force of nature, irresistible and overwhelming, and collapsing suddenly as if it had never been. Their fearless disregard of casualties and their mass sacrifices of prisoners terrified the Romans.

While this invasion occupied Roman attention for decades afterward, other Germanic groupings had been more peacefully seeping south into the territory that later took their name, pushing Celtic culture south and east over the Rhine. In about 70 B.C., the chieftain Ariovistus was the first to be named as a "king of Germans" in Latin sources when he crossed the Rhine and invaded Gaul. It was partly to stop such Germanic encroachment on Gaul that Julius Caesar decided to conquer it in the 50s B.C. Caesar stopped at the Rhine. His successors wanted to conquer "free Germany" and extend the Roman border to a line following the Elbe River, the Sudeten range of hills west and south of latter-day Bohemia, and along the March River to the Danube below modern Vienna. This attempt ended when a chieftain of the Cheruscan tribe, whom Tacitus named Arminius, trapped and destroyed a 30,000-man-strong Roman army in A.D. 9.

Arminius was a Roman citizen with the rank of knight and could look forward to a lucrative career if Rome conquered free Germany. He chose to defect for two very Germanic reasons: honor and luck. These were fundamental categories of character, motive, and behavior in ancient Germanic society. "A man's honor is his total integrity, his bodily, mental, material, and spiritual strength and wholeness. He who has honor is 'hale,' he owns luck, good fortune. He who loses his honor, also loses his luck and becomes 'fey,' that is, marked for death."[6] Arminius belonged to a divided royal family. If he did not assert the power of his branch of the family and destroy those who threatened it, whether Roman or Cheruscan, he would be without honor, in which case rank and privileges under Rome would mean nothing. To assert his honor he needed to prove his luck. An ancient German playing a high-risk game could prove his luck by matching it with that of the most powerful male around. In Arminius's Germanic world, that male was Maroboduus, a chieftain of the Marcomanni who had demonstrated great honor and luck by assembling a substantial kingdom along the Danube, including some later famous nations such as the Goths and the Lombards, and centered in Bohemia, the "home of the Boii," another tribe under his control. To match your luck against that of a king who had already won great honor was a desperate gamble: either you lost, losing your own luck and enhancing his, or you won, in which case you were the prime male—for a while.

And so it went. Arminius returned to his people, raised a rebellion, trapped and destroyed the Roman armies, and confirmed his luck and honor among the Cheruscans. He then assembled a new army and attacked the Marcomannic kingdom. His first attempt failed because his uncle, who belonged to the rival branch of the Cheruscan royal family, defected to Maroboduus with a large part of the Cheruscan host. On the next attempt, in A.D. 19, Arminius defeated Maroboduus and expelled him from his kingdom.

The deposed king, his honor and luck gone beyond recall, fled to Roman territory, where, according to Tacitus, he spent his last eighteen years in Ravenna as a happy and well-fed pensioner, disturbed only, the Roman historian reported, by an excessive appetite for sex. Back in the land of luck and honor, Arminius, "grasping for the crown," fell victim to the inevitable assassin. Tacitus granted him the epitaph *haud dubie liberator Germaniae* (beyond doubt the liberator of Germany). The name Arminius was Roman; ironically no one ever discovered his Germanic name. Five of eight other members of the Cheruscan royal family known to sources had names starting with *Sigi-*, "victory," giving rise to the romantic legend that Arminius was the original Siegfried, the invincible hero who was slain by treacherous relatives before he could reach the pinnacle of glory.

The populations of the western Roman empire were to become thoroughly familiar with the world of Arminius and Maroboduus, but not for several more centuries. For over four hundred years, from the time of Caesar to the early fifth century A.D., the Germans were held on the Rhine. German pressure during these centuries struck the middle and lower Danube, as in the time of Marcus Aurelius in the 160s or when, in the 250s and 260s, armies of Goths, an eastern Germanic people, pushed into the Balkans and Greece. In the fourth century whole communities of Goths entered the empire across the Danube. The tribes on the Rhine, the Franks and Alemanni, entered Gaul around 406, and by the mid-fifth century the Rhine frontier was no more.

No one in these tribes, Goths, Franks, or others, thought of himself as German. The term was used by Latin sources as a name for the invading tribes who shared Germanic speech. The community of identification was the nation, or tribe, and its king. Such identification was strong; the Visigothic, Ostrogothic, Burgundian, Skirian, Vandal, Frankish, or Alemannic groupings were national communities in a sense not wholly dissimilar to later medieval or modern feeling. A common Germanic nation or identity hardly developed, except in regard to outsiders, that is, speakers of non-Germanic languages. From an early period, Germans of all tribes referred to speakers of Celtic or Latin, such as the native inhabitants of Gaul, as *volcae*, strangers. This word in English became *wealas*, which was the Anglo-Saxon name for all the Celtic-speaking inhabitants of the British Isles, and which in modern times became restricted to just one of the several Celtic peoples of Britain, the Welsh.

By the end of the fifth century, the Franks were the dominant Germanic nation within the old Roman frontiers. Over the next few centuries, they shaped and largely manned the political, cultural, and religious elite of Gaul, which eventually became the land of the western Franks, western Francia, and, later still, France. To what extent these Franks, or "free men," brought freedom to Roman Gaul, what freedom might mean in the context of the Germanic migrations and the end of Roman power, and how this Germanic freedom shaped the later West were the questions that the Enlightenment Germanic model claimed to answer.

The settlement of the Franks in Gaul completed the division of the Germanic tribes into two main groups: those living on ex-Roman territory in Gaul and Spain and those living east of the old Roman frontier. The latter group included the eastern Franks, the Alemanni, and the groupings that took shape in the seventh century and later as the Bavarians, the Saxons, and the Swabians—the historic "tribes" or regions of medieval and modern Germany. How these "tribes" related to the earlier tribes or nations of Goths, Vandals, Skirians, and the others was hotly disputed by historians for much of the nineteenth and twentieth centuries; the conclusion, after the smoke of scholarly battle cleared, was, no one knew. But one thing was certain: neither in the time of Arminius nor during the migrations of the fourth or fifth century was there a Germanic nation, a common feeling of identity among the various peoples of Germanic speech and culture. Those who asserted such an identity, whether because they admired or hated the Germans of a later day, were making it up.

A sense of national identity among the two separate groups of Germanic peoples, those within the old empire and those outside it, hardly existed before the eleventh century. By that time the western Franks had blended with the native Romano-Celtic population of Gaul to form the people of France, and the eastern Franks, Bavarians, Swabians, and Saxons had begun to coalesce into the German nation. The process of nation building was in both cases a long and arduous one, and never reached a final point for the simple reason that the criteria of nationhood kept changing. The Germans of the modern era, when the Germanic model was being formulated and fought over, had no national history in common with the tribes or nations that invaded the Roman Empire. Whether they had a history of values, culture, or ideals in common was a highly politicized question.

The Enlightenment model of the Germans as the authors of Western freedom and the decisive third party in the Christian-Roman synthesis was invented not in Germany, as one might expect, but in France, Britain, and America. The reason was not the same in these three countries. In France, the model grew out of a long-standing argument within the French nobility and among French antiquaries about the origins of the French nation and monarchy. On the one side stood those who believed that the Franks had become wholly assimilated to the native Roman population of Gaul. All Frenchmen had a common national origin in this melting pot, which meant that the French monarchy was ultimately a gift of the people, and that noble rank and privileges were mere rewards for service, practical measures that could be granted or withdrawn according to the needs of the state and nation. This one-nation ideology also implied that anyone who fulfilled the practical requirements of wealth or merit could rise to noble rank.

On the other hand stood those who believed that the ancient Franks, the "free men," were the direct ancestors of the highest nobility of France, the *noblesse d'épée*, or sword nobility. The Franks had conquered Gaul; they had divided its lands, resources, and inhabitants between them; and their descendants, the sword nobility, held their lands and privileges therefore by right of conquest and not by gift of anyone, king or people. This was an ideology of aristocratic freedom, modeled in no small part on early Rome, as portrayed in the seventeenth century in the Roman dramas of Corneille. The Frankish doctrine was directed against the commoners and the second-rank nobility, the *noblesse de robe*, or nobility of the gown, who wanted access to the top privileges reserved for the sword nobility. It was also directed against the absolute monarchy, which threatened to emasculate the sword nobles and reduce them to being merely a top class of state servants. It found expression in such magnificently haughty phrases as the motto of the dukes of Rohan: *Roy ne puis, prince ne daigne, Rohan suis* (king I cannot be, mere noble I deign not to be, Rohan I am).

Historically, the Frankish doctrine was not as far-fetched as it sounded. The top tier of French nobility was unusual in Europe in that it was a small and closed group, and most of its member families were very ancient. The point in the eighteenth century, however, was not whether the doctrine was true as history, but that it produced, in Montesquieu, a member of the sword nobility who took pride in his three hundred years of noble descent, but who was also his era's leading political theorist and a founder of liberalism. Montesquieu took the aristocratic doctrine of Frankish freedom and turned it into a liberal doctrine of general republican liberty under law that would resume, in the modern world, the liberation of resources and spirits begun by his Frankish forefathers in Gaul twelve hundred years earlier. The source of both kinds of liberty, that of the Germanic Franks and that of modernity, was the conquest of the Roman Empire: "The Goths, in conquering the Roman Empire, everywhere founded monarchy and liberty." Before the conquest, the inhabitants of the empire lived in misery, under an unbalanced regime that combined the worst features of autocratic despotism and arbitrary local misgovernment by uncontrolled provincial governors and, in the later phases, military commanders. The Germanic invasions brought the seeds of freedom, because the conquerors established monarchies based on ordered and law-governed hierarchies of nobility, security of ownership of land, and responsible administration that encouraged agriculture, commerce, and useful arts. Montesquieu's great insight, which was taken up by economic historians in the twentieth century, was that freedom was not opposed to order, but dependent on it. "The political liberty of a citizen is that tranquillity of spirit which stems from the idea that each has of his own safety, and in order to enjoy this liberty, the government must be such that a citizen does not have to fear another citizen."[7] The type of government that secured such freedom was one in which the legislative and executive powers were divided, and which consisted of representatives of the citizenry. The origins of divided, representative government were to be found, so he concluded, not in Greece or Rome, but among the Germans.

Looking around the Europe of his day, Montesquieu identified England as the country with the constitution most friendly to liberty. It was the best because it consisted in a mixture of monarchical, aristocratic, and democratic or popular elements, a mixture that granted the subject greater freedom of thought, action, and behavior than any other in Europe. Montesquieu departed radically from the Frankish doctrine of his fellow-aristocrats in France. He castigated them for having sunk beneath the noble liberty of their ancestors. Having given in to the blandishments of the absolute monarchy, they lived lives of waste, expending the resources of their lands, giving nothing in return, and exploiting the people. According to him, it was the English who had best preserved the Germanic freedoms, whereas in France the nobility, who ought to have maintained it, had gradually surrendered it over the past two hundred years. Montesquieu concluded that the origins of English freedom went back to the Germanic invaders of Gaul and Roman Britain, who brought the spark of liberty "from the Germanic forests." Thus, the Germanic forests, the tribal society of the prehistoric German nations, was the birthplace of the freedom that was destined, in Montesquieu's view, to sweep the world. The reason that freedom was born in the forests of Germany was that the northern climate and challenging physical environment drew out the best in people. The argument paralleled that of Demaratus, who claimed, according to Herodotus, that the Greeks loved freedom because they were poor, wise, and subject to laws that were strict but fair.

Montesquieu's praise of England won him many friends in that country and stimulated a British and American version of the Germanic model of freedom. This version started not from an ideology of aristocratic freedom or from a romantic view of the Germanic invaders, but from the doctrine known as the Ancient Constitution. This was the idea, first coined by Edward Coke in the early seventeenth century, that England had from the time of the ancient Britons been a mixed monarchy, in which the king always governed with the advice and consent of his nobles in parliament. Whenever a king broke the Ancient Constitution and governed alone, he was a despot and could justly be resisted or overthrown by the nobles, whose task was to restore and guard the Ancient Constitution and its laws. During the turbulent era of the Civil Wars of the 1640s, English antiquaries "built up a historical 'myth' according to which the English monarchy had always been implicitly contractual. Even the rude fact of the Norman Conquest had not interrupted this good old Anglo-Saxon tradition, for William the Conqueror (they said) had accepted and perpetuated the existing constitution. And this constitution had been preserved intact ever since."[8]

The philosopher David Hume exploded the myth of the Ancient Constitution in his historical works of the 1750s, but that did not prevent its living on both in Britain and America as alleged evidence of the remote birth of modern liberty in the Germanic forests and in the government and society of the early Anglo-Saxons. It was not politically significant that the Ancient Constitution never existed, and that modern English liberty was growing under people's noses and was not just a surviving legacy from the Germanic past. What was significant was that Montesquieu and Hume both diagnosed and praised the birth of modern liberty in the commercial and undespotic society of Britain, and that they both anchored this liberty as a cornerstone of the West. Hume in particular denied that the synthesis of Rome and Christianity constituted the West; for him, freedom was the key, and freedom was incompatible with domination by either of the other two forces: government inspired by Roman models or Christianity as a political and social factor. Montesquieu and Hume, in effect, developed the notion of ancient Germanic freedom into a notion of modern Germanic freedom, located in the Anglo-Saxon nations.

The very coinage Anglo-Saxon emphasized the Germanic origins of the English and the eighteenth-century Americans, since it named two of the three Germanic peoples, the Angles and the Saxons, who invaded Britain in the fifth century, just as the Franks had invaded Gaul. During and after the revolution, Americans adopted the Germanic model of freedom because it seemed to suggest that their own claims to independence were rooted in history as their ethnic heritage. John Adams, the second president of the United States, was not stating an eccentric opinion when he praised "the Teutonic institutions" as "the most memorable experiment, merely political, ever yet made in human affairs. They have spread all over Europe and have lasted eighteen hundred years." Thomas Jefferson, his successor as president, took pride in his "Saxon ancestors," who, after conquering England, had applied a federal form of government. "All Europe" was therefore "beholden to the Northern nations for introducing or restoring a constitution of government for excelling all others, that we know in the world."[9]

The Enlightenment Germanic model claimed that the critical feature of Western civilization was liberty. This liberty was independent of both Rome and Christianity, for it was not discovered or introduced by either of those two entities but by the Germanic tribes who invaded the Roman Empire and who were, by native constitution, free before they invaded and before they became Christian. The Enlightenment model was therefore the ideal substrate of the liberal Grand Narrative, or so one would have thought. When the liberal narrative assumed its definitive form, America happened to be at war with modern Germany, a nation whose leaders in both world wars claimed to be descended from and inspired by the ancient Germans, but which actually had only tenuous links to them. Therefore, the Enlightenment model never achieved this role. Instead, the liberal narrative borrowed a much less appropriate definition of Western identity, ironically enough from the very Germany that America was fighting, namely, the definition of the West as descended from the Greeks.

The Enlightenment model of the Germans was an optimistic and harmonious one. Its authors, such as Montesquieu and Jefferson, believed that the Germanic tribes contributed liberty to the West and little else. Like much else in Enlightenment thought, this perspective was partial, narrow, and deeply colored by a faith in progress and improvement. The Germanic contribution to the West was broader, richer, more significant, and more ambiguous than the model suggested. The Germans and their culture were the third element in the western synthesis, along with Rome and Christianity. But they did not bring only liberty; they also brought the values of Arminius—honor and luck—the values of the warrior.

Ancient Germanic society was based ethically on the notions of luck and honor and institutionally on the "three k's": cults, kings, and companions.

The oldest traceable groupings were people of common descent who worshipped the same gods in the same way. The Germans conceived of their original tribes, such as the Cheruscans and the Marcomanni, as groups of people all of whom were related by blood and who lived and sacrificed in the same place and according to the same ritual. Tribal life had two fundamental purposes, worship and war. Priests and priestesses directed the former, kings and chieftains the latter. The king normally belonged to the royal family, which was distinct from other families in the tribe in being descended from one or more gods. An outsider of exceptional luck and honor might sometimes usurp the throne, thereby introducing his lineage and its magic to the tribe and extending its power.

Tacitus reported that the Germans had no writing but preserved memory and customs in song. According to these songs, many of the Germans claimed a common and ultimate descent from the earth-god Tuisto and his son Mannus, "the man." Mannus in turn had three sons who were the forefathers of three aboriginal communities of Germanic speakers, the Ingaevones, Hermiones, and Istaevones. Others, notably the Suebi and the Vandals, asserted a rival genealogy. Whatever the particular names, the tribes shared a uniform notion that what bound them together was common descent and a particular relation to a particular deity.

Kings had magical powers that demonstrated the honor and luck, but were not divine. Germanic customs and memory revealed no trace of the Oriental, Hellenistic, and Roman practice of divinizing rulers, either in their lifetime or after. Germanic kingship changed in Roman times. When Caesar arrived at the Rhine, he found that some of the Germanic tribes no longer had kings but were led by a council of warriors. In anthropological terms, what was happening was that the tribes closest to civilization, that is, to Rome, were moving from a sacred kingship, in which the kings had mainly ritual functions alongside the priests and ruled only a small area, to a more meritocratic form of rule. The criterion of merit in Germanic society was, of course, a military one: can he win battles and repel attacks? The first stage of this meritocratic rule was one of competition, in which men of various lineages fought, either physically or in the council, to demonstrate their luck and honor. By the time of the great migrations, the stage of competition was largely over, and the new, larger tribes that invaded the empire had, once again, kings. Unlike the earlier small-scale cultic kings, these were monarchs of large groupings and vast territories—the constitutional and ritual ancestors of the monarchs of Europe.

Kings, especially the new-style territorial and meritocratic monarchs, could not govern alone. The ancient sources referred often to the council that governed the tribes and to the heated, sometimes murderous arguments that took place there. Tacitus in particular took an interest in these proceedings, for he considered that the Germans were innately disputatious and irascible, unorganized and unwilling to accept command and direction. This, to him, was a saving grace, for as long as the Germanic warriors were busy competing with one another and refusing to take orders, they would not be able to mobilize their inherently great energies to attack Rome. When the Goths, Franks, and other tribes successfully invaded in the fourth and fifth century, they had evidently solved this problem.

By the time of the invasions, the council of warriors had shaken down to what the sources came to label the companions, the *comitatus* or, in modern German, the *Gefolgschaft* of the king. The companions were free men whose duty was to follow, obey, and protect the king, who incarnated the power and good fortune of the people. "Those who command the companions fight for victory, the companions for their master," Tacitus noted. The companions and their king followed a strict ethic: win together or die together. Evidence from a thousand years revealed that this ethic was often obeyed.

One late but striking example, because it involved a Christian king, was that of Olaf the Fat, king of Norway. He belonged to the ancient royal lineage, but his power was insecure. Canute the Great, king of Denmark and England, also wanted Norway. Throughout the 1020s, Olaf defended himself against various attacks. Many nobles deserted him, bribed by Canute, who, by his wealth, persistence, and great power as king of the North Sea area, was proving his superior luck. In 1030, Olaf faced the enemy coalition of Danes and Norwegian defectors at Stiklastadir, near modern Trondheim. Before the battle, Olaf prayed to God, but he also had his bard recite the *Bjarkamál*.

This poem—*Bjarkamál* means "the tale of Bjarki"—already ancient in Olaf's day, praised the dutiful follower who died with his lord. No Old Norse version has survived, but the twelfth-century Danish monk and chronicler Saxo Grammaticus provided a Latin version as well as the complete story that lay behind it. This legend told of Rolf Krake, the "weedy," a king of Lejre in Denmark. It was a well-known story throughout the old Germanic nations, and Rolf and his uncle Roar, or Hrothgar, also appeared in the Old English epic *Beowulf*, composed probably in the eighth century, and which told of the monster, Grendel, that harried Hrothgar's hall until Beowulf killed it and its mother.

Rolf was blessed with great luck but he had gravely challenged the gods by killing his weak-willed cousin and usurping the kingdom. His chief enemies were the Swedes. On one occasion Rolf and his companions visited the Swedish court. They were ostensibly paying a courtesy visit, but in fact Rolf wanted to steal the treasure of Adils, the king of Sweden, which included the magnificent golden arm-ring Sveagris, "adornment of the Swedes," a semimagical object that embodied the luck and power of the kingdom. The Danes managed to lay hands on the treasure, but could not immediately leave because that would rouse the Swedes' suspicions. They were therefore compelled to remain for the great feast that was to take place in the evening.

Adils suspected foul play but could not accuse Rolf to his face in case Rolf was innocent, for he would then have put himself in the wrong and suffered a loss of face fatal to his own position. He thus determined to put the Danes to the test. At the feast, he sat the Danes on a bench right before the great fire in the middle of the hall and ordered his men to keep piling wood on the flames. For some hours the Danes suffered in silence. Just when his companions were about to give in and beg Adils for mercy, which would have meant ridicule and a loss of face on their part, Rolf drew his sword and sprang over the fire, crying "To leap the fire is not to flee it!" In the resulting melee, Rolf and his men escaped.

The Swedes followed and pressed the Danes so hard that, to delay pursuit, Rolf had his companions scatter the treasure as they rode across the Fyris-field. As Adils stooped from his horse to collect his gold, he heard the Danes laughing at his greed.

Rolf kept the ring Sveagris, and this earned him the Swedes' undying hatred. Many years later, Rolf's treacherous cousin, Hjarvard, determined to win the kingdom from Rolf. In this enterprise, he found eager allies in the Swedes, who provided him with an army. The Danes were outnumbered. Knowing they were doomed, Bjarki, Rolf's closest friend and the head of the companions, composed the poem that bore his name and that Olaf of Norway heard before the battle of Stiklastadir. In later versions of the story, Bjarki was a magical character. His name meant bear, and he was a shapeshifter, a were-bear, but had agreed to keep his human form and lay aside his magic to serve the king. The poem as Saxo reported it, and as Olaf probably heard it, consists of a dialogue between Bjarki and another of Rolf's chief companions, Vögg, who asks Bjarki for reassurance. Bjarki gives none and instead states the heroic ethos of sacrifice for one's chief.

At the end of the day, Rolf, Bjarki, and all their companions lay dead, except for Vögg, who went to the victorious Hjarvard and offered his service. Delighted that one of Rolf's followers was willing to honor his new luck, Hjarvard held out his spear, asking Vögg to swear fealty to him on its tip.

Vögg said he would gladly do so, but he would prefer to do it in the manner of Rolf's court. "What manner is that?" asked Hjarvard. "Well, in Rolf's time we always swore by the haft of the spear," said Vögg. "Very well," said Hjarvard and handed Bjarki the spear. "Thank you," said Vögg, "I hereby take vengeance on Rolf," and ran him through.

This was the poem that Olaf asked to hear before the battle in which he and many of his companions fell. Not long after, when the Norwegian royal house returned to power, he was canonized as the patron saint of Norway. In this guise his images adorned churches throughout Scandinavia. Saint Olaf, as he became, was portrayed with a big red beard and holding an ax, the preferred Viking weapon. He looked, in fact, remarkably like the popular image of the pagan god Thor, lord of thunder. Saint Olaf remained hugely popular until long after the Protestant Reformation supposedly abolished saints and their images. As late as 1915, a Scandinavian immigrant in America sent a petition asking Saint Olaf to intercede for his health. The petition was sent to the last church in Scandinavia where an image of Saint Olaf could still be found in its original location.[10]

Rolf, Bjarki, Hrothgar, and other figures of demonic or heroic grandeur appeared in stories throughout the Germanic world. Long after they had settled in Gaul, Britain, and elsewhere in the former empire, Germanic peoples retained a sense of common kinship, a remote legacy perhaps of their ancestral belief that a nation was a kinship group. In the eighth century, the English monk Winfred, better known as Boniface, the apostle of Germany, quoted a Saxon in England saying of the Saxons on the Continent that "we are of the same bone and blood."

The author of *Beowulf* would have agreed. Although an Old English poem, its subject was pagan people living in and near the lands from which the Anglo-Saxons had originally come to Britain. Like Saint Olaf, *Beowulf* looked in two directions, to Christianity and to the ancestral norms. This, in outline, was its story:

A powerful warrior from the land of the Geats (a Scandinavian people dwelling in southern Sweden) travels to Denmark to do battle with a man-eating ogre who is killing King Hrothgar's thanes in a series of nocturnal attacks. Beowulf rids the Danes of their tormentor and returns to Geatland, where he puts his great strength at the service of his own people in their wars with hostile neighbours. Eventually, he becomes King of the Geats, and years later, when he is an old man, he gives his life in the course of slaying a dragon that had threatened to destroy the nation.[11]

A scene in the first part of the poem presented the Germanic heroic ethos in its pure form. After killing Grendel, the ogre, Beowulf retires for a well-earned rest. While he is away from the hall, the ogre's mother appears from her lair beneath a gloomy lake to avenge her son. She enters King Hrothgar's hall and kills his favorite thane, or companion. When Beowulf comes, the king laments his companion's death and describes the haunted and eerie lake where the monsters live. He declares that Beowulf, once again, is his only hope if he is to save his people from being destroyed. If Beowulf kills this second monster and survives, he will reward him richly.

Beowulf replies:

Ne sorga, snotor guma! Selre bidh æghwæm,
þæt he his freond wrece, thonne he fela murne.
Ure æghwylc sceal ende gebidan
worolde lifes; wyrce se the mote
domes ær deathe; þæt bith drihtguman
unlifgendum æfter selest (1384–89)

Rendering this dense and laden passage into modern English is difficult, since each phrase carried to its original listeners complex echoes of the ancient ethos. A rough paraphrase: "Have no care, good lord! It is a better thing for a man to avenge his friend than to sit in mourning. Each of us must face the end of life in this world. Therefore, let him who is able achieve fame before death, for such fame is the only afterlife that a warrior will have, after he is dead."

The word *drihtguma* literally meant "man of a lord," companion. He belonged to the *comitatus*, the men who lived with and for the king and for their joint fellowship. The poet of *Beowulf* was a Christian and therefore meant his listeners to feel a special poignancy at the thought that these pagan men, when dead, would have no afterlife other than the memory of their deeds. Not having heard the Christian message, they had no way to eternal life. The core of the heroic ethos was the command to do memorable and noble deeds in this life, "let him who is able achieve fame before death," for only by such deeds would a man's memory live. Not all were able; some had not the luck or the honor. The mark of a true king's companion was that you were indeed able to achieve fame.

The author of *Beowulf* was looking back from the Christian era to a world of other values that were his own and yet no longer his own. This doubleness survived deep into the Middle Ages as two faces of the Old Western synthesis of Roman, Christian, and Germanic elements. Geopolitically, the synthesis took on concrete form in the era when *Beowulf* was composed, the era of Boniface, Pope Stephen, and Charlemagne.

Boniface and his activities held a special place for those who saw in the eighth century the Magic Moment when the West made its appearance. Such a one was the German historian Theodor Schieffer, who subtitled his study of Boniface "the Christian foundation of Europe."[12] Boniface was one of the new breed of Anglo-Saxon missionaries who, coming from a recently converted land, restored order to the troubled churches of the Continent and preached Christianity to new tribes. Second, the fact that his mission was authorized by the pope and favored by the Franks confirmed the emerging order of spiritual and political power in the West, an order resting on the pope, the Franks, and the energy of the Anglo-Saxon missionaries.

Boniface's activities coincided with the geopolitical shift whereby the popes abandoned the eastern empire and chose the Franks as the nation with whom to seal the great bargain that founded the West. In this shift, the popes had two sets of allies, the Franks and the missionaries. These were mostly Anglo-Saxon, but the Anglo-Saxon church itself drew heavily on the discipline, learning, and commitment of Irish monks and missionaries in the period since the sixth century. In 1994, an American author, Thomas Cahill, published a book describing how, in his view, "the Irish saved Western civilization." Cahill's book was the last of a tradition of works in the twentieth century pointing out that the Carolingian cultural revival that helped to confirm the *translatio imperii* rested largely on the classical and Christian learning preserved in the monasteries of Britain and Ireland, whereas it had become largely lost in the former cultural centers of the Continent, thanks to invasions, wars, and general collapse.

The idea was this: in the early fifth century, the Gothic, Vandal, Frankish, and other invasions of the western provinces had disrupted, if not the economy, then at least the urban literate culture of antiquity. Saint Augustine dying in Hippo Regius under Vandal siege in 430 was the emblematic figure of this end. Augustine had absorbed the classical curriculum of his culture, but also knew that it would not be reproduced and would not be very significant or valuable after his own time. For all his own love of classical learning, he also believed, as a Christian, that much of it needed to be fundamentally transformed and renewed. His own works were in large part descriptions and defenses of the culture he considered fitting for a post-classical, Christian world.

In the century or so following Augustine, missionaries carried this renewed classical learning and Christian doctrine beyond the old imperial boundaries. One of the places they reached was Ireland. By an accident of history, the Irish monasteries, established with amazing speed after Christianity had arrived, became the repositories of learning and of traditions that were lost on the Continent. In the seventh century, this learning migrated to Britain, which was itself recovering from its pagan and barbarian interlude, and on to Europe. Using the metaphor of the "desert" as the place of withdrawal and contemplation preparatory to one's return to the world, one historian of education noted that "it was in the desert that the West rethought its culture."[13]

The theme of exile and return was almost as influential and as powerful in Western cultural mythology as that of exile without return—the case of Aeneas, the legendary ancestor of the kings of Rome in Greek and Roman mythology. In the 1930s and 1940s a number of Europeans involuntarily faced exile without, always, much hope of return. One of them was the Austrian scholar Ludwig Bieler, an expert on the handwriting of early medieval manuscripts, of the manuscripts of classical authors written during the darkest of the Dark Ages and from which all later manuscripts and therefore all later knowledge of Greek and Roman literature depended. Driven from Austria by the National Socialists, Bieler spent some years in Ireland studying the particular Irish script and some of the literature that only survived thanks to Irish monks. Partly as a thanks to his temporary hosts and partly in homage to the Irish contribution to preserving the classical legacy, Bieler wrote what became the most famous book in the Hibernophile tradition, *Ireland: Harbinger of the Middle Ages*.[14]

The learning of the Irish in the seventh century and of their intellectual descendants in England in the eighth was genuinely astounding. When knowledge of Greek was lost elsewhere in Europe, it remained in the offshore islands. Classical authors virtually unknown in Europe between the fifth and the fifteenth centuries were copied, read, and commented on at the monasteries of Kells, York, Jarrow, and Winchester. Perhaps because Latin to them was a foreign language, the Irish paid particular attention to grammar and rhetoric, a tradition continued by men such as Boniface, who was much more than a mere preacher of doctrine and theology. He wrote grammatical treatises and, with his associates, founded the monasteries that became the cultural and intellectual centers of Germany for the next seven centuries.

Nevertheless, Western civilization was saved not by the Irish alone but by the bargain of church and state that sealed the Old Western synthesis. The background to the bargain, as to all momentous events, was a mixture of long-term trends and immediate contingencies.

In the seventh and first half of the eighth centuries, the eastern Roman Empire, based in Constantinople, retained a foothold in Italy, and for much of that time the popes were themselves easterners, Greek or Syrian. Until the 720s, the popes looked east, as loyal subjects of the empire. A gulf was opening up between the papacy, the pinnacle of Christian hierarchy in the West, and Western society itself. Then, in the 720s, the emperors provoked a breach that was to lead, by the year 800, to the Westernization of the papacy and the restoration, by the popes, of a western Empire.

In 725, emperor Leo III decided to forbid religious images on the grounds that they were sacrilegious and detracted worship from its proper object, the invisible Deity. This was a doctrinal innovation, and the popes objected. The emperor, used to obedience from all his clerics, including the Roman bishops, sent men to persuade the pope to change his mind. The pope, Gregory II, refused. The emperor, enraged, sent more men, this time with orders to kill the pope. Gregory II was a Greek, but somewhere along the line he had acquired the notion that he belonged in Rome, that he was head of the Western church and that this meant something more than doing the emperor's bidding. He wrote to Constantinople that he could not in good conscience enforce the imperial edict against images, because it was contrary to doctrine and to Western practice. The Roman populace, all 30,000 of them, were rioting in defense of images. Gregory II took the opportunity to explain to the emperor what it meant to be pope of the West: "The whole West has eyes on us . . . and on St. Peter . . . whom all the kingdoms of the West revere . . . We go out to the most distant corners of the West to seek those who desire baptism . . . and they and their princes wish to receive it from us."[15]

For indeed, what was happening in the eighth century was that the empire, the one and only, was becoming more Greek, more eastern, more preoccupied with holding off the Muslims and minding its own eastern diplomacy and strategy. It was, slowly but surely, ceasing to be universal and starting to be simply the great power of the eastern Mediterranean. More ominously for the unity of Christendom, it was starting to become, from the Western viewpoint, heretical. What began as a simple shift of the East-West line in the early centuries A.D. was now taking shape as an unbridgeable cultural, theological, and civilizational divide.

Conversely, the papacy was becoming Westernized. In the 750s, another pope, Stephen II, took the next step. He transferred his political allegiance from the empire to the king of the Franks, who lived north of the Alps, who had recently defeated the Muslims who were invading from Spain, and who had distinct advantages over the emperor as protector of the church: he was Western, he was Catholic, he was energetic, and he was geopolitically in the right place. In the winter of 756, Pope Stephen made a dramatic and dangerous journey across the Alps to Gaul. Here he and the king of the Franks sealed a bargain that shaped European history for a thousand years: the bargain of church and state.

Church and state? According to tradition and theology, the bargain should be, as it was in the days of Constantine, between church and empire. But the empire was in Constantinople, it was heretical, and it was not at all a good idea to be associated with it. The pope had too many roots in the West for that. The answer was blindingly obvious: create a new, proper, Catholic empire in the West to be the partner for the church.

The idea that the eighth century was the crucial epoch, the time when the synthesis of Roman, Christian, and German truly coalesced into something new, owed much to the work of a Belgian historian, Henri Pirenne. In the 1920s and 1930s, he developed the so-called Pirenne thesis, which held that antiquity did not finally end until around the year 700. The thesis was an argument about economic history, trade, and communications. According to Pirenne, the ancient Mediterranean should be understood as a lake and the inhabitants all around it as members of a common culture. In antiquity, the north African had more in common with the Syrian, the Greek, the Italian, and the Spaniard than with the tribesmen south of the Atlas Mountains that rose immediately behind the coastal plain. Likewise, the Roman had more in common with the north African or the Syrian than with the German living across the Alps. Communication in antiquity, and before railroads generally, was easy by sea, slow and difficult by land.

The end of antiquity, therefore, did not happen with the Germanic invasions or the end of the western empire. It happened only when the economic and cultural unity of the Mediterranean was broken, and that was the result not of the Germanic but of the Muslim invasions of the seventh century. By 711, Muslims controlled the entire north African shoreline and Spain. The result was a geocultural transformation of immense significance. It created the West by laying the equivalent of an iron curtain lengthwise through the Mediterranean and along the Pyrenees that separated Gaul from Spain. Henceforth, the Mediterranean was not the heart of one civilization but the border zone of three: the Middle Eastern, Arabic, and Muslim civilization to the south and east, and, to the north, the Western and Byzantine civilizations.

Pirenne based his thesis on the archaeological knowledge of his time about trade to and from sites in western Europe. Finds from across the Mediterranean appeared in Gaul until the late seventh century and then stopped. Trade altogether seemed to stop for several centuries.

Historians since the 1930s undermined the thesis. No one in the 1990s would maintain it as strictly as Pirenne did. But even though economic interaction perhaps did not cease as suddenly and as completely after the Muslim conquests in Africa as Pirenne had maintained, his thesis held up much better as an argument about religious and constitutional change. The popes shifted the geopolitical axis of the West from one running from Rome to Constantinople to one that ran from Rome to northern Gaul, centered on the Rhone and Rhine Rivers. This ninety-degree turn and northward movement created the West as a physical entity.

The popes' shift and the bargain they concluded with the Frankish kings also set the seal on the religious synthesis of papacy and secular power. The year zero of the West, if one were to fix such a date, was 800, when the pope created a new western empire by crowning Charlemagne, the Frankish king, emperor in Saint Peter's basilica in Rome. For Pirenne, Charlemagne was, as his contemporaries named him, the "father of Europe." But Pirenne was a Belgian, a Romance-speaker, and a Europeanist. His Charlemagne was the supranational, benevolent ruler imposing order on violent tribes and thus prefiguring the constant attempts since his time to construct a cultural and commercial, not a nationalistic and militarily competitive, Europe. In the 1930s an old and ridiculous argument between French and Germans about Charlemagne's nationality and stature as founder of the West reached its apogee. In the interwar years, French nationalists annexed Charlemagne as they had annexed Virgil, as defender of the West, not for all of Europe, but against the German threat. The Germans for their part had abandoned Charlemagne. Spengler did not know quite what to make of him. He called him a Byzantine, Oriental ruler, whose rule was "a superficial episode," something "accidental and without consequences." Meanwhile, "the Germanic-Western proto-culture advances slowly and subterraneously.[16]

In the liberal narrative, Charlemagne appeared as a beacon in the darkness, leading a noble but doomed attempt to restore a transnational order to western Europe. In the Enlightenment Germanic model, he appeared as the king of Franks, the "free men," who graciously accepted a burden he did not really want, that of emperor, to devote himself to protecting the church, promoting education, and harnessing the Germanic vigor and independence of his ancestral nation to the cause of a new Western civilization.

What neither narrative liked to think about was that Charlemagne was also a bloodthirsty Germanic war chief who had tens of thousands of Saxons massacred in the 780s and 790s to instill terror and secure the Saxon territory northeast of the Rhine.

Charlemagne was a Christian prince and a Germanic warrior. The Germanic Christian hero was the missing character in the rational story, even those versions of it that incorporated Germanic freedoms as part of Western identity. Yet a story of the West that did not include that figure as part of the old Western synthesis would be defective and misleading. The fact of the matter was that the Germanic freedoms were not distinct from the warrior ethos, something that could be daintily removed by Enlightenment ideals and placed at the head of the West as an alternative to the Christian story. Germanic freedom and the heroic ethos were two aspects of the same thing. The true early history of the Western synthesis was the story of how the Germanic warlike love of liberty married the Christian ethic of sacrifice, producing what amounted to a Western doctrine of holy war.

One of the most characteristic expressions of the early holy war ideal was the *Song of Roland*. The *Song* in its extant version dated from shortly before the First Crusade in the 1090s.[17] Its hero was modeled on a historical figure, a margrave of Brittany and a companion of Charlemagne. According to Charlemagne's biographer Einhard, who wrote in the later ninth century, one Hruotlandus, or Roland, led the rearguard of the royal Frankish host as it was returning in the year 778 from a raid into Muslim territory in northern Spain. A band of Basque raiders ambushed Roland's force in the pass of Roncesvaux in the Pyrenees and destroyed it to the last man. The episode, minor in itself, soon became the subject of song and story, in the traditional Germanic manner, just as Arminius's defeat of the Romans in A.D. 9 was remembered in song by tribesmen three generations later, according to Tacitus.

In the *Song of Roland*, the hero is the bravest and strongest of all the knights of Charlemagne, who is called *Carles li reis, nostre emperere magnes*, "Charles the king, our great emperor." The emperor has twelve chief companions or peers, who are equal, except for Roland, his nephew, who is more powerful, noble, and devoted than the rest. The minor action in the Roncesvaux pass becomes, in the epic, a battle of many tens of thousands. The war between Charlemagne and the Spanish Moors is described as a crusade, which was anachronistic if applied to 778, but accurate about the holy war ideals of the poet's own day. The Muslims, who are consistently called "pagans," are hard-pressed by the Franks. Their king, Marsile, asks the advice of his own knights on how to stop the Frankish offensive that threatens Saragossa, his capital. The Muslim knights propose that Marsile send a message offering peace and hostages to gain time and save Saragossa.

At Charlemagne's court, the emperor and his knights debate how to respond to this message. One of the pairs, Roland's father-in-law, Ganelon, argues that the message is in good faith and should be accepted: "When king Marsile sends a message saying that he will become your man," that is, do feudal homage, "and that he will hold Spain of you, accepting the law that we follow, then he who proposes that you reject this pact has no care for the death we will die. A counsel of pride should not prevail. Let us leave the fools aside and follow the wise!"

Another knight suggests sending an ambassador to Marsile to find out more about the Moorish king's proposal. This seems a dangerous task. What if the perfidious pagans break the rules that protect envoys and kill the ambassador? Roland offers to go. "You shall certainly not go," says Roland's best friend, Olivier, because you are too hot-headed and may provoke the pagans into killing you (255–58). The emperor asks his knights to choose another. "Ganelon, my father-in-law," says Roland. But

> count Ganelon is seized with great anguish,
> From his shoulders he casts off his ermine coat,
> And stands in his silk shirt alone . . .
> He said to Roland, "Madman, what rage has seized you?
> Every man knows I am your father-in-law,
> And you have designated me to go to Marsile!
> If God should grant me to return
> I shall do such great harm to you
> That it will last your whole life." (277–91)[18]

This episode is of a common type in legendary tales of disaster, in which the villain warns the noble hero to avoid a course of action that will lead to his death. But in the *Song*, Ganelon is not a villain before this scene. It is his hurt surprise that Roland would immediately think of him as the envoy that triggers what may have been a long-standing resentment of his brilliant son-in-law into active treachery. Roland responds to this outburst by again offering to go himself. But Ganelon is now in a huff: "You shall never go for me. You are not my vassal, and I am not your lord. Charlemagne is commanding me to do him service, I shall therefore go to Saragossa, to Marsile," he stiffly insists, adding that he is so furious that he will doubtless do some damage (296–301).

Roland, in a classic display of hubris, laughs at the older man's rage. Suddenly cold, Ganelon says, "I love you not. You have imposed this ill choice on me. Just emperor, you see me present here. I shall carry out your command" (306–9).

Ganelon thus arrives at Marsile's court resentful and furious. It is not hard for him to convince himself that it would be a great deed in the service of peace if he could bring about Roland's death, the hot-head whose pride and arrogance, so Ganelon begins to think, is the only reason the war is continuing. "Please let someone kill him. We shall then have peace entire" (390–91). Ganelon, "who has thought long," subtly changes Charlemagne's message. Instead of offering to negotiate, Ganelon presents the message in terms of a double threat: you have two choices, he tells Marsile. Either you become a Christian and accept half of Spain as your fief from the emperor, or you will be taken and brought to Aix, there to die a horrible death. The pagan knights are about to attack Ganelon and kill him, when he adds that, of course, none of these ill choices need arise if Roland dies, for he is the emperor's most warlike and aggressive companion. They then hatch the plot by which Ganelon will encourage the emperor to move ahead with the Frankish main army as it departs Spain, leaving Roland in command of the rearguard. Marsile will stealthily bring up his own host and overwhelm the rearguard. Roland will fall, and both sides will have peace.

The plot succeeds. Roland fights long and bravely, but finally falls, unwilling to save himself from the defeat of his army. As he dies, angels from heaven appear to carry his spirit away. The rest of the poem describes Charlemagne's campaign of revenge against Marsile, and, almost at the end, Ganelon's capture and terrible punishment. Though he is a forsworn traitor, a knight nevertheless offers to fight for him, but he is killed, and the Franks take this as divine judgment. Ganelon is torn apart alive between four horses. As the poem ends, we see the emperor weeping at the news that the Moors, despite their dreadful defeats and losses, are again on the march.

The author of the *Song* was a clergyman, and the story turns on the idea of holy war against unbelievers in which the outcome of battle is a judgment of God. Clergymen fight, like archbishop Turpin:

Through the camp goes Turpin the archbishop,
never did priest chant mass,
who with his body performed such prodigies.

He said to the pagan, "God send you all evil!
You have killed one whom my heart mourns."
He forces his good horse forward
and strikes the pagan so hard on his shield of Toledo steel
that he falls dead on the green grass (1605–12)

The courage of the Christian warriors is fired because they are fighting under "Saint Peter's banner which is called Romaine," by which the poet meant that the legendary banner of Charlemagne was given him by the pope. Being "Romaine," it contained both the mythical power of Rome and the sacred power of having been blessed by the pope. At the time the *Song* was composed, banners were starting to achieve the symbolic and emotional value they held for much of Western history and that made them a characteristic element of Western political mythology.

The holy or magical banner was a Germanic idea. The Viking armies often fought under banners that had appropriate names, such as "Landwaster," the banner of the Norwegian king Harold Hardrada. He fell fighting the English at Stamford Bridge in August 1066, obedient to the Germanic code that forbade the king and war chief to survive defeat. The English took his banner. According to tradition, Landwaster remained in the north of England, where it was later seized by the Scots in a raid and ultimately found its way to Dunvegan Castle on the Isle of Skye, home of the McLeod lairds. Here, in 1994, visitors were shown an aged and torn linen cloth of an off-white color known locally as *am bratach sidh*, the fairy banner, and a good-luck totem of the clan, and claimed by the lairds to be none other than Landwaster itself.

Twice in the poem, Charlemagne conquers a Saracen city; twice we hear that all inhabitants are baptized or killed. Confronting the Saracen emir who ambushed and killed Roland, Charlemagne states that "I owe pagans neither peace nor love," *Pais në amor ne dei a paien rendre* (3596). Whether Germanic or Christian in origin, such a doctrine contradicted strict Christian teaching. Rather, it contradicted ancient Christian teaching. Thanks to the Germanic warrior element, it became very much a part of Christian holy war doctrine in the Middle Ages.

It was a historian working in Nazi Germany who provided one of the most penetrating analyses of the Western way of war, which descended in part from the Germanic and Christian idea of holy war as a religious duty. Carl Erdmann, who died as a result of combat wounds in Zagreb, Yugoslavia, in early 1945, had published ten years earlier a study of how the crusading mentality arose in the West and of its intimate relation to Christian ideals. War was a constant presence in all civilizations throughout history. In the West more than in other cultures, war had often been justified by denouncing the enemy as not merely the Other, but as an evil force that it was morally worthy to suppress and extirpate. Erdmann's book of 1935 was not merely an exploration of the link between faith and war, but an implicit critique of his own times and of the regime in power in his own country, which preached violence and crusading conquest of other nations.

Erdmann asked how Christianity, which began as a religion that forbade its members to fight and preached peace even at the cost of defeat and enslavement, could arrive at the point when, in the eleventh century, it conceived, mobilized, and launched crusades against nonbelievers? In terms of the idea of the West, Erdmann was asking, how did the idea of crusading warfare arise, and how central was it to Western identity?

One line of argument was to trace the origins of the Christian warrior ethic and holy war doctrine in Germanic culture. Erdmann was not inclined to look in this direction. This was not only because Hitler's regime, in power when he wrote, exploited the Germanic warrior image, because in fact the regime did not do so very consistently. Hitler and his followers were ambivalent about the Germanic legacy, because it had a barbarian reputation, and they wanted to portray themselves as defenders of civilization against Jews and Bolsheviks. That was why Hitler identified the Greeks and Romans as the "true Germans," whose legacy was represented by the new Germany. Erdmann was rather thinking of his academic colleagues, many of whom enthusiastically glorified the ancient Germans, their warlike spirit, and their ethic of sacrifice and obedience to their lord. The Germanic legacy was for him poisoned territory. Though he did not wholly discount that legacy in holy war doctrine, it was, he argued, only one of several factors and not necessarily decisive.

The early church, Erdmann explained, condemned war and accepted warriors only as penitents. By the third century A.D., Christians were praying for the pagan emperor and serving in his armies, although war itself was at best morally neutral. When the Roman emperors became Christian in the fourth century and adopted Christianity as the religion of the state, they intended also to acquire the new religion's support of their military needs. By the end of the fourth century, theologians had developed further the biblical distinction between the things of God and the things of Caesar: the emperor had competence in his own sphere, including the competence to wage war, but war was ultimately a flaw in the world caused by sin.

At the same time, Christian theologians developed the idea of *militia*, strenuous effort on behalf of some goal beyond oneself. One could exercise *militia Dei*, effort for God's sake, and *militia saecularis*, effort on behalf of worldly things such as a king or glory. Until the tenth century, Christian doctrine in the West kept the two distinct, arguing that effort on God's behalf was superior.

The change came with the parallel rise of feudal knighthood on the one hand and the reform movement in the church and especially in monasticism. These developments were post-Carolingian and marked the resurgence of culture in western Europe after the disruptions following the end of the Carolingian revival in the 800s. In northern France, and in particular in Normandy, monastic writers began comparing monastic effort, as exercised in the movement for reform, and the martial valor of knights. Knights were assimilated to monks and given almost sacred status as defenders of the church and as persons devoting themselves to a noble purpose greater than themselves.

Two particular factors, in Erdmann's view, helped to provoke this new way of comparing and combining divine and military effort. First, in the chaotic century after Charlemagne, the Scandinavian invaders and plunderers that descended on the coastlands of western Europe often attacked churches and monasteries because, to paraphrase a modern bank robber, "that was where the gold was." The churches thus became battlefields in the literal sense, and their priests and abbots often found themselves taking up the sword in violation of Christian doctrine, which forbade ordained persons to fight. Second, in the early tenth century Scandinavian invaders settled the province that later became known after them as Normandy. They brought with them from the north an older Germanic tradition of respect for the warrior. As Normans in Normandy, the descendants of the Northmen upheld their martial traditions and the honor paid to the warrior, and this honor coalesced with the changing views in the church of fighting and its legitimacy.

Thus, by the mid-eleventh century, the time of William the Conqueror, the Normans had produced a coherent, consistent doctrine of battle that gave it moral standing close to that of the priesthood, at the summit of social prestige. The warrior, moreover, was bound by a code of conduct that again assimilated him to the priest: to protect the weak and in particular the church. In the words of Christopher Dawson, who set Erdmann's thesis about the origins of Christian holy war into the broader context of the rise of the West, "the ancient barbarian motive of personal loyalty to the war leader was reinforced by higher religious motives, so that the knight finally becomes a consecrated person, pledged not only to be faithful to his lord, but to be the defender of the Church, the widow and the orphan."[19] The warrior and his banner were blessed in church before he set out; his task was hallowed and drawn into the embrace of Christian doctrine. The result was the priest-warrior symbiosis of the crusader. In France, "the doctrine of defense of the Church, the ecclesiastical symbolism of the life of the warrior, and the important connection of these ideas with the cult of the saints provided the decisive impetus." The church "approached war and weakened her objections to it."[20]

Thus, the perceived needs and threats of the time, and the new status of the warrior, noble in both social and moral terms, combined with the assertive reform movement to sanction the idea of holy war against the enemies of the church. The first such holy wars were those in which the reform popes of the 1050s and 1060s launched Norman expeditionary forces against Italian princes perceived as threats to the economic and political autonomy of the papacy. By the 1070s, these Norman adventurers had established their own principalities in the south of Italy and became in turn prime suppliers of labor power and ideology to the Crusades to Palestine that began in the 1090s.

From the viewpoint of the pacifist 1990s in the West, it was sometimes hard to realize how positive the imagery of crusade and of holy war still was at midcentury. Many Americans possibly remembered that Douglas MacArthur—descendant of Scots lairds—presented himself as a Christian warrior, or that the Supreme Allied Commander in the European theater in World War II, Dwight D. Eisenhower, entitled his war chronicle *Crusade for Freedom*, and in 1989 a military historian entitled his own excellent history of World War II *The Great Crusade*.[21] World War II lent itself to such imagery since, in the words of that same historian, it was indeed in part a war about "fundamental values" against "powers that were committed to the realisation of unlimited ambition and to the enslavement and degradation of man." But of course these powers committed to "enslavement and degradation" also cast their efforts in the imagery of crusade from time to time and sought to mobilize support on that basis. German recruiting posters for Norwegians, Frenchmen, Belgians, and others to join the fight against the Soviet Union habitually used the symbolism and imagery of holy war, often drawing an explicit analogy between the medieval Crusades to the Holy Land and the defense of Christian Europe against Bolshevism in the 1940s.

It was this sort of exploitation of holy war imagery that Erdmann tried indirectly to subvert by showing how the original crusading ideology arose out of specific social, cultural, and doctrinal conditions of the eleventh century. Erdmann was too good a scholar to pass moralistic judgment on the churchmen and knights of the Middle Ages, but he was explicit on the point that holy war was not the prerogative of any particular nation, such as the Germans, and that the distinctive feature of the crusading doctrines of the eleventh century was that they combined the notion that defense of the church justified war and the notion of knightly service and self-sacrifice.

After his book was published, Erdmann was not popular with his more nationalistic colleagues. That was one reason he was not exempted from war service in World War II even though he was born in 1898 and had lost two brothers in World War I. Thus we find him in a combat unit in the Balkans at age forty-seven, writing to his sister shortly before his death: "I for my part am all done and for what is left of my life am beyond fear and hope . . . As a genuine humanist one must be able to say yes to the end of life and know how to die *en philosophe*. In the end it is only in the face of death that one sees if one really believes in one's ideals or not. So I intend to depart without hatred and with all good cheer."[22]

Carl Erdmann represented an ethic of sacrifice that arguably bore more relation to that of the ancient Germans in the tradition of Arminius and Roland than to the peculiar notions about the Germans that his nationalist colleagues proposed. Erdmann saw in the medieval West a complex synthesis of Christian teaching about service, a Christian ethic of sacrifice, and the Germanic warrior ethos. The nationalist vision of the Western synthesis among Nazi academics was cruder: the West was the creation of the Aryan race, culminating in the Germans. Although most of this ideology was of recent vintage in the 1930s, one strand of it had a longer history: the idea of the noble savage.

Far from being Rousseau's invention, the theme or cliché of the vigorous and innocent barbarian dated from Roman times. The very word *barbarian* underwent an interesting evolution. In the original Greek, *barbaros*, Latin *barbarus*, meant someone who spoke stutteringly or incomprehensibly. By the time of Herodotus, *barbarian* meant any alien or hostile non-Greek. This sense expanded in Roman times to mean anyone alien to Mediterranean society and culture and to Roman political norms. But starting in the third century, the Romans recruited ever more such "barbarians" into their armies.

Others continued to refer to these men as barbarians. Whether as an ironic gesture or simply by acculturation, the barbarian soldiers at some point began referring to themselves as barbarian. As their share of the total army continued to grow, the word *barbarian*, in the short form *brabus*, eventually came to mean simply "soldier," and since soldiers were often both courageous and jolly fellows, at least in popular legend, it acquired a connotation of courage as well. This sense descended into the Romance languages and gave rise to Italian *bravo* (fine, spirited) and via French to the English word and meaning *brave*.

Tacitus in his *Germania* painted a picture of the Germanic world that never lost relevance. According to Tacitus, the illiterate and barbarous Germans were undisciplined, emotional, disorderly, immoderate, and superstitious; to these chaotic qualities corresponded virtues: courage, honesty, love of freedom, devotion to family. They were capable of great generosity as well as cruelty; they were passionate in civil disputes and in war displayed extreme rage and fury, the *furor teutonicus,* or Germanic rage, that became another catchword of writers throughout later ages.

The *furor teutonicus* was not so named by Tacitus but by another Roman writer, the poet Lucan. From the eleventh century on, it reappeared in Europe, mostly in writers who wanted to describe the ancient Germans. Petrarch in the fourteenth century was among the first to apply a similar phrase to contemporary Germans. He spoke of the *furore de lassù,* or "fury from the north," which he contrasted to the *virtù,* or manly, that is, mature vigor of the more civilized Italians.[23] He needed a strong phrase to describe and condemn the German invasions of Italy in the early fourteenth century, when various German pretenders to the supreme office of the Holy Roman Empire tried to fight their way to Rome, their putative capital. Petrarch did not believe in the empire nor that, if there was an empire, the Germans should control it.

Tacitus's work was rediscovered in the 1450s, when the north-south split in Europe had grown deeper since Petrarch's day. Many Germans resented what they considered Roman domination, exercised through the church, its institutions, tithes, and control of land and local politics. The humanist movement of rediscovery of classical learning reinforced this incipient German patriotism. Writers like Konrad Celtis, Ulrich von Hutten, and the founder of Protestantism, Martin Luther, belonged to and promoted this national humanism, arguing in elegant Latin as well as in German that contemporary Germans should throw off the Roman yoke of culture, spiritual oppression, and economic extortion. A simple, primitive life close to the soil such as that described by Tacitus was to be preferred to the artificial habits and decadent practices imported from the south.

The cliché of the vigorous, innocent barbarian thus joined forces with hostility to the Roman legacy in its religious form, the Catholic Church. The German humanists of Luther's day forged a composite image of simple, patriotic virtue and national independence maintained by barbarian vigor that survived many incarnations and was exploited by many interests until the culmination in the National Socialist dictatorship.

Montesquieu's idea that Western liberty was born in the forest of Germany began among the fifteenth-century humanists who rediscovered Tacitus. The German humanists had a problem: their only evidence for the ancient virtues of their race was a Roman author, Tacitus. The Germans themselves had left no independent records. This was a problem because humanism was a literary movement, and texts were its lifeblood. Resting patriotic doctrine on the claim that the Germans were superior because they were ignorant and illiterate was not pleasing logic to the humanists.

Rescue came from Scandinavia. In the 1540s, two Swedish brothers, Olaus and Johannes Magnus, published two books, one a history and one an ethnographic account of the high north of Europe. Both were Catholic and both lived in exile in Rome, because Sweden had become Protestant. They were therefore not writing to support anti-Roman sentiment. Neither did they disavow their country for having become what they considered heretical. They took it upon themselves, rather, to provide the Nordic peoples with a history of their own, as good as that of the Greeks, Romans, and Jews. The Magnus brothers maintained that the art of writing was discovered in the north "before the Deluge or immediately thereafter," and as evidence they pointed to the runic inscriptions found throughout Scandinavia and believed to be of immeasurable antiquity.

The two brothers also maintained that martial vigor had its original home in the north, because the Gothic tribes who defeated Rome came originally from Sweden, the oldest literate people and the bravest. This combination swept Europe in the 1630s and 1640s, when Swedish armies defended Protestantism and enriched themselves across central Europe. The Swedish military onslaught was supported back home by a vigorous campaign of "Gothicism," which was the Magnus doctrine in ideological form, now turned against Rome and yielding the argument that original liberty in the world was at home in Scandinavia, and that therefore it was only right and just that liberty against the pope and the emperor should be defended by the Swedish king. John Russel, an English poet, praised the Swedish victories over the imperial forces in 1632 by alluding to the heroic ancestors of king Gustavus Adolphus:

The warlike Goths, once of renowned fame,
Whose Ancestours with fire and sword did tame
Great Rome it self.[24]

The Swedish conquests in defense of religious liberty against the pope and emperor produced a short-lived Swedish empire, supported ideologically by a crowd of Gothicist writers drawing on the Magnus brothers and the German humanist tradition. One of them was Olaus Rudbeck, who produced a ridiculous book alleging that the Swedes were the source of all culture in the world; they hailed originally from Atlantis and were the ancestors of the Greeks. Thus, Sweden was the source not only of Nordic vigor, independence, and strength, but also of classical civilization. Rudbeck, in turn, became a source of Montesquieu's assertion that the freedom of Europe was born in the forests of Germany.

The shift in Gothicist doctrine, from locating all original good qualities in the North to saying that it might also be found in prehistoric Germany, was fateful. It was seized upon by Johann Gottlieb Fichte, the idealist philosopher and a main source of modern German nationalism, and from Fichte's day to that of Adolf Hitler the confusion of "Nordic" and "German" continued. German ideologues asserted that Germans were superior because they were more vigorous and honest, but also because they were more civilized; the evidence, for the latter assertion at least, went back via Montesquieu to the Gothicists, who were talking not about Germany, but Scandinavia.

So it was that a generation of German historians and anthropologists from the later nineteenth century through the time of Spengler at the end of World War I to the end of the National Socialist regime in 1945 could claim that the ancient Germans were morally and culturally superior, and that they owed this superiority to a miraculous combination of cultural skill and barbaric vigor, or, to use the language of the time, of "state-building power" and "heroic ecstasy." The Apollonian-Dionysiac polarity was being driven here to and beyond its limits.

The quoted phrases were coined by Otto Höfler, a historian of religion who built his career in the Third Reich by arguing that the ancient Germans derived their culture and their political skills not from the use of reason, but from passionate fanaticism. In the argument between civilization and barbarism, Höfler stood proudly on the latter's side.

His theory of culture and Germanic superiority rested on three claims. First, that culture was not to be equated with high culture, with literature, education, or art, but rather with "the evolution of popular ways of life." Culture was not a matter for the elite, but for the whole people. Second, culture evolved not by exchange and communication between ethnic groups, but solely by the vigorous and defiant preservation of one's own identity, which, remember, was populist and universal. Precisely because Höfler's idea of culture was anti-elitist, it was essential to him that it be preserved as a matter of national or ethnic identity. A corollary of this populist view of culture was that nations needed to preserve their "defensive and political social practices." These practices, thirdly, were maintained among Germans—and this was again an example of their superiority—in secret brotherhoods, fellowships, sacred lodges. Höfler built an entire theory of cultural continuity on the claim that German culture had been preserved through the ages in the secret practices, memories, and rituals of such brotherhoods.

Höfler's imaginary reconstruction of Germanic ethnic customs and culture died along with Hitler's regime; his populist view of culture, ethnic particularity, and the need for defiant assertion of diversity did not.

The trail from Montesquieu's Germanic freedom to Höfler's Germanic ethnic virtues was neither necessary nor even very plausible, except in hindsight. While some were treading it, others were warning of its likely destination and drawing opposite lessons from Montesquieu's argument. A contemporary and compatriot of Höfler's, the church historian Johannes Haller, stood at the opposite pole to the Nazi ideologue when, in a masterly five-volume history of the papacy from its origins to the fifteenth century, he presented the classic version of the Enlightenment Germanic model as applied to the history of the church, namely, the argument that medieval Europe and the modern West were the synthesis not of Greece or Rome alone but of the synthesis of classical civilization and barbarian vigor.

In this view, Christianity conquered a Roman Empire that was already in decline. The Christians were not subversives; they did not plan the Fall of Rome, but they were unable to fend it off, and in some respects their commitment to church over state promoted it. The barbarian invasions and settlements, although initially destructive, appeared providential. By Christianizing the barbarians, the last Romans did the only thing possible to preserve what was possible of classical culture. They obtained pious, devoted, vigorous allies;

they pacified the "Germanic rage" and turned it to useful ends; they laid the foundations for the medieval synthesis.

Western freedom and the ethic of individual assertion and courage were thus the joint children of the Germanic invasions and the psychological and cultural core of the Old Western synthesis. We have seen how that synthesis manifested itself in *Beowulf*, the *Bjarkamál*, and the *Song of Roland*. We have seen how individualism and devotion could appear both as self-sacrifice and as holy war—the two being not distinct but parallel. This ambiguous legacy of the synthesis was displayed on a much larger canvas in the imperialism and the spirit of conquest of the later Middle Ages. At that time, it also acquired another and surprising dimension—the dimension of doomed, passionate love as the most sublime expression of individual personality. To these further elements in Western identity we now turn.

CHAPTER SIX

Faith, Passion, and Conquest

Love conquers all; let us, too, give in to love
—Virgil

Before entering upon the conquest of a country, your Majesty
must find out for sure if it is inhabited and by what sort of
people, and what is their religion and their rites, and what
they live on, and what there is to be found in the earth
—Hernán Cortés to Charles V

The Old Western synthesis of classical, Christian, and Germanic elements appeared symbolically complete when, on Christmas Day, A.D. 800, the pope, Leo III, made Charles, king of the Franks, emperor of the Romans. Contemporaries recognized the decisive character of the event and of its protagonist, whom they immediately labeled as "the Great"—Charlemagne—and "father of Europe." In performing that act, the pope was using a privilege that, he claimed, had been conceded to the papacy for all time by the emperor Constantine in the early fourth century.[1] God alone could make or unmake emperors; but God needed an earthly delegate to pronounce his choice, and that delegate was the bishop of Rome, successor to St. Peter as the vicar of Christ. In the papal political theology as Leo applied it, only the pope was competent to make the discerning judgment of whom God had chosen to be emperor, and to perform the ritual that turned a pretender or an emperor-elect into the real thing. This political theology was laid down in the document known as the Donation of Constantine.

The Donation was a weapon in the papal political arsenal that, for centuries, carried the heavy weight of papal claims to jurisdiction and authority in the West. Although it was in fact produced not long before 800, it claimed to be a document in which the emperor Constantine, after his victory at the Milvian Bridge in 312, stated that "we transfer and relinquish to the most blessed pontiff and universal pope Silvester . . . the city of Rome and all the provinces, places, and towns of Italy and of the western regions, and by ordinance in due and proper form we decree that they may be disposed of by him and his successors and that they shall remain under the jurisdiction of the Holy Roman Church." The Donation, which constituted the foundation of the medieval canon law, the papal laws of church administration and jurisdiction, rescinded the ancient Roman law whereby the emperor was elected by the Senate and people of Rome. Instead, it granted the papal see "power and glory and dignity and imperial force and honor," declaring that the popes rightfully had "the power of a greater pre-eminence than our own clement and serene imperial majesty appears to have."[2] The Donation, carefully worded to avoid the impression that Constantine was giving the pope a power that only God could give, put words in Constantine's mouth whereby he recognized the pope's preexisting and inherent superior authority as the final arbiter of power in the West and the only source of imperial authority. The emperor's power was no longer autonomous. Though he had independence in his own sphere, his power was, in effect, delegated by the pope, and no emperor could therefore nominate or crown himself. This papal universalism, or as modern scholars called it, this hierocratic principle of government, reached its fullest expression in the early thirteenth century in the metaphor of pope Innocent III, who said that the papal power was like the sun, which was the source of its own light and splendor. The imperial power was like the moon, its light was not its own but was borrowed from the sun.

When Leo III crowned Charlemagne, he wanted to show, as the forged Donation claimed, that the spiritual authority of the pope was above the temporal power of the emperor and that since the West belonged to the pope, he could at any time delegate political authority over it to an emperor of his choice. The papal doctrine claimed an absurdity: that the popes, as rulers of the West, were superior, even in the temporal sphere, to kings and emperors. Charlemagne himself is supposed to have been unpleasantly surprised by the coronation, because it seemed to confirm the papal claims, but also because he saw himself as more than just a candidate for emperor in Roman terms, but as a Germanic chieftain whose power and authority owed nothing to the papacy.

Far from setting in concrete a particular balance of church and empire, the particular synthesis represented at St. Peter's on Christmas Day 800 was short-lived. For the next several centuries, the three elements—classical, Christian, Germanic—modified one another and produced new political and social realities. The most important of these was the idea, derived from the early Germanic kingdoms, especially that of the Franks, of the Christian nation, the Christian ethnic group under the collaborative authority of a secular—military and administrative—and a religious head. Christian ethnicity was the continuation of Germanic nationalism, shaped and adapted by the late antique legacy of Roman Christianity, of the Christian Roman Empire. In the end, it was Christian ethnicity that undermined the Carolingian ideal of a Europe-wide, Western Christian Empire. By the fifteenth and sixteenth centuries, the West consisted not of a single empire, but of a number of kingdoms and principalities. The Holy Empire retained a shadowy authority and legitimacy, and the dream of a universal empire died hard, but the political reality of pluralism, conflict, and rivalry triumphed. In the sixteenth century, this pluralism spread to the religious sphere, when the Protestant Reformation broke the theological and ecclesiastical unity of the West and created the national churches that, in hindsight, seemed to be the natural concomitants of the emerging national states.

That the synthesis failed as a political project did not mean that it ceased being an element of Western identity. Throughout the modern period, rulers from Charles V to Napoleon and Adolf Hitler dreamed of recreating the supposed lost unity of the West by force. Philosophers and idealists, by contrast, claimed that behind the political pluralism, the wars, and the balance of power lay a spiritual and cultural unity. Thus was born, ultimately, the idea of Western civilization as the set of beliefs, customs, values, and principles that defined this unity. At the dawn of the third millennium of the Christian era, when wars between Western powers were a thing of the past, the major stake in world politics for Western peoples was whether this alleged Western identity in fact existed, and if it did, what that should mean in practice.

The old synthesis was not, therefore, of merely historical interest. In its own time, from the ninth to the sixteenth centuries, it was part reality, part inspiration. It was also a stage—the first and most basic—in the evolution of Western identity. The modern, liberal, and democratic West was also a synthesis, and this modern synthesis was rooted in the old. The idea, popular in some quarters in the post–Cold War era, that this modern synthesis of democracy, capitalism, and science was a historical abstraction that could be used to promote a universal humanistic civilization without regard to culture, tradition, religion, or the particular history of other regions was false and misleading precisely to the extent that it ignored the debt that the modern synthesis owed to the old. The West might have much to offer the world of the twenty-first century, but what it had to offer would be Western rather than universalist.

That is why it is useful to recall the political and intellectual history of the original synthesis and some of the ways in which historians and ideologues understood and exploited that history. Looking at it shows, for one thing, why universalism misrepresented Western identity, but also why it was a constant temptation. This was chiefly because church and empire formed the political and spiritual poles of the old synthesis, and each was universalist. If the emperor did not rule all humankind, he ought to, in accordance with the biblical prophecies and the Four Empires doctrine of world order. If all men were not Catholic Christians, they ought to be, in accordance with the New Testament command to baptize all peoples. From these original, rival universalisms descended the secularized universalism that was such a crucial part of modern Western identity.

What supporters of that modern identity forgot was that medieval universalism, whether of church or empire, was mostly ambition and ideology. Neither church nor empire was ever truly universal, a fact recognized even in the titulature of the Roman pontiff itself. On the one hand, he called himself vicar of Christ and universal pastor; on the other, he was styled bishop of Rome and patriarch of the West—not of the human race or even of the universal church, but of the West. Moreover, the ethnicity of the Western peoples, manifested in the Germanic contribution, denied the universalism of both popes and emperors. Including the Germanic element in its proper place as a constituent element of the Old West brings this neglected aspect to the fore, because it shows us that, throughout the history of Western identity, the universalism of church and empire was subverted and denied by Christian ethnicity and its modern successor, nationalism. Modern Western universalism was the secular and rationalist descendant of these two elements, but the Old West was not exclusively universalist. Rather, it was two-faced, with both universalist and particularist manifestations. This schizophrenia underlay much of the perplexity among Western leaders and publics as they approached the twenty-first century. Universalism, which dominated elite opinion in the United States and in much of the European Union, was taken to be the essence of the West, defined as democracy, human rights, and a market economy. But the illusion that the modern West had escaped from history and had become merely a carrier of universal principles was precisely that, an illusion. The universalists of the 1990s thought they had abandoned their history, whereas in fact they were reenacting one of the two basic scenarios of Western identity, the universalist scenario. Isolated from its particularist, ethnic, and religious counterpart, however, universalism risked discredit and disaster.

Universalism was a bad guide not just to policy but to history, because—like the Grand Narrative—it saw in the past only those reasonable, calm, peace-loving, and dispassionate elements that pointed forward to modern Enlightenment rationalism. But the history of the West in the era of the old synthesis was not only a history of reason; it was also a history of faith, passion, and conquest. For centuries, emperors tried to recreate the *dominium mundi*, lordship of the world, which they believed existed in the time of Augustus. The popes fought them, and since the popes had few armies of their own, they mobilized all those, whether kings, princes, or communal governments, who, for their own reasons, opposed the imperial universalism. The result was that the forces of particularism—the kings and cities of western Europe—defeated the emperors, but this did not serve papal primacy, for the fall of one universalism also undermined the other. The people who risked life and limb to prevent a German imperial hegemony were no more inclined to submit to a papal hegemony perceived increasingly in national and economic terms, as Italian exploitation of the north and west of Europe.

The idea that the West, properly defined, began not with the Greeks or the early Christians, but in the time of Charlemagne and after, was popular in that strong countercurrent of historians and philosophers who did not share the Grand Narrative's philhellenist and rationalist premises. In his *Decline of the West*, Oswald Spengler proposed that Western civilization, which he called Faustian, defined by the spirit of discovery, conquest, and acquisition, began in the tenth century. According to Spengler, all civilizations were dynamic for about a thousand years and then declined. Since the point of Spengler's book was to show that the decline of the West was becoming universal in his own day, around 1900, it was necessary to fix the beginning of the West a millennium earlier. The same metaphysical doctrine that civilizations were healthy for a thousand years determined what otherwise seemed Spengler's odd claim that ancient civilization began to decline in the age of Caesar and Augustus, because it had then, by his definition, existed for a thousand years. The intervening millennium, encompassing the Roman Empire, late antiquity, and the first half of what historians according to the Three Ages scheme called the Middle Ages, had no proper identity in Spengler's philosophy; it was simply the long period in which the decline of ancient civilization blended into the prehistory of the West.

The thousand years of Western civilization were, Spengler famously held, coming to an end in his own day, as the original Faustian spirit faded into conformity and stagnation, as the will to discovery and conquest became the administration of material and spiritual investments already made, as the West became a society of intellectual rentiers rather than cultural entrepreneurs. The Grand Narrative tried to contradict Spengler, but its centrist liberalism and faith in progress were weak reeds that shriveled at the first serious assault after 1968. As an intellectual design, the Grand Narrative spectacularly confirmed Spengler, for what was it other than a list of past ideas appropriately predigested for the tender stomachs of the late modern era? This was precisely the kind of intellectual life Spengler predicted for a West in its final phase.

In Spengler's cyclical and deterministic theory, the Western spirit of conquest and discovery remained always the same, until its inevitable decline. The West was dynamic, but it was a strange dynamism, always churning, never changing. The Faustian spirit, Spengler said, sought extension and expression in sustained activity, leading to such masterpieces as the cathedral of Chartres or J. S. Bach's *Art of the Fugue*. But according to Spengler's own philosophy, inspired by Goethe and Nietzsche, sustained activity of this kind could never really change the world, never produce any permanent impact. Building cathedrals and writing works of music were doomed attempts to create eternity in the material world, and this was impossible, for the material creations were ultimately transient; they crumbled into dust or, more fatefully, became incomprehensible when later generations forgot what they meant and how to understand them. Thus the ceaseless busyness of the Western world was, according to Spengler, only the Faustian spirit's heroic but doomed attempt to "make itself at home in its own endless solitude."[3] Thus, Western civilization, in Spengler's book and in his philosophy, was like a permanently idling engine, roaring and bellowing, but never actually able to go anywhere, and finally sputtering into stillness. Such a theory might accurately portray an aspect of the West, but it was fundamentally unhistorical, a modern myth of eternal return.[4]

Spengler's diagnosis of the West's beginnings was not unreasonable. The Carolingian Empire was short-lived. In 843, in the Treaty of Verdun, descendants of Charlemagne agreed to divide the empire among them. Although this treaty did not create France and Germany, as patriotic historians held in the nineteenth century, it did mark the beginning of a process that, by the mid-ninth century, produced two rival monarchies, each representing early versions of Christian ethnicity—the East and West Franks, later to become the German and French nations.[5] It was around the year 1000 that the Germanic, ancient, and Christian elements crystallized into a more enduring and recognizable pattern called Christendom, or the Old West.[6] In preceding centuries, since the formation of the relatively short-lived Christian Roman Empire in the fourth century, the synthesis had been shifting and uncertain. The Germanic invasions of the West brought Germanic traditions and, if Montesquieu was right, Germanic liberty to the heartland of ancient culture, but at the same time these invasions largely destroyed that culture. The Enlightenment Germanic model of Western development emphasized the new freedom that followed Roman rule, but with characteristic optimism ignored the price paid in lost literacy, living standards, and civility. But the Enlightenment model did have the great advantage over the later, Greek-based model of the liberal Grand Narrative that it focused attention on the actual political and constitutional history of Western nations and regions and proposed an account of the West in terms of that history and not in terms of a metaphysical transmission of great ideas from the Greeks to modernity.

By the late tenth century, the East Frankish or Saxon emperors of the Ottonian dynasty began to conceive of the western empire as a new entity, the Holy Roman Empire, with its own legitimacy as a force for order and partner in the grand bargain with the church. The rulers of the Carolingian Empire founded its legitimacy on the claim that it was the old western empire restored. Their successors legitimated it by the manner in which it incarnated the ideas of Rome and of empire in the West, not merely because it was Rome, but because of how it was Rome.

According to the dominant Four Empires doctrine of world history, God granted universal dominion to the Romans as the last of the four; no further empire could arise until the world's end. Therefore every new empire in the West had to be identified as a *renovatio*, a renewal, of the Roman Empire, for to imagine a new, independent, fifth empire was cosmologically impossible, a sacrilege and a blasphemy that could only be the devil's work.[7] All agreed on this; where emperors, popes, and propagandists differed was in how they saw the balance between empire and church, Roman law and church law, and, later, nationality and religion. As it happened, the years immediately before and after the year 1000 marked a turning point both in imperial ideology and in philosophy. The emperor, the young Otto III, adopted the hitherto unusual title of "august emperor of the Romans," where his predecessors had simply called themselves emperor. This showed that Otto saw himself as a new Augustus or Constantine, a Roman world ruler and not a Frankish emperor. He also appointed his own pope, the philosopher and inventor Gerbert of Aurillac. Gerbert took the name Silvester II, the same name as that of the pope who, in 312, supposedly received from Constantine the supreme power in the Western world. Otto's title and Silvester's name signified a program of joint renewal of the world under the guidance of two equal and supreme powers.

In theology, literature, and ethics, the synthesis produced, in the years around 1000, the remarkable phenomenon of the Christian Germanic hero, both in real life, in people like Saint Olaf of Norway, and in poetry, in characters like Roland. The Germanic community of cults, kings, and companions became the Christian community of loyal warriors bound by a double ethic of sacrifice: the Germanic and the Christian. This powerful combination yielded a Christian doctrine of holy war that drew on the Germanic principle of loyal service and the Christian ideal of striving for and proving holiness of life and thereby pleasing God by taking on dangerous and violent tasks. This double dose of moral and ideological energy reached its maximum effect in the eleventh and twelfth centuries in the Norman campaigns to recover southern Italy and Sicily from the Muslims and in the Crusades. While these ultimately failed as geopolitical endeavors, they not only left behind romantic memories in song and story, but also the idea, which would have appalled or at least disturbed Christians in late antiquity, that piety and soldiering, faith and conquest, heroic and Christian precepts not only need not conflict, but could mutually reinforce each other.

The new understanding of empire, the crusading ideal, and the characteristic literature praising the Christian hero all manifested themselves around the year 1000, building the political, theological, and psychological structure of the Old West. At the same time, western Europeans were, on the local as well as the geopolitical level, starting to develop the social and economic practices that, centuries later, evolved into democracy and capitalism. In the early eleventh century, autonomous urban communities "where," in Montesquieu's words, "several governed," and who saw themselves as independent-minded members of an active political body, reappeared for the first time since late antiquity. Or, more correctly, they appeared as new phenomena, for Roman cities never developed self-government or particular political identities based on the citizens' mutual interest in liberty. The democratic cities of ancient Greece were not an exact precedent either. Greek democracy, for adult males, was total and equal. The self-governing towns of medieval Europe were not democratic in this sense, for they were organized into guilds and hierarchies of power, and governed, usually, by oligarchies, by "several," to be exact, not by all. But in another sense they prefigured modern democracy more closely than the Greeks, because they offered the first experiments in representative government, a concept unknown to antiquity but fundamental to the modern world.

Economic development also accelerated in the eleventh century. The towns whose inhabitants wanted self-government were centers of expanding trade and production. Various factors came together to launch a period of growth and expansion that lasted several centuries and undergirded the optimistic and ambitious European civilization of the twelfth and thirteenth centuries, the era of the Gothic cathedrals, the rationalist and Aristotelian theology of Thomas Aquinas, the administrative systems of Edward I in England and Philip the Fair in France, and the Christian cosmology of Dante's *Divine Comedy*. Population was growing, and people were living longer and better. Europe was less exposed to invasions and sudden military disaster after the Vikings, the Hungarians, and the Slavonic nations east of Germany settled down and began to organize their own kingdoms, churches, and trade networks on Western lines. The climate was favorable, offering marginally better conditions for crops than either before 1000 or after 1300, the period of the so-called Little Ice Age from 1300 to 1750. Government was more secure and less arbitrary. Kings decided they needed better government, and better government increasingly meant not noble companions who would die for you in battle, but administrators capable of maximizing and mobilizing the resources of the land.[8] Administrators, unlike companions, had to be educated. Education therefore revived, producing experts in law and administration who compiled law codes on the basis of national customs and Roman law, codes that, for the first time, created conditions of work and production that encouraged innovation and growth. By a number of important measures, then, the West took definitive shape starting around the year 1000.

Two great developments shaped the early centuries of the synthesis, laying the groundwork for the pluralism, expansionism, and rationalism of modernity: the struggle of church and empire in the eleventh to thirteenth centuries, and the Western invention of doomed passion as the highest expression of individuality—and therefore, of individuality as suffering—around 1100, which added a new dimension to the shape and impulses of war, violence, and conquest in the West.

When Otto III made Gerbert of Aurillac pope in 997, he was, in a sense, repealing the Donation of Constantine. According to that piece of papal political theology, the popes, as vicars of Christ, held a divine mandate to choose the emperor from among the available candidates and to confer on him the divine grace that alone made him an emperor. But Otto knew his history and knew that the Roman Empire was older than the papacy. The emperor Augustus had not been chosen by any pope, even though Christians considered him a providential ruler, because it was thanks to the order he created in the Roman world that Christianity was able to spread. In Otto's imperial political theology, the emperor's authority was the divinely sanctioned instrument of Christian order on Earth, and it had a separate dignity not subject to papal choice. Or, to put it differently, the popes were not the only ones able to determine the rightful emperor.

In the early eleventh century, it looked as though this imperial theology was going to prevail, and that the emperors would resume the senior position they had held in the fourth and fifth centuries. But this was not to be. The papacy recovered and reasserted the claim first manifested in the coronation of Charlemagne, that the popes were the senior party, and that only they had the key to the divine mandate that conferred imperial authority. The brief Ottonian *renovatio* of imperial ideology was succeeded by two further acts in the great rivalry of church and empire, a rivalry that undermined the universalist legitimacy of both and cleared the ground for the triumph of Christian ethnicity, religious pluralism, and the modern balance of power.

The first was the Investiture Contest of the late eleventh and early twelfth century, and the key to understanding it lay in Otto's homeland. The administrative, legal, and economic structure of the church in Germany was, for historical reasons, unlike that elsewhere in the West. German nobles owned the churches of their territories and had the right to appoint, or "invest," incumbents: priests, bishops, abbots. By a natural theological confusion, this right had come to mean also the right to confer spiritual authority. This confusion was all the more plausible as German nobles and German kings retained much of the archaic chieftain-magic of pre-Christian times. The king, duke, or count was, first and last, the war leader of the folk, a function that remained, well into Christian times, girded about with supernatural awe. It was not surprising that such men should feel that they had power direct from God to confer authority on ministers of the church.

The popes disagreed. Ironically, one reason the popes disagreed was that the papacy, after a bad patch in the tenth century, had been reformed and bashed into some sort of reputability by none other than the German emperors, who were embarrassed that the heirs of St. Peter, the vicars of Christ, were conducting themselves like delinquent teenagers. The emperors had marched in, deposed a pope here, appointed another there, and made sure that pious men with strong managerial skills occupied St. Peter's chair. Now, it turned out that the reform popes had taken the lesson to heart. They were no longer willing to bow to the emperors in the matter of investitures. The ironic result of the church reform promoted by the German emperors was that the popes learned the skills of organized power all too well. Despite Charlemagne and his revival, the Western empire founded in 800 never established administrative and institutional cohesion comparable to that of the old Roman Empire. The papacy, however, did so; invigorated by the reforming popes appointed by the German emperors, the papacy recovered its institutional memory, which was both more literate and more solid than that of the Frankish or Saxon empire. Thus, as Dawson wrote, "it was not the Empire but the reformed Papacy which was the real heir of the Roman tradition of universalism and international order."[9]

The struggle lasted forty years, but the conclusion was foregone. The archaic magical powers of the German chieftains was no match for the theology and logic of the popes. The emperor Henry IV marched barefoot in the snow to the pope's citadel at Canossa in northern Italy to do penance for his arrogant sin in claiming the right to investiture, and he was still excommunicated until his deathbed. In 1118, pope and emperor sealed a new bargain, the Concordat of Worms. The old bargain, that of Leo III and Charlemagne, was restored with a new emphasis; the popes confirmed what had been merely implicit in 800. They held the whip hand in matters of spiritual authority, specifically, in the matter of deciding whether to crown a German king emperor, and second, in the matter of investitures of bishops anywhere in the West.

The second of the two succeeding acts in the drama was the vain but spectacular struggle of the emperor Frederick II in the thirteenth century to establish a secular empire on the Roman model in the teeth of papal jurisdiction and theology. Frederick was no archaic magic-wielding tribal chieftain. He was an educated agnostic, a man of the Enlightenment five hundred years before his time. His learning and his pride as emperor, the son and grandson of emperors, convinced him that his authority should rest on itself, on his own sheer power and on the memory and revived reality of Rome. He deduced his imperial rights not from superstition and atavistic prestige, nor from the papacy, but from history, logic, and Roman law. "For him, the emperor was the very source of law itself, not by divine inspiration, nor because he was able to draw on the traditional laws of his people, but because he was the living law on earth, the son and, at the same time, the father of justice, its creature and its creator, intrinsically endowed with a power of rational discernment which allowed him infallibly to determine justice and to establish the rules of human social existence."[10] Frederick built a lay, authoritarian state ruled by inflexible justice. He also built castles and fortresses and decorated them with statues modeled on Roman portraits. He constantly reassured the popes of his devotion, but they were unimpressed as well as fearful of his power: he controlled both Sicily and the south of Italy, his maternal inheritance, and northern Italy and Germany, his paternal and imperial inheritance.

To show that he understood how a great emperor upheld the bargain with the popes, he promised to lead a crusade to recapture the kingdom of Jerusalem, which had fallen to Saladin in 1187 and which was Frederick's by marriage. When he delayed, pope Gregory IX excommunicated him. Frederick nevertheless set out on the crusade that he was excommunicated for postponing. He captured Jerusalem, but could find no priest willing to crown him as its king, since to do so would be to incur the same excommunication that lay on Frederick. Undaunted, Frederick marched to the church of the Holy Sepulchre, took the crown of Jerusalem from its altar, and crowned himself, on March 18, 1229.[11]

The gift of Jerusalem did nothing to appease the popes. Gregory IX denounced him as the Antichrist. Frederick's supporters in turn denounced the popes as unworthy priests, greedy for money and worldly power. In 1241, Frederick laid siege to Rome itself as Gregory, aged 99, lay dying within its walls. In 1244, Innocent IV repeated the excommunication and continued his conspiracies to persuade Italian towns to rebel and undermine Frederick's power. The emperor, who now called himself "lord of the earth," died in 1250 on a hunting trip, a brief respite from his endless campaigns to reduce Italy to obedience and to complete the never-ending and impossible task of the German emperors—to hold a continuous body of territory from the city of Rome itself, their notional capital, to the forests of northern Germany, their home.

The struggle of empire and church was not a struggle between agnostics or unbelievers and Christians. It was a struggle among Christians over who should define the West and how. The imperialists believed that the empire was as legitimate, ancient, and authoritative as the papacy or, in the stronger version, that the empire had political priority, because the Roman Empire was older than the church. It was therefore the right and duty of the emperor to be the monarch of the world, under the spiritual, but not the political, guidance of the popes. The person who most concisely justified this imperial claim was the poet of the medieval Christian vision, Dante Alighieri.

Of all Western poetry since Virgil, T.S. Eliot recognized only Dante's *Divine Comedy* as approaching the status of a "classic in a modern European language."[12] In his 1929 book on Dante, Eliot had gone further and proclaimed the Florentine as "a master—I may even say, *the* master—for a poet writing to-day in any language."[13] But here Eliot was writing as a craftsman, and in 1944, he implied that Dante could not be the classic of Europe because his purposes and his style were alien and particular to Christendom, and therefore not universal, not valid outside his own culture. Dante's mastery of the *terza rima* made this verse his and none other's; it was particular to him, and reading it took you into Dante's world, not through it to your own. His religion was no longer that of Europe. His purpose was not to tell an epic story but to present the medieval supernatural universe of damnation and salvation. The "modern mind," Eliot said, might respect but could never fully understand such a purpose. Modern literature was about personal emotions and their reasons.

> It is difficult [Eliot wrote] to conceive of an age . . . when human beings cared somewhat about the salvation of the "soul," but not about each other as "personalities." Now Dante, I believe, had experiences which seemed to him of some importance; not of importance because they had happened to him and because he, Dante Alighieri, was an important person who kept press-cutting bureaux busy; but important in themselves; and therefore they seemed to him to have some philosophical and impersonal value.[14]

Dante's experiences were both political and spiritual. He was a Florentine patriot who had to spend the last twenty years of his life in exile from the city he loved but whose rulers, who had banished him, he hated. He belonged to the White faction of the Guelph party. The Guelphs were pro-papal, but the White faction included those more inclined to question or resist papal political or jurisdictional claims. In 1301, the thirty-six-year-old Dante, who was a member of the supreme governing council of Florence, was sent to negotiate with pope Boniface VIII about some of those claims. While the mission was away, the Black, more radically pro-papal party staged a coup in Florence and seized power from the Whites. Dante was called to stand trial and, when he did not appear, sentenced to perpetual exile on pain of death if the Florentines ever caught him.

Dante lived in an age when empire and papacy were succumbing to mutual exhaustion. By 1300, the German emperors were not much more than the leaders of a party, namely, that party of German magnates and administrators who believed in the ideology of empire, as opposed to those who preferred to build up their regional power. The last convincing emperor in the West had been Frederick II, a hero of Dante's. Frederick officially ruled Germany and much of Italy from 1212 to 1250, although his control was contested for much of that time. Disregarding reality, Frederick constructed his own ideology of empire both in words and in stone, in the shape of his castles, fortifications, statuary, and emblems scattered throughout his domains. Larger-than-life statues of Frederick and his ministers in Roman dress, using Roman portraiture as models, adorned his buildings. Historians since the mid-nineteenth century had argued that Frederick's obsession with the idea of Rome and also with the reality, that is, with control of the city of Rome and of Italy, fatally undermined imperial authority in Germany itself. Thus, in 1237, after defeating an alliance of towns in northern Italy fighting for self-government, Frederick sent the Milanese *carroccio,* or war wagon, the symbol of civic pride and self-government, to the people of Rome as a gesture of respect for their ancient right to elect the emperor.

Dante, in exile, became convinced that the empire was necessary to defeat papal arrogance and reestablish the terms of the ancient bargain, which he saw as a bargain between a Roman world ruler supported—but not dominated—by the head of the church. In 1310, the German king Henry VII visited Italy to obtain the imperial crown. Dante, in accordance with Ghibelline, that is, imperialist, doctrine, suspected that the Donation of Constantine was a fake and considered that Henry VII was already emperor by virtue of his election, without need of papal sanction. He hailed Henry as the champion of peace, order, and justice. Unfortunately, Henry deceived Dante's hopes for an imperial restoration and made his peace with the pope on the latter's terms. Shortly after these events, Dante composed his great defense of imperial universalism, the *De Monarchia* (On Monarchy). As Dante explained, he had not chosen to call his work "On the Empire," because empire, *imperium*, could also be spiritual, and he wanted to explain and justify the universal political rule of one man. "The temporal monarchy, commonly called 'Imperium,' is that sole principate which is above all other principates in the world, relating to all questions of the temporal order."[15]

The most important of these questions was how to maintain peace, and Dante believed that this required a world monarchy: "in order to prevent wars and to remove the cause of them through all the earth," he argued, "there must be one Prince who, possessing all, and not being able to desire more, holds the kings content within the limits of the kingdoms, so that peace may be between them."[16] Only in peace could men live happily and devote themselves to their highest calling, learning and knowledge. The world empire or universal monarchy was the political means to establish civilization and to permit people to build up a single community of knowledge bound together by a universal religion, but a religion whose priests would have only spiritual, not political, authority. Just as humankind had one spiritual head, Christ, so it should also have only one worldly and political head, an emperor. Pluralism of authority in either the religious or the political sphere violated divinely willed order and was a form of sin.

Dante knew that his vision of a single world state was anachronistic, but he devoted all his energy to presenting the dream of a single system of order serving a common good not just in the *De Monarchia* but in the *Divine Comedy* itself. As a Florentine citizen, he grew up in a world where proto-capitalist exchange and the practical reason of government, business, and commerce were shaping both life and consciousness. He objected to the political forces behind this new movement and was exiled, but he understood its force. His response was to construct a mystical, prophetic vision of future unity that he transmitted through his poetry to the world and, in particular, to the modern revivalists. In this prophecy, the church would retreat from its claims to political authority and renounce power, whereas a purified empire would arise from the wreckage left behind by Frederick II and his ephemeral successors.

The second great development within the Old West—next to the dualism of church and empire—was the discovery, or invention, of doomed passion as the essence of selfhood, the means by which men and women became most truly themselves in a fatal act of love. While the long conflict of popes and emperors was approaching its culmination in the twelfth and thirteenth centuries, a few people in a corner of Europe arrived at an original definition of passion and its demands that changed forever the Western understanding of love and war. That definition produced a new code of chivalry and self-sacrifice that reinforced and renewed the Germanic legacy of militant faith, holy war, and loyalty. In subsequent centuries, this code fed both the rituals of war and the missionary fervor of conquest in the New World. Disparaged, despised, or forgotten by the centrist liberalism of the Grand Narrative and its critical successors, the Western code of chivalry, love, and sacrifice was, for most of Western history, one of the crucial expressions of Western identity.

As Denis de Rougemont tried to show in his epochal and influential 1939 book on *Love in the Western World*, the emotions and the torment unleashed by the new notion of insatiable romantic passion starting in the twelfth century defined not only the Western view of love but much of the Western way of war as well, and therefore also the impulses behind the era of Western expansion and conquest that began in the late fifteenth century. Rougemont's claim was nothing less than that "the West is above all an idea of love," an idea he summarized in what he called "the myth of the West."

Rougemont belonged to the same movement of post–World War I Western revival as T.S. Eliot, the German Francophile Ernst Robert Curtius, the Virgilian mystic Theodor Haecker, and Christopher Dawson. But Rougemont was not like the others. First of all, he was a natural optimist. Where they saw decline and despair, he saw opportunity and challenge. Where they retreated into medievalism and mysticism, he joined the movement for European political and cultural unity where he labored, undaunted by disasters and disappointments, until in the 1960s and 1970s he could say that his efforts had not been entirely useless.

His book propounded an original, subversive, and exciting theory of Western identity. According to Rougemont, the myth of the West was a story of love as passionate and doomed, as fulfilled only in the extreme moment of death, and as being in constant conflict with the demands of society and religion. The Western idea of love, he claimed, was unique; if we understood its origins, history, and logic, we would be able to explain other ways in which the West differed from other civilizations, including attitudes to war, heroism, and politics.

Rougemont's work acquired a prominent place in the debate on the West not because his historical research was in all or even most respects impeccable, but because he provided an extensive audience, especially in the United States, with a plausible explanation of what appeared in the 1930s and remained in the 1990s, for many, psychological truths. "It is," Rougemont commented in a postscript written in 1970, "a question of listening and not of written evidence or sources to be verified, a question of intuition and receptivity, not of demonstration."[17]

His "intuition," often derided but just as often tacitly assimilated by professional medievalists, was that the myth of Western love was a remarkable, paradoxical, implausible invention that first appeared in the early decades of the twelfth century in the poetry of the troubadours, or courtly poets of southern France. This myth, radically different from ancient or non-Western conceptions, established a dichotomy between the "Passion of Night" and the "Norm of Day," between romantic desire and the obstacles to its fulfillment, between the fleeting and bitter joy of illicit love stolen at Night and the mundane world of Day. Only in the West was a love story supposed to have a tragic ending. Only in the West could a storyteller ask his audience, "Would you like to hear a story of love and death?" and receive an enthusiastic response. "Happy love has no history in Western literature," Rougemont stated. The great discovery of the West, appearing first in the verse of William of Aquitaine in the 1120s, was "mutual unhappy love." Romantic passion, in this Western form, was by definition unfulfillable. If it could be fulfilled, it was not love. All later Western literature, Rougemont argued, used and exploited the myth of desire and passion as that which could not be achieved, or, if it was, would thereby immediately come to an end.

His prime illustration of his myth was the story of *Tristan and Isolde*, which existed in various versions of the later twelfth century. It was a "song of love and death," and it was this conjunction of love and death that first piqued his curiosity, because, although it seemed unsurprising from within the West, it must have seemed very peculiar from outside. In the story, Tristan and Isolde have several chances to fulfill their love. They never seize them, or if they do, they soon reject their freedom and return to a situation where only tragedy can result from their continued passion. The obstacles to desire are not wholly outside the lovers; often, it is they themselves who reject happiness. Why? Because the myth of passion, or so Rougemont argued, rested partly on a belief that only in pain or unhappiness were you truly yourself; happiness was and must be an illusion. And this in two senses. Only in the Night could you find joy, for only the Night opened the gates of transgression and allowed you to find your true being. But the Night was also the time of phantoms and dreams. The joy found there could never be more than illusory. Day, on the other hand, was an illusion in a different sense, because mundane reality denied man, and woman, their only chance of becoming truly themselves through joy, which was found only at Night.

Men and women were fated to despair, either because the love they briefly won at Night was doomed or because their mundane life of duty, family, and social obligations by Day was vain. This mundane life could never give the fulfillment available only, and at fatal cost, at Night. The myth of passion was a myth of salvation by denial and pain. A life of shared happiness was, within the myth, a lie and a sin. Nor was the myth only a myth in story; Rougemont's point was that Westerners had tried for eight hundred years to live, that is, to suffer, by this bizarre code. "Drawn by an irresistible force I go to my perdition with open eyes," wrote a real-life lover, Benjamin Constant, in 1800.[18]

This was Rougemont's original discovery: that in the archetypal code of Western love, the Tristan and Isolde story, the lovers refused permanence and sought only that which made permanence impossible. Their mutual unhappy love existed only as desire, not as fulfillment. It was as though a love capable of fulfillment would not be true love and would therefore not be truly theirs, but something imposed from outside. What was truly theirs was doomed, and its realization could only happen in death.

> Why [asked Rougemont] does Western man want to undergo this passion which wounds him and which his own reason condemns? Why does he want this love whose dramatic result can only be his suicide? Because he knows and senses himself only as the object of vital menace, in suffering and on the threshold of death. The third act of [Richard] Wagner's drama [*Tristan and Isolde*] describes much more than a fictional catastrophe: it describes the *essential catastrophe* of our sadistic genius, this repressed taste for death, this desire to know oneself to the limit, this taste for self-discovery in violent collision which is undoubtedly the most ineradicable of all the roots of our instinct for war.[19]

To explain why this myth of doomed love took hold in the West when it did, Rougemont traced a panorama of pagan survivals and Near Eastern mysticism arriving by hidden paths to erupt in the courtly poetry of the troubadours. "*Passionate love appeared in the West as one of the reactions to Christianity (and especially its doctrine of marriage) in minds where a natural or inherited paganism still survived*," was his conclusion.[20]

The Christian doctrine of marriage as shared fidelity and happiness between man and woman was modeled on the mutual love (*agapé*) of God and his church. In this doctrine, happiness was to be found in self-sacrifice and being with the Other. Underlying the doctrine of marriage was the basic Judeo-Christian dogma that the world was good, though marked by sin, and not an evil place of expiation and pain. But precisely this opposite teaching was common in the ancient Near East in the so-called dualist sects. In dualist teaching, similar in this respect to Buddhism, the purpose of life was extinction. The world was evil, made by an evil god. All that served to make the world bearable was a lie; the only path to redemption, in dualism, was to reject the world and seek salvation through pain and suffering in this life in order to hope for a better life after death, in the realm of the good god.

Rougemont noticed that the courtly poetry of the troubadours constructed a world in which the man served his lady as a knight served his master, but in love, not in war. However, courtly love, in its ideal form, did not seek consummation. The whole teaching of the poetry was of a discipline by which the lover, in pain and anguish, awaited what he would never have. In much troubadour poetry, the lady was actually not a real woman at all but "the Lady of imagination, the Platonic idea of the feminine principle, the cult of Love against marriage."[21] Courtly love, or *cortezia*, became a complicated set of rituals designed to prove the lover's passion and show the obstacles to its fulfillment. The troubadour Marcabru wrote,

> Of *cortezia* let him be proud who knows how to keep *Mesure* [moderation] . . . The well-being of lovers consists in joy, patience, and moderation . . . I cherish the fact that my lady makes me wait long and that I will not have of her what she has promised me.[22]

In Rougemont's theory, the troubadours took the inspiration for their doctrine of love from a dualist faith, namely, the heretical Catharite religion known to have been widespread in southern France in the twelfth and thirteenth centuries. Catharism posited a radical distinction between the material world, which was evil, and a supernatural world, to which one could aspire by denying the material world. Catharism played an important part in troubadour society, which was furthermore nourished, so Rougemont claimed, by influences from Islamic mysticism, in which again a world of Night and passion was contrasted to the evil and mundane world of Day with its false and tawdry illusions, as in the poetry of the Muslim mystic Jalal'al-Din Rumi:

> Your soul is a hero this night.
> How quiet. Others sleep . . .
> God and I are alone this night.
> What a roar! Joy arises,
> Truth with gleaming wing shines forth this night!

Do not sleep, friend,
Were I to sleep until morning,
I should never regain this night![23]

The night, not only in Islamic mystics but transmitted through the myth of passion to Western literature, became the place of "intuitive knowledge, spiritual truth beyond the reality of objects. Tristan and Isolde find day a delusion and fulfillment only in the night."

The myth did not die with the tradition of courtly poetry but became pervasive in Western literature to such a degree that, by the nineteenth century, a story, poem, play, or novel featuring or praising mundane happiness as a plausible or noble theme was hardly conceivable. From *Romeo and Juliet* through *The Red and the Black* to *Madame Bovary* and David Lean's film *Brief Encounter*, the myth of doomed passion and of self-realization through pain dominated the serious and popular literature of the West. Uncounted Western love poems began at dusk and assumed that the ecstatic union of the lovers was, and had to be, doomed, fleeting, and bitter. One example among hundreds: in 1911, the composer Arnold Schönberg presented to the public the most successful work of his career, the late romantic, post-Wagnerian *Gurre-lieder*. In this lush and opulent work, Schönberg set a short cycle of poems, *Songs of Gurre*, by J.P. Jacobsen, a Danish poet who died of consumption in 1885. The *Songs* recount an old folktale—a "story of love and death"—of the illicit love of a king for Tove, a beautiful peasant girl. The poem opens, of course, at dusk, with the words "The blue dusk mutes now all sounds from sea and land." The king is riding to meet his love, urging his horse along in impatient longing. Impatiently, she waits. But when they meet, their conversation is a series of eerie passages, in which they describe their love as of the moment and looking only to death. The king says, "My lips murmur, 'My time is now!' But . . . I shall walk, a dead man, at midnight, clutching my shroud against the cold winds . . . and, sinking, sigh, 'Our time is gone!'" Tove: "Let us, then, drink to great, ennobling death; thus we go to our graves as a smile, dying for a blessed kiss."[24] Only death can confirm their love, for only death will seal its fatal glory, only in death will it be immutable and unchanged. The poem describes how the king's vengeful wife kills Tove. The king, echoing the Cathars who saw the creator god as an evil demon, accuses God of tyrannical behavior. The second half of the cycle tells how, centuries later, the dead king and his dead companions gallop through the summer night. Tove has become a spirit of nature, inhabiting the lake, the mist, the trees, and the grass.

Rougemont concluded,

it is far from the case that the passion and the myth of the passion are only active in our private lives.

The *mystique of the West* is another passion whose metaphorical language is
sometimes oddly similar to that of courtly love.

Our great *literatures* are in good part laicized forms of the myth, or as I
prefer to say, successive "profanations" of its content and its form.

Finally, *war*, in the West, and all its military forms, until 1914, have maintained by the very fact of their origins in chivalry . . . a constant parallelism to
the evolution of the myth.[25]

Three strands came together to make the Western way of war: the idea of ascetic effort as the way of the warrior; the idea of chivalry as a form of ritualized,
valuable achievement by self-denial, whether in *cortezia* or in battle; the myth's
desire of death by passion, of passion meaning, literally, suffering.[26] "Our notion of love . . . we thus find linked to a notion of *fruitful suffering* which darkly
flatters or justifies, at the very back of the Western mind, the taste for war."
War, in short, was the deliberate hunt for pain, confirming Paul Valéry, who
once wrote, "Man has only himself to fear—his capacity for pain."[27]

For example, there were perhaps many reasons that Americans in the late
twentieth century continued to demand stories and films about their Civil
War. But why were they so often, when engaged in these stories, sympathetic
to the South, which was not only the losing side but the side fighting for
slavery, which no one could endorse? Americans, in the words of George C.
Scott in the opening scene of *Patton*, "love a winner. They will not tolerate a
loser." But that was simply not true when applied to Americans' endless love
affair with the Confederacy. The South was the greatest loser of them all, yet
enjoyed perpetual grace from its sins on the screen and in story. Why did so
many people forgive the South its ultimate failure to be American—to lose
the war, and to have supported injustice?

In terms of Rougemont's arguments, the answer was that the reality and
legend of the South corresponded perfectly to the demands of the myth in
its guise as a myth of suffering and chivalry in war. The South was, from the
beginning, outnumbered and out-produced. It could not win, yet it fought
bravely to the end. The South was also, in all of America, the land of
chivalry, its pretenses as well as its reality. Military historians pointed out
that Southern commanders were often notably more reckless and daring
than their Yankee counterparts; some attributed this to the Celtic strain in
Southern culture. Rougemont would have found in this hypothesis delicious

confirmation of his thesis that the myth of passion among the troubadours, and in particular the *Tristan and Isolde* legend, derived not only from Catharism but from Celtic roots, and argued that much in ancient Celtic culture shared the dualist love of night and fear of day, cult of passion and rejection of the mundane.

The key to linking the two aspects of the myth, love and war, Rougemont found in the way that the language of chivalry and battle entered the language of love poetry: the lover "lays siege" to his lady, delivers "assaults of love," tries to "turn her defenses," until she "cries mercy." But then, an odd reversal takes place. After his victory, it is the lover who suffers pain. He, not she, becomes the "prisoner"; it is he who is the "vassal" of his "sovereign mistress." The rules of feudal warfare for the defeated party apply to him, not her. Victory, in short, is not pleasant, it is nothing other than defeat.[28]

Courtly love and its curiously turned military metaphors transformed "sensual passion into an ethical or quasi-ethical self-denial . . . The expression and fulfillment of this desire, which seem to be unobtainable, are replaced and elevated to the dream of heroic deeds for love. This immediately posits death as an alternative to fulfillment, and satisfaction is, so to speak, thus guaranteed in either direction."[29]

If the language of battle and chivalry informed courtly poetry, so did the poetry's myth of passion inform feelings about and desire for battle. This was true even in details of convention, for example, the idea that the victor in battle was the one who was able to stay the night on the battlefield. The custom of the tournament and, later, the duel were further social manifestations of the cult of suffering.

From the sixteenth through the eighteenth centuries, Western thought on war centered on attempts to limit its destructiveness, or, in Rougemont's terms, to limit the power of the myth of passion in political conflicts. In the eighteenth century, the ideal commander was he who never had to fight a battle but could win entirely by maneuver and negotiation. This restraint of war ended in the French Revolution, which reopened the doors of myth. War, after the revolution, was again a matter of emotion and passion. The scope for satisfying the desire for death or achievement through pain widened enormously.

In Rougemont's perspective, World War I was both the culmination and the reversal of the myth of passion in politics. In that war, combat took place not as part of chivalrous exchange or from passion, but as part of mechanized, total war, in which death and emotion were divorced. In World War I, the historic link in Western culture among sex, violence, and death was cut.

Rougemont reported studies claiming that World War I soldiers were not un-usually active sexually. The French birthrate, never high since Napoleon, did not rise during or immediately after the war, which was contrary to all histor-ical experience. The war, Rougemont concluded, was no longer "the dis-charge of passions, but a sort of enormous castration of Europe."

Writing in 1938, Rougemont saw in the totalitarian states of Continental Europe the logical result of separating war from passion. Modern war threat-ened all of society, not just the soldiers. This threat encouraged people to seek safety in dictatorship, but this solution was, in his view, temporary. "Po-lice measures do not make a culture, slogans do not constitute morality. Be-tween the artificial framework of the great states and the daily life of people there is still too much play, too much anxiety and too much uncertainty. Nothing has *really* been resolved." Therefore the future would be either one of total and final war, or of peace, in which the tensions of the myth "will reappear in the totalitarian countries, just as it unceasingly bothers us in our liberal societies."[30]

Rougemont's account of the Western myth of passion and war, inspired by Sigmund Freud and deconstructing Nietzsche's nihilism as evidence of displaced emotional energy, was one of those hypotheses that, if one accepted it, found confirmation in every detail of daily life. Published in English by T.S. Eliot's house of Faber & Faber in 1939, *Love in the Western World* en-joyed greater success in English-speaking countries than on the Continent. One reason was that Rougemont provided an explanation of the crisis of middle-class marriage. The philosopher Allan Bloom once wrote that Amer-ica took the somber philosophies of Europe and gave them an optimistic turn. Thus, for example, Freud's scepticism about human nature and progress became, in America, the idea of therapy to cure precisely those prob-lems that, to Freud, were incurable. Rougemont said that Western man wanted to immolate himself in unfulfillable desire, and that to fulfill that de-sire was to end it. The goal was suffering, not achievement. The American version of the myth was to say, in direct denial of the original version, that great passion was not only possible, it was a generic human right that must and could be fulfilled in marriage. But this created a new problem. If, in the American version, every man and woman had a right to the great passion, and if marriage should rest on such a great passion, what then if in real life it did not? Then, of course, the unhappy party or parties would, by the very terms of the myth in its American, optimistic shape, have the right to divorce in order to seek that ever-elusive goal of true love.

In his postscript of 1970, Rougemont commented on what he called the "bourgeois romantic" version of the myth and its error, "wanting to *found marriage on passionate love*, that is to say, on that which denies it from the beginning. A hardly less fatal error would be to *exclude passion from marriage*." The only solution capable of sustaining any society, Western or other, was to seek "the combination of opposites and the tension of contrary poles . . . The couple is the original cell of society, whose constitutive forces are two beings of singular, different natures but who choose to form a 'union without fusion, without separation, and without subordination' . . . while the conflict of Eros [passionate love] and Agapé animates their days and their dreams."[31]

At the end, Rougemont rejoined his optimistic point of departure that was to explain the West to itself in order to help prevent the disasters of totalitarianism and total war, not to contribute to a Nietzschean or Spenglerian prophecy of doom or to a nostalgic revivalism without future or social purpose. Rougemont was a good liberal free of despair. Others, in his time, saw less hope than he for the future of a liberal West, and were even inclined to see in liberalism the very denial of the true West.

Love in the Western World gave an account of what happened when the medieval warrior ethos of sacrifice, with its Germanic and Christian roots, met the dualist religion of radical pessimism in the south of France. Later scholars disputed this thesis, and were never able to agree how far troubadour poetry was in fact influenced by Catharism. Nor did Rougemont's argument that the myth of self-sacrifice in love determined the Western way of war find universal favor. In the 1980s and 1990s, an American classicist, Victor Hanson, proposed another explanation of why Western societies usually believed that the right way to wage war was, in the words of an American field manual, "to close with the enemy and destroy him." The standard model of war in the West, Hanson said, was a model of mass mobilization and a quick campaign ending, as soon as possible, in "a single, magnificent collision of infantry." Western armies and public opinion defined war as "the ability but also the *desire* to deliver fatal blows and then steadfastly to endure, without retreat, any counterresponse."[32] Hanson traced this model to ancient Greece and the citizen armies of the archaic towns in the seventh and sixth centuries B.C. In these towns, the citizens were also the soldiers; wars were fought by those who lived in the towns and tilled the ground, not by mercenaries. Citizen armies had two great advantages: they were cheaper than mercenaries and they were, usually, highly motivated to fight, as Aeschylus said, "to free your country, free your children, your women, the temples of your ancestral gods and the graves of your forefathers."[33] On the other hand, they also had a handicap: they could not tolerate long campaigns of attrition, because the citizen could not afford to be away from his farm for more than a short time. Therefore, the Greek citizen army learned to plan for and expect the decisive battle, and therefore the idea of the decisive battle as the only right way to wage war descended to the West.

Hanson's theory did not contradict Rougemont, because one could certainly imagine that the reason that Western societies were for so long prepared to offer their young men to death in decisive battles was that the myth of sacrifice and of self-realization through death was so powerful. But Rougemont argued that the Western way of love and war began in the Middle Ages, whereas Hanson traced the idea of the decisive battle to ancient Greece. Moreover, Hanson linked the Western way of war to citizen armies, whereas most armies in the West were not, in the Middle Ages or later, citizen or national armies until the French Revolution and its wars, with a few exceptions such as the Swiss, or the Swedish armies in the early years of the Thirty Years' War. Where the two might agree was on the nationalist wars fought between 1792 and 1945 by citizen armies seeking decisive battles and informed by the ethic of sacrifice.

Rougemont's theory of doomed passion as the myth of the West provided a background to the political, ideological, and constitutional struggle of the rival universalisms, a struggle that defined the history of the Old West from the eleventh to the eighteenth centuries. Papal universalism, basing its claims on the Donation of Constantine, both won and lost the struggle with the emperors. It won, because the popes succeeded in subverting the emperor's subjects and allies and in convincing other kings of Christendom that the German emperors were dangerous and should be resisted. Thus reinforced, the popes defeated those emperors who hoped to establish their own hegemony over Christendom. But in another sense the popes lost, for the political battles they fought undermined their credibility as spiritual masters of the West. When the struggle with the empire was over, the papacy found itself deprived both of an enemy and of its own moral and political authority.

When Dante died in 1321, few outside Germany took imperial universalism seriously as a practical proposition. Neither the popes nor, for different reasons, the kings of France, England, and other countries were prepared to subordinate themselves to the man whom a group of German princes and bishops happened to elect as their king and prospective emperor. Yet, for three centuries after Frederick II failed in his final attempt to subjugate the papacy, the emperors retained a symbolic and ritual dignity as the first lords of Christendom. Of Charles IV, who ruled from 1346 to 1378, Gibbon wrote:

> An hundred princes bowed before his throne, and exalted their own dignity by the voluntary honours which they yielded to their chief or minister. . . . Nor was the supremacy of the emperor confined to Germany alone: the hereditary monarchs of Europe confessed the pre-eminence of his rank and dignity; he was the first of the Christian princes, the temporal head of the great republic of the West: to his person the title of majesty was long appropriated; and he disputed with the pope the sublime prerogative of creating kings and assembling councils. The oracle of the civil law, the learned Bartolus, was a pensioner of Charles the fourth; and his school resounded with the doctrine, that the Roman emperor was the rightful sovereign of the earth, from the rising to the setting sun. The contrary opinion was condemned, not as an error, but as an heresy, since even the gospel had pronounced, "And there went forth a decree from Caesar Augustus, that *all the world* should be taxed."[34]

The reality was sometimes less flattering than the ritual. Gibbon also reported that the same Charles IV was once "arrested by a butcher in the streets of Worms, and was detained in the public inn, as a pledge or hostage for the payment of his expences."

By the time of Charles IV, most people in the West had in any case other preoccupations than asserting or defying imperial universalism. From 1315 to 1322, famine swept Europe as three harvests in a row failed. Nothing on that scale had been known since the long-forgotten dire days of the Germanic invasions. The bad years were a harbinger of the worsening climate that lopped a decisive few days off the growing season, reducing both yields and the amount of land available for crops. Iceland, northern Norway, and other areas at the edge of the zone of cultivation ceased being able to support grain. Swiss mountain peasants huddled in the valley bottoms as snow replaced what used to be fertile fields. In 1348, bubonic plague arrived from south Asia, killing around a third of the population in its first visitation, and thereafter returning every generation or so to cull those who had been born since the last epidemic. Of those who caught the plague, fewer than half lived. The plague solved the food crisis and, for survivors, reversed the balance of economic power between peasants and landlords. Until the famine that began in 1315, the population of western Europe had been growing, probably somewhat more rapidly than the food supply. Europe around 1300 was full of landless laborers willing to work for a pittance. Peasants were increasingly tenants, not owners, and at the mercy of landlords who could evict them and find more docile tenants without difficulty.

The plague changed this. Surviving peasants found themselves fewer and more in demand. Landlords suffered losses when their tenants died and, unable to meet their obligations, were willing to pay more to have their land tilled and rents paid. Peasants who received better conditions were more often able to buy their land. Free peasantry recovered in parts of Europe where it had been extinct for centuries.

In the midst of this era of crisis began the period known as the Renaissance. In the Grand Narrative, the Renaissance was the reawakening of the West after its long medieval slumber. Peter Gay, one of the most profound historians of the modern Western personality, called the Renaissance the first Enlightenment, the first glimpse of what a humanist, liberal civilization could be. This judgment of the 1960s was often repeated in popular accounts that derived from the Grand Narrative's model of the West, but, taken on its own, it was as misleading as saying that the Greeks were the first Westerners. By the 1990s, many historians rejected the traditional idea of the Renaissance as an era of individualism, creativity, and confidence. The period known by that name, from the later fourteenth to the mid-sixteenth century, was not, in this interpretation, an era of optimism and recovery, but rather an era in which the Four Horsemen—famine, war, pestilence, and untimely death—rode freely and often across Europe.

Indeed they did, but frequent wars of the limited kind known to premodern Europe were never incompatible with cultural creativity, whereas famines were probably less frequent, at least in Italy, in the fifteenth century than earlier, simply because the Black Death had temporarily reduced population pressure. The problem with the liberal vision of the Renaissance as propounded by Jacob Burckhardt in the 1860s and carried on in the Grand Narrative was not that it ignored famines, plagues, or war. For that vision was correct when it showed artists, poets, and philosophers in Italy in the fifteenth century creating a unique era not only of renewal and rebirth of classical civilization, but of faith in progress beyond the limits of past achievement. Where the liberal vision was wrong, however, was in assuming that the Renaissance emerged suddenly, in a burst of originality, as the first and splendid act in the drama of the modern West. The contrary was true: the Renaissance was not the revolutionary first act of modernity; it was the flowering of tendencies rooted deep within the heart of the Old West.

Take the key idea of the Renaissance, the idea of humanism. In the Renaissance itself, a humanist was someone who studied the texts of Greek and

Roman civilization, realizing that they were separated from him by time and custom and therefore needed methodical analysis and interpretation to yield their wisdom and their lessons for his own age. The humanist believed the ancients to have established the highest standards in all branches of study concerned with the practical human condition—history, poetry, moral philosophy, grammar, and the practical arts of medicine, agriculture, and law. The ancients were, in a word, classical—that is to say, alien, yet perfect; distant, yet comprehensible. In a broader sense, a humanist was one who took human reason and human liberty as legitimate sources of judgment, who did not defer to supernatural authority, but tested all claims and arguments by whether they were plausible, consistent, and in accord with other evidence.

With the key idea went, in the liberal view of the Renaissance, a key text: Giovanni Pico della Mirandola's *Oration on the Dignity of Man*, written in 1486. Generations of students of the Grand Narrative were taught to take this document as the emblematic statement of humanism in the twentieth-century sense, of a commitment to human dignity, reason, and freedom, in direct opposition to medieval asceticism, superstition, and submission of reason and will to theology and metaphysics.

Parts of the *Oration* certainly read as though they are meant to defend such a modern, secular view. Pico starts by defining man as "a most fortunate animal, worthy of all admiration," who is "justly considered to be a great and marvelous miracle." Contrast this to the penitential Christian view of man as a fallen creature who constantly needs to be forgiven for past sins and evil desires and to be warned of hellfire lest he sin constantly. In the Middle Ages, people composed treatises "on the miserable condition of mankind"; now, in the bright sunshine of fifteenth-century Florence, the unabashed Pico della Mirandola contradicts this entire tradition and launches the modern, rationalist, and liberal praise of human abilities and aspirations.

A closer reading of the *Oration* shows that reading it as a founding document of secular liberalism, opposed to medieval dogmatism and misanthropy, is thoroughly mistaken. For one thing, texts in praise of human dignity were hardly unknown in the Middle Ages. Lothar of Segni, who wrote the most famous and popular of all treatises *On the Misery of the Human Condition*, did not mean it to stand alone; he intended to write its necessary complement, "On the Dignity of the Human Condition," but was unable to find the time because he was elected pope at age thirty-seven as Innocent III. St. Augustine, whom secular liberals considered to be the most dour and misanthropic of all Christian theologians, next to St. Paul himself, not only wrote that "man is truly a great phenomenon . . . because he excels the beasts in the glory of his rational spirit," but declared in one of his sermons to his flock at Hippo Regius that "God wants to make you God."

Literary compositions in defense of human dignity were thus nothing new in the Renaissance; indeed, the recovery of the "medieval sources of Renaissance humanism" was one of the more fruitful areas of intellectual history in the 1960s and 1970s.[35] Nor was Pico original in his praise of human reason and autonomy; the idea that medieval societies before his day were universally characterized by submission to authority, by discipline, and by superstition is utterly mistaken. The different legacies of freedom in the Old West, of the Germanic tribesman and of Christianity, combined in many interesting ways to generate climates of independence, critical thought, and hardheaded rationalism, especially in the larger towns and monastic centers of western Europe from the twelfth century on.

If Pico had wanted merely to praise human autonomy and dignity, he would thus have been following a venerable and deeply Christian tradition, one exemplified by hundreds if not thousands of sermons and treatises from the preceding millennium. Had this been his purpose, his *Oration* would have been a forerunner of secular liberalism, but so would the similar writings of many leading theologians and philosophers of the Middle Ages. In fact, the *Oration* is a much odder document than its liberal reputation suggests. When Pico praised human dignity, he was not rejecting the authority of Christian religion or fomenting any supposed pagan revival. He was, rather, advocating an anthropology of human nature as linked both to heaven and earth, as a microcosm of the universe, that which joined and embraced both the higher and the lower. This was not rational, secular liberalism; it was an exaltation of human obligations and human possibility in the realm of philosophy, esoteric theology, and mysticism. Piling together references to Plato, Aristotle, the church fathers, the Jewish Cabala, and the esoteric doctrines known by the name of Hermes the Thrice-Great, Pico was pleading for a return to the original knowledge of divine reality found in all these thinkers and traditions. The *Oration*, in short, was nothing less than an "introduction to a synthesis of universal knowledge."[36] Pico himself was neither a rationalist nor a forerunner of the Enlightenment. He was, in fact, the greatest of the Christian cabalists and was considered a magician by his contemporaries. When he was born, a legend held, a ball of fire appeared in his mother's room. His memory was so great that he could recite long poems after seeing them once. At the age of twenty-three he proposed nine hundred theses "concerning all things known," stating his belief that he could summarize universal knowledge. This knowledge was not only of things seen but especially of things unseen, of the esoteric reality underlying the appearances of the mundane world. The Cabala was a teaching that promised to initiate its adepts into the universal knowledge of the world hitherto held only by God and his angels. Pico wanted to adapt that teaching and broaden it to encompass other mystical traditions, such as those of Plato and "Hermes," whom Pico and his contemporaries believed to have been the author of ancient Egyptian wisdom. In this perspective, the title of the *Oration* takes on a significance rather different from that assumed by modern liberals who thought "dignity of man" meant emancipation of reason from superstition. In fact, Pico borrowed the title from another cabalist. It did not imply that human dignity lay in the autonomy of reason, but that the human figure and the human imagination were the focal points of a universal wisdom, of the supernatural truth of the cosmos, waiting to be recovered from the ancient traditions.[37]

Pico's example shows that the Renaissance was neither a clean break with the past nor, in any simple sense, a "first Enlightenment." Many of its leading thinkers and artists were, as he was, in search of mystical illumination and esoteric wisdom; some would call such desires superstitious. This temperament was more typical of the fifteenth-century Renaissance than simple rationalism. In fact, the secular, quantifying approach to reality associated with the productive, capitalist, acquisitive, exploratory, and scientific aspects of the New West began, not in the Renaissance but in the preceding centuries, more precisely—according to the historian Alfred Crosby—in the thirteenth and early fourteenth centuries.[38]

Renaissance humanism was, therefore, anything but liberal, agnostic, and opposed to clericalism and church authority. Most humanists were not against Christianity or even the papacy; they were against fictitious claims that they proposed to dissolve by rational criticism to provide better defenses for a purified church. The rational, calculating, and quantifying mentality was not a breaking away from the Old West, but lay at its very core, though it took centuries for it to crystallize out of the original, early medieval synthesis. The Renaissance, with its hankering for pagan mysticism, Neoplatonism, and a theology beyond all theologies, was in some respects a colorful detour into magic, astrology, and superstition. In other respects, the period known as the Renaissance pursued and strengthened the calculating, quantifying, rational impulse. The most important of these respects was the study of ancient and medieval texts—the field of activity of humanism in the original, Renaissance meaning of the word.

The earliest and one of the most spectacular examples of methodical reason applied to textual criticism, and the opening shot in the modern, critical analysis of documents, was Lorenzo Valla's exuberant denunciation of the Donation of Constantine, probably the most devastating piece of scholarly sarcasm ever published and "the cornerstone of the modern critical method."[39] The basic principle of that method was the distinction, so seemingly obvious since, but revolutionary then, between authentic and secondary, derived, or forged information. Authentic information about an event was that of eyewitnesses or contemporary sources that might be mistaken, but were of a different category than secondary sources. Valla maintained that the Donation, which the popes claimed was authentic and contemporary with its supposed participants, could be determined on internal evidence to be later, and once shown to be later, it could also be shown to have been a false representation of history. Before the time of Valla, authentic meant *confirmed by indisputable authority*. Valla changed that to *verified by critical method*, by internal and external evidence. "For the knowledge of authority he substituted the authority of knowledge."[40]

Valla was a Renaissance humanist and philologist, that is, someone interested in ancient texts because they were texts from a culture perceived as classical, distant, and in need of recovery by careful methods and trained insight. The philologists were those who first understood that the classical past had become a foreign country, and who embarked on the double task of recovering the past and building up the present as a new age, the modern age, with its own legitimacy that was neither that of the ancients nor that of the universalist powers who had administered and quarreled over the great bargain—church and empire. The philologists "were less interested in reaching out to antiquity over the head of Christendom than in discovering how societies evolve and vary and how the past becomes an object of knowledge."[41] Valla, who was born in 1407, not only knew Latin, as did anyone with any education, but Greek, which was much less common. Later in life he produced the first translations into Italian of Thucydides and Herodotus. Unlike some other humanists, he was interested not only in ancient, but in Christian and medieval texts, and in distinguishing the moral force of the papacy from its sordid territorial and financial interests. Thanks in part to his anticlerical opinions, he found employment at the court of king Alfonso V in Naples, who, like other kings with interests in Italy, opposed the temporal power of the popes. His expertise in textual criticism, his theological interests, and his opposition to the papacy of his own time came together in his best-known work, *The Mendacious Donation of Constantine Falsely Believed to be True*, written in difficult circumstances in 1439, disseminated in manuscript, published in printed form to general European acclaim in

1502, and put on the index of books forbidden to Catholics by the Council of Trent in 1563.

The emperors and their supporters, the imperialists, had long disliked the Donation and many, like Dante, suspected it was fishy, but could prove nothing until Valla wrote his denunciation. In the twelfth century, the emperors had rediscovered Roman law, in the form of Justinian's code, which included the old Roman rule that the emperor was created by the Senate and people of Rome, who in a deliberate, legal act granted the emperor his power. On this principle of popular sovereignty and on the indisputable historical fact that the empire was older than the church, the German kings of the Saxon and Staufen dynasties, from Otto III to Frederick II, claimed that their election as kings in Germany was in itself evidence of divine favor and therefore of their right to be made emperors. The imperial power, in this view, was not a privilege granted by the popes but autonomous. And that power, once conferred over a thousand years ago on Augustus, was universal. The imperialist lawyers loved to quote two Roman tags: "Whatever pleases the emperor has the force of law," and "The emperor is not bound by laws." The emperor was the "living law," the universal legislator holding universal authority on Earth, "including as to property," as one lawyer claimed.[42] In the papal view, all these ambitious arguments were trumped by the Donation, whereby Constantine rescinded all the ancient Roman rules of popular sovereignty and transferred to the vicar of Christ, the pope, the sole right to find, nominate, and judge the emperor and to depose him if he violated divine law.

Valla's denunciation used textual analysis to show that the Donation could not possibly date from the time of Constantine. In one respect he looked back: he was the last of the medieval imperialists, who defended the emperor's autonomy and privileges in the centuries-long battle with the popes. In another, he faced the future. Because he had learned Latin and studied Roman culture like a philologist, because he knew the ancient world was not his own and required explanation and understanding, he could show that the author of the Donation had misunderstood and misapplied ancient Roman political and ritual terms, that its Latin was anachronistic and confused. He could show that when the Donation referred to royal insignia given by Constantine to the popes, it was revealing its later date, for everyone knew that the Romans hated the idea of kingship, and no real Roman emperor would have spoken, in a formal document, of his distinctions as "royal insignia."

Valla embedded his analysis in a much wider argument against the consequences of believing the Donation to be true. Relying on it, the popes had claimed a bargain with the imperial power, whether Roman, Frankish, or German, that made the popes the superior partner in the political system of the West. This entanglement, Valla held, was a betrayal of "Christian freedom," the freedom promised to the church in her scriptures. Only by abandoning the Donation and its corrupting effects could the church return to her pristine condition, which was also a condition of recovering her theological and moral authority. This was a line of argument later adopted by the Protestant reformers.

The Donation, Valla concluded, was not written by Constantine, but was invented by papal propagandists to justify papal claims that had no basis in fact, law, or history. Later scholars confirmed this and concluded that the Donation was most likely manufactured in the later eighth century, at the time when the popes were making their grand bargain with the Frankish kings. The papal side wanted to demonstrate that they held the whip hand. In doing so, they had an advantage over the Frankish kings, who had few literate advisers, no archives, and no information on which to rest their case that imperial power was equal to papal power. All they had was intuition and ancestral custom. When the later emperors introduced Roman law as argument against the papalists, they failed to make their case because the Donation was assumed to override all earlier Roman law.

Lorenzo Valla began the tradition of humanistic textual criticism of ancient texts and hence of modern classical scholarship, and also the tradition of scrutinizing medieval documents to see whether they were genuine. Over the following centuries, this antiquarian art of documentary analysis developed into an elaborate technique for classifying charters, that is, documents stating, describing, or confirming a legal right, by type, age, and purpose, and hence into a technique for judging the various claims of kings, nobles, or churches to land, taxes, exemptions, or other privileges. Many of these early textual scholars were priests. In the seventeenth century, the study of documents from the Frankish era, the centuries after the invasions, reached a high point at the Benedictine monastery of Saint Maur in Paris under the guidance of a humble and indefatigable priest, Dom Jean Mabillon. An admiring contemporary wrote that "Father Mabillon claims to have discovered the art of distinguishing genuine ancient charters from those that only appear to be so. The rules of this novel art consist in describing, so to say, all the marks of a genuine charter, and in stating in detail what should be its paper, ink, shape, style, signature, seal, date, etc.," and then comparing what, from years of training and deduction, you knew to be the right form to what you had before you. "This art of distinguishing true charters from false ones is doubtless of the utmost consequence, whether it be in judging in the courts the right of parties that usually rests on ancient titles, or whether it be in guiding the learned on obscure points of history or chronology."[43]

Wars and the fates of kingdoms might depend on such erudite research and the ability to mobilize it in the right political interest and at the right moment. A marvelous example of this is the opening scene of *Henry V*, where Shakespeare shows the archbishop of Canterbury and the bishop of Ely complaining that Parliament is about to pass a law depriving the church of much of its income. How to persuade the king not to sign that bill? By providing him with another and even better source of revenue. What might that source be? The kingdom of France. The archbishop of Canterbury whispers that he has, in his erudite research, come upon good arguments in support of Henry's

> true titles to some certain dukedoms,
> And generally to the crown and seat of France,
> Derived from Edward, his great-grandfather.

Henry summons the archbishop and asks him to lay out these arguments, but warns him not to

> fashion, wrest, or bow your reading,
> Or nicely charge your understanding soul
> With opening titles miscreate, whose right
> Suits not in native colours with the truth.

Straight-faced, the archbishop proceeds to demolish the French argument that Henry's claim to France was void, because it descended to him through a woman. The basis of the French case was

> this, which they produce from Pharamond:
> *"In terram Salicam mulieres ne succedant"*—
> "No woman shall succeed in Salic land"—
> Which "Salic land" the French unjustly gloss
> To be the realm of France, and Pharamond
> The founder of this law and female bar.

The archbishop explains that the French were not entitled to use this Salic Law to deny Henry's claim.[44] For one thing, the "Salic land" was no part of France, so royalty in France was not subject to the Salic Law. For another, the French themselves by their actions admitted this, because royalty in France on several occasions had descended through women. Third, the male ancestor of the current French line was Hugh Capet

> who usurped the crown
> Of Charles the Duke of Lorraine, sole heir male
> Of the true line and stock of Charles the Great.

A claim derived from a usurper was not a good claim, and Hugh Capet's descendants strengthened it by asserting that they were in fact descended from Charlemagne. But to do so, they had to admit that royalty could descend through a woman:

> Also, King Louis the Ninth,
> Who was sole heir to the usurper Capet,
> Could not keep quiet in his conscience,
> Wearing the crown of France, till satisfied
> That fair Queen Isabel, his grandmother,
> Was lineal of the Lady Ermengarde,
> Daughter to Charles, the foresaid Duke of Lorraine;
> By the which marriage, the line of Charles the Great
> Was reunited to the crown of France.
> So that, as clear as is the summer's sun,
> King Pépin's title and Hugh Capet's claim,
> King Louis his satisfaction, all appear
> To hold in right and title of the female;
> So do the kings of France unto this day,
> Howbeit they would hold up this Salic Law
> To bar your highness claiming from the female,
> And rather choose to hide them in a net
> Than amply to embar their crooked titles,
> Usurped from you and your progenitors.

Satisfied, the king goes to war and wins his new kingdom.

By the early eighteenth century, powerful men in both church and state had become disillusioned with erudite research, partly because, as Shakespeare showed, it lent itself easily to political abuses. Some church leaders believed either that learning was vain and led to intellectual arrogance, or that people so well trained in judging early medieval charters might turn their attentions to the historians of early Christianity or to Sacred Scripture itself. In the eighteenth century, erudite research came under attack from the secular intellectuals of the radical Enlightenment as well; but one who acknowledged his debt to the antiquarians was Edward Gibbon, who confessed on several occasions in his *History* that he could not have found his way through the mazes of late antiquity and the early Middle Ages but for them.

The age of Valla and Pico was an age of extremes. Neoplatonic mysticism coexisted with hardheaded rationalism, with the ambitious attempt to measure and understand the physical universe. In the hundred years that followed, the most dramatic expression of the impulse to measure, quantify, and control was the series of discoveries and conquests that began with the Portuguese sailors of the mid-fifteenth century and reached its first culmination in the voyages of Columbus and the Spanish discovery and conquest of Mexico in 1519–21. This territorial expansion gathered the strands of the Old West in an explosion of courage and violence, generosity and exploitation. The era of expansion was the era of the last attempt at imperial universalism in Europe. It was also the eruption, beyond Europe, of a combination of energies, derived from the Germanic hero, the Christianized idea of holy war, the sublimation of doomed passion, and the universal motivator of all conquest from ancient Assyria on, *auri sacra fames*, the "demonic hunger for gold."[45] That eruption, however, was crucially enabled by the calculating and quantifying impulse that was itself one expression of the old synthesis.

Another enabling factor was the demographic recovery of the West after the middle of the fifteenth century. Although epidemics continued to recur throughout the sixteenth and seventeenth centuries, their virulence declined after around 1450, and by 1500 the population of Europe was again rising. A rapidly growing population, here as elsewhere, was a young population, and a young population, a flat demographic pyramid, was always part of the recipe for social unrest, political and cultural radicalism, and war. So it was in the sixteenth century, when, for the last time, an emperor, Charles V, made a bid for the universal monarchy of the West, when that emperor's subjects conquered and destroyed the Mexican and Inca cultures, and when the Protestant Reformation and the later Renaissance shifted the rudder of Western civilization from the path laid out by the old synthesis to a new path. Where this new path led, few dared say. The Enlightenment, emphasizing the quantifying impulse and giving it a secular twist, provided one answer: it was the path of reason, democracy, and economic development, the path that, until the last third of the twentieth century, defined the modern West. But even within the Enlightenment, as we shall see, two opposed spirits struggled for mastery: a spirit of sceptical curiosity and respect for history, embodied in Montesquieu and his identification of freedom as the key principle of the West, and one of revolutionary radicalism and impatience, embodied in Rousseau, Voltaire, and those who sought justice and equality. The former spirit sought Western identity in history, the latter in universalism. This schism, which defined the dilemma of Western identity and the stakes of the battle to define it at the end of the twentieth century, still lay far to the future in the era of exploration.

"Charles the Fifth, by the grace of God Roman emperor, perpetual enlarger of the empire, king in Germany, Castile, Aragon, Leon, both Sicilies, Jerusalem, Hungary, Dalmatia, Croatia, Navarre, Granada, Toledo, Valencia, Galicia, Mallorca, Seville, Sardinia, Cordoba, Corsica, Genoa, Algarve, Algeciras, Gibraltar, the Canary and Indian Islands, the mainlands across the Ocean Sea, etc., archduke of Austria, duke of Burgundy, Lorraine, Brabant, Styria, Carinthia, Carniola, Limburg, Lützenburg, Geldern, Calabria, Athens, Neopatras, and Württemberg, etc., count of Habsburg, Flanders, Tirol, Goricia, Barcelona, Artois, Burgundy, count palatine of Hainault, Holland, Zeeland, Pfirdt, Kyburg, Namur, Roussillon, Ceretano and Zutphen, lantgrave of Alsace, margrave of Burgau, Oristani, Gotiani, Holy Roman Imperial prince of Swabia, Catalonia, Asturias, etc., master of Frisia, of the Wendish March, of Portenau, Biscay, Molina, Salins, Tripoli, Malines, etc."—this was the imposing titulature inherited and displayed by the man elected master of the empire in 1519 in an unusually contested election. His grandfather, Maximilian, the "last of the knights," succeeded his own father as head of the house of Habsburg and king in 1495. The wars that ravaged Italy starting in 1494 made it impossible for him to contemplate an expedition to Rome to be crowned emperor. Even though the emperors had for centuries been German kings and princes, the legacy of Rome and the idea of empire were so powerful that it remained inconceivable that an emperor could be crowned in any other way than by the pope and anywhere but in Rome. Maximilian's actual power was no less than his father's; in fact it was somewhat greater because he was a better manager of his inherited lands and a better administrator of the complex machinery that the empire had become. Yet, in deference to that element of the ancient bargain that said that the electors could nominate an emperor, but only the pope could confirm the choice, he always called himself "Roman emperor-elect," never plain emperor.

Maximilian was brilliantly lucky in his dynastic policy, which was driven by two goals: expand the wealth and power of the house of Habsburg and contain France. He married the heiress of the dukes of Burgundy, adding a claim to large parts of France and the Low Countries to his other titles. His son and heir to his expanding rights and territories, Philip the Handsome, married Juana, daughter of Ferdinand of Castile and Isabella of Aragon. Within a few years of their marriage her siblings were all dead and she, like Philip, was the sole heiress to several kingdoms. Philip soon died, in 1506, and Juana became insane—"la Loca"—but not before the two had, in 1500, engendered Charles, the scion and heir of two mighty conglomerations of power, prestige, and influence: the German and the Spanish monarchies.

Charles, who since 1506 was duke of Burgundy and since 1516 king of Spain, was the likely but not certain choice of the seven electors. Francis, king of France, was another serious candidate, and although no Frenchman had been emperor since the ninth century, when the French were not yet French but still western Franks, his prospects were not insignificant, since several of the electors were concerned at the rising Habsburg power. Giving the empire to a different family for a change might not be a bad idea. A French emperor, however, would have meant a strategic revolution. The emerging Spanish, Burgundian, and German encirclement of France, incarnated in the person of the young king and duke Charles, would have been reversed, as French power allied with the resources of the empire formed a geopolitical bloc across western and central Europe. Spain, instead of being linked to a great empire, would have remained in remote isolation, with unimaginable consequences for the history both of Europe and of the Americas.

Both Charles and Francis lobbied the electors in eloquent statements prepared by the most skilled rhetoricians available. Charles based his application on the merits of his house as a loyal German dynasty, and asked for election "not for his own advantage, but purely for the love and fealty [he] bears to the honor and welfare of holy Christendom, the Roman Empire, and the German nation, considering that the holy Empire was founded to support the Christian faith, that its rule, honor, and dignity were brought to the German nation by [his] German ancestors by their deeds of knightly valor and much bloodshed and maintained in that nation for 700 years, and that thereby the German nation kept its liberty." In this imperial vision, Charlemagne, as the first emperor of the German nation, received the *translatio imperii*, the transfer of the one and only fourth world empire, from the heretical and unworthy Greeks. The real Charlemagne was a Frank and the German nation did not exist for 300 years after his time, but that was unknown in 1519, when Charles of Spain flattered his electors by saying that "the Empire, from the time of its transfer, has been dedicated solely to the keeping of the German nation and that of your princely graces."

Where Charles offered national flattery, Francis suggested that the matter of "granting the rule of the whole world" was such a serious affair that one should consider not nationality but quality. Charles was young and vacillating; he, Francis, offered the virtues of the greatest of the ancient Roman emperors, in particular the valor and resources necessary to oppose the Turkish power that threatened to overwhelm Europe.[46] Thanks in part to lavish bribes and campaign spending, financed by the Fugger house of bankers and merchants in Augsburg, Charles defeated his rivals and received the empire, which had been known officially since 1512 as the Holy Roman Empire of the German Nation. Charles had to accept a capitulation, a list of guarantees limiting his power. He had, for example, to promise to include the estates of the empire in the government. The estates were all the people, such as bishops, dukes, or counts, or entities, such as free cities, whose territories constituted the empire, and who had no superior between themselves and the emperor. In the constitutional law of the time, the estates, together with the emperor, were the empire; neither could govern legitimately without the other. Charles had also to promise to appoint only Germans to senior posts, to protect the estates against papal interference, and to renounce any hereditary claim to the empire for his relatives.

Charles sought election as a German, but, once elected, he governed as though he intended and hoped to become a world ruler as he believed his namesake, Charlemagne, had been. Shortly after his election, his closest adviser, Gattinara, wrote him a confidential memorandum, arguing in words borrowed from Dante's *De Monarchia* that "God the creator has shown you the grace of raising your dignity over all Christian kings and princes by making you the greatest emperor and king since the division of the Empire of Charlemagne, your predecessor, and by setting you on the path of the rightful monarchy of the world, so that the whole circle of the earth should be united under one shepherd." The emperor, not the pope, was the driving force in Gattinara's version of the ancient bargain. "Pray God," he advised the young emperor, for grace and understanding, so that Charles might exercise his office "in promoting all Christendom, so that with the help and aid of the holy apostolic see you may attain the benefit of universal peace, which cannot be achieved in any other way than by the imperial monarchy."[47] Charles took every part of this seriously. He was the last of the medieval imperial universalists, but he added to ancient claims a resource base that far exceeded what was available to the Frankish or German emperors before him. Unlike them, he controlled Spain, and Spain controlled the New World.

Charles's lifelong purpose, however, was not exploration or overseas conquest, but to put an end to the seven-hundred-year debate between church and empire by establishing a universal empire in Europe and restoring Christian unity. The struggle of the emperor Charles V with the popes in the 1520s in retrospect seemed futile for both parties, for both were being overtaken by events they could neither control nor understand: the Reformation, the opening of the world to exploration, exploitation, and colonization, and the rise of national states—of Christian ethnicity in political form—that made the old bargain of church and empire increasingly irrelevant for European and Western political and cultural life.

Charles was king of Spain, emperor-elect of the Holy Roman Empire, duke of Burgundy, and ruler of a number of other minor principalities in western Europe. He was young, ambitious, and orthodox. In 1521, he declared Martin Luther a traitor to the empire at the Diet of Worms, because the monk from Wittenberg would not retract his theological opinion that the pope was in error and that the Church of Rome was the harlot of Babylon. Charles expected praise and recognition from the pope; at the very least, he expected the pope to crown him in Rome, as tradition demanded, and to accept him publicly as the defender of Catholic faith in a Europe ridden with error and heresy.

The popes were not up to it. The papacy in the early sixteenth century was the patron of art and scholarship, but morally and doctrinally it was in one of its bad patches, not as bad as the tenth century but within hailing distance. Times had changed, and the emperor could no longer march to Rome and clean up the papacy's Augean stables. The papacy was too strong and too well entrenched for that. It needed reform but had become too powerful, too well organized, and too bureaucratically inert for any outsider to impose change. Moreover, the popes were politically allied to the kings of France and to Italian princes hostile to the emperor. This was an old story: whenever the popes felt the German emperors were becoming too powerful, they had, since the thirteenth century, leaned toward France. In a sense, this French connection was merely the latest incarnation of Stephen II's journey to Gaul in 756. That journey had ultimately led to the western Empire of the Franks. Since the tenth century, the western empire had belonged to the Germans. From then on, the connection with France was no longer the same thing as a connection with the empire. This gave the popes geopolitical options. It also confused the politics of Europe, contributed to Franco-imperial or Franco-German rivalry, and stimulated competition from other embryonic national states.

Charles V became impatient and worried; he was an emperor and the head of the Habsburg dynasty, and he did not want to see French power grow. His notion of a balance of power in Europe was a pyramid with him at the head and the other kings obediently arranged on the lower steps, with the pope hovering in the background. This notion, in the sixteenth century, was several hundred years out of date. The West had moved on.

Charles waited, and the pope, Clement VII, dithered. In the end, Charles sent an army to Italy which marched on Rome, captured Rome, and sacked Rome worse than the city had been sacked since Alaric and the Visigoths in 410. The sack of 1527 was worse, for Rome in 1527 was a richer, more beautiful, and more fragile city than in 410. One would think that this expedition would make the popes the enemies of the Habsburgs forever. Not so. In 1530 the pope crowned Charles emperor of the Romans—the last such coronation—and confirmed his role as the last defender of the Catholic religion against the pullulating heretics.

Charles V and Clement VII fought against the background of a Europe that, by expanding across the oceans, was outgrowing Europe and, by conquest, conversion, and colonization, becoming the West. When they were young, the Old, or in Three Age terms, the medieval, West still existed. When they died, it had gone beyond recall.

The New World was not yet the factor it later became in Charles's thinking at his election or in Gattinara's description of the obligations and power due to Charles as universal monarch and peacemaker. It was not until 1520 that the first letter of Hernán Cortés arrived from Mexico, containing the first serious indication that the American mainland was a vast territory full of people to conquer and convert and, possibly, of treasure to exploit. Later in the century, Mexican silver, according to some historians, ruined the Spanish economy by producing inflation, undermining crafts and agriculture, and creating a class of military and civilian parasites that could not be sustained except by the unreliable and varying infusions of silver. But that was far in the future in the 1520s, when the conquest of New Spain offered Charles V a new empire with which to bolster his claim to universal dominion and his resources in the geopolitical battle for Europe. The New World empire made that battle global, for the winner, if there was one, would rule not merely Europe, but what people not long after started to call the West.

The Spanish claims to America, which Charles inherited, rested on the papal bulls issued in 1493, when Christopher Columbus returned with the information that there was land across the Atlantic. He misidentified these lands as parts of Asia, but that only made the bulls more urgent, for the pope knew that the Portuguese were exploring the coasts of Africa and that they hoped to reach Asia by sailing south and east. Inevitably, if Columbus had found Asia across the Atlantic, Spanish and Portuguese explorers would clash. To avoid conflict, the pope granted Ferdinand and Isabella, Columbus's Spanish sponsors, the right to occupy such lands as they might discover on the westward path. By 1504 at the latest, when Amerigo Vespucci published an account of the voyages that forever attached his name to the new continents, curious Europeans knew that America was not Asia.

The postmodern and multiculturalist antinarratives condemned the conquest of Mexico more than any other event in Western history. Such condemnation expressed a logical confusion, since the antinarratives were explicitly relativist and asserted that moral judgments were illegitimate. History, they said, could not be constructed as a Grand Narrative, and people of any age, place, and culture should be judged in their own terms and not in others. The antinarratives violated both these premises and adopted a primitive moralism, of the kind they denounced when it was used in favor of the West, in blaming the conquistadores for destroying Mexican culture and introducing the diseases that, in a single generation after the conquest, killed, by most estimates, about ninety percent of the native American population.

These illogical but vehement condemnations created an impression that the conquest had hitherto been admired and praised as evidence of Western religious, cultural, technological, and military superiority. This was not true. The Grand Narrative, written by North American Protestants and Jews, and not by Spanish Catholics, labeled the conquest a necessary disaster, necessary for the rise of the modern West and its heartland, the United States, but a disaster for its victims. In fact, pity for the Indians and denunciations of Spanish cruelty and greed were much older than the Grand Narrative. Michel de Montaigne in the 1560s anticipated the 1992 denunciation of the "conquest of paradise" by American leftists when he contrasted what he described as the innocent Golden Age of the Indians with its destruction at the hands of the violent and boorish Europeans: "I feere that by our contagion, we shall have directly furthered his [the Indian's] declination, and hastened his ruine . . . so many goodly citties ransacked and razed; so many nations destroyed and made desolate; so infinite millions of harmlesse people of all sexes, states and ages, massacred, ravaged and put to the sword."[48]

The regulations of the Spanish crown for the government of New Spain repeatedly demanded fair treatment of the Indians. This attitude was as old as the discoveries themselves. In 1494 Columbus, whose own image of the Indians had become harsher over the preceding year, suggested that the ships that brought cattle from Europe to the New World should bring Indians as slaves back to Europe, at least until the explorers discovered the gold for which they were hoping. Isabella and Ferdinand objected; they preferred tax-paying subjects to slaves. Columbus returned to the idea as governor of Hispaniola in 1498, when, still short of gold, he proposed to compensate the Spaniards who came to settle in Hispaniola with native slaves whom the settlers could then sell in Spain, thereby deriving some financial advantage from coming to the Caribbean. In 1530, Charles V, in a formal order, forbade settlers from enslaving Indians under any circumstances, and from "keeping any Indian in slavery on the pretext that he was acquired in a just war, by repurchase, purchase, or barter, or under any designation or pretext whatever, including those Indians whom the natives of these islands and these continental lands themselves hold to be slaves." The popes agreed: "The Indians, being true men . . . cannot in any way be deprived of their liberty or of their belongings."[49]

Against such decrees and intentions stood the conquistadores themselves and those whom Montaigne denounced for bringing "contagion" and "declination" to the hapless natives. Many of them were not interested in philosophical arguments about whether the Indians were fully human or not, but in land, power, gold, and conversion, not necessarily in that order. Bernal Diaz, who, as an old man, wrote his memoirs of the conquest of Mexico in 1519–21, described his goals and those of his fellows as "the service of God and of His Majesty, and to give light to those who sat in darkness, and also to acquire that wealth which most men covet."[50] Three basic motives for the "spirit of conquest" as it manifested itself in the discoveries explained much of why decrees from distant Europe did not always produce humane behavior by the conquistadores and settlers: lust for power, hunger for gold, and religious commitment.

The imperial and papal decrees defending the rights of the Indians and denouncing the cruel behavior of the settlers revealed two sides of an argument that split the West then and that returned, in milder form, in the aftermath of the Grand Narrative at the end of the twentieth century. The argument, in the sixteenth century, was this: was there a single human race and human nature such that anyone who belonged to it had certain rights, virtues, and qualities that no one could take away and no one rightfully deny? Or were there, as Aristotle had taught, two kinds of human being: one free by nature, and one a slave by nature? The argument in the late twentieth century was the argument between classical liberalism on the one hand and multiculturalism or postmodern liberalism on the other. The former insisted that human nature was uniform, that all people deserved the same rights, and that some social arrangements were better suited to human beings, who all shared the same basic traits, than others. The latter modernized Aristotle and divided humankind not into natural slaves and those free by nature, but into ethnic, racial, and national communities each with its own norms, identity, and legitimacy, none of which were commensurable with the others.

The settlers, even allowing for exaggerations, killed and massacred to a degree that astonished and appalled many contemporaries in what was not, by modern standards, a sentimental or pacific age. In 1519, a group of Dominican friars submitted a report on events they had witnessed on the Caribbean islands under Spanish rule to the Spanish crown. This, the earliest catalogue of atrocities by settlers, mentioned, for example, "some Christians who met an Indian woman who was carrying an infant whom she was nursing. As the dog that was with them was hungry, they tore the child from its mother's arms and threw it alive to the dog, which began to tear it to pieces before the mother's eyes." In 1550, the bishop of Yucatán, Diego de Landa, who was not particularly friendly to the Indians, reported that "the Spaniards committed unheard-of cruelties, severing the hands, the arms, the legs, and the breasts of women, throwing them into deep lakes, and beating the children with sticks because they were not walking as fast as their mothers. And if those whom they were bringing along with collars round their necks fell ill or could not move as quickly as their companions, they would cut their heads off in order not to stop the column and untie them."[51] Such cruelties were not as extraordinary as these reports implied; history before and after offered many parallels. They did, however, strike many contemporaries as unusual and arbitrary. The Aristotelian notion that some people were born to be slaves might be a partial explanation, but it was incomplete, because a rational slave owner did not destroy his property. Something else was at work that also helped to explain why Columbus failed to conquer a kingdom while Cortés succeeded.

Columbus and Cortés shared two ambitions: to win land and riches, and convert the heathen. Columbus was idealistic and stubborn. His idealism pushed him to assemble his original expedition in 1492, to sail despite its shortcomings, and to continue sailing when others gave up hope of finding land. It also convinced him that he was seeing Asia long after others decided that what he had found was not the easternmost edge of Asia but a new continent. His obstinacy sustained his energy and courage, but was also part of an outlook that was eager to find the new only in order to name, classify, and interpret it according to a precise schema. Columbus was an extreme example of the calculating, quantifying Westerner. He sailed to find new lands to conquer and to convert, and was prepared to discover the unexpected. But when he actually met the unexpected, it had to fit his preconceived schema. If the reality did not match his first identification of it, he was disappointed. For example, at first he saw the natives as good and generous, as people who had only recently left the state of original innocence. "To such a degree are they devoid of artifice and generous with what they own that no one would believe it who had not seen them," he wrote in a letter in early 1493.[52] Such innocent people were, he thought, ideal candidates for conversion. Within a year, he was calling the same people cunning and devious and recommending that they be enslaved. Because he could not see the reality he encountered in its own terms, Columbus remained a prisoner of his elaborate code of interpretation of the world around him. He could not make the world conform to his ambitions, which were to conquer and spread the faith.

Cortés, by contrast, conquered the Aztec Empire of Mexico with a few hundred companions. He was able to do so not only because he was brave, which he was, or had superior equipment, which he had, although the equipment was often unusable. Cortés won because, unlike Columbus, he was able to use language and communication to make the world conform. Conversely, the Aztecs lost because, to use their language, the gods stopped speaking to them. Like Columbus, they had a complicated code for interpreting the world, which was made up of divine messages. But they had no code for understanding a world where the fundamentally unexpected happened and where the key to success was the ability to communicate successfully not with the gods but with other human beings. The unexpected was not supposed to happen; if it did happen, they tried to ignore it, as Montezuma, the Aztec king, tried to ignore Cortés and his men. At first he refused to allow Cortés to come to him. He sent repeated envoys to the Spaniards telling them to stay away, meanwhile increasing the rate of human sacrifices to obtain advice from the gods of war and the underworld, Tezcatlipoca and Huitzilopochtli. Montezuma wanted the gods to tell him what to do about the Spaniards, but they remained silent, despite the sacrifices, until Cortés showed up in Tenochtitlán and ultimately destroyed his empire.

Cortés did not listen to gods but to what people told him, and he in turn dosed his messages to produce the desired response. Bernal Diaz reported a striking example of this from the early stages of the march up country from Vera Cruz to the valley of Mexico. At the town of Cempoala, Cortés and his men found welcome from the local tribe, the Totonacs, and their chief, whom Diaz called "the fat *cacique*," who hoped that the Spaniards would help him rebel against the Aztecs. The Cempoalans were recently conquered and resented having to pay tribute to Mexico. With the help of his interpreter, Doña Marina, Cortés offered to help the Totonacs. While these talks were taking place, five of Montezuma's tax gatherers arrived in Cempoala. Diaz continued:

> As soon as they had dined, the tax-gatherers sent for the fat *cacique* and the other chiefs and scolded them for having entertained us in their villages, since now they would have to meet and deal with us, which would not please their lord Montezuma. For without his permission and instructions they should neither have received us nor given us golden jewels. They continued to reproach the fat *cacique* and his nobles for their actions, and ordered them to provide twenty Indians, male and female, as a peace-offering to their gods for the wrong that had been done.

Cortés, being told what the tax-gatherers said, ordered the Totonacs to arrest them and to send messages to all the villages of the tribe saying that the Totonacs were now free of Aztec rule and would cease to pay tribute. The Totonacs obeyed, but they were amazed at what Cortés had done.

> The act they had witnessed was so astonishing and of such importance to them that they said no human beings dared to do such a thing, and it must be the work of *teules*. Therefore from that moment they called us *teules*, which means gods or demons.
>
> To return to the prisoners, all the *caciques* were of the opinion that they ought to be sacrificed, so that none could return to Mexico to tell the tale.

This seemed rational in both Indian and Spanish terms. Imprisoning the Aztec officials was a hostile act that seemed to declare that Cortés was joining the enemies of the Aztecs. But Cortés had a devious plan.

> Cortés said that they should not be killed, and that he would take charge of them. He set a guard over them, and at midnight summoned the soldiers of this guard to instruct them: "Choose the two prisoners that seem to you the most intelligent, and loose them. Then bring them to my quarters. But do not let any of the village Indians see what you are doing." When the prisoners were brought before him, he asked them, through our interpreters, why they were prisoners and from what country they came, as if he knew nothing of the matter. They answered that the *caciques* of Cempoala had arrested them, with the aid of their followers and ours, and had held them prisoner. Cortés replied that he knew nothing about this and was very sorry. He ordered food

to be brought to them, and talked to them in a very friendly way. He then told them to return at once to their lord Montezuma and tell him that we were all his good friends and entirely at his service.

The Spaniards then released the two prisoners. The next morning, the Totonacs were naturally terrified, thinking that the two Mexicans had escaped and would now bring vengeance on Cempoala for their imprisonment.

The *caciques* of this village and of Cempoala and all the Totonac dignitaries who had assembled asked Cortes what was to be done, for all the forces of Mexico and of the great Montezuma would descend upon them, and they could not possibly escape death or destruction.

Cortes replied with a most cheerful smile that he and his brothers who were with him would defend them and kill anyone who tried to harm them; and the *caciques* and their villagers one and all promised to stand by us, to obey any orders we might give them, and to join their forces with ours against Montezuma and his allies. Then in the presence of Diego de Godoy the notary they took the oath of obedience to His Majesty.[53]

A classic Machiavellian display of how to win friends and influence people. Cortés spoke not to describe the world or the divine messages found in it, but to achieve a practical goal. His understanding of the new world in which he found himself was more flexible than that of Columbus because it accepted surprise and the unexpected, always interpreting it in accordance with his desired purpose. Cortés represented the militarily and psychologically effective variant of the measuring, controlling impulse; he wanted to categorize and quantify not to satisfy an aesthetic or philosophical need, but to conquer and rule. Unfortunately for him, he was so good at this that he aroused fear and suspicion in Spain, among those who thought that a man so gifted in the skills of manipulation and conquest was not likely to become a submissive administrator. So, while he remained honored for his achievement in the conquest, he never became the ruler of New Spain.

The Spaniards won because their kind of communication, from person to person, was more effective in changing the world than Mexican communication, which went from gods to men and consisted, on the human side, in reading the signs to be found in the world in order to detect the messages of the gods. Mexican culture, defined by ritual, produced a different kind of violence than the society of the conquistadores, defined by improvisation. The Mexicans sought to read the world as a code; the Spaniards sought to understand context. Sometimes the Mexican code told them to sacrifice 80,400 prisoners to dedicate a new temple. The code of sacrifice had specific rules. One could not sacrifice someone from a distant tribe, for he would be indigestible to the gods. Nor could one sacrifice someone from the same town as oneself. Prisoners from neighboring tribes were the best solution. By being made prisoners and kept for a while, they were partially assimilated, but never so much as to become ineligible for sacrifice. Brave warriors were a more valuable sacrifice, more pleasing to the gods, than undistinguished people.

The Spanish atrocities, by contrast, seemed to follow no code, no reason, not even a cruel one. They were not religious or ritual murder, but lawless murders, murders at the margin of normal behavior. They represented a "civilization of massacre" contrasted to the Mexican "civilization of sacrifice." Massacres were anarchic phenomena, evidence of weak social bonds, occurring by preference in remote locations. The victims of massacres were anonymous and casual; their identity was irrelevant, whereas for the Aztecs the identity of sacrificial victims was highly relevant. Massacres were "atheistic murders," and the murderers were not men who had fallen back to a bestial condition, but modern men who, far from home, had shaken off the shackles of religious and social sanction and realized that, suddenly, "everything was permitted."[54]

The sharpest critic of the Spanish massacres was the Dominican friar Bartolomé de Las Casas, who after the conquest was bishop of Chiapas. He published several works in the 1530s and 1540s protesting ill-treatment of Indians on the grounds that such treatment violated "natural law and custom and the rights of men." Las Casas was making an explicitly Christian argument that the Indians, like all human beings, were created in God's image and hence capable of and entitled to conversion. In 1520, in a speech in front of Charles V, Las Casas stated that "our Christian religion is equally suited to all nations of the world, and it is open to all in the same manner; and, depriving no one of his liberty or sovereignty, it places no one in a condition of servitude and makes no distinction between free men and those who are slaves by nature."[55] Thirty-one years later, in a five-day disputation in Salamanca with the humanist and classicist Juan Gines de Sepúlveda, Las Casas had subtly changed his mind. He now argued that the Indians deserved better treatment not because they were potentially Christian and because they were not, as the Aristotelians claimed, natural slaves, but because their society and customs, however horrible, expressed a desire for the good.

Sepúlveda had, on the basis of his classical learning, constructed a defense of colonial conquest of peoples who were by nature inferior. The Indians, he determined, were by nature submissive; they committed the evil acts of cannibalism and mass human sacrifice; they were ignorant of Christianity. These points singly and together justified the war of conquest. Las Casas, in 1551, decided to attack Sepúlveda's argument not at its weakest point, the Aristotelian claim that the Indians were by nature subordinate, but at its strongest point: the claim that any means available were justified in putting a stop to the absolute evil of mass human sacrifices. Las Casas began by noting that while it was true that cannibalism and human sacrifice were bad in themselves, that did not necessarily entitle one to go to war to stop them, for such a war might be a worse evil than the evil it was supposed to remedy. He then claimed that, for the Aztecs, human sacrifice was the law of the land, and all people were required, by natural justice, to obey the law of their land.

Las Casas then entered upon an anthropological and philosophical argument that was sensational for its time. He concluded that using force to stop human sacrifice was wrong. He used two avenues to reach that conclusion. The first was that several instances in the Scriptures proved that God did not necessarily find human sacrifice detestable. Nor was cannibalism unheard of among Europeans, in case of dire necessity. The second avenue of argument was the more elaborate. This consisted in saying that the Indians, like all human beings, had an inborn and instinctive sense of God. All people, granted this inborn sense of a supreme power, worshipped this supreme power according to their manner and devotion. The greatest gift one could make to the supreme power was the gift of life:

> The most powerful manner of worshipping God is to offer him a sacrifice. This is the only act by which we show him to whom it is offered that we are his subjects, who are under obligation to him. Further, nature teaches us that it is right to sacrifice to God, whose debtors we are for many reasons, precious and excellent things, because of the excellence of his power. Now according to human judgment and truth, nothing in nature is greater or more precious than human life, the human being himself. That is why nature herself teaches and instructs those who have neither the faith, nor grace, nor doctrine, those who live by natural understanding alone, that without any positive law to the contrary they are bound to sacrifice human victims to the true God or to the false god whom they consider to be true, so that by offering him a supremely precious thing they can express their gratitude for the many favors they have received.[56]

Few Enlightenment thinkers were as radical as the Dominican friar who concluded from Christian premises that human sacrifice had noble and worthy religious causes and that the Spaniards had no right to eradicate it by force, just as they had no right to impose themselves on the Indians other than by free and mutual agreement.

Las Casas won the debate although his victory did little to help the Indians. It was nevertheless symbolic of the failure of Charles V's bid for universal empire that the ideology of conquest and just war in defense of Spanish interests, as stated by Sepúlveda, failed to convince those asked to judge the debate in 1551. Charles V lost the ideological battle at Salamanca as he had already lost the political battle in Europe, to the Protestants and to France. His universalism was modern in its global reach but anachronistic in its medieval imperialism. In claiming universal monarchy and aiming at world government, he alarmed not only France, his major rival in Europe, but also many of the estates within the empire who might have supported him against the rebellious Protestants, who by the end of Charles's reign in the mid-1550s represented half the population of the empire. While Cortés was improvising his way to the conquest of Mexico, Martin Luther and others had fatally undermined the world-emperor's ambitions in Europe.

CHAPTER SEVEN

From Christendom to Civilization

in societies where several govern . . . the greater surety of property . . . leads to enterprise; and, because men are secure in what they acquire, they dare to risk it to acquire more; the risk they run affects only their means of acquisition; and they expect much of their fortune . . . in a nation which is under despotism, people work rather to hold than to buy. In a free nation, people work rather to buy than to hold

—Montesquieu

Multitudes of people, necessity, and liberty have begotten commerce

—David Hume

In the story told by the Grand Narrative, the New West was the true West, and it emerged from the Old in a series of radical breaks echelonned through the centuries of European and North American history from around 1500 to 1850. At the beginning of this period, Columbus and Vasco da Gama launched European expansion, while back in Europe, in the heartland of the Renaissance, Pico della Mirandola exalted human dignity and reason, and Niccolò Machiavelli sought in history and political action, rather than in religion and moral philosophy, lessons for statesmen and princes who wanted to know how to master Fortune rather than be mastered by her. The Renaissance, on this reading, introduced the ideal of civic human-ism—the principle that the purpose of political action was to establish and defend a just and free society for its own sake, and not as part of a journey to God and eternal life. Taken together, as products of the same era of energy and expansion, the overseas discoveries and civic humanism began the found-ing of the New West as a dynamic, secular civilization of potentially universal scope, for justice and liberty were not inherently limited to any one region of the globe, just as the rational approach to knowledge that made expansion possible was not available only to members of the culture that first applied it in a systematic way. In the phraseology of the Enlightenment, Europe moved from Christendom, which was particular, to civilization, which was universal.

The idea that the New West was a cumulative series of breaks, resulting in a civilization that was incommensurate with all that went before as well as with all other civilizations in the world, was not invented by the Grand Nar-rative, but was part of its intellectual heritage. Winckelmann and Goethe turned to the Greeks to find the standard of absolute perfection and used them to establish models for the future to replace the exhausted symbols of Christendom. Although they ostensibly turned to the past, it was the future they wanted to build: a future liberated from the metaphysical and moral shackles of a thousand years. Their cult of Greece had a message for the pres-ent, which later became the Grand Narrative's Greek model, its notion that the sources of identity of the modern, future-oriented, and liberal West were to be found not in the Old West but in ancient Greece.

The most important source of the Grand Narrative's version of Western identity was, however, not Winckelmann and Goethe, but the Enlighten-ment itself, the intellectual, psychological, and philosophical movement of the eighteenth century that founded modernity, or the West, as progressive, forward-looking, rational, secular, and individualist. In particular, the En-lightenment established the true Western identity as distinct from and op-posed to its past. Defined as the new, the rational, and the worldly, Western identity in this Enlightenment version was also universal, for it belonged equally to all.

In fact, the Enlightenment included more than one definition of Western identity. The one that survived to shape both the centrist liberal Grand Nar-rative and its radical liberal successors was secular and universalist. But the Enlightenment also included a definition of Western identity that sought that identity in history—in the Old West, as well as in the transitions to the New. Adherents of both definitions saw the essence of the West as freedom, but whereas radicals and progressives saw freedom as a political task, something to be constructed according to conscious goals, the sceptics saw freedom rather as something inherent in Western history. To the radicals of the Enlightenment and their revolutionary, Marxist, feminist, and multiculturalist successors, freedom was to be established by denying an imperfect or evil past and enforcing a perfect future. To the sceptics, freedom was a manifestation of that very past. The intellectual and political task of the present was therefore not to break with the past, but to understand the conditions that permitted freedom to grow.

The Grand Narrative borrowed from both aspects of the Enlightenment, but since its fundamental approach—the Greek model—was ahistorical, it obscured its own access to those parts of Western history that could explain the growth of freedom. Throughout its intellectual hegemony, from the 1920s to the 1960s, it was always tempted to see freedom as the radical Enlightenment defined it, as a break with the past, something to be created by political will. This weakness was one reason that the Grand Narrative, and the centrist liberalism on which it rested, so easily succumbed to the radical and multicultural antinarratives of the late twentieth century. At century's end, many of those who still preached the Grand Narrative had merged with the radical agenda and were advocating a postliberal universalism that rejected the historical West in favor of an impossible, global humanism that was both individualistic and multicultural.[1]

To see the New West as a radical break, begun in the fifteenth and completed in the nineteenth century, was to deny that its roots lay deep in the Old. To progressives and radicals, the secular, rational freedom of modernity was inexplicable as a fruit of the past; it was the original creation of the bold spirits of the Enlightenment and the era of revolution. Such a definition ignored the triple legacy of Western freedom—from the Greeks through the Romans, from Christianity, and from the Germans. Of that legacy, the most controversial element was the second. That Christian freedom could be in any way responsible for the modern understanding of political and social liberty was abhorrent to those Enlightenment radicals for whom freedom was to be asserted against Christianity, against the censorship, ignorance, superstition, and irrationalism of a hierarchical church and its theological apparatus of justification. The whole point of modernity, for Voltaire and his many followers in the twentieth century, was that it had abandoned the particularism and narrow-mindedness of Christendom for the progressive universalism of civilization. Ironically, however, one of the most powerful analyses of how the New West emerged from the Old, that of the German sociologist Max Weber, agreed that the New was decisively different, yet argued that the essence of the New—rationalism, capitalism, and faith in progress—derived directly from the Christian essence of the Old.

Weber's case was that long-term economic growth, a phenomenon unique to the West until the twentieth century, depended on individual behavior that, at first sight, appeared irrational. Growth required capital, but the only way to accumulate capital was for many individuals to save rather than spend. People had to defer consumption to accumulate capital, and in the uncertain world of early modernity, the chances were that he who accumulated would not live to enjoy. Nevertheless, throughout Europe, starting in the later Middle Ages, people began to save and invest. What drove this irrational behavior, Weber argued, was two things: Christian asceticism and the early Protestant idea that the ability to make money was a sign of divine favor. The combination of these two ideas promoted capitalist behavior, the success of which proved divine favor, but also saving and accumulation, which followed from the asceticism that the Protestant denominations inherited from the monasteries of the early Middle Ages, where the commandment was "pray and work." But the monasteries had never been sources of sustained growth, for even though they accumulated vast capital, they did not make this capital available for investment, but used it on conspicuous religious consumption—churches, vestments, art, and libraries. It was the Protestant turn toward the secular realm that captured ascetic accumulation for capitalist ends.

Weber had part of the story right, though not all. He did, however, focus attention on the Protestant Reformation as the first and most decisive stage in the transformation of the West—the two others being the Enlightenment and the French Revolution. What, then, was the place of the Reformation in the evolution of Western identity?

The Reformation, which began in Germany around the time that Charles was elected emperor in 1519, was both easily predicted and utterly unpredictable. For centuries, reformers within the established church had called for a simpler religion, a return to early Christianity, more influence for the laity, less corruption, and a better fit between the morality preached and the morality practiced. The humanistic and classical scholarship of Lorenzo Valla and others stimulated interest in the early Christian theologians, the fathers of the church, and in the text of the New Testament itself. Philosophical currents of the fifteenth and early sixteenth centuries urged men to use practical reason to unmask and denounce hypocrisy, abuses, and metaphysical double-talk. Nationalism, especially in Germany, stimulated by the rediscovery of Tacitus's *Germania*, legitimated resentment at paying tithes to Rome and at the supposed exploitation by the Church of Rome of the pious Germans.[2] Finally, the spread of the printing press after 1450 and the rise in literacy urged many more people than before to read the Bible and the church fathers for themselves and to judge the discrepancy between the church they described and contemporary Holy Mother Church.[3]

All these factors indicated that an explosion might come and that the Church of Rome might find it difficult to retain its moral, economic, and cultural control in the manner to which her leaders had become accustomed since the thirteenth century. Gianfrancesco Pico della Mirandola, a God-fearing Florentine humanist and nephew of the author of the *Oration on the Dignity of Man*, warned Pope Leo X in 1516 that "if you fail to heal these wounds, I fear that God himself, whose place on earth you take, will not apply a gentle cure, but with fire and sword will cut off those diseased members and destroy them; and I believe that He has already clearly given signs of his future remedy."[4] Still, the explosion that actually happened was more powerful, extensive, and revolutionary than anyone expected. Although some sort of widespread, literary, humanistic, and national reform movement was in the cards, it was thanks to Martin Luther and John Calvin that it took the form it did, resulting by the 1520s in the religious and political division of the West, a division as radical and, in the event, vastly more bloody than the East-West division that split Europe from 1945 to 1989.

The Protestant claim was that faith and study, not sacraments and hierarchy, built the true church. The former showed the believer that he was saved despite his ineradicable sin; the latter, so the reformers, were vain attempts to guarantee salvation that could come only directly from God, not through any mediating practice or person. The claim went back to Martin Luther's famous realization, in his study in the tower of the Augustinian abbey of Wittenberg, that the justice of God was gracious, not vindictive. According to his own later and marvelously dramatized account, he was struggling with St. Paul's meaning in Romans 1:17, quoting Habakuk 2:4: "For the justice of God is revealed in it [the gospel], from faith to faith, as it is written, *The just man liveth by faith*":

> I hated this word "justice of God," for by the usage and teaching of all the doctors I had learned to understand it philosophically, as a so-called formal or active justice, by which God is just and punishes the sinners and the unjust.

Although my life as a monk was irreproachable, I felt I was a sinner before God with a most uneasy conscience, and that I might not trust to appease Him by my effort of penitence. And so I did not love this just God who punished sinners, rather, I hated Him. Silently and powerfully, though maybe not blasphemously, I grumbled against God: "Is it not yet enough that the poor sinners, eternally damned by original sin, must labor under every kind of evil by the law of the Ten Commandments? Must God even in His good news add pain to pain and pour out His justice and His anger upon us in the gospel?". . .

Day and night I pondered until by God's mercy I discerned the connection in the wording, namely, "the justice of God is revealed in it [the gospel], as it is written, the just man liveth by faith." I then began to understand "the justice of God" as one by which the just person lives as by God's gift, that is, out of faith, and I realized that this was the meaning: by the gospel the passive justice of God is revealed, by which the merciful God justifies us through faith, as it is written, "the just man liveth by faith." Now I truly felt quite new-born and as though I had entered through open gates into Paradise itself.[5]

Luther's reading was not original; it was highly orthodox. But he thought it was new, and that made all the difference. The original "tower experience" probably took place in 1512. Luther concluded from it, as he explained, that "God justifies us through faith," but whereas Catholics understood this to mean justification in and through a community of faith—the church—which was itself divinely created, Luther saw justification as something given gratuitously by God to isolated individuals. This individualist reading moved him to his decisive conclusion, which he had reached by 1517, that the human will and the human person by themselves were wholly sinful, wholly corrupt; that their only hope of justification was through this free gift of God to the particular sinner. Any idea that an earthly community could mediate the gift or that the gift was to be understood as a gift to the community as well as to its members was, to him, abhorrent. In 1517, he was still willing, in his Ninety-Five Theses, to grant the pope a spiritual and pastoral primacy. By 1521, he concluded that the pope and the hierarchical church were not merely neutral but harmful, in that they prevented man from appreciating his complete nullity and sinfulness, his utter dependence on the gift of faith that alone could justify him. His conviction that he was only restating the truth of Christianity made him seem both arrogant and humble: "I do not pretend to be a saint, and am not arguing about my own life, but about the teaching of Christ," he said, quoting Matthew 10:34: "I came not to send peace, but the sword." And so, summoned by Charles V, the Holy Roman

Emperor, to defend his views before the assembled estates of the empire at Worms in 1521, Luther concluded his defense in the famous words:

> If I am not refuted by Scripture or clear evidence of reason—for I believe neither pope nor councils, since it is evident that they have often erred—I am bound only by the passages of Scripture I have quoted, and by my conscience, which is bound by the Word of God. I neither can nor will recant anything, for it is neither safe nor becoming to do anything contrary to conscience. I can do no other, here I stand, God help me. Amen.[6]

By the mid-1520s, Germany and Europe were divided, as Luther and his allies launched a religious, political, and social revolution. The Protestant claim that Christianity meant faith and study, and not the political Christendom geopolitically incarnated in the Church of Rome and the Holy Roman Empire, the two poles of the ancient bargain, had profound economic and political effects. It meant, for one thing, that the church should not be a landowner, an organization of magnates playing the game of power within the empire or within Europe. Grateful for this message, and convinced by Martin Luther's doctrinal arguments, princes across the continent confiscated church lands and issued ordinances arrogating education and social discipline to the prince and his officials and reducing the clergy to the role of teachers and preachers. "Schools are necessary," proclaimed Ottheinrich, count palatine in Heidelberg, for "providing good clergy, officials, and heads of household"; they therefore required close supervision. His *School Ordinance* of 1556 prescribed a detailed curriculum. Wednesdays and Saturdays, for example, "a lesson from Holy Scripture will be presented and explained. The schoolmasters shall, as part of the exposition, diligently set forth the grammar and distinctly tell the boys the one and actual meaning and not introduce foreign disputations."[7]

Luther's anxiety and theological struggles were part of a broad movement in the church to get back to basics. Many who did not follow him into open schism and defiance agreed that the Church of Rome drastically needed repair. Pope Hadrian VI launched what historians later came to call the Catholic Reformation when, in 1522, he had his legate (envoy) to Germany issue a confession of guilt: "We know that at this Holy See many abuses in the spiritual realm have occurred, commandments have been violated, and much has been wrong . . . We and the men of the Church have all 'gone aside,' we 'are become unprofitable together: there is none that doth good, no not one' (Psalm 13:3)." Hadrian VI was a sad man, as well he might be; he was some years too early for his call to have serious effect in his own church, and it was already too late to heal the split in Germany, which was fast spreading across Europe. Admitting that the head of the church, the papacy, was sick and had spread contagion to all her members, he promised "to expend all efforts to reform the papal curia [court] first, from which all the evil has gone out. And as corruption flowed thence to all below, so also from it shall healing and reformation issue to all." But it was "a very old disease, not simple, but various and manifold."[8] Therefore the cure must be careful and gradual.

It was not. In 1526, the army of the most Catholic emperor Charles V invaded Italy to meet the army of his mortal enemy, the most Catholic king of France. The popes supported France as a counterweight to the empire; ever since Charlemagne the popes had been anxious lest their partner in the grand bargain become too strong. Charles, therefore, was not too happy with the pope either. In the spring of 1527, the imperial army, unpaid and with the enemy at its back, decided to march on Rome. Many soldiers shared the Germanic national and anti-Roman ideology, although many of them were Catholic. Others wanted plunder, since they had not been paid. As described in the last chapter, the army captured and sacked Rome in May 1527. The *sacco di Roma* divided time just as the Reformation had divided space. It was a shock to all Christendom as nothing had been since the earlier sack of Rome by the Visigoths under Alaric in 410. As Alaric provoked Saint Augustine to create the idea of Christendom in his book *The City of God,* so the emperor's drunken and blasphemous mercenaries provoked the Catholic Reformation and put a sudden and shocking stop to Renaissance optimism and libertinism.

In 1530, the pope crowned Charles emperor in Bologna, the last imperial coronation in Italy. Allied again, the powers of the grand bargain began to reform their church, to mobilize energies against the Protestants, and to produce, by the 1560s, the well-oiled and efficient machine of propaganda and reconversion known to later historians as the Counter-Reformation Church. One result of this double process of reform was the wars of religion that raged in France from the 1560s to the 1590s and in the empire in the Thirty Years' War—conflicts that terminally wounded the prestige and power of the emperors and arranged the geopolitical map of Europe into the state system familiar to political theory and to history from the peace of Westphalia in 1648 to the end of World War II in 1945.

The religious and cultural division of Europe and of Europe's central nation, Germany, was the first crucial geopolitical fact of Western history in the centuries after 1520; by some measures, it remained central until 1990, when the most recent version of German division came to an end. During the centuries when the West was shifting from the old to the new triad of identity, the division of Europe, which was specially marked in Germany because it was a division within a nation and not between nations, produced a vacuum of power and energy at the physical heart of the European continent. The Enlightenment and the revolutionary era replaced religious conflict with political and ideological struggle, and the split, so bloody in the sixteenth and seventeenth centuries, appeared after 1789 rather as a split in literary and cultural temperaments.[9]

The second crucial geopolitical fact of Western identity was the rise, from the mid-sixteenth century on, of England and the Netherlands as the economic core region of the West. The Grand Narrative treated this, as it treated the Renaissance and the Reformation, as a development that shaped the future rather than as the result of long-term evolution. In fact, the conditions that stimulated economic development in England and Holland were not new in the sixteenth century, but had been slowly maturing for several centuries, and the dynamics of that earlier evolution provided a critical hint about what was wrong with the progressivist idea of the West.

Reducing Western identity to the New West meant seeing its critical economic ingredient, capitalism, as an exclusively modern phenomenon, something that emerged by lucky chance at some point after the Renaissance and Reformation. Capitalism, in that perspective, became one of the criteria that marked the New West off from its past as well as from other civilizations, one of the instruments of liberation and rational universalism, one of the ways by which the New West dissolved its own historical identity before going on to dissolve the historical identity of other cultures.

The real story of how capitalism—sustained economic development—got going in its core regions, England and Holland, is more complicated and demonstrates, once again, that the New West did not spring like Athena from the brow of Zeus, but was the slowly maturing fruit of practices, institutions, and cultural forms rooted deep in the Old West and the early medieval synthesis. The critical practices supporting the rise of capitalism were property rights and the incentives they gave individuals to act in ways that yielded both personal and social gain. People in all civilizations always sought material gain; the difference that began to distinguish the West from other cultures in the later Middle Ages was that such individual behavior began to have sustained social effects. That was the conundrum that needed to be explained by any economic history that looked beyond the progressivist image of the capitalist and rationalist New West as a recent and fortuitous creation.

Two theorists, Douglass North and Robert Thomas, proposed in 1973 that the secret of long-term growth was "effective organization" and the key to effective organization was "institutional arrangements and property rights that create an incentive to channel individual economic effort into activities that bring the private rate of return close to the social rate of return."[10] The social rate of return was the shared benefit that a given society derived from an activity; the private rate was how much the "economic unit"—individual, workshop, family, or other group—gained. In crude terms, the private rate was net profit.

In early medieval Europe, governments hardly existed, and where they did exist, had neither the interest nor the ability to encourage or protect innovation. Most economic activity took place on the land, within the feudal hierarchy of lord, tenant, subtenant, down to the actual worker of the land. The first breakthrough to higher productivity happened when European peasants moved to the three-field system, where a given plot of land was divided into three parts cultivated in rotation every year. Economic historians had long realized that this shift increased food production by almost half in the areas where it occurred and that it was a necessary precondition for the population growth of the high Middle Ages that accompanied the technological and commercial changes and the impulse to exploration that marked the beginning of Western ascendancy.

North and Thomas noted that the three-field system was introduced very slowly. If it was obviously better, why was it not more quickly adopted after it was first invented in northern France, probably in the tenth century? They pointed out that the three-field method yielded higher returns only where land was scarce and labor cheap, which did not happen until the thirteenth century in most areas. Where land was plentiful and labor relatively scarce, there was no incentive to produce more, because, in the barter economy of the feudal manor, no one could buy more anyway. Both values of the economic equation, supply and demand, had to rise at the same time. This did not begin to happen until two other conditions began to be fulfilled: the peasants had to be permitted to keep more of the fruits of their labor, so that they could buy more; and the early medieval economy of barter and tenancy had to change in the direction of markets and freehold.

Population growth in the eleventh through thirteenth centuries "created a foundation for the enormously expanded trade, stimulating specialization in production, extending the basis for commerce, reducing transactions costs and encouraging more use of the market mechanism to exploit special-ized resource endowments. Productivity obviously benefited."[11] This growth affected mainly the towns. It is true that thirteenth-century Europe had more and denser towns than ever before; the Low Countries and northern Italy, in particular, had more people living in towns than on the land, which was unprecedented in human history. Taken as a whole, most Europeans lived on the land, and here productivity did not increase. Instead, the popu-lation rose too fast for the food supply. Most peasants were tenants and had no incentive to improve agricultural productivity, as they would not retain enough of any benefits to make it worth while. Until about 1200, the way to increase food supply was to put new land under the plow, but by the thir-teenth century western Europe had little new land left that was worth till-ing. Given that productivity on existing land did not increase, per capita food supply stagnated. Peasant incomes, in kind and money, fell. Europe entered a "Malthusian trap," the condition described by Thomas Malthus in 1798 and assumed by him to be a law of social development, that popu-lation would always rise faster than the economic means to support it. Ac-cording to North and Thomas, Malthusian traps were not facts of nature. The economic means of supporting the population did not have to stagnate; if they did, it was because producers had no incentive to raise production and to innovate because they could not capture the gains for themselves. The private rate of return was too low, and in such conditions the social rate was irrelevant; too few people would act to maximize it. And the reason for that, North and Thomas concluded, was that property rights were too ill de-fined, too vague, and too much subject to arbitrary change to encourage people to innovate and trade.

Plague, deteriorating climate, wars, and other social crises brought stagna-tion for a century or more after the Black Death first struck Europe in 1348. By the later fifteenth century, a second wave of production growth and in-creasing demand began. This time, not only agricultural but craft production rose, and so did productivity and innovation. The reason was that govern-ments and lords were beginning to protect property rights not just in land but in methods and inventions. Some of them, notably the kings of England, discovered that it was in their interest to protect producers and inventors, be-cause by increasing the total wealth of the society such people also increased the king's own revenues and thereby the power of the state. Having felt their way toward this insight, the new monarchs began to grant protection to craftsmen, letting them keep some of their profits instead of expropriating them. Moreover, "differences in the performance of the economies of Western Europe between 1500 and 1700 was in the main due to the type of property rights created by the emerging states in response to their continuing fiscal crisis."[12] The needs of the state and in particular how states responded to those needs drove accumulation.

North and Thomas ended where Weber began; they explained not why Calvinism encouraged economic rationality and accumulation, but what social arrangements had to exist for accumulation to occur. That these arrangements emerged first in regions marked by Calvinism might be an accident or it might not. What was certain was that, in the Netherlands and later in England, "a fortunate conjunction occurred between the interests of the state and the interests of the progressive sector of society."[13] Markets in land, products, and capital developed under the protection of laws that protected property rights and the profits of innovation. This process was not inevitable; much of Europe never shared in it; some regions, such as parts of Germany, Italy, and France, began to grow and then stopped, as the state authorities failed to create incentives to innovate. Governments might, for any of a variety of reasons, follow policies or introduce new rules that undermined the precarious balance of property rights and protection of private rates of return that led to the "rise of the Western world."

The rules and protections identified by North and Thomas as early stimulants to long-term economic development had another feature that they did not emphasize: they represented significant niches of liberty in a political landscape otherwise characterized by hierarchy, feudal subordination, and the rival universalisms of church and empire. Another way of putting the argument that people would not engage in economically innovative and socially beneficial behavior without protection was to say that they would not engage in such behavior without the freedom to dispose of their resources and the freedom to secure at least some of the benefits to themselves.

That freedom was the wellspring of economic development was the insight of Montesquieu that "where several govern . . . the greater surety of property . . . leads to enterprise"; but although he was the first to formulate the relationship so clearly, he was not the first to sense that a measure of liberty was essential to the security and prosperity of a society. One of the earliest places where that connection became clear was in England during the Civil War of the 1640s.

The idea of English liberties as something unusual, valuable, and necessary for the independence of England as a kingdom was already old by the

seventeenth century. Debunking historians in the twentieth century generally ignored these sentiments, ascribing them to patriotic Victorians' mis-
reading of a history that, so far from giving evidence of liberty, was in fact a
tedious tale of inequality and oppression. Many of these debunkers, however,
confused the modern, New West idea of liberty as something absolute, universal, and individualistic with the historical reality. An important clue to the
difference was that the traditional English discourse on freedom spoke just
as often of "liberties" in the plural as of "liberty" in the singular. It was the
liberties of Englishmen that were special, not liberty in the abstract. These
liberties were communal and status-specific. They were laid down, most im-
portantly, in the Magna Carta of 1215, which provided that the king could
not proceed in law against a subject except for just cause, that no subject
could be convicted of any charge without judgment of his peers, and that his
property was secure against arbitrary sanction. It was true that the free subjects of Magna Carta were only a small proportion of the population, and
that most of its provisions described the rights of landowners, but it was
equally true that no other medieval document limiting the power of kings
was as comprehensive or reached as far down the social scale.

The reign of Elizabeth I (1558–1603) marked an outpouring of national
ideology, describing England as a uniquely fortunate "empire," ruled by a
Virgin Queen who represented divine favor. The architects of Elizabethan
patriotism referred to a verse of Virgil:

iam redit et virgo, redeunt Saturnia aeva

[Now the virgin returns, and now returns the age of Saturn]

The "age of Saturn" in Roman legend was the mythical age of prehistoric
bliss when Saturn, the father of Jupiter, ruled the world, when all was peace,
none were needy, and no one exploited or oppressed anyone else. As the historian Frances Yates documented in her studies of early modern political
mysticism, the Elizabethan patriots identified their queen with the mythical
virgin of the poem, who visited Earth only at times of exceptional good fortune. She was shy and vulnerable and would withdraw to her heavenly home
if men abused her friendship by engaging in war and oppression.

Elizabethan patriotism received its greatest boost in 1588, when Sir Francis Drake and his motley flotilla defeated the Spanish Armada. Here again,
the nationalist Victorian view was that this was a heroic victory fought
against heavy odds, a miraculous deliverance from papist and Spanish domination. The king of Spain, Philip II, had a legitimate claim to the English

throne through his wife, Mary Tudor, Elizabeth's half-sister, who had died in 1558. During her five-year reign, she and Philip were joint monarchs of England. When she died, he claimed the right to succeed, but was immediately rejected by the English Parliament in favor of Henry VIII's last surviving legitimate child, Elizabeth, who not only belonged to the royal line but was a Protestant. Philip was ruled ineligible as a foreigner, as someone whose claim was by marriage only, and above all as a Catholic—three distinct reasons that merged into one, as patriotism, Protestantism, and loyalty to the house of Tudor came together to define the Christian ethnicity of the nation that more than any other straddled the divide of Old and New West in the sixteenth century. Elizabeth herself sensed and consciously enacted this Christian ethnicity, and she and her people were well aware of the stakes at issue in the conflict with Spain. Her speech to the assembled troops at Tilbury was a ringing statement of the new patriotism of a rising commercial nation as well as a statement of the Protestant imperialism of the Tudors, a doctrine that mobilized monarch and people together against the enemy.

> I have always so behaved myself that, under God, I have placed my chiefest strength and safeguard in the loyal hearts and good will of my subjects, and therefore I am come amongst you as you see at this time, not for my recreation and disport, but being resolved, in the midst and heat of the battle, to live or die amongst you all, to lay down for my god, and for my kingdom, and for my people, my honour and my blood, even in the dust. I know I have the body of a weak and feeble woman, but I have the heart and stomach of a king, and of a king of England too, and think foul scorn that Parma or Spain or any Prince of Europe should dare to invade the borders of my realm.[14]

Revisionist historians argued that the Armada was not that significant; that its defeat was more or less inevitable, because the Spanish ships, despite their size and number, were no match for the skilled coastal navigators in Drake's fleet; and that the whole exercise meant far less to Spain than self-important Englishmen believed. In the 1990s, a counterreaction had set in. It now appeared that the Armada was anything but an empty threat, and that the storm that first prevented it from taking on board the Spanish army waiting in the Netherlands and then drove it through the Straits of Dover and into the North Sea was truly providential for the defenders.

While Spain certainly survived the defeat of the Armada, that wasted operation was one more nail in the coffin of Spanish and Habsburg global power. Although Spain continued to receive silver from Mexico, the Spanish economy—notoriously lacking in the niches of freedom that North and

Thomas identified in England and Holland—continued its long-term decline. And English poets and philosophers were in no doubt that their survival as an independent state was both providential and magnificent. It confirmed the divine favor already manifested in the very person of Elizabeth and justified the commercial liberties and relative prosperity that, in her reign, spread with increasing speed from the old landed estates to the propertied classes of the towns.

The Civil War of the 1640s was actually a complicated set of wars between a number of different groups allied in shifting coalitions. There were the Civil Wars proper, of 1642–46 and 1647–48, between king Charles I and his supporters—the Royalists or Cavaliers—and Parliament—the Roundheads. But these wars were also, at times, national wars among the English, Scots, and Irish, with the Scots siding first with the English Parliament, then with the king, and also having their own civil war within Scotland. Finally, the wars were religious wars, with the Royalists supporting the established, Protestant but episcopal, Church of England, and most of Parliament and the Scots supporting Presbyterianism, that is, an ecclesiastical system without bishops, with a minimum of sacramental ritual, and with ministers chosen by and closely identified with their particular congregations. Presbyterianism rejected hierarchy and sacraments, but was intensely concerned with doctrinal orthodoxy—as defined by the leading ministers and theologians. Increasingly during the wars, a third, more radical religious faction, known as the Independents, gained ground. These were people who refused all doctrinal hegemony, whether it be that of bishops or that of the Presbyterians. The Independents had other grievances against the other factions: they were mainly farmers, artisans, and simple workmen who were excluded from undertaking profitable work by the guild system of the towns, which was dominated by men sympathetic to Parliament.

In terms of economic interest, therefore, one can speak of a fourth war, between the Royalists, who believed that the king should have extensive control of national finances and should have the right to determine the rules of economic activity; the Parliamentarians, who were prosperous urban businessmen and merchants, who wanted fewer controls by the state, but at the same time wanted to guarantee that they would not have to face competition from poorer and possibly more productive rivals; and, third, the Independents, who wanted religious, economic, and political freedom. Their most famous leader was the man whose military reforms and generalship delivered the final blow against the king in the first Civil War—Oliver Cromwell.

The paradox of the English Civil Wars in the history of Western identity was that the Independents swore to a religion that was anarchic, often mystical, and very often apocalyptic, a type of Christianity more reminiscent of some of the sects of late antiquity than of anything in contemporary Europe. But on the other hand these same Independents were men of the New West in their capitalist individualism, for they demanded the free right of enterprise, production, and exchange. To them, economic, religious, and political freedom were not separate, but identical—in that, they were true heirs of the Elizabethan patriots.

The Independent understanding of freedom as something both rooted in national history and promising universal betterment found pregnant expression in the Putney debates that took place in late 1647 among representatives of the victorious army, which was at that point the leading social and political force in the realm. An important group of Independents, known as the Levellers, presented a document known as *The Agreement of the People*. The mainstream Parliamentarians had conducted the war as a defense of traditional liberties—one of their leaders, Fairfax, invoked the Magna Carta as "what we all fight for"—but, to the Levellers, these traditional liberties looked too much like interest-group privileges that they were determined to break. How to do so? Parliament, victorious in the war against the king, was not likely to infringe the privileges of its most influential supporters, at least as it was then constituted. With radical logic, the Levellers therefore demanded a new method of choosing the members of Parliament; this new method amounted to universal manhood suffrage to be granted to "all housekeepers of twenty-one who had not aided the King or impeded the Army," with the exception of "persons on alms, wage-earners or servants." The Parliament elected in this fashion would be the absolute sovereign in the realm; it would appoint the government—a Council of State—establish courts as needed, and make laws of universal and general application. It would also reform religion "to the greatest purity in doctrine, worship and discipline according to the Word of God" and provide, out of taxation, for maintaining the ministers, buildings, and other establishment of this purified church.

Unlike the French revolutionaries a century and a half later, the Levellers did not pretend that their demands would inaugurate a new era of freedom. They claimed, rather, that the freedoms they demanded were the historic rights of Englishmen, established in Anglo-Saxon times and stolen from the people by William the Conqueror and his Norman lords. The oppression of the king and the protectionism of Parliament were both examples of this confiscated liberty, which the Levellers intended to reestablish. The Leveller colonel Thomas Rainborowe struggled to explain this new idea of political liberty in terms of universal suffrage, the idea that just government must rest on the explicit consent of the governed, in words that vividly revealed the effort of his mind to conceive and state the hitherto inconceivable:

> The poorest he that is in England hath a life to live, as the greatest he; and therefore truly, sir, I think it's clear, that every man that is to live under a government ought first by his own consent to put himself under that government; and I do think that the poorest man in England is not at all bound in a strict sense to that government that he hath not had a voice to put himself under. . . . I do hear nothing at all that can convince me, why any man that is born in England ought not to have his voice in the election of burgesses. . . . I do think that the main cause why Almighty God gave men reason, it was that they should make use of that reason, and that they should improve it for that end and purpose that God gave it them. . . . I do not find anything in the Law of God, that a lord shall choose twenty burgesses, and a gentleman but two, or a poor man shall choose none: I find no such thing in the Law of Nature, nor in the Law of Nations.[15]

The time was not yet for democracy on this radical model. Oliver Cromwell and his supporters attended the debates, but argued that "it is our duty as Christians and men to consider consequences" of such far-reaching proposals. But the critical objection, which essentially held the field in English politics until the liberal breakthrough of the 1830s, was put by Cromwell's son-in-law Henry Ireton. Responding to the Leveller claim "that every man that is an inhabitant is to be equally considered," he said:

> For you to make this the rule, I think you must fly for refuge to an absolute natural Right, and you must deny all Civil Right . . . For my part I think that [the notion of natural rights] no right at all. I think that no person hath a right to an interest or share in the disposing or determining of the Kingdom, and in choosing those that shall determine what laws we shall be ruled by here, no person hath a right to this, that hath not a permanent fixed interest in this Kingdom.[16]

This was the dividing point in the evolution of democracy: Ireton declared the "natural right" of all to share in government by electing the government to be incompatible with the "civil right" of those who, by being property owners, had "a permanent fixed interest." The Leveller grievance was in part that they had no opportunity to acquire a fixed interest, because they were excluded by the guild privileges of the wealthy Parliamentarians from making money and buying the assets that would make them property owners. Seeing no easy way to break the guild monopolies, they proposed to subvert the political system that upheld those monopolies by demanding suffrage for all—property owners or not. To Ireton and Cromwell—who at this point deserted his Independent followers—the notion of complete democracy was tantamount to chaos and anarchy, which they had just spent blood and treasure to stop. Typically, in arguing the impossibility and incoherence of democracy, Cromwell referred to Switzerland, the only known example in seventeenth-century Europe of a society in which democracy based on universal suffrage was even partly practiced. As everyone knew, Cromwell said, the Swiss lived in "utter confusion," for the democratic decision of the people of one canton might not be in accord with that of another. The idea of binding majority decisions and of representative government as the institution capable of reconciling majority rule with consistent and responsible policy had not yet matured.

The Levellers lost the debates, but the pressure of productive people with no outlet for their energies could not be permanently suppressed. The second English Revolution—the Glorious Revolution of 1688–89—established the supremacy of Parliament for the second time, but also began the process by which groups outside the guild circles that dominated the Civil War Parliament began to gain ground, economically and politically. The history of England and Scotland in the eighteenth century was the history of how a Western identity defined by the goals of peace and profitable commerce began to take hold.

The rise of peaceful commercialism in the Netherlands and England in the later seventeenth and eighteenth centuries introduced a new kind of universalism, distinct from that of the medieval church and empire. This commercial or capitalist universalism was, for long, less politically powerful than the forces of conflict and pluralism that drove the military and hegemonic rivalries of the European powers. In the end, however, it proved victorious. Its message was that peace, order, and economic development went together, and that this correlation, first realized in Europe, was of global relevance. It was the intellectual ancestor of the liberal democratic universalism of the Grand Narrative and of its reincarnation after the Cold War.

The phenomenon of the English Independents, whose religion was lurid, dramatic, and colored by visions of judgment and the end of the world, but whose economic and political insights seemed uncannily modern, directs our attention once again to Max Weber's analysis of the origins of the modern West. We can now recapitulate that argument in more detail, while adding to it one crucial twist that Weber did not include, but that explains the logic of the Levellers' seemingly incoherent position.

The key text is Weber's 1905 essay on "The Protestant Ethic and the Spirit of Capitalism." Its argument spawned a whole tradition of theories focusing on the psychological and social factors that encouraged capitalist behavior, rather than on the legal and political factors emphasized by other models. Weber wanted to explain why the most prosperous, liberal, and rationalist regions of the world in his own day were also those regions where Protestant religion had taken hold during the Reformation. Where did capitalist rationality begin, and where did the notion that the purpose of money was to be saved and invested and not to buy power come into the world? Studying the matter, he realized that it was not even the case that all Protestants were equal in their prosperity. Growth was fastest and subsequent prosperity greatest not among Protestants in general, but mainly among people belonging to what were called, variously, the reformed, dissenting, or free churches, that is, among Calvinists, Presbyterians, Methodists, rather than among Lutherans or Anglicans. The refined form of the thesis thus stated that capitalist accumulation of economic resources and economic growth occurred first and fastest among members of the most extreme, consistent, and radical Protestants. Was there a connection or only a correlation?

Weber thought there was a connection, and he found it in the theology of the reformed churches. The Protestant Reformation as a whole began when discontent with Roman doctrinal, social, institutional, and partly economic hegemony over Christians in Europe reached boiling point in Martin Luther and a few other German biblical scholars, humanists, and princes. These people had many grievances, but the important one from Weber's viewpoint was that the reformers objected to what they considered an erroneous belief in "good works," the idea that you could save yourself by prayer, fasting, penance, giving alms, asking saints for intercession, and fulfilling church discipline. On the contrary, Luther said, man can do nothing to save himself; he must recognize that he is a helpless sinner but that he is simultaneously justified by Christ. Faith in salvation was the only human prerequisite for salvation; if that faith was whole, God would save the believer.

The Lutheran doctrine of justification of, or by, faith disengaged worldly life and striving from heavenly reward. In medieval Catholicism, the two moved in tandem like engaged cogwheels: the more you did the good works of fasting, penance, and the like, the more merit you accumulated in your heavenly bank account. The Reformation separated the cogwheels: the individual could do nothing for his salvation. This might at first glance seem to work against Weber's thesis. What would be the point of hard work in the world, being a good provider, feeding the poor, and caring for the sick, if God was not keeping a ledger on you? This was where Weber's thesis became both original and problematic. According to him, it was the very fact that Protestantism disengaged the gears of salvation from the ratchets of worldly work that made worldly work important for its own sake. Weber pointed out that the "good works" to which Luther objected were not actually displayed in worldly accomplishment, but mainly served the church. Giving alms and fasting were not activities that accumulated wealth on Earth. Precisely because the Protestant had no reason to worry about the state of his soul he was freed to do his best in the world.

So much, Weber said, for the Lutheran origins of the movement. Going now to the Calvinists and in particular the Puritans, Weber made two further connections. One was that the Calvinists added to the general Protestant condemnation of religious "good works" the idea of predestination, that God, before the beginning of time, had chosen those to be saved and those to be damned. The individual could do even less to change this judgment than, according to Luther, he could to improve his chances in this life. Because the Calvinist individual could never know whether he was among the damned or among the saved, he was a naturally anxious, uncertain, and uncomfortable individual. In practice, Weber pointed out, Calvinist and Puritan theology considered that even though the individual could never know God's decision for certain, there were certain secondary signs of election visible even in this world. One of these was a pious and moral life; the person capable of living such a life might hope that this ability was a sign of election. Another was to fulfill one's public obligations as scrupulously as possible. The consequences of trying to live up to these signs of election was the "Protestant ethic," combining ascetic habits with rigid attention to duty in work. A consequence of this ethic, theologically unintended but socially and economically significant, was that ascetic habits and duty in one's *Beruf*, or calling, tended, all else being equal, to make one better off. Consequently, in what one might call vulgar Calvinism, a third sign of election appeared: the individual who was saved could expect to enjoy God's favor on Earth, manifested in the prosperity that was the result of trying to follow the two original signs, by being ascetic and fulfilling one's obligations. In vulgar Calvinism, then, a sign of God's favor was that one devoted all one's energies to work, and that this devotion resulted in prosperity.

The second connection between Calvinism and capitalism was that

Calvinists who lived in this way were not supposed to spend any of their wealth. The point of what Weber called "piety within the world" was to make as sure as possible of one's signs of election by working to and beyond one's limit and saving the proceeds. It was this determined accumulation of resources, Weber said, that constituted the basis of capitalist growth, because growth was a long-term process that took generations to get started and centuries to complete. The accumulation of wealth, according to Weber, began as a paradoxical reaction to a faith that told its members they could not save themselves:

> What can they do?
>
> The only strategy available to them is to look out for signs of their own Election. They cannot logically *bring it about*, for the die has been cast long ago. They cannot purchase it by manipulation or propitiation. Their ethos discourages attempts at bribing the divine; their sense of order precludes it; the dismantling of spiritual hierarchy deprives them of the mediators who could have solaced and reassured them and would have received the appropriate prestations. They are dreadfully alone in their anxiety.[17]

Weber thought he had identified a "Protestant ethic" in the precise sense of a new, rational attitude to life, derived at bottom from theology but growing far beyond its theological foundations. This ethic commanded work for its own sake, because either God would reward you, which would indicate that you were saved, or he would not, in which case you should still work hard, because you never knew if you might not anyway be saved.

In his own program of trying to devise a modern science of society, Weber was interested not so much in the economic consequences of Calvinism as in how social institutions and social norms encouraged particular kinds of people to come to the fore and rewarded certain forms of behavior. His own philosophical point of departure was Friedrich Nietzsche, but Nietzsche stopped short after defining the modern individual as nihilistic and as having no core desire, self, or purposes other than "the will to power," that is, survival and control of things in this world. Weber agreed that reason, and the sense of self in which it rested, were precarious things, but wanted to know for precisely that reason why and how rational, productive people arose, what institutions they created, and how those institutions in turn encouraged future generations to act, live, and plan. Weber learned from Nietzsche that Western rationality was fragile. He also knew that, once prevalent in the world, it was a force of tremendous and, he considered, generally beneficial economic and social change. But if reason of this kind was fragile and came into the world only by accident, would it not be good to know how and why, given its advantages, so as to know how, if possible, to preserve it?

The reason Weber focused on religion was that he realized that economic rationality, of the kind that led to growth and beyond that to modern science and indirectly to democratic freedoms, was not self-explanatory. In an earlier society, being economically rational according to nineteenth- or twentieth-century standards would be, literally, quite irrational. Anyone who planned, worked, and saved to accumulate great riches was a fool, because he would arouse the envy either of the king and his tax collectors or of his neighbors. They would assume that he was collecting wealth to buy power and would conspire against him. The tax collectors would assume the same thing and try either to take away his wealth or co-opt him. And if the rich man let himself be co-opted, he was no longer saving riches in order to save, but was doing what rich people had always done in history until the early modern West, namely, use money for power, either for its own sake or as a safeguard against being victimized and expropriated. It was only in parts of the West, and only in particular circumstances, which Weber tried to understand, that a few people began acting in an entirely irrational way:

> From the viewpoint of those first engaging in it, there was nothing in the least rational about capitalist activity: on past form, the fruits of industrial labour were destined to be taken away from them by those endowed with political power. This did not, however, bother puritan entrepreneurs, for they had turned to the new economic ethic not in the hope of wealth, but only in the surreptitious hope of finding evidence for their own salvation.[18]

That this peculiar form of behavior ultimately paid off in the sense that Western nations became rich could not have been known to the first accumulators nor, if they had known it, would they have considered it especially meritorious.

In the decades after his essay appeared in 1905, critics found many flaws in it. The most common complaint was that his "Protestant ethic" was not sufficient to explain what he wanted to explain—capitalist rationality. Alternately, some said that it was a mere accident that growth happened in those parts of the world inhabited by dissenting Protestants and not, say, in Catholic or Lutheran countries, in Arabia, India, China, or the Americas. Other factors, not religion, determined whether a region or a people were able to accumulate riches over the generations.

Weber himself thought further about the origins of capitalism before he died in 1920. His later ideas changed the emphasis from the 1905 essay, which focused on the logic of predestination and the paradoxical behavior it encouraged. In his last writing on the subject, he began by noting that it was a universal human need to look for explanations or justifications of happiness or misfortune. There were three logically possible answers to the question "why am I lucky?" or its more common opposite, "why do I suffer?" The first, that of the Cathars and other dualists, was that there were two equal powers in the universe, a principle for good and one for evil. The evil principle had created the world and governed it, which was why the good often suffered and the evil prospered. The second was the Calvinist answer, predestination; God made the world and our fates as he did, and we cannot know why. The third was that of the reincarnationist religions of the East, in which the good or evil fortune of individuals was to be explained by karma, by responsibility or merit incurred in earlier lives.

In all three answers, the world was a sorry place, full of evil. The good man must reject the world. This, again, could be done in two ways, by mystical withdrawal or by the "inner-worldly asceticism" of the Calvinist capitalists. In societies where mystical withdrawal predominated, such as India or the medieval West, capitalist accumulation had no chance. In the early modern West, the Protestant ethic of inner-worldly asceticism rejected mysticism and ritual means of salvation. Weber's point in his second essay on the subject was that Calvinism tended to win over those groups particularly suited to turn the ethic into capitalism, such as artisans, tradesmen, and builders— who were free of the natural hazards and economic constraints of agriculture. Weber concluded, as he had done in his 1905 essay, that the practical and moral effect of Calvinism was that to live well and to work well became both signs of election and guarantees of economic success.

Unfortunately for this neat and convincing theory, it could never explain what it promised to explain. Weber claimed to explain how capitalism and the rational outlook that it entailed began in the early modern West. If, however, one defined capitalism as entrepreneurs producing according to rational methods and seeking to sell their products for profit in markets, then capitalism was never unique to the West; entrepreneurs, rational production, profits, and markets were found not only in the earlier West, but in China, India, ancient Greece and Rome, Mesopotamia, and elsewhere. If, on the other hand, one defined capitalism as the large-scale production and mass markets of the Industrial Revolution of the eighteenth century and after, its links with Calvinism were likewise thin or nonexistent; industrial capitalism flourished in Catholic, Confucian, Buddhist, Hindu, and other societies. At most, Weber's two ingenious essays explained certain features of Dutch, Scottish, or North American capitalism. Since, however, most of the influential economic historians of the West were American, they failed to notice that Weber's theory did not explain what it claimed to explain. It was therefore understandable that Weber's theory accompanied the twentieth-century discussion of the West as an economic civilization based on a fragile and vulnerable rationality that was supposedly specific to a certain time and place.

Weber's theory that a particular form of religion spurred capitalism was not wrong, merely inadequate. It was true that Calvinism generated capitalism, but so, evidently, did a number of other things. Which of them were decisive? And was capitalism the preeminent trait of the modern West, or was it part of a larger pattern? Just as Weber had tried to trace all of capitalism to Calvinism, so others, long before him, had tried to trace another Western feature, freedom of thought, to Puritanism, on its face an implausible descent. In economic rationality, Weber claimed, it was the extreme puritans who, in worldly terms, were foolish enough to store up wealth without using it, at least not in all cases, to buy power.

In the matter of personal and political liberty, it was the extreme sectarians who helped to bring about modern liberty. The logic was identified by David Hume in an essay of 1741 on "Superstition and Enthusiasm." Hume noted that, in his day, strong state churches characterized by elaborate ritual and hierarchy, such as the Catholic Church in France or the Church of England, tended to go along with strong monarchical government and not to tolerate civil dissent. This was true even where the strong state churches were relatively tolerant of religious dissent. Hume called this combination of established, hierarchical religion and social power "superstition." On the other hand, societies with many radical religious movements, like Scotland, Holland, or New England, tended to have more civil freedom. Why? Not obvious, because religious radicals, what he called "enthusiasts," were usually very sure of themselves, of how to be saved, and how to believe. One would not expect such people, in power, to extend liberty to others.

Yet the opposite happened. The reason, Hume argued, was that

> religions, which partake of enthusiasm are, on the first rise, more furious and violent than those which partake of superstition; but in a little time become more gentle and moderate . . . Enthusiasm being founded on strong spirits, and a presumptuous boldness of character, it naturally begets the most extreme resolutions; . . . produces the most cruel disorders in human society;

but its fury is like that of thunder and tempest, which exhaust themselves in a little time . . . When the first fire of enthusiasm is spent, men naturally, in all fanatical sects, sink into the greatest remissness and coolness in sacred matters; there being no body of them among them, endowed with sufficient authority . . . Superstition, on the contrary, steals in gradually and insensibly; renders men tame and submissive; is acceptable to the magistrate, and seems inoffensive to the people: Till at last the priest, having firmly established his authority, becomes the tyrant . . . of human society.

Hume was thus able to make the paradoxical conclusion that "*superstition is an enemy to civil liberty, and enthusiasm a friend to it.*"[19] Enthusiasts who were losing their fire, like the Covenanters in Scotland in his own day, the puritans of the Massachusetts Bay Colony, or the relaxed Calvinist burghers of Amsterdam, were the best friends to liberty. Such men remembered why freedom was precious, for only freedom allowed their forebears to proclaim their radical faith; freedom remained precious, for without the fire in their bellies the later generations were not sure what beliefs and habits to punish and which ones to reward. So to be safe in their consciences and their interests, they became tolerant.

Hume's argument applied to the Levellers of 1647, though not, interestingly, to the Presbyterians at that time. The latter were riding the crest of their power and were not inclined to grant any freedom whatever to those they considered to be in the wrong. The whole point of the Leveller *Agreement of the People* was that the Presbyterians who dominated Parliament protected their own interests and would not admit the popular control that might threaten their political, economic, and religious privileges. The Independents, and in particular the Levellers, presented the unique picture of religious enthusiasts oppressed and, so they held, unjustly treated by other, more powerful enthusiasts, so that they became democrats.

Of such paradoxes was the New West made. The point, however, goes deeper, and it is the point reiterated throughout these chapters: that the New West was not a radical turn from the past to the future, but the maturation of long, slow developments that began within the Old West—sometimes, as in the case of Leveller religion, very far back indeed.

The English Civil Wars coincided with the final phase of a much greater conflict that convulsed Germany in the first half of the seventeenth century: the Thirty Years' War of 1618–48. On one level, the Thirty Years'

War was simply another stage in the 1,100-year rivalry of the two power centers that dominated European politics throughout the era of the Old West and well into the era of the New—one power center located in France and one in central Europe. By the seventeenth century, this rivalry had taken the form of a struggle between the Habsburgs, who held the title of Holy Roman Emperor and controlled much of Germany, and the Valois kings of France. But into this rivalry came the religious and political conflict precipitated by the Reformation within the empire itself, that is, within Germany. The Habsburg emperors were Catholic and refused permanently to tolerate the religious liberty and political standing of the Protestant estates—those dukes, counts, and other princes who ruled the Protestant territories of northern, eastern, and south-central Germany.

The Thirty Years' War began as the attempt of the emperor to revoke the rights reluctantly granted to the Protestants in the preceding century and to restore Catholic and Habsburg hegemony in all German lands. The Protestant estates resisted and when, despite Swedish aid, they were on the verge of defeat, they found an ally in France, governed, under Louis XIII, by the cardinal-soldier Armand Jean Duplessis de Richelieu. Playing a double game that involved suppressing Protestant political power within France while supporting Protestant power in the empire, he took the opportunity to assert the perennial French interest against the empire. The result was the peace of Westphalia of 1648, which guaranteed the religious freedom of Protestants within the empire and granted France and Sweden a right of oversight and intervention, should the Catholic emperors ever dare to violate the settlement.

When the smoke of religious and national battles cleared after the peace of Westphalia in 1648, the philosophers of Europe first looked with pleasure on the prospect of peaceful development, the spread of reason, and economic prosperity. Then, as the Enlightenment took hold in the eighteenth century, some of them were seized with panic that the promising new world would not be correctly organized, not have the right ideas, not educate its citizens properly. Since different people worried about different things, they produced rival programs and ideologies to ensure the good society. Because the stakes were great—nothing less than future human happiness—the programs were as uncompromising as they were incompatible. Thus, the panic of intellectuals in the century and a half from Rousseau through Marx to Lenin and Hitler produced incomparably deeper hatreds and wars more bitter than even the religious wars, confirming the gloomy foreboding implicit in the words of the poet Friedrich Klopstock, contemplating from his home in Hamburg the revolutionary wars of the 1790s:

Once, to me, the worst of all horrors
Was thunderous war fought to settle this question:
What is the path to bliss everlasting?
No less dismay now troubles my spirit
For every life taken, every breath failing
To find the right road to joy in this world.

The road from war holy or heroic to commercial peace and back to ideological war was simple in outline, complex in practice and in the millions of lives and fates that, by taking that road, shaped it. An interesting stage on the road, and one not much studied by adherents of either the Grand Narrative or the antinarratives, was made up of those people who, in the age of the early modern state and the rise of commercial society, preserved the heroic ideal by, in effect, dissolving the synthesis that Carl Erdmann diagnosed in the early Middle Ages, the synthesis of Christian asceticism and the Germanic hero that produced Roland, Saint Olaf, and the holy wars of the Crusades. In the France of Louis XIV, the demographic and geopolitical center of gravity of Western civilization, supremely serious men and women endeavored to restore the original ideal of an aristocratic *militia Dei*, war-service for God, a service purely ascetic but nevertheless heroic, one that only the strongest and most noble characters could dare to undertake.

Two factors shaped the religious and political situation in seventeenth-century France. One was the state's interest in maintaining the integrity of the realm and the loyalty of its subjects. The church hierarchy constituted a powerful group of subjects constantly tempted by overarching loyalties, namely, to the papacy. Keeping the church loyal and national was a basic principle of French reason of state, manifested in the doctrine known as Gallicanism, which stated that the pope's writ ran in France only through the king and by his leave. France was "the eldest daughter of the Church," but that very rank gave France special responsibilities in the defense of Christendom, responsibilities best understood by the king and not by the pope. The second was the movement of piety that spread in France after the wars of religion and as a reaction to the libertinism of the court, the philosophers, and some of the noble houses. The two factors sometimes converged and sometimes conflicted. In the 1640s, for example, the religious revival known as Jansenism spread through the educated elite of Paris. One family in particular, the Arnaulds, devoted many members and all its energies to establishing houses of prayer, retreat, and devotion. The Jansenists held that human nature was incurably corrupt and opposed, in particular, the aristocratic idealism of the French church and court, as represented most spectacularly by Richelieu. Neither the established church nor the government could accept this gloomy and stringent doctrine and collaborated in suppressing it.

The ascetic version of aristocratic heroism therefore did not find its most striking expression in the Jansenists, who rejected the heroic ethos and its presupposition that man could and should act nobly. Rather, it was a man of the lesser nobility who in the later seventeenth century came to represent the most extreme asceticism and who put into radical practice a heroic model of *militia Dei* in a manner that would have seemed quite familiar in the seventh and eighth centuries. This was Armand-Jean Le Bouthillier de Rancé, the reforming abbot of La Trappe, a Cistercian abbey near Paris that, thanks to him, became the mother house of the Trappist order of strict observance. That Rancé shared the name of Richelieu was no accident, since Richelieu was his godfather.

Nothing in Rancé's birth or upbringing predicted his astonishing history. As a boy, he learned the classics and at the age of twelve, in 1638, published a translation of the archaic Greek poet Anacreon. Like many young nobles, he held various church benefices. These were simply entitlements, distributed by the government, to receive a third of the income from a particular ecclesiastical property. One of these benefices, however, was that of La Trappe. His older brother, who died young, was beneficiary abbot of La Trappe, and on this boy's death, Rancé's father persuaded Richelieu to waive a provision that would normally have prevented him from inheriting his brother's benefice. It was thus by accident that Rancé inherited, as a source of wealth, the asset that he was to make his own in a manner quite different from what he or his peers envisaged.

As Rancé grew up, he participated in the festive life of the capital and the court and appeared to share fully its aristocratic, worldly values. At the great Parisian houses of the Lafayettes, the Richelieus, or the Albrets, he rubbed shoulders with the political and cultural elite of the most powerful and confident nation in the West. "Here, Rancé discovers modern aristocratic civility, rich in politeness and conventions, fond of categorizing the passions and dissecting feelings," such as "the nine categories of esteem, the twelve categories of sighs, the eight categories of beauty." He learned to speak, write, and cherish the language of sentiment and its presumption that the self could be refined and directed to nobility of feeling and action. "While England discovered the black habit and Puritanism, France followed fashion and invented the psychology of the passions. What Rancé met in this first part of his life was not the power of duty to constrain instinct, but rather pride, the daring of the aristocratic self, the passions and satisfactions of desire. The movement that bore him along was the movement that bears the noble man from desire to pride and from a pride that regards itself to a pride that displays itself in spectacular action, in other words, in glory."[20] A typical Rancé statement of this period, in answer to the question "where are you going?" was "This morning I shall preach like an angel and this afternoon I shall hunt like a devil." Rancé was ordained priest in 1651, but remained the worldly aristocrat.

From 1648 to 1652, French aristocrats rebelled against the growing power of the absolute monarchy in the confused, violent, and catastrophic civil war known as the Fronde. Famine and disease followed the feuding armies, and, in Jules Michelet's imagery, "impoverished nobles not deigning to beg, died on beds of straw . . . people ate lizards, dogs dead for eight days." Rancé emerged from the Fronde a close ally of the cardinal de Retz, who protected him from reprisals against the rebellious families with which Rancé was associated. In particular, he was linked to the great family of Rohan, leading rebels and, what was worse, Protestants. The link was intimate: Rancé's mistress was Marie de Montbazon, the widow of a much older member of the Rohan family, who had died in 1654 aged eighty-eight. By the universal consent of her contemporaries, she was beautiful, intelligent, and lascivious. "I never met anyone who kept in her vices so little respect for virtue," de Retz, no stranger to sin himself, wrote in his memoirs. Others insisted that it was only after her aged husband died that she "gave herself a little more liberty," as one put it. Since her husband was both a libertine and forty-six years her senior, her patience might well be termed virtuous. Her impact on Rancé was devastating while she lived, even more when she died. The turning-point in Rancé's life occurred, in fact, at the time of her death, in April 1657.

Two versions of what happened circulated in Rancé's lifetime. According to the first, generally accepted by later writers, Marie fell ill with smallpox and, fearing the worst, sent for her Armand. At her deathbed, the older woman and her younger lover spoke of death and damnation, vanity, and misfortune. She received the last sacraments and died. Leaving her body, Rancé left the world. He went to his abbey of La Trappe and became its head in fact as well as in law.

The other version was more dramatic but less plausible. It ran like this:

The abbot of La Trappe was a gallant and had several intimate affairs. The last of them to break out was with a duchess famous for her beauty and who, having happily escaped death in crossing a river, encountered it a few months later. The abbot, who often visited the countryside, was there when this unforeseen death occurred. His servants who were aware of his love took care to hide from him the news of this sad event, which he did not learn of until later. [Returning to Paris,] he went straight to the duchess' apartments, where he was always admitted at any hour. The first thing he saw, instead of the pleasures that he thought were awaiting him, was a coffin. He knew it for that of his mistress when he saw her bloody head which had fallen, as if by accident, from beneath the sheet with which it had been carelessly covered, and which had been detached from the rest of the body. This was done because the coffin available was too short, and the carpenters had wanted to avoid having to make a new one.[21]

Whatever the true story, and historians made it boringly clear that the story of the bloody head and the undersized coffin was almost certainly a canard, it took Rancé six years to untangle himself from the world. When he had done so, in 1662, he entered La Trappe, never to leave it again. The abbey was in ruins, with only six monks who led an undisciplined and debauched life. Rancé paid them off and introduced Cistercians of the strict observance, which included a special vow of absolute silence—a vow that Rancé himself perpetually violated, for he was not only one of the most prolific religious writers and correspondents of his day, but also received frequent visitors, whom he consulted, advised, harangued, and preached at from his cell.

In 1672, Rancé published the new constitution of the abbey, centered on the four practices of withdrawal, detachment, humiliation, and mortification. The thrust of the new rules was to destroy the will and replace it with obedience. Rancé transferred all his noble values and daring to the task of achieving a unique, superhuman degree of what a secular age would call mindless self-flagellation. "Exercise on yourself the charitable hatred of self that Christ recommended," he wrote. Sick monks were not exempt from any duties, for "this should be the care of all Christians when they are ill, not to change anything in their devotional practices." Good Friday observance was particularly strenuous. The monks stood, fasting and barefoot, from four in the morning until two in the afternoon, chanting psalms in adoration of the cross in a dank and gloomy building. Every year, this exercise cost lives. Intellectual work was banished, for knowledge, even in monks, was vanity, and the more you knew, the more you had to reject and repent. This doctrine was the exact opposite to that of the Maurist monks, who were, in these same years, perfecting their science of diplomatics—the study and interpretation of medieval documents. In the 1680s and 1690s, Rancé provoked a controversy with the Maurist Jean Mabillon, the leading antiquarian historian of the age, and probably of any age. Perfection, to Rancé, was destruction of self in an incessant and unremitting act of aggression. To Mabillon's question whether it was not a good and useful thing for religious to employ themselves usefully in study and reading, Rancé retorted that "monks are not destined for study, but for penitence. Their rightful condition is to weep and not to teach, and God's design in raising up solitaries in a Church was not to make doctors, but penitents."[22]

The controversy of Rancé and Mabillon ended in a peaceful reconciliation of the two monks in 1693. The proud and aristocratic hermit and Mabillon, who was a humble peasant's son, agreed to disagree. For the moment, French culture agreed with the scholar. But half a century after their deaths in 1700 and 1707, respectively, the rising Enlightenment condemned both the hermit and the medievalist. The mental universe that produced both Rancé's final version of *militia Dei* and Mabillon's antiquarian erudition had disappeared forever. Both figures, however radically opposed in values and philosophy, belonged to the Old West, not just because both were monks, but because their striving had a common goal: mortification, the sacrifice of self at divine command. The Enlightenment did not seek divine commands but the authority of reason. The civil war within the West since the Enlightenment was not a war between those who listened for the voice of God and those who obeyed pure human reason, but between different interpretations of reason and its commands.

I n 1971, an American historian, Edward Whiting Fox, became one of the pioneers of a new economic and geopolitical approach to the history and identity of the modern West. He did so in a short, dense book that appeared to be mainly an analysis of party politics in France in the late nineteenth and twentieth centuries.[23] His problem was to explain the levels of support for differing political parties and alliances in various parts of France. He discovered that to understand people's political allegiances it was necessary to go deep into history and uncover the simultaneous existence of two Frances: a territorial France and a commercial France. The territorial state was administered centrally and followed the rules and incentives of centralized, bureaucratic government. Commercial France, while politically subject to the same authorities as territorial France, consisted of the people living in the major trading and producing cities of eastern and northern France. These people had always favored free trade and liberal politics, whereas the inhabitants of Paris and of much of the interior of the country favored protectionism and politics which were conservative, socialist, or communist.

Whiting Fox's book established two basic criteria for the new literature on the economic rise of the West. First, it had to investigate incentives for growth and the location of growth. Why and where did growth and civil liberties occur? Were they related, and if so, how? Second, it had to combine economic and historical with geopolitical analysis. It was not enough to show the legal, cultural, or administrative framework of growth; a theory with claims to originality had also to relate growth to the geographical environment, that is, the combination of natural conditions and human influence on those conditions that encouraged the triad of economic growth, political liberty, and rationality.

While Fox took a geopolitical approach to understanding liberalism and political conflict in the modern world, economic theorists and historians approached the origins of capitalism from another direction. Trying to explain not personality types but material outcomes, they looked for reasons why long-term economic growth took off in Europe in the eighteenth century.

In 1981, Eric Jones, a British historian working in Australia, refined the economic argument on the rise of the West by going further back in time than North and Thomas and adding new and crisscrossing chains of causation. Jones concluded that "the European miracle" that continued in higher gear in the modern United States was a combination of many factors, of which efficient markets were only one. The common denominator of all the factors making for ultimate expansion, growth, innovation, and spreading prosperity, Jones found, was variety—the physical variety of the western tip of Eurasia, that is, of Europe, divided by mountains and highlands into fertile river valleys leading to navigable seas. Physical and climatic variety precluded political unity; the Holy Roman Empire from Charlemagne's day until its abolition in 1806 was always more a federation than a monarchy, and no single power ever succeeded in uniting the continent for more than a decade or so at a time. Political variety meant conflict, but it also meant differing jurisdictions and different rules that welcomed different kinds of people, encouraging different types of activity. Social and institutional variety encouraged competition among small groups, including the competition that consisted in the voyages of exploration and the trade and exploitation of global resources after 1500. While not attributing overwhelming importance to profits from overseas expansion as did, for example, some Marxist scholars, Jones found that new foods and new crops, such as cotton, that came from America and Asia had a trigger function in releasing pent-up energies. "What had happened" by the eighteenth century "was that the Europeans had discovered an unprecedented ecological windfall. Europe was sufficiently decentralised and flexible to develop in response, and not merely content to consume the raw gains. This conjunction of windfall and entrepreneurship happened only once in history."[24]

Jones combined Weberian, economic, environmental, political, and cultural explanations of an outcome that was both unique and multicausal. For example, one reason that rulers, in North and Thomas's account, found it useful to encourage innovation was that they were powerful, but not that powerful. Unlike the monarchs of vast empires in Asia, European kings, dukes, and princes had to make do with less. Faced with competition and threats from abroad, they had to defend themselves and secure their "state," their splendor and reputation. But they had to do it on the cheap; the large-scale exploitation and opulence of Asian courts were not within their grasp. Thus European rulers, in their own interests, learned early to make efficient use of their resources. European travelers to Asia noted in the sixteenth century how much greater economic inequalities were in the East, how much richer the rulers, and how much less, therefore, the economic activities of their subjects.

Nor could European rulers waste manpower. As soon as they discovered how to use labor power efficiently, they began doing so. In this as in all other areas, Jones found that the key to growth was not only variety, but balance between extremes. Too few people could not provide a productive base no matter how clever the individuals; too many created what a historian of China called a "high-level equilibrium trap," in which population grew too quickly to encourage the labor-saving and innovative processes that, more than mere invention or resource extraction, led to long-term growth. An odd feature of western Europe from a very early date was that the population, within the overarching constraints of disease and famine, was self-regulating to a higher degree than elsewhere in the world. The anthropologist Jack Goody and the demographer Richard Schofield earlier noted this tendency to a relatively low birthrate. They explained it in terms of the Western nuclear family structure that encouraged fewer births to keep assets in the family. In the West, too many people in the younger generation meant conflicts of interest; in Asia, more was better because each new member was a potential producer whose gains would accrue to the extended family as a whole. More important, many regions of Asia were more exposed to climatic disaster and earthquake than Europe. The threat of disaster encouraged people to have as many children as possible as insurance. Asians maximized numbers "as an adaptation to frequent mortality peaks, so that some might hope to survive catastrophes," whereas Europeans "had less to gain from producing the maximum number of progeny" and therefore controlled fertility, which in turn "improved the quality of the human capital." According to Schofield:

> What is remarkable about the populations of pre-industrial western Europe is that they not only evolved a set of social rules, which effectively linked their rate of family formation with changes in their environment, but also managed to secure such low fertility that they achieved both a demographically efficient replacement of their population, and an age-structure which was economically more advantageous than the age-structures generally to be found amongst non-industrial societies today.[25]

Jones avoided environmental and climatic determinism by stressing that what counted was the response to conditions as well as the conditions themselves. His broader message was somewhat more confident than Weber's. Where Weber had seen a fragile and contingent alliance of beliefs and conditions, Jones saw a rich tapestry of interacting physical, mental, social, cultural, and behavioral features, resulting by the nineteenth century in a robust system capable of withstanding severe shocks in any one of its many parts without suffering collapse.

The Protestant ethic, religious toleration, legal protection of property rights, and geopolitical pluralism were all aspects of the liberal, productive, and technological West. But were they also explanations? Was there a way to tie these disparate pieces together? Such a general theory would have to embed the Faustian and modern West together in a general view of human nature and motivation, explaining why the factors that shifted the Old West into the shape of the New West occurred when, why, and where they did.

As we have seen, the New Western triad of democracy, capitalism, and reason had deep roots in the behavior, political structures, personal values, and social formations created by the Old Western synthesis. Hints about what drove the transition came from Max Weber and the economic historians. Geopolitics offered other suggestions: the competitive international system of five to ten major players, as it existed from the fifteenth to the nineteenth century, stimulated development within each state toward power sharing. This was because, as the English example showed, a system "where several govern" created the niches of liberty that induced more people to engage in behavior that was socially as well as individually advantageous. An oligarchical, as opposed to a strictly absolutist or despotic state, might seem less powerful, because power was less centralized; in practice, however, such a state was capable of mobilizing more resources over a longer term than its despotic rivals. Acting on this insight, the most rationally self-interested rulers, in turn, allowed just enough incipiently democratic space within their kingdoms and principalities to launch the engine of sustained capitalism, first by trade, later by mass production and mass markets.

One of the most comprehensive attempts to understand the emerging identity of the New West was that, already alluded to, of Montesquieu, who was the mainspring of the sceptical Enlightenment—the Enlightenment that saw the West not as a project to be realized, but as a historical reality to be understood, and one in which liberty was a pervasive principle, but also a fragile good.

The Grand Narrative put Montesquieu on a lower pedestal than Rousseau or Voltaire, which reflected its secularist and progressivist bias. The radical antinarratives that took the field after the 1960s were even less inclined to pay much attention to Montesquieu, whose arguments seemed arcane and conservative and to have more than a taste of the erudite antiquarianism that Voltaire despised. The difference between them, however, is that whereas Montesquieu wanted to understand the West for what it was and how it had evolved, Voltaire wanted to show what the West should be.

Charles-Louis de Secondat, baron de la Brède et de Montesquieu was born—as mentioned earlier—of three centuries of nobility, in the southwest of France. Unlike Voltaire or Rousseau, he did not reject institutional Christianity and remained—despite disagreements with aspects of the institutional church—a practicing Catholic, perhaps an indication that he did not share his fellow-philosophers' great idea that true civilization had to rest on a single, all-pervading principle, but that pluralism at the deepest level was perhaps one of the guarantees of the freedom that he, like they, sought to understand and defend.

His first famous writing was the *Persian Letters* of 1721, in which he parodied French urban society and in particular the court of Versailles following the death of Louis XIV in a book pretending to be written by two Persian travelers. He was soon identified as the author and, on the strength of his skills as a satirist, was elected a member of the French Academy in 1728, aged thirty-nine. He then embarked on a tour of Europe, which included a stay of several years in England that proved crucial for his development and for his understanding of Western identity. It was to be some years before that understanding matured. In 1734 he published *Reflections on the Causes of the Grandeur and Decline of the Romans*, in which he presented the argument, which Gibbon later popularized, that Roman power began to ebb when Rome became a despotic empire and lost its original republican liberties. He was fascinated by the apparent paradox that Roman power began to decay precisely because it had become so great.

His main life's work, which gave him the claim to be considered the first modern sociologist as well as one of the most profound investigators of Western identity, was the *Spirit of the Laws*, which occupied most of his later years and appeared in 1748, with a defense against critics issued in 1750. His purpose was to understand the sources of the different kinds of regime and administrative arrangement found in the world, mostly in the Europe of his own day, but including frequent references to the New World, Asia, and Greek and Roman antiquity. While using all the erudite research and historical information available, he went beyond his sources in his conclusions, of which three were especially significant.

The first was that regimes, or governments, could be divided into three types. Such a classification was not new; it was Aristotle who first divided polities into monarchies, aristocracies, and democracies. Montesquieu made a different distinction: his three types were the republic, the monarchy, and despotism. Next, he focused not on the constitution as such, but on the spirit that informed it. Thus he concluded that the test of a republic was whether its animating spirit was virtue, that is, whether people in the society were disposed to act responsibly for the common good; in a monarchy, the guiding principle—as Rancé showed—was honor; whereas people under despotism were guided, or driven, by fear. The difference between this and all previous classifications was that it rested not on where power was officially located, but on how the regime in question habitually formulated and conducted its policy; it was dynamic, not static.

Montesquieu's second important argument was that the separation of powers was the source of liberty, which he identified, in chapter 6 of book 11, a passage written during his stay in England, as the common principle of European, or Western, political identity. The three types of power, according to him, were the legislative, executive, and judicial power; only where each was confided to different individuals with different interests would their interplay produce the niches of liberty that, in other passages, he identified as the source of security and prosperity. His third argument, much noted at the time but largely neglected since, was his account of how climate—the physical environment—influenced the temper and manners, or, in modern parlance, the values, of a society. Some read this as climatic and geographical determinism; Montesquieu in fact argued against determinism, saying that it was the task of the responsible ruler and administrator to counteract negative effects of the environment and put positive effects to best use.

Montesquieu's historical and sociological vision was in two respects accurate and in advance of most later theory for two centuries. In the chapter on English liberty, he identified the constitution of the Germanic tribes as a critical source of political liberty in subsequent Western history. This was the liberty that spurred the Germanic heroes of the medieval songs and stories, the aristocratic magnates of Europe and that, in his own day, inspired the British constitution that divided power and gave subjects avenues of independent and creative activity, both cultural and commercial. Second, he identified the particular conditions that allowed the faint traditions of ancient tribal freedom to revive and become the foundation of commercial and capitalist development.

Montesquieu believed he had found a key to unlock human history. It was not a history with a predetermined end, for he realized that what he considered good laws, the kind that promoted liberty and commerce, were not fated to exist; all he could do was to show what such laws were like and indicate the conditions that favored their appearance. Montesquieu did not reject the West as Christendom; he wished to show how a liberal West, a West of sturdy entrepreneurs and laws that restrained both greedy rulers and despotic bureaucrats could, and had, come into existence. How such a liberal West adapted, adopted, or kept its distance from its predecessor, the West as Christendom, was, for him, a matter of free debate.

His contemporary Voltaire, the most famous of all the Enlightenment thinkers, inaugurated a different way of thinking about history. In Voltaire, the turning of the West from Christendom to Enlightenment, from the ancient to the modern triad, was sudden and decisive. Voltaire's guiding principle was reason, which was cosmopolitan and international, not, as in Montesquieu, incarnated in actual people with mixed motives and varying intelligence. For Voltaire, culture was reason's escape from superstition, force, and intolerance. Those factors, for Montesquieu, were inescapable, the task was to understand them and know under what conditions their effects could be minimized. Voltaire thought they could and should be crushed.

Voltaire began, as did Montesquieu, by admiring the English for their liberties, but where Montesquieu focused on commerce, policy, and the values of a society that produced niches of liberty, Voltaire picked on another English trait as crucial—the religious toleration that followed the Glorious

Revolution. From an early age, his focus was freedom of thought and intellectual progress, not social and historical understanding. His forthright religious scepticism earned him censure, and in 1726, aged thirty-two, he left French territory to avoid prosecution. He spent much of his life traveling; his most famous journey was the one he took to the court of Frederick II of Prussia, where he lived for three years in the 1750s, hoping that he had found the enlightened autocrat who would illustrate in practice the precepts of Voltaire's own rationalist, secular, technological philosophy.

After writing a number of theatrical works, Voltaire made his mark in the 1730s with two works, the *History of Charles XII* and the *Philosophical Letters*. The former was a documented narrative of the extraordinary career of Charles XII, king of Sweden, one of the last monarchs of Europe to fight sword in hand in his own battles, a nationalist dreamer and cynical pragmatist rolled into one who came near to toppling the Russian monarchy of Peter the Great, until he was himself defeated at Poltava in 1709. Voltaire drew a philosophical moral from the tale: the warrior king, for all his courage, brought desolation, whereas the military threat from outside impelled Peter to embark on the modernization of Russia, turning it into a European empire. The *Letters* continued this argument, that the great rulers are those who further civilization, but most of them are devoted to a defense of toleration, such as Voltaire had seen it in England. He then moved on to attack Blaise Pascal, the mathematician, ascetic, and Catholic puritan, who had argued that nothing in the world was of greater value than surety of salvation. Voltaire retorted that the purpose of life was not to reach heaven by ferocious penitence or any other method, but to support and ensure progress in science, technology, and learning. This was the New West taking disdainful leave of the religious core of the Old.

Appropriately, Voltaire's model of social and political development was pedagogical—a prefiguration of the Grand Narrative. Progress was measured in information and technology. The educated citizen was necessarily a moral and reasonable citizen who would not be subject to unreason. Similarly, the Grand Narrative told a story of the West as a story of reason expanding to ever more control of its environment and of the conditions of human life and social existence. Montesquieu would not have disagreed, but would have added with Hume that reason was often the slave of the passions, that is, that human beings were very clever at inventing good reasons for doing what their interests suggested they do. The path of reason was not straight, and its deviations were not the fault of enemies, but of ourselves.

Voltaire anticipated the Grand Narrative in another, even more crucial sense. He invented the idea of history as the history of civilization. The anti-quaries of the seventeenth century raised the science of documentary analysis to a level of sophistication never since exceeded. To Voltaire, this was dust and nonsense. "Curse details . . . this vermin that kills great works." He wanted to know not how the laws of France were established or by what right the king claimed allegiance from the Bretons, but "the radical vice and the dominant virtue of a nation; why she was strong or weak at sea; how and up to what point she has become prosperous over a century . . . how the arts and manufactures are arranged . . . the changes in values, habits, and laws will be his great subject. Thus we shall have the history of human beings instead of a small part of the history of kings and courts."[26]

The radical Enlightenment, whose two leaders were Voltaire and Jean-Jacques Rousseau, rejected Christendom in its two aspects, as an ancient unity of originally incompatible elements that still set bounds for what was allowed and what was commanded, and as a discipline of historical and social study. They wanted to know not how the Germanic invasions introduced a certain idea of liberty to the peoples of Rome and thereby created the West, but how the human race as a whole was and ought to be progressing from darkness to light, folly to reason, superstition to unfettered freedom of thought. This, of course, was the model of the Grand Narrative. In his history of the age of Louis XIV, Voltaire identified four Magic Moments in human history, "when the arts were perfected and which may serve as epochs in the greatness of the human spirit as examples to posterity."[27] These were Greece in the fifth and fourth centuries B.C., the age of Pericles, Plato, Phidias, and Aristotle; Rome in the age of Lucretius, Cicero, Livy, and Virgil, that is, the first century B.C.; the Italian Renaissance of the fifteenth century; and the age of Louis XIV. From Plato to Louis?

Montesquieu remained closer to the idea of the West as Christendom, be-cause he retained the idea of natural law, of the basic rules of human nature and society that made it possible to explain, for example, the rise of com-merce and liberty in terms of laws and institutions. In Voltaire, the critical factor was not institutions, which might be old, irrational, and difficult to ex-plain, but education. And by that criterion, "the major part of the human race has been and will for long be mindless and stupid," he wrote. "And the most mindless are those who have tried to find some meaning in those ab-surd stories and to temper folly with reason."[28]

For Voltaire, education was the sign of progress. Since most people were not educated, progress was fragile and uncertain. History was an arena of force, fraud, and stupidity. In their different ways, both Montesquieu and the historians of Christendom had detected true development in history, the former in the spread of freedom-permitting institutions and power sharing, the latter in the rise of Christian ethical and social teaching on the ruins of the Roman Empire. Voltaire rejected such confidence, preferring to divide history into a few moments of light and vast tracts of darkness. The age of reason, if one was to exist, would commence a new history, different from what had gone before. Thus, Voltaire launched not only the model of the Grand Narrative but the even more radical idea that the New West was wholly distinct from the Old.

One of the pervasive lines of division in the post-Enlightenment West was between those who held, with Montesquieu, that human nature and natural law indicated the conditions of liberty and progress, and those who agreed with Voltaire that history was mostly the story of idiots doing stupid things, but that the future might be different, if only reason and not emotions governed policy. Montesquieu replied that this was not the point; policy would always be governed by a mixture of reason and emotion; the point both of scholarship and policy-making was to devise arrangements that would, so far as possible, encourage reason and minimize the political harm done by emotions.

The French Revolution that began in 1789 politicized the major division in the modern West between those who looked for guidance to history and tradition as well as reason and those who trusted in reason alone to define the good society and the ways to reach it. This was a division among scholars, philosophers, and elites, not kings, politicians, or bureaucrats. When the enemies of revolution took back power in France in 1814, they did not install a regime of respect for tradition mixed with reason, such as Benjamin Constant set forth in his proposed constitution, but a regime of reaction, censorship, and arbitrary autocracy. But the thought and writings of elites legitimated or condemned the political practices during the two centuries of the West's civil wars.

The revolution was the seminal event of modern Western politics, overshadowing in its effects the significance of the other late-eighteenth-century revolution, the American. The French Revolution became the political model for all those who took their cue from the radical Enlightenment of Voltaire and Rousseau, the Enlightenment that proposed education, or ideology, as the crucial element of progress, and that saw freedom as the goal of such pedagogy. Its political history traditionally fell into two parts, the moderate, liberal revolution of 1789–91, followed by the radical, Jacobin revolution of 1792–94.[29] The fall of the leading Jacobin, Robespierre, was then succeeded by five years of lingering oligarchy, until Napoleon Bonaparte marched in to become first the consul, and then the emperor, of the French state. In fact, the distinction between a moderate and a radical phase became hard to sustain once one looked closely at the events of 1789, which included many bloody episodes. Rather, at least two revolutions coexisted throughout those five dramatic years of 1789–94: a liberal impulse that sought to free national energies from injustice, coercion, and exploitation, and a harsher, ideological current deriving its energies rather from hatred and suspicion than from hope for the future.

The classic optimist vision of the revolution was that of the historian Jules Michelet, who wrote his *History of the French Revolution* in the 1840s and 1850s. He was the sickly son of a Jacobin artisan who grew up to be the most prolific historical writer in French literature. Although he wrote dozens of volumes on French medieval and early modern history, the revolution was his first and last love, which he regarded with all the passion of a lover, refusing to hear ill spoken of it. According to Michelet, the essence of the revolution was "the interior conquest of France by herself, *the conquest of the land by the worker.*"[30] The revolution, in Michelet's view, took property from the few and gave it to the many, from whom it had been unjustly taken by legal fictions and devices over the previous centuries. The essence of this revolutionary change was a transfer of property rights; for Michelet, the revolution was about giving the many a stake in national identity and independence, a stake that they would have only if each family owned its own corner of France. In prerevolutionary France, most land was held by absentee landlords or by the church; this, according to Michelet, was both unjust and inefficient. As for the church, he was not anti-Christian—nor, for that matter, were any of the leading revolutionaries, including Robespierre—merely anticlerical. Church property was an obstacle to true Christianity, for it gave the church worldly interests. True Christianity was not about suffering, but about joy and health, and should therefore serve human purposes. In this, Michelet's outlook resembled the progressive deism of Voltaire.

Michelet also had an explanation of why the extreme wing of the Jacobins took power in 1792. They did this in a national emergency—France was being invaded by the hostile armies of the First Coalition—and were able to do so because a remarkable apathy had spread through the population, particularly the population of Paris. It was in an attempt to rally people to defend the Revolution that Danton, Robespierre, and their associates mobilized the Jacobin clubs throughout Paris and the provinces. Once they had become the centers of political action, the clubs also became the places from which members of the Convention—the revolutionary government—were chosen; by early 1794, their delegates were dominant.

The Jacobin revolution was an attempt to enforce a vision of the good society and was thus the first act in the ideological drama of modernity. The particular vision of the good held by the Jacobins owed much to Rousseau, although, as the historian Simon Schama noted, one could at best describe the Jacobin ideology as "Rousseau in a raucous voice." Starting with Benjamin Constant himself, one of the founders of classical liberalism, anti-Jacobin writers tried to pin the Great Terror of the Year II (1793–94) and other tyrannical deeds on Rousseau as their ideological inspiration.

Rousseau's fundamental doctrine was that "man is born free, yet everywhere he is in chains." Human nature in its original condition was good. Civilization represented a fall from this happy state of innocence, introducing dishonesty, competition, vice, and ambition, which led to inequality, the great evil of society and the cause as well as the consequence of the psychological trap that prevented people from breaking free and returning to their true natures. In civilization, man is a divided creature, his original goodness obscured and dominated by a persona of greed and insincerity. The political task therefore was to find a way to restore man to his pristine state.

The doctrine of original human goodness overlaid by a vicious civilized nature was a politicized, secular version of Christianity, or rather, of the Calvinist Christianity of Rousseau's homeland Geneva. In his *Confession of Faith of a Savoyard Vicar*, a part of his pedagogical novel *Émile*, Rousseau spelled out his political religion. As in his earlier writing on the origins of inequality, he began by positing an original unity of the human spirit. Inequality and divisions between men were the source of all social and personal evils, but they were acquired habits and could therefore be abolished. By introducing inequality, vice, and ambition, civilization also corrupted reason, which always found ways of justifying inequality. Therefore, we should trust our emotions rather than our reason, for our emotions were a link to the state of nature, to original innocence. Nature, or God, was the source of harmony and goodness, whereas civilized man was capable only of chaos and confusion. Rousseau agreed with Saint Paul that people desired the good but did what was evil. But Rousseau then claimed, a little paradoxically, man remained free and able to break the bonds of civilization and inequality. The inner voice of emotion and conscience, the voice of nature, had not wholly died. Informed by conscience, reason would be able to recognize the good, and human freedom would be strong enough to choose it.

The fatal division in man between a pristine nature and a corrupt persona, or civil personality, had also, Rousseau said, fatally undermined religion. Christianity was in essence good and true, but Christians had committed a fatal mistake when they distinguished what was God's from what was Caesar's. In distinguishing religious from civil obligation, the churches in effect instituted two religions: a personal religion of charity and a civil religion of obedience to the powers that be. But such a split was immoral and intolerable, like the split in the human soul between original innocence and corrupt convention. The task of the wise legislator and reformer was to heal both breaches, to restore the unity of human beings and the unity of their religion. The goal of political action, Rousseau held, was to build a society of good people whose religion would also constitute their social norms and civil obligation. The wise legislator should have the right to enforce good behavior and right belief. If any citizen refused to accept the rules that true, uncorrupted human nature indicated, he should be banished. If any citizen accepted the rules but then showed by his actions that he did not believe them, he should be executed, because he would then have committed the greatest of all crimes, that of deceiving the law.

Rousseau rejected the classical liberal philosophy found in embryonic form in Montesquieu, namely, that human nature, history, and society were a blend of good and evil, reason and emotion, liberty and coercion. He wanted unity and coherence. The good society for Rousseau was not one where people were free to pursue their particular interests, but one that forced them to be free according to what he knew was their deepest, uncorrupted desire, the desire of the state of nature for harmony and equality. The good society united the best part of individual wills into "the general will," a common purpose and policy that would be the immediate reflection of what each individual knew, deep down in his or her conscience, was right. The good society, in short, would recreate the original unity of the human race by a political act.

As Benjamin Constant pointed out, since creating the good society was necessarily a moral demand, no one could morally refuse to participate. Those who had discovered how to achieve the good society, in which citizens had the right desires and the correct morality, had, by Rousseau's doctrine, an incontrovertible license to coerce in the name of the general will, which by definition was always in the right and ought always to prevail over the corrupted, private, individual wills, caught as they were in the illusions of ambition and the temptations of inequality. Rousseau desperately wanted to elide what he saw as the fatal gap in man's social life, the gap between what people knew, or should know, to be good and what they actually did. The practical attempt to elide that gap never failed to lead to mass murder and war, whether in the relatively mild form of the 1790s or the more catastrophic versions launched by the Bolshevik and National Socialist revolutions of 1917 and 1933, respectively.

Rousseau truly believed that "man was born free, yet everywhere he is in chains." As Montesquieu would have said, that was a profoundly unhistorical and naive idea. Neither part of the sentence was historically or philosophically coherent. That man was born free was a metaphysical postulate that begged the definition of freedom. That he was everywhere in chains was a judgment that depended for its meaning on the same, absent definition of freedom. And the relation between the two statements, the "yet," implied yet a third metaphysical and moral postulate—that a bad thing had happened to reduce man from the asserted original state. As well might one say, "Sheep were born as carnivores, yet everywhere they eat grass."[31]

The American Revolution was the product of Montesquieu in the same inexact but revealing sense that the French Revolution was the product of Rousseau. Montesquieu described the conditions of liberty and prosperity; these were divided power, the government of several rather than of one or of all, and the incentive that such power sharing and secure laws gave to men to produce and invest, to make money, finance inventions and new methods, create employment, and raise the total prosperity and potentiality of their society. He identified Britain as the society with the best conditions for enterprise and liberty, which were two sides of the same coin. He died twenty years before the Declaration of Independence and thirty years before the American Constitution, but he would have understood and endorsed James Madison's hopeful but, in the main, accurate definition of America as a great commercial republic. A commercial republic was exactly what Montesquieu identified as the best framework for individual and social liberty, as well as for prosperity.

The most striking feature of the stormy and often imperiled history of political and social liberty in the West from the days of the late antique synthesis through the grand bargain of church and empire, the Renaissance, and the Reformation was its marriage to Christian ideas of freedom. A marriage less made in heaven would, at first glance, seem hard to imagine. Germanic freedom was the freedom of aristocratic warriors to decide the actions of their tribe or nation; a freedom tinged with the heroic ethos of self-assertion and self-sacrifice. Christian freedom was freedom from the world, fulfilled in humble service of God and without regard to one's social or economic state; male or female, slave or free, Jew or Gentile. Yet the marriage took place, and produced the *militia Dei*, the war service of God, of Boniface the martyr and of the Carolingian warriors, of the eleventh-century reformers of the church and their contemporaries, the crusaders. Blood and holiness were close in those days, as the *Song of Roland* demonstrated. Turpin the archbishop brained a Moor with Toledo steel, and the poet told us in the same breath that "no man chanted a better mass." The Muslims understood; this was as close to jihad, the holy striving to do God's will, as Christendom ever got.

The commercial republic that Madison saw growing around him in America partook of Montesquieu's original freedom but also of its history. What the French baron for all his perception did not fully see was that the commercial and social liberty of his own time was the modern, pacific, debellicized face of the Dark Age marriage. The piecemeal, partial pacification of Europe after 1648, itself the result in part of better expectations of life and less patience with wars, holy or political, turned the energies of the West from *militia Dei* to trade, commerce, and invention. The modern triad did not spring into being in the late eighteenth century; it was present in embryo in the eleventh-century Rhineland.

The French Revolution chose a different path, obscuring the commercial option and choosing the option of a modernized *militia Dei*, now called patriotism. Jefferson and the other Americans knew what that was; it motivated their political and religious rebellion against their dread sovereign lord, His Britannic Majesty King George the Third, Defender of the Faith. But the distance and the commercial orientation of the American Republic delayed for eighty-five years the military explosion that tested American patriotism to its limits and thereby forged it anew: the Civil War. The French Republic was born in a fever of populist hate against aristocrats, and then, with an eye to the foreigners who were not three thousand miles away but across the Rhine and the Alps, in a fever of a different and more urgent kind of patriotism, one that defined the patriot as the mobilized and armed *citoyen*. The task of the French revolutionaries was to forge a mobilized and defensible nation that would at one and the same time be able to constitute itself as a self-governing body politic, and maintain itself against the attack of hostile monarchies.

The Americans won their liberty thanks in part to patriotic fervor; they could then lay down their arms and constitute themselves into a free republic.

The French first constituted themselves into a political nation and then had to defend themselves. The first sequence made militant patriotism an emergency feeling, not necessary in the important task of political creation. The second sequence, the French, made militant patriotism into the essence of political creation, for the two were not separated by time and space but run together. The Jacobin and Girondin majority of the National Assembly proclaimed the republic in September 1792 and found *la patrie en danger*, France at war. The Americans had been at war, and were at peace, when their republic was instituted. The opposing sequences by no means fully explained why the Jacobins thought it necessary to employ terror to enforce their Republic of Virtue; but it made the Jacobin impulse in the French Revolution, and its temporary success in 1792–94, more comprehensible.

Mirabeau, one of the leaders of the early phase of the revolution, defined popular sovereignty as made up of two parts: "the power of willing, and the power of acting."[32] The legacy of Rousseau to the Jacobins was that they thought they had to merge the two, that the democratic people had to be at the same time its own master and the executor of its own laws. Rousseau prescribed that the free community of individuals must constitute itself as sovereign, because only the people that knowingly liberated itself was in a position to create and maintain liberty by healing the fatal breach in human social nature between the good and the artificial, the true and the corrupt, the noble and rightly guided general will and the wayward, particularistic, and selfish individual will. Because the Jacobins believed this, and because they found themselves engaged in the impossible task of forcing their people to be themselves, that is, free, in the midst of war, they turned to terror.

The revolutionary era launched the divided identity of the New West, with one part, the universalist and progressive impulse, denying history, and the other studying it for clues to the growth of freedom and security. Edmund Burke, who defended the Americans against George III in Parliament, was often classed as a conservative because he opposed the French Revolution, which he defined as "a Revolution of doctrine and theoretic dogma" in which "a spirit of proselytism makes an essential part." As early as 1790, when the atmosphere in Paris was still one of national solidarity and optimism, Burke predicted "transmigrations, fire, and blood." To call Burke a conservative, however, was to misunderstand his commitment to "liberty connected with order," which "inheres in good and steady government, as in its substance and vital principle."[33] Burke, like Montesquieu, detected the forces that shaped the interests, and hence the behavior, of large social groups like nations. He warned against playing with those forces or ignorantly conjuring them. But, again like Montesquieu, his constant focus was the real freedom, the niches of liberty, found in the history of the Old West and taken by him to define its identity. He rejected the false promise of absolute freedom held out by the radical revolutionaries in France, for he saw in it a denial of the Old West and a denial of the idea of reasoned progress into the New.

The battle between the advocates of reasoned progress based on history and of radical change based on hope and the claims of justice defined the internal conflict and the schizophrenic identity of the New West from 1789 on. The conflict between universalists and sceptics in the 1990s demonstrated that the conflict had not been concluded.

CHAPTER EIGHT

The High Tide of Liberalism

This is the real struggle, therefore the real force of the future—the force of work, intelligence, efficiency, which really achieves things; not the force of arms, which achieves nothing
—Norman Angell

The entire idealism of humanity up to this point is on the verge of tipping over into nihilism, into faith in the absolute loss of value, that is, of meaning
—Friedrich Nietzsche

When the twenty-two-year-old Napoleon Bonaparte, recently commissioned first lieutenant in the royal army of France, left his unit in late 1791 to visit his family on his native island of Corsica, he found that his great uncle was dying. The old man gave his last messages to each of the eight Bonaparte siblings. To Napoleon, he said, *"tu poi, Napoleone, tu sarai un omone"* (as for you, you're going to be a big shot)."[1] Within eight years, the little Corsican was dictator of France, first as consul, then as emperor. Six years after that, he won his most brilliant military victory over the superior forces of Russia and the Holy Roman Empire at Austerlitz. Eighteen months later again, he had wiped off the map the kingdom of Prussia, the most feared military state of

Enlightenment Europe, and had forced Francis I, "by the grace of God elected Roman emperor," to dissolve the thousand-year-old empire of Charlemagne, Otto III, Frederick II, and Charles V. Like the earlier dissolution in 476 of the western Roman Empire of Julius Caesar, Augustus, and Constantine, the collapse of 1806 was, to many contemporaries, an overdue nonevent. Since the seventeenth century, observers like the legal and constitutional theorist Samuel Pufendorf had repeatedly pointed out that the empire lacked sovereign authority, strong central institutions, and most other attributes of a normal European state. But for a century and a half after the peace of Westphalia devolved much imperial power to the constituent parts—the estates—of the empire, the ancient confederation refused to die. It was not until Napoleon in 1804 broke the ancient rule that the West could have but one emperor and had occupied and redistributed half the territory of the empire that the old structure lost its last shreds of credibility. Napoleon had done more—he had violated two other principles of the ancient compact of the West. The Holy Roman Emperors were, in theory, divinely appointed and supranational; the empire was not a national state but the living memory of the old bargain that divided the emerging West. At his coronation in Paris, however, Napoleon had taken the crown from the pope and put it on his own head, and he had done so not as Roman emperor, but as emperor of the French.

So while the old empire had long seemed an erratic block of archaic symbolism, its end was more than a casual accident, a cleaning-up of old business. Wounded in 1648 by the principle of religious toleration and by the national interests of the new European states, it fell in 1806 to the aggressive nationalism of France and the balancing nationalism of Germany, whose leaders saw it as an obstacle in their attempts to create a modern national identity. The timing may have been fortuitous; the event itself, like that of 476, was not. On each occasion, Western identity turned a corner: in 476, it began moving out of the late antique synthesis of the Christian empire; in 1806, it left behind the last remnant of the Old Western attempt to build a supranational political system.

In 1807, Napoleon stood at the pinnacle of his power. In place of the ancient bargain of church and empire, first proposed by Constantine and renewed more lastingly by Leo III and Charlemagne, he proposed a new bargain based on the modern forces of nationalism and geopolitics. According to his own self-serving recollections, he had never wanted perpetual war. No, his dream was to unite the great nations of Europe in a peaceful and prosperous federation, one in which the distinct virtues of the different nations would work together for the common good:

> One of my greatest ideas was to bring together and assemble those same geographical nations which had been torn and fragmented by revolution and politics. Thus, you find scattered across Europe thirty million Frenchmen, fifteen million Spaniards, fifteen million Italians, thirty million Germans. I would have wanted to turn each of these peoples into one single national body. How beautiful it would have been, with such a parade, to advance into posterity and the blessings of the centuries. I felt myself worthy of such glory! . . . it would then have been possible to give oneself to the effort of [bringing about] the beautiful ideal of civilization; in such a state of affairs one would have found the most chances of promoting everywhere the unity of laws, of principles, of opinions, of feelings, of attitudes, and of interests. Then, perhaps, by the favor of universal Enlightenment, it might become possible to dream, for the great European family, of going the way of the American Congress . . . what an outlook then of power, of glory, of well-being, of prosperity! What a great and magnificent spectacle![2]

Nationalism and geopolitics were here allied in Napoleon's imagination; what was notably absent from his pageant was liberty and individual rights. The pieces in his picture were not men and women but the nations, conceived as giant entities, who, at the end of the day, were all going to think alike, act alike, and dream alike in a "unity of laws, of principles, of opinions, of feelings." The height of absurdity was to imagine that these homogenized nations could somehow come together in a United States of Europe on the model of the American Congress. Quite apart from the question of who would represent them, such a vision completely ignored the most important point about the American Congress, which was that it was a delegation of free individuals gathered to develop the constitution of a free people. So unconsciously revealing was this vision of Napoleon's totalitarianism that it probably represented his true beliefs. He was too artless to conceal his dictatorial nature. The whole vignette reminds one of nothing so much as an energetic little Corsican boy manipulating his large family, marching platoons of loving cousins back and forth across the map until they all are moving in the same direction and with the same smile of doglike devotion on their faces.

In July 1807, Napoleon held a summit meeting with the only other ruler in Europe whom he could call a peer—Alexander I, czar of all the Russias.[3]

Since Peter the Great a hundred years earlier, Russia had become a European great power and its ruler was accorded, in his own titulature as well as in diplomacy, the rank of emperor. The Russian ruler was exempt from the rule against plural emperors, because he was, in a sense, the heir of the eastern Roman, or Byzantine, emperors, who had coexisted with those of the West until 1453, and whose claim to the title was arguably better, since imperial authority in the East had never lapsed, as it had in the West between 476 and 800. The last eastern Roman emperor, Constantine XI, who fell defending Constantinople against the Turks in 1453, was the direct heir, in unbroken succession, of the first Constantine, the first Christian emperor, and through him of Augustus and Julius Caesar. When the princes of Moscow adopted the imperial title in the sixteenth century, they were not, therefore, stating an absurd pretense, but resurrecting what, to them and to all Orthodox Christians, was a necessary element of the political cosmos—a Christian emperor who was not, like the Westerners, a heretic and upstart, but a representative of the true Roman and ancient Christian legacy.

Nevertheless it was not ancient history or the bipolar political theology that—grudgingly—accepted one emperor for Catholics and one for the Orthodox that concerned Napoleon when he met Alexander at Tilsit in Prussia, on the Memel River that separated German, or west European, from Russian territory. As the quintessential self-made man, Napoleon represented two new principles in Western identity: the revolutionary meritocracy that permitted a man of low rank to rise above the ranks reserved for the highly born and to destroy them, and nationalism, which fed his armies and confirmed his victories. For a brief moment it looked as though Europe might settle into a new sort of bipolarity, in which an expanded Western conglomeration of power centered on France and its new empire that was based on the ideology—not the reality—of popular sovereignty faced an eastern empire that, despite its eastern Roman and Orthodox legacies, was also becoming a national community, expressed in the Christian ethnicity of Russia.

But bipolar geopolitical systems are inherently unstable, because each of the two parties always needs to worry that the other is aiming for supremacy. Therefore, each will try to pre-empt or deter such ambitions, forcing the other to a similar course of action. Bipolar systems inevitably end either in a general conflict that destroys one of the parties as a contender for supreme power or in a collapse of bipolarity, after which the system reverts to its multipolar norm. That Napoleon was unable to rest content with dividing power in Europe, but was compelled by his character and desires to destroy all rivals, merely hastened the collapse of an arrangement that might have seemed greatly to the advantage of both Russia and an imperial France exhausted by wars and in need of peace and consolidation.

Napoleon was defeated not only by his own inability to stay put, which created new enemies where none existed, but also by a third modern principle that, unlike revolutionary meritocracy and nationalism, worked against him rather than for him. This was the capitalist liberalism of England and of the global economy of the high seas and of intercontinental commerce, which not only gave Britain the resources to stand alone against a Europe dominated, in 1807–9, by the Franco-Russian bipolar coalition, but also outcompeted the Continental powers in efficient use of resources and in geopolitical scope. Command of the seas allowed Britain to intervene in Europe where the French could not easily respond, yet where the risks to Britain were minimal. By the back doors of Spain, the Mediterranean, the Black Sea, and the Baltic, British power first pricked French power and then, in alliance with Russia, defeated it. Only at the very end, at Waterloo in June 1815, did British forces engage the main French army under Napoleon himself, when France was bled white by twenty-three years of war, whereas Britain, with less than half the population, still had the best of its human resources to draw on.

The economic historians pinpointed incentives to efficient use of resources as the key to economic development in the West. But efficient resource use not only stimulated the economy, but was the fruit of those niches of liberty—collective and individual, religious and political—that, as Montesquieu and Hume suggested, cumulatively defined Western identity from the age of the Germanic invasions on. And as the niches of liberty provided and promoted incentives to efficient use of resources, so the advantages of efficiency fed back to the niches of liberty, justifying, strengthening, and expanding them. No account of Western identity focused on only one side of the equation, on either capitalism or liberty, on material incentives or libertarian idealism, is adequate. It was the inextricable correlation of both motivations that drove the combined engine of democracy and growth. For a thousand years, the scattered communities "where several governed" provided intermittent evidence of the material as well as spiritual advantages that could result from political and social pluralism, until, in the era of Napoleon, the long prehistory of Western liberal democracy met the challenge of a rival modernization.

The British world power that outmaneuvered Napoleonic France, wearing down her energies until she was ripe for defeat in open combat, was preeminently power based on parsimony and efficiency. One reason that Edmund Burke and, with him, other British political thinkers were not overly downcast when Britain lost most of her American colonies was that Britain had, in those same years, acquired a far more populous and prosperous empire in India—and not by committing the resources of government in the way that government tried to stop American independence, but by private initiative supported at critical points by minute doses of public spending. To keep a relatively small number of unprofitable, unwilling subjects at the cost of much public treasure seemed irrational when vast new provinces with great scope for trade and profit were available at minimal public cost. The end of the American empire of Britain thus coincided with the rise of her Asian empire based on India—and it was noteworthy that this second empire also began to pall, around 1900, as it ceased being a commercial, and increasingly became a geopolitical and administrative operation.

Parsimony also characterized Britain's war against Napoleon. France sacrificed over a million men—out of a population in 1792 of some twenty-eight million—and suffered irreparable economic, social, and demographic damage to acquire, to defend, and then almost immediately to lose Continental hegemony in Europe. At Trafalgar in 1805, Britain denied France that Continental hegemony and confirmed her own much broader, global hegemony for a century at the cost of 449 casualties. Napoleon's bid for power applied nationalist fervor to the centuries-old mobilizing abilities of the centralized, sovereign state, producing enormous energy but yielding only disaster. The British containment of Napoleon used nationalism to give a final, sharp edge to the strategically deployed but limited military means available to a commercial, trading state—a state defined not by the size of its government or its ability to mobilize the masses, but by how its institutions, including judiciously applied power, encouraged and enabled its subjects to manufacture, sell, invest, and reap the profits. And not just to reap profits, for that was the aim of all merchants throughout history, but to reap them in ways and in amounts that maximized the social, as well as the private, benefits of economic activity.

The Congress of Vienna called to settle the political system of Europe in 1814–15 thus met in the shadow of conflicting interests and forces: revolutionary nationalism, which had appeared in 1792 as a volcanic transformation of Western identity, political, social, and international; defensive, dynastic conservatism, which wished to return to the world of 1789 or, if that was not possible, to enforce a Europe-wide police state that would learn from the past to suppress, effectively, any new stirrings of the volcano; and finally, the force that was both the oldest and the most modern of all, the capitalist liberalism that was the slowly maturing fruit of centuries of political and social evolution—mainly, but by no means exclusively, in Britain—and that, now finally ripening, was about to become the core of the West.

Surprisingly, the Congress succeeded in mediating among these interests and the more immediate interests of the more than two hundred separate states, principalities, cities, and corporate entities represented in its deliberations. Liberal historians, including the Grand Narrative, typically shrugged off the congress as a reactionary assembly of autocrats determined to turn back the clock to 1792, when the first revolutionary war began, and to stifle liberal currents throughout Europe. This was in several ways a caricature. Had the congress really tried to reimpose the frontiers and the regimes of 1792, it would have failed, and any settlement would have been short-lived. The congress settlement of Europe lasted for ninety-nine years, which was a better record than any international peace conference either before or since. Europe during that century was not entirely free of war, but the wars that did break out—in 1848, 1854, 1864, 1866, and 1870—were brief and limited. More important: no Western state during that century either hoped or attempted to subvert the system and acquire hegemony in the manner of Napoleon. For another thing, the liberal historians overestimated the strength of political liberalism in 1814. The idea that the nations of Europe were waiting impatiently for democracy was simply anachronistic. The congress settlement—the so-called Concert of Europe—was less a matter of imposing unpopular regimes than of giving both rulers and ruled much of what they all wanted—ordered government and the prospect of a durable, international peace. If liberalism grew in the following decades to become a doctrine of national as well as individual and group autonomy, this was in no small part due to the peace and tranquillity offered by the concert. Nor were the congress decisions always in favor of restoration, authority, legitimacy, and solidarity among the monarchist regimes. Where one might have expected high-handed treatment of small or weak nations, such as the Swiss, the Dutch, or the Norwegians, the congress mediated conflicting interests in ways that preserved peace longer than if it had simply sought to establish a mechanical balance among the great powers. Finally, in another gesture that none of the conservative powers would have made in 1792, the Congress attached a declaration condemning the slave trade to its final act, thereby serving one of the great liberal causes of the age.

The conventional, progressive, and liberal definition of the congress settlement as a restoration—of authoritarian monarchy and the balance of power—was therefore misleading. Its most knowledgeable late-twentieth-century historian, Paul Schroeder, convincingly refuted that understanding and proposed that, so far from being backward-looking, the congress was

> progressive, oriented in practical, non-Utopian ways toward the future. In fact, another term might substitute for "restoration": revolution. It has now become possible, even fashionable, to doubt that the French Revolution revolutionized domestic politics and society in France and Europe. If it remains in the long term the source of liberal and democratic ideals, it may in the short term have set them back. . . . Only in one arena in 1789–1815 can one speak unequivocally of progress, breakthrough, even revolution: in international politics. Here there was unmistakable structural change. A competitive balance-of-power struggle gave way to an international system of political equilibrium based on benign shared hegemony and the mutual recognition of rights underpinned by law.[4]

The congress and its system, the concert, were the victims of their own success. Because they created international peace in Europe for several decades, Western societies were able to evolve free of the burdens of war. That benefited liberalism and permitted liberal movements to grow until, in the 1830s and after, they were able to dispute the legitimacy of the existing regimes. The concert was indeed revolutionary, in two senses: it constructed a durable peace, where previous settlements had mostly rewarded winners and punished losers, and thus launched Europe into an era of social, economic, and political development that never could have taken place under conditions of endemic war.

The image of the Congress as purely reactionary was wrong in another way as well. It ignored the differences between its many members. At one end stood Britain, already markedly pluralistic in domestic politics, at the other, the Habsburg monarchy, which was itself a result of the revolutionary wars. Had it insisted on restoration, it would have had to abolish itself and resurrect the Holy Roman Empire. When Francis I dissolved the empire in 1806, he retained the title of emperor, but of Austria rather than of Rome. This Austrian empire lasted until 1918, and for the first four decades of its history its leading statesman was Clemens von Metternich, a native of the Rhineland, where his family had held lands on the left, or western, bank of the Rhine since the thirteenth century. He was born in 1773; when the French revolutionary armies invaded the western Rhineland in the 1790s, he declared his opposition to the revolution, to national self-determination, and to popular sovereignty. In 1809, he became Austrian foreign minister and for the next thirty-nine years the dominant figure not only in the Austrian government, but in the entire conservative wing of the Concert of Europe. The so-called Metternich System sought to stabilize the concert by suppressing internal dissent, especially liberal and nationalist movements. But even Metternich did not believe in thorough restoration: he had no intention of trying to bring back the Holy Roman Empire, nor of restoring the many German princes who had lost their lands and their sovereignty in the revolutionary wars. He believed that the peace of Europe required government of the great powers by monarchs supported by established churches, and therefore, also, that peace required internal order, to be obtained, if necessary, by censorship and persecution.

The Metternich System began to collapse in 1830, when an alliance of reforming monarchists and liberals overthrew Charles X, the last king of France who had been crowned with all the pomp and ritual of the medieval tradition, and who, unfortunately, believed that he ought to govern as his ancestors had. His attempts to do so provoked the July uprising—the one immortalized by Delacroix in his painting of the bare-breasted goddess of Revolution brandishing the *tricouleur* and inspiring the sons of the people defending the barricade. The July revolution in turn established the liberal July monarchy, which lasted until the next French revolution, that of February 1848.

The nineteenth century was the high tide of classical liberalism, of the belief that political liberty and economic development were complementary, that both were destined to grow and to spread, and that the purpose of statecraft and policy was to help them do so. Liberals were not wrong in this diagnosis, which the third millennium may, in the end, prove right. But classical liberalism appeared to fail in 1914, when it did not stop World War I; in 1929, when it did not stop the Great Depression; in 1939, when it did not stop World War II; and in the decades from 1917 to 1989, when it did not stop the totalitarian regimes of the Soviet Union and National Socialist Germany. Starting in the 1880s, front-line thinkers of the West increasingly assumed that liberalism was destined to fail and that progress was either an illusion or carried too great a price. For much of the next century, many of those who defined Western identity considered liberalism inadequate or downright harmful. Others—such as Robert Maynard Hutchins, Will Durant, or the authors of the Columbia Grand Narrative—resurrected a liberal Western identity, but they did so defensively and with a sneaking sense that the critics of liberalism were right, that liberalism really was not enough. The result of this effort was the centrist liberalism of mid-twentieth-century America, which fell to the radicalized, collectivist liberalism of the 1960s and after because it had never been really sure of itself in the first place.

Classical liberalism began in the sceptical Enlightenment and in opposition to the Jacobin elements in the French Revolution, but lost its confidence as it developed weaknesses that vitiated its twentieth-century descendants— and that continued, in the post–Cold War era, to vitiate the optimists who advocated a new universalism. The first of these weaknesses was the illusion of newness. Many liberals saw their political and economic beliefs, and the successful principles of government of the most prosperous societies of the West, as an original body of thought and practice never before seen and that emerged, with great speed and almost miraculously, out of the revolutionary era, whereas in fact capitalist liberalism was but the latest, developed fruit of the classical, Christian, and Germanic legacies, and therefore of the religion, institutions, and social practices of the Old West.

The second weakness was that nineteenth-century liberals increasingly saw freedom in purely economic terms, as a doctrine of minimal government, free trade, and laissez-faire—literally, "let them act," meaning the capitalists and investors, the men with money. Liberalism shrank from being an understanding of ordered liberty as promoting civic virtue as well as economic development and became an ideology—the bourgeois ideology—of economic liberty, of wealth as an end in itself.[5] This economism invited the egalitarianist retort that free trade and laissez-faire for the few meant exploitation and misery of the many. Liberals who had abandoned the original, political and moral core of their philosophy had no answer to this retort, which, in the egalitarian political universe of modernity, gave them a permanently bad conscience.[6] Unnecessarily so, for bourgeois economism sold liberalism short and, in particular, distorted the teaching of Adam Smith, universally acknowledged as a founding father of liberal thought. Smith was, and intended to be, a moral, as well as a political philosopher and economist. To him, all three elements were equally indispensable for a comprehensive understanding of the social world. To define social man as a utility-maximizing creature driven mainly by material incentives—by greed—was an individualistic and materialist distortion of Smith's analysis and of the original richness of the liberal tradition. For the same reason, the liberal decision to place Edmund Burke in the conservative camp had fateful consequences for liberalism, for his thought faithfully represented the historical roots of Western liberty and thus belonged rather in the ancestry of a comprehensive liberalism than in that of conservatism. No true conservative would argue, as Burke did, that "a disposition to preserve and an ability to improve" was the criterion of sound policy, for "improvement" was not a value in the conservative lexicon. No conservative would place liberty and justice, as Burke did, at the heart of his political philosophy, in preference, for example, to order, obedience, or faith. No conservative, finally, would condemn the French Revolution for undermining genuine, particular liberty in the name of an absolute, never-before-seen universal liberty, but rather as a rebellion against the divinely ordered social hierarchy. The true conservatives of the counterrevolution, Joseph de Maistre and Louis de Bonald, condemned the revolution and liberalism not as excesses of a good thing—freedom—but condemned political freedom itself as a heresy against Catholic doctrine.

The economic fixation or pathology of liberalism was not so much a weakness as a tendency that had always been part of the liberal outlook but that, if allowed to dominate, turned it into a caricature of itself. Economic development in the systematic fashion that came to characterize the West from the later Middle Ages on required specific habits of mind and behavior, habits of quantification, planning, parsimony, and caution.[7] People displaying such habits and reaping their benefits often came to see them as ends in themselves, and to see all reality, including other people, in terms of their use-value; as Benjamin Franklin—no misanthrope—said, "time is money." There was, therefore, within the liberal outlook a tendency to economism, to narrow utility maximization, to greed and exploitative behavior that came to the fore in the nineteenth century, producing the negative image of the bourgeois as Ebenezer Scrooge or Old Man Potter in Frank Capra's *It's a Wonderful Life*, the penny-pinching, patriarchal, joyless, black-clad figure who considered his employees and customers solely as instruments of revenue and his money, his capital, as an end in itself and not as the means to serve other ends—pedagogical, moral, aesthetic, erotic, or religious. "Bourgeois civilization," wrote one of its historians, "is essentially one in which only those goods count that belong to a quantitative and abstract order, interchangeable and anonymous goods, which confer no responsibility of any kind—such as real estate and investments—and where the goods that make up a fortune are considered not in terms of their use, but in terms of their market value; that is to say, above all, as elements of account; everything becomes merchandise, and the merchant imposes on society as a whole the character of his profession. As a result, one owns goods which in themselves evoke no human feeling of affection or preference, and which remain abstract, even though they are emphatically material."[8]

That capitalist liberalism included a tendency to bourgeois inhumanity, to an imperialism of the market, did not, as the socialists believed, make it a uniquely flawed political movement. All political movements had their characteristic pathologies; that of capitalist liberalism was precisely this acquisitive mentality combined with the tendency to view everything through quantitative, economic spectacles, to consider economic value the only value, and to see profits and revenue as ends in themselves, to be pursued at all costs and beyond all limits. Economism and exploitation were the temptations of capitalist liberalism, as theocracy and intolerance were the temptations of Christianity.

The third and most fundamental weakness of liberalism was the ambiguity of the idea of freedom itself. To Montesquieu and the early British liberals, freedom was tangible; it consisted in secure ownership and the right to dispose of one's property as one wished, with minimal despotic interference. The British Civil Wars of the 1640s were fought to determine whether the king would be able to override the ancient rights and liberties of Englishmen and Scots, in particular the right of religious freedom, and the right to decide on the crown's demands for taxes. Freedom resting on secure ownership encouraged self-reliance and responsibility; it built character, confidence, and civic virtue. It did not begin as a general principle but as the specific liberties—in the plural—of specific communities. It was freedom as the absence of coercion, and its most characteristic material expression was private property. Security of property demanded the rule of law and of impartial justice, which benefited both rich and poor, for only under the rule of law could the poor hope to better their condition and become, in their turn, owners of property. The greater a proportion of a people to hold property, the more secure their liberties and the more just and prosperous the society. This chain of logic underpinned Jules Michelet's great paean to the French Revolution, which he saw as a shift from arbitrary to just and rational government, from an era in which property was a revocable privilege to one in which it was an irrevocable right.[9]

Against this idea of freedom as property, as something asserted against arbitrary government, stood the idea of freedom as self-realization, as the ability to shape one's own life. The former idea, in the words of Isaiah Berlin, was negative freedom, the niche of liberty that individuals could assert for themselves against those who would restrict or deny it. Negative freedom focused on the external threats to freedom and posed the question "who is master?" Positive freedom focused on the well-being of the individual and asked "how far am I master?"[10] As soon as the focus shifted from external threats to personal autonomy, however, the very thing that underpinned negative freedom, namely property, became an obstacle to positive freedom. In the 1650s, the Leveller Gerrard Winstanley argued that property was the root of all evil, because it gave some people power over others, and that therefore no one could be truly free as long as it existed. Abolishing property would abolish both the temptation to exploit and the danger of being exploited. A century later, Jean-Jacques Rousseau argued that injustice entered history the moment someone fenced a field and said "this is mine." In the 1820s, the German philosopher G. W. F. Hegel took from the French Revolution and from Napoleon the lesson that the key to history was the idea of freedom, which he defined as autonomy and self-realization. In the ancient Near Eastern despotisms, only one, the ruler, was free; in classical Athens, a few, the male citizens, were free; in the modern West, all were potentially free, but only when each realized that his own autonomy depended on the equal autonomy of others. State power, he predicted, would be essential to secure this autonomy.

The weaknesses of liberalism were not fatal. On the contrary; the popular notion that liberalism was a failure because it did not stop the wars of the twentieth century—a notion that undermined the Grand Narrative from the start and gave American centrist liberalism its bad conscience—was profoundly mistaken. In the United States and Britain, a political culture permeated by the capitalist liberal understanding of human nature and its flourishing dominated for over a century, leading to a sustained and largely unbroken history of economic development, material improvement for the masses, and expanding personal autonomy. On the Continent, where most of the serious thinking about Western identity took place, the story was different. There—in Germany, France, Italy, and the smaller countries—liberals consistently failed to seize political power. Because liberals were rarely exposed to the challenge of politics, they took refuge in what they were good at—making money and producing economic growth for their societies. This produced the apolitical liberalism of the later nineteenth century, a liberalism strongly marked by its bourgeois, acquisitive pathology, as well as by another, nationalism.

Nationalism was the social force that was not supposed to happen.[11] When the Napoleonic Wars ended in 1815, Europeans and, later, Americans turned to social, cultural, and economic development and, by 1850, were fully engaged on the complex process of industrial, financial, and institutional modernization of their societies and communities. Economic and political liberalism looked to a future of harmony and collaboration between nations, in which, as Montesquieu and Benjamin Constant had predicted, trade would replace war as the focus of social energy. Karl Marx did not like trade or liberalism, but he, too, insisted that wars between states were a thing of the past; the time was coming, instead, for class warfare and for the expropriation of the expropriators, by which the impoverished proletariat would turn society on its head and become the one and only ruling class of the new communist society. Neither the liberal vision of harmony and trade nor the communist vision of conflict left much room for nationality, national feeling, nationalism, or national conflict.

Evidently, however, neither economic development nor class conflict satisfied the social needs of the growing and diversifying Western national communities. National identities grew more, not less, pronounced as the nineteenth century passed. Nationalism, the idea that one's own nation was not only good and worth defending, but endowed with unique qualities making it superior to others, satisfied the need for community and fellow feeling undermined by urbanization and, paradoxically, by the very forces of economic development and class conflict that, according to liberals and to Marx, were supposed to make national feeling superfluous. People bunched in or near cities, hoping for economic betterment and mobilized for improvement in trade unions, derived, in many cases, little emotional fulfillment, little sense of identity, from these activities. Nationalism supplied the lack. For millions across the West, it was not economic activity or proletarian activism but nationalism that replaced the social void that was the inevitable consequence, as well as the motive, of modernization.

But neither work and trade, nor the labor movement, nor even nationalism could wholly remove or cancel the scepticism that also spread in the wake of the victorious march of the liberal triad of democracy, capitalism, and science. The practical rationalism of the sceptical Enlightenment, hoping to reconcile the Old and the New West, began to slide toward nihilism, as the pressures of modernization and the temptations of nationalism swallowed up people in a modern maelstrom of ideologies and emotions, increasingly far removed from the ageless certainties of the old synthesis and the ancient bargain of church and state.

The most perceptive of the nineteenth-century diagnosticians of Western civilization in its modern version, of the liberal age and especially of its pathologies, were, in order of birth date, Giacomo Leopardi, Alexis de Tocqueville, Søren Kierkegaard, and Friedrich Nietzsche.[12] What these very different men had in common was the prophetic ability to see that what was happening in the West was not merely that long-standing trends toward popular sovereignty in politics, personal autonomy in culture and morals, widening prosperity in economics, freedom of thought in religion, and mass participation in social life were crystallizing into new forms of public and personal existence, that of liberal democracy, capitalist exchange, and mass education and production. They realized that the West itself was becoming a world, an outlook, and a culture that no longer wanted or needed tradition. The West by World War I was, for many, and particularly for the urban elites that designed the culture, not a civilization that had lost its traditional moorings, which one could perhaps restore or at least rediscover and describe. It was a civilization that rejected moorings of any sort. The essence of the modern West was coming to this: that it had no essence, no heritage, no tradition. Tradition had become not the missing center of culture, but something that the culture increasingly regarded as its enemy.

During the twentieth century, those who tried to define the West and its essence all shared, openly or not, a double, or false, consciousness. On the one hand, many represented honest, sincere, often highly sophisticated attempts to define the essence of the West in terms comprehensible to modernity. On the other, they were waging an impossible battle, because they were trying to give the culture what that culture, by its very definition, did not and could not want. Some ignored this contradiction and plunged on regardless; this was the case for the explicitly traditionalist proposals. Some understood the contradiction but objected that, willing or not, the West needed tradition because without tradition it would die, that the experiment of casting off one's moorings and drifting on the high seas was inevitably fatal.

The concordance between the four figures was striking. All were pessimists, that is to say, all rejected the facile confidence of a purely economic and progressive liberalism, whose adherents believed that knowing the good was a simple matter and achieving it a straightforward political and economic task.[13] In a deeper sense, they were pessimists because they understood on the one hand that liberalism was the destiny of the West, and on the other that this set of doctrines was unable and unwilling, by its very nature, to restore the sense of self, of continuity, of belonging, and of tranquillity that they considered essential to any civilization with a pretense to last. Why, for example, should people act with social responsibility in a secular age?

Considering how people live nowadays and their opinions, considering that hardly anyone any longer shares the beliefs on which one might found moral principles, that all those opinions without which it is impossible that justice and honesty make sense, and that the exercise of virtue seem worthy of a wise man, are virtually extinct, considering also that the politics of modern states makes virtue seem useless while vice seems decidedly useful, considering these things it is undeniable that the survival of society seems due rather to chance than to any other cause, and it does seem truly marvelous that it can happen among individuals who hate each other, plot against each other, and seek in all ways to harm each other. The chain and brake of the laws and of public force, which is the only thing remaining to society, have long been recognized as utterly insufficient to restrain people from evil and to encourage them to good. All know, with Horace, that laws without good habits are not enough, and on the other hand that good habits depend on and are determined by and principally founded on and guaranteed by opinions.[14]

This was a harrowing diagnosis of the pathology of a liberalism in which the political and moral element were lost, of a liberalism deprived of political power and therefore reduced to a doctrine of selfish acquisitiveness, to the bourgeois pathology. The crisis of Western identity at the end of the liberal age was the crisis of this pathology, but it affected also those societies, notably Britain and America, where liberalism was part of the political culture, and where its religious and medieval roots were not ignored.

Leopardi was an Italian aristocrat and poet who died relatively young in 1837, having spent all his life in a nation that was not a nation and a culture that, so he saw, had left the Old Western synthesis behind, but without bringing its moral and political legacy along as ballast with which to find its place in the New. A society that was becoming liberal and capitalist without that Old Western ballast was a society of timid, bourgeois cynics, incapable either of great passion or of great joy. As he wrote, "this century presumes to re-do all skills and institutions, because it actually does not know how to *do* anything."[15] Happiness, he believed, could come only from the sense of achievement, of having created something, overcome real challenges. In the age of faith, of Christendom, religion posed both the absolute challenge—of following Christ—and the absolute reward. Living under judgment, men conceived life as an adventure, and their vivid imaginations conceived great tasks—sometimes bloody, cruel, and murderous—and impelled them to surmount great challenges. Hernán Cortés conquered Mexico for God, gold, and glory, and only a mundane imagination would distinguish these impulses, for they were one and the same. In the liberal age, great desires, great efforts, and great risks were banished, but "the man who does not desire for himself and love himself is not good to others."[16] He is a Potter or a Scrooge, in other words. The modern age was the age of the selfish calculator, not that of new freedom. Leopardi's diagnosis of the simultaneous decline of faith and of aristocratic liberty was strikingly similar to Tocqueville's. Contrary to the conventional wisdom that men in the Old West were otherworldly and timid, these two thinkers insisted that faith and the personal search for glory were not mutually exclusive, but two sides of the same mentality—the mentality of the Christian Germanic hero, of Beowulf, Roland, and Bjarki.

Curiously, though Leopardi and Tocqueville never had anything to do with each other, both used the exact same example to argue that the Anglo-Saxon nations had somehow managed to cross from the Old West without abandoning the morality of achievement or forgetting the intimate connection of liberty and responsibility—which was another word for the effects of ownership. The example was the American penal system and philosophy of punishment, which was the immediate reason behind Tocqueville's journey to America in 1831–32. Leopardi had observed in 1824 that in Europe "it is no shame to be or to have been wicked, nor to have committed crimes, but rather to have been punished," whereas "in the United States of America, public opinion attaches no disgrace to punishment, and the felon who has been punished and re-enters society is just as free from obloquy as one who has never been sentenced, because (1) he is considered to have expiated his fault along with his punishment," and because, second,

> people judge—and generally rightly—that the penalty, which is there considered and called penitence (the prisons are called penitentiaries), along with the measures taken during it to cure, with physical and moral remedies, the morality of the felon, will have corrected and reformed his character, his habits, his inclinations, and his principles, and returned him to the straight path, so that he returns entirely, in law, in fact, and in public opinion, to the standing and the level of other citizens.[17]

American prisons in the nineteenth century were institutions of moral cure and rehabilitation, resting on the Christian principle of repentance and self-improvement, combined with the modern principle that freedom and responsibility were two sides of the same coin—principles that, Leopardi sensed, had lost credibility in Europe.

What was a brief insight in Leopardi became the starting-point of Tocqueville's great work on American democracy and its global significance. The Norman aristocrat found in America a unique blend of ancient and modern liberty and a widely diffused sense of responsibility, expressed specifically in the penitentiary system but more generally in American self-government, in the absence of hierarchy and regulation, and in the spontaneous commercial creativity of the people. He also found a vigorous, Protestant Christianity, and this, he argued, following Montesquieu and Burke, was no accident. Religion and democracy, he argued, needed each other. Democracy was not only secularized Christianity, it needed religion to survive: "I doubt whether man can ever support at the same time complete religious independence and entire political freedom," he noted in terms strongly reminiscent of Burke. Democratic liberty and especially democratic equality stimulated "the taste for well-being," which, if indulged for itself, produced its opposite: the bourgeois pathology of Potter and Scrooge, who destroyed their own well-being in their desperate search for material security. A cool, liberal religion, which persuaded men "to enrich themselves by none but honest means," was the best way to temper the taste for well-being with responsibility, thereby preserving liberty. In America, the clergy did not condemn democracy and its psychology of well-being, but turned them to responsible uses. "By respecting all democratic tendencies not absolutely contrary to herself, and by making use of several of them for her own purposes, religion sustains a successful struggle with the spirit of individual independence which is her most dangerous opponent."[18]

Thus, in Tocqueville's analysis, Christianity and liberal democracy, religion and social structure, were interdependent, and Christianity had throughout its history—throughout the Old West—worked slowly but surely in favor of the niches of liberty, of individual responsibility, and hence, ultimately, of political freedom. "Christianity, even when it commands passive obedience in matters of dogma, is still of all religious doctrines the most favorable to liberty" as well as "the most favorable to equality," and it was precisely the remarkable symbiosis of liberty and equality, grounded in Christianity, that struck Tocqueville as the key to American prosperity and well-being and, more generally, to that of a moderate, humane liberalism.[19] Liberalism in this comprehensive sense, seen at its best and not in its pathological, bourgeois excesses, was secularized Christianity and the modern age therefore a child of the church, of the Old West:

> Religion perceives in civil liberty a noble exercise for the faculties of man, and in the political world a field prepared by the Creator for the efforts of mind. Free and powerful in its own sphere, satisfied with the place reserved for it, religion never more surely establishes its empire than when it reigns in the hearts of man unsupported by anything save its native strength.
>
> Liberty regards religion as its companion in all its battles and its triumphs, as the cradle of its infancy and the divine source of its rights. It considers reli-

gion as the safeguard of *mœurs* [customs, habits, culture], and *mœurs* as the best security of law and the surest pledge of the duration of freedom.[20]

However, Tocqueville, who of the four was the most sympathetic to liberalism and who understood how a democratic society gave its members autonomy, choices, liberty, and dignity, balanced his praise of democracy with concern that it might ultimately turn out to be a self-defeating proposition. And those passages in which he expressed concern for the fate of freedom under democracy were stylistically and rhetorically the strongest, the ones where passion and conviction showed through the most.

Freedom in danger: was that not a contradiction? If the modern West was essentially a doctrine of maximum freedom, how could one be concerned for freedom as the modern West grew in strength and power? Because, all four diagnosticians replied in chorus, the freedom of liberalism was at best a pale shadow of genuine freedom and at worst its opposite. A common theme of their thought was that liberal hegemony inevitably deadened people's desire and ability to act, love, suffer, perform, and make ambitious plans. Liberal doctrines appeared reasonable and just. They were hard to argue against; they made opposing positions seem ridiculous, arbitrary, or even sinister. The search for truth under liberalism seemed simple. Democratic equality gave people the right and, with prosperity, the opportunity to focus on their own desires, but it undermined the aristocratic ambition to do noble things on a grand scale, for the community, for the ages, or for God. *Militia sui*, to coin a phrase, acquisitive effort for one's own benefit, replaced *militia Dei*, the war effort for God.

Liberalism made truth and achievement painless. But truth and achievement, the four agreed, were not painless. By concealing this, democratic beliefs betrayed and diminished the dangers of life. "Nature," to quote Leopardi again, "is an imposture against man and does not make his life either desirable or tolerable, unless principally by means of imagination and deception."[21] The democratic deception was to make life and nature a matter for planning and calculation. It undermined the "imagination and deception" necessary for survival. Then, when truth broke it, as it inevitably would, liberalism stood defenseless, having undermined "imagination and deception" in the name of reason, progress, and science.

The barrier against this invasion of a cold, secular truth, in which the bourgeois pathology made more sense than moderation, was, again, religion. But in the final sections of *Democracy in America*, Tocqueville gave reasons to believe that this logic of democratic individualism might prove more powerful than all opposing forces. Individualism was not merely an impulse to well-being, a psychological state, but also the sociological result of modernization. In the 1820s, one of Tocqueville's friends and mentors, Pierre Paul Royer-Collard, had argued, following Burke, that the fall of the old regime in the revolution had destroyed "that crowd of domestic institutions and independent magistracies" that, in effect, constituted niches of liberty within a hierarchical, authoritarian state. Where Jules Michelet had seen them as arbitrary and tyrannical, making invidious distinctions between classes of people at the whim of the powerful, Royer-Collard and Tocqueville saw them as valuable guardians of local, communal identities. When they were gone, "the Revolution has left only individuals standing." The revolution produced "an atomized society," and an atomized society invited centralization. "Where there are no independent magistrates, there are only agents of central power. That is how we have become an *administered* people, under the hand of irresponsible civil servants, themselves centralized in the power of which they are agents."[22]

In America—and by extension, in any society that evolved toward an individualistic liberalism—the principle of atomization would not, at first, be a powerful state, but individualism itself, the citizens' desire for equality and conformity. This desire would tempt citizens to surrender political power over their lives to a government that promised to protect them. The vigorous virtues of self-reliance, communal independence, and patriotic solidarity would wither. "Equality places men side by side, unconnected by a common tie." By seeking equality in the name of individual well-being and liberty, democratic societies risked succumbing to "democratic despotism," a despotism that would be managed by a maternal, therapeutic government:

> I want to imagine under what new traits despotism will appear in the world. I see an innumerable multitude of similar and equal people who turn incessantly in search of petty and vulgar pleasures, with which they fill their soul. Each, standing apart, is like a stranger to the destiny of the others; his children and personal friends forming for him the entire human race. As for the remainder of his fellow citizens, he is beside them, but he does not see them. He touches them, but does not feel them. He exists only in and for himself, and even if he still has a family, one can say that he no longer has a country. Above these people rises an immense and tutelary power, which alone takes charge of assuring their pleasures and looking after their fate. It is absolute, detailed, regular, foresighted, and mild. It would resemble paternal power, if,

like it, its object was to prepare men for maturity. But it only seeks, on the contrary, to fix them irrevocably in childhood.[23]

Well might Tocqueville conclude that "the sight of such universal uniformity saddens and chills me." He ended *Democracy in America* on the ambiguous note that democratic despotism was not an inevitable fate, warning also that to abandon a vigorous commitment to liberty was also to abandon well-being; that to surrender to democratic despotism to ensure well-being was a false bargain, for the despot could promise only poverty: "The nations of our time cannot prevent the conditions of men from becoming equal; but it depends upon themselves whether the principle of equality is to lead them to servitude or freedom, to knowledge or barbarism, to prosperity or wretchedness."

In 1848, revolutions broke out again in Europe. For several years, economic recession and hunger had provoked food riots in parts of Germany and France. By early 1848, almost a third of the workers of Paris were unemployed. In February, as the crisis rapidly worsened, the Parisians rose and overthrew the July monarchy. By the spring, uprisings had taken place in Berlin, Munich, Frankfurt, Rome, Warsaw, Vienna, and Budapest. In June, desperate because the new government had failed to provide either food or work for many of them, the workers of Paris rose again. The republican assembly responded by calling in the army, which put down the insurrection, executed hundreds, and deported hundreds more without trial. The French Assembly was controlled by a loose alliance of agrarian, financial, and liberal interests. By summer, a constitutional assembly was meeting in Frankfurt to prepare a liberal constitution for a national German state. Within a year, however, royalists and conservatives had divided the liberals, marginalized the few socialists and radicals, and reinstated the previous regimes in Germany and Austria. In France, a nephew of Napoleon, Louis Bonaparte, became president of the Second French Republic, then, in 1852, emperor, prompting Karl Marx to reflect that "all facts and personages of great importance in world history occur, as it were, twice," but "the first time as tragedy, the second as farce."[24]

The revolution of 1848 broke out a few days after Karl Marx and Friedrich Engels had published the *Communist Manifesto*, declaring that the "specter of communism" was haunting Europe and calling for "the forcible overthrow of all existing social conditions" to replace "the old bourgeois society, with its classes and class antagonisms" with "an association in which the free development of each is the condition for the free development of all."[25] The events were not related, and, with the partial exception of the June uprising in Paris, the revolts of 1848 were not proletarian uprisings, for Europe as yet hardly had an extensive working class—except in Britain, where no revolution took place. They were, rather, liberal and democratic movements aiming to seize political power for the new middle classes. When this attempt failed, Continental liberalism split, with a minority holding fast to the original principles of liberalism, those described by Tocqueville: liberty and responsibility, the nexus of property and freedom, and a majority abandoning the immediate hope of political power and liberty in favor of nationalism and bourgeois acquisitiveness. The 1850s were known in Germany as the *Gründerzeit*, the "age of the founders," the age when the great businesses and conglomerations of German capitalism were established. The *Gründer* were the bourgeois liberals without political power but with the nationalist beliefs that made them acceptable junior partners to the alliance of large landowners, officials, and military men who ran Germany, as they ran most of the European Continent.

Marxism was the doctrine of radicals who interpreted 1848 and its failure as the inevitable result of the balance of power among the social classes of Europe. Unlike the liberals, Marxists were not interested in political liberty as the absence of coercion, and still less in its connection with property. They belonged rather to the lineage of Gerrard Winstanley, for whom property was the root of evil, and of Hegel, who defined history as man's journey to absolute freedom—not the freedom to exercise responsibility in a real world of constraints and scarcity, but freedom to become one's real self, a self alienated and disguised in all existing societies:

> In history up to the present it is certainly an empirical fact that separate individuals have, with the broadening of their activity into world-historical activity, become more and more enslaved under a power alien to them . . . a power which has become more and more enormous, and, in the last instance, turns out to be the world market. But it is just as empirically established that, by the overthrow of the existing state of society by the communist revolution . . . and the abolition of private property which is identical with it, this power . . . will be dissolved; and that then the liberation of each single individual will be accomplished in the measure in which history becomes transformed into world history.[26]

Marxist doctrine rested on two concepts: the idea of alienation and the idea of history as an inevitable evolution, through class struggle, to the point at which alienated humankind rebelled against alienation and established the kingdom of freedom. The alienation of man from his true self was incarnated in private property, which so far from being the gauge of freedom was, for Marx, its greatest obstacle. Property expressed the tragic fact of history, which was that in all existing societies, the labor necessary to wrest subsistence from nature took place within certain "relations of production," in which a minority controlled the conditions under which the many expended their labor. In the words of the leading late-twentieth-century historian of communism,

> For Marx, beginning with *The German Ideology* of 1845, the human condition is one of alienating dependence on nature, and alienating division into warring social classes, a sundering of humanity's primal unity created by the division of labour necessary to master nature. Marx's idea of emancipation from these dehumanizing forces, therefore, does not mean individual freedom; it means, rather, liberation of the species as a whole, and will come about only over the long haul of history.[27]

History, according to Marx, proceeded in distinct stages, from the primitive communism of the Stone Age, before society reached a stage requiring the division of labor, through slavery, serfdom, and wage labor, "the progressive epochs in the economic formation of society." All these stages were necessary for the human race to accumulate the productive capacity to free itself from nature and from class divisions. But the final leap "from the kingdom of necessity to the kingdom of freedom" would not take place until the fatal contradiction of capitalism had come to fruition: the contradiction between maximum productivity, maximum potential wealth, and extreme inequality.[28] "The bourgeois relations of production are the last antagonistic form of the social process of production" and "brings, therefore, the prehistory of human society to a close."[29]

Marx stressed that the communist revolution, the shift from prehistory to history, could not happen unless the conditions of universal plenty were assured, for "without it want is merely made general."[30] The logic of capitalism pointed in the right direction. On the one hand, productivity was rising at an increasing rate. On the other, capitalist relations of production inevitably turned more and more people into wage laborers, and those in turn into proletarians—people whose only asset was their labor, and who were the helpless victims of the capitalist terms of exchange under which they sold that labor. This logic would, at a late stage, begin to eat into the bourgeois ranks as well. Capital would become centralized in ever fewer hands, as the lesser capitalists themselves were turned into wage laborers and proletarians. All the while, production would be increasing:

> Hand in hand with this centralization, or this expropriation of many capitalists by few, develop, on an ever-extending scale, the co-operative form of the labour process, the conscious technical application of science, the methodical cultivation of the soil, the transformation of the instruments of labour into instruments of labour usable only in common, the economizing of all means of production by their use as the means of production of combined, socialized labour, the entanglement of all peoples in the net of the world market, and with this, the international character of the capitalistic regime. Along with the constantly diminishing number of the magnates of capital, who usurp and monopolize all advantages of this process of transformation, grows the mass of misery, oppression, slavery, degradation, exploitation.

At this point, the stage would be set for the final denouement:

> Centralization of the means of production and socialization of labour at last reach a point where they become incompatible with their capitalist integument. This integument is burst asunder. The knell of capitalist private property sounds. The expropriators are expropriated.[31]

And the kingdom of freedom would be established, under the slogan "from each according to his ability, to each according to his needs."[32]

Marxism despised and rejected both the liberal idea of freedom as noncoercion and the bourgeois capitalist. To Marxists, Scrooge was not a pathological variant of a fundamentally sound doctrine of human nature and its flourishing, but the typical representative of the last stage of an age-old order, one not subject to individual will, but nevertheless evil, for it deprived man—in the abstract—of his true nature. Marxism was the overwhelmingly most powerful expression of the Hegelian idea of positive freedom. As a philosophy of revolution and of such absolute freedom, it sought to redefine Western identity more radically than any previous body of ideas: that identity was now to be found in the future, when revolution had ended exploitation, the hallmark of "prehistory," and inaugurated the true history of the socialized, universal human race.

The political success of Marxism for most of the twentieth century exaggerated its originality in the 1840s. At the time, its ideas were neither especially original nor, indeed, as opposed to the logic of bourgeois capitalism as Marx liked to claim. For example, he accepted the idea of property as something absolute and exclusive, definable in terms of its relation to labor and capital, which was exactly as it was defined by his bourgeois targets. "The very bases of historical materialism"—which was Engels's name for the predictive theory of history in Marxism—"are taken exclusively from the history of the bourgeoisie, which introduced into society the notion of classes founded essentially on distinctions of fortune and not on differences of function."[33] That is to say, Marxism pretended to offer a "science" of universal history, but the materials for this "science" were drawn from the immediate context of early-nineteenth-century Europe, and more specifically, from radical debates rather than from political and social reality. This affiliation indicated that Marxism, as political practice, would reproduce, to an extreme degree, the materialist, inhuman, cynical, and exploitative pathologies of bourgeois liberalism, without even the hope or expectation of liberty.

Marxism was the most comprehensive version within the New West of a political philosophy that denounced the democratic core of liberalism as a fraud and identified its bourgeois pathology as its true face, as the enemy to be conquered. On the opposite side of the spectrum, the counter-revolutionary judgment that liberalism was a heresy against Christianity likewise received its final statement in the wake of 1848. To conservative Catholics, Western identity was that of the Old West and the political alliance of throne and altar. Like the Marxists, they denied that the liberal synthesis of freedom and economic development was a legitimate and promising evolution of that identity. Where the Marxists proposed to await the collapse of capitalism to install the true history of humanity, the so-called ultramontane or integralist Catholics proposed to return, not to the Middle Ages, but to the Counter-Reformation.

That the central hierarchy of the Catholic Church should come down on the side of the enemies of liberalism for a century after 1860 was by no means fated. In the first half of the nineteenth century, when liberals and patriots throughout Europe made common cause against the Metternich System, many of them believed that because their aims seemed so obviously in the interests of the poor and the many, they ought to be able to enlist the church on their side. This liberal, national movement was especially strong in areas, such as Italy, that did not already constitute national states.

The leading figure of the literary, political, and theological movement for Italian national unity, the Risorgimento, was Giuseppe Mazzini, considered by Metternich in the mid-1840s as "the most influential revolutionary in Europe."[34] At the time, Mazzini was living in exile in London, devising revolutionary projects for Italian unification. He was a remarkable blend of utopian and pragmatic, revolutionary and liberal; his ideal was an enlightened nation, moral and moderate in its foreign policies, egalitarian and progressive in its social structure. Like the socialists, he turned against the materialist and bourgeois tendencies of liberalism, but without the hatred of Marx; Mazzini believed, rather, that individual rights had been essential to break the hold of the old regimes in the eighteenth century. The complex modern societies resulting from the revolution and from industrial change, however, demanded less individualism and more solidarity. "He hoped," wrote his leading biographer, "that the future would establish more clearly that society had rights and duties which should modify selfish individualism. In particular, an Italian nation would hardly come into existence unless the clash of individual rights was transcended by a readiness for self-sacrifice and a greater assertion of collective responsibility. The desire to satisfy material interests might lead to riot or rebellion but never to the real revolution in society that was needed."[35]

One of Mazzini's ideas for Italian unity involved asking the pope to be the first president of an Italian republic. In 1846, he and other leaders of the Risorgimento thought they had a friend in the Vatican when Pius IX became pope; he was supposed to be sympathetic to liberalism and in particular to the ideas of a group of younger priests and theologians who argued that the only long-term hope for Catholicism in Europe lay in adapting to democracy and putting the church at the head of progressive liberalism. Like Tocqueville, these thinkers considered Christianity a source of modern freedom and also necessary to temper this freedom from sliding into the materialist, selfish, bourgeois pathology. For the first two years of his reign, Pius seemed sympathetic to these ideas. He introduced a new constitution for the Papal State abolishing some of the oppressive laws and threatening the corrupt oligarchy of senior clergy and their retainers who governed Rome and exploited its revenues. In late 1847, Mazzini wrote Pius asking him to step forward to lead the movement for unification, "because with you at its head our struggle will take on a religious aspect and liberate us from many risks of reaction and civil war."[36]

In 1848, the Italian nationalists, led by the Piedmontese in the north, rose in rebellion against the various monarchs and princes of the peninsula. Some of them, including the pope, granted their subjects democratic constitutions. Encouraged by this, the liberal patriots believed that the pope would willingly surrender his sovereignty in the Papal State to a united national government. The elected Roman assembly demanded that the pope take a stand in favor of Italian unification and against the oppressive feudal powers that stood in its way. The pope, however, abandoned Rome and refused to heed the elected government's calls for his return. Early in 1849, the assembly of Rome formally deposed the pope as ruler of the city and established a republic, inviting Mazzini to be one of its three heads. The pope asked for help in putting down the republic and received it from an unlikely quarter: the French Republic, ruled by Louis Bonaparte, who was soon to call himself Napoleon III. Restored to Rome by French guns, after much fighting and heroic resistance on the part of the Roman republicans, Pius IX, the progressive pope, became Pius IX, the reactionary enemy of Italian nationalism in particular and of liberal nationalism in general.

The revolutions of 1848–49 ended in defeat, but nationalism was not dead and returned in the 1850s and 1860s in a less liberal and more authoritarian form. In 1860, the anticlerical adventurer Giuseppe Garibaldi, accompanied by the later founder of theosophy, Helene Blavatsky, and riding on a donkey he had named "Pionono" after the pope, marched with his "thousand" from Palermo to Naples and, backed by the Piedmontese prime minister, Camillo Cavour, completed the unification of Italy, except for the Papal State, which remained under the pope's control. Pius had become determined that this remnant of political jurisdiction was essential to the papacy. He angrily rejected offers of a settlement from the new Italian government, calling reconciliation as likely as a pact between Christ and the devil. The papacy, as of 1860 at the latest, was aligned against liberal nationalism, the mass movement of Europe. By denouncing it as anti-Christian and demonic, the Vatican implied that only a retreat to authoritarian theocracy could save the West from the destructive, popular forces that were taking it over.

In 1864, Pius IX issued a comprehensive statement of all that was wrong with the modern world, thereby again defining his own position and that of his church as antimodern, which to most Americans and Europeans meant anti-Western. Liberal democracy, popular suffrage, and a scientific, tolerant world view had become elements of Western identity for the overwhelming majority of elites on both sides of the Atlantic. Education, the media, literature, scholarship, political doctrines, and ideas about life, progress, and value—all reflected an optimistic, secular outlook that could only laugh at what seemed the pope's quixotic rearguard action.

The document was the *Syllabus of the leading errors of the present age* and consisted of eighty statements assembled from various earlier pronouncements of Pius IX. Each statement represented a widely held opinion or belief, and each was condemned as wrong and to be rejected by Catholics. The *Syllabus* included propositions about rationalism, science, socialism, communism, the right to freedom of judgment, marriage, social ethics, the pope's civil power, and liberalism. The following statements, for example, were declared to be errors:

6. Faith in Christ offends human reason, and divine revelation not only serves no purpose but moreover stands in the way of human perfection.

15. Every human being is free to embrace and profess whatever faith he, by the light of his reason, considers true.

20. The ecclesiastical power ought not to exercise any authority on its own without the permission and consent of the civil government.

39. The state being the origin and the source of all rights, itself enjoys a right that knows no limit.

55. The Church should be separated from the state, and the state from the Church.

58. One should not accept the existence of other forces than those contained in matter, and the sole rule and principle of honest conduct is to accumulate and to gather riches by any means and to satisfy the desire for pleasure.

80. The Roman pontiff can and should make his peace with and reconcile himself to progress, liberalism, and modern culture.[37]

One of the strongest endorsements of the *Syllabus* was that of a Protestant minister who defined it as "the ultimate and the grandest monument by which the West is trying to tame the rising tide of barbarism."[38]

Many liberals agreed that the West in the later nineteenth century faced threats of barbarism, but hardly of the same kind. To the Catholic hierarchy of the Vatican Council of 1870, the liberals were the barbarians, with their heretical doctrines of human rights, democracy, and individualism. To sober liberals like the Swiss historian Jacob Burckhardt, the potential barbarians were the masses of Western societies, who, unable to exercise responsible freedom in Tocqueville's manner, were increasingly likely to be tempted by demagogues, dictators, and militarist or racist ideologies.

The political failure of liberalism on the Continent in 1848 was one of the profound causes of the weakness of democracy in the next hundred years. Liberal leaders surrendered to the bourgeois pathology or developed a nationalist variant of their doctrine that allowed them to accept political subordination with equanimity. Into the gap left by democratic liberalism, as defined by Montesquieu, Burke, and Tocqueville, stepped various antidemocratic teachings that purported to combine economic betterment with social solidarity. One of the most influential was that of Arthur de Gobineau, a young friend of Tocqueville who proceeded to develop a doctrine of racial hierarchy and collectivism that appalled his older friend.

Gobineau's starting point was that the Enlightenment had overcome and discredited Christianity by showing that morality, and especially social morality, was independent of religion; that religion was an obstacle to progress. The radical Enlightenment—for this was Gobineau's source—had left behind Christianity's immature obsession with individual souls in favor of discovering the social laws of mass improvement. Now, in the nineteenth century, Gobineau argued, science and morality together demonstrated that the goal of politics should be to maximize welfare. "I shall no longer take pity on the unfortunate in order to give him some temporary relief," he wrote. No, "instead I shall . . . put the government in a condition to destroy misery and to turn every man into a worker serving in the interest of social utility." In the new, scientific society beyond both Christianity and democracy, *"everyone has an equal right to work."*[39]

To Gobineau, and after him to many others, Christianity was a conspiracy of the weak against the strong, of the poor against the rich. Its doctrine of human equality was not, as it was for Tocqueville, a foundation of modern liberty and an essential condition of modern social progress, but an obstacle to realism. In the 1850s, Gobineau took a further, radical step. He was at this point in Persia for the French foreign service. Although he rejected Christianity because of its debilitating social effects, he had become rather taken with Islam, which struck him as a manly, sensible religion, resting on an explicit, strict code of law, committed to ethnic purity, and unaffected by the individualism and fragmentation of the West. All these various impulses came together in the work that made him notorious among liberals, the *Essay on the Inequality of the Human Races* of 1855, which advanced two arguments: that miscegenation was the source of most social evils, especially of democracy; and that the races of the world constituted a hierarchy, with the Aryans—the white Europeans—at the top.

Although Gobineau's idea that Christianity was a conspiracy to sap the unitary will of Western nations might resemble the views of Friedrich Nietzsche, the two were poles apart, and not just because Nietzsche rejected doctrines of racial hierarchy as he rejected anti-Semitism. Nietzsche's objection to Christianity was to its practitioners, to its social and cultural reality, not to its message of individualism and personal dignity. It was because Christianity in practice seemed, to him, to deny personal dignity that he scorned it, saying "there has only ever been one Christian, and he was crucified."

Nietzsche's diagnosis owed much to that of his older friend and mentor Jacob Burckhardt. Like him, Nietzsche feared the masses, not out of contempt, but because he agreed with the Swiss historian that the failure of liberalism in Continental Europe was leading the Western nations into a trap—a trap composed of wealth and power on the one hand and lack of democracy on the other. In such a situation, the democratic ambitions of capitalist liberalism could only breed cynicism and nihilism, the faith in the absolute loss of meaning. Nihilism became Nietzsche's key political category and the fate he predicted for the politics and the political thought of the West.

Part of the reason for nihilism was that the scientific search for truth about nature or society created the illusion of knowledge, and when those who searched for knowledge made the inevitable discovery that it was not to be found by means of their doctrines, they would lapse into nihilism. Uniformity of habits, expectations, and values, less advanced in the 1830s or the 1880s than a century later, was both the expression and the cause of nihilism. According to Nietzsche and Spengler, nihilism was the symptom and the empty core of the declining West, the reason it rejected tradition and the reason that tradition could not be recovered. In the modern West, nihilism was "a normal condition." The formerly highest values "devalued themselves." Liberal doctrines and scientific truth-seeking subverted religious and moral certainties. People not only stopped believing in such certainties, they stopped wanting to believe.

This state of affairs was "passive nihilism as a sign of weakness. The power of the spirit can be exhausted, worn out, so that the goals and values hitherto honored are [found to be] inappropriate and unconvincing." In response, some might adopt an "active nihilism" that "can be a sign of strength: the power of spirit can grow so much that it finds earlier goals, convictions, and doctrines inappropriate." Such active nihilism "reaches its high point of relative power as a violent power of destruction." Another term for this in Nietzsche's vocabulary was the "will to power" as the only surviving source of social and political energy.

Since Nietzsche and the other pessimists had already cast doubt on the possibility of truth itself, nihilism, as the recognition that there was no convincing truth, was not wholly negative or destructive. "The extremest form of nihilism would be this: that every faith, every belief that something is true, is necessarily false, because there is no *true world*." The true measure of vigor in the culture, Nietzsche suggested, was how far its members dared to recognize that culture needed lies to survive, while at the same time recognizing that they were lies, how far they dared "to admit to ourselves the plausibility, the necessity of the lie without perishing. In that sense, nihilism, as the *denial* of a truthful world, of being, might be a divine way of thinking."[40]

Psychologically, nihilism prevailed when people lost faith in their own intrinsic value as people, and this happened when they realized that the very idea of value was an invention by people who wanted to claim it for themselves. A manifestation of nihilism was, therefore, that people realized that power, position, doctrines, and convictions were created by people for a purpose and not given in the nature of things. There was no such thing as a fixed personal identity firmly rooted in the world; identity, personality, and belief were fragmentary and mutable. Here was the source of the breakdown of meaning signaled by Eliot.

In 1885, Nietzsche stated that "I take the 'I' as a construction of mind" that enabled us to "imaginatively impute some sort of permanence, hence familiarity to the world of becoming."[41] Since the world of becoming was the real world and was not in fact familiar or knowable outside the human desire to make it so, any certainty about it was impossible. The fundamental postulate of Western metaphysics since Plato, namely, that by appropriate methods one could arrive at true knowledge as opposed to mere opinion, suffered its final defeat. The death of true knowledge was the manifestation in philosophy of the death of tradition in the culture, for the notion of tradition and its justification was simply the cultural, historical manifestation of belief in truth and in values above the struggles of the day.

Nihilism was, for some, mediated or softened by the liberal story of the West as descended from the Magic Moment of Greece. In the 1760s, Winckelmann and Goethe had begun to deconstruct the Christian West, proposing instead worship of Greece and of an ideal humanity rooted in Greek art, literature, and aesthetics. In liberal Britain, George Grote, starting in the 1820s, turned the Greek axis of Western evolution into an article of faith that rehabilitated Athenian democracy by reference to modern liberalism and modern liberalism by its remote descent, along an axis of time outside history, from the Greeks. Later in the nineteenth century, Ulrich von Wilamowitz Moellendorf deconstructed these Greeks, showing who they really were, and while retaining a religious awe for them, sought them not as otherworldly models but as creators of their own unique and individual culture. Oswald Spengler then deconstructed the idea of the West's classical origins, showing that classical and Western civilization were morphologically parallel, not continuous, and that the West was entering a phase of decline equivalent to that of ancient civilization in the Hellenistic and Roman periods.

Among them, Nietzsche, Spengler, and Sigmund Freud deconstructed the very idea of the West as a civilization, arguing that modern liberal man and his preferred political system, democracy, rejected any substantive core, and that the modern West was defined by nihilism, by its rejection of tradition and of meaning. In the mental and political world of modernity, civilization had no essence, no heritage, and no legacy; it was merely the technical administration of things.

The nihilist revolutions of the twentieth century—that of the Bolsheviks in Russia, of the National Socialists in Germany, and of their various allies and imitators—defined the history of that century until 1989. They posed the question whether they represented the inevitable future of the modern West, whether the liberal triad was fated to end in nihilism, violence, genocide, and war, or whether they were a deviation, some kind of vast but temporary accident, after which the modern triad of liberty, economic growth, and science could reassert its central role as shaper of the world's desires. The pessimists said the former, the neo-optimists of the post–Cold War era said the latter, and the Grand Narrative, constructed to maintain Western courage in the totalitarian era, said little either way.

Before these revolutions broke out, the West suffered what many considered its fatal blow in World War I. The war, like the Reformation of 1520, had, in one respect, so many causes that it was unthinkable that it should not break out at some point, and yet, when it happened, it changed everything. When it began, most expected a quick war, an explosive readjustment of the balance of power along the lines of the Franco-Prussian War of 1870–71. Few recalled that there had been another war in the nineteenth century, a long, bloody conflict driven by passion and technology: the American Civil War of 1861–65, and few considered that this war, rather than any of the brief European conflicts, was a more accurate precedent for what started in 1914.

The men who unleashed the war of 14 . . . saw this war as an evil, but an evil known, classified, controllable, compatible with weighing or wagering gains and losses. They rightly relied on the patriotism of citizens, this most natural of virtues to the inhabitants of the old nation-states of Europe. In doing so, they entered, in the name of what they knew, into a history that they did not know, which is of course what usually happens. Yet, in this case, an abyss separated the political universe that framed their decisions from that which was so soon to be born of this war, whose revolutionary nature they could not imagine. They each thought they would remain within the stream of their national history. In fact, they represented the end of an era; they opened the first episode of the European tragedy.[42]

Sidney Hook, the American political philosopher, socialist, and anticommunist, was the opposite of a religious believer. In his memoirs he explained that he lost his faith at the age of about six when he realized that no one could answer the question, "Why does an all-powerful and loving God permit evil?" The only situation to which he was ever known to apply religious language was the outbreak of World War I, which he, and many with him, called "the second fall of man."

World War I, or the Great War as it was called until 1939, was a second fall in two senses. It seemed to contradict every premise and assumption of Western liberal and progressive opinion of the preceding half-century. According to the English liberal writer Norman Angell in 1909, for example, it was a "great illusion" to believe "that economic advantage goes with the exercise of military force," that military force and control of territory were advantageous to nations. Power and prosperity were increasingly dependent on trade and economic activity, both of which would be harmed by war. The main danger of war, Angell said, came from the atavistic beliefs of those who still thought in terms of national honor, prestige, and territorial control, and who measured power by arms, and security by the will to defend. One of these was the British admiral Sir John Fisher, an old sea dog of humble origins who never minced his words:

> I am not for war, I am for peace. That is why I am for a supreme navy. Did I not write in your autograph book at the Hague, "The supremacy of the British Navy is the best security for the peace of the world?" My sole object is peace. What you call my truculence is all for peace. If you rub it in both at home and abroad that you are ready for instant war with every unit of your strength in the first line and waiting to be first in, and hit your enemy in the belly and kick him when he is down, and boil your prisoners in oil (if you take any), and torture his women and children, then people will keep clear of you.[43]

This, to Angell, was an example of the great illusion that military power could yield security. For Jack Fisher overlooked the fact that his counterpart in Berlin might be thinking exactly the same thoughts—though no doubt expressing them less vividly. And if each side thought that only it was brave, and its maximum force necessary to deter war, then the result would be "the blind bulldog piling up of armaments on both sides to the limit of the resources in each case—a solution . . . which, if unchecked, will lead with every probability to war."

Angell hoped that the great nations of the West would never go to war with each other, for they were linked by too many ties of financial, commercial, and political interest. International trade had grown so large and so essential to the prosperity of individual nations that business leaders and governments would never permit anachronistic territorial and diplomatic conflicts to provoke actual war. Everyone in positions of power or influence knew that their own well-being depended on economic growth for the masses, so they ought to do nothing to harm that growth. Peace, Angell concluded, made more sense, even to nationalists and advocates of national power, for nowadays, in 1913, and unlike earlier times, the economic and political interests—indeed, the security itself—of nations demanded peace. Power and peace, liberals believed, had come to be synonymous. What Benjamin Constant wrote in 1814 appeared to be coming true:

> The single goal of modern nations is peace and quiet, and with peace and quiet, affluence, and as the source of affluence, hard work. War is, with every passing day, an increasingly inefficient way of attaining that goal. Its chances no longer offer either individuals or nations benefits that equal the results of peaceful work and regular exchanges. . . . War has thus lost both its charm and its utility. Men are no longer drawn to it, either by interest or by passion.[44]

This was true—in liberal societies. But the tragedy of the nineteenth century, from the viewpoint of pacifist, commercial-minded liberals such as Angell, was that a politically dominant capitalist liberalism, whose leaders recognized that power was no longer to be achieved by military force, was a relative rarity in the West, and was indeed to be found only in the Anglo-Saxon nations. Other societies were not governed by the assumptions that seemed self-evident to liberals, most crucially the assumption that making money in peace was a better way to occupy one's time than in assembling arms and planning war. Many people in the West, including many in the liberal Anglo-Saxon democracies, believed that war was a test of national manhood and that periodic wars were necessary to purge the nation of degeneracy, which tended to spread if peace lasted too long. Angell recognized these ideas, but assumed they would die out and become unacceptable, just as, for example, the slave trade had become unacceptable to Europeans in the space of a single generation at the end of the eighteenth century. In the past, values had changed, sometimes quickly, and in modern society, value change was becoming quicker still. Therefore, those who spoke of "unchangeable human nature" and insisted that war was a permanent fact of life, were—according to Angell—mistaken.

Where Angell—and his numerous successors in the arms control business over the following century—went wrong was not in their analysis of power and security as resting on economic strength and hard work rather than on guns and belligerence. Nor were they wrong that whole societies could change their minds about such things as honor, power, militarism, or pacifism within a generation. They went wrong, rather, because they forgot, or chose to ignore, that states might nevertheless have incompatible interests, and that not everyone would agree with the liberal view that military power was henceforth only an "illusion." Clearly, the German government in 1914 did not agree with Angell. The Germans did not go to war because they misunderstood the value of military force as against that of economic activity, but because they wanted the status of a global power, and Britain was not about to concede it to them.

For Hook, a lifelong socialist, the fall of man in 1914 had particular poignancy in a further sense. Whereas liberals held that economic self-interest made peace secure, socialists believed that the ruling classes of the West might well be tempted to war as competition for resources intensified. In socialist theory of the time, capitalism could not yield permanent growth but must at some point collide with falling rates of return and diminishing resources. At that point, the rulers of particular nations would want to grab as much of the remaining pie as they could for themselves. War, according to socialism, was by no means an unlikely option for capitalists. In the words of the French socialist leader Jean Jaurès, capitalism carried war with it "as the cloud carries the storm."[45]

However, the capitalists would not be able to unleash this war, because the instant they tried to do so, the working classes of the world would unite in a general strike, paralyze the economies of the leading nations, and thus force the capitalists to keep the peace. For socialists, peace was essential, because only in peace could they advance toward the socialist transformation of economic relations. The socialists needed peace as much as did business and government, according to Angell, although for radically opposed motives.

Whether by trade or by socialist solidarity, therefore, peace was safe.

These two beliefs were disproved in the space of five days from July 31 to

August 4, 1914. On July 31, the German government mobilized its army to stop what it feared was a Russian attack, which in its turn was motivated by Russia's support for Serbia, threatened by Germany's ally, the Austro-Hungarian Empire. On June 28, 1914, a Serb patriot had assassinated the heir to the Austrian and Hungarian thrones in Sarajevo, then under Austrian control. The date was symbolic, for it was the Turkish defeat of the Serbs on the Field of Blackbirds on June 28, 1389, that, in Serb national memory, created the Serb nation in the hour of its defeat. Five and a quarter centuries later to the day, Gavrilo Princip undertook to rattle the power that was aspiring to succeed Turkey as the hegemon of the Balkans, namely, Austria. Austria demanded reparations and invoked her alliance with Germany in support. The Germans, with some misgivings, gave their full backing to Austria, because they feared that if Austria could not coerce tiny Serbia, then all the nationalities of the Austrian Empire would start to demand independence. A collapse of the Habsburg monarchy raised the specter of unacceptable chaos in Europe and of increased Russian power. So the German government supported Austria in the interests of transnational order in southeastern Europe.

During July, the counterbalancing alliances established over the previous two decades came into play, aligning Russia, with French and British backing, in support of Serbia against Austria and Germany. When Germany mobilized against Russia on July 31, the government knew that a clash with Russia would mean general war with Britain and France as well.

The international trading interests of the capitalist ruling classes did not manifest themselves to prevent this. What about the socialists? On August 4, with general war a fact, the German government asked the parliament for war credits. According to socialist predictions, the socialists, who since 1912 constituted the largest party in parliament, should vote no. This would have deprived the government of war finance and would have made sustained war impossible. The socialist delegation, with three exceptions, voted for the government's request. Emperor Wilhelm II thanked them in the words, "Today I know no socialists or conservatives. I know only Germans."

The second fall of man, then, was the triumph of nationalism and war over socialism, liberalism, and peace. But if that were the whole story, the liberal narrative that emerged out of and as a response to the war, in the Columbia Contemporary Civilization course in America and in equivalents in secular schools in Europe, was right to draw its simple moral: nationalism bad, liberal democracy good; militarism bad, arms control good. World War I demonstrated not so much that nationalism trumped socialism or liberalism, but that these three forces could, in the right circumstances, coalesce.

The socialists who voted war credits for their governments in August 1914 were not violating socialist solidarity; they were replacing international solidarity with national solidarity, but it was still a socialist solidarity, a solidarity with the common people threatened with attack and invasion. World War I was, in a precise sense, the war of the common man. As for liberalism, 1914 proved that Constant and Angell remained, for all their lucid common sense, futurists and not sociologists. The fact was that the common man, and the rich man, for that matter, did not love or want war, but regarded it as a fateful necessity, a part of the life of nations, "the proving ground of courage and patriotism, the ultimate test of civic virtue." Liberal societies were not yet so affluent that their common members enjoyed the gains from hard work that Constant assumed. War, for the masses, was not a destructive distraction but, in the beginning at least, a relief from drudgery, a test of the values of self-sacrifice and duty upheld by the overwhelming majority of Western peoples. "They did not have so comfortable a civil existence that they refused in advance the chances and discomforts of the soldier as unacceptable. These farmers, craftsmen, workers, bourgeois, were raised in their families and schools to be patriots. They belonged to an old moral civilization which preserved many aristocratic traits within democracy."[46] World War I, to repeat, did not mark the victory of an irrational ideology, nationalism, over the reasonable doctrines of liberalism or socialism, but the remarkable, explosive symbiosis of the three. Tocqueville would, sadly, have understood; 1914 was the last revenge in the West of the aristocratic spirit in democratic dress.

At the end of the war in 1918, Western self-confidence seemed broken forever. Impoverished, bled white, deprived of the bravest and most ambitious of their young men, ruled by aging cynics and disillusioned mediocrities, the Western nations staggered into a twenty-year period of economic and political crisis that ended in a second and greater war.

Oswald Spengler's book erupted into the fear and bitterness of 1918 with what seemed to many the force of revelation. "Decline of the West," was that not precisely what the war meant? Socialism and liberalism had not stopped the war; in fact, though this was less clear at the time, they had fatefully enabled it, and enabled it to continue long after both sides lost the chance of easy victory. Its survivors now saw, some with anguish and some with defiance, what a nationalism charged with socialist solidarity within nations and liberal reason in the service of strategy and arms production had accomplished: death and ruin. Most who heard of Spengler took him to be saying that the war was the beginning of the end of the West, a fall from a prewar condition of cultural health and vigor.

But Spengler did not write to explain, justify, or assuage the destruction of the war. He coined his title in 1912 and wrote the bulk of his book before 1914. His purpose, generally misunderstood and ignored in 1918, had nothing to do with the war, the specifics of which he was no more able to predict in 1912 than Norman Angell in 1913. It was to explain how and why the West was coming to an end in a process lasting centuries, a process that began around 1800 and would, in his opinion, become universal only in the twenty-first century. The war in no way started the "end of the West," which was no single event. It was the inevitable playing out of social, philosophical, cultural, and political processes embedded in the very essence of the West, and which were analogous to similar processes in other civilizations, such as Greece and Rome, India, China, or Islam.

"End" or "disappearance" are better translations of *Untergang*, which, unlike the English word *decline,* did not necessarily imply a value judgment, simply a statement of the fact that something was ending. The problem with using the word *end*, though, was that it implied something definite and short-term; Spengler's point was that the process of ending for the West would take centuries.

Spengler's "decline" was not a value judgment but rather a way of saying that he was describing a set of long-term trends. In society, the trend was urbanization—the movement to towns and cities and the lifestyles, expectations, and behavior appropriate to large concentrations of people. Politically, Spengler saw decline in the rise of mass movements and of the belief that society and government could or even should be changed. All modern political ideas for making the world better, whether liberal, socialist, or reactionary, were symptoms of decline.

In culture, art, and philosophy, decline manifested itself as a change from inner, immediate, and unself-conscious experience to the search for objective knowledge of cause and effect, for particular aesthetic styles, for ideas of natural law and human rights. A civilization before decline, Spengler held, did not have a need for natural rights, because its members had their own particular, historic rights. Natural rights were an example of precisely the sort of universal ideology that, for Spengler, was the very epitome of a declining civilization.

Healthy civilization, according to Spengler, was organic, cohesive, natural. People accepted their lives as fate and did not reflect upon them. They had no "values" and "ideals," since what they believed was part of themselves.

Decline began when people started constructing ideologies and programs to explain the world and institutions and infrastructure to improve it. Now, they thought with their brains, not their souls. Progressive ideologies, machines, scientific thought, social policies, philosophical systems, cities—all these were symptoms of decline. "The metropolis itself lies in the midst of a cultivated landscape as an extreme type of inorganic structure; it unties humanity from its roots, draws it to itself and consumes it."[47]

The beginning of the end of the West, as of all other civilizations, according to Spengler, was that certain people began acting as though thinking about life was more important than living it. "All world-improvers, priests, and philosophers agree that life is a matter for the most serious reflection"; however, "only the acting individual, the man of fate, lives in the *real* world, in the world of political, military, and economic decisions, where concepts and systems do not count." Such theoreticians were tempted to think "that their place was at the head and not the tail of great events."[48]

This philosophy, praising vitality and deploring its loss from the West, appealed to the despairing elites of the West after World War I. Even though they themselves were the targets of Spengler's sarcasm, they accepted his harsh verdict and looked around feverishly for grounds of hope. And Spengler was not a lonely voice. Many Western intellectuals in the interwar years sought a more usable past for their own times, a past that was both genuinely Western but that would also, in its own qualities, be an appropriate ground of support for the dangerous present.

The trauma of the war made this search for a viable tradition both urgent and problematic. Urgent, because many Western intellectuals believed that their world needed to find roots in a better tradition than that which had led to the war. Problematic, because the prophets of relativism had shown that there was no such thing as a valid tradition beyond the particular needs of a given cultural moment. Greece and Rome were not the West's ancestors except in particular respects. Civilization was not a single story of progress, but a set of defeats, and the West was becoming one of that set.

Spengler himself wrote within the broader embrace of Nietzsche, and we can look to him for the reason that the search for tradition was both urgent and problematic in the 1920s, when those who saw themselves as teachers of the West—poets and intellectuals—shared not merely a political or cultural pessimism, but that basic fear for meaning itself that T.S. Eliot expressed in his poem "Burnt Norton," that words themselves were about to fall apart, "slip, slide, perish, decay with imprecision." Language itself would no longer "stay still."

Nietzsche, writing in the 1880s, long before Spengler and World War I, anticipated the problem facing those who wanted to reconstruct a tradition for the West after World War I. This was that to reconstruct a tradition and have it make sense, you needed to know what a tradition was and that it was valuable. And it was precisely this knowledge that had become both discredited and implausible by 1920.

World War I showed that progress was not inevitable. Oswald Spengler argued that the West was not descended from the Greeks and Romans, but was its own culture with its own life history, now coming to an end. Contemporary art and philosophy affirmed that certainty was not possible, that the strong self assumed in earlier Western thought was an evanescent, fragmented being. Meaning itself, as Eliot noted, seemed fragile. In this morass of doubt and confusion, might Western roots be found?

The search for a firm grounding of Western identity dominated the interwar years. For many, the search led to the new experiment of the Soviet Union, in which the Marxist realm of freedom was taking shape. Communism promised both a radical break with an unredeemably flawed history, with privilege and the bourgeois pathology of property, exploitation, and greed, and a reassertion of the best of the West, as the left saw it, of the promise of the French Revolution to bring about a regime of freedom that was just, rational, secular, and democratic. For others, the search led not to the future but to the past, to attempts to resurrect some form of the Old Western synthesis. This second group spawned no political force comparable to the communist movement in the West and its supporters. There was no conservative international of advocates of Western restoration. Nevertheless, the spectrum of Western identity was broader in the interwar years than it became after 1945, when it followed the polarization of the Cold War.

CHAPTER NINE

The Totalitarian Trap

[T]he world is very evil, the times are waxing late; be sober
and keep vigil, the judge is at the gate
—Bernard of Morlais

I am not a follower of Spengler at all. I don't believe in the decline of the West
—Adolf Hitler

Schmitt, as the former "crown jurist" of the "Third Reich,"
obviously only now realized that he had, in the end, been
working to undermine the very idea that had been his guiding
image, the idea of the West
—Andreas Koenen

In 1914, as the war was beginning and everyone hoped for a quick victory, Élie Halévy, a French historian of English society, predicted that
"we have before us 10 or 15 or 30 years of war. Thus, the second, the last
part of our lives will hardly resemble the first part."[1] Halévy was not predicting thirty years of continuous fighting, but thirty years of instability, wars,
armistices, revolutions, and tyrannies. His schedule proved exact. In 1945, at
the end of World War II, France and the rest of western Europe and America
emerged from the thirty years of nationalist and ideological warfare with

their democratic constitutions and the modern triad battered, but intact. The same was not true for eastern Europe or for Russia. The end of thirty years of Western civil war in 1945 did not end the war that the communist regimes waged against their own citizens unremittingly from 1917 to 1989. Rather, the end of World War II gave the Soviet Union and its supporters renewed legitimacy in their long struggle to discredit and overthrow liberal democracy, which they denounced as bourgeois exploitation. Conversely, the end of World War II in 1945 also constituted the political and strategic West defined as North America plus those parts of Europe lucky enough to be occupied by the Americans and the British and not by the Soviet Union.

The communist and fascist movements inherited and intensified the mass mobilization that made World War I possible.[2] Thus the national solidarity of 1914 merged into the ideological solidarities of the interwar years and the years of World War II. The entire period, as Halévy foresaw, took on the character of a second Thirty Years' War. Within the West, even in those countries where domestic development and modernization continued, the second Thirty Years' War divided elites and parties between those who, actively or passively, agreed with the totalitarian claim that the modern liberal West was defunct and those who hoped that it was not.

From the Russian Revolution of 1917 to the fall of National Socialism in 1945, four forces, of unequal weight, contested the definition of Western identity. The most powerful was the Soviet Union and its numerous supporters throughout the West, whether communist or procommunist, all those who shared two basic beliefs—that the most urgent task was to realize the promise of the French Revolution for universal equality and justice, and that the Soviet Union, the first workers' state, was the leader and guide in this task, despite its faults and errors. The most remarkable ideological fact in the West for most of the twentieth century was this attraction, this drawing power of communism even on many who were not members of communist parties, who rejected communist practice, but who nevertheless identified the cause of progress and humanity with the interests of the Soviet Union and who, conversely, regarded those who opposed the Soviet Union as enemies, whether witting or unwitting, of peace, humanity, and progress.

A second and much smaller group, of minimal political importance compared with the communists and their allies, was that of the interwar revivalists, people such as T.S. Eliot, Theodor Haecker, Ernst Robert Curtius, or Christopher Dawson, who accepted Nietzsche's and Spengler's interpretation of the modern West as a civilization of nihilism, but refused to accept the logical consequence, which was resignation. The revivalists concluded from

World War I that the modern triad of liberty, capitalism, and science was self-defeating. They dove into history—medieval or ancient—to locate times, places, and people that incarnated a better, fuller, stronger Western identity, and retrieved them to construct a historical and literary pedagogy of re-Westernization of the nihilistic West. The revivalists responded to the political challenge of communism and of the other antidemocratic movements by insisting that the West had a coherent past, and that this past could be recovered and mobilized to yield a Western future that avoided both the tragedy of liberalism and the trap of totalitarianism.

Third came those who agreed with Nietzsche and Spengler that the West had become nihilistic, who blamed liberalism and the idea of progress for this, but insisted that the solution was not to complain weakly, but to forge ahead strongly and build a new world order beyond democracy and liberalism. They sought a return to Western identity by moving through nihilism toward an authoritarian restoration of the political framework of the Old West. Some in this group saw the regimes of Hitler and Mussolini as the best chance to achieve such a restoration, ignoring Hitler's nationalist appeal and hoping to persuade him to act the part of a latter-day Holy Roman Emperor.

The fourth and final force was the grand narrative, the optimistic version of Western identity derived by Will Durant, Robert Maynard Hutchins, and the Columbia professors of 1917–19 from a reading of the past that emphasized the Greeks and all those since the Greeks who anticipated modern democratic liberalism. The fourth force was native to the United States, where liberalism as a political culture was dominant, where its success seemed certain, and where Spengler and the advocates of nihilism had little credibility. These interwar liberals constructed the grand narrative to deny pessimism and to teach young Americans that the West was comprehensible as a single story, that this story began in Greece, that it was a story of progress and growing universalism, and that its concluding stage of liberal democracy was the logical result of history, was durable, and was in conformity with man's social needs and deepest political feelings. In the interwar years, this optimistic version had few takers in Europe; its heyday was the first two decades after 1945, when it dominated American higher education and popular culture, and recruited many new allies in Europe as the covering philosophy of the Cold War West.

Of these four, the first three were the most politically significant in the era of the world wars. Each demonstrated the risks of rejecting liberalism, whereas the fourth embraced liberalism in its centrist, midcentury, procapitalist form, while asserting a false genealogy for it, tracing it to Greece rather than to the

Old West. Their weaknesses and fallacies left a vacuum at the heart of Western identity that was not filled either by the radical antinarratives of the last third of the century or by the hectic neo-optimism of the 1990s.

On October 24–25, 1917, according to the Julian calendar, some soldiers and sailors in Petrograd, inspired by the Bolshevik minority on the Soviet, or Council of Workers' and Soldiers' Deputies, "found power lying in the streets and simply picked it up." Russia in October 1917 had no central government, an army in complete dissolution, and the vast bulk of her population, the peasants, were busy seizing the land on which they lived and worked from its owners, the gentry and aristocrats. The military collapse was a result of Russian defeat in the war and of the February revolution, which abolished the monarchy and encouraged many soldiers to hope that peace was at hand. Since most soldiers were peasants, they also hoped that the new regime would give them land. During the spring, summer, and fall of 1917, soldiers left the front in growing numbers and walked home to seize the land. This peasant movement became the largest source of mass support for the Bolsheviks, although it was not inspired by them, but by the Social Revolutionary party. October 1917 was not a revolution, for the actual Bolshevik coup had no mass support; it was not a national uprising, for very few Russians had ever heard of the Bolsheviks; and it was not an action of workers, for Russia had few workers, and they stayed home. October represented, rather, "a conjunction of the greatest military mutiny of all time and the greatest peasant jacquerie in history," combined with a Bolshevik drama staged in Petrograd as a pale imitation of the Paris June uprising of 1848, which—unlike the event in Russia—had been a genuine urban uprising of workers.[3] Nevertheless, by agreeing to the redistribution of land, the new regime in Petrograd quickly won the all-important support of the peasants, and such was the vacuum of power in Russia that no force rose to challenge the Bolsheviks until it was too late. The peasants were not to know that Lenin and his comrades had no intention of letting them keep their land, for that would violate the fundamental Marxist dogma, that private property was illegitimate. They were not to know that thirteen years later, the Bolshevik regime that guaranteed their land would take it away, killing or starving some fifteen million of them in the process. In 1917–18, their support was strategically necessary, and Lenin, who was always a realist, did what was necessary to secure it. Thus began the Soviet Union.

The October revolution opened the breach at the heart of the modern

West between those who, following Montesquieu, the American Founders, and the classical liberals, continued to believe that the modern Western triad was viable, and those who, leaning toward Rousseau and Marx, accepted the totalitarian argument that democracy and liberalism were weak, evil, and doomed, and that the future belonged to those who could seize it in the name of a healed, perfected, disciplined, and mobilized humanity. The Russian Revolution was carried out by Bolsheviks, who claimed to be Marxists, yet their success violated the prediction of Marx that the proletarian revolution would take place first in the most advanced industrial economy. Russia was not an advanced industrial economy; though its economy and industry were expanding in the years before 1914 at the fastest rate in Europe, it had far to go to reach the levels of industrial employment, production, transportation density, and education achieved in Germany or Britain some twenty or thirty years earlier.

That the first Marxist revolution took place in a largely agrarian society was, as the Marxists themselves were fond of saying, no accident. Lenin, the master of the Russian Revolution, bridged the gap between theory and practice when he asserted that Marxism would win first in the country that represented the weakest link in the capitalist chain; that country for Marx was Germany, for Lenin, it was Russia. This formulation stood Marx on his head, as he had stood Hegel on his head. For Marx maintained that it was only when a mode of production had exhausted all its internal possibilities, when a society and economy had reached their fullest potential, that the deep forces of history would mobilize to transform that society and that economy into its opposite, that is, into the next-higher stage of historical development. Thus, feudalism replaced ancient slavery, and bourgeois capitalism replaced feudalism, not when slavery and feudalism were new, weak, or undeveloped, but when they were at the end of their course. Lenin, by a rhetorical device, overturned this fundamental element of Marxist doctrine, asserting that, in the most important case of all, the transformation from bourgeois capitalism to socialism and communism, the transformation had begun, not where bourgeois capitalism was most developed, but where it hardly existed at all.

If Lenin stood Marx on his head, he did it with permission. Marxism in one aspect claimed to be a scientific, that is, objectively true and verifiable, account of historical development, in which forces beyond human control changed the lives of millions and to which it would be as silly to apply moral judgments as to an avalanche or an earthquake. In another, Marxism was a prophetic call to the wretched of the earth to arise, seize their own destiny, and liberate themselves. In this, second, millennialist and prophetic aspect,

Marxism was both sentimental and moralistic. As a call and prophecy, Marxism painted a vivid picture of historical change in which the worse things got, the closer was salvation. It was a big jump in logic, but a small one in sentiment, from this to say that where things were worst, there was salvation closest. It was a sentiment remarkably similar in form to that expressed, on behalf of Western civilization generally, by Friedrich Hölderlin in 1801:

wo aber Gefahr ist
wächst das Rettende auch

[where there is danger
there also grows that which will save us]

But where was that? Obviously in those countries where the most were the poorest. To Lenin, being Russian, the country was Russia. Therefore, by a link of feeling rather than logic, and by appeal to the prophetic aspect of the doctrine, Lenin was able to assert that it made perfect sense for Marxism to win first in the country that represented the weakest, the least-developed link of capitalism, when the scientific aspect of the doctrine would have predicted that Marxism would win first in the country that was the strongest, the most developed link.

A requirement of the Leninist inversion of scientific Marxism was, however, that revolution had to be forced; it would not happen by itself. The Russian Revolution thus introduced a two-pronged puzzle into all Marxist thought: why did we win first in Russia, and how was revolutionary activism possible when the theory said that activism before its time was folly? This puzzle affected Western Marxism more than Russian or Soviet communism or the communism of the rulers of the post-1945 Soviet empire in eastern Europe. The Soviets and their east European retainers were not in the first instance theoreticians, but people interested in power to a degree not seen since ancient Assyria. If a theory could be constructed to justify their power, their killings, and the corruption they used to undermine dissent, so much the better, especially if the theory could be used to gain goodwill, allies, and money. But the power was primary, and every word, syllable, and comma of the doctrine existed solely to serve power.

In western Europe, by contrast, communist and socialist ideologues wanted to justify their own policies in Marxist terms, whether scientific or prophetic or, preferably, both. At the same time, they wished to understand the Russian Revolution because that revolution had created the first Marxist state, which was therefore the true homeland of all Marxists anywhere. The

Russian Revolution had to be made to fit into a scheme that justified and explained both that revolution itself and the efforts of Western Marxist parties to produce revolutions in their own countries.

The most effective solution was to marry the prestige of the Russian Revolution, its heroic aspect as the revolution that happened against the odds, to the preexisting legacy of the French Revolution and the Jacobins, which had never died in western Europe and which World War I helped to revive. Enrolling the Bolsheviks in the Jacobin tradition served to make them more European and Western, better models, more comprehensible, and more deserving of attention, respect, admiration, and emulation. Toward the end of 1918, the French Human Rights League, a prestigious association of scholars and intellectuals formed on the occasion of the Dreyfus affair in the 1890s to defend Alfred Dreyfus and, by extension, all victims of prejudice and injustice, met to debate the Bolshevik revolution. The evidence that the Bolsheviks were hostile to democracy was plentiful. Yet the distinguished members of the league, democrats to a man, concluded that "the Revolution was entirely good as to its declared aims, whereas its actual evils were due to external factors: a mechanism of exculpation which is the foundation of the 'republican' account of the dictatorship and the Terror of the Year II as caused by 'circumstances,' but which can also be extended to the benefit of the October revolution, as the victim of the inertia of the Russian past (illiteracy), of civil war and soon of foreign war."[4]

The Jacobin reading of Leninism proved an ideological success story in the West, for it was in that guise that the Russian Revolution mobilized sympathy and support far beyond the ranks of the communist parties themselves, support that reached far across the Western left and, on occasion, into the Western right as well. Long after the Western communist parties had, in many cases, shrunk from defections and disillusion caused by Soviet genocides and other atrocities, the Western left as whole continued to offer the Soviet Union the benefit of the doubt in major questions, such as who began the Cold War, who was aggressive in international politics, who was for peace, who was fundamentally, and despite all appearances, on the side of humanity. That the answer, on the left and, in America, the liberal left, to the first two questions was "the United States," and, to the two last, "the Soviet Union," was due ultimately in no small part to the success of Lenin and his early Western supporters in presenting the Russian Revolution as the second and final stage of the French Revolution, which was, as the left unanimously agreed, a revolution for liberty, democracy, equality, and fraternity.

The Russian Revolution and the Soviet Union represented the voluntaristic and, in their Western echoes, the sentimental side of Marxism. These echoes produced not only seventy-five years of illusion about both Marxism and the Soviet Union—the illusion that these were humane, democratic, and peaceful forces—but also established an enduring paradigm of leftist and left-leaning thought, the paradigm of the victim class or classes, those deemed, by various elites, to have been the losers in history, but who deserved to be winners, and in historical justice would be winners.

Marxism in its Leninist form was a "narrow, fanatical, almost primitive idea," and was therefore supremely well fitted to provide the strategy and the doctrine of a total seizure of power in an undeveloped society.[5] The common denominator of Marxist revolutions was that they took place in agrarian societies with a minimal civil society, and under the impact of devastating war. No Marxist revolution ever occurred in a society firmly within the orbit of the modern Western triad of reason, liberty, and prosperity. Yet it was within the liberal democracies that Marxism scored its greatest intellectual success, for in those countries men and women became Marxists or Soviet sympathizers through the free use of their reason, which, after 1917, was not possible where Marxists held power.

The Russian Revolution posed anew a question that many had asked since the Russian czar Peter the Great joined the European balance of powers in the early eighteenth century, namely, was Russia part of the West? The Cold War, from 1945 to 1989, defined the West as America plus that part of Europe outside Soviet control and so denied the question. Rome's geopolitical shift of the East-West line to the Adriatic preemptively excluded Russia from the West. Yet Russia had established its own medieval synthesis of Orthodox Christianity, the imperial model of East Rome or Constantinople, and a Russian ethnic culture that was itself a blend of Slavonic and Nordic elements. As part of his Westernization program, Peter adopted the imperial title, not to compete with the western emperor who was, by the eighteenth century, a figurehead president of the German estates, but to establish a superior pedigree: the pedigree of Moscow as the Third Rome, a name granted in the late fifteenth century by a Russian theologian, who observed that the first Rome had fallen to heresy, that is, to Catholic Christianity; the second, Constantinople, to the infidel Turks. Moscow, after 1453, was the last bastion of Orthodoxy and therefore the rightful heir of what was best and true in the first and second Romes. This theory was Russia's answer to the Western doctrines of the Four Empires or, later, the Three Ages. Russia, it held, was the end point of secular history. Nothing beyond it could or should be imagined.

Russia was bigger, more agrarian, and less urban than western Europe, but was not separated by an unbridgeable gulf from the West. Rather, if the Atlantic seaboard of Europe represented the leading edge of advance of the modern triad, the countries to the east formed a slow gradient of culture, from bigger and denser towns to fewer and smaller, from evolved civil societies to ones in which almost nothing lay between the prince, the landowner, and the serf. Eastern Europe, including Russia, was not unable to modernize, but unlike the western edge of the continent or America, the eastern nations did so via the state and not, as Montesquieu noted in Britain, by dispersed power and the synergy of competing entrepreneurs, rulers, and administrators. And whatever development Russia showed in Western terms by 1914, which was by no means insignificant, it was cut short and derailed by the revolution, which thus accomplished what seemed a supreme paradox: in inflicting on Russia a Western doctrine of historical development, it de-westernized Russia for almost three generations, at unimaginable human cost. But it was no paradox: the crude and violent form of Marxism devised by Lenin was, as he well knew, the one form of revolutionary strategy that could succeed in Russia, and Russia was eminently suited to be its victim.

The gnostic essence of twentieth-century communism was the claim that man lived at the mercy of a hostile, alien force: capital. This was the central feature of the ideology, the idea that human life was governed by an evil force and that salvation consisted in defeating this force. Capital, in communist theory, was overwhelming and irresistible. Communism, like all gnostic world views, was a deeply pessimistic doctrine, springing from the same nihilism diagnosed by Nietzsche as the justified and understandable response of the West to its own condition in the nineteenth century. Capital and its political face, liberalism, represented history, progress, and change; communism denied these things and sought by force to stop them; that is, to stop history. For the supposed destiny of Marxism, the kingdom of freedom, was not achievable within history, and the attempt to reach it amounted, in practice, to a never-ending effort to deny history, because it persistently refused to move in the right direction. The purpose of communism thus became, in effect, stagnation, and the most typical manifestation of its "kingdom of freedom" was the Siberian concentration camp—a world without property, individuality, or hope.[6]

Communists sought support as long as they needed it by claiming to defend peace and progress, universal education, the interests of the poor, and economic progress and equality. In fact all these claims were instruments of achieving power and had no independent value. Many people supported communism believing that it stood for more and better liberty, for human rights, for education, and for any number of other things valued by liberals. Communists welcomed their support, but advancing liberal goals was never part of their agenda, which was a gnostic agenda of total reversal of the existing world. Western supporters rarely saw this; what they thought they saw was that the Leninist regime had abolished profit, the curse of history, and installed instead the regenerate human being of the future. John Maynard Keynes, the economist, who was no friend of the Soviet Union, perceptively commented in the 1930s that when Cambridge undergraduates "made the inevitable pilgrimage to the Holy Land of Bolshevism," they were not disappointed to find it poor and ruinously ill-managed. No, they expected that; it was what they had come to find, for it was the material evidence that history and society were here, in the Soviet Union, being reversed.[7]

History and society, in the new West of science, democracy, and capitalism, were to many people inadequate, unsatisfactory, or immoral. The romance of Western communism was, in the first instance, the romance of those who felt keenly Rousseau's wound and who wanted to believe that something better was possible. Such people were not impressed by the Soviet Union's fraudulent claims of greater economic performance; not emotionally impressed, for while they might, for purposes of argument, brag about Soviet strength, what truly appealed was the idea that here the split, fragmented, and morally ambiguous legacy of history was being transcended in a new wholeness that was not a going back to primitive unity, but a brave forging ahead. What truly appealed was the idea of the genuine human community.

Thus it was not surprising that a considerable contingent of sympathizers and fellow travelers in the West came from the Catholic Church. In 1864, Pius IX had denounced modern democracy and liberalism. Although many Catholics in the twentieth century considered this position reactionary and disreputable, they shared its basic hostility to the West of the liberal triad. Pius wanted to return to the Christendom model of the West. The leftist Catholics of the *Esprit* circle in France of the 1930s and 1940s ridiculed that model, but they, like it, opposed the moneygrubbing, alienating, exploitative, capitalist West. They yearned for community, understanding it in a romantic Christian sense as "a social universe where the activities of individuals are organized to serve the common good, as foreshadowed in the divine will and in the sacrifice of Christ." This romantic vision of community was, in its own way, as reactionary as Pius's theocratic doctrines; it was merely egalitarian and antihierarchical. But even though it was, in some ways, turned toward an ideal past, the leftist Catholic vision of community agreed with the future-oriented socialists of the interwar years that "modern market society was too corrupted by bourgeois individualism ever to be the foundation of a genuine social order." The purpose, for both the *Esprit* group and the sentimental socialists of the 1930s, was to "reconstruct, on the wreckage of individualism, a fraternal world of human beings associated for a common purpose." In the simplistic political theology of the young Emmanuel Mounier, editor of *Esprit*, human nature was open to God and the Other, and a society that discouraged or repressed that openness and turned generosity to greed was evil. "To capitalist society, the mechanical aggregate of isolated individuals, Mounier opposed the living and free community of associates, spiritually alive, drawn as by a magnet to creative emulation of the common good." Mounier's Rousseauist ideal society was "incompatible philosophically with communism, but shared with the communists the hostility to capitalism and a militant spirit, which nourished dialogue and permitted common action."[8] On this kind of pattern was built, in the interwar years, the popular fronts of France and Spain, and the constant attempts of communist parties to infiltrate and subvert democratic politics by pretending to share certain humane and unexceptionable goals: peace, liberty, free expansion of the person in a free community of equals.

One of the earliest and most consistent critics of communism as the final stage of nihilism was the Russian writer Aleksandr Solzhenitsyn. In several stories and novels, but above all in the three volumes of *The Gulag Archipelago*, he described the Russian communists as committed from the first day of power to destroying everything they could not control. The Soviet regime, as he saw it, was from its very first day a regime based not on any positive program of change, but on terror, the invention and the tool of men driven by unfathomable hatred of the world and of all who resisted their will to power. Subverting the legend, popular among socialists and some liberals, that Josef Stalin had suppressed a moderate, early communism that held genuine promise of progress for the Russian people and for the world, Solzhenitsyn argued that Stalin was no less a characteristic product of communist doctrine than Lenin, Trotsky, Brezhnev, Andropov, or any other of the Soviet leaders over the decades. The Soviet Union was the instrument of power of the party, whose controllers recognized no limits to their claims or to the means for achieving them. From day one, Solzhenitsyn held, the regime engaged in deliberate genocide of its own subjects to terrorize the remnant into total obedience. Brutal, anti-Semitic, anti-Christian, and hostile to all autonomous or creative expressions of culture, it lived a cancerous existence at the expense of the Russian people and the world.

The regime expelled Solzhenitsyn in 1974, and after he visited various countries he settled in the United States. Here, in a speech at Harvard University in 1978 on "A World Split Apart," he denounced the West, in its most potent, American incarnation, as having lost religious faith and therefore being in danger of falling under the same temptations of power, arrogance, and inhumanity as had taken over his own country. The reason was that Americans had become too free, or rather, they had forgotten that aimless and morally ungrounded freedom risked leading to its opposite. Freedom without faith, said the Russian prophet, risked a "tilt of freedom toward evil." By giving this "Harvard speech," Solzhenitsyn cut the few cords that still bound him to the Western progressive consensus. Its members had been happy enough to welcome him to democratic freedom; they were less happy to hear him attack them as agents of corruption in the West itself. Solzhenitsyn retired to his farm in Vermont and continued to write his multivolume history of the Russian Revolution, part novel, part philosophy, and part political analysis. He continued to maintain that "if I were called upon to identify briefly the principal trait of the entire twentieth century, here too, I would be unable to find anything more precise and pithy than to repeat once again, 'Men have forgotten God.'"9

In 1994, he returned home to a Russia under the thumb not of a communist party but of the nomenklatura, the former owners of the party, who remained in control of assets and therefore of people's livelihoods. Trained by their past and character to a criminal, exploitative view of their fellowmen, these former apparatchiks found great scope for their acquisitive instincts in the new Russia. The end of communist power did not bring democracy, because democracy, as Montesquieu and Tocqueville suggested, required a base of law and religion. It brought, rather, a superficial freedom importing the worst bourgeois pathologies of the West to a nation ruined by seven decades of communism. Solzhenitsyn labeled this "the Westernist conversion" of Russia, distinguishing "Westernism," the superficial caricature of Western freedom, from valuable aspects of the West.

Solzhenitsyn's reminder, from an eastern Orthodox standpoint, that Western identity needed Christianity if it was to avoid slipping into a nihilistic secularism, caused much offense in a political culture that, in the 1970s, was moving from a centrist liberalism toward the late-twentieth-century version, which combined universalism and multiculturalism as two principles that might seem to contradict each other, but that both rejected the historical identity of Western civilization, the identity composed of liberty based on property and political pluralism, Christianity, and the spirit of discovery. He raised hackles for another reason as well. The prestige of Marxism as representing the best of the West, the hope of justice and equality, remained strong among scholars and intellectuals. In this respect, the Marxist temptation proved stronger than the three other proposals for a rejuvenated Western identity—the revivalist, the National Socialist, and the Grand Narrative.

The revivalist dream of Western identity was, unlike communism, an affair of scholars and poets, and claimed no political power. Its adherents did, however, hope to have an effect on culture and pedagogy. Their entire proposal amounted, in effect, to reform elite teaching in Western nations in order to emphasize what they considered to be the essence of the West. It was the medieval synthesis of Christian and classical learning, pedagogy, and philosophy that struck them as the unique feature of European, or Western, civilization. This legacy, if recovered and properly taught, would show that the West was more than liberalism, and especially more than its bourgeois pathology. The revivalists traced both the bourgeois pathology and the antidemocratic ideologies of left and right to a neglect by Western elites of their own proper heritage. In the 1920s and 1930s, they wrote under the growing shadow of both communism and its National Socialist and fascist adversaries; the hour was indeed late, and the times evil.

The revivalist argument was that there was more to the West than either liberalism or nihilism. It had antecedents among the romantics, in the highly unhistorical and unrealistic nostalgia for the Christendom version of the West, for a unitary Western civilization, of the short-lived poet Novalis, best known for his *Hymns to the Night*, which was his contribution to Rougemont's Western myth of self-immolation in the land of darkness. In an essay written a year before his death at twenty-eight, Novalis lamented the loss of "those splendid times when Europe was one Christian country, when *one* Christendom inhabited this humanely ordered part of the world; *one* great common interest connected the most far-flung provinces of this widespread, spiritual realm." In those unitary and harmonious times when, as in Dante's ideal world, empire, church, and world were united, "*one* head guided the great political forces." Wise, saintly ministers directed the labor and learning of all, so that "individuals reached unheard-of heights in all the disciplines of the sciences of life and the arts," whereas "blossoming trade in spiritual and earthly goods spread from Europe to the farthest reaches of India."[10]

The most important twentieth-century revivalists were T.S. Eliot in England, Ernst Robert Curtius in Germany, and Christopher Dawson in America. They looked to the European Middle Ages as a source of tradition. They
also looked, through the Christian Middle Ages, to Rome and in particular
to the poet Virgil, defined by Eliot in 1944 as the one and only truly classical
poet of the West. A classic poet, Eliot explained, must display maturity of
style and manners and be cosmopolitan and polished. By such criteria, all
languages had their classic poets. What made Virgil the classic for all Europe,
an absolute rather than a relative classic, was that his work was fundamental
and decisive not just for the Latin language but for all Western languages:
"His comprehensiveness, his peculiar kind of comprehensiveness, is due to
the unique position in our history of the Roman Empire and the Latin language; a position which may be said to conform to its *destiny*." Rome built
the universal empire that enriched and transmitted the Greek and Christian
heritages to the West. The classic of the West therefore had to be the poet
who best and most completely expressed the ethos and mission of Rome.

A classic must hold in itself not merely the universe in which it was composed but later universes as well. It must have personal and psychological
meaning for later generations; it must be living, not dead. Eliot further argued that Europe, the West, needed a classic, a core referent that would not
dominate but liberate contemporary culture from its political and spiritual
bondage to the trivial, the violent, and the merely confusing. Finally, he said,
the *Aeneid* was that classic for Europe because it did, in fact, contain the universal meaning in the particular story required by the definition. It balanced,
precariously, on the edge between maturity and decay. It was the rich harvest
of centuries of ancient culture without any of the preciosity, decadence, and
self-absorption of later Roman literature. Virgil portrayed a "world of dignity,
reason and order" without sentimentality or false pride. In the *Aeneid*, he

> acquires the centrality of the unique classic; he is at the centre of European
> civilization, in a position which no other poet can share or usurp. The Roman
> Empire and the Latin language were not any empire and any language, but an
> empire and a language with a unique destiny in relation to ourselves; and the
> poet in whom that Empire and that language came to consciousness and ex-
> pression is a poet of unique destiny.[11]

To the revivalists, Eliot in particular, the Roman Empire was crucial. Virgil would not have been a classic if his story of loss, wandering, and hope was
merely an epic quest like the *Odyssey*. What was necessary was the political
and spiritual vision of a world order. "Both classic and empire exist within

history," noted Charles Martindale, "but also transcend history, evincing both permanence and change and enabling us to grasp, or at least to experience in practice, the relationship between them."[12]

Nostalgic imperialism as a remedy for nihilism and the disaster of the West in World War I was without doubt a quixotic and, in hindsight, impossibly paradoxical scheme of cultural restoration. One can only imagine Nietzsche's withering put-downs, had he lived to witness it. For one thing, the vision of empire largely, and perhaps deliberately, did not distinguish between myth and history, between the timeless ideal of an empire of the West and the actual empires of history. Theodor Haecker stated that "now as before, we live in the Roman Empire, which according to the prophecy of Daniel will not end until the end of the world," a phrase echoed, with a small but significant difference, by Eliot in his 1944 lecture, when he said, "We are all, insofar as we inherit the civilization of Europe, still citizens of the Roman Empire." Haecker was a Catholic political mystic; Eliot, though a confessed Christian, was speaking the language of secular culture and so stressed "civilization" as the link binding the men and women of culture in 1944 to Rome and Virgil.

This merely cultural link was not enough for Haecker. His imperialism was not an idea that if we all studied Virgil and hoped for Western unity, something good would happen; it was a sustained, passionate lament for the fall of the medieval European order, consisting of a supranational political institution, the empire, guided by a universal spiritual institution, the church. Although the Roman Empire was without end, "we live no longer in the Holy Empire, *it has come to an end*, alas, it will never return," and in his view it was blasphemous or nonsensical to think that any German empire without that spiritual guidance was worthy of the name.[13]

He was writing in 1932 and thinking of the empire of Bismarck and Wilhelm II, but he was also thinking of the idea of a "third Reich" popularized in the 1920s by the so-called conservative revolutionaries in Germany and appropriated by the National Socialists. The idea of a "third empire" after those of Alexander the Great and Rome had been a marginal figure of Western political mythology since the Middle Ages. Spengler revived it, significantly enough in a discussion of socialism and of socialist man as the final incarnation of the West. The socialist, said Spengler, wanted "permanence," wanted to plan, order, and govern the future. In this sense, socialism was the future of the West, and in particular of Germany. "*The third Reich is the Germanic ideal*," he wrote, combining the socialist desire for planned labor with Germanic-Faustian ambitions for a perfect future.[14] It was precisely this sort of anti-Christian, nihilistic activism that appalled Haecker. Without the pope, that is, without Rome, such an empire would be mere power. And given the political reality of Hitler's "Third Empire," it would be hard to deny that the impractical dreamer, Haecker, was right to be appalled.

Nostalgic imperialism had two sources. The first was Virgil, who made the hope of empire the reason that the exiled Trojans, in the *Aeneid*, need not despair. They had lost their homes; but far in the future, their descendants would bring peace, order, and justice to a suffering world. In the famous words put into the mouth of Jupiter, father of gods and men, in book 1:

his ego nec metas rerum nec tempora pono:
imperium sine fine dedi

[I set no bounds of space or time for them [the future Romans]: I have granted them an empire without end]

In an angry essay of 1962, the poet and philhellenist Robert Graves ridiculed "The Virgil Cult," saying of these two lines, "This heady doctrine, to which as a young Romano-British imperialist I too was asked to subscribe a few years later, Mr. Eliot still cherishes."[15] Less sarcastically, that ambiguity again illustrated Haecker's emotional point, that the 1920s and 1930s plans to build a new empire in Germany bore little relation to the nostalgic dreams. The Latin word *imperium* was itself ambiguous; legally, it denoted the absolute authority within his allotted sphere of a Roman commander. By definition, *imperium* was total, whether exercised over an army, a province, a political process, or, as in Rome after Augustus, the whole Mediterranean world. The Romans invented *imperium* for the precise reason that they wanted to create spheres of administration and action exempt from the usual processes of law and appeal available to citizens in normal circumstances. That was why Augustus's settlement, hailed by Virgil, was revolutionary: it completed a century-long process of extending the extraordinary practice and methods of *imperium* to the whole society.

But *imperium* in Virgil, Augustan ideology, and later nostalgic imperialism implied that the total authority of the *imperator*, the holder of *imperium*, was also fair, just, orderly, and respected by the people. The problem, in Rome as later, was that there was no way to secure a continued supply of fair, just, respectable, and responsible *imperatores*. Hence Haecker's vision of secular *imperium* subordinated to the church. In the actual history of Europe, that balance worked only intermittently; inevitably, conflicts of interest and personality undermined the ideal alliance, so that by the fourteenth century, both parties—the Holy Empire and the papacy—were exhausted and discredited. In their place, Europe got the territorial states with their wars, their competition, but also their ability to stimulate growth and economic activity.

Another source for imperial nostalgia was Dante. Without Dante's own idealistic imperialism, which confirmed that of Virgil, the twentieth-century revivalists could not claim that the idea of empire, Roman or Holy or both, was a plausible foundation of the West. In his defense of empire, the *De Monarchia*, Dante proposed that just as humankind had one spiritual head, Christ, so it should also have only one worldly and political head, namely, an emperor. Pluralism of authority in either the religious or the political sphere violated divinely willed order and was a form of sin. Dante knew that his vision of a single world state was anachronistic, but he devoted all his energy to presenting the dream of a single system of order serving a common good not just in the *De Monarchia* but in the *Divine Comedy* itself.

Dante's political mysticism and his hope against hope for a restored universal empire was virtually designed to appeal to the interwar revivalists. The most comprehensive statement of that revival and of Dante's role in it was not Eliot's but that of Ernst Robert Curtius. Where Eliot sometimes tied Western hopes to religion, and in particular to his own Anglo-Catholic religion, Curtius, although not irreligious, wrote as a humanist and a pedagogue, to present a practical program of educational and literary recovery.

Nostalgic imperialism, medievalism, a need for hope: these were the common ground proposed by Eliot, Curtius, and their fellows. Their problem was not merely to disprove a philosophy or spread light and comfort in the midst of social and political disaster. It was to rescue tradition in a world that did not want it and, given its assumptions, could not want it, except in the optimistic and unhistorical form presented in the Grand Narrative. "We fight for lost causes because we know that our defeat and dismay may be the preface to our successors' victory, though that victory itself will be temporary; we fight rather to keep something alive than in the expectation that anything will triumph."[16] So wrote Eliot in 1939 to explain his work as a critic of modern culture and a defender of Christianity. A similar belief inspired others who in the years between the world wars sought a viable tradition for the uncaring West. Some looked to antiquity, others to the Middle Ages. It was notable, however, that the revivalists, unlike the philhellenists of the eighteenth and nineteenth centuries, almost never looked to Greece. It was the cosmopolitan Roman Empire and its medieval successors that provided their mental map of where the West was to be found, and when.

Virgil was a gratifying figure to use in this project of defiance. So popular was he in the interwar years that one literary historian in the 1990s described the period as an *aetas Virgiliana* (Virgilian era). Classicists, poets, and others found in him a "prophet of modernity . . . a message of compelling relevance for the morally chaotic and socially anarchic present."[17] Not because Virgil reveled in decline and nihilism—on the contrary. The idea was that "we stand now, as Virgil stood, among the wreckage of a world; he can give light and guidance to us in the foundation of a new world upon its ruins."[18] The poets of 1920, like Eliot in *The Waste Land*, could only lament; Virgil was, at least in the view of the time, a builder and an optimist, not a defeatist. In the words of the literary historian Theodore Ziolkowski:

> The reception of Virgil in the decades embracing the worldwide bimillennial celebrations in 1930 can be understood as a specific case of the general Roman analogy that was invoked by many thoughtful people in Europe and the Americas in response to the pervasive crisis of history precipitated by World War I. In the effort to bring meaning into the world of the 1920s and 1930s the Roman poet was invoked, who two thousand years earlier had succeeded in distilling beauty and order from the political and social horror of his own age.[19]

Publius Vergilius Maro, or Virgil in English, was born near Mantua in what is today northern Italy, traditionally on October 15, 70 B.C. His family were Roman citizens, which was noteworthy if not unusual for the region, because in 70 B.C. the Po valley and Lombard plain, where Mantua was located, was not part of Italy but rather of the province of Cisalpine Gaul. His father was a potter and had a small farm; Virgil was supposed to have inherited the bearing, physique, dialect, and slow speech of the peasant. Both he himself, his contemporaries, and his modern admirers made much of the contrast between Virgil's humble origins in a family that held fast to the ancient republican virtues and the corruption and violence of Rome itself. All of his poems directly or indirectly praised country life in opposition to the seductions and moral ambiguities of the city: *fortunatus et ille deos qui novit agrestes* (lucky is he who has known the spirits of the field). His sense of values, to use a modern term, was firmly rooted in the soil.

When Virgil was born, the Roman Republic was at the halfway mark of its final century, the century of twelve civil wars that ended when Augustus designed the settlement that established the empire. At an early age, Virgil was sent abroad for schooling, first to local towns and then to Rome. His family intended for him to become a forensic orator, a lawyer; in its decadence the republic produced and rewarded many such. But his rustic manner and shyness stopped that career and soon he began composing poetry. His first surviving poems were the ten *Eclogues* dating from around 40 B.C. These were idylls of pastoral love in the manner of the Hellenistic Greek poets, though Virgil introduced material foreign to his models, contrasting rural bliss to political insecurity and rural values to urban immorality.

One of these *Eclogues*, the fourth, became the key to Virgil's popularity in the Christian Middle Ages. In it, he prophesied that the civil wars and turmoil of the present would soon end and that a prince of peace would bring harmony back to the world. Scholars have referred these words to various possible Roman figures; the point here is that they were taken throughout the Middle Ages and beyond as evidence that Virgil was a pagan prophet of Christ and therefore a seer of magical powers. So great was this faith that the collected works of Virgil were often, like the Bible, used as oracles: you opened a passage at random and interpreted what you read to fit your question and provide guidance.

The medievalist-Virgilian revival returned to this poem and redeployed it to bring Virgil back in as "father of the [Christian] West." Speaking of the fourth *Eclogue* and its prophecy of a future savior, Theodor Haecker wrote:

> It is not Roman, it is a mythical intimation of a divine history of salvation that came to him in Naples out of the East and, seizing his heart pining for peace and completion, inspired his genius to prophetic verses that fall quite outside the rest of his work . . . Virgil was no prophet like Isaiah . . . but he shaped a mythical material linked to the eternal truth of the angels and patriarchs and prophets, at a time that not he, but providence decided, providence, which again had appointed him in particular to be the shaper of this material in the advent atmosphere of paganism, because he was eminently the *anima naturaliter christiana*. . . . only when possessed of these Messianic hopes and eschatological expectations was Virgilian man fully and truly himself and open to the future, a light and transparent readiness, no end, but a way.[20]

In these ecstatic terms, the Christianization of Rome and the foundation of the West—the West imagined by the revivalists—were hardly matters of history, but of divine action.

The *Eclogues* brought Virgil fame in Rome. "On one occasion the people, hearing in the theatre a performance of Virgil's verses, rose and acclaimed the poet, who was present and watching, as though he were Augustus himself," wrote Tacitus.²¹ The young Augustus seemed not to mind the poet's popularity. Part of the future emperor's political program was to end the civil wars; but he would then be stuck with thousands of landless soldiers without work. Augustus proposed to settle them on land confiscated from his enemies. To provide the ideological backdrop for this policy and in general to support a restoration of old civic virtues, Augustus paid lip service to rural values and the stable and stabilizing life of the countryside. He was therefore gratified that Virgil's next work was the four books of *Georgics*, which combined detailed descriptions of farm work with praise of agriculture and country life, contrasting the everlasting cycle of the seasons and their demands to the ugly world of politics with its *tot bella per orbem* (all the wars in the world), that took the farmer from his field and forged plowshares into swords. The Irish poet and socialist Cecil Day Lewis translated the *Georgics* into English in time of war, in 1940, and saw in them, not in the romantic imperialism of the *Aeneid*, the key to Virgil's greatness and his appeal to modernity:

> Virgil . . . chiefly dear for his gift to understand
> Earth's intricate, ordered heart, and for a vision
> That saw beyond an imperial day the hand
> Of man no longer armed against his fellow
> But all for vine and cattle, fruit and fallow,
> Subduing with love's positive force the land.²²

The praise of toil in the *Georgics* was unusual and subversive in antiquity. Greeks and Romans considered earning your bread by the sweat of your brow dishonorable; not having to work was the mark of the full citizen. In such a culture, Virgil's praise of the *iustissima tellus*, the most just earth, which yielded its fruits only to hard human labor, was original. Virgil's message in the *Georgics*, that all human life depended on the soil and therefore on labor, was, with Christianity, one of the reasons the later West turned the classical order of social and economic values upside down. Thus, where antiquity despised the man who had to work to buy his leisure time, the West, and especially America, regarded such a man more highly than the rentier, the "man of leisure." Work, in the West, ennobled the worker; in antiquity, it degraded him and made him unfit for the highest civic callings.

Virgil's greatest work was the *Aeneid*, on which he worked in the final decade of his life. He died suddenly in 19 B.C. at Brindisi, in the south of Italy, and was supposed to have ordered the papyrus rolls containing the poem destroyed. He was buried in Naples; his famous epitaph named the stations of his life and the themes of his work:

Mantua me genuit, Calabri rapuere, tenet nunc
Parthenope. Cecini pascua, rura, duces.

[Mantua bore me, Calabria took me, Naples holds me
Now. I sang of meadows, fields, chieftains.][23]

The *Aeneid* was not destroyed, but the poem remained unfinished. The *Aeneid*, in twelve books, told the mythological story of how Rome came to be founded by Aeneas, a prince of Troy, who escaped from the city when it was captured by the Greeks. The first six books described how Aeneas and his followers made their way from the ruins of Troy to Italy, the last six the struggles faced by the Trojan exiles in Italy until they established themselves by defeating the native king, Turnus, and won the territory on which their descendants would found the city of Rome.

The idea of the proto-Christian, or "adventist," Virgil derived not merely from the mysterious annunciation of a coming savior in the fourth *Eclogue* but more generally from the Messianic flavor that permeated all his works. Writing from the standpoint of his conservative, rural values in a time of turmoil, and hoping that his poetry would help sustain Augustus's policy of order, Virgil used every opportunity to contrast present unhappiness with future bliss and to show how his characters' suffering had a noble purpose. That life today was part of a divine design for future greatness and order was a recurrent theme in the stories he told. The *Aeneid* in particular was the story of a chosen people, the Trojan exiles, who could never return to their ancestral hearths but whose descendants would enjoy the peace and power that they themselves would never know again. Loss and promise, a journey from ruin to hope, the duty to proceed, set against the constant temptations to give up the quest—such themes became foundations of Western literature and legend. In particular, the idea of a journey from which you could not turn back or deviate, the idea that "you can't go home again," and the related idea that "the journey not the arrival matters,"[24] entered the Western psychology as deeply as the heroic virtues of Roland or the ascetic virtues of a real-life Rancé.

Americans in particular identified with Virgil's story of Aeneas and his Trojans as a saving remnant carrying the best of the old westward to a new world, and with their heroic struggle to establish themselves there against traitors, fatigue, and natives both friendly and hostile. In his early novel *The Cabala*, the story of a young American in Rome in the 1920s, Thornton

Wilder had his protagonist literally invoke the shade of Virgil on the eve of his departure back to the United States. Virgil's shade reassures the young man that his voyage home to the New World is justified, because New York is the new Rome: "The secret is to make a city, not to rest in it. . . . Oh, in the pride of your city, and when she too begins to produce great men, do not forget mine." And the novel concludes, "The shimmering ghost faded before the stars, and the engines beneath me pounded eagerly toward the new world and the last and greatest of all cities."[25]

In 1930, scholars and not a few politicians celebrated Virgil's two thousandth birthday. As a response to that occasion there appeared in 1931 one of the more remarkable productions of the interwar *aetas Virgiliana*, the book *Virgil, Father of the West* by the German Catholic writer and teacher Theodor Haecker, on whom Eliot drew in his own work on Virgil. Haecker belonged to a generation largely ignored in the happy days after World War II, the generation of unorthodox Catholic social and cultural thinkers that included Jacques Maritain in France and Hans Kuhn and Reinhold Schneider in Germany. They were unorthodox because they read and treasured non-Catholic thinkers at time when obedient Catholic writers were not supposed to do so. Haecker, for example, found his chief inspiration and consolation in the Protestant Kierkegaard, as well as Virgil. As Catholics, they felt the crisis of the West in a different way than secular thinkers such as Spengler. He was able to analyze with scholarly detachment the coming end of the West and its origins. For them, the essence of the West was Christianity and its manifestation the Catholic Church; they still swore by the old triad, holding that the new triad of reason, liberty, and prosperity could not, as World War I had seemingly shown, survive on its own. They could not contemplate the final fading of the old triad with equanimity, and their religion forbade them to fall into despair. Thus, the crisis of the West was to them not a matter for reflection but one of passion, urgency, and personal commitment. If they were German, as Haecker was, the 1930s and 1940s brought the additional shame and terror of belonging to a nation that, whatever its leader claimed, was promoting the work of destruction at a speed and with a consistency of purpose that even Spengler had not foreseen.

Haecker's attitude to the National Socialist regime was unambiguous, and he paid for it with prison sentences and censorship. For example, in his diary for May 19, 1940, at the height of the German victories, he noted:

> The automaton voice of the "German radio" today proclaimed one of its master's thoughts. The vigor and fighting spirit of the German soldiers who over-

ran Holland and Belgium can only be compared to the impact of the French soldiers of the revolution who overran all Europe and spread the ideas of the French revolution. Those ideas are now outdated; the ideas of National Socialism are young. . . . Let's see: the ideas of the French revolution were liberty, equality, fraternity. They were ideas stolen from Christianity and partly poisoned and falsified. But in themselves they were, rightly, understandably, and in human terms, thrilling ideas. What then are the ideas of National Socialism? Beyond all doubt, the polar opposite. *In*equality, not equality, because the whole movement derives from an essay by Gobineau on the inequality of races. *Unfreedom*, not freedom, because one man, the Führer, decides all, including science, art, and above all the first thing for man, religion and faith. *Non*-fraternity, not fraternity, because there is *one* race which is superior to all others and certainly cannot show those others any fraternity; there are even peoples, like the Jews and the Poles, who are *racially*, compared to the "Aryans," *subhuman* and therefore not brothers. These, then, are the ideas that we are bringing to the nations and to the world. They will be so delighted they won't know where to turn. But it is also a fantastic claim that our soldiers are such good soldiers on behalf of these ideas.[26]

A later age might consider such thoughts simplistic; yet both in 1940 and later many remained unable to arrive at such a clear appraisal.

Haecker's book on Virgil was a defense of the "adventist" Virgil, the idea that Virgil was an *anima naturaliter christiana*, a "naturally Christian spirit." Haecker's was not a literary, aesthetic, or philological study, rather it was a sustained paean to Virgil as the divinely guided prophet of the West. For example, the *Aeneid* was the epic of how Rome came to be and a call to the Romans of Virgil's own time to remember what they shared and to join in bringing Augustus's great work of pacification to completion. The result of Augustus's policy and Virgil's poetry was the Roman Empire, of which all later empires and great European nations were the spiritual and in some cases the territorial heirs. Now, providentially, Augustus's work made Christianity possible by bringing peace to the Mediterranean. So, without Virgil, no empire; without the empire, no Christianity; without Christianity, no West— therefore Virgil was the father of the West.

The amazing thing about this sequence, Haecker argued, was that the Romans became Christian not as victims or sufferers, but as victors, as the rulers of the great empire. Why did these proud people accept this religion of slaves and outcasts? Again, Virgil was responsible. "I say that the most complete, inner, natural explanation for this is Virgil and the Virgilian personality in the poetic incarnation of Aeneas, whom the best of the Romans recognized as the ideal Roman, drawn from reality, called into reality." The clue was that Virgil constantly described Aeneas as *pius*, which was more than "pious"; it meant honoring duties assigned by your fathers and painstaking in complying with divinely ordained ritual, which incarnated "the *principle* of an outer form, without which there is no durable *true* religion among men, nor any *pietas*."

But the West, consisting of sinful and fallible men, did not always live up to Aeneas's *pietas*. Too often, the West took *pietas* as a call to rebellion against the divine order in the name of service to humankind, or power. "Both the Titanic and the Promethean, the rebellion from envy and that from compassion, belong to Western man, but it is only an ingredient, which one recognizes spontaneously or gradually as injustice, as sin, and whose bearer is punished. . . . This should be noted, especially by Germans, who have renewed the Promethean and the Titanic in the Faustian, at which even the old Goethe at the end of his life and his drama shuddered a little."[27]

Haecker's presentation of Virgil as the "father of the West" was directed to Europe at large, but in particular to his compatriots. In Germany, the Virgilian revival was also a revolt against the "tyranny of Greece" introduced by Winckelmann and Goethe, and which Spengler denounced when he called the Greeks alien to the West. Before Winckelmann, "the German of the Holy Roman Empire. . . . knew, in common with all good Europeans, that Virgil is a fixed star, a radiant star of the first order."[28] In Germany, the rediscovery of Greece yielded not merely cultural knowledge but virtually an ersatz religion. Winckelmann and the other philhellenists found, in an age of declining Christianity, what they regarded as a more perfect, more humane, and more universal religion in Greece. This inflated worship of Greece cut off Germany and the West, according to Haecker and Curtius, from its own descent through the Latin Middle Ages from Virgil. In fairness to old Wilamowitz one might note that the eighty-two- year old scholar commented on the occasion of the Virgilian bimillennium in 1930 that "it ought to be time . . . to do justice to the great artist," while also noting that Virgil was perhaps more important to the Romance-speaking cultures than to Germany.[29]

The Romantic vision of Greece, which seemed universal to Goethe, no longer had the same power after Spengler and World War I, whereas Virgil, who seemed artificial and overcivilized to Goethe, had, after the advent of nihilism, reacquired the universal appeal his work enjoyed in the Middle Ages. One reason was that Goethe wrote not merely out of his own serene and supremely secure personality, but out of a serene and self-confident age, that of the Enlightenment, the birth of liberalism and of modern freedom. An age, in short, not unlike the *Saturnia regna* of peace, prosperity, and humane values invoked by Virgil. The German Hellenists sought in Greece what their own age lacked: energy, originality, the vigor of the dawn of time. By the 1920s, war and nihilism had sapped Western serenity. It was C.S. Lewis who, as a young man of eighteen in 1916, on arriving at the western front, said to himself, "This is war. This is what Homer wrote about." If you lived in a Homeric age rather than dreaming about it, you might perhaps seek inspiration in its opposite, in the world of Virgil.

Thus, each epoch chose its opposite as its ideal. Goethe, the Virgilian man par excellence, found true humanity and the roots of the West in Homer.[30] Eliot, Haecker, Curtius, Lewis, and other early-twentieth-century men, living unwillingly in an age of Homeric passion and war, found true humanity and the roots of the West in Virgil.

Given the real or imaginary analogies between the Dark Ages and the decades after World War I, it was not surprising that scholarship on the Middle Ages, and in particular on the transmission of ancient literature, flourished in the interwar years, and much of this scholarship fed the revivalist project. One of its chief proponents was the literary historian and conservative intellectual Ernst Robert Curtius, professor of Romance languages and literature at the University of Bonn from 1928 to his death in 1956. As a lover and teacher of French literature, Curtius saw his world end in 1914 when the war, and the passions and bitterness it left behind, made communication and understanding between France and Germany all but impossible. As a humanist Curtius had a feeling for change and continuity and difference, although he, too, considered literature as offering a "timeless present."[31] Faced with the "heap of broken images," Curtius set out not to unbreak them, while leaving them in a heap, but to set them back into their original order and rank. His attempt was no less doomed than that of the other revivalists, but he had, or rather acquired along the way, an additional political motivation, namely the Hitlerite regime in Germany and its attack on humanistic culture.

In the 1920s, Eliot and Curtius saw themselves as fighting the same battle. Curtius translated *The Waste Land* into German in 1927 and, in the same year, Eliot published an essay by Curtius in his journal. In this essay, "The Restoration of Reason," Curtius made the revivalist plea for recovery of common culture and against nihilism. In 1932, in the midst of economic crisis and with right- and left-wing extremists fighting for power in Germany, Curtius published a short book on the "danger" threatening the

"German spirit." This danger was not National Socialism or communism—Curtius failed to foresee what would happen when Hitler took power—but ignorance of history and contempt for tradition. He found this contempt concentrated in the social sciences with their faith in quantification and their ahistorical methods.

Curtius had begun his career as a teacher of French literature. After World War I, he continued to argue that French and German culture were parts of a common whole, but with a few exceptions he was snubbed in France, where a defensive, arrogant nationalism set the agenda. For example, the right-wing thinker André Bellessort wrote a book on Virgil in 1920 in which he likened the French victory over Germany in 1918 to Augustus's defeat of Mark Antony and Cleopatra at the battle of Actium in 31 B.C. Virgil might be the father of the West, but in the interwar cultural crisis nationalism often dictated the definition of the West. In France, the West was anti-German; in Fascist Italy, it was defended by Fascism, and there were Germans under Hitler who believed that the Third Reich was the highest incarnation of the West. Giovanni Gentile, the Italian philosopher who served Mussolini as minister of education, managed to align both Nazi Germany and Mussolini's Italy in the battle for the West when he said, in March 1944, only four weeks before he was killed, that the place of Italy was at the side of Germany "for her honor and her destiny, facing in common the fearsome struggle for the salvation of Europe and of Western civilization."[32]

It was precisely this sort of ideological deformation of the idea of the West that Curtius was determined to subvert. Finding that French nationalists wished to appropriate Virgil and the West, Curtius remarked that "whoever cuts off the road to Paris must open the road to Rome," and began from the later 1920s on to look to Rome, both ancient and medieval, as the only source of European cultural unity and of Western restoration. He was a conservative but, or rather, therefore no National Socialist. He distinguished a southwestern from a Slavic-northeastern orientation in Germany, "a Berlin spirit—among both bureaucrats and writers—and a German spirit."[33] The truly German spirit, in Curtius's view, was a spirit open to the Latin world and the West. He saw in Hitler's movement the denial of this genuine German spirit and its necessary roots in the European tradition in its variety and transformations. One could only know and love that tradition by knowing and loving every one of its provinces, languages, styles, periods, and temperaments. Therefore, in the years of dictatorship and World War II, Curtius prepared his own counterstroke to the powers ruling his world, his own statement of defiance against those who would deny tradition and the common values of the West. This statement was his work on *European Literature and the Latin Middle Ages* of 1952, described by Eliot as "the best book to be published this year and for many years."

In his masterpiece, Curtius deployed a method peculiarly apt to an age that both misunderstood and rejected the very idea of tradition. This was to describe not particular writers, periods, or ideas but the "topics, *communes loci* that provide the building blocks, in a manner analogous to letters in an alphabet," and that appeared, in various shapes and to various purposes, in Latin literature and its vernacular offspring from the eighth to the sixteenth century.[34] To undertake his work, Curtius had to be intimately familiar with epic, fable, lyric, chronicles, and philosophy not just in the dominant Latin language, but in the growing literatures in Italian, French, German, Spanish, and English, as well as with their uses of each other and the past. He had also to develop a sense for the interesting "common places," the ideas, figures of speech, perspectives, and feelings that writers of the medieval past had traded among each other. Some of his examples were the consolation speech, nature as goddess, metaphors of life and fate as navigation and drama, the portrayal of heroic figures, landscape descriptions, uses of theology, the symbolism of the book. Tracing these notions and their use through seven to eight languages and ten centuries—a task requiring the learning of lifetimes, one would have thought—demonstrated that European literature was a "spiritual unity" with a Latin core and reservoir of images, tradition, metaphor, and subjects.

One of his purposes was not to let nationalism, whether German or French, undermine the recovery of Virgil and his meaning for Europe. For Curtius, Virgil was the "genius" and the "prophet of the West," not only in himself, but in Dante's encounter with him and in the resulting synthesis of ancient and Christian worlds:

> The conception of the [*Divine*] *Comedy* rests on a spiritual encounter with Virgil. In the whole circle of European literature there is little that can compare to this phenomenon. The reawakening of Aristotle in the thirteenth century was the work of generations and was carried out in the cool light of conceptual scholarship. The awakening of Virgil by Dante is an arc of flame springing from one great spirit to another. The tradition of the European spirit knows no situation of comparable grandeur, tenderness, fruitfulness. It is the encounter of the two greatest Latinists. Historically: the sealing of the bond that the Latin Middle Ages forged between Antiquity and the modern world. Only when we become able to understand Virgil again in all his poetic greatness, which we Germans have lost since 1770, shall we be able to give Dante his proper due.[35]

T.S. Eliot's hope for the West consisted in recommending that Westerners seek the empire that would never exist in the world and that, for the Christian Eliot, was found in the realm of faith. "The World is trying the experiment of attempting to form a civilized but non-Christian mentality," he wrote in 1931. "The experiment will fail; but we must be very patient awaiting its collapse; meanwhile redeeming the time: so that the Faith may be preserved alive through the dark ages before us; to renew and rebuild civilization, and save the World from suicide."[36] This was not a practical program of action, but a call to contemplation and resigned patience, behind the walls of an imaginary monastery. The Virgilian revival and the interwar counterattack on nihilism invoked the old idea of the West as Christendom, but they produced no political results, nor, arguably, were they intended to.

Others in the interwar years both intended and achieved substantial political results. The two decades from 1918 to 1939 remained marked by fundamental paradox. On the one hand, in America, Britain, Scandinavia, and France, liberal and socialist forces allied, more or less reluctantly, to formulate and put in place the social policies that abated the worst effects of the great Depression and launched the modern welfare state. The interwar years were also, in those countries and elsewhere, the years of architectural and literary modernism. On the other, the communists, both those in power in the Soviet Union and those fighting for power in the West, and their fascist and National Socialist rivals and enemies, seized power in some of the most powerful states of the West, and seemed to demonstrate that energy, dynamism, and the future rested with the antidemocrats. It was necessary, these new movements claimed, to forge ahead, to cross the threshold from the fragmentation of liberal democracy and the remnants of superstition to a new and higher reality, a reality of power, unity, and solidarity.

The dividing line between those who leaned to the communists and those who leaned to Hitler was not always clear. "The affliction of those times is that, whereas anti-Semites could always feel a weakness for Hitler, it was not necessary to be anti-Semitic to be tempted to search for solutions in Fascism. It was enough to be at the same time non-communist and anti-liberal; which defined a large zone of intellectual opinion from right to left. I deliberately write 'non-communist' and not 'anticommunist': the anti-liberal passion, the rejection of the bourgeois lie, were sometimes strong enough in themselves and to merge, in many minds, the attraction of Fascism with the weakness for communism."[37]

The antidemocratic noncommunists were a large family, including Catholic supporters of Franco, atheistic Italian Fascists, and right-wing Germans who saw in Hitler the savior of the West. They had some ideas in common. One was that they refused to see liberal democracy as the destiny of the West. They found no satisfaction in recalling a liberal story that pointed toward secular enlightenment or revolution as its end. They saw, rather, a besieged culture in crisis and looked for forces that could hold the defenders together as long as possible. They declared that if the West was no more than secular liberalism, it ought to be rejected. But at the same time they were not defeatists. They were not content to escape into esoteric mysticism. They wanted to assert an active West, first to beat off the assault, then to construct an authoritarian political system as the framework of a new culture. Tradition, in their view, was not something to be laboriously recovered by an intellectual elite, as in the case of the Virgilian revivalists, but was the permanent and necessary center of any viable civilization. To respect tradition was, in Virgilian terms, to show *pietas*, that is, to recognize that human will neither could nor should shape life, society, politics, or hope for the future.

In this space, that of antidemocratic noncommunists, one found the third grouping of thinkers proposing to reshape Western identity. These thinkers shared with Nietzsche and Spengler the diagnosis that the liberal West was defunct, killed by its own bourgeois pathology and by World War I. Like the communists, they considered the new Western identity as something to be actively shaped by a creative political will, and like them, they saw the political aspects of this identity as something collective, superhuman, and supranational. But on the other hand, they agreed with the revivalists that the clue to this new Western identity was to be sought in the past, specifically in the medieval empire and in the ancient bargain of Leo III and Charlemagne. The emblematic figure of this movement, this third force of Western identity, was the German legal philosopher Carl Schmitt.

From the 1910s to the 1950s, spanning the two world wars, Schmitt propounded what amounted to the most consistent antiliberal account of the West and its crisis conceivable after both Nietzsche and liberalism. At bottom, Schmitt read that crisis in the same way as Joseph de Maistre and Pius IX, as a heretical rebellion against the divine political and cosmic order. In the West, that order had two elements, a supranational empire as the focus of temporal power, and an orthodox papacy as the focus of religious authority. Liberalism, to Schmitt, was a lie and a fraud, for it undermined order in the name of discussion, deliberation, pluralism, and democratic rights. One of the sources of this liberal disease, according to Schmitt, was "political romanticism," of which its author considered liberalism to be the classic example. The basic illusions of political romanticism were that it was possible to arrive at the truth by democratic discussion, and that it was possible to institute the good society by asking people what they wanted.

Schmitt's influence did not end when, in 1945, he lost his chair of law at the University of Berlin and was relegated to an impoverished retirement in his native town of Plettenberg. Though he never taught in public after 1945 and rarely published, his students from the 1920s and 1930s continued to occupy, well into the 1970s, leading positions in German law schools and in the civil service. Until the 1970s, he was an unseen presence largely among conservatives, which in postwar West Germany meant people who were sceptical of the welfare state. But from the mid-1970s on, Schmitt—who lived until 1985—began to acquire an amazing reputation on the left as a critic of bourgeois liberalism whose ideas were far from incompatible with the account given by Marxism. His leftist admirers hoped "that his ideas will be critically evaluated in terms of their content."[38] This influence was often unacknowledged, and the one thing most people who had ever heard his name knew about him was that he had been a National Socialist; in the words of his former friend and later enemy, the Russian-born political philosopher Waldemar Gurian, he was "the official advocate of the Third Reich."[39]

Schmitt illustrated, for those who studied his case, the maxim that a little knowledge was, if not dangerous, then at least highly misleading. His case was surrounded by a great deal of misinformation, owing in no small part to the fact that his legacy was contested by left and right, for different purposes. Three reasons suggested themselves for reviewing it. First and most important, Schmitt was the leading spokesman for an idea of the West that, in the 1920s and 1930s, rivaled liberalism and that he judged superior, because it was more faithful to history and to Christianity. The two other reasons had to do with Schmitt's support of Hitler.

It was an article of faith in the liberal West of the 1990s that Hitler's regime was the moral nadir of human history. The more relativist and post-modern the Western elites became, the more they clung to one remaining moral certainty, which their own philosophy ought to have debarred them from holding: the certainty that Hitler was uniquely evil and all who served him contaminated by that evil. It would be easy, but also disingenuous, to reply that, as relativists, postmodern liberals had no standing to use moral language of any regime or action or to call them evil. Whether or not Hitler and his state were the most evil in history, they murdered millions of people, unleashed a world war, and caused, albeit involuntarily, the division of Europe into a democratic and a Soviet-ruled part. One did not have to be a moralist to find that these actions amounted to objective damage to people, culture, and peace on a vast scale.

Substantively, the National Socialist issue demanded attention because, as Schmitt himself demonstrated, the antimodernist idea of the West had some connection with that ideology. He joined Hitler's movement because he had decided that it met his requirements for the sort of political system and authority needed to save Europe and the West. He was neither an opportunist, nor a national chauvinist, nor a superficial thinker. It was precisely the strongest and most coherent elements in his philosophy of law and politics, and in his religion, that produced his fateful decision to join.

Most traditionalist interpretations of the West had nothing to do with Hitler or his movement, but some did, and in a more general sense those who held illiberal and antimodern ideas of the West of the 1920s to 1940s generally looked if not with favor then with understanding on National Socialist Germany. The problem with 1990s liberal prejudice was not that it was disingenuous, applying morality to history when it rejected morality in the present, nor that it raised questions about people who supported or agreed with Hitler. The problem was that it painted all such with the same black brush, as though all traditionalist conservatives who ever said a kind word about National Socialism were thereby coresponsible for killing six million Jews between 1940 and 1945. Precisely because discussion of the Hitler regime had become, in the 1990s, a matter of clichés and of demonstrating one's own credentials by indulging in ritualistic condemnation, it was essential to differentiate and distinguish, and that could be done only by engaging the issue. It was a valid point that one could not judge attitudes of the 1930s with the supposedly superior hindsight of the 1990s. All the more reason to try to understand the dimensions and implications of positions on the West in the 1930s.

The final reason for including an account of Schmitt's Nazi period was that doing so illustrated aspects of his life and thought that were essential to understand the often ironic and surprising relationships among ideas, ideologies, and politics of his age. Schmitt was not a thug or a killer, and his personal behavior was no worse than that of many other academics and certainly more in accord with liberal values than that of some, then as later.[40] But he was, for a time, a follower of Hitler. Why?

Schmitt and Eliot, to take just those two, had much in common. They were born in the same year, 1888. They grew up in a rapidly modernizing and changing world, yet both shared a longing for and a deep belief in tradition, which to them in the West meant Christianity, a longing that in later life brought Eliot to Anglo-Catholicism and kept Schmitt a lifelong and devoted Catholic, faithfully carrying out all the demands of ritual and habit, which were substantially stricter in the early twentieth century than they became after the Second Vatican Council of the 1960s. Both Eliot and Schmitt encountered modernist poetry around 1910, and both were captivated. Schmitt tried his hand at verse similar to that of the young Eliot in what Stephen Medcalf called his punk, nasty phase. Both loathed romanticism. Both shared a temperament not uncommon in their generation: outwardly formal, always neatly dressed, and well spoken, they inwardly despised convention, stuffiness, what a later generation would call uptightness. They flirted with Dada and surrealism in the years around World War I. Both found in literary modernism and surrealism accurate, liberating, and necessary responses to nihilism, war, and the absurdities and trauma of rapid social and economic change. Both despised the superficial liberalism that tried to carry on after 1914 as though nothing had happened, as though citizens could still be mobilized under the old banners of progress, prosperity, and individualism. They saw in a revived authoritarian state the only solution to ideological conflict that otherwise would destroy civilization. Both, and this was the gravamen of many liberal charges, were, at least in certain periods, anti-Semites. Neither gave much if any thought to the question: assuming the authoritarian state really was necessary, what recourse would the citizen have if that state could not or would not protect him; if indeed it persecuted and attacked him? Both thought themselves hardheaded, realistic, and free of romantic illusions; both were profoundly romantic in their belief that strong and good intentions created reality. Both thought they understood politics; both were innocents in the political world.

There were, of course, important differences as well. For one thing, Eliot was a poet, and whatever his political ideas were, he was never in a position to do harm to Jews, even assuming he really wanted to, and assuming his anti-Semitism was more than posturing. Schmitt was something different, a public and political figure. In 1933, he was perhaps Germany's most distinguished professor of law of the younger generation. Although he never held a central post in the National Socialist regime, he clearly wanted to, and he was delighted when asked to advise Hitler's first government on constitutional matters. He joined the National Socialist party in May 1933, not to keep his chair of law, but from conviction.

In 1934, after Hitler and a few close aides had personally murdered Ernst

Röhm and the other leaders of the SA (storm troopers), who, Hitler claimed, were plotting to seize power, Hitler had his tame parliament pass a law consisting of a single clause: "The measures taken in putting down treasonous attacks on June 30 and July 1 and 2, 1934, are lawful, having been taken in emergency defense of the state." There were no "treasonous attacks" except in Hitler's propaganda; most of the SA men were shot in their homes or barracks. Schmitt wrote an article in the leading German legal journal defending the murders, in which he argued that "the Führer protects the law against the worst kind of abuse, when in the moment of danger and by the power of his leadership he creates immediate law as the highest master of justice.[41] . . . The true leader is also always a judge. From leadership flows judgeship. . . . Truly the Führer's act was genuine justice. It comes under no other jurisdiction, but was itself genuine justice. . . . The judgeship of the Führer springs from the same source of law as does all law of every people. . . . All law stems from the right to life of the people."[42]

In his account written after the war at the order of the U.S. Military Government in occupied Germany, Schmitt explained this article as follows: he was not providing Hitler with a license to kill, but rather making two points. One, that Hitler as head of state had the obligation to protect the state, and that all his actions must serve that end. Declaring the murders "highest law" was not meant to encourage Hitler to go on making more law by killing more people, but rather to say to him: "You have killed these people. You claim they were dangerous threats to order. Very well, let us admit that; but accept your obligation as head of state not to break the law you have now created which specifies the act of treason." Two, that by delineating the murders as "law" he was at the same time allowing them legal standing and prohibiting further arbitrary violence. If they were lawful, they were also unique; and by making them lawful the regime—so Schmitt in 1946—had implicitly outlawed any subsequent, similar acts. Schmitt was, if one were to believe him, using a form of what Old Testament scholars called the "prophetic indicative": you stated as a fact what you hoped was the case. The statement "the Lord hears the needy" was the prophetic indicative; it stated a fact, but in reality no one knew whether the Lord heard any particular needy person or not; it was a pious hope. In the same way, so Schmitt in 1946, his article in 1934, stating that "Hitler is the law and will act accordingly" was a pious hope, betrayed by events.

Schmitt demonstrated in over forty other articles in the first three years of Hitler's regime his "readiness to assimilate unconditionally." In a semiofficial text of late 1933 containing "principles of legal practice," that is, a text directed not only to academics but to practicing lawyers, Schmitt defined one such principle: "In managing and applying law, judges, attorneys, guardians and teachers of law are bound immediately and exclusively by the principles of National Socialism," because

> The ruling viewpoints and ideas of value of a people are always manifested in the prescriptive viewpoints and ideas of some leading group or movement. Viewpoints and ideas do not rule, direct, or guide in general, but only the ideas of people of a certain kind. In the German state today, the National Socialist movement rules. On its foundations therefore we must decide what good customs, faith and credit, acceptable demands, public security and order, etc., are. . . . It would be pure subjective whim and a political operation directed against the National Socialist state, if anyone were to put forward viewpoints other than, alien or even hostile to the National Socialist viewpoints of the German people.[43]

Those who knew enough about Schmitt to realize that he was an important legal and political thinker and who were embarrassed by his pro-Hitler stance also usually knew that he fell out of favor with the Nazi party leaders in 1936. In the fall of 1936, the SS, the elite political organization of the party, denounced him in two articles as an agent of "political Catholicism," that is, of a power alien and hostile to National Socialism. When Alfred Rosenberg, the chief ideologue of the party, learned that Schmitt might be appointed to a senior post in the German ministry of justice, he and the SS launched a "pincer attack" on Schmitt, who was completely blindsided. By December 1936, the plans for a government appointment had disappeared into thin air. Schmitt was not executed, never went to prison, and was not fired from his chair of law at the University of Berlin, but he ceased to have any influence in the regime. His political career was over.

Nothing like the forty-odd articles justifying and praising the National Socialist revolution appeared from his pen after the end of 1936. But to conclude that he fell out of favor because he was a dissident, or that his articles praising the regime were mere acts of expediency, would be wrong. The first irony in the Schmitt case, if case it is, is that he fell out of favor because he was too enthusiastic in what, to Hitler and his aides, was the wrong cause. Schmitt saw Hitler not primarily as the leader of an ideological, political movement, but as something vastly more significant: as the last emperor of the West. Schmitt's own personal doctrine of world history was a charged, antimodern, antiliberal version of the Old Western triad of church, empire, and Germanic, well, not liberty but certainly martial vigor. Schmitt, the last

Ghibelline, the last believer in the Western world empire, yearned for the ancient bargain. Hitler and the Reich, the empire, were going to defend the West and contain the Antichrist of chaos, liberalism, communism, and parliamentary democracy. That, in a nutshell, was the version, in the prophetic indicative, of Schmitt's philosophy and theology of history.

There was something else, too, behind his sudden fall from high favor in 1936. In late 1932 Schmitt had never had the least contact with Hitler or any other leading National Socialist. In fact, he never managed to meet Hitler, and it is doubtful whether Hitler ever knew his name. Schmitt was a clever man, but he had no sense of the real importance—that is, the nonimportance—of his type of aristocratic intellectual in a radical revolution. He really did believe that ideas mattered, and that reality would eventually conform. Therefore, men of ideas, such as himself, mattered. He thought he could write his way to a position of influence in the new regime and bend it to his Ghibelline, romantic imperialist ideas of what was necessary for Germany. Whereas in fact Hitler and his henchmen had only contempt for intellectuals, and especially for lawyers.

Schmitt irritated the Nazi bosses not just because he was an intellectual but because he had not, like they had, done his time in the trenches. His contact to the regime was lateral. In 1932 he was known as a prominent critic of the democratic Weimar republic's inability to deal with civil strife and extremist activism, and an advocate of strong central government. The German Reich, or "realm," as the state was officially called, was a federation composed of states with considerably more autonomy in legislation and policy than the American states at that time or later. The chancellor, Franz von Papen, wanted an authoritarian centralized government. In July 1932, Papen's Reich government, by virtue of a clause in the federal constitution, unilaterally suspended the democratically elected government of Prussia, the largest state in Germany, on the grounds that the Prussian government had shown itself unable to keep the civil peace. This was true enough: right-wing and communist gangs were fighting each other and beating innocent bystanders. But the real reason was that the Prussian government was a left-liberal government and opposed to Papen's right-wing cabinet, which had not been popularly elected and which the Prussians suspected, rightly, of leaning toward giving power to Hitler's movement, the National Socialist German Workers' Party.

The Prussian government appealed to the German Supreme Court for a judgment that the Reich's action was unconstitutional. Schmitt was called in as counsel on the Reich's side. In October 1932, the court declared that the coup against Prussia was unconstitutional, but that the caretaker government installed by Papen should nevertheless be allowed to continue. The case, where Schmitt presented in court his view that emergency conditions authorized extreme measures to keep order, strengthened Schmitt's ties to the right-wing cliques who ran the central government in the last months before Hitler and who handed power to Hitler.

Schmitt followed the crowd and greeted the change. But he had no personal power base and few strong backers in Hitler's party. His real political friends were Papen and the other right-wingers who were soon neutralized by Hitler. Why, the Hitlerite veterans said, should this law professor from nowhere be allowed to set himself up as some sort of semiofficial legal spokesman of our movement, when we have worked years to achieve our revolution? Why should he get recognition, awards, preferment when most of us are unemployed, poor, and more deserving than he? Germany in 1933 had six million unemployed; many of them had joined Hitler's movement, often at some cost; they expected victory to bring them long-awaited chances at good jobs. They had little patience with those who jumped late on the bandwagon and thought themselves entitled to go to the head of the queue.

Precisely this feeling among leading National Socialists, and Schmitt's lack of a power base from which to fight back, were among the deeper reasons his star began to fall in 1936. Not that he stopped being a convinced National Socialist; they did not want him. In particular, they did not care for his irritating insistence that what mattered was the state, not the movement.

Evidence that this was the order of events, that Schmitt was pushed away, rather than that he had become a dissenter, was to be found in his anti-Semitic writings that culminated in his lecture on "Judaism in legal science," given in late 1936. Even as the SS was tightening the noose, not around his neck but around his ambitions, he was telling an audience of lawyers that "a purely emotional anti-Semitism is not enough, we need reliably founded certain knowledge. . . . We must liberate the German spirit from all Jewish distortions, distortions of the idea of spirit. . . . We have the racial doctrine to thank for our understanding of the difference between Jews and other peoples."[44]

The SS bill of ideological indictment against Schmitt made for ironic reading. It contained five counts of accusation, five reasons that he should not be trusted with a senior position in a National Socialist government. First, he continued to invite Jews to his house after Hitler seized power in 1933, and one of his partners in the Prussian case had been a Jewish colleague, Erwin Jacobi. Second, before 1933 Schmitt had called the National

Socialist party an illegal association. This was both true and a constitution-ally correct judgment on his part. Third, Schmitt had been the ally of Papen and other right-wing politicians at a time when they were still trying to keep Hitler from power. Fourth, he was a habitual turncoat and might be expected to reject National Socialism if "conditions changed." Fifth and most serious were his ties to political Catholicism, which were "incompatible with any sort of authentically ethnic [*völkisch*] world-view."

The SS man who wrote down these points probably had not the least inkling that the last charge was correct in the precise sense that Schmitt, as a neo-imperialist, saw Hitler's movement as a tool to restore the imperial power in the West for the struggle against the Antichrist, and not as an end in itself. In other words, Schmitt did not object to National Socialist terror against Jews or dissidents, provided that terror would help to sustain the last empire of the West. But in reality, despite Schmitt's prophetic indicatives, Hitler and his party had not the least interest in performing in a romantic play with reminiscences of Dante, Charlemagne, Otto III, and Frederick II. The medieval emperors were not necessarily *personae gratae* in Hitler's Ger-many. In a final irony, the SS classified Schmitt with one of his greatest oppo-nents in legal thought, Hans Kelsen, as a representative of the defunct liberalism against which Schmitt had written his most famous works.

So much for the record of Schmitt's involvement in Hitler's regime. Judg-ments about it were no more conclusive in the 1990s than they were at the time. Why did a thinker of Schmitt's stature give his wholehearted support to Hitler's regime?

Schmitt was not actually a very clever opportunist. Had he really wanted to enter and stay in the center of power, he would have gone about it differ-ently. Furthermore, since when was ideological opportunism a crime for aca-demics? It seemed rather an occupational characteristic. A credible charge of opportunism against Schmitt by other intellectuals must go to the direction of his alleged opportunism, his support of Hitler, rather than the fact of adaptation. And here again the critics had weak standing. First, Schmitt's support was determined by his theology of history, in which Hitler was a possible hero, and not by any strong interest in party ideology. Second, some of Schmitt's critics supported the Soviet Union far longer and more consis-tently than Schmitt supported Hitler; many in the 1990s still seemed to be-lieve that regimes claiming to be progressive deserved moral exemptions that did not apply to others. Finally, the attacks on Schmitt lacked credibility to the degree that they excused others who served Hitler later and in more seri-ous posts than Schmitt ever held. For example, the nuclear physicist Carl

Friedrich von Weizsäcker, who became a kind of guru of the 1980s green and pacifist movements in the West, was prepared until 1940 to try to build an atomic bomb for Hitler. He later explained that he did so because he hoped thereby to become such an essential figure that Hitler would have to talk to him, and he would then have the chance to persuade the dictator to make peace.[45] Few attacked Weizsäcker for his activities in National Socialist Germany, though he was more involved with the regime than Schmitt. But then Weizsäcker had become a public opponent of nuclear weapons as early as 1957 and so won the pardon of the postwar left.

Second, if Schmitt was no opportunist, what was he? His biographer gave six reasons for his "seducibility." First his generation, that of the Germans defeated in World War I and who saw in Hitler's movement the chance to heal the wounds left by that war. Second, his error in believing National Socialism to be, not so much a party and an ideology, but the representative of the strong state and of social harmony. Schmitt's whole philosophy of politics was based on the need to strengthen the political decision-making authority, the state, against postliberal and nihilistic ideologies. What he did not realize soon enough was that the Nazis were not at all interested in a strong, neutral state, but in using state power to further their ideological aims. Third, the flattery involved in being included, as he thought, in the centers of power, when he was asked to help draft the Hitler government's law on the government of the federal states and was appointed "councillor" of the Prussian government. Fourth, the example of trusted friends who joined the new regime. Fifth, his self-aggrandizing error in believing he could imprint Hitler's raucous and plebeian movement with his own aristocratic notions of power and authority. After the war, he stated that "I felt immeasurably superior to Hitler intellectually. He was so uninteresting to me." Sixth, his religiously based anti-Semitism, which the regime seemed both to confirm and to exacerbate.

What this biographer largely ignored was the political theology that underlay and explained most of Schmitt's writings and actions under the Hitler regime. This theology had its immediate origins in the Benedictine abbey of Maria Laach in the Eifel district of the Rhineland, not far from Schmitt's deeply Catholic native region of Sauerland. Here, in the aftermath of World War I, a group of philosophers and historians with whom Schmitt soon became associated developed the idea that the only hope for the West was to restore the *sacrum imperium*, the holy empire of the Middle Ages. These men were, in medieval terms, Ghibellines—people who supported the claim of the German ruler to be emperor of the West, and who considered such an emperor cosmologically necessary to defend the order of the universe and to keep the balance with the popes. The war had shown the bankruptcy of liberalism, of the new triad of the West; only the old triad, and in particular the ancient bargain of church and empire, remained. The medieval empire was the "unquestionably valid, or at least, in the twentieth century, the only possible form of existence for the German."[46] The empire was an act of will, an act of sacred history, taking the anthropological given, the state, and turning it into a particular kind of state, a missionary state, a state that would defend the shreds of the West against liberalism, pluralism, interest groups, and democratic confusion and error.

In his *De Monarchia*, so these latter-day Ghibellines held, Dante described the two poles of the West: the spiritual pole of the papacy and the political pole of the empire. Misguidedly, the church put Dante's book on its index of literature forbidden to Catholics until 1880, because of its open criticism of papal political claims. Now, in the aftermath of liberalism and under the threat of communism, the most responsible forces in the church and in Catholic Germany should reunite around Dante's program of a revived imperialism, around a Third Empire or a Third Reich. This phrase, which was popular among conservative and Catholic Germans in the 1920s, was not one popular with Hitler, even though by a curious irony it became a common name for Hitler's Germany.

The designation Third Reich implied a particular political program. The first empire was that of Charlemagne, created by united action of the pope and the Frankish king, or so the ideologues claimed, in A.D. 800, as a recreation of the Roman Empire in the West. This first empire ended temporarily in 887, when the last Carolingian died, but was re-established by Otto I in 962, and extinguished only when Francis I unilaterally abolished the empire in 1806 to appease Napoleon and France. The Second Empire began in 1871, when the member states of the German Federation, victorious against France, proclaimed the king of Prussia as emperor and head of the federation. This empire constitutionally still existed, but had since 1918 not had a monarch at its head and was, therefore, literally and metaphorically leaderless. The idea of the Third Empire meant that a new leader would come and re-create ancient glories by renewing the idea and the reality of empire from the ground up. The Third Empire was a political and theological category and was not easily compatible with Hitler's own program, which was why he disliked and in 1939 forbade the phrase to be used.[47]

It was, then, a reasoned decision and an emotional predisposition that made Schmitt see in Hitler the savior of order in Germany and the protector of the Third Reich. Both the decision and the predisposition were shared by many others who, in the interwar years, saw the only salvation for the West in authoritarian or totalitarian movements without necessarily sharing Schmitt's peculiar Ghibelline political theology.

The decision was that liberalism and parliamentary democracy were dead or dying, and that instead of keeping order they were becoming reasons, or excuses, for disorder. And disorder was a greater danger than before because the West no longer had any shared metaphysical idea, no common ground on which to build political society. The only way to achieve stability and stave off disaster was through a strong, neutral state power, separated from all sectional interests, political parties, and ideologies about what was good, bad, desirable, or undesirable in society.

The predisposition was, in Schmitt's case, his enormous self-confidence, which led him to believe that he could ride the tiger, could help to turn the ideological movement of National Socialism into the foundation of a renewed empire. He believed himself "immeasurably superior to Hitler intellectually." Yes; but what about politically? He never realized until too late that he had overreached himself, that the National Socialists did not share his interest in depoliticizing power and decision, but on the contrary intended to continue in power their ideological battle against all those they labeled as their enemies. He forgot that National Socialism meant what it said—that it intended to establish a nationalist German regime on collectivist, or socialist, principles, a regime that would restrict the universal solidarity of socialism to the members of the privileged nation, namely, Germany.

People like Schmitt illustrated one response to the dilemma of the West in the early twentieth century—the crisis of authority after World War I. They fell for Hitler, and others for Mussolini in Italy, because they saw in these leaders the only possible political answer to the crisis of authority. Since you could not go back and reconstruct the shattered metaphysical basis of the West—the belief in the coherent self, the coherent political program of modernity, and the coherent notion of what was good—the only way forward was through nihilism and out the other side. The problem was that whereas a few intellectuals such as Schmitt thought this way, Hitler did not. He was quite happy being a nihilist and had no interest or desire in moving forward to a new and viable basis of stable authority, and he certainly had no intention of acting as the tool of papists and romantic imperialists.

A common complaint among some conservatives after World War II was that Hitler perpetrated a fraud on them. He had presented himself as a defender of the most minimal common interest of the West, namely, political power, but had in fact shown himself to be the enemy of the West because he was neither able nor willing to seek stability, but remained in constant, destructive movement until he destroyed himself and half of Europe. The complaint was understandable but disingenuous. Hitler never hid his aims or his lack of interest in bourgeois pacification. When he said that he was not a follower of Spengler, he was being consciously ironic. He knew perfectly well that Spengler had predicted that the future of the West would consist, politically, of a succession of dictators who alone would be able to control the centrifugal forces unleashed by the postliberal and nihilistic human consciousness. He was saying that he did not want to play Spengler's role. Hitler's notion of the West was of violent resistance to everything that came out of the liberal revolutions of the eighteenth century and the idea of progress of the nineteenth, and in particular to communism. He represented the extreme end of the antimodernist response to crisis, a response that wanted not to solve the crisis but to make it worse and turn it into a global conflagration.

Schmitt's diagnosis of the modern world and its crisis emerged in two stages. First, as a young man reacting to, hating, despising, and fearing the direction of his times, he produced his devastating attacks on liberalism and parliamentary government and his defense of dictatorship, the power of decision, and of political Catholicism in the 1920s. Second, after Hitler and in obscure and penniless retirement, he produced his last major works on international relations and international law, offering assessments of the ending West that were both farewells to what he considered gone forever and prospects on the future.

The key to both the early and the late Schmitt was threefold: that he was an utter pessimist about human nature and politics; that he was a believing Catholic; and that he hoped to restore a modern equivalent of the medieval empire. The third point followed, so he maintained, from the two others. All worldly actions, desires, and designs were irredeemably tilted toward evil, but each was also unique, unrepeatable, and under the shadow of judgment. To Schmitt, the world was so rotten that it was a miracle God had not long ago put a stop to it. His religious sense of imminent apocalypse colored, indeed shaped, his political sense of rising chaos that needed to be put down by force, brute force if needed. Political action was both vain and essential—vain because it could never "raise man's estate," and essential because some force in the world had to stave off the apocalypse as long as possible. Schmitt accepted the diagnosis of nihilism as the essence of the modern West but refused to accept its consequence, an empty liberalism of material progress and technical power. By an act of will, he decided to believe that the power of the individual creative mind could stave off the end of the world, deny and overcome nihilism, and, from within itself, generate the forces that would say "stop!" to the age and force a political and cultural rebirth. "The spirit conquers doubt; the final negation yields the victory over all relativity, which is transcendence."[48] Truly, this was an attack on nihilism using its own weapons.

The sentence quoted came from Schmitt's study of a long, mystical, and expressionistic poem, *Nordlicht* (Northern Light), by Theodor Däubler, a six-foot-six Bavarian with a huge beard and huge appetites, who befriended the short, shy, formal Schmitt and introduced him to the Bohemian world of Munich, where early expressionism, modernist poetry, and antibourgeois aesthetic radicalism held sway in the years before World War I. Däubler's poem was a colossal experiment in language and mythmaking, an attempt to force a new world into being by sheer linguistic creativity. It presented a gnostic history of humankind. The metaphor of "light" was fundamental to gnosticism; light was the source of life and of the mystical insight into divine reality. Light in this sense was not merely visible light, but the illumination of the spirit that allowed it to soar above mundane reality, to escape materialism and nihilism. In *Nordlicht*, Däubler described how, at the beginning of time, the earth separated from the source of light, the sun. Only the "northern light" remained on the earth as a memory of original unity and as a call to the remaining divine spark in man. The poem recounted a series of attempts by humanity to attain the "northern light" and true knowledge. The journey toward the light was both a geographical journey, from the heart of Asia to the north of Europe, and a spiritual journey, at the end of which stood "the spiritualization of earth," the end stage of mystical history when matter and spirit came together.

To Schmitt, who called *Nordlicht* "the poem of the West," it affirmed the tradition of poetic communication with the ultimate reality from which all power flowed, which he in his essay on Däubler called "the *gnosis*, the vision of God." To understand the journey toward the northern light was to understand the gnostic, the secret path and the hidden stages by which true progress was measured.

Schmitt's reference to "*gnosis*" implied that links to the divine and therefore true understanding was not something available to the masses, but only to the spiritually energetic few, but that these few would be able to derive from the divine the strength to carry out their work of renewal. He was touching here on a matter of fundamental importance for all traditionalist and antimodernist ideas of the West. Should a traditionalist appeal to the mainstream Christian tradition and try to revive it? Or should he conclude that liberalism and nihilism had so subverted that tradition that it had no vitality left? In that case some form of gnosticism, of belief in a specific, narrow revelation available only to the specially deserving was a logical alternative. Gnosticism became in the twentieth century one of the mainstays of non-Christian traditionalist thought, drawing in the 1920s and 1930s on Islamic mysticism and, from the 1950s onward, increasingly on Buddhist and other Oriental religious traditions.

Schmitt's first serious work of political thought was his attack on political romanticism, which appeared in 1919. The subject might seem remote from the postwar concerns of Germany and the Western world, but was in fact of vital relevance. Schmitt denounced the romantic temperament that took its cue from life experiences, from "occasions." Novalis had written: "All accidents of our lives are materials for us to make of what we choose."[49] This was what Schmitt absolutely despised: pretending that life was a pick-and-choose game, in which the generous mind constructed its own kindly reality. Romanticism in politics was feel-good politics, politics by personal impulse, politics, ultimately, of self-gratification of the policymaker.

According to Schmitt the purpose of politics was not to make the policymakers feel good or to gratify generous impulses, but to preserve the state, the national community, or civilization. In the atmosphere of world war, civil war, and ideological confrontation of the early 1920s, it seemed to Schmitt that for a government to serve its function of guaranteeing national survival, it had to be able to do two things: determine who its friends and enemies were, and second, in order to restrain its enemies, who might well be domestic enemies, it had to be able to call on all its resources at any time. This was why Schmitt, in publications of the 1920s, devoted attention to the problem of crisis and the state of emergency. He concluded that the fundamental political power was the power to determine the state of emergency, that is, decide when it existed, act accordingly, and terminate it. Hence his famous definition of the sovereign as "he who determines the state of emergency."[50]

Schmitt's emerging political philosophy, which he considered not a philosophy but a recognition of reality, was analogous to his religious outlook at this early stage. In religion, Schmitt indicated that revelation required effort, energy, and perhaps election. In politics, he argued in the 1920s that successful government required the head of state, the sovereign, to recognize the true path through the thicket of legal, constitutional, and customary prescriptions that conspired to stop him in his necessary task of saving the state. In both cases, understanding was the result of mental effort and mental power.

An important part of his work consisted in defending the Catholic Church as a political institution. Schmitt coined in 1922 the term "political theology," which became popular in an entirely different sense after the 1960s, namely, as the demand that theology and the church serve left-wing political purposes. In Schmitt's usage, the term meant that theology, that is, questions of truth and error, necessarily governed politics and that to deny the fact was a typical modern, romantic fallacy that ought to be pointed out and if possible eradicated. "The metaphysical image that a given age makes for itself of the world has the same structure as that which appears plausible as the shape of its political organization." Political beliefs reflected the same assumptions and understandings as beliefs about ultimate reality. To take an example: liberalism believed in improving the world because it had a metaphysical belief that human nature was perfectible and would improve as conditions improved.

The little book *Political Theology* contained the essence of the younger Schmitt's diagnosis of the West. It amounted to an attack on the ideals of the French Revolution—on liberalism and parliamentary democracy—and to the claim that the only possible response to these errors was a return to the counterrevolutionary doctrines of a union of ecclesiastical and political power. What Schmitt was here saying was keener, but not that different from what Eliot would soon be saying in England about the need for a "Christian society" and that those who governed such a society should have the power to decide who belonged and who did not.

The diagnosis reached its sharpest edge in phrases such as these:

> The exception is more interesting than the normal condition. The normal condition proves nothing, the exception proves everything; the former only confirms the rule, but the rule itself lives only on the basis of the exception . . .
>
> The liberal bourgeoisie wants a God, but he must not become active; it wants a monarch, but he must be impotent. . . . It abolishes the aristocracy of blood and family and yet permits the rule of the aristocracy of money, the stupidest and crudest form of aristocracy . . .
>
> Donoso Cortés defines the bourgeoisie as a discussing class, *una clasa discutidora*. Thereby it stands condemned, because that implies that it wants to evade decision.[51]

To understand Schmitt's attack on liberal philosophy and politics and his advocacy of decision and dictatorship, one had to remember that, to him, "the history of the world is like a ship careening aimlessly through the sea, manned by a bunch of drunken sailors who scream and dance until God thrusts the ship under the waves so that there will be silence."[52] Schmitt did not accept that well-meaning government made the least difference in the world or that humankind ever had or ever would progress to some more enlightened stage either of personal conduct or of government. To believe that was to fall into a "Satanic temptation." All that could be done was to resist the tide of disorder, and for that you needed state power and a political authority that also included the theological authority of distinguishing truth from error.

Schmitt's name for a power capable of stemming the tide of chaos and postponing the inevitable apocalypse—God's hand pushing the boat under—was the Greek word *katekhon*, literally, "he who restrains" or "holds off" the enemy, the Antichrist, the end of the world. The word came from an obscure passage of St. Paul, in which he warned the Thessalonians to stand fast against a figure he called "the man of lawlessness." Paul told his correspondents, "You know what is restraining him now," *to katekhon*. Ever since, mystically inclined exegetes had constructed a whole apocalyptic politics around their guesses as to what, or who, this "restrainer" might be.

In Schmitt's historical theology, the medieval empire had been the *katekhon* of its time. Its rulers knew that it was not permanent; they lived and acted under God's sentence of doom. But within the terms of that doom they strove to hold off the Antichrist as long and as effectively as possible, as "powers of order." Only in the knowledge of the imminent end of the age would rulers retain the responsibility and the seriousness to act with power and justice, and this was as true for a Third Reich as it had been true for ancient Rome and for the medieval empire. The purpose of the empire was not to build the kingdom of God on earth; rather, the empire, as "the divinely willed political institution," was necessary only because, if it did not exist, then "mankind, fallen through original sin into enmity," would go under in "chaotic fratricide." To prevent this, God in his mercy had called into being a power for order that would channel the fratricidal energies into "a struggle that creates history and is responsible for history."[53]

In 1925, a Catholic group in Cologne launched the periodical *Abendland*, meaning "the West," in response to Spengler's sentence of doom of seven years earlier. Cologne lay in the Rhineland, the scene of bitter conflict between the German population and French occupying forces after 1919. Cologne was also the heart of Catholic Germany, its cathedral the mother church of German Catholics. The editors proclaimed in a founding statement that they hoped to turn their experiences as occupation victims and members of a defeated nation to advantage; these things had directed their attention to "a generative force . . . *the West*. For it we have decided. On it we shall test our new-found will, our highest loyalty. . . . We are convinced that the *people* and the *state* of the Germans will find new strength and fulfilment by organically entering into the Empire of order that we see afar. In all Western nations, and especially among us Germans, a *movement* must arise from native strength which will develop the Western principle as an idea and as a force and will hammer it into our awareness."[54] Schmitt was an inspirer of this group, which included several of what at the time were his close friends, though some took their distance to him after 1933. In particular, he supported their nostalgic imperialism, their antiliberalism, and their wholehearted support of a political, Germanocentric version of the old Western triad.

Schmitt's most famous and misunderstood idea seemed to have little to do with his imperialist eschatology. This idea, which summed up his entire outlook and diagnosis of liberal modernity, was his "concept of the political," formulated in an essay of 1927, then in a short book of 1932, and revisited in many of his later writings. The third thing that most people who had heard of Schmitt thought they knew about him, in addition to his National Socialist activities and his falling-out with the party in 1936, was that he supposedly defined politics as the war of all against all, as the amoral effort to identify and destroy your enemy. The second irony about the Schmitt case was that his intention was the exact opposite: to show how to avoid war.

The starting point was that liberal democracy, and in particular parliamentary democracy, was unable to handle radical opposition, because it depended on a preexisting consensus about goals and methods. Faced with those who denied any common ground and who insisted on a fight to the death, liberalism had no response other than to continue talking. Schmitt called this "to refuse decision." But continued debate was inadequate unless those who conducted the debate were also able to identify what, at bottom, they were for, and what they were against. Without that ability, liberal democracy moved from one fashion to the next; while each fashion was dominant, its terms controlled the debate. Thus, in the United States in the 1990s, all were in favor of a greater role for market incentives and against "welfare as we know it." The background belief, or fashion, created a consensus within which debate took place; no one stepped outside the consensus to define the real oppositions.

Schmitt's critique of liberalism was a critique not only of its failure to identify conflict but also of its failure to take itself seriously, because taking yourself seriously also meant taking sides, demarcating your position, and identifying friends and enemies. There was more than a shade of Kierkegaard here, with his pity and contempt for those who refused to "step into their own character" and recognize who they were and whom they were against. One might also recall Valéry's devastatingly superior judgment of modernity, that "modern man is satisfied with little." Schmitt thought the modern age deserved better, for the sake of its own dignity and for the sake of its survival.

Politics, Schmitt said, was not about identifying your enemy in order to destroy him, but about identifying the conflict and restraining it so that it did not degenerate into civil war. The concept of the political was the concept of that realm of human action where the task was to limit destruction by identifying and delimiting conflict. Liberal democracy, despite its best intentions, risked civil war precisely because it refused to prepare for struggle by making the critical identification, which was the essential preliminary to keeping political differences from erupting into civil war. Those who were ignorant of the conflict, or denied its reality, were helpless to stem it when it moved from words to guns and bombs.

So far from being a nihilistic philosophy of war, Schmitt's theory of the political was, in his view, the only theory of politics that was able to prevent war. Liberalism had undermined the shared metaphysics of the Western world. Fine, he said, there was no going back. But the end of shared metaphysics did not mean the end of politics; it just meant that political struggle was now potentially limitless, unbounded, terminally destructive. It was therefore necessary to move forward, since both going back and standing still were impossible and suicidal. And the only way forward was through a nonmetaphysical but also nonliberal and nonnihilistic understanding of the essence of political action, so that political action could fulfill its greatest task: to manage conflict and keep the peace, and to reserve the right to make war to recognized authority, not to gangs of ideologues. To find this way forward was urgent, because ideologues were tearing apart the states of the West, but also because "the era of state government" itself was ending; Schmitt in 1927, when he drafted his theory, foresaw the era of supranational geopolitics and supranational ideological conflict that constituted international relations after 1945.

Schmitt's later phase began with a lecture in April 1939 on "The ordering of large-scale spaces in international law." His idea was that the national state as the actor in international law and international relations was fading. The transnational powers both of governments and of forces such as free-trade liberalism meant that traditional state sovereignty and the role of the state as the focal point of international relations were losing their former central significance. Instead, world politics would be shaped, Schmitt argued, by supranational regional orders—"large-scale spaces"—directed by hegemons such as the United States in the Western hemisphere according to the Monroe Doctrine, and now Germany in Central Europe. The talk was certainly in part a geopolitical revival of his political theology of the West that he evolved in the 1920s and tried to make into the official policy of Hitler's regime in 1933–34. The talk was also an attack on the U.S. position as being in reality a moralistically camouflaged attempt to impose a liberal, which in this case meant free-trade, order on the world as a whole. His critique of the early history of the modern liberal states went further and anticipated some of the anti-Western arguments heard in connection with the quincentenary of Columbus in 1992. "No government, neither the Portuguese nor the Spanish, French, Dutch, or English, respected the rights of the natives to their own soil."[55]

In difficult circumstances Schmitt completed the summa of his geopolitical thoughts in 1950. His book *Nomos der Erde* (*The Nomos of the Earth*) was a lament for a bygone era of European international law and limited war, and a sketch of how the new masters of the world, the United States, would need to act to secure their own survival. The Greek word *nomos* meant "law," "order," but also "ordered division into parts." Classical international law recognized a community of members limited to those states capable of civilized intercourse, which could be both commercial, that is, peaceful, or violent. The point of classical international law from the seventeenth to the nineteenth century had been to limit interstate violence within this community of members. This was done by removing from war the emotion of destruction—Rougemont's myth of passion and pain. If war could be reduced to a necessary act to restrain a threat, rather than be inflated to a moral act required to destroy an evil enemy, then war would be less destructive.

By 1900, two developments came to a head that between them undermined the classical international order. The first was that the West became oceanic and global. Beginning in the fifteenth century, the West had expanded by exploration, colonization, settlement, imperialism, trade, building of new nations, and export of political systems. By 1900, the West was no longer European but had its center of gravity in the Atlantic, between Europe and America. This disturbed the equilibrium of the old European international order and opened the way to the *nomos* of the whole earth, the age when every corner of the globe was in the hands of political actors.

The second development was the re-ideologization of war. This began in the French Revolution, whose leaders combined ideological and national fervor, identifying the fate of the revolution with that of France. Thus when the revolutionary government ordered mass mobilization in 1793, it called men to arms not to repel an invasion but to destroy a morally inferior enemy.

In the world wars of the twentieth century, the effort to limit war turned into its opposite: total war, and the total denigration and demonization of the enemy. Schmitt, ignoring his part in supporting a regime that vigorously demonized its enemies, advised the American hegemons that, in the new world order, they would have to take up again the old task of limiting war, for under the new conditions of global *nomos*, in which all the world had become politically active, and with the new weapons of mass destruction, an unlimited, emotional war like the two world wars would mean final destruction of civilization.

Schmitt thus ended his advice to the West with a mild set of recommendations that read like the philosophical preamble to a manual for arms control negotiators. He had lost nothing of his contempt for liberalism; he accepted as a realist that a liberal superpower, the United States, dominated the West and the world. By virtue of its economic and technological strength and its victory in World War II, the United States was the closest thing the political world of the second half of the twentieth century had to a *katekhon*, a power capable of holding back chaos and delaying the apocalypse. Given, then, that the new dominator—the "master of the state of emergency"— needed peace and order to carry out its task, he considered it relevant to explain how to limit conflict and prevent it from degenerating into the type of military and ideological struggle that had destroyed the old Eurocentric geopolitical order.

A liberal might respond that to speak of a *nomos*, a division of the world, and of geopolitical dominance was neither desirable nor necessary, because the world had, since 1945, an authority that was both moral and political, the United Nations. The Western allies had fought World War II to defeat an immoral regime and to establish a moral world order. Schmitt, of course, believed none of this. The United Nations was liberalism on a global scale with all the faults he identified in the 1920s: endless discussion, false consensus concealing deadly enmity, inability to put a stop to any really serious conflicts. According to him, the United Nations would have the net effect of making conflicts worse and less manageable, not better.

World organization was no way to achieve world peace, he concluded once again in his last philosophical writing, an essay published in 1978. Better that the world have a few identifiable political authorities, capable of defining their interests, identifying their enemies, and seeing to it that ideological conflicts did not break out into war. Regional hegemons like the United States would actually be more able to depoliticize conflicts and restrain them, because doing so was in their immediate interest of survival.

Schmitt's final teaching returned to his old problem of the 1920s—how to tame ideological conflict and how to depoliticize the center of authority, whether that be the national state or a supranational entity, by distinguishing it from the ideological movements that fought to control it. One could argue, without too much exaggeration, that his philosophy of the political and his geopolitical analysis provided a truly multicultural approach to peace in an era characterized by clashes of civilizations. For the essence of Schmitt's doctrine was to remove authority and peacekeeping from parochial ideological and cultural interests. His whole purpose was to separate passion from power while recognizing the reality of both. He had considerable sympathy for Third World claims that the West was hypocritical, concealing its own interests under the cloak of "common security," "peacekeeping," and "the interests of humanity." Such phrases were danger signals to Schmitt, indicating that those who proclaimed them had an ideological agenda, were trying to politicize and control the centers of decision while claiming to do the opposite. Whenever "humanity" took the place of identifiable enemies, he held, then the only possible enemy was "inhuman." The liberal ideology of common interests forced anyone who did not match those interests into the role of immoral opponent of humanity, that is, into the role of a subhuman enemy to be destroyed without mercy. The American culture wars provided rich, if often farcical, illustrations of this apparent law of human political nature.

Schmitt's contribution to a traditionalist vision of the West was as unorthodox as it was substantive. He prided himself on seeing things as they were and calling them by their name; he refused nostalgia and nihilism with equal intensity. His most significant contribution was his Ghibelline imperialism, which proposed to restore a Germanocentric Christendom under an empire acting as regional hegemon in social order, culture, and politics. In this grandiose scheme, the church herself and the popes played a modest role, which was exactly in accordance with Dante's *De Monarchia*, which allotted a purely spiritual and sacramental hegemony to the popes, leaving politics and order in the widest sense to the secular partner in the ancient bargain. Yet Schmitt did not take a purely instrumental or positivist view of the church, such as did the head of the most influential movement of political Catholicism in the twentieth century, Charles Maurras, the head of the nationalist and anti-Semitic *Action française* party. Maurras and his followers had three enemies: individualism, Protestantism, and Judaism. They had three goals: monarchy, Catholicism, and nationalism and protectionism for France.

Maurras formed his party in the wake of the Dreyfus affair, which split French political society in the 1890s. Alfred Dreyfus, a Jewish officer in the French army, was framed and convicted on a charge of betraying military secrets to the Germans. In fact the guilty party was a dissolute officer who was being protected by powerful friends because he was an aristocrat, whereas Dreyfus, as a Jew, was an outsider. Dreyfus was eventually, after years of debate, argument, and conflict, exonerated. The Affair mobilized all of what one might call Enlightenment France—liberal, progressive, and freethinking—behind Dreyfus and anti-Enlightenment, counterrevolutionary, monarchist, and conservative France against him. Even after his innocence was proved in court, the anti-Dreyfusards persisted in attacking him, for even if he were not in fact guilty, as a Jew and therefore an alien he was morally guilty.

So virulent was the anti-Semitic agitation of some anti-Dreyfusards that it rivaled the worst denunciations heard in Germany even under Hitler. Maurras exploited this feeling in mobilizing support for his new party. Religious belief was by no means either central or important to him. It was the idea of France as a Mediterranean, Latin, Catholic culture, and not Christian faith, that formed the core of his political ideology and mission. Maurras believed that a strict Catholicism was part of French national identity, and moreover a good idea as a spiritual bond and as social discipline. It was necessary that all citizens of his ideal France belong to the church, but faith itself was irrelevant, and he himself was a nonbeliever. "Religion," as Louis Menand wrote, "was an instrument not of personal salvation but of national cohesion" for Maurras.[56]

It was this strategic use of Catholicism for political purposes that led to pope Pius XI's condemnation of the movement in 1926. The papal decree caused a crisis among right-wing French Catholics, many of whom supported Maurras without fully realizing that he did not believe that France needed Catholicism because it was true, but because, in its authoritarian form, it was useful. That same year, Henri Massis, a follower of Maurras, tried to square the circle of politics and religion by arguing, in his book on the West and its fate, that Western civilization was not a place, or an institution, but a "spirit":

> By the West, let me say it once more to take away any confusion, we mean to describe a *spirit*, for the West is more a region of the human spirit than a part of the world. That which characterizes this spirit is the *Christian element*, and for that reason the word West cannot be captured by geographical definitions.[57]

By identifying the West and Christianity, Massis hoped to remove the threat of papal censure from the *Action française*. Instead of advocating Catholic discipline and culture because it strengthened France, Massis broadened the argument to one that claimed that Western culture and the church stood or fell together. The question whether religion was valuable because it was true or because it kept people disciplined and gave them a cultural tradition to fall back on in times of change was evaded.

The strategy failed, not only because the Vatican proceeded to condemn Maurras, his party, and his writings as "pagan" and contrary to Catholic belief, but because a younger philosopher and convert to Catholicism, Jacques Maritain, had recently arrived on the French philosophical and cultural scene with a different interpretation of the role of religion in society and of the relationship among Catholicism, liberalism, and the West. Maurras, the nonbeliever, defended religion, or, rather, theocracy, as a political necessity; Maritain, the believer, defended the liberal state and society, as Tocqueville had done, as the best environment for religion.

To Maurras, as to Schmitt, the demands of the political trumped all moral questions. The emergency facing the state and Western culture meant that whatever could serve to sustain the culture against the forces of subversion had to be deployed. Hence, Maurras had only contempt for what he called the "theistic hypocrisy" and the "poison" spread about by those who, like the pope, wanted to subject the state and the political to moral judgment.[58] The irony of Maurras's position was that it claimed to be spiritual, to be in opposition to the enemies of culture who were materialistic, worldly, corrupt, and self-interested. He said, in effect, the West is threatened by Jews and secularists; let us mobilize Catholicism as the ideology of an authoritarian, revived, and purified West. In fact, the *Action française* ideology was itself wholly materialistic, because it wanted to exploit religion for the political purpose of shoring up its own vision of culture. Maurras, even more than Schmitt, relativized religion in the service of his god, the national state. Maritain, by contrast, tried to remind the members of *Action française* that, according to

Christian teaching, they had it backwards: it was not for ideology to relativize faith, but for faith to relativize all political doctrines, designs, and desires.

It was in that context, and in specific response to Henri Massis and his doctrine of "the West as a region of spirit" marked by "the Christian element," that Maritain retorted in the same year, 1926, that "Catholicism is not a Westernism." Massis was no more a Catholic than Maurras; he was just as ready to use any tool that came to hand to uphold a nationalist, chauvinist, and anti-Semitic ideology. The last point was of particular relevance to Maritain, as his wife, Raïssa, was Jewish. Maritain saw a great danger both for the West, as he conceived it, and for the church in the way *Action française* confused Catholicism and cultural chauvinism. Maurras and his followers considered the church useful for their purposes; Maritain subordinated politics, including the politics of Western survival, to Christianity. Thus he was able to go on to argue, as he did in later writings, that although the church and the West were not the same thing, and although the era of European domination in the world had passed, nevertheless the West was "the only culture where reason has almost succeeded" and that this was due, in no small part, to what Massis rather dismissively called "the Christian element."

One reason Maritain emphasized the distinction between Christianity and the West was to point out and denounce what, to him, was a particularly egregious abuse of religion by the *Action française*. To Maurras, the Jews were evil, among other things, because they represented an alien, "Oriental" way of life, which he considered the font of evil and of corruption. Maurras had little direct influence on the German National Socialists, but they, of course, shared this anti-Semitic prejudice that they expanded to include Christianity, which, according to Hitler, was merely the spiritual consequence and most complete expression of "Oriental corruption." But, Maritain asked in the 1920s and again in the 1930s and 1940s, how could you uphold Christianity as the foundation of culture against Jews, when Christianity itself displayed the same elements of "Oriental corruption" as they? Without Judaism, no Christianity. The idea of a Christianity purged of its ties to its parent had been a constant temptation in Christian history, but had also been just as regularly condemned as heretical—starting with the condemnation of the second-century theologian Marcion, who argued for a radical distinction between Old and New Testaments, even going so far as to claim that the Jewish God of the Old Testament was a different and less benign being than the God incarnated in Jesus Christ. But, Maritain said, only distortion and hypocrisy could deny the common root and common ground of the two religions, and only ill will would attempt to sow discord between them today.

Thus, one of Maritain's lifelong preoccupations was to demonstrate both theologically and in practice the moral, logical, and doctrinal impermissibility of a Christian anti-Semitism. It was, he argued, quite literally nonsensical.

What Maritain and Western liberals considered the German onslaught on the West in the shape of the National Socialist ideology produced many instances of Jewish and Catholic collaboration to identify, analyze, and condemn a common enemy. One example was Carl Schmitt's erstwhile friend, the Russian-born political thinker Waldemar Gurian. He performed the collaboration in his own person, inasmuch as he was born a Jew in St. Petersburg in 1902, but was converted to Catholicism along with his siblings by his mother, when she left her husband and took her children with her to Germany in 1909. In the 1920s, Gurian was for a time a pupil of Schmitt in Bonn. He shared Schmitt's diagnosis of liberalism as too feeble to preserve political peace, but could not follow him to the degree of seeing Hitler's movement as anything other than an even greater danger. Gurian rejected Maurras's instrumental use of the church, and by 1933, when he left Germany, had arrived at a diagnosis of the age that classified both National Socialism and communism as antiliberal and anti-Catholic. Later, as professor at the University of Notre Dame in the United States, Gurian refined his analysis of both the totalitarian ideologies and came to consider Nazism as "the German form of Bolshevism." To him, "the Bolshevik and Nazi regimes were products of the crisis of bourgeois Europe which had died between 1914 and 1918 because it could not go beyond itself." Gurian was no liberal and could not disagree with the nihilist diagnosis that said that liberalism had failed in World War I, but he was equally unable to accept either of the two antidemocratic doctrines that arose after that war and promised solutions to the crisis of modernity.[59]

Another example of collaboration in the shadow of war promised a more optimistic message than Gurian's bleak analysis. In June 1939, a young French philosopher, Raymond Aron, Jewish by birth but a nonbeliever by conviction, spoke in Paris on "Democratic and totalitarian states." By totalitarian, Aron meant Germany and Italy, not the Soviet Union. He argued that Hitler and Mussolini were the enemies of the West rather than of communism, with which they shared a revolutionary, antiliberal outlook. Aron had no great faith in liberalism, but he was not at all prepared to exchange it for any antidemocratic doctrine. Just because liberalism had failed to stop war in 1914 and had been discredited by that war was no reason to jettison democratic ideas as the basis of Western culture: "We cannot today," he said in June 1939, "save the bourgeois, humanitarian, or pacifist illusions. The rise of irrationalism does not in any way disqualify the effort necessary to question the ideology of progress, abstract moralism, or the ideas of 1789. Democratic conservatism, like the idea of reason, cannot save itself unless it renews itself."[60]

A close personal friend of Aron's at this time was the Jesuit priest Gaston Fessard. The two formed part of a remarkable group of brilliant thinkers, most of them young, who used to meet during the academic year in Paris to hear the Russian émigré philosopher Alexandre Kojève analyze Hegel. In 1935, Fessard wrote an analysis of Fascism, arguing against Maurras that "politics rests in the final instance on morality," because politics is the art of determining and pursuing the common good, and therefore, "all political conduct is commanded by a [prior] spiritual choice." Fessard and Aron, unlike most of the others who listened to Kojève, agreed with Maritain that morality could not be separated from politics, and that if the political thinker or actor taught himself, like Schmitt, to despise morality, he would ultimately destroy himself.

Maritain's answer to the problem of the West in a postnihilist age differed from that of Gurian as well as from that of Schmitt. Gurian saw no hope in liberalism but likewise rejected the totalitarian solutions. Schmitt believed that the apocalypse was so close, and the political emergency so dire, that the moral law itself had been undermined, had effectively ceased to have any purchase on social and political reality. The only hope was to re-create the empire, and the first step toward doing that was to identify the force willing to rule the state against its enemies. Maritain, by contrast, argued that "the moral law must never be given up, we must fasten on to it all the more as the social or political environment becomes more perverted or criminal. . . . Reason must never abdicate. The task of ethics is humble but it is also magnanimous in carrying the mutable application of immutable moral principles even in the midst of the agonies of an unhappy world, as far as there is in it a gleam of humanity."[61] It was that gleam that Schmitt no longer saw, except perhaps in the mystic vision of a Däubler, and that Maurras arguably never recognized in the first place.

One possible response to the crisis of the West after World War I was to reject all solutions, to glory in destruction. This was, of course, the final consequence of Hitler, although he presented his ideology as one of national restoration. On a different level was the French surrealist writer Georges Bataille, another member of Kojève's audience, whose own sympathies lay with the extreme left but who denied that either the extreme left or liberalism could or should do anything to stop chaos. The antifascists of the 1930s he ridiculed as "sorcerers fighting the hurricane," but he welcomed the "hurricane" because, if it did nothing else, it would surely destroy the last remnants of liberal, bourgeois society. Bataille belonged to that group of Western nihilists who not only shared Nietzsche's cool assessment that the West had become nihilistic, but who actively hated the liberal, bourgeois order. Anything that promised to destroy that order, whatever its origin, was to be welcomed. Bataille's writings of the 1930s demonstrated, one critic wrote, "a cold, deadly violence" in their gleeful proclamation that Enlightenment was dead, and good riddance.

During a few years in the late 1930s, Bataille formed part of a small group of thinkers of radical, anarchist, or communist persuasion called the *Collège de sociologie*. The name should not confuse: these were not sociologists; they used the word in the sense of Émile Durkheim, as the investigation of the sources of belief that made people form societies. None of the group held any very coherent political doctrine, but all shared a fascination with gnostic ideas. Bataille was driven in his life by one basic political emotion: hatred of the middle class and contempt for its liberal, progressive ideology. One could call this gnosticism: the world was unredeemably evil and inadequate, and the only hope for improvement was by preliminary, total destruction.

The *Collège* group accepted another gnostic idea, that social life must rest on a sacred source, a belief in some driving force that was both creative and destructive. They were groping for a type of outlook that became quite common in the West in the 1960s and after, namely, the cult of the sacred self. For people who could not accept liberalism and who saw no hope either in communism or Fascism, because they really were not looking for hope at all, the only remaining source of faith or of the sacred was the self.

Gnosticism was thus the final answer of the traditionalist, religious spirit to the crisis of the West. If orthodox Christianity offered no satisfaction, if no political ideology was satisfactory, and if no decisionism à la Schmitt could credibly fill the void at the core of the nihilistic West, the last recourse was necessarily mystical and esoteric. And it had to be gnostic, because the answer to nihilism had to take nihilism into account in two ways: first, the essence of Western nihilism was the belief that there was nothing to believe. Therefore, no answer to it could rest on a shared belief, a shared metaphysic. Second, nihilism implied that life was controlled by alien forces, that life was an aimless journey, that it had no meaning in itself. But if meaning was lost, some one or some thing must be at fault. If happiness and harmony had been lost, something had taken them. This "something" was the modern equivalent of the classic gnostic evil god, the creator of the world and oppressor of humanity. The only way to escape the evil god and find both true knowledge of one's state and true happiness was by a secret, interior journey of discovery. At the end of this journey, and under appropriate guidance, one would overcome the tragic dichotomy of self and world, of aspiration and reality. In the words of a historian of contemporary religious feeling, at the end of the gnostic journey of enlightenment, the traveler would find his "name in the book of the living," thanks to the "vision of the eyes of fire," the vision granted by the "northern light" that was beyond all earthly lights.[62]

Decisionism, National Socialism, communism, perverse despair—these were painful answers to the crisis of the liberal West. Fessard's and Maritain's Catholic liberalism and pro-Semitism seemed easier. But were they not too easy? Were the nihilists not right? Did the political history of the twentieth century not confirm Nietzsche and Spengler, and was there really no hope for the West except, perhaps, in some form of dictatorship, some last, harsh *katekhon* staving off disaster?

The end of World War II destroyed National Socialism and, with it, the credibility of the noncommunist, antidemocratic regimes of the West. Some of them, like that of Franco in Spain, survived many years, but had few public supporters outside their own ranks. The true victors of the war in terms of the power to define the battle over Western identity were all those, communists and sympathizers, who defined the battle as that between "antifascism" and its enemies. The communists had always maintained that Hitler's regime had more in common with the liberal democracies than either would admit. Both, in the communist perspective, were capitalist, and capitalism, with its private property, was the permanent enemy. After 1945, the antifascists within the West no longer had any rivals in their opposition to capitalist democracy. In the interwar years, left and right shared a contempt for liberalism and what they considered its pathetic democratic pretenses, and agreed that the true face of liberalism was the bourgeois pathology of individualistic materialism. The war demonstrated the true face of the National Socialist regime, which was genocide. No matter that communism counted several times as many victims; they were unknown or obscure. Absolute evil became the prerogative of Germans, who "paid for the whole world, and for all the crimes of the century."[63] Moreover, the Soviet Union was the chief victim of Hitler, and received therefore an immense bonus of goodwill in the West that canceled its crimes.

For these reasons, the Soviet Union and its supporters who shared the antifascist temper and ideology acquired a double privilege in 1945, as true democrats, and as guardians of the moral high ground of anticapitalism. But this strategic and ideological privilege was not in itself enough to explain the long triumphal reign of antifascist beliefs among Western intellectuals, and to permit them to define so profoundly a Western identity against or beyond capitalist democracy. To secure their stronghold in Western culture, a stronghold that was by no means overthrown when communism itself fell, the antifascist beliefs needed something beyond the reputation of the Soviet Union or its democratic credentials. What they needed was the secularized religious impulse that impelled political and intellectual leaders to continue the search for the perfect society, for the revolutionary transformation of all existing conditions, for the place and the moment of the leap into the kingdom of freedom. As François Furet wrote:

> In this sense, the war of 1939 completed what the war of 1914 began: the stranglehold of the great political religions on European public opinion. But, of those religions, it destroyed one and crowned the other, thereby increasing its power tenfold. Victorious antifascism did not subvert the moral and political terrain on which it grew. Rather, it aggravated the crisis of the democratic idea, even while claiming to have resolved it. That was the great illusion of the era.[64]

In the face of this renewed ideological onslaught, democratic liberalism remained, in Europe, on the defensive. Surprisingly so, on a superficial level, for it was the productive power of democratic liberalism and the commitment of its leaders—Franklin Roosevelt and Winston Churchill—that won the war for democracy and ensured that at least part of Europe would escape communist rule. And again on a superficial level, it might seem that democratic liberalism was not as defensive as Furet's account suggested. In America, the Grand Narrative and its political counterpart, the centrist liberalism of the Cold War, held the high ground in culture and education for at least two decades after 1945. Moreover, this Grand Narrative of the West as the axis of democracy, human rights, and liberalism, growing from Greece into modernity, spread throughout the West as a vulgate of mass higher education.

The Grand Narrative and its centrist liberalism were, however, less vigorous than met the eye. The moral victory of communism and its antifascist penumbra of supporting ideas and feelings permeated even American liberalism, giving it a bad conscience, directing its attention to the flaws and imperfections of American democracy. However productive the liberal regimes, and however broad their freedoms, they remained under the judgment of history, as defined by communism, a judgment that found them wanting, unjust, artificial, inhuman, and condemned to extinction.

This dilemma, of vigorous liberalism in practice, faced with vigorous antiliberalism in the sphere of political religion and political emotion, marked the history of Western identity in the Cold War. In the course of that history, American liberalism changed its own identity in obedience to the judgment of history, abandoning the Western legacy in favor of new, supposedly more moral ideas, such as universalism, feminism, or multiculturalism. All of these were, ideologically speaking, pleas before the great court of history. They were motions to convince the judge that Western liberalism was not really all bad, measured by the antifascist criteria. Of course, all these motions were denied; Western liberalism would never be forgiven unless it abandoned itself completely. It could never live up to the demands of the antifascist canon of values—positive freedom, self-realization, equality. As long as it held fast to its original essence as the combination of negative freedom, property, and pluralism, it would be judged always lacking, always immoral, always tainted by its sinful link to the imaginary fascism of the leftist mindset—the link of capitalism and private property.

The history of the fourth twentieth-century bid to define the West, the bid offered by American Cold War liberalism, was therefore, from the beginning, vitiated by self-doubt and guilt. It did not help that its main historical self-description, the Grand Narrative, was itself flawed, asserting an ahistorical continuity from Plato to NATO that ignored the real history of Western identity and Western freedom.

CHAPTER TEN

The Cold War West

American civilization's stock of utopian tendencies assumes
the prior departure of Europeans from Europe. Furthermore,
in its reality it is too tied up with Christian faith and too confident in the spirit of free enterprise to seduce all those who
cannot imagine the future of democracy except as distinct
from both Christianity and capitalism: the innumerable children of the French Revolution.

—François Furet

Liberalism produces the total authoritarian state as its accomplishment at a higher level of development. The total authoritarian state brings with it the organization and theory of
society that correspond to the monopoly stage of capitalism.

—Herbert Marcuse

Liberalism is the ideology of Western suicide

—James Burnham

In September 1938, as Britain and France were preparing to give the
German-inhabited parts of Czechoslovakia to Hitler in the hope of securing, in the words of the British prime minister, "peace in our time,"
another British statesman, Winston Churchill, issued a statement to the

press. "The partition of Czechoslovakia under pressure from England and France," he said, "amounts to the complete surrender of the Western democracies."[1] By "Western," Churchill meant the two remaining major democracies of Europe, Britain and France. This minimal usage of the term became increasingly common in the 1930s, as politicians and journalists refused to accept communist Russia and National Socialist Germany as members of the community called "the West." It implied that to be Western, it was not enough to be geopolitically European. In order to be Western, a society had to be also democratic. On that definition, the West in 1938 had indeed retreated to its final ramparts.

When the United States joined World War II in 1941, the political West, the alliance of democracies at war, expanded immeasurably. In 1945, this enlarged, democratic West stood as victor, but it was a flawed and partial victory. Its victory would not have been possible without the Soviet Union, which upheld an ideology that did not divide the world between democracy and totalitarianism, but between communism and capitalism. World War II, from the communist point of view, had been a temporary alliance of communism, the force of justice and freedom, with some capitalists—America and Britain—against Germany, which was also capitalist. In the long-term perspective of Marxism, what Germany, America, and Britain had in common, namely, capitalism and private property, was more important than their temporary falling-out in 1939–45. The defeat of Germany in 1945 meant that the capitalist camp was once again monolithic. The essence or truth of capitalism, however, was what communist rhetoric called "Fascism," a term that permitted communists and their allies to argue, after 1945, that the global struggle, of communism against Fascism, continued.

The purpose of the term *Fascism* was to elide the distinction between democracy and dictatorship, to paint the defeated Germans and the victorious Western democracies in similar colors, and to conclude from this that the defeat of Fascism in 1945 was only apparent, for, as the Western Marxist Herbert Marcuse said in 1967, "liberalism produces the total authoritarian state," as in Germany in 1933 and in America in the 1960s. The bourgeois democracies of the West remained class societies, enemies of the higher and more genuine democracy represented by communism. Therefore, to be a true democrat was to be antifascist, and the purpose of true democrats after 1945 was to continue the struggle for a revolutionary transformation in the West, in alliance with the Soviet Union. In this new episode of the struggle, the fascist enemy was no longer Adolf Hitler and his Germany, but the democratic nations of the West:

> Fascism thus outlives itself as a latent menace until the day of socialist revolution, the only thing which can destroy its conditions of possibility. The antifascist union of 1945 is superior to the Popular Front of 1936 in that it opens the way to an anticapitalist democracy, conceived as a stage on the road to socialism. This ideological construct . . . gives politics a negative purpose—antifascist, anticapitalist—and simultaneously avoids a debate on democracy and a debate on socialism. It makes believe that antifascism necessarily entails the collective appropriation of the means of production; that anticapitalism is necessarily democratic. It tends to mask both the idea of revolution and the idea of democracy.[2]

Public opinion within the democracies was vulnerable to this line of argument. While the war was continuing, few disputed that the war showed the true dividing line in the world, the line dividing the forces of freedom from the forces of despotism. But as a victim of German aggression, the Soviet Union in 1941 acquired democratic credentials in the West that its earlier policy of alliance with Hitler had to some extent undermined. Thus, from 1941 on, the Soviet Union stood with the West on one side of the line, Germany and Japan on the other. That the Soviet Union was as despotic as National Socialist Germany, and many times as murderous, was something that only gradually dawned on some Western statesmen and was never accepted by its scholars and intellectuals. Only a few intellectuals, outside France and Italy, were members of communist parties, but almost all were among the "innumerable children of the French Revolution," who could not envisage the future of democracy except as distinct from Christianity and capitalism—that is, as distinct from the historic legacies of the West. They therefore easily accepted the communist argument that Western democracy was a sham, that liberalism was defined by its bourgeois pathology, that Fascism was a continuing danger, that the purpose of political activity was to combat the forces of Fascism in the West, and that the Soviet Union, in that struggle, was on the side of humanity, justice, progress, and genuine democracy. Thus, the victory of the West in 1945 was ambiguous. It was contested by the communists, by geopolitics, and by the bad conscience of the West itself.

The progressive mindset—of sympathy for the Soviets and suspicion of America and of capitalism—was all the more prevalent in the West after 1945, because it corresponded to deep-seated beliefs of the progressive elites, beliefs that predated World War II. As François Furet noted, the ultimate origin of those beliefs was the French Revolution, or, rather, the image of the radical, Jacobin revolution as a new dawn of justice and democracy that echoed down the years as an unfulfilled promise, long after the realities of the revolution had been forgotten. A more immediate and powerful stimulus to the antiliberal and antibourgeois bias of progressive, antifascist opinion, however, was the Depression of the 1930s. Even in the United States, where capitalist liberalism was more deeply rooted than in Europe, leading thinkers, such as Sidney Hook, seriously wondered in 1932 whether democratic capitalism was finished. In Europe, the economic crisis discredited capitalism all the more thoroughly, in that capitalism had never been as solidly based in the culture as it was in America. The Depression powerfully strengthened the bias of European elites against free enterprise, seen as responsible for the crisis, and against bourgeois democracy, seen as inadequate to solve the crisis and as morally stunted in its supposed worship of selfish individualism.

So it was that the end of World War II signaled to these antifascist elites not that the hour of democratic capitalism had come again, but that the defeat of militant Fascism in alliance with the Soviet Union created new opportunities to finish the task of abolishing the more insidious Fascism operating under the guise of Western bourgeois democracy, a task begun in the 1930s but that the war had interrupted. The historian Alan Taylor, a British intellectual who was in this respect typical of his class and generation, smugly asserted in 1945 that "nobody in Europe believes in the American way of life—that is, in private enterprise; or rather those who believe in it are a defeated party and a party which seems to have no more future than the Jacobites in England after 1688."[3] Comparing market liberals to the Jacobites was intended to be particularly cutting and patronizing, for everyone knew how pathetic were the diehard supporters of James II, how out of tune with the progressive England that emerged from the Glorious Revolution, and how unrealistic their chances of a comeback.

Against this conviction of the intellectuals and opinion shapers in post–World War II Europe stood the reality of American capitalist democracy, a reality that, even in America, was not always appreciated for what it was—a unique civilization that was not a fruit of modernity, but rather its cause, with roots deep in the Old Western crucible of Christianity, liberty, and economic development. But as Taylor's self-satisfied, ignorant, and bigoted statement indicated, forthright Americanism—the assertion of American capitalist democracy and its particular civic virtue as a new, adequate

Western identity worth understanding and fighting for—had few chances among the progressive intellectuals who had the cultural power to write the script of Western identity after 1945.

The intellectual underpinning of the Cold War West that was the closest thing available to a coherent response to the ideology of antifascist democracy was something less than full Americanism; it was the Grand Narrative. But the Grand Narrative, although committed to liberal, pluralist democracy and, less certainly, to the market economy, suffered from the weaknesses of liberalism: the illusion of newness, economic reductionism, and an inability to choose between the negative and positive ideas of liberty—the idea that saw liberty as freedom from coercion versus the idea of liberty as self-realization. The Grand Narrative shared with the antifascist consensus a tendency to see perfect justice and democracy in the future, as something always to be worked for, and not as something that would never be perfect, but whose imperfect reality needed urgent defense. Its advocates were unwilling to risk the Cold War coalition by defining the West in any controversial way, by referring to the Old West, for example, and its Roman, Christian, and Germanic legacies. It was far safer to focus entirely on the misleading, Greek-centered model, and to define the West as an ahistorical set of great ideas migrating, unsullied by history and passion, from Plato to NATO.

The Cold War West was a lowest common denominator capable of rallying support across a broad spectrum. As such, it was politically effective for some two decades after 1945, but because of the internal fissures in its supporting coalition, it was never able to present as convincing an account of the world as its procommunist, antifascist rival. An essential part of the story of Western identity during the Cold War was, therefore, the story of its ambiguities, for only they explain why that identity was so quickly and successfully overturned by the antinarratives about the West that erupted in the symbolic year of 1968.

Of course, sturdy Cold War liberals had no doubt of the merits of liberalism and saw through the ideological smoke screen of antifascism to its cruel core, which was to destroy liberal democracy. Their definition of the West as the democracies opposed to totalitarianism, whether German or Soviet, began to take shape even before the United States entered World War II. Its origin was Churchill's definition of the West in 1938, which received a dramatic and decisive amplification in August 1941. In that month, the president of the United States, Franklin Roosevelt, met Churchill on a

U.S. battleship in Placentia Bay, off Newfoundland. Britain had been at war with Germany for almost two years, and Germany had, two months earlier, invaded the Soviet Union. This act threw the Soviets into alliance with the democracies and eventually produced the progressive mindset of 1945, but the Atlantic Charter, the document that emerged from Placentia Bay, was still largely free of it. The charter was, rather, the last statement of the interwar Western identity and the first statement of the Cold War West, in its commitment to the negative freedoms of suffrage, property, exchange, movement, and belief.

The meeting took place in Canadian waters, and Canada, as a British dominion, was, like the mother country, at war with Germany. So on a neutral vessel in the waters of a belligerent state, the political heads of the world's richest and its oldest democracy declared the goals that they both professed to be seeking, the one in war, the other as a prospective ally. These goals took the form of three principles that, they believed, would and should govern international relations when Germany was defeated, an event they could as yet only hope for. The principles, laid down in the Atlantic Charter, were more than principles of foreign policy. They also contained specific implications about the domestic politics and social arrangements that, Roosevelt and Churchill stated, should prevail in all countries of the world after the ongoing war. The principles—self-determination, free trade, and collective security—were not invented in 1941. They expressed, rather, the insights of the sceptical Enlightenment about what made societies prefer peace to war.

The first goal, self-determination, had both a domestic and an international aspect, as well as a moral one. Domestically, the two countries agreed that one purpose of the war was to secure the right of nations to establish themselves as nations and to choose their governments freely. In August, 1941, self-determination was a promise held out to the nations under German domination in Europe, starting with the Poles; it was when Germany attacked Poland in September 1939 that Britain declared war, on the grounds that Germany had violated Poland's independence and right to self-determination. Internationally, the democratic statesmen believed that nations enjoying self-determination were more likely to be satisfied, less likely to be aggressive, and so more likely to live in peace with one another. Self-determination also implied democracy, which meant that governments were answerable to the people. Since the people rarely wanted war, democracy would be a barrier to aggression and conflict, as Immanuel Kant argued in 1793, when he stated that what he called "republics"—democratically governed societies—were inherently the most peaceful kind of regime. Therefore, the more of the globe that consisted of democracies, the fewer wars there would be. German aggression was, in this view, due largely to the fact that Germany had been ruled since 1933 by a dictatorial regime that did not respect self-determination, either in Germany or elsewhere. Self-determination was thus both a policy objective for the conduct of war, specifying that the war was fought to restore self-determination where it had been lost and to extend it where it had never prevailed, and part of a world view that hoped to end the war by creating a world safe from war.

The goal of open markets and free trade rested on a similar analysis of the causes of conflict and a similar idea of what a desirable postwar world should look like. Open markets meant free flows of capital and commodities. Recalling the Depression and how protectionism had made it worse, Roosevelt and Churchill believed that if the war effort was to produce a durable peace, it would have to include solid action to prevent the sort of competitive and self-destructive protectionism that, in their view, had undermined the fragile peace of 1919.

Collective security was the third policy aim of the Atlantic Charter. By that, Churchill and Roosevelt meant an arrangement more durable than the League of Nations of 1919, which had notably failed to stop the rise of totalitarian regimes and war. Collective security was, like self-determination, both an idea and a hope. The idea was that World War I happened, and the League of Nations failed in its turn, for two reasons. Governments had not cooperated to solve their problems, but had aligned themselves into opposing camps. And governments had not cooperated in large part because they were not the governments of commercial republics, not governments that represented the true economic and social interests of their people, but governments of nationalist cliques and narrow ruling classes, pursing goals of power politics and ambition rather than policies that were in the genuine, that is, democratically defined national interest. The hope behind collective security was that a postwar world of commercial republics would both want and be able to exercise collective security, that the peoples and governments of such a world would prefer, as Churchill later put it, jaw-jaw to war-war.

The Atlantic Charter diagnosed important causes of war and stated the means to obviate those causes in the future. Its main institutional prescription, collective security, proved unachievable. Its result was not a world composed of commercial republics, united in a collective security arrangement, but a world divided among those governments that subscribed to its principles and those that did not. Alliances and alignments dominated postwar international relations as they had dominated them before 1914, though that was not Churchill's or Roosevelt's fault. It was not until the final years of the century that it became realistically possible, once again, to envisage collective security as a practicable instrument of deterring war.

The spectacle of heroic Soviet resistance to the German invasion appealed powerfully to the Western public, especially to emotional Americans, always prone to moralize conflicts and to conceive of democracy as a mission rather than a practice. The heroic Soviets were fighting evil; therefore, they were good, and since all good people were by definition democrats, the Soviets, including their ruler, Josef Stalin, were cast, by American opinion, as members of the party of progress and humanity. The tendency to see democracy as a mission, which in America had religious origins, was vulnerable to the antifascist ideology, which insisted that the bourgeois democracy of the West was inadequate and that true democracy required revolutionary change.

The slippage from the realistic freedoms of the Atlantic Charter to the nebulous moralism of the progressive consensus was already evident in American debate. Earlier in 1941, leading American public figures had formed a Commission to Study the Organization of Peace, which formed three hundred study groups across the United States. One of the guidelines of the commission was to seek proposals, including the proposals of religious groups, on how to overcome the "outmoded" principle of national sovereignty—the very principle enshrined in the first goal of the Atlantic Charter. A few months after the charter, the Japanese attacked Pearl Harbor and threw America into the war, creating the Grand Alliance of the United States, the Soviet Union, and Britain. The nature of the attack reinforced American political moralism to a boiling point. In January 1942, representatives of twenty-six nations agreed in Washington, D.C., to "fight the Axis until final victory in the name of life, liberty, independence, religious freedom, and justice"—a rousing list perhaps, but vague and open-ended, not like the specific and measurable goals of the charter.

President Roosevelt dubbed the twenty-six nations represented in that declaration "the United Nations." During 1942, the secretary of state, Cordell Hull, threw himself wholeheartedly behind the idea of a United Nations Organization to preserve the moral and political goals of the wartime alliance, a plan endorsed by the U.S. Senate in November 1943 by 85 votes to 5. One of the 85, a democratic senator, spoke of the drive for a postwar world organization as "the greatest crusade since Jesus sent out his twelve disciples to preach the brotherhood of man."[4] Such overcharged moralism was constitutionally unable to resist the progressive appeal to go beyond prewar practice in search of a better world, a world defined by the new struggle, which was not that of democracy against totalitarianism but that of a superior, progressive democracy against crypto-fascist liberal capitalism.

German wartime propaganda about National Socialism's being a bulwark of the West undermined any idea of the West in the democracies itself that was not compatible with the Grand Alliance ideology of a common front of the liberal democracies and the Soviet Union. For such an idea to be credible and worthy after 1941, it had to exclude both Christendom and capitalism, for these were incompatible with a West that included the Soviet Union, and seemed all too compatible with the racist and genocidal West represented by Hitler's Germany. It was thus necessary after 1945, in order to build a political consensus for the Cold War West, to construct a liberal Western identity that avoided looking too far into the past for its roots, for looking into the past risked uncovering the common ground of liberalism and totalitarianism. But even within that identity, the two basic options remained: the option of seeing liberal democracy as imperfect but genuine, and hence worth understanding and defending for its own sake, and that of seeing it as imperfect and in need of radical reform, as suggested by the progressive left. Those who took the former option looked to America as the core of the West; those who took the latter sought the path to a better West in the doctrines of the European left, in the many variants of Marxism adapted for Western European use. The postwar schism within the West, the argument over Western identity, was thus between those who identified the West with America—the commercial republic with its Christian foundations—and those whose idea of the West rejected Christianity and capitalism and looked rather to the ideals of progress and social transformation that they believed had been at least partly realized in the Soviet Union.

The arrival of the Americans in Europe in and after World War II as members of the Grand Alliance, but soon after as enemies of the Soviet Union, put the schism at the center of Western politics. The Americans were, in the European perspective, emissaries of a unique edition of the West distinct from Europe and its ideological battles and parties. There was no American nihilism, Bolshevism, or Fascism. The Americans, according to François Furet,

had invented a society so original and so powerful that it constituted, by itself, a distinct species of modern democracy, different, by definition and purpose, from everything that existed in Europe, and which had furthermore deliberately kept itself apart, as long as it could, from the politics of the Old

Continent. The Americans never ceased to be true to the decision that defined them as a nation: they had left the shores of Europe to found a new social contract on the other side of the ocean. Taken by millions in the course of recent centuries, that decision also implied abandoning the European revolutionary model: whatever American civilization contained in the way of utopian tendencies assumed the prior departure of Europeans from Europe. Furthermore, the reality of American civilization was too tied up with Christian faith and too confident in the spirit of free enterprise to seduce all those who could not imagine the future of democracy except as distinct from both Christianity and capitalism: the innumerable children of the French Revolution.[5]

The arrival of the Americans in Europe thus complemented the Soviet expansion and added confusion and controversy to the battle for the West. The Soviet Union represented, to "the innumerable children of the French Revolution," an idea of the West as anticapitalist and, certainly, non-Christian, a model that owed little to either of the two ancient versions and everything to the Jacobin tradition and, behind that, to Rousseau. The postwar left in Europe, broadly speaking, enrolled the Soviet Union in its logic of Western history, which was a logic that necessarily led beyond capitalism and Christianity. In this logic, the Soviets, with the prestige of the Grand Alliance and as the major force behind the victory over Hitler, stood, however imprecisely, for the true West. This was a West that defined the modern triad in a fundamentally different way from the Americans: not as science, democracy, and capitalism, but as science, equality, and rational planning. The Americans, by contrast, appeared in this logic as reactionary interlopers, emissaries from a superseded stage of the West, the stage of liberal, bourgeois capitalism and of Christianity.

To the other side, by contrast, and to themselves, the Americans represented not a marginal oddity or a reactionary conspiracy, but the very essence and heart of the West and the core of its future greatness: they were the heirs, not of Rousseau, but of the American Revolution, the revolution of political freedom and individual rights, the revolution of the commercial republic, the revolution according to Jefferson, Montesquieu, Hume, Burke, and Locke. The American presence in Europe after 1945 brought back to Europe something that most Europeans no longer recognized as theirs: the modern liberal triad of science, democracy, and capitalism, with an Old Western dosage of religion, but without the Old Western bargain of church and empire that Schmitt tried to resurrect as a mission for National Socialist Germany.

The Cold War thus realigned the forces contesting the identity of the West in new ways. Within Western elites, the democratic consensus was divided between socialists and liberals, some looking East and some across the Atlantic, for the true definition of the West. The American presence also introduced a geopolitical shift comparable to that of the Roman Empire, in that the Americans asserted that it was they, and not some European constellation of forces, that represented the genuine West. From the American perspective, those "children of the French Revolution" who admired the Soviet Union and rejected Christianity and capitalism therefore appeared not only anti-American but anti-Western, part of the enemy lineup. Since this lineup included a large part of the intellectual elite, particularly in France, Italy, and Britain, the battle for the West during the Cold War often seemed to the defenders of the liberal triad as a two-front war, a war with both the Soviet Union and with domestic opponents.

In 1946–47, most European and American policymakers came to realize that the Grand Alliance was finished, that Stalin's purposes in Europe and the world were incompatible with the interests of the democracies. The Cold War was the result of this insight, and the Cold War West was thus born as the set of states and people who shared that insight and who did not wish to become part of Stalin's world order. The Cold War West, however, included incompatible elements, which was one source of its intellectual fragility over the next decades. The fact was that the alignment in 1944–45 of Western elites into, roughly, an American party and a Soviet party, a party of the classical liberal triad and a party of its socialist transformation, gave way, in 1947, to an ad hoc alliance within the West between the American party and many who favored economic planning and collectivism and who were therefore critical of American capitalism and religiosity. Many of the children of the French Revolution preferred to develop their revolutionary ideology in the shelter of NATO and of American weapons. Léon Blum, the French socialist leader, was the head of a government in 1936 that included communists and represented the high point of the interwar popular front strategy that sought to align communists and liberal democrats. In 1946, Blum took a very different view of the Communist party, defining it as a "foreign nationalist party," repudiating the popular front ideology, and aligning himself with the forces resisting Soviet power in Europe and communist power at home.[6] But such declarations did not mean that socialists like Blum or the many leftist intellectuals of the West were willing to surrender their Jacobin instincts or their belief that, at bottom, Rousseau was right, that existing society was fatally flawed and that this flaw could be remedied if all the individual wills of human beings could be brought into harmony with the general will, which promised equality, justice, and happiness.

Thus the covering ideology of the Cold War West had to remain a lowest common denominator. It could not contain any substantive definitions of liberty or democracy, for no such substantive definitions could command general agreement. Some read liberty as meaning the right and the ability to work, trade, and become rich; others, as the result of the state redistributing income and resources, so that those who would not or could not work, trade, and become rich could nevertheless live to their fullest potential. Some read democracy as the sharing of power at the top, as alternating government, and as a pluralistic constitution permitting free individual activity to the largest possible extent. Others read democracy as a guarantee of equality and as the way by which the poorer majority restrained the rich minority, extracting from it its surplus to be distributed to all. The elites were divided, with many, especially in Europe, favoring Rousseau, collectivism, and equality, and many, especially in America in the early years, favoring Montesquieu, enterprise, and ordered liberty. To enroll such contradictory ideas in a common front required that the distinctions be ignored or elided.

The difference between the two main groupings within the Cold War West boiled down, in practice, to different answers to two critical questions: what was the Soviet Union, and what was the United States. Both questions haunted Western political and intellectual elites for the entire duration of the Cold War West, that is, from 1947 to 1989. During the early years, until the symbolic date of 1968, the question of the Soviet Union took priority; the answer you gave to that question was the important answer that determined your overall political stance and also largely determined your answer to the question about America. Starting in the 1960s, during the Vietnam War, Western elites, both in America and Europe, began giving priority to the question about America, and the answer to that then came to determine how one defined the Soviet Union. Thus, during the second half of the Cold War, the Soviet Union played, in most Western circles, a secondary and derivative role. This lack of primary attention to the basic nature of the Cold War West's geopolitical and strategic opponent was one reason that much of the political debate within the West in the 1970s and 1980s came to seem parochial and divorced from reality. The West argued with itself, ostensibly about fundamental matters of identity, morality, and policy, but most participants in the argument paid only intermittent attention to the question that was the precondition for all the others. The question about the Soviet Union was also the question about the conditions of Western survival, and before that was clarified, discussions of Western purpose, identity, and morality might seem secondary.

The question about the Soviet Union had, ever since 1917, two basic answers. The first was that the Soviet Union was a revolutionary socialist regime that had inherited the French Revolution's promises of liberty, equality, and fraternity. Despite all deviations and mistakes, the Soviet Union remained fundamentally on the side of the angels, of humanity, progress, and peace. Therefore no purely anti-Soviet policy could be moral or legitimate, and any legitimate policy must include understanding of, and perhaps even cooperation with, the Soviet Union. The second answer was the answer in terms of totalitarianism. Despite superficial appearances, the Soviet Union had nothing in common with Western traditions of liberty, equality, and fraternity. The supposed resemblance was a Western illusion; in fact, the Soviet Union was, like Hitler's Germany, a regime conceived in diametrical opposition to liberal democracy and had nothing in common with it. It was the enemy of the West and, even though temporary and short-term dealings were possible, it shared neither goals nor methods with the West.

The former answer emerged from the Grand Alliance and, behind that, from the antifascist ideology of the 1930s, the ideology that stated that the Soviet Union and liberal democracy were part of a common alignment of modernity, against the forces of reaction represented by Fascism and National Socialism. The Soviet war effort and the spread of Soviet power to Central Europe vastly enhanced the prestige and influence of the antifascist mentality. It dominated the Western left, which came, as time passed, to include substantial portions of American liberalism; for these groups, the Soviet Union improved as time went on and the memory of the early Cold War years faded.

A t the heart of the progressive case against liberal democracy was the argument that liberal democracy was potentially fascist because it was capitalist. Western identity based on liberal democracy was therefore also tainted. As such, the case was nonsensical. Italian Fascism and German National Socialism did not arise in the most, but in the least liberal and least democratic of the Western nations. Liberalism on the Continent, including Germany and Italy, had never achieved the political hegemony that it enjoyed in Britain and the United States. The nexus of liberal democracy and Fascism was not only not proven, it was absurd.

A different form of the progressive case against a Western identity based on liberalism made more sense. This was the argument that since Fascism and National Socialism arose in Western nations, therefore these ideologies had some relationship to Western identity, and therefore a restored democratic Western identity that did not acknowledge its own totalitarian temptation risked obfuscating history and evading its own responsibility. It was easy after 1945 for the Cold War West to embrace all those who now called themselves democrats without conducting an examination of its own conscience to trace the roots, within the West, of totalitarianism as well as of liberty.

The answer to this criticism was to admit that modern totalitarianism—whether Marxist or anti-Marxist—was indeed Western and could be understood only as a particular, radical, and antiliberal response to the modernization and democratization that were part of the transition from the Old to the New West. But while this answer might hold good in theory, the practice of the Cold War West often left gaps of logic and responsibility that disturbed many people who were not necessarily members of the progressive, antifascist intelligentsia.

An example of one such ambiguity of the restored West occurred at the Bayreuth Festival in Germany in June 1951. The Bayreuth Festival was the annual celebration of the music of Richard Wagner, established by the composer himself in 1876. From its beginning, the Bayreuth Festival became a symbol of German nationalism and, increasingly, of anti-Semitism. Friedrich Nietzsche, who worshipped Wagner's music as a young man, broke with the composer when the idea of the festival began to take shape and when the philosopher noted that the music that to him was a liberation from petty bourgeois piety and convention was being used to justify a nationalistic and anti-Semitic rhetoric that, so Nietzsche felt, appealed to the worst and most narrow-minded aspects of German bourgeois society. Wagner's own anti-Semitism was relatively mild and intermittent compared with that of his long-lived widow, Cosima, and of some of the hangers-on of Bayreuth, notably, the Englishman Houston Stewart Chamberlain, who married Wagner's daughter.[7] By the 1920s, Bayreuth and the Wagner family home, Wahnfried, stood for a revanchist nationalism and for the idea that the Jews were an alien and unassimilable element in German society. The Italian conductor Arturo Toscanini—a political liberal who exiled himself from Mussolini's Italy—was asked to come to Bayreuth, which he, as an admirer of Wagner, considered a unique honor. When he came, he found not a sanctuary of music, but, as he put it, "a barracks." He left and never returned.

Another conductor who did not refuse to work at Bayreuth was Wilhelm Furtwängler, who was often accused after 1945 of supporting the Hitler regime because he not only stayed in Germany, but retained his prestigious post as chief conductor of the Berlin Philharmonic, the country's leading orchestra. Furtwängler also worked at Bayreuth in the years when the Wagner family welcomed Adolf Hitler at Wahnfried, excluded Jewish artists, and continued to present Wagner's music as the essence of German ethnic identity and of a new civilization purged of Jewish and other non-German influences. In 1942, he conducted what Wagner himself considered the most patriotic of his operas, the *Meistersinger*, as the main attraction of the final season at Bayreuth before war conditions forced the festival to close.

Nine years later, the Bayreuth Festival reopened under new management and with a completely revised philosophy of presentation and dramatization of Wagner's works. Gone were all references, in sets, costumes, or effects, to German national identity; gone were all the former, heavy-handed attempts to prove that the stories on stage confirmed German chauvinism or prefigured the *Volksgemeinschaft*—the ethnic community—of National Socialism. The great dramas—*Tristan and Isolde, The Ring of the Nibelung, Parsifal*, and *Meistersinger*—were instead to be presented as archetypal dramas of love, fate, power, and temptation. The psychologist Carl Jung, who argued that the myths and stories of various civilizations retold the essential truths of individual human development, inspired the sets and costumes, which were spare, anonymous, deprived of any topical reference or content. The stories were to speak for themselves, not as tools of chauvinist propaganda.

The festival authorities nevertheless invited Furtwängler to conduct, giving him his first chance to appear in public since before the end of Hitler's regime. He was not asked to conduct one of the operas—that was politically impossible. But he was given another, in some ways an even more conspicuous task to mark his rehabilitation. He was asked to conduct a special performance of Beethoven's Ninth Symphony, the work that both he and Wagner considered the greatest piece of music ever written, and that Wagner himself had chosen to conduct at the opening concert of the first Bayreuth Festival in 1876. The performance, captured on disc, was, in the words of one critic, "a mystical moment in the history of the West."[8] Beethoven's troubled, ominous, yet finally exalted setting of Friedrich Schiller's "Ode to Joy," a setting hailed in the 1990s as the "anthem of Europe," conducted in Wagner's temple to himself by the greatest conductor of the age, as a sign of reconciliation and Western revival—a "mystical moment" indeed. Except that the mystical moment elided the recent history of the West, just as the Cold War definition of the West as antitotalitarian democracies did. For the fact of the matter was that the 1930s and 1940s had been years of conflict within the West between two competing principles of Western identity, the democratic and the totalitarian. That the democratic principle won, temporarily at least, was perhaps always the most likely outcome, though it did not seem so at the time. But this victory of democracy was not fully appreciated if it became an excuse to ignore that recent history and to consider all latter-day democrats equal in the star-studded nighttime of a "mystical moment."

When Furtwängler picked up the baton at Bayreuth in June 1951, the North Atlantic Treaty and its organization, NATO, were two years old. The treaty was also known as the Washington Treaty, for it was signed in the U.S. capital in April 1949 by representatives of most of the democratic nations of Europe and one nondemocratic one, Portugal. The main purpose of NATO was mutual defense, enshrined in article five of the treaty, which bound all signatories jointly to help any member that was attacked. The reason for NATO was that the western European democracies, struggling to recover economically and politically from World War II, could not organize a credible defensive alliance on their own. This was a problem because, starting in 1947, most responsible European and American statesmen believed that the Soviet Union, which had advanced into Central Europe when Germany was defeated, was a direct military threat to the independence of the western European states. The Europeans had signed their own mutual assistance treaty in 1948, but everyone agreed that this treaty would not deter Soviet attack unless it was backed by American power. The main purpose of European diplomacy in 1947–49 was, therefore, to convince the Americans to return once again to Europe, only a few years after the victory of 1945, and to stay indefinitely to prevent Josef Stalin's USSR from gaining control of the European landmass.

The Atlantic Alliance, as NATO was often called, was more than just a treaty of mutual military defense. It was intended to be a community of joint interests and values, dedicated to the principles of the Atlantic Charter—self-determination, open economies, and collective security—and to increased mutual understanding among the democratic societies of its members. As time wore on, the military dimension tended to be all any outsider ever saw of NATO, and as Western elites increasingly began to resent American predominance, this dimension was criticized as unnecessarily provocative, or as a cloak for American interests that had nothing to do with deterring a mythical Soviet threat and more to do with protecting American investments and hegemony.

In 1949, however, and for at least a decade and a half—until the Vietnam War—NATO constituted more than a symbolic bond across the Atlantic. A Western counterelite, devoted to liberal democracy and sceptical of the progressive, antifascist outlook that met Soviet policies with understanding and

American policies with suspicion, emerged in Europe, even, to a modest extent, in France and Italy, the countries where communist parties were the strongest and where communists and their sympathizers controlled much of the academic, media, and professional worlds. NATO played a significant role in democratizing West Germany, first by providing military security and then, after 1954, by admitting the Federal Republic of Germany as a member, recognizing its new democratic substance, and committing its other members to promoting and nourishing the new German democracy.

Within the Western community itself, NATO's political and cultural role as the institutional cement of what people began calling Atlantic civilization was more important than its military role. In fact, NATO's members decided quite early, in 1952, that they were not able to afford the massive conventional rearmament that would be necessary to deter the Soviet Union, which retained, all through its history, a substantial preponderance of conventional military force in Europe. Instead, NATO relied on American and, to a lesser extent, British and French nuclear weapons to provide the "existential deterrent" of the Soviets, inducing the fear, however tiny, that a Soviet conventional attack would not be immune to a Western nuclear response that would trigger mutual annihilation, rendering any Soviet gains illusory. Such, at least, was the calculation, and insofar as the Soviets never actually attacked, it succeeded.

As the political manifestation of an alleged Western community, NATO was from the beginning contested in Europe, primarily by the progressive elites, who saw in it an instrument of bourgeois capitalism designed to delay socialist revolution in the West, and as the militaristic and oppressive true face of liberalism, which, as Marcuse said, was "the total authoritarian state." Even those who supported and used NATO did not always agree on its value or purposes. To American governments, it was mainly a military institution, and its purpose was to prevent the Soviet Union from occupying western Europe, a development that would tip the geopolitical balance decisively against the United States. To the British, at least until the later 1960s, NATO confirmed Britain's residual great-power status, a status bolstered by the British nuclear deterrent. Thanks to NATO, Britain retained a relative military hegemony in Europe and some remnants of preferred rank in dealings with the United States. To the French, and especially to Charles de Gaulle, who incarnated French resistance to Germany in 1940 and governed as president of France from 1958 to 1969, NATO was an unwelcome necessity, and one that de Gaulle himself, who was a conservative nationalist, came to see largely in the left's terms as an instrument of American hegemony. Acting on this belief, he ordered all military installations under NATO out of France in 1965 and withdrew France from the joint military activities of the alliance. Although later French governments, especially after the Soviet Union dissolved in 1991, sometimes indicated that they might want to return to the military cooperation of the alliance, they never did so.

The NATO West, which existed from 1947 to 1989, was, unlike the earlier versions of the West, defined increasingly in purely political terms, as the sum of those states and peoples who were members of the alliance, and their shared interest in resisting Soviet power. The NATO West, short-lived as it was, dominated the imaginations both of its friends and of its enemies during its existence to such an extent that people tended to forget that there ever had been other versions of the West. The NATO West was neither the West of Christendom nor the West of the modern triad of science, democracy, and economic development, though it contained simplified and schematized trace elements of both. It was, as understood by politicians, journalists, and public opinion, a crude precipitate, derived for comprehensible strategic and diplomatic reasons, of the older and richer definitions whose adherents had argued and fought over the preceding sixteen hundred years. Its ideological predominance within its own sphere rested on the Grand Narrative, which came to its final flowering and the height of its influence in the early years of the NATO West. The narrative gave the NATO West a prehistory of Magic Moments starting with the Greeks and ending with the final Magic Moment of the Atlantic Charter. The Plato to NATO scheme drew an ahistorical axis across two and a half millennia. Neither the Christendom model of the late antique synthesis and the grand bargain of church and empire nor Montesquieu's and Jefferson's model of the West as ordered liberty started by the ancient Germans, revived by economic enterprise and promoted by political pluralism, played much part in shaping the NATO definition of the West. The Cold War West was a by-product of postwar liberalism, but one undermined by the inner split within that liberalism among its historical, institutional identity, which went back to the Old West, and its modern identity as a universalist doctrine of individual freedom. This modern identity invited the criticism of the progressive position, which stated that the liberal West would be more truly itself if it adopted the progressive ideology of anticapitalism and secularism. The split had many causes; one of them was certainly the reversal of 1941, when the Soviet Union became the ally of the democracies.

W hen Hitler and Stalin joined forces in August 1939, people in the democracies could legitimately see the resulting war as a war between democracy and tyranny. The democracies, in this view, represented the West as the joint fruit of two long histories: the history of Christendom and the slow growth of liberal institutions and civic virtue out of the niches of liberty, the economic growth they encouraged, and the gradual spread of pluralist and democratic institutions and practices through the national states of the early modern West from the fifteenth to the nineteenth centuries.

The war thus first appeared to many as a war of Western civilization against its totalitarian and technocratic enemies. One of these was the Catholic convert and sarcastic caricaturist of modern, secularized existence, Evelyn Waugh. In his *Sword of Honour* trilogy, he follows Guy Crouchback, the mild-mannered scion of an ancient West Country recusant family.[9] As the story opens, Crouchback is living as an expatriate in Italy, in a house built by his great-grandparents near the tomb of an English crusader from the twelfth century. He has left England because he finds himself out of sympathy with the fashions and beliefs of his contemporaries in the 1930s, notably their leftism and what he sees as their lack of seriousness and moral purpose in life. He is an Old Westerner in a diminished and cynical age; he seeks a cause to follow but finds the causes of his friends tawdry at best, inhuman at worst. When he hears the news that the National Socialist regime of Germany and the communist regime of the Soviet Union have signed their treaty in August 1939, he is exhilarated and relieved:

> Just seven days earlier he had opened his morning newspaper on the headlines announcing the Russian-German alliance. News that shook the politicians and young poets of a dozen capital cities brought deep peace to one English heart. Eight years of shame and loneliness was ended. For eight years Guy, already set apart from his fellows by his own deep wound, that unstaunched, internal draining away of life and love, had been deprived of the loyalties which should have sustained him. . . . He expected his country to go to war in a panic, for the wrong reasons or for no reason at all, with the wrong allies, in pitiful weakness. But now, splendidly, everything had become clear. *The enemy at last was in plain view, huge and hateful, all disguise cast off. It was the Modern Age in arms.* Whatever the outcome there was a place for him in that battle.[10]

Guy's "deep wound" was that his wife, Victoria, had left him for other husbands, a betrayal made existential because Guy, as a Catholic, considered marriage a sacrament and was therefore unable to seek a divorce (in the third volume, a needy, though not contrite, Victoria, thrown off by her third husband and pregnant by a lover, returns briefly to Guy before she is killed by a flying bomb).

This war he will gladly join, because it will be a war of the West against its enemies. "He was packed and dressed for a long journey, already on his way back to his own country to serve his King." Before leaving his Italian village, he goes to the old crusader's tomb and asks the old knight to "pray for me . . . and for our endangered kingdom." Our kingdom: in 1149 and 1939. When Crouchback learns on June 22, 1941, that Germany has attacked the Soviet Union, he is disappointed. His crusade for chivalry and nobility, already somewhat dented by the self-seeking incompetence he encounters in the British army, has lost its point:

> Now that hallucination was dissolved . . . he was back after less than two years' pilgrimage in a Holy Land of illusion in the old ambiguous world, where priests were spies and gallant friends proved traitors and his country was led blundering into dishonour.[11]

For example the dishonor, briefly alluded to, of British officers in 1945 handing over two million soldiers and civilians, natives of countries occupied by communists, people who had been in German prison camps or factories, but who were anticommunist and educated, who had fallen into British captivity through the fortunes of war, and whom Britain's communist allies—Stalin and the Yugoslav dictator Josip Tito—demanded to have extradited. Appeasing Stalin and Tito was a closely enforced British policy in 1945, and it required sending these two million civilians back, many of them "to certain execution."[12]

Guy is last seen, at the end of the final volume, as a successful but disillusioned postwar businessman-farmer, turning into what, in 1939, he hated: a complacent, self-deluding member of a declining civilization without the courage of its convictions or a justified sense of identity—because it sold that sense of identity down the road when, during the war, it lost track of who was its enemy. The title of the last volume, *Unconditional Surrender*, describes Guy, but in a larger sense it describes his country, surrendering to dishonor and materialism and—so Waugh's Catholic imagination suggested—to their inevitable consequence, despair.

Guy Crouchback had many real-life counterparts in the 1930s; fewer after Hitler unwittingly laid the groundwork for the Grand Alliance when he attacked Stalin in 1941. One of the more famous was the exiled German novelist Thomas Mann, who left Germany a few days after Hitler became head of the government in 1933 and who, in 1939, was living in the United States, more specifically, in southern California, where, in the 1940s, he wrote the most German of all his novels, *Doktor Faustus*. In a diary entry of

September 11, 1939, he lamented that Germany, with the Hitler-Stalin pact, had finally "abandoned the West, perhaps for ever, and joined the East." This, to him, was "the end of Germany." The National Socialist regime was, Mann held, a "revolution with profound consequences; it completely *de*nationalized the country, as far as any traditional notion of German character is concerned, by giving itself 'national' appeal. The Nazi Bolshevism has *nothing* to do with German national character. The new barbarism has quite naturally found common ground with a Russia to which it was apparently opposed."[13]

This was no new idea for Mann. As early as 1933, he described Hitler's regime as a "German Bolshevism," inspired by and secondary to both Leninist communism and Mussolini's Italian Fascism. The diagnosis was noteworthy for several reasons, not least the fact that, in the form of the totalitarian hypothesis, it became an object of ideological controversy after World War II and remained able to stir strong feelings as late as 1986. One of the earliest philosophical elaborations of it was that of the Jewish-Catholic political theorist Waldemar Gurian, a pupil of Carl Schmitt who was forced to leave Germany in 1933. In 1935, he published in Switzerland a short book entitled *The Future of Bolshevism*. According to Gurian, Bolshevism could not be properly understood either as denial of Christianity, nor as an egalitarian revolution against private property, nor even, as Oswald Spengler argued, as a symptom of the West's inevitable slide into barbarism. Soviet Bolshevism, Gurian held, was not the issue; in 1935, when he was writing, Soviet power and prestige were weak. The issue, rather, was that Hitler had reproduced, in Germany, a far stronger, more thorough, and more dangerous form of Bolshevism in the most powerful and technologically advanced Western state. It was this German Bolshevism, and not the relatively weak Bolshevism of Russia, that represented the true revolution of nihilism and the true emergence of the new phenomenon, the party-state, with its declared mission of total transformation by force and destruction of the existing order. The fact that this impulse to destruction, nihilism, and concentrated force had adopted Marxist rhetoric and ideology to seize power in Russia was secondary. Marxism was an ideology of the nineteenth century, appropriate to a backward society like Russia. In Germany, the forces of nihilism could not use that old doctrine; they wanted not to undermine the state but to make it infinitely strong. They therefore adopted a rhetoric of nationalism and anti-Semitism directed against both liberalism and Marxism; but behind this apparent conflict of National Socialism and Soviet communism lay what they had in common, the radical project of total power.

According to Gurian, then both the red and the brown revolutions were revolutions of nihilism, both were against the West in both its Christian and its liberal models, but, again from the viewpoint of 1935, the National Socialists were both more consistent and more powerful, because they controlled a modern society; they, therefore, were the true Bolsheviks.

To Thomas Mann in 1939, it seemed as though the two allied monsters, Hitler and Stalin, were destined to win. Would the West, would civilization be able to defeat them? The democracies seemed weak and disorganized, without the common purpose that was the hallmark of what few people as yet referred to as the totalitarian regimes. Mann was here returning, ironically and with opposed purpose, to a position he abandoned after World War I. During that war he had written a nationalist and anti-Western tract in which he opposed German *Kultur*, strong, rooted, personal, and authentic, to Western "civilization," which was cosmopolitan, liberal, weak, divided, and superficial. In 1939, unlike in 1917, he found himself hoping that this weak Western civilization, which he had despised and condemned as a German nationalist, would prove after all to be strong enough to resist and overcome the forces that had overwhelmed both Russia and Germany.

Belonging to the antifascist mindset dictated responses and reactions to a number of events in the Cold War West, not least the attitude to the second of the two basic questions, the question about America. From the 1930s on, the antifascist mindset included both initial sympathy for the Soviet Union as, all things considered, a force for good, and some distrust of American capitalism and some doubt concerning the essential justice and fairness of the American system. In the 1930s, the antifascist mindset dominated progressive intellectual and academic circles in the West and was one of the forces motivating the treason of men like Guy Burgess and Anthony Blunt in Britain or of Alger Hiss in the United States. Such men were not downtrodden proletarians but the flower of the liberal elite of their societies, recipients of the best education and, by their merits, the rightful heirs to leading positions. They came out of their education and into their high positions with fundamental doubts and guilt about their own societies and just as fundamental sympathy for what they considered the only true force for progress, the Soviet Union, which in the 1930s appeared to them weak, embattled, at risk, and in urgent need of help. It was for the sake of justice and humanity that they used their positions to collect information and reveal it to the Soviet regime; their purposes were moral in the extreme.

Perhaps the most famous of all antifascists, the guru of the European left for several decades, was the French philosopher Jean-Paul Sartre, who in the 1930s and early 1940s, under German occupation, wrote novels and plays in which he presented what became known as the existentialist theory of liberty. Civilization and society offered no valid codes, traditions, or values, Sartre held. Therefore, the free individual was not the one who accepted any of the codes or values on offer on their own terms, for these were all fraudulent, all designed to co-opt people into supporting some particular interest or cause. Rather, the free individual was one who made a choice, a decision to be free of all constraints and codes. In such a condition of absolute liberty the individual could then choose a code, for it would then be his own in a deep sense, not something accepted or handed down.

After the war, Sartre exercised his choice in favor of Stalinism. He never joined the Communist party but served its interests more slavishly than the majority of its cadres, and more effectively thanks to his reputation as an independent and profound thinker. The single consistent principle of Sartre's Stalinism was that Stalin, and the party, were always right. In 1948 he wrote that "in Stalinism . . . the working class recognizes its own image, its work, the provisional repository of its sovereignty. You claim that this minority [the party] is harming the working class. But how could it? It draws its power from the proletariat."[14] It was, in Sartre's world view, impossible for the Communist party not to represent freedom, for communist doctrine said that the party "draws its power" from the proletariat, and if the doctrine said so, it must be true. Everything that the communists said, Sartre took at face value; everything the liberals or the Americans said had a cynical purpose and was to be deconstructed and disbelieved. His contemporary, the liberal philosopher Raymond Aron, who was one of the very few French intellectuals never to partake in the fashionable antifascist and procommunist ideology, recalled many years later that the young Sartre exclaimed in 1929 that any adult, thinking person had the moral duty to be a revolutionary, for "this society" was immeasurably evil and corrupt.[15] Sartre, as such comments revealed, was not really, as he claimed, an amoral existentialist, but a deeply moralistic heir of Rousseau and Robespierre who believed that history had a purpose and a moral, that this purpose rested with communism, and that everything that resisted or opposed that purpose was utterly evil.

The antifascist tendency married, in France, a national tradition, descended from the revolution, of believing that history had a grand design, embodied in a particular political movement, which was therefore excused any and all crimes because it served the logic of history, which was universal emancipation. This faith in history was purist and intolerant. It allowed no legitimacy to the West as a historical phenomenon, nor was it concerned, as Montesquieu had been, with the conditions of actual freedom. The faith in history, which combined Jacobin revolutionary ideals with Marxism, believed in an abstract, universal freedom as the destiny, not of real people, but of "man." Its adherents, like Sartre, were supremely uninterested in how the spread of power or the rise of democratic practices had encouraged both liberty and economic growth in the real West. Such liberty and growth were contemptible phantasms, which had benefited only the rich and the exploiters. The point was not to protect and extend these fragile and genuine pockets of liberty, but to annul all history in a revolutionary transformation that would bring about real freedom. This transformation would also, of course, abolish private property, for in the Marxist and Sartrean world view, private property was not an enabler of liberty but its enemy.

This latter-day, late-twentieth-century Western Marxism grew strong in the West even as communism, as the doctrine of power in the Soviet Union and Central Europe, lost legitimacy among its victims. This was a third paradox of the Cold War West: how an attenuated, primitive, and simplistic blend of Rousseau and Marx conquered the citadel of the commercial, capitalist West, the United States, starting in the 1960s. Before that time, during the first two decades of the Cold War, the American consensus remained, for both politicians and intellectuals, largely that of Cold War liberalism, which was the mobilized and battle-ready variant of the classical modern triad according to Montesquieu and the American Founders. During those decades, Cold War liberalism and its pedagogical counterpart, the Grand Narrative, dominated American culture.

From the beginning of the Cold War until the Vietnam War, the Cold War liberals accepted the totalitarian analysis and rejected antifascism as an obscurantist and ideological confusion, dangerous to Western self-confidence and a barrier to understanding the real differences between liberal democracy and its enemies. Cold War liberals were the main representatives in the 1950s and early 1960s of the West as the liberal triad, in which democracy meant individual liberty and prosperity rested on free enterprise and not on planning. Through such links as the Congress for Cultural Freedom, the Cold War liberals tried to find allies in Europe and to promote the classical liberal definition of the West. They conceived this work as comparable to mobilization for war; it was urgent and highly political, not a matter merely of philosophical analysis. Outside America, however, Cold War liberalism won only few supporters. European academics and intellectuals remained overwhelmingly within the antifascist mentality. "At a time when the American intelligentsia had massively converted to anticommunism," François Furet wrote, "most European intellectuals had difficulty following its reasons." The United States, although its version of the West owed almost everything to the moderate Enlightenment, returned to Europe as almost an alien force, brandishing an "almost religious affirmation of the individual." American democracy, although authentically a product of Western history, "remained too capitalist for the Europeans not to suspect that it concealed the domination of money under the slogans of freedom." Europeans, therefore, remained largely unconvinced and continued to share the antifascist intuition that "what was bad in the USSR was not to be attributed to the system, but to circumstances, whereas it was the opposite for the United States."[16] America, though seemingly democratic, was really fascist; the Soviet Union, though seemingly totalitarian, was really progressive and on the side of humanity. That America represented an idea of the West that combined democracy and economic liberty remained largely incomprehensible to the heirs of Rousseau, who dominated European universities, newspapers, bureaucracies, and culture.

There was one exception, at least until the 1960s, and that was West Germany. Over ten million inhabitants of West Germany had fled their homes in eastern Germany before the Soviet army in 1944–45; other millions had left communist-ruled East Germany in the 1940s and 1950s, until the Berlin Wall made escape impossible in 1961. Soviet power appeared to most Germans decidedly hostile and dangerous, and the idea that this power was at bottom a force for peace and justice was a difficult idea to swallow for those who had personal experience of it. But West German solidarity with the American model of the West was not necessarily an advantage for that model elsewhere. The antifascist mentality thrived on the belief that Fascism was not dead; Germany had been the most powerful, aggressive, and destructive fascist country; therefore, it was tempting to conclude that Germans were anti-Soviet not because they were democrats, but because they remained at bottom fascists. From a Cold War liberal perspective, German support of the American model of the West confirmed the totalitarian thesis; to be democratic was to be opposed to both kinds of totalitarianism, and the Germans thus proved that they had become genuinely democratic. From the antifascist perspective, German support of the Cold War West confirmed that Germans were not truly democratic, for if they were, they could not be so adamantly anti-Soviet.

Hitler's Germany fought the Soviet Union and presented its war against Stalin as a war of fundamental significance, a war for the West against Bolshevism and Judaism. Democratic West Germany resisted Soviet power and understood this resistance as a necessary consequence of democracy. The anti-Soviet position was justified in one way by Hitler and in another by the democratic leaders of West Germany, but both positions were anti-Soviet and anticommunist. And if the antifascist intuition was correct that the Soviet Union was essentially good, and that Fascism was still a danger, then the continuity made perfect sense. The Germans had not changed; they had just become more cunning, since after 1945 they concealed their inhuman ideology in democratic slogans, whereas until 1945 they had been openly fascist.

The question was whether this continuity of anticommunism was the most significant thing about Germany, or whether the Cold War liberals were right who said that Hitler's Germany was anticommunist for the wrong reasons, whereas democratic West Germany was, like America, anticommunist for the right reasons. Those who suspected German credentials and who shared the antifascist intuition could point to continuities not just in anticommunism but of anticommunists. In the 1920s and 1930s, the members of the *Abendland* circle argued that Germany's role was to reconstruct the ancient bargain of church and empire. They represented a political theology of the West that assigned to an authoritarian German regime the main responsibility of rescuing the West from democracy and liberalism. In the 1950s and 1960s, some of these people resurfaced with a democratic version of this political theology that assigned pride of place to America and to the values of democracy and Christianity. Regardless of whether their conversion to democracy was sincere, what did such continuity say about the legitimacy of the Cold War liberal position? Did it not show that the liberal triad of science, democracy, and capitalism was hopelessly corrupt by its affinities and entanglements, and that the only morally acceptable West was one that entered into the Marxist logic of history by looking ahead to a glorious, antifascist future of technology, equality, and the planned society?

Anticommunism, like antifascism, contained many subgroups and temperaments, not all of them compatible with each other. From the interwar battle against nihilism emerged both the hard-core, authoritarian political theology of a Carl Schmitt and the democratic, liberal, and humane cultural vision of Western unity of an Ernst Robert Curtius. One of the internal controversies of the Cold War West in the 1950s was that between the heirs of these two positions.

Five years after Curtius published his great work, *European Literature and the Latin Middle Ages*, West Germany, France, Italy, the Netherlands, Belgium, and Luxembourg signed the Treaty of Rome in 1957 and launched the Common Market, known in the 1990s as the European Union. The political and the intellectual events were not unconnected. Curtius had written his book as a response to nihilism and despair and in particular against the cultural nationalism of the 1920s and 1930s, which, in his view, constituted inappropriate and harmful answers to the decline of the West. By a considerable irony, however, his book in the 1950s became one of the sources of a quite different, more optimistic, yet historically and philosophically peculiar ideology.

The proponents of this ideology, known in German as *Abendländlertum*, or "Westernism," claimed that World War II created an unprecedented danger as well as an opportunity for the West. With communist power advanced to the Elbe and Berlin and representing the utter denial of the West, the remaining West was reduced, in Europe, to its early medieval core of the Rhine and Rhone valleys and adjacent regions. This was the Europe of Charlemagne's empire in the eighth and ninth centuries, a Europe that stopped not far east of the Rhine and extended from Rome in the south to the English Channel in the north. The Soviet threat to this rump of Europe should, it was said, force the survivors of World War II to forget the war and to recall what they had in common: the Roman and Latin legacy symbolized in the cities and monuments scattered across this remaining Western territory. The Soviet advance was in two senses providential, the Westernists held: it forced Western Europeans to recall their common culture and join forces, and it also generated the alliance with the United States and created the only West capable of survival: the NATO West of North America and Carolingian Europe.

The *Abendland* ideology rested on a solid base of truth. Carolingian Europe was the common origin of the later West geographically, economically, and culturally. The Soviet advance into Europe following the defeat of Germany had indeed reduced democratic Europe, roughly, to its Carolingian dimensions. Likewise, it was undoubtedly a good idea for Europeans, if they wanted peace and order, to recall what they had in common and to abandon nationalism and ethnic prejudice. Finally, the American commitment to defending this rump of Europe, which was also a consequence of World War II, certainly benefited transatlantic political, economic, and cultural contacts, promoted mutual interests, and kept a sense of Western identity alive.

All this was true, yet the 1950s refrain that "we're all Western now" and the chorus of universal support for "Western values," whatever they might in practice be, seemed easy coming so soon after a world war in which the world in general and Europe in particular had been divided into warring camps, all of which claimed to be defending "civilization" and the West. The Soviet conquest of Central Europe and nearly half of Germany up to the Elbe was not an act of God but mainly a consequence of Germany's attack on the Soviet Union in 1941 and of Hitler's policy of war against the rest of the world. Westernism required that Europeans and Americans forget that ten years earlier, they had been in opposite camps not just militarily, but ideologically, and that they hark back a thousand years or more to recover their grounds of identity. Westernism obscured the immediate past and emphasized the remote past as the binding force.

As Curtius had shown, common culture there was, and in great riches, but his book was about the Middle Ages, even though some chapters ranged into the seventeenth century. In the 1950s, that more distant common culture had been overlaid for two centuries, and most dramatically in the World Wars of the twentieth, by hatred, war, mass murder, and violence. The Westernist doctrines took for granted that the old common culture was viable and capable of being rebuilt and redeployed, while likewise assuming that the hatreds and wars of much more recent vintage could easily be swept aside.

A particular feature of Westernism was that some German historians who, in the Nazi years, had written works implicitly or explicitly praising National Socialism as the wave of the future and the foundation of European civilization, turned around in the 1950s and wrote works of equal size and sophistication arguing that the war had shown that no nation could stand alone and that the West must now join forces, recall its common values, and defend itself against the Soviet Union. Some of these had been party members out of opportunism or nationalist fervor; in the 1950s, they rediscovered the virtues of democratic liberalism as a better weapon against communism than Hitler had provided. A more interesting case was that of Carl Schmitt's friend, the Catholic historian Albert Mirgeler, who, in the 1960s, received the *Karlspreis*, the Charlemagne prize of the city of Aachen (Aix-la-Chapelle), where Charlemagne was crowned, and which was given for outstanding services to the cause of Western civilization. In the 1920s and early 1930s, Mirgeler was one of the most enthusiastic advocates of the political and theological program of restoring the Catholic empire as the answer to nihilism and its causes, liberalism, and democracy. "If there remains any life instinct and any European calling left," Mirgeler wrote in 1928, then such forces needed urgently to come together and forge European unity to avoid the "American hegemony," for that hegemony was intolerable, since it meant anarchy and "the determination of the political by the economic."[17] This was what Arnold

Toynbee later believed, but with a Catholic and authoritarian edge: the threat to the West was American capitalism.

In 1933, Mirgeler, like Schmitt, discovered another and even more insidious enemy of the West—the Jews. Anti-Semitism, and not primarily nationalism or anticommunism, drove Mirgeler and Schmitt and their theological allies to supporting Hitler. The Jews were incompatible with the theocratic order of the future Third Reich; moreover, they had killed Christ. The Germans and the Jews, Mirgeler wrote, had been competitors in the history of salvation, but the Jews had rejected the Messiah and put themselves irremediably in the wrong. Then, in the early modern age, the Holy Roman Empire of the German Nation had come to an end, thereby "dissolving the foundations of that kingdom of God that the people of the West had labored to build." What followed was the un-Christian modern age, in which "Christian culture was deposed from its former dignity and rule" and replaced by "another faith . . . another understanding of the origin and destiny of man and his relationship to the other visible and invisible beings." And who benefited from this dethronement, who was responsible for the modern, heretical, idea of man? The Jews, whose "social power" rested on "their economic and financial position, which they construct and promote by virtue of their earthly version of the Messianic idea in the form of a kingdom of general fleshly love and earthly happiness." Consequently, a politico-theological restoration of the empire must "raise up the Christian name" and the power of the "ecclesiastical association" to stop the ongoing plan by which "the emancipation of the Jews is only the mediating transition to the subjugation of the Christians."[18]

In 1933, then, Mirgeler believed that the salvation of the West required eliminating the Jews from public life, rejecting American economic imperialism and the Anglo-Saxon commercial world view, and restoring the Holy Roman Empire. In the 1950s, Mirgeler's extensive works of history took an entirely more relaxed view of these matters, so relaxed, in fact, that the Jews made only a peripheral and sympathetic appearance. In his narrative of European history from 1954 and his philosophical interpretation of it from 1971, Mirgeler mentioned that Charlemagne, who had always been the central figure of Western identity both for liberals and antiliberals like the younger Mirgeler, modeled his kingship on that of David in the Old Testament. Had Charlemagne wanted to copy his Roman predecessors, he would have had to fight the eastern, or Byzantine, emperor, for in Roman imperial doctrine there could be only one emperor or at most some agreed division of responsibilities. Since Charlemagne had not been delegated to the West by the Byzantine emperor but was independently crowned, he was technically a usurper under the Roman rules. By adopting the legacy of King David, Charlemagne tried to evade the whole question of his precise status in terms of Roman ideology; he was, Mirgeler insisted, not just a Roman emperor in the tradition of Augustus, but the supreme lord of his people, the chosen people of the new covenant and, therefore, theologically the heir of David as much as of Augustus.

Mirgeler never gave his readers an explanation of how Jewish influence could help to found Christian Europe in A.D. 800 when, in 1933, he had carefully explained how the Jews were busy destroying the remnants of Christian Europe and establishing their own rival, fleshly, and earthly dominion of ideas, based on materialism, socialism, and nationalism. But as an ideologue of the Westernist tendency, Mirgeler illustrated what one might call its dark side or, more neutrally, its unfinished business. The irony of his fate in Hitler's Germany, as of Schmitt's, was that their political theology of a restored empire was too strong and precise for the National Socialists, who were modern totalitarians, not pseudomedieval hierarchs. But the anti-Semitism was common, and equally sincerely held on both sides.

The Jews, however, were not an element in Mirgeler's postwar work. Rather, the role of villain and corrupter of the true Western character and institutions was now taken not by a group of people, but by an anonymous force: technology. Mirgeler quoted Arnold Toynbee for saying that Western civilization emerged from its cocoon of Christendom in the seventeenth century and engendered a new, secular version of itself, in which technology replaced religion as the highest purpose and interest of Western man.[19] He could also have quoted the philosopher Martin Heidegger, who, like Mirgeler, had seen great hope in the National Socialist revolution of 1933, only to find himself disappointed a year later. Heidegger had no interest in the political theology of a restored empire; his reasons for supporting Hitler were modern, not medieval. Like Schmitt and Mirgeler, however, anti-Semitism was a crucial source of attraction for him in Hitler's regime, and if he, like his fellow-Catholics, soon withdrew, it was not because Hitler was anti-Semitic, for that they supported; it was because Hitler would not play the part they each had allotted him in their personal cultural scenarios.

Heidegger decided, in the 1950s, that technology was the great sin and evil of the Western world, which had tempted man from the path of being to the path of making and domination; this path, Heidegger solemnly declared, led only to ruin and despair; he provided two horrifying examples of this despair, which in his mind were equally nihilistic, equally inhuman. One was the assembly line of the Ford Motor Company in Detroit; the other was the extermination camp at Auschwitz. To overcome the nihilism of the modern technocratic and bourgeois world, Heidegger explained, it was necessary to go back beyond Plato, back to before the Greek philosophers started trying to understand and master the laws of nature, an effort that led directly to the nihilism of science, technology, mass democracy, and liberalism. All this found enormous favor with a wide range of late-twentieth-century thinkers, from the pro-Stalinist Sartre in Paris to disillusioned liberals like John Gray in 1990s Britain. None of these admirers of Heidegger drew the political consequences that he had drawn, consequences that seemed to follow rigorously from his denial of value to liberal democracy. In 1933, Heidegger welcomed the National Socialist revolution in Germany as the political proof that nihilism could be overcome by an act of will, by a "national uprising" expressing the truth of Being—*das Sein*—against the lie of democracy. The carriers of this lie were, above all, the Jews, the rootless people who were the furthest removed from true Being. Heidegger never repudiated his political statements, which at least made him more consistent than his later admirers, who believed that one could denounce liberalism as nihilistic while continuing to enjoy its protections.

"The effort to understand European history is an indispensable part of our task of locating and defining ourselves within the spiritual and social anarchy engendered by the revolution of the last few centuries," Albert Mirgeler loftily pronounced in 1971.[20] His philosophical account dealt in detail with the late antique and Carolingian synthesis of the West, with the rise of political pluralism in the later Middle Ages, and with the wars of religion and the beginnings of modern political rationality that opened the modern era. But after about 1650, everything ran together in one long, pervasive technological revolution, a dark night of the soul in which all ideological cats were equally gray. Rousseau's vision of healing the human spirit, Montesquieu's and Jefferson's vigorous Anglo-Saxon liberties, Marxism, and Fascism were all roughly the same, all equally degenerate results of the fall from Western greatness.

In such a broad and impossibly general perspective, the crucial threshold of the modern West whereby the triad of science, democracy, and capitalism was born by the spirit of discovery and war out of the older triad of Rome, Christianity, and the Germanic liberties, was completely obscured in a general condemnation of modernity. How this antitechnological pseudomedievalism related to the Westernists' professed loyalty to the Atlantic Alliance, which depended on American capitalism and technology for its survival, they did not explain. Toynbee was useful to such people, for he belonged to the democratic side, was certainly an opponent of Hitler, but, especially in his later years, lapsed into a peculiar combination of hostility to the modern, technological, and capitalist West and optimism about a religious revival that perfectly suited the twilight climate of the Westernists. Also, although they diligently avoided the Jewish issue themselves, the formerly pro-Hitler Westernists could not have been disappointed in Toynbee's own anti-Semitism, which he expressed the more openly as he felt no guilt for the Holocaust. To Toynbee, the Jews were pretty much what Heidegger and Mirgeler had condemned in 1933, though the genteel, ecumenical Englishman was never as forceful as the two German Catholics. Jews represented the brash, arrogant side of modernity, and particularly as a nation-state, in Israel, they continued the worst aspects of Western colonialism and oppression. In 1961, Toynbee was, if not the first, one of the first prominent Westerners to compare Israeli actions against the Arabs to German actions against the Jews in World War II; some of the "massacres by Israeli armed forces in Palestine," he said in a debate with an Israeli diplomat, "do compare . . . in moral quality with what the Germans did."[21]

The history of Western identity during the Cold War fell into three parts, with the dividing line between the first two corresponding, symbolically, to the "year that changed everything: 1968." The first two decades, from the late 1940s to the late 1960s, were traditionally labeled conservative, family-oriented, and somewhat puritanical. Certainly this was an era when duty and self-sacrifice were still taught and, by and large, learned by young people. The era also acquired a reputation for optimism; also largely true, as the prevalent versions of the Grand Narrative taught in thousands of Western civ courses suggested: the democratic, free-market West was the best thing going—the logical result of thousands of years of social evolution—and it was the best combination of Greek ideas of liberty, modern representative democracy, and modern technology.

Behind the optimism, the 1950s were also an era of doubt and cultural pessimism. No Spengler appeared to pronounce the end of the West, but instead José Ortega y Gasset, Arnold Toynbee, and James Burnham revised Tocqueville's and Nietzsche's warning that modern liberal democracy was headed into a cul-de-sac of soul-destroying regimentation and mediocrity, to which Burnham added the rider that this would ensure its defeat at the hands of the more purposive and determined communists. And for those who did not read Ortega, Burnham, or Toynbee, the espionage cases of the decade provided evidence that at least some highly educated people in the democratic West had no faith in it, but had placed their moral and ideological bets on the Soviet Union.

The trial of Alger Hiss in 1950–51 was a symbolic moment in American history and the history of the Cold War West. Hiss had been cleared of charges of espionage at an earlier trial, but was then accused of having perjured himself at that trial. In particular, he had denied owning a typewriter that was known to have been used to compose messages containing secret information that had, in the late 1930s, been passed illegally to Soviet agents. At his trial for perjury, his main accuser was his former friend Whittaker Chambers. The drama of the modern West rarely found such contrasting protagonists as those two. Hiss, the son of the elite, suave, elegant, and well-spoken, faced Chambers, a neurotic, overweight, troubled individual of common social origins who, by his own confession, had been a communist and who had then, as he himself put it, deserted the winning for the losing side. For, by the time of the perjury trial, the antifascist mindset had been transformed from what it was in the 1930s, when Hiss decided to help the cause of humanity. Then, helping the Soviets was helping those who were in danger of being crushed by the forces of inhumanity and reaction. Now, in 1950, the Soviet Union had crushed National Socialist Germany, controlled half of Europe, and represented not only moral and ideological power, but strategic and political force. The antifascist mindset was not the mindset of those who sympathized with a threatened regime, but that of an onrushing, triumphant power. Chambers sincerely believed that the Soviet Union was on the side of history; his personal tragedy at the time was that he had lost his faith in the Soviet Union's credentials.

The prosecution was able to show, to the court's satisfaction, that Hiss had indeed perjured himself and that he had owned the famous typewriter. He could not be sentenced for espionage, for that would have been double jeopardy, but he was convicted of perjury and spent time in prison. From his release until his death in 1995, his supporters never ceased to insist that he was innocent or, when that became difficult in the face of argument and evidence, that he was framed by the forces of evil, by agents of a reactionary American government.[22] The Hiss case divided American intellectuals as few cases before or since, with most of those who defined themselves as progressive believing that he was innocent, and those who believed Chambers defined as reactionary and as enemies of peace and justice.

When he accused Hiss and brought to a New York courtroom a whiff of the conspiratorial atmosphere of prewar American communism, Chambers had, as he said, said good-bye long ago to the historical optimism of Marxist doctrine and had thrown in his lot with America and the West. Even as an anticommunist, however, Chambers continued to believe in the dogma of history so characteristic of communism, the dogma that said that history had only one direction, that this direction led to communism, and that resistance was both immoral and futile. The only temporary exception to this pessimism in Chambers's postcommunist experience happened when, in 1947, he discovered Arnold Toynbee and his theory of universal history. In March of that year, five days after the American president, Harry Truman, asked Congress to support the governments of Greece and Turkey against Soviet subversion, *Time* magazine ran a cover story on Toynbee and his *Study of History* under the headline "Our civilization is not inexorably doomed."

Toynbee had come to *Time*'s attention during the war, when the founder and editor of the magazine, Henry Luce, met Toynbee and concluded that the British historian had discovered laws of historical development that not only gave a full account of all past history but also pointed the way to the future, a way that, so Luce and later Chambers hoped, gave the West the opportunity to avoid the fate of all other civilizations—decline, disruption, and collapse. In the issue of March 1947, Chambers tied Toynbee's supposed lessons to the immediate situation in south-eastern Europe, which was "a crisis in Western civilization," which could be remedied if the United States would "consciously become what she had been in reluctant fact, since the beginning of World War II: the champion of the remnants of Christian civilization against the forces that threatened it." If the Americans were to shoulder this burden, they would have to understand it, and that meant understanding both history and the Judeo-Christian view of evil. "But most Americans had no more idea that there is a problem of history than that there is a problem of evil."[23] This they could now learn from Toynbee and from his theory of universal history as summarized in the magazine and available in bookstores in the shape of the two-volume condensation of *A Study of History* that had just been released in America.

Toynbee's theory, in effect, was Spengler plus facts and a dash of religious hope. The German thinker had mechanistically allotted a thousand years to each civilization. As his title indicated, he had also concentrated largely on the West, which he described in philosophical and psychological terms rather than through an interpretation of political and cultural history. Toynbee shared two basic intuitions with Spengler. First, that civilizations had real existence, that they were, in fact, the "smallest intelligible units of study" in human affairs. This meant that one could not make sense of political or any other history unless one understood the nature of the civilization to which that history belonged. Second, that civilizations rose and fell, and that it was possible to detect, in all civilizations, the forces of creation and destruction, which were analogous across time and space. Toynbee spoke respectfully of Spengler, but always denied that he owed his theory to him. According to Toynbee, he gained his basic insight into the laws of history when World War I broke out in 1914, years before Spengler published his book. What Toynbee realized as that war began was that he was witnessing the analogy in Western civilization to what happened to ancient Greek civilization in 431 B.C., when the Peloponnesian War between Athens and Sparta opened. Just as the Peloponnesian War marked the beginning of the Time of Troubles of ancient civilization and the end of its golden age, so, in 1914, the war that was then beginning marked the beginning of the West's Time of Troubles and the end of its most creative era. Toynbee did not mention that it was a German historian, Otto Seeck, who had speculated in 1898 that the Peloponnesian War marked the fatal turn to decline in ancient civilization; but even if he had acknowledged borrowing that part of his idea from Seeck, the notion that the West and antiquity were at the same point of their cycles, that the experience of Europeans in 1914 was in some fundamental sense the same as the experience of Greeks in 431 B.C., was his original contribution.

When Toynbee visited America in 1947 and was put on the cover of *Time*, he was almost done with his great project. In the course of it, he had developed concepts and phrases that historians continued to use long after most of them derided and neglected his work. One was the idea of the Creative Minority; the idea that every civilization owed its rise and its particular kind of excellence to a few gifted and often marginal individuals and groups. Another was the notion of Challenge and Response, the idea that a civilization at some point in its early history was spurred to progress and growth by challenge; that societies that enjoyed too easy a natural or a human environment failed to produce great civilizations. Conversely, if the natural or human challenges were too daunting, as for example in the Arctic regions, the human groups living there would be completely occupied in meeting those challenges and would also not be able to develop civilization. The challenge had to be just right, no more, no less, to evoke the creative response. A third notion was that of the Internal Proletariat, the idea that an advanced civilization, after its Time of Troubles, took the political form of a universal state encompassing most of the societies that comprised it. Within such a universal state, large numbers of people would be alienated from the civilization economically and culturally; these groups formed the Internal Proletariat. They were always a sign that the civilization was nearing its end, and their descendants would often constitute the Creative Minority of the next, or daughter, civilization; thus, the Christians were an Internal Proletariat in the Roman Empire but became the Creative Minority of the daughter civilization of the West.

If Toynbee had maintained his initial, rigorous pessimism about the West there would have been little mileage in his theories for Luce or Chambers. However, Toynbee had, as he wrote, become increasingly religious, in a generally but not doctrinally precise Christian sense. In the second half of his *Study*, therefore, he revised his original insight of 1914. The civilizations existing in the world of the twentieth century, he said, including the West, might not be destined to die as had their predecessors. The key to survival was religion. As the voice of God on earth, religions were not bound by civilizational life cycles. If the peoples of the world would turn to religion and realize their ultimate unity in God, they might then be able to overcome the death sentence of history and produce a world culture without the disruptions and evils that would normally await them in their Time of Troubles.

This was what appealed to Henry Luce, who believed that "man could collaborate with God in his own evolution towards higher stages of life on earth, towards an approximation of the City of Man to the City of God."[24] But neither Luce nor Chambers had read Toynbee carefully if they thought that he looked to America and to American Christians as the people who would lead humankind out of the trap of history and into a universal and immortal civilization. Toynbee, increasingly as he grew older, criticized America strongly; in 1967, he stated in *Playboy* magazine that "Madison Avenue is more of a danger to the West than Communism."[25] The major challenge of world politics, he believed, was to give satisfaction to the poor and exploited nations of the world, and this meant a change of heart in the West.

Toynbee represented a different kind of anti-Americanism than the pro-Soviet "children of the French Revolution" in either America or Europe. Like them, he believed that a decent West excluded American capitalism; but unlike them, he did not believe it implied a Marxist logic of history; rather, he hoped that a European West could survive, a sort of "third position" between both American capitalism and Soviet communism. This idea of a third position or a third way was a dominant thread of political and cultural thought in Europe throughout the twentieth century, nor did it wither after the Cold War and the collapse of Marxist regimes. It had a conservative, religious variant, as in Toynbee, and a social democratic political variant in the policies and beliefs of the millions who voted for social democratic parties and welfare state policies on the grounds that such policies undermined the appeal of communism and helped create a more egalitarian Europe, offering precisely a third option. On the left, the idea of the third way merged into the philo-Soviet and antifascist mindset; on the right, it merged into conservative and religious ideas that were often not only anti-American but antidemocratic.

Many people who were not as critical of capitalism as Toynbee appreciated the fundamental liberal intuition that ordered liberty and economic freedom were symbiotically linked, and that the art of Western liberty was to prevent either of the two poles from dominating: if the economic pole dominated, a society risked the bourgeois pathology, turning everything into a commodity, encouraging greed and speculation, and making chrematistical economic activity the yardstick of social purpose rather than a means to other ends. If the pole of personal liberty dominated, it would encourage hedonism, license, and irresponsible selfishness. The moral of both the ancient synthesis in the time of Christendom and of modern synthesis in the age of liberalism was to maintain the balance, not to push any of the elements to an extreme. Between the aesthetic anticapitalists like Toynbee and the political "children of the French Revolution" like Sartre there stood, in the 1950s and 1960s, a group of sceptical liberals who wanted to rescue the moral core of liberalism from revolutionaries and anticapitalists, but also from individualists and hedonists. One such was the Spanish philosopher José Ortega y Gasset.

Ortega's political philosophy was existentialist and decisionist, but in an optimistic and liberal mode wholly different from that of Jacobin moralists like Sartre or interwar nihilists like Spengler. It was different, also, from much of his own earlier thought. In the 1930s, in his best-known work, *Rebellion of the Masses*, Ortega took a somber and pessimistic view of the rise of the masses to political influence and control in the Western world. His analysis in that work was Tocqueville with the hope left out: mass society ran the risk of dictatorship and collectivism, and these dangers could be restrained only where the elite remained liberal. But he gave few grounds for hope that this would be the case, nor could he explain why Western elites ought to remain liberal.

The postwar Ortega had strengthened his faith in democratic society, but his epistemology was the same as before. The only source of knowledge available to man, Ortega held, was historical. We could know who we were only by reflecting on our past, our emergence, and what knowledge experience gave us of our capabilities, hopes, and dangers. Life could not be known in its entirety either by revelation or logic. It could be known only partially in the light of "historical reason." One of Ortega's favorite principles was that "man has no nature, only history," and that "in order to understand something human, whether it be personal or collective, it is necessary to tell a story."[26]

The difference between the earlier and the later Ortega was that the earlier thought that this undefined nature of man, this absence of reliable knowledge in human life, was a temptation to ideology, because the masses could not live with uncertainty. The later Ortega turned the weakness into a strength. The existential uncertainty of human life and knowledge became, in the 1950s, the reason that liberalism was the only possible political doctrine compatible with peace, progress, and the greatest happiness of the greatest number. Still, even the optimistic Ortega retained some fear of the masses; his liberalism was meritocratic. But, all told, it was a philosophy that eminently suited the early phase of the Cold War West. It turned out to be a transitory and brief period, in which the facade of international and domestic harmony concealed internal contradictions, the most important one being the contradiction between expanding mass higher education and the use some of the educated would make of their knowledge.

Another characteristic product of the post-1945 wave of liberal, philosophical reflection on the West was the series of books entitled "World Perspectives," edited by a multicultural board that included natural and social scientists, philosophers, and religious leaders. In a number of short works of what the French called *haute vulgarisation*, leading political, religious, and scientific practitioners and thinkers exemplified the cautiously optimistic liberal and progressive world view of the era. One of the works included in this series was a book by Denis de Rougemont on "the intellectual adventure of Western man," in which the Swiss philosopher of love and federalism explained the West in Weberian terms as the state of mind, the character, and the achievements in science, technology, politics, and art of a certain kind of person. This kind of person was one who sought adventure and change, driven by a "fundamental restlessness" and by the need "to run ever greater risks, always putting in question acquired certainties and securities." Rougemont declared that the West had no particular origin, no Magic Moment, but was rather the result of certain "fundamental choices, both initial and final, which determine the kind of adventure or Quest which a certain human group engages in." Every choice defined the future problems to be solved in politics or science, and thereby defined also what would count as solutions.

Rougemont popularized Max Weber's idea that the key to social change was personality type, that is, the question to ask of history was what kind of person emerged in a given society. He also, in his 1957 book, proposed an optimistic version of Spenglerian morphology. Ancient civilization had moved through a series of social, religious, and psychological stages from tribalism and magic through city-states and the Hellenistic era of aesthetic and philosophical individualism to the grand collective society of the empire. Analogously, medieval and modern Western civilization had moved from an age of religious faith and life in small groups through the Renaissance era of city-states, the individualism of the Enlightenment, and the collective movements of nationalism and revolution. In each of these stages, the human person, "the fundamental and specific category of the West," was tempted by a dialectic between two poles of understanding and action. In the stage of tribal or village society, for example, the dialectic was between the sacred and magic. In that of the city-state, the poles were the official worship of the community versus a purely secular focus on civic rights and virtues. The choice for the present, he concluded, was between totalitarian universal ideologies like communism and a federal world state that would balance personal liberty, community, and international peace.[27]

Standing a ways apart from these efforts in political pedagogy and social philosophy was a work that came at the end of the unitary phase of postwar political and international liberalism and reflection on the West. This was the Chicago historian William McNeill's summa of world history, *The Rise of the West*, subtitled *A History of the Human Community*. The title sounded chauvinistic to a later age, rather like the Durants' *Story of Civilization*. It was not meant to make a case, but to state a fact, namely, that the growing tendency of the past five hundred years had been Western dominance. As McNeill explained it in a retrospective essay published twenty-five years after the book:

> In retrospect it seems obvious that *The Rise of the West* should be seen as an expression of the postwar imperial mood in the United States. Its scope and conception is a form of intellectual imperialism, for it takes on the world as a whole, and it tries to understand global history on the basis of the concept of cultural diffusion developed among American anthropologists in the 1930s. In particular, *The Rise of the West* is built on the notion that the principal factor promoting historically significant social change is contact with strangers possessing new and unfamiliar skills. A corollary of this proposition is that centers of high skill (i.e., civilizations) tend to upset their neighbors by exposing them to attractive novelties. . . . .A second corollary of the proposition that contact with strangers is the major motor of historical change is that contacts among contemporaneous civilizations ought to be of key concern to a world historian.[28]

The reason that the West rose, McNeill argued, was the same reason that explained the rise and decline of other cultures. Sometime around 1500, the

West, largely because it had been good at borrowing others' skills, acquired a critical mass of technology, resource mobilization, and political control, which enabled it to influence others more than it was itself influenced; then, for the next five centuries, "the grain of world history" ran in a single direction. Like all powerful civilizations, the West destroyed as it rose, and the rise of the West brought losses as well as gains, by a wide variety of measures. McNeill also refrained from judging the future. That the West had grown in power, reach, and ability for the past centuries said nothing about the future; he was concerned to explain how the world of his own day emerged, not to recommend or predict its future fate. But McNeill was unapologetic about the course of world history, as he deduced it. The overall tendency of world history, he said, was "humankind's accumulated capacity to control the natural and social environment and shape it to our wishes. Profiting from such skills, as everyone constantly does, including the poorest populations alive today, we must, I think, admire those who pioneered the enterprise and treat the human adventure on earth as an amazing success story." That was written in 1988, when the intellectual climate in America and particularly in McNeill's profession of history was hostile to praise of the past, particularly the Western past. In 1963, his ringing conclusion to the original text was even more forthright:

> Men some centuries from now will surely look back upon our time as a golden age of unparalleled technical, intellectual, institutional, and perhaps even of artistic creativity. Life in Demosthenes' Athens, in Confucius' China, and in Mohammed's Arabia was violent, risky, and uncertain; hopes struggled with fears; greatness teetered perilously on the brim of disaster. We belong in this high company and should count ourselves fortunate to live in one of the great ages of the world.[29]

The "rise of the West," McNeill explained in 1963, was a reasonable shorthand description of the upshot of human history, for "the cosmopolitanism of the future will surely bear a Western imprint." This was because even if non-Westerners became globally dominant, "they could do so only by utilizing such originally Western traits as industrialism, science, and the public palliation of power through advocacy of one or other of the democratic political faiths."[30] One of the big questions of the 1990s and 2000s would be if this remained true—if modernization by means of industry, science, some form of popular sovereignty, and a market economy inevitably, sooner or later, entailed Westernization. If the West was no more than a set of instrumental methods of achieving political and economic power, then Westernization would indeed be universal, but would also mean very little, no more than that these methods had become dominant, and would imply nothing about the culture of the societies that adopted and used those methods. Such a narrow definition of the West struck many in the 1990s as inadequate, and is contrary to the entire thrust of this book, which is to argue that the West was more than its instruments, but was rather the nexus of religion, culture, passion, and mentality that created those instruments.

McNeill's reasoned optimism about world history as the growing control of the social and physical environment for human ends contrasted, in the 1950s and 1960s, with a type of despair about the prospects of liberal democracy that was in origin neither traditionally communist nor culturally anticapitalist. This despair was rather that of those who began as strong supporters of the American version of the New West but concluded that it could not stay the distance, that it was destined to succumb to the democratic despotism that Tocqueville warned against. The paradigmatic example was that of the American social philosopher James Burnham. His fate included the added twist that he came, originally, out of communism, not the orthodox Leninist variety but that of Leon Trotsky, who stressed the role of the organized, revolutionary will in forcing change, and who preached permanent revolution, a constant churning of creative destruction, which would raise postrevolutionary humanity to peaks of genius and power never before seen. Though Burnham abandoned Marxism as a political doctrine in the 1930s, he retained from it a grasp of the vast movements of history and the deep dynamics of social and cultural change that gave his works in defense of the liberal West a peculiar urgency—he had been the enemy and knew his strength and his unremitting determination to win. In 1941, Burnham published *The Managerial Revolution*, which predicted that power would lie with societies that learned to command the skills of mobilizing creativity. In 1950, he predicted the defeat of communism in the global struggle, giving capitalist liberalism the edge in the ability to mobilize resources. By 1963, however, in *Suicide of the West*, Burnham arrived at a pessimistic diagnosis, derived from that of Tocqueville's final chapters in *Democracy in America*, but without the coda that left fate to human desire and free will. "Liberalism," Burnham stated, "is the ideology of Western suicide." Why? Because liberalism presented a false idea of human nature as good and of all social problems as the result of ignorance or prejudice. To this, liberalism added guilt—a common human feeling, but one for which liberalism had no religious solution. Therefore, it adopted political solutions. Liberalism's false anthropology, combined with its use of guilt, led it to propound supposedly universalist values of peace, equal rights, and justice. But in reality, Burnham argued, the global universalism of peace and justice meant the suicide of the West, the inevitable contraction of Western power that began in 1914 and that, so he predicted, would end in Western self-annihilation by the end of the twentieth century. The critical moment would come when the United States surrendered completely to liberalism, a process already far advanced in his own time. Once America had succumbed, the rest of the West would soon follow.

Liberal societies, then, lacked the lung power for the deep breath and the long haul, where communism, inured to poverty and suffering, had the decisive advantage. Burdened by guilt and by a false view of human nature, "liberalism is not equipped to meet and overcome the actual challenges confronting Western civilization in our time."[31] And Burnham borrowed another key idea from Tocqueville and the other nineteenth-century diagnosticians—that democratic liberalism undermined the heroic virtues and the heroic idea of liberty that alone could motivate great sacrifices, such as were needed to survive the communist onslaught. Even though communism offered no freedom and much misery, the greatest spirits would choose it because it gave history significance—as, according to him, liberal democracy could never do. Burnham thus ended in despair, for he was an American patriot, and unlike Toynbee he understood the logic of civic virtue and productivity, property, and freedom.

Burnham represented rational despair. Although the postwar decades were decades of technological optimism and faith in the value of science and scholarship, irrational despair, or at least irrationalist judgments against the West, had not died out. Many such ideas only blossomed back into mass popularity after the rise of irrationalism and the various New Age movements from the 1960s on. But it was a mistake to suppose that these movements came from nowhere. Their roots were in the late-nineteenth-century soil of mysticism, theosophy, and occult political philosophy fertilized by the more enthusiastic followers of Richard Wagner and by many others, especially but not exclusively in Central Europe, who wanted to cut through secularism and liberalism to a new birth of a post-Christian and yet at the same time atavistic faith.

For example, starting in 1977, the *Star Wars* film saga broadcast a popular mythology of heroism, growth, light and dark sides, wise old men, and evil tempters concocted by the California filmmaker George Lucas. Much of the inspiration came from the teachings of Joseph Campbell, a comparative mythologist whose inspiration went back to Oswald Spengler and other early-twentieth-century irrationalists, and whose best-known work was *The Hero With a Thousand Faces*, published in 1949. The argument of this book was that the great stories of all cultures were not dead and lifeless, but were being reenacted daily in modern society, because they were not simply stories but representations and explanations of what it meant to be human, to grow up, to become who one was. The source of myth, and this point was crucial, was not some external, divine, or supernatural reality, but the human psyche. All myths, including Christianity, were stories created by and describing ourselves. "The 'monstrous, irrational and unnatural' motifs of folktale and myth are derived from the reservoirs of dream and vision," Campbell wrote around this time. "But clarified of personal distortions and profounded—by poets, prophets, visionaries—they become symbolic of the spiritual norm for Man the Microcosm. *Mythology is psychology*, misread as cosmology, history and biography. Dante, Aquinas and Augustine, al-Ghazali and Mahomet, Zarathustra, Shankârachârya, Nâgâryuna, and T'ai Tsung, were not bad scientists making misstatements about the weather, or neurotics reading dreams into the stars, but masters of the human spirit teaching a wisdom of life and death."[32]

Campbell had rejected his cradle Catholicism in favor of a transcendental cult of the human truth in all mythology. He wrote in 1955 that "clearly Christianity is opposed fundamentally and intrinsically to everything I am working and living for."[33] The problem with Christianity, as Campbell put it, was that it separated consciousness from "the root of the soul." This attitude, as well as the belief that mythology and psychology were coextensive, derived from Carl Gustav Jung, the second most influential psychologist of the twentieth century and a man who, in Richard Noll's sensationalized account, invented for himself and his followers a neopagan, polygamist religion of which he was the demiurge or "Aryan Christ." In his published work, Jung, unlike Campbell, was careful to remain distantly respectful of Christianity. Noll suggested that Jung developed his psychological theories as the outerworks of his own, new religion, one purpose of which was to liberate the psychic forces repressed by Christianity and bourgeois society, and another to redeem God, that is, to rescue God from his Judeo-Christian distortions. "He regarded his life as a mission, to serve the function of making God conscious," wrote one of his collaborators. "He had to help God to make himself conscious, and not for our own sake, but for the sake of God." According to his English translator, the psychologist Richard Hull, "everything vital and creative came to him out of the depths of his pagan unconscious." Noll concluded about Jung "that, as an individual, he ranks with the Roman emperor Julian the Apostate (fourth century C.E.) as one who significantly undermined orthodox Christianity and restored the polytheism of the Hellenistic world in Western civilization."[34]

Noll relied on a text from 1916 in which Jung himself supposedly announced his new religion. However, another scholar, Sonu Shamdasani, showed that this document was not written or inspired by Jung and argued that so far from launching a new cult, what Jung wanted was to understand the psychology of existing cults and religions.[35] This discovery fatally weakened Noll's case, which henceforth rested on anecdotes about Jung's personal beliefs and behavior at a particular stage in his life, on scattered evidence from some of his followers that his mythology-based methods and interpretations amounted to a new faith, or on unwarranted extrapolations from some of Jung's own esoteric writings.

Those writings were not those of an orthodox Christian, as many before Noll had realized. For example, in that same year of 1916, Jung wrote a strange text that he called "The Seven Sermons to the Dead." It began with the words "The dead came back from Jerusalem where they did not find what they sought. They asked me to let them in and begged me to teach them, and so I taught them."[36] If "Jerusalem" symbolized mainstream Judaism or Christianity, then one might read those words as saying that these traditional faiths were empty and vain. Jung, however, wrote the "Seven Sermons" not in his own name but in that of the second-century gnostic Basilides of Alexandria, "the city where the East touches the West." Noll disregarded this point, as he disregarded the fact that Jung, in his professional writings, which included works on alchemy, gnosticism, and astrology, as well as psychology conventionally understood, stressed that what he sought was not a system of belief but "a science of the soul." He came to believe that to understand the soul one had to understand all manifestations of the psyche in mythology and belief. Among the most important of such manifestations were alchemy, astrology, and gnosticism, all of which Jung understood as embodying traditional teachings about growth, change, and development—the fundamental conditions of human life and hence of human psychology. Jung's final word on Christianity, from an essay written in 1957, was that "in the present state of the world, it is not Christianity, but rather the way it has hitherto been conceived and understood that is antiquated. The Christian symbol is a living being that carries the seeds of further elaboration within itself."[37] Change and transformation were the destiny not only of individual human beings but of their faiths and beliefs, and it was to understanding the nature and process of such change that Jung devoted his life.

Joseph Campbell was for decades the channel by which a modified version of Jung's revision of all religion into mythology and psychology penetrated to the reading public. His was an interesting case, for even though in later life he found allies on the left, among the New Age heirs of Rousseau, his criticism of the bourgeois New West was not a typical example of liberal guilt for imperialism, colonialism, and oppression. He first turned against Christianity because he came to despise the purposes and practice of missionary activity, but his real grievance against both Christianity and the West was that they were spiritually empty, focused on materialism and fatally tempted by political power. Oswald Spengler had made a tremendous impact on the young Campbell, who found himself agreeing profoundly with Spengler's diagnosis of the Faustian West as concerned solely with physical power, scientific understanding, technology, and space. He equally admired what Spengler called the Magian cultures, which were concerned with the spiritual world, mythology, and an understanding based not on scientific method or technology but on access to higher realities. Magian cultures were places where people knew that beyond the natural, material, observable plane of existence there were at least two others: that of ultimate reality, God, or the life force, and an intermediary plane where the characters and forces of myth and legend existed and from which they influenced or controlled the material plane.

From Spengler, whom he "spent two years reading," Campbell also drew the idea that the fate of cultures was determined and irrevocable. Because the Faustian West was obsessed with the material plane and with power over external reality, it was by that same drive doomed to sterility, which was another word for decline. "These things proceed like glaciers," Campbell said in conversation in the 1980s. "These cultural events go mathematically, there's nothing you can change about them, and once the three Caesars have appeared, everything goes downhill in an absolute genuine and clear way and it's all laid out." Who were "the three Caesars?" Emblematic figures who appeared at a certain point in the determined cycle of ancient and of Western civilization, evidently, and their appearance was the visible sign of the end time approaching. In the West, the three Caesars were "Hitler, Mussolini, and Franklin Delano Roosevelt." And "once the three Caesars have appeared there's no sense in doing a political act, it makes no sense at all. Don't waste your time, because everything is disintegrating."[38]

In 1940, when he suspected that Roosevelt was plotting to bring America into the war against Germany, he gave a talk at Sarah Lawrence College, where he taught, on "Permanent Human Values." These were endangered by the passions of war. Nationalism and self-righteousness threatened the world of scholarship, and more than that: the political passions of the age made it hard to remember that "permanent things . . . are not possessed exclusively by the democracies; not exclusively even by the Western world." When American academics defined the war as one "between beasts and human beings," Campbell was enraged, because he knew that Western nations were themselves founded on bestial brutality. He praised the disinterested work of scientists and historians, which must continue despite war and across the political divide separating the democracies from their enemies. He denounced the capture of religion by political passion: "the ministers of religion are always, always, always ready to deliver God into the hands of their king or their president. We hear of it already—this arm-in-arm blood brotherhood of democracy and Christianity." Let us, he concluded in tones of Spenglerian Schadenfreude that his young female hearers probably missed, not worry if, in this war, "Europe and America were to be blown away entirely." Because there would still be many good "subtly disciplined human beings—who might even feel relieved to see us go!"[39]

Campbell was impatient with leftists, but shared many of their anticapitalist and anti-Christian prejudices. His anti-Westernism was of the Toynbee variety, inspired by Spengler, fed with irritation at American smugness and self-satisfaction, and enriched with a substantial dose of glee at the imminent prospect of Western self-destruction. Also like Toynbee, he increasingly found spirituality and wisdom outside the West, reducing Western mythology to a poor relation tainted by the political and colonialist misdeeds of Western conquistadors, capitalists, and missionaries.

New Age and the myth-cult of Campbell were odd bedfellows. New Agers typically saw themselves as heirs of the liberationist and self-realizing youth movement symbolized by 1968, or perhaps more accurately by the summer of love in 1967. Politically, these people were on the side of Rousseau and the Jacobins, desiring to heal the hurt in their souls and in that of society by recovering their true deep natures. Campbell served this interest by keeping silent about his youthful sympathies and digesting all the myths of humankind into a bland, easily digestible stew in which everything symbolized everything else, and everything contributed to the inner growth, maturation, and development of that sacred figure, the Great Modern Self. Serious students of myth and of Spengler and Jung, the two thinkers who gave Campbell most of his hints about how to analyze myths and modernity, realized that serious myth-cult was not compatible with the New Age generation's political preferences or for that matter with mainstream liberal democracy. Religion, myth, and the deep structures of the psyche were far more serious, interesting, and dangerous preoccupations than politics. Their content and meaning long predated liberalism and would long outlast it.

The second phase of the NATO, or Cold War, West was the phase of the Vietnam War and the intellectual and cultural upheavals symbolized by the events of 1968. When people spoke of these events, they meant, in the first instance, the demonstrations and upheavals led by university students in Paris, Frankfurt, Berlin, London, New York, and Berkeley, and on a number of university campuses that were not in large cities, such as Cornell University in upstate New York. Much more was happening than student demonstrations, however.

Western public opinion no longer thought much about the Cold War in 1968. Indeed, if one had asked, one would have been told that the Cold War had ended some years earlier, after the Cuban Missile Crisis of 1962. Within a year of that crisis, the United States and the Soviet Union had signed the Nuclear Test Ban Treaty, soon to be followed by a treaty against proliferation of nuclear weapons to states that did not possess them, and then by the arms control negotiations that ended in the Strategic Arms Limitation Treaty of 1972. Also in 1963, a new political word, détente, began to be heard in policy and media circles in the West. The word literally meant "relaxing tension" and had been used by historians to describe periods of diplomatic history in which jaw-jaw, as Churchill said, prevailed over war-war. By the mid-1960s, it had spread beyond the ranks of historians to become a commonly used word to describe a particular state of relations between the superpowers in which talks of some kind were taking place and the presumption was that these would continue and that the rocket-rattling threats of the 1950s would no longer be used. "Détente" was held to have superseded "Cold War," a phrase used to describe the periods of heightened tension from 1947 to 1953 and from 1958 to 1962. The 1990s usage, which labeled the entire period from 1947 to 1989 as the Cold War, would have seemed incomprehensible to Western public opinion in the 1960s. That opinion ignored that for the Soviet Union, the Cold War had not ended—but one of the features of the post–Cold War feeling of the 1960s and the 1970s was that what the Soviet Union thought and did no longer mattered much to Western public opinion.

In this post–Cold War atmosphere of the 1960s, students, who had the leisure, and intellectuals, who had the desire, returned with fresh energy to the old antifascist, anticapitalist agenda of the 1930s and 1940s. One reason for the fresh energy was demographic. The rising inflow of young people to higher education that prompted the Columbia Contemporary Civilization course in 1919 was exceeded many times over starting in the 1950s and continuing in the 1960s. The number and proportion of college-age Americans was growing as was the proportion of those age cohorts attending college or university. A second reason was prosperity. The political West enjoyed from 1947 to 1973 a continuous rise in individual and family living standards. The 1990s image of this period as one of uninterrupted growth and wealth was false; there were recessions and many people in the 1960s were not, either by the standards of the day or of the 1990s, especially well off. But most people in the political West came to expect, and receive, both secure and rising incomes. To many, these goods came to seem virtual facts of nature; not least members of the 1968 generation itself often operated on the assumption that growth and, with it, new personal freedoms were automatic rights, not fragile and hard-earned achievements.

In America, the Vietnam War gave a particular impetus to the new antifascism, now often labeled anti-imperialist, liberationist, or simply anti-American. The Vietnam War, according to the left, showed the United States in its true colors as oppressor of nonwhite people and cynical supporter of client dictators. The rising student numbers, their self-confidence bred of prosperity, and the sympathy of the many veterans of progressive ideology among their teachers combined to produce a series of dramatic explosions, echelonned through a short decade from 1964 to 1972, in which the spring of 1968 was the high point.

In the fall of 1964, students at the University of California launched the Free Speech Movement, which, in hindsight, consisted of a series of extremely polite sit-ins in university buildings by neatly dressed young men and women in ties and skirts, all obediently listening to a couple of Bay Area Italian-Americans, Lawrence Ferlinghetti and Mario Savio, reciting what at the time passed for obscene poetry. In the fall of 1965, the torch of this hitherto well-bred rebellion passed to Berlin, where more well-dressed and short-haired students disrupted courses, mostly in political and social science, in protest against the Vietnam War. One reason that Berlin became one of the hot spots of university activism in these years was that West Berlin, as a city directly under Allied occupation and not administered by the West German government, was not subject to the German draft. Therefore, young West German men who wanted to avoid the draft went to West Berlin. The easiest way to live in West Berlin as a young man was to be a student, for in that case you were paid a stipend by the same West German government whose draft law you despised. Also, until the 1970s, admission to university in West Germany—including, for this purpose, West Berlin—was open to anyone who graduated from the German equivalent of high school. The university of West Berlin, the Free University, thus became a magnet for left-wing youth, a self-selected group of draft opposers who were also likely to oppose other aspects of the political West, such as NATO or the presence of American troops, which was especially obvious in Berlin.

Berlin quieted down a little after the spring semester of 1966, but a year later erupted again when police accidentally shot a student who was part of a mass demonstration against the shah of Iran, who was on a state visit to Germany. This was one of the very few deaths attributable to the university upheavals. For the rest of 1967, the social and political science faculties at Berlin were essentially out of commission. In the spring of 1968, student activism in Germany culminated, as it did in France, Britain, and the United States. From February to May 1968, the focus of events was Paris, where the more enthusiastic students saw the chance of a broad alliance of students and workers against the "total authoritarian state" that they had been taught to detect under the camouflage of liberal democracy. The idea that students and workers—two mythical entities—had identifiable common interests and that these common interests were revolutionary, progressive, and anti-capitalist was one of the most fruitful of the legends peddled by the Frankfurt school of Western Marxists, led by Max Horkheimer, Theodor Adorno, and Herbert Marcuse. These three Jewish intellectuals had emigrated from Frankfurt, where they ran a left-wing social science think tank in the 1920s and early 1930s, to the United States, from which Horkheimer and Adorno returned to Frankfurt in the 1950s. Observing that Western populations were becoming less rather than more revolutionary, and that prosperity was spreading, but at the same time holding fast to their progressive ideology of a better democracy beyond private property, the Frankfurters inspired a critical number of students and younger teachers with the heady idea that they were the intellectual and political vanguard of the long-delayed revolution in capitalist societies.

In May 1968, it seemed for a moment as though the alliance of students and workers was coming to pass. Student demonstrations, which at first demanded that the radical activist minority of students be given power to censor teaching, control appointments, and design the curricula, became general demonstrations against the government and the president, Charles de Gaulle. In late May, some of the leading trade union organizations called a general strike. De Gaulle left the capital and for over a day was nowhere to be found; it later appeared that he had gone to the French army in Germany to confer with its commander about using the army to restore order. In fact, the student-worker alliance was never close to success, for the most powerful trade union movement, that of the Communist party, refused to play along. De Gaulle returned without the army, the general strike collapsed, and the students went home on vacation.

In America, 1968 symbolized the rise to cultural power of the New Left. Before 1968, the totalitarian model of the Soviet Union defined Soviet hostility to the West as inevitable and normal. That model was largely accepted in American pedagogy and emphatically in American politics. After 1968, the primary question that Western elites asked was no longer, what is the Soviet Union like but what is wrong with America? The diffuse philo-communism and antifascism of the European intelligentsia mobilized into the New Left, invaded America, and put the Cold War West on the defensive. The New Left introduced to America the Jacobin and Marxist presumption that history pointed away from capitalist democracy and toward something better, more absolute, more perfect. To the New Left, the West became radically flawed, in need of drastic correction in favor of students, women, blacks, other minorities, oppressed peoples, or the environment. The question about the Soviet Union, which was in reality the question of how the West could survive, was relegated to the second rank and usually answered, by the New Left, with the doctrine of moral equivalence. Both sides were equally at fault, only the West was slightly more guilty; both were oppressive, America somewhat more so; both conducted violent and inhumane policies, mostly the Americans; and both, especially the United States, were a danger to world peace and to the hope for universal emancipation. The New Left was less interested in understanding the Soviet Union than in finding fault with America, and its fault finding followed the schema of the old progressive mindset of the 1930s and 1940s. Like its intellectual forebear, the New Left repudiated the notion that capitalism and liberty were mutually necessary, which had been the central principle and belief of the mainstream West from Montesquieu and Hume on.

The New Left differed from its forebear in that it rejected tradition and history more decisively, believing that tradition was not the avenue to insight and understanding, but a prison to be broken out of. Benjamin Barber, an American social historian of New Left persuasions, wrote that he hoped to found social cohesion by "forging a new art of politics capable of holding together and giving meaning to beings emancipated from the roots that once imprisoned their spirits even as it grounded their values."[40] He could nourish such a hope only if he understood roots as imprisoning, as rendering immature and dependent. The contrary view of tradition was that of the English Catholic writer and Old Westerner Gilbert Chesterton, who defined tradition as "the democracy of the dead." The New Left insisted on seeing roots as confining and rejected not only the Old Western triad of Christianity, Rome, and Germanic liberty, but also the New, for its inventors, from Locke and Montesquieu to the American Founders, understood themselves as the heirs of a long tradition and did not suppose that the liberties and the life chances that they cherished would long survive without respect for and critical obedience of tradition.

The 1968 generation did not take immediate power in any Western country. Nevertheless, the cultural revolution soon affected the policies of the political West. A symptom of this was that the ubiquitous Western civilization courses disappeared from American campuses or were subverted into something very different. Western elites in the 1970s and 1980s pursued a policy of appeasing the cultural revolution without ever agreeing entirely with it. One net result was that by the early 1980s, the liberal West was on the defensive, not just in American higher education but in American culture generally. Those who wished to define or defend the West swaddled their remarks in phrases designed to buy off hostile enemies: for example, that the West had previously been racist, sexist, and exploitative, but was now improving; or that the West invented science, modern medicine, and technologies of food production, but that these had any number of bad side effects; or that the West was prosperous, but that this prosperity came at the cost of the poor of the Third World or even the poor within the West itself.

One striking result of the cultural revolution in America was the redefinition of liberalism or, perhaps better, of liberals. In its late medieval origins, the word *liberal* used of a political or social persuasion described a person of broad views and generous instinct, someone who enjoyed life and who wanted to see others enjoy it. Soon after, in Machiavelli, the word first appeared with a political connotation: a liberal was someone who loved freedom. By the time of the French Revolution, liberal had acquired the additional meaning of being in favor of economic freedom and against crown or state control of economic activity. In this sense liberalism became the doctrine of political parties across Europe and America whose members feared and suspected any concentration of power and who supported and demanded freedom of trade, contract, and exchange.

What liberals wanted was autonomy of the individual, and it was the notion of autonomy and how to secure it that led to the divorce between American and European understandings of the term in the 1960s and to the reversal in its American definition. In Europe, liberal parties from the 1920s onward were overtaken on the left by socialists. No longer were the liberals the party of freedom, but the party of free markets and of capitalism, which socialists denounced as unfair. Liberal doctrine was on the defensive in Europe from the 1920s to the 1980s, not only because socialists seized the moral high ground of being in favor of ordinary people and of fairness, but also because liberalism was condemned by philosophers for being no more than its bourgeois pathology. If liberalism, as socialists said, only protected the freedom of the strong, then what use or moral value could liberalism have?

After 1945, liberal doctrines of trade, production, and social order influenced policy in most countries. In America, liberalism became a widely held doctrine, with the important difference that whereas European liberals sought autonomy through freedom from the state, American liberals sought to give their fellow citizens autonomy by using the power of the state to combat discrimination, poverty, and unfairness. By the 1960s, American liberalism was the name for economic policies of state subsidy, redistribution, and regulation of individual behavior that in Europe would have been called social democratic. But American liberalism was still the authentic descendant of the transatlantic Western liberal tradition, because its demand for autonomy rested on the belief that freedom was better than coercion; that the purpose of liberal policy was to set people free to be themselves, to exercise that freedom.

One clue to why American liberalism changed from a philosophy of minimal government to one of expansive government was that American liberalism was shedding the negative understanding of freedom as absence of coercion in favor of a positive—Hegelian and Marxist—understanding of freedom as self-realization. Nowhere was this shift more obvious than in the obsessive focus of American liberal political philosophy in the late twentieth century on the idea of rights. Where traditional liberals, from Montesquieu via Tocqueville to Friedrich von Hayek and Jean Baechler, discussed history and institutions, seeking to trace the logic and the psychology of self-reliance, productivity, and confidence to the nexus of political liberty and its protection of property, American liberal thinkers of the later twentieth century, such as John Rawls, Ronald Dworkin, Michael Sandel, or Amy Guttmann, discussed abstract principles of legal or political philosophy to arrive at the best possible, universally valid description of how equal rights for everyone squared with the equal liberty of everyone. Of these thinkers, Rawls was the most influential and was indeed regarded worldwide as the leading philosopher of universalist liberalism. But to a traditional liberal, Rawls's account of the good society was ahistorical, bloodless, and devoid of practical relevance. In fact, for a philosopher who claimed to present a political liberalism, Rawls was stunningly apolitical.

In his 1971 book, *A Theory of Justice*, Rawls argued that the best way to arrive at a universally valid set of ethical principles for a good society was to imagine yourself behind a "veil of ignorance." You had the task of devising the good society, but the veil of ignorance hid from you any knowledge of the status, income, rank, sex, age, or other material aspect of your existence in that society. How would you design it?

Rawls suggested that you would design it to allow maximum liberty to all to pursue their interests and values. This would result in inequality; and the one constraint you would want to impose was that the inequalities should always benefit the worst off; that is to say, inequalities would be allowed only if reducing them meant making the poorest worse off. An inequality that could be reduced by redistribution that benefited the poor must not be permitted.

This egalitarian obsession alone disqualified Rawls's ideas as liberal in any historically recognizable sense. Classical liberalism was not concerned with inequalities but with how to limit force, coercion, and the corrupting effect of governmental power and interest group politics. Montesquieu did not ask if the distribution of resources that resulted from the niches of liberty led to equality; of course it did not. He asked what were the political conditions that permitted people to use and multiply resources in the first place. The ability of a few to save and invest and become prosperous was the historical condition of many doing the same. The distributional result at any given moment in time of democratic government was never of primary concern to liberals—although most of them granted that in modern conditions of prosperity it was perfectly possible for governments to redistribute without imperiling the bases of prosperity.

But of such real-world phenomena there was no trace in Rawls. On the other hand, Rawls took his egalitarianism a step further than merely demanding redistribution of "unnecessary" inequalities. Since, he argued, personal attributes such as intelligence, a pleasant personality, or beauty, which might give you an advantage in social relations and hence in income, were not earned but given, they were not yours to exploit. Rather, social status and income acquired by means of such unearned attributes was not your own, but could justly be expropriated by the collective. Such an argument was not unfamiliar in the twentieth century; it was, however, a totalitarian argument and not a liberal one. The retroactive enrollment of John Rawls in the ranks of liberal thinkers was one of the mysteries of political debate in the later twentieth century.

Rawlsian collectivist liberalism, which dominated the academic and intellectual discussion of political philosophy in America from the 1970s on, was ahistorical and apolitical not only in its egalitarianism, but in its rationalist belief that people given a set of universally valid ethics would act according to it and never succumb to passion, irrationality, envy, or the desire for power. Such rationalism was incompatible with a historically informed liberalism that sought to trace the thread of liberty through the minefields of cruelty, violence, and passion that constituted human history. Constructing abstract models of an impossibly equal—and utterly oppressive—society was as far from the original endeavor of liberalism as might be imagined. The history of liberty in the West and as part of Western identity was not a list of bloodless models, but the slow spread of a set of practices and institutions, often threatened and destroyed, but always reappearing, which, out of the Old Western nexus, gradually yielded growing islands of liberty. These islands were not the fruit of abstract reflection by dry, dispassionate thinkers, but the result of political choices, particularly the choices of rulers who realized that in their own interests and in order to mobilize the resources of the societies under their control, they ought to protect and expand the niches of liberty, the rights and privileges of property, for doing so would benefit them—with resources, soldiers, wealth, and prestige. Liberty grew because it served the interests of power. That was the happy paradox of the West.

Rationalism, universalism, and ahistorical intellectualism were the besetting sins of academic liberalism after 1968. They led American political philosophy, and much American political practice, into a cul-de-sac from which the global revolutions of the 1980s and 1990s failed entirely to extract them. For the main American response to those revolutions was not to rediscover and reassert the virtues of the West, but to preach the same ahistorical universalism that had already proven unable to give an account of Western history. Or, worse, the American response was to preach a West defined as such an ahistorical universalism.

Not surprisingly, these new postliberal American liberals rejected the Grand Narrative of the West, which was in fact a story about how the West was born in Greece and matured through a series of stages to its most complete stage in American democracy. This old liberal story, for all its flaws and misplaced Magic Moments, was a confident story of progress and hope. The new liberals did not want to hear or tell a story of progress and hope, but—and here again they came to resemble European leftists—one of abstract principles to be enforced in some future never-never land of perfect liberty. In this, they resembled not so much the historically robust older liberals, but the anticapitalist progressives of interwar and postwar Europe, the children of the French Revolution, who believed that genuine democracy could be realized only beyond the historical conditions that had accompanied the only real democracy the world would ever know—Christianity and the private property of capitalism.

Liberalism thus found itself in the 1980s in the peculiar position of not wanting to explain, and not being able to explain, either liberty or the identity of the West, even while liberty won global victories and a historical account of Western identity was more necessary than ever. This predicament was not due only to liberals. Since the 1960s, they had had to defend a shrinking legitimacy against the antinarratives of feminists, multiculturalists, environmentalists, and others who argued—in the spirit of the progressive ideology—that the West was flawed and inadequate, carried a heavy burden of historical guilt, and could redeem itself only by shedding all its historical identity and becoming something new, shining, universalist, and abstract, a set of ethical principles useful to all and every new ideology.

CHAPTER ELEVEN

Battle in the Heartland

Slowly the sun fell from the sky down into the West. A smoke
seemed to rise up and darken the sun's disc to the hue of blood,
as if it had kindled the grass as it passed down under the rim
of the earth.

   "I see a great smoke," said Legolas. "What may that be?"

   "Battle and war!" said Gandalf. "Ride on!"

   —J.R.R. Tolkien

Postmodernism is nothing other than a sign of retreat of a
sickly Western civilization

   —Bassam Tibi

For the West, especially the United States, the issue is whether
the time has come to stress the shoring up of shared values
and to set some new limits on autonomy

   —Amitai Etzioni

Some time in the gray dusk of November 9, 1989, a group of angry and
confused men in the communist sector of Berlin made, by accident,
a fateful decision. These men were senior members of the German
Communist party, officially known as the Socialist Unity Party of Germany.
The men, and a few women, who controlled this party had also, for exactly
forty years, run their own state, the so-called German Democratic Republic.

They had individually and collectively derived great benefits from this operation. As absolute rulers of sixteen million subjects, the party chiefs controlled everyone's work and movements and, through a vast network of full- or part-time informers, sought detailed knowledge of everyone's private thoughts, habits, and opinions. In particular, the party chiefs controlled economic and personal contacts with the West. Thanks to this control, the communist chiefs were able to skim off substantial amounts of hard currency and to finance a style of life unavailable to even the most hard-working of their subjects, though by no means extravagant by the standards of rich people in West Germany, much less the United States.

By the late 1980s, collecting hard currency had become the main purpose of power for the German communists. As the Soviet Union itself began to question its totalitarian past and to move toward liberalization, the frontline German communists found themselves engaged in a race with time; their task now being to convince the West to continue giving them money. They had two sources of money: the second-rate goods their forty-year-old economy produced and the ransom money they were able to extort by the simple means of putting dissidents and imaginary dissidents in jail and then waiting for a softhearted West German government to pay generous ransoms in hard currency. This trade in people provided the East German party chiefs with a reliable supply of hard currency without requiring any productive input. In that sense it was the ideal form of communist economy.

But in November 1989 they knew that this lucrative game was likely to have a short life. Mikhail Gorbachev, their Soviet colleague, had told them so the week before. Gorbachev was engaged on a desperate, flailing gamble of his own to save Soviet communism by giving it a human face and hoping the Cold War West would thank him by rescuing the communist system from its self-inflicted economic catastrophes. In Gorbachev's disillusioned, mercenary perspective, East Germany was no longer, as it had been in the days of the true Cold War, a bastion of offensive weaponry and propaganda directed against Western public opinion and Western military strategists. Rather, East Germany was an asset, a piece of strategic real estate that Gorbachev could exchange for lots of cold cash.

The Germans of East Germany, sensing change without realizing its direction, were weekly on the streets demanding democracy and human rights. The party chiefs were in a bind. If they fell back on standard communist practice from the past and let their tanks and machine guns decimate the demonstrators, Gorbachev might not like it, because it would spoil his careful game of looking good to the West. And because Gorbachev would object to a hard line, so would Western governments, who, at the time, regarded Gorbachev with little short of adulation. If, therefore, the German communists let the tanks roll, they faced not just verbal censure, which they could ignore, but an end to hard currency transfers, which they could not.

The party chiefs meeting in Berlin in that November twilight discussed these questions for some time, aimlessly, until one of them suggested that lifting the ban on East Germans leaving East Germany might take some of the pressure off the popular discontent. It had been twenty-eight years since the communists raised the wall that split Berlin and stopped individual movements from the communist to the democratic sectors of the city. No one had any inkling what it would mean to lift the ban. The party chiefs thought that they could lift it partially and temporarily. Having no experience with partially open borders, they did not realize that letting their subjects out was not like letting steam out of a pressure cooker; it was like lighting the fuse under their own hitherto unshaken power.

So it was with some vague idea of shoring up their own legitimacy—not something they had felt they needed before—and gaining some popular support, as well as time, that they called a press conference on the political situation in the GDR, which was transmitted live on official television. At exactly 6:53 P.M. Central European Time, one of the members of the Politburo, the executive organ of the party, read out a hastily prepared statement allowing any citizen of the German Democratic Republic to leave the communist state without prior authorization or permits. Until that moment, only certain categories of people, mostly pensioners who cost the state money, had been allowed to leave. Now, all would be allowed to leave, without prior clearance. "When will these rules take effect?" someone asked. "At once, immediately," replied the spokesman.

As soon as the Berliners heard these magical words, they began streaming in their thousands to the checkpoints and to the Wall itself. By midnight they were dancing atop the Wall in front of the Brandenburg Gate and clogging the main streets of West Berlin, and still the East Berlin guards kept quiet. At that moment, the Cold War ended, even in its extended form, and, though it staggered on for almost another year, so did the communist regime of East Germany. Barely two years after the communist chiefs of Germany inadvertently hastened their own retirement, the Soviet Union, too, was gone.

The end of the extended Cold War removed the Iron Curtain as the physical symbol of an artificial East-West line imposed across Europe by the Soviet Union in 1945 and accepted by the Western allies. The West, riven for two decades or more by internal dissent and confusion of purpose and identity, found itself in the unexpected position of seeming to have won the secular conflict with its former ally and later adversary, the Soviet Union. The internal critics of the West were temporarily silent; instead, the neo-optimists and universalists stepped confidently forward, announcing that the Cold War was indeed a victory for the West; that the West consisted of democracy and capitalism, or free markets; and that these practices, and therefore the West, were destined to be universal, all-powerful, and without rival as the organizing principles of a new world order.

The universalists dominated the worlds of policy-making and the economy; in the media, universities, churches, and other opinion-making institutions, they never held the high ground. The liberal West that won the Cold War was divided about itself, its legitimacy, and its identity. Indeed, the failure of liberalism, in its late-twentieth-century version, in its apparent hour of victory was the most striking ideological and political fact of the 1990s in the West. The changes that took place in Central and eastern Europe starting in 1989 marked the transition, in the history of the West after 1945, to a new phase. The first phase, which ran until 1968, was the heyday of the centrist liberalism of the Grand Narrative and of the NATO West. The second, which replaced the first around 1968, was the era of cultural and social conflict, in which antinarratives about the West began to replace the standard story and propelled its liberal defenders to various fallback positions, which could all be described as "appeasement liberalism." Starting in 1989, a paradoxical situation began to emerge: in the former communist countries, liberal democratic ideas of a rather old-fashioned stamp, which would have been recognizable to Tocqueville and Montesquieu—especially the ideas about division of power—won broad acceptance. But in America, and to a lesser degree in Western Europe, the antinarratives and other expressions of profound self-doubt strengthened their grip on the culture. Appeasement liberals who, in the twenty years since the late 1960s, had conceded point after point to the critics—about the innate racism, sexism, and environmental rapacity of the West, for example—now gave in and joined their opponents. Martin Bernal, Kirkpatrick Sale, and the curriculum activists on many campuses found that they had few energetic enemies. Their critical story of the West permeated and largely replaced the hollowed-out Grand Narrative in short order.

The argument of this book is that the idea of the West embodied in the Grand Narrative and its centrist liberal underpinnings was partial and inadequate. It raised the great books and ideas of the West onto a pedestal from which it was all too easy to pull them down. In trying to ignore history, it fell victim to it in the shape of the antinarratives, all of which shared one basic claim—that they were telling unpleasant truths concealed by the Grand Narrative's defensive ideology of white male privilege. And so, in a sense, they were. The Grand Narrative was bad history because it created an artificial, ahistorical identity of the West that could not stand up to serious assault.

In that perspective, the paradox of the 1990s was that the new democrats in the former communist states were recovering an older liberalism that had not forgotten its history, in particular the fact that liberty was always relative, limited, and contested, and needed to be nourished in the face of power and interests, while in the West itself, the liberals had turned their backs on history in the pursuit of universalism. Against the ideological attacks of the antinarratives, the appeasement liberals had two choices. One was to join the critics. The other was to try to run even faster away from history and to construct, out of the ruins of centrist liberalism, a new, optimistic universalism. This new universalism accepted much of the radical attacks but said, in effect, that the attacks were now irrelevant, because the point was to enforce a global order of democratic values, which could be done without risk of infection by the bad history of the West. For much of the 1990s, this universalist solution to the liberal loss of nerve was both popular—especially in American policy-making circles—and seemingly effective. But it could not last, for it had not cured, but exacerbated, the great weakness of its centrist ancestor, namely, the lack of history, in particular, the link from the New to the Old West. Neo-optimist universalism thus became not universal at all, but merely one, and not the most convincing, of a series of proposals about the future of world order. Its etiolated, bloodless version of the West as universalist democratic values and universalist free markets represented not a new, viable Western identity, but the final abrogation of any such identity. And by this departure from the ground of history into the thin air of incantatory ideology, the universalist idea of the West ironically deprived itself of any real ability to defend either of its two alleged values—democracy and capitalism. For they were not universalist but fruits of Western history and identity, and if they were to survive and spread—especially in non-Western cultures—they could not be handed out as culture-free packages, but needed to be recovered and understood.

The cultural landscape of the 1990s thus presented an efflorescence of various versions and narratives of the West, ranging from the universalist to conservative arguments—derived, in most cases, from Spengler and

Toynbee—to the effect that, since the West had become technocratic and universalist, it no longer had a future. What was missing from the public arena was a strong and confident reassertion of the main line of Western identity, the line that led from heroic freedom, through holy war, discovery, and conquest to democracy and capitalism, understood not as magic solvents of culture, but as the core legacy of the Old West to the New.

The arguments in play in the 1990s could be divided into four teams, each occupying a corner of the contested arena. The first team was that of the optimistic universalists, who took the Grand Narrative's ahistorical West several steps further. The second was that of the postmaterialists and postmodernists, who were not especially impressed with Western science, democracy, or capitalism, but who predicted their own variety of pluralistic universalism. Team three was the communitarians, who wanted to have their universalist cake and eat it too, for they warned that liberalism had overreached itself in its individualism and hedonism, but refused to return to the Old West to find the rules of order that they admitted were desirable. Finally, in the fourth corner were the critics and enemies of the liberal West who thought, in the manner of Spengler, that it had exhausted itself, as well as those who thought that its only possible future was that of a restored, authoritarian order. In this camp were found, notably, the environmentalists, a group that included both leftists with a postmodern bent and right-wingers who, in the manner of Toynbee, deplored the results of mass consumerism.

One of the clearest statements of the universalist view, which drew on both the sceptical and the radical Enlightenment, had been published a few months before the German communists opened the Berlin Wall. In his article "The End of History and the Last Man," the American policy analyst and political philosopher Francis Fukuyama presented a thesis that the events in Berlin seemed eminently to confirm. The thesis was that "liberal democracy may constitute the end point of mankind's ideological evolution and the final form of human government." Other forms of regime, such as Marxist socialism, "were characterized by grave defects and irrationalities that led to their eventual collapse," but liberal democracy, uniquely, was free of such basic contradictions. They might have problems, but these problems "were ones of incomplete implementation of the twin principles of liberty and equality on which modern democracy is founded." Therefore, "the *ideal* of liberal democracy could not be improved on."[1]

The reason the communists in Germany opened the Wall, if one followed Fukuyama, was that they had no choice. Their regime had reached the end of its economic as well as ideological tether. It had become nonviable, not just because Gorbachev had decided to sell out the GDR to the West, but be-cause the very fact that he chose such a course proved that he, and other communists with him, had lost confidence in their own doctrines and their own future. The opening of the Wall was merely the most dramatic of all demonstrations of the "enormous weaknesses at the core of the world's seem-ingly strong dictatorships." These dictatorships, whether communist, fascist, or merely militarist, seemed to dominate modern history from 1917 on. They convinced many people that the Enlightenment West of progress, whether in its liberal and American version or its Jacobin, French, collectivist, and social democratic version, was a limited and threatened enterprise, which was cer-tainly not destined to dominate the globe and which might well prove weaker than its totalitarian enemies. One of the Enlightenment West's major modifi-cations of the old Christendom version was the idea of progress or of History as a progress toward more liberty and more well-being, thanks to the synergy of technology and economic development. The antidemocratic regimes that dominated much of Europe and the world, starting with the Bolsheviks in 1917, had seemed to deny or pervert this story of democratic progress. They hijacked the notion of History, turning it into a doctrine of inevitable prole-tarian or Aryan domination and presenting the disheartened remnants of the Enlightenment with a ghastly caricature of their original, optimistic vision. By 1989, the presumption that these antidemocratic regimes were on the side of History emphatically no longer held. Did the end of the twentieth century, Fukuyama then asked, mark the return to "a coherent and directional History of mankind that will eventually lead the greater part of humanity to liberal democracy?"[2] His answer was yes; History was back, not as a partial or dis-torted tale but as a true story with a universal subject: humanity as a whole. As the century ended, Fukuyama held, the distortions were revealed as such, and the original democratic and capitalist direction of the story resurfaced.

Fukuyama gave two reasons for believing that History's true shape was benign, and that it was now reasserting itself. The first was the power of science, applied reason, the first leg of our modern triad of the West. "Modern natural science," Fukuyama argued, "is the only important social activity that by common consensus is both cumulative and directional, even if its ultimate impact on human happiness is ambiguous. The progressive conquest of nature made possible with the development of the scientific method in the sixteenth and seventeenth centuries has proceeded according to certain definite rules laid down not by man, but by nature and nature's laws."[3] Cumulative scientific knowledge permitted a vastly expanded range of technological invention and application. The latter in turn enabled industrial production and global communications, leading to the information and knowledge societies of the late twentieth century. Science, technology, and their economic effects were similar in every society, and necessary if a society wanted to industrialize and compete. They were thus one manifestation of a universal History.

But science and technology were only one proof of History. "The logic of modern science," Fukuyama said, "can explain a great deal about our world: why we residents of developed democracies are office workers rather than peasants eking out a living on the land, why we are members of labor unions or professional organizations rather than tribes or clans, why we obey the authority of a bureaucratic superior rather than a priest, why we are literate and speak a common national language." But in themselves, science, technology, and capitalist production were not the whole of History. The other aspect was the universal rise of liberal democracy, and this Fukuyama attributed to a universal human need for recognition. Plato in ancient Greece and the philosopher Hegel in the early nineteenth century were the two thinkers who had most clearly formulated this need. People, they said, sought

> recognition of their own worth, or of the people, things, or principles they invest with worth. The propensity to invest the self with a certain value, and to demand recognition for that value, is what in today's popular language we would call "self-esteem." The propensity to feel self-esteem arises out of the part of the soul called [by Plato] *thymos*. It is like an innate human sense of justice. People believe that they have a certain worth, and when other people treat them as though they are worth less than that, they experience the emotion of *anger*. Conversely, when people fail to live up to their own sense of worth, they feel *shame*, and when they are evaluated correctly in proportion to their worth, they feel *pride*. The desire for recognition, and the accompanying emotions of anger, shame, and pride are parts of the human personality critical to political life.[4]

Throughout history, and long before History became possible, people fought to achieve recognition. This was the main cause of wars, empires, and culture. The liberal and democratic revolutions of the late eighteenth century in America and France raised the struggle for recognition to a new and unprecedented level; they made it possible and desirable not just for a few, but for many to aspire to and fight for recognition. And the condition of this struggle for recognition in the democratic era was that it had to be a political, that is, a peaceful struggle, for wars and empires undermined the universal hope for recognition by restricting it to a few, something that the many, after the revolutions, no longer accepted. Now the great change of the later twentieth century, Fukuyama held, was that the History represented by science, technology, and economic development was merging with the History of democratic freedom launched by the revolutions, so that for the first time the human race as a whole could look forward to a collective, global History of liberty, underpinned by the material progress made possible by science, technology, and markets. The promise of this progress was in itself a force of tremendous political significance, for it tempted everyone to adopt similar behavior and strategies to gain a share in the prosperity that had become the sole criterion of political well-being and power. "The enormously productive and dynamic economic world created by advancing technology and the rational organization of labor has a tremendous homogenizing power. It is capable of linking different societies around the world physically through the creation of global markets, and . . . creates a very strong *predisposition* for all human societies to participate in it, while success in this participation requires the adoption of the principles of economic liberalism."[5]

The emerging History would be, as Immanuel Kant had suggested in the eighteenth century, a "Universal History from a cosmopolitan point of view." Moreover, as Kant also predicted, this "Universal History" would be one of societies governed increasingly according to liberal and democratic, or, as Kant called it, republican principles. These republics would be more concerned with wealth and knowledge than with war; their people would indeed come to realize that war was an inferior method of acquiring wealth, knowledge, or power. The liberal and democratic world would therefore also be a peaceful world. It would not necessarily be a more moral world. The thesis of the end of History in no way entailed a thesis of moral progress. "One can recognize the fact that modernity has permitted new scope for human evil," Fukuyama observed, "and yet continue to believe in the existence of a directional and coherent historical process."[6]

Fukuyama argued that liberal democracy was the end state of human political invention and that it faced no serious rivals as the starting point and the generally recognized ideal form of political organization, just as democratic and egalitarian behavior, however defined in particular cases, had become the obligatory mode of conduct of *homo democraticus*, the democratic human being, or more precisely, the democratic personality, who was no longer a Western species but one who would ultimately prevail across the globe. If this slow but inevitable spread of liberal politics and liberal values—liberal taken here in its classic sense of favoring autonomy, self-reliance, and tolerance— was really to take place, one might then say, sometime in the twenty-second or twenty-third century, that the world had become the West, or that the idea of the West had become meaningless because it would then be synonymous with the way the world lived, imagined, thought, built, and believed.

Spengler's end of the West would receive its most remarkable confutation, a confutation that would also be a confirmation. For his speculative chronicle of the future in many respects anticipated Fukuyama quite precisely, which was no surprise, since both drew on Hegel and Nietzsche for the substance of their idea that the end of history (or of the West) was a state of society in which no one any longer undertook outward, dramatic, conquering action, but rather contented themselves, as last men, with analysis, administration, technical advances, and therapy. True civilization, Nietzsche and Spengler held, required that life be limited by a horizon of beliefs, by some mental and spiritual rules by which the individual, to use Nietzsche's terms, endured the pain of life. The end of history would be the condition when the veils of culture could be torn away, leaving human life free of illusions, but this revelation would no longer be a threat, because the causes of pain would have been lost along with the beliefs. Reality would no longer be unendurable, but simply another set of facts to be acknowledged and assimilated.

The argument was more plausible than many critics wanted to accept, but it nevertheless rested on some premises that might not, in the twenty-first century, prove as solid and as durable as Fukuyama assumed. For example, the end of history depended on and in turn encouraged universal education and universal enlightenment, that is, a rational understanding of all things. "Modern education, that universal education that is absolutely crucial in preparing societies for the modern economic world, liberates men from their attachments to tradition and authority . . . That is why modern man is the *last* man: he has been jaded by the experience of history, and disabused of the possibility of direct experience of values."[7]

Within Fukuyama's Hegelian and Nietzschean scheme of political and psychological finality, such might well be the function and role of education. But what if the West chose, as had America, by some measures to dis-educate itself? It might well be true, as Fukuyama said, that modern education in the politics, culture, and history of the important nations of the world, in economics, in scientific method, and in information technology, was "crucial in preparing societies for the modern economic world." If he rested the end of history on the education levels of America, however, one was entitled to suspect that he, or his descendants, would have to wait a long time indeed; in fact one would have to say that, if being educated was a criterion, America was closer to the end of history in 1968 than in 1998.

The big change in the trajectory of education in America occurred when, over the decades since the late 1960s, those responsible decided that the purpose of education was no longer knowledge, competence, or cultural literacy but self-esteem. Such a change was what one would expect in a world of "last men" who, lacking sturdy virtues of their own, sought to recapture "the direct experience of values." To confer such experience, educators removed what they considered dry facts and information, things that were moreover corrupted by their Western and European origins and epistemology. Instead, experience, feeling good about oneself, and collective self-congratulation became the criteria of success. One saw this change not merely in schools and colleges but in, for example, the heritage industry exhaustively analyzed by the historian David Lowenthal. Heritage, as opposed to knowledge of history, fulfilled an emotional and psychological, rather than a cognitive function. By supposedly re-creating the past of particular groups, cultures, and peoples, heritage brought a faint shadow of "direct experience of values" to flickering life for the timid yet demanding "last men," while at the same time recreating a sense of solidarity, continuity, and tradition for people plagued, or so the litany went, by insecurity, change, and the never-ceasing challenges of late or postmodernity. But of course, as Lowenthal pointed out, "'experiencing' the past is not learning about the past. . . . Empathetic role-play and reenactment feed the illusion that heritage experience suffices to know the past."[8] It was, moreover, not clear how indulging in a false traditionalism geared wholly to confirming present-day prejudices, parochialism, and intolerance toward others could very well serve the educational needs defined by Fukuyama as essential for those who wanted both to maintain a rational understanding of their identity and to live and prosper in the global society of the twenty-first century.

The sabotage of American primary, secondary, and higher mass education by America's own elites was a story to itself. It impinged on the question of the West at the point where Fukuyama made the level of knowledge a critical variable in determining that liberal democracy was in the world to stay, to expand, and to become the final condition of all. If the West of the year 2000 included, at the minimum, the modern Western synthesis of reason, liberty, and prosperity, then the geopolitical center of the West, America, was in two minds about whether to stay Western.

At the end of his book, Fukuyama used the metaphor of the cultures and societies of the world as a series of wagons strung out in a long train, crossing plains and rivers and finally a narrow pass in the mountains, to arrive at the same ultimate destination. The farther from the pass, the more each driver would be able to believe that there were many destinations and many roads to each. Once through the pass and in sight of the city that was the final stop, each driver would find it hard, if not impossible, to deny the evidence of his eyes that he was indeed going in the same direction as all.

But to stay within the metaphor, what if a wagon party should decide, not to reverse direction, not to stop for an extended stay at trail side, but to get out of the wagon and begin deliberately to disable it, so that it could neither keep up with the others nor ever reach the town? Such seemed to be the insistent goal of many in the Western elites, either because they thought the wagon so robust that removing a few wheels would not impair its operation, or because they really despised the fellow members of their party and wished to strand them in the desert forever.

Critics of Fukuyama, misled by his title, claimed that the rise of nationalism, the fragmentation of states, and the many small or great conflicts that erupted after the Cold War disproved his thesis. History, they said, so far from ending, was resuming its erratic and purposeless course after the ideologies of the "short twentieth century" of 1914–91 had imposed their false schemes.[9] Their history was indeed over, but not that of wars and conflicts, which would continue forever. Nor, they argued, was there much evidence that liberal democracy was destined to be the universal type of political regime, and capitalism the universal form of economy.

At one level, these critics missed their target. Nothing that happened in the course of a few years could prove or disprove Fukuyama, who thought in centuries and millennia. At another level, they had a point, though it was not the point that many of them thought they were making. This point was whether Fukuyama, as a universalist, was right, not just about the world in general, but about the West. Even as liberalism and market economics won adherents across the globe, their value and legitimacy were challenged within the West by the powerful coalition of anti-Western Westerners who seized the cultural and, to some extent, the political hegemony in the decades after the symbolic year 1968. When the Cold War ended, the Cold War West had been for some time the scene of intense political struggle over the merits of the modern triad of science, democracy, and capitalism. This struggle was one reason to doubt Fukuyama's prognosis. Also, Fukuyama derived his analysis and predictions from his philosophical and psychological understanding of human nature. This understanding, the idea that people acted fundamentally to gain recognition from themselves and others, was certainly plausible. Likewise, Fukuyama's idea that the Universal History of humanity, driven by the struggle for recognition, was taking over again after the aberrations of ideology, was an advance over the old Grand Narrative. Yet something was missing—two things, in fact. One was that he did not make it clear whether democracy and capitalism adequately defined the West and whether their spread meant that the West, so defined, was becoming the universal civilization. The other was that, following Hegel and Nietzsche, he tagged the breakthrough to Universal History to the American and French Revolutions. But where did they come from? Were liberal democracy and market economics merely fortunate accidents that happened to appear, or were they more deeply grounded? If one could answer that question, one could also answer the broader question of the likely future fate of these arrangements, and their relation to the West.

Fukuyama's argument was primarily about social psychology under democratic and egalitarian conditions, and not an analysis of recent history or a diagnosis of future politics, though his theory had implications for both. His purpose was to explain why the liberal democratic synthesis of economic and technical progress would not be challenged by any fundamentally different political vision, such as communism or National Socialism.

In the second corner of the arena stood the postmaterialists and postmodernists. In their own way, they were also universalist, but they differed from Fukuyama in saying that the universal principle of culture and politics was that there were no longer any overarching principles, such as science, democracy, or capitalism.

Postmodernists saw America, and the West, as crossing from a modern era characterized by rationality, technology, and belief in Grand Narratives of history and culture to a postmodern era in which Grand Narratives had become unconvincing or illegitimate, in which the truth of theory was a matter of choice or rhetoric, and the Western triads, whether in the Christendom version or in that of classical liberalism, had lost their validity. Jean-François Lyotard, the best-known postmodernist, recommended in 1979 "scepticism towards all metanarratives." Metanarratives, or Grand Narratives, in Lyotard's definition, "are the supposedly universal, absolute or ultimate truths that are used to legitimize various projects, political or scientific. Examples are: the emancipation of humanity through that of the workers (Marx); the creation of wealth (Adam Smith); the evolution of life (Darwin); the dominance of the unconscious mind (Freud)."[10] The postmodernists were not merely uninterested in whether any one of these Grand Narratives was more true or just than the others, they denied that the question of truth had any meaning. By this means, they elided the distinction between the sceptical

Enlightenment's historical analysis of the West, which to them was merely another Grand Narrative, and the radical Enlightenment's political demands for change. All Grand Narratives, Lyotard held, had purely political purposes; none of them revealed more than any other about real history or real social evolution, which were meaningless notions. The Columbia model of the Grand Narrative of the West from the Greeks to modern liberalism seemed a good example of the kind of ideological construct that postmodernism condemned. But its fate was actually an ironic disproof of the postmodernist position that no history was more true or false than any other. The late liberal and multiculturalist heirs of the radical Enlightenment did not throw out the Columbia model of the Grand Narrative because there was no truth, but because they believed they had a higher and fairer truth than the allegedly Eurocentric and biased version of the Grand Narrative. That was not a postmodernist argument, but a highly moralistic modern argument. A further irony of the fate of the liberal Grand Narrative was that, as history, it was, as the radicals claimed, partial and inadequate, though not for the reasons they alleged—Eurocentrism and male chauvinism—but because it was an unhistorical representation of the West.

In postmodernism lurked the fear, or hope, that Western civilization and its emphasis on reason and liberalism had come, or was coming, to an end. Postmodernism, which was a word first used in the 1870s but which became widespread only in the 1970s, implied both fear and hope: "the negative feeling of coming after a creative age or, conversely, the positive feeling of transcending a negative ideology."[11] Starting as a critical term of architecture, art criticism, and literary theory, postmodernism spread to politics and culture, where it defined a vaguely voluntarist, subjectivist, and moralistic attitude. Although its adherents claimed that they rejected all existing political narratives, many of them denied this belief in their own behavior and opinions, which usually conformed to left-liberal progressivism, which was one of the narratives that postmodernism supposedly had undermined. Thus, according to Jacques Derrida, a leading light of postmodern theory, reason had been delegitimated by technology, for example, the atomic bomb, and tyranny, for example, the Holocaust. As a typical French intellectual of his generation, Derrida shared the antifascist mindset that refused to identify Hitler's Germany and Stalin's USSR as totalitarian, but rather attributed Hitler's evils to the West while holding Stalin to a lesser standard so as to save Marxism as a promise of redemption. Despite his claims to originality, Derrida was in fact deeply conventional in his fashionable mistrust of the sceptical Enlightenment West of science, democracy, and capitalism and his yearning for a radical change.

Postmodernists pretended to be the ultimate sceptics; in fact, most of the leading spokesmen of the movement were moralists in the tradition of Voltaire and Rousseau, thereby demonstrating that they were not postmodern at all, but consistently in the mainstream of one branch of modernity, that of the radical Enlightenment and its totalitarian heirs. They added to this radical legacy a touch of intellectual nihilism, but most of them fell miserably short in this respect of the man who, of all thinkers, was their intellectual ancestor; one of the heroes of the radical Enlightenment, the Marquis de Sade. Nothing written by a twentieth-century postmodernist expressed the movement's claim to nihilism as precisely as he had done in 1781:

> Similar to the concepts of virtue and vice, [the concepts of justice and injustice] are purely local and geographical; that which is vicious in Paris turns up, as we know, a virtue in Peking, and it is quite the same thing here: that which is just in Isfahan they call unjust in Copenhagen. Amidst these manifold variations do we discover anything constant? Only this: . . . self interest . . . is the single rule for defining just and unjust.
>
> Justice has no real existence, it is the deity of every passion. . . . So let us abandon our belief in this fiction, it no more exists than does the God of whom fools believe it is the image: there is no God in this world, neither is there virtue, neither is there justice; there is nothing good, useful, or necessary but our passions, nothing merits to be respected but their effects.[12]

But if postmodernism was merely nihilism, it offered nothing other than a new name to distinguish itself from the more serious and better-defined nihilism analyzed by Nietzsche and Spengler, and feared by the interwar revivalists. And if postmodernism concealed, under a facade of nihilism, yet another version of the radical attack on the legitimacy of the West, that again was nothing new, merely a tedious and repetitive recital of the same alleged grievances and errors denounced by Rousseau, Marx, and their followers for two centuries. The sole contribution of postmodernism as a label or a movement was to sow further confusion by combining anticapitalist and antimodern resentments. By the 1990s, the label had become so broad that some critics defined Fukuyama and his theory of history as postmodernist, which was utterly absurd, since Fukuyama claimed that the modernity of liberal democracy and capitalism was not only not ending but destined for global victory. He was the polar opposite of a postmodernist, and if he could be included in that description, its advocates had certainly arrived at terminal incoherence. As an ideology, moreover, postmodernism constructed an enemy, modernity, which it defined as including both "capitalism and the command economy, Western democracy and totalitarianism, liberalism and communism," all of which, according to postmodernism, were equally dated and equally defunct.[13] In terms of the sceptical Enlightenment and its attempt to understand, rather than to praise or denounce, the West, postmodernism was neither original nor interesting but primarily significant as a barely camouflaged anti-Western ideology demanding, as its predecessors had done, a moralistic and tyrannical dictatorship of virtue.

Postmodernism, however, was not just a movement, however incoherent and dishonest about its motives and suppositions. It was also the atmosphere generated by that movement and by the sense, common to many who did not consider themselves postmodernist, that the victory of the Cold War West paradoxically coincided with a crisis of Western legitimacy and of modernity, defined as liberalism, rationalism, and market capitalism. Alasdair MacIntyre, a moral and political philosopher, wrote in the early 1980s that both the sceptical and the radical Enlightenment had self-destructed. Both posited a rational model of a liberal society; the fact that one tradition derived this model from history and the other from principles was, to him, less significant than the shared assumption that it was possible to define the criteria of justice, rationality, and moral behavior, in short, to define virtue. Modernity, the result of the Enlightenment, was the appeal to unaided human reason, not divine law or revelation, as the criterion for judging both history and politics.

"Each moral agent," MacIntyre wrote, "now spoke unconstrained by the externalities of divine law, natural teleology or hierarchical authority; but why should anyone else now listen to him?" This, in a nutshell, was the question of legitimacy within the modern West. Legitimacy in the modern West rested, MacIntyre argued, on rights claims, but the rights were themselves defined within the modern, individualistic, and rationalist universe. They had no external foundation in natural or divine law. Therefore, these rights claims were mere statements made by agents who wanted to obtain some good or advantage. They could have no objective basis, for modernity denied the possibility of such an external objective basis. Consequently, for MacIntyre, modernity was not a move forward, but a move backward, not an escape from Christendom to a higher stage, but a retreat from it to a lower stage, the stage of barbarism such as prevailed in the early West after the late antique synthesis had been overrun by the Germanic nations and before the Germanic nations had themselves become civilized enough to reconstruct the West as medieval Christendom. Today, MacIntyre said, "the barbarians are not waiting beyond the frontiers; they have already been governing us for quite some time."[14]

MacIntyre was not a counterrevolutionary in the tradition of Juan Donoso Cortés or the *Syllabus of Errors*, but he believed he had identified the terminal decline of the West as the self-destruction of the Enlightenment, and he recommended that defenders of culture form beleaguered communities, like the monastery of Cassiodorus in southern Italy in the 580s, where the highest ambition was to keep the monks literate so they would at least know the world they had lost and could try to keep the flame alive until conditions again permitted cultural activity. It remained to be seen whether a historical and sociological analysis derived from the sceptical Enlightenment justified such a bleak conclusion.

The burden of the postmodernist case, as indeed of the antitechnological and environmentalist case, was that the West was self-destructing. A sophisticated defense of that position grounded in history was that of Stephen Toulmin. In *Cosmopolis*, Toulmin argued that what he called "High Modernity," that is, essentially, the classical liberal West, consisted of two "timbers," two sets of beliefs, one about nature and one about man, or human nature. High Modernity believed that "nature is governed by fixed laws set up at creation" and that "the objects of physical nature are composed of inert matter." There was no spirit in nature, which was the domain of laws discoverable by scientific reason; these laws had operated in the same way throughout the history of the universe. As for human nature, "the 'human' thing about humanity," in the world view of High Modernity, "is its capacity for rational thought or action," whereas "emotion typically frustrates and distorts the work of reason."[15]

This High Modernity and its associated personality type was what Nietzsche had declared dead in the 1880s with the advent on the one hand of nihilism as the core belief, or lack of belief, of the West, and on the other of the small-willed and timid "last men," seeking knowledge, sophistication, and pleasure but without energy or enthusiasm. For Toulmin, High Modernity had not ended in the nineteenth but in the twentieth century, under the onslaught of the world wars, psychoanalysis, antidemocratic doctrines, and science itself, which, at least in the popular understanding, abandoned certainty and reason in favor of uncertainty and ambiguity. Toulmin disputed Fukuyama's claim that science was by "common consensus" cumulative and directional. No longer, said Toulmin. According to him, the effect of these political, psychological, and cultural changes was not that the West abandoned science and reason, but that its elites "reinvented" humanism, a movement "for a reintegration of humanity with nature, a restoration of respect for Eros and the emotions, for effective trans-national institutions . . . pluralism in the sciences, and a final renunciation of philosophical fundamentalism and the Quest for Certainty."

Toulmin shared, in a moderate way, some of the beliefs of the anti-Western Westerners, although he himself insisted that the end of High Modernity did not mean a "farewell to reason," only to "the exclusively theoretical agenda of rationalism." In the neohumanist age that was his benevolent and optimistic reading of the consequences of 1968, of the end of ideological confrontation, and the end of the liberal West, modernity would "come of age" in a new set of commitments to egalitarian politics and to environmentalism, feminism, multiculturalism, and other projects dear to the hearts of many in the 1990s, especially of those who held the West to be gravely misguided and in need of expert assistance.

Toulmin conceded much ground to the 1968 generation and its criticism of the West as hyperrational, scientific, unfeeling, hierarchical, and exploitative. He belonged to that large group of Western academics who hoped, either naively or sincerely, that enough of the liberal triad would survive to guarantee progress in medical science and in prosperity to secure their own well-being and that of their children, while meanwhile giving ground rhetorically and politically to the "new humanists" who denied the value or the future of the West as understood by the sceptical Enlightenment. Critics like Toulmin on the one hand demonstrated that Max Weber was right in considering his rational, productive West fragile but on the other hand insisted on considering it less fragile than it was. Despite his talk about a new, egalitarian and environmentalist form of reason, one must doubt whether Toulmin or the many other, far more daring and radical critics would wish to reject a fairly rigid Weberian rationality when it came to their own personal economic decisions, or when it came to trusting in the "exclusively theoretical agenda of rationalism" in building the airplanes they flew in or the computers they used.

The third team of contenders was the one that, for a short moment in the mid-1990s, seemed the most energetic and influential. This group was that of the communitarians, believers in the possibility of recreating humane social bonds without abandoning liberal individualism. Their apotheosis was the New Labour government of Britain elected in 1997, which promised an implausibly painless combination of social solidarity, prosperity, equality, and optimism. The basic thesis of New Labour under Tony Blair was that it was possible to use government to restore some of the social and cultural bonds allegedly swept away by the hurricane of market forces that invaded Britain—as they invaded America—in the 1980s. This superficially plausible thesis ignored that government, under Margaret Thatcher, had not shrunk appreciably; in fact, it had grown. To believe that government had pulled back from society such that there was now, in 1997, available a large margin of government spending power to redress the inroads of market liberalism was to believe an illusion. To believe that government, no matter what its spending power, could re-create communities dispersed by the culture of the market was to believe another illusion. The likely fate of Blairite communitarianism, therefore, was higher taxes, lower growth, and frustration.

But what did communitarian thinkers—as opposed to politicians who used their ideas—actually say? The starting-point of communitarianism was the observation that "after a point, the quest for ever greater liberty does not make for a good society." The leading communitarian, the sociologist Amitai Etzioni, advocated an equilibrium of tradition and modernity as the "golden rule" to which societies should conform—authoritarian societies by liberalizing somewhat; anarchic and nihilistic societies, such as late-1990s America seemed to many to be, by becoming somewhat less permissive and tolerant. Communitarians advocated a social reconstruction in three stages: first by relegitimizing and constructing small communities: kinship networks, towns, school support groups, churches, local professional associations, local political parties. Next, by establishing a "thick shared framework" of mutual recognition and tolerance with other groups in one's region. Finally, by acknowledging that the whole society, the United States, for example, constituted a "community of communities" within which the same rules and the same thick shared framework should apply as applied within the particular communities. A reconstruction of America based on a mutual recognition of rights and duties, autonomy and obligation, freedom to act and responsibility to others, would, the communitarians argued, lead to a regeneration of America, contrary to the predictions both of doomsayers and of sociologists like Max Weber, who argued that once the social fabric of a society started to fray, it would unravel before some new social formation arose out of the ashes of the old.

Etzioni suggested seven "core elements" of the "thick shared framework," principles and practices to which all members and all communities within the community of communities would have to subscribe. They were democracy as a value, the U.S. Constitution and Bill of Rights, layered loyalties, neutrality and tolerance, a limit to identity politics, continuous dialogue, and reconciliation. Layered loyalties might sound obscure; Etzioni meant that people almost always were loyal to several entities at the same time, for example, the United States, one's home state, one's church, one's favorite sports team, one's professional ethics. The list was unexceptionable, however; as analysts of the culture war pointed out, it was precisely because Americans could not agree what such core elements meant or should entail that they were engaged in the battle to define America. The communitarians tended to sound like rational people for whom reason was not the slave of the passions. They had great faith in what Etzioni called "the moral voice," which was similar to but more specific than the generic Judeo-Christian notion of an individual conscience; the moral voice was the source of the norms of a particular community. But "the ultimate moral arbitrator" for communitarians was not the community, the core elements, or tradition, but "the members." Communitarianism was, in the end, a wager that it was possible to put a kindly face on the radical, subjectivist Enlightenment, for nothing in communitarian doctrine delegitimized the kind of politics or ambition released by Rousseau and Marx. It was also not a historical doctrine, though its authors were social scientists. They did not define the conditions of survival of the liberal West and ask whether contemporary America was meeting them but idealistically offered the America of the culture wars a recipe for order. But the culture war was not about order, but about the power to define political morality and American identity, and communitarianism had no purchase on that conflict.

Communitarianism had a considerable vogue and addressed some real problems. Its reach was strictly limited, though, by its voluntarism. Freely chosen bonds of community were by definition not bonds but temporary agreements; they did not step outside the limits of the individualistic liberalism that the communitarians wanted to dampen. But if the communitarians had suggested that certain bonds, of family or faith, for example, partook of the nature of "piety," that is, they were unchosen but not therefore unbinding, they would have been accused of conservative ideology and would have lost most of their audience. This they would and could not do. "The basic social virtues," wrote Etzioni, "are a *voluntary* moral order and strong measure of bounded individual and subgroup autonomy, held in careful equilibrium, the new golden rule."[16]

Another problem with communitarianism was that it claimed to address the decline of civil society under the threefold pressure of expressive individualism, of the market, and of intrusive and domineering government. For the first of these problems, intense expressive individualism, it proposed that people give a little ground in their demands and return to the "core elements" that would allow communities to be built and survive. But for the second and third threats to civil society, from the market and government, communitarianism had little more than sweet words and mild exhortation. It presupposed an interest in and a commitment to civil society that, according to some social scientists, was lessening in America. Exactly why this should be so was unclear; longer workdays and stagnant incomes for the middle class, where most Americans belonged and where, therefore, civil society found what Burke called its little platoons, did not seem to be the whole reason. Whatever the role of each factor, it was clear that many Americans worked longer hours, watched more television, spent more time on personal pursuits and on defining individual identity rather than giving their effort to the kind of collective working and learning activities in parties, movements, and churches that taught democratic and communitarian habits. As a result, by the mid-1990s,

> weakness is the general, if uneven, feature of associational life in today's America; any program for political renewal must start from this reality. Unions, churches, interest groups, ethnic organizations, political parties and sects, societies for self-improvement and good works, local philanthropies, neighborhood clubs and cooperatives, religious sodalities, brotherhoods and sisterhoods: American civil society is wonderfully multitudinous. Most of these associations, however, are precariously established, skimpily funded, and always at risk. They have less reach and holding power than they once did.[17]

Measuring this decline was tricky; some experts found contrary evidence that American philanthropy and volunteerism were alive and flourishing. But if it was true, as Tocqueville had argued, that American democracy and democratic culture grew from the "social capital" produced and absorbed by citizens working together for particular purposes in the small platoons of civil society, then a weakening accumulation of this social capital was ominous for the commercial republic of America. Social capital, in turn, was created not by the wealth-maximizing egotists known to economic theory but by persons possessing and driven by what the British scholar Shirley Letwin called the "vigorous virtues." The vigorous virtues were habits of life and behavior that made for responsibility as well as energy. A person of vigorous virtues might be prosperous, but his prosperity would be the fruit of a broader set of qualities and not an end in itself. Letwin coined the phrase "vigorous virtues" in the course of arguing that the government of Margaret Thatcher marked more than a mere change of government. Thatcher, in Letwin's view, sought not only to improve British economic performance but to restore to respect the qualities of character that built the original liberties and prosperity of the West:

> The individual preferred by Thatcherism is . . . upright, self-sufficient, energetic, adventurous, independent-minded, loyal to friends, and robust against enemies. . . . There is nothing substantive, that is to say, no description of the individual's profession, level of education, achievements, wealth or poverty, position in society, marital status, proficiency in particular skills, political views, aesthetic sensibilities, religion, likes or dislikes. It is, in other words, possible for a person to conform to the Thatcherite conception and yet *be* any one of an infinite number of different kinds of person. This is because the list contains *virtues* . . . they can be described as the *vigorous* virtues.[18]

The vigorous virtue of strong individuality that did not need to express itself aggressively but sought satisfaction rather in accomplishment and generosity was the true core element of pluralist democracy as well as of economic development and was the psychological foundation of liberty. The vigorous virtues in action constituted the social capital of the Western heartland of America, and a plentiful supply of people displaying those virtues was a necessary precondition of all parts of the triad: science, democracy, and economic development. The scholar who looked most closely at the loss of social capital in America of the 1990s, Robert Putnam, had previously investigated the joint origins of local self-government and economic development in the Old World, more specifically in Italy. As Montesquieu first suggested, the two went together; where several governed, as in the medieval and Renaissance city-states of Lombardy, Emilia-Romagna, and Tuscany, there also laws, customs, and incentives motivated people to collaborate in both political and economic enterprise; collaboration discouraged cheating and rewarded those who contributed to the joint efforts; the result was both liberty and prosperity. But the symbiosis of incipient democracy, nonarbitrary laws, enlightened self-interest, and economic enterprise took centuries to evolve. It could not be established by fiat, which, so Putnam held, was the main reason for poverty and political lethargy in southern Italy. The symbiosis that ultimately produced Western capitalist democracy was centuries in the making. Conversely, social capital was easier to pillage and exhaust than to build up; hence his warning signals to America.

Communitarianism recognized some of the danger signals. But although its proponents were social scientists, they recommended that people choose to work together rather than offering a sociological diagnosis of the conditions enabling or hampering such collaboration. The movement was, in its kindly and well-meaning way, analogous to well-meaning green policies or well-meaning policies of redistribution as a response to inequality and stagnation. Such policies did not question their own presuppositions or take in the available evidence in the relevant areas and therefore were likely to make the perceived problems worse, not better. Communitarianism was also a weak defense of the West because, like almost all other participants in the culture war and culture debates of the 1990s, it misdiagnosed the contemporary West as resulting from the victory of modernity, alias the radical Enlightenment, over tradition, alias the bad old Christendom version. But if modernity was not the result of a struggle but itself the historical and social development of deep-seated and long-standing factors lodged at the very center of the Christendom model, then the communitarian diagnosis of the contemporary crisis of modernity would also yield a wrong prescription.

The fourth set of contenders was the most disparate; some of them would no doubt disapprove of being lumped together. In this internally divided camp, then, one found various enemies of the late liberal West. They differed, however, in what aspect of the West they disliked, in their prognoses, and in the remedies that some of them advocated.

Neither the Old nor the New West had much credibility in the eyes of critics like Agnes Heller, who wrote in 1991 that "the most superficial investigation shows that the conceptual and geopolitical myth of the West has lost its validity now that communism has collapsed."[19] Heller, a former Marxist who wrote penetrating and devastating analyses of communist regimes during the Cold War, adopted a mirror image of the Marxist and antifascist mindset, according to which the West after 1945 was defined by its opposition to communism, rather than the other way round. The antifascist mindset viewed communism with sympathy, believing its claims and disregarding its reality. Heller denounced the reality and unmasked the claims, but ignored the modern West's classical liberal structure that long predated communism and was in no way defined by it. Thus she could claim that the West was a strategic idea designed to contain the Soviet Union. Heller would not have known what to make of Curtius and Eliot and their nostalgic revivalism, or indeed of Carl Schmitt and his desperate search for the restrainer of the Antichrist, the *katekhon*.

Oswald Spengler argued that the end of the West, not the end of history, was beginning in the liberal age. He did not deny that after this end was completed, some new civilization might arise on an entirely different basis and start the cycle anew. In the immediate aftermath of World War II, the idea of an end of history cropped up again. The Belgian social thinker Henri de Man—not to be confused with the more famous literary critic Paul de Man—argued in the early 1950s that industrial society had created institutions that were too large to be understood or managed by any individual, and that had therefore acquired a momentum of their own. De Man believed that this momentum was going to lead to even greater wars than those that had just ended in 1945; he thus linked large-scale social organization to large-scale violence and to cultural decline. One of his readers, the German philosophical anthropologist Arnold Gehlen, coined the word *posthistoire* (posthistory) around 1950, meaning that history had ended and that the West, or the entire world, was now living in a posthistorical condition without knowing it. This idea of posthistory was one of the sources of postmodernism.

According to de Man, the political shape of the last stage of history was that of conflict ending in nuclear war. Others concluded that atomic weapons had made large-scale war impossible, which left a world state as the most plausible framework of the end of history. The German writer Ernst Jünger came to accept this belief after World War II. Jünger, who died aged 102 in 1998, and whose last name meant "pupil" or "young man," was a novelist, travel writer, entomologist, comet watcher, author of fables, and soldier. He was one of the last warriors in Western culture. He was a veteran of both world wars and, while in the first, had received in 1918 the highest decoration given for valor by the king of Prussia, the cross of the military branch of the Pour le mérite order, known as the "blue Max." In World War I, the king of Prussia was the same person as the German emperor, Wilhelm II, and Prussia was not an independent state but part of the German Empire. Nevertheless, the order was a Prussian order, founded by Frederick the Great in the eighteenth century, and only Prussian subjects could be admitted to it. At his death, Jünger himself was its last living member, since the order ceased to admit new members when the Prussian monarchy was abolished in 1918.

In 1920 Jünger published his first and, in the English-speaking world, best-known book, *Storm of Steel*, a memoir of his life in the war. What upset many people then and many more people since was that Jünger liked war. It was not so much that he described war and combat as positive, valuable experiences, as that he completely avoided making any judgments at all. The war simply happened; it was the backdrop and the reason for the narrator's experiences.

Along with many other veterans, Jünger at first welcomed Hitler's regime as a welcome end to the frustrating incompetence of the republican democrats, but he withdrew his support and retreated into dissent. In his works of that time a sinister, dictatorial, violent, and mysterious figure known as the "Head Forester" sometimes appeared, usually in the background; perhaps an allegorical version of Hitler, but who could tell? Jünger was a mystic and a fantasist and not a consistent philosopher.

When, after World War II, he declared his support for the idea that history had ended, it might therefore be seen as yet another turn by an author who had never held a consistent viewpoint, had it not been for the fact that he was picking up ideas popular in many quarters after 1945 and giving them his own powerful literary expression. In various essays and stories of the 1950s, Jünger argued as follows.

The history of the world until the mid-twentieth century was determined by the clash of East and West, Asia and Europe, or, in the German terms, *Morgenland* and *Abendland*, literally, "morning country" and "evening country." The West symbolized and incarnated reason, light, moderation, and freedom; the East, magic and secrecy, wild energy, despotism. The Greeks were the first to break out of the embrace of Asia and the Great Mother goddess and to seek a freedom that began as curiosity about the world and themselves. In the Persian Wars, the Eastern claim to absolute power failed to subdue the Greeks, fortified by their sense of liberty.

The idea of freedom and reason survived in the West but had become a "tower of Babel," an exaggerated and inhuman cult of technology, mass organization, and rationalization of every domain of human life. Western man, originally free, absorbed the Eastern qualities of despotic power and energy. Thus, war in the modern world became unlimited, passionate, emotional, whereas in earlier European history it was limited by codes and regulated by chivalrous or monarchical custom. The losers, in the old days, were not discriminated against; in modern times, they were enslaved and exploited.

At this point it might seem that Jünger was arguing that the modern world was becoming increasingly barbarized and violent, and that this would, by some catastrophic reversal, bring about the end of history, either in a final war or in a world state. But before making any such argument, Jünger first modified his scheme of history, whereby the human race was becoming both more technically powerful and wilder, by the combination of Western and Eastern traits. We were told that history was cyclical, comparable to the waxing and waning of the moon, or to the millennial rhythms of climate, from Ice Age to warming phases and back to ice. Nothing new under the sun, then?

Not quite, because Jünger then moved back to technology and asked whether technical progress had an "end phase in which space collapses" into nothing, as in late-twentieth-century communications that Jünger could only imagine in the 1950s. Technology and the shrinking of space, which Jünger called "great dreams," meant that "all peoples are now entangled in the fate of the West. The old Russian, the Turk, the Japanese, all these withdrew in fear from that entanglement," which had become fact in the twentieth century.[20]

This Western technological supremacy, displayed in two world wars, required that war and technical power be limited. Domination henceforth was not external, over lands and peoples, nor exercised by force and machinery, but must become an inner discipline directed by sacred and earthly laws. The forceful, dominating person would want to escape from these bonds; technology attracted those who would use it. In the future, the "taming of the titans" of technology and war would become the main tasks of political thought and action. Here Jünger harked back to Nietzsche and to the polarity of Apollonian and Dionysiac. The Apollonian impulse was the impulse of order, grand designs, and the taming of the titans; the Dionysiac was the energy of the titans themselves. Their final alliance would found the "world state," a world of technical perfection and abundance. The infinite quantity of technical products available to all would ultimately bring about a change in the quality of the human spirit and human relationships, so that the Dionysiac impulse to war would be restrained forever.

The end of history, in this vision, was a consequence of technology and of the human psychology that, at the end, could not avoid being modeled in its rational, benevolent, helpful image. Jünger's vision turned de Man's nightmare scenario on its head: technical organization and the vast dimensions of social institutions and social power led not to war but to its opposite.

End of history visions of this kind, which were not uncommon in the 1950s, especially in Germany, derived either from Spengler and Nietzsche or through them from Hegel, who was also Fukuyama's inspiration. Along with his psychologically more elaborate and politically more egalitarian and democratic vision, they belonged to a tradition that sought the end of history in the end of grand designs and revolutionary upheaval.

The diagnosis of the West as technocratic and soulless was a common denominator of the fourth group, which included the environmentalists. One who phrased this diagnosis elegantly, if unconvincingly, without being an out-and-out Green, was Václav Havel, the playwright, former dissident, and later president of the Czech Republic. In February 1992 he addressed the World Economic Forum, an annual gathering of business and government leaders from across the world held in the Swiss town of Davos. Here, in the first year after the end of the Soviet Union, Havel the philosopher-statesman took the opportunity to present a critical perspective on "the modern age" that, he said, had now come to an end.

The modern era, which had come to a final end with the fall of communism, had been, said Havel,

> dominated by the culminating belief, expressed in different forms, that the world—and Being as such—is a wholly knowable system governed by a finite number of universal laws that man can grasp and rationally direct for his own benefit. This era, beginning in the Renaissance and developing from the Enlightenment to socialism, from positivism to scientism, from the Industrial Revolution to the information revolution, was characterized by rapid advances in rational, cognitive thinking.

As criticism, this was fervent and sincere. As intellectual history or as a presentation of Western identity, it was a caricature. Had Havel listened to the sceptical Enlightenment, he would have realized that the rise of science and rationalism was part of a general change in politics, economics, and culture, which produced not a narrow and single-minded rationalism, but the complex mixture of entrepreneurship, technology, political experimentation, and modern religious faith that constituted a historically grounded, liberal Western identity. But, like so many others, he had adopted the radical Enlightenment's ahistorical moralism even while condemning its results. He continued his list of evils. The modern era, by which he meant the modern West, had believed that the world was wholly knowable.

> This, in turn, gave rise to the proud belief that man, as the pinnacle of everything that exists, was capable of objectively describing, explaining and controlling everything that exists, and of possessing the one and only truth about the world. It was an era in which there was a cult of depersonalized objectivity, an era in which objective knowledge was amassed and technologically exploited, an era of belief in automatic progress brokered by the scientific method. It was an era of ideologies, doctrines, interpretations of reality, an era in which the goal was to find a universal theory of the world, and thus a universal key to unlock its prosperity.

Again, a sincere list of grievances, but one little related to the imperiled, fragile construction of liberty, reason, and prosperity described by Max Weber or the more sophisticated West defined by the economic historians of the 1970s and 1980s. No doubt some technocrats, managers, and politicians in the West believed some of the things Havel listed. But they were precisely the "nullities" described by Weber who had never really given thought to where they came from and what they stood for. They had never understood the West in any serious sense other than technocratic power. Some such people certainly existed. But it would be difficult, if not impossible, to find any great scientist, poet, statesman, inventor, or entrepreneur of the past two centuries who subscribed to such simplistic notions. Havel's catalogue was the catalogue of an intellectual who, somewhat against his will, found himself in a position of political responsibility and who imported into that position the unworldly stance of the critic without responsibility. But it was also the stance of one who, for whatever good reasons, had never bothered to acquaint himself with what scientists, philosophers, and even technocrats and quantifiers thought about their own work or believed about its status in the hierarchy of things.

The best reason for Havel's ignorance and for his misrepresentations was that he had lived most of his life as a dissident in a communist society. And it was precisely the communists who more than anyone represented the caricature of Western ideas that made up Havel's list. He mistook the inhuman and moronic political ideology that ruled his wretched country for its opposite. Hence his plausible, but nonetheless philosophically unforgivable, identification of communist ideology as merely the highest stage, rather than the complete denial of, the West:

> Communism was the perverse extreme of this trend. . . . The fall of communism can be regarded as a sign that modern thought—based on the premise that the world is objectively knowable, and that the knowledge so obtained can be absolutely generalized—has come to a final crisis. This era has created the first global, or planetary, technical civilization, but it has reached the limit of its potential, the point beyond which the abyss begins.

One hoped, as in Toulmin's case, that Havel's fear of objectivity did not extend to a refusal to accept medical care or travel in modern vehicles, which after all functioned only because the laws of energy and motion were objectively true.

Havel's errors were as profound as they were understandable, given his history. He attacked an enemy that did not exist except in the distorted form of Marxism, in both its Soviet and its antifascist, formerly fashionable Western European and American variants. Its errors, as ideology and as practice, were two: first, Marxists believed that they had discovered the key to human behavior, the scientific answer to the question of history: where did it come from? where was it going? This was exactly what Havel condemned, the false search for a "universal theory of the world." But it was only Marxism, and those Western doctrines infected by it, that succumbed to this temptation. The whole point of modern science and of modern politics properly understood, that is, as understood, for example, by Max Weber, was to know that you could not know human nature and politics the way a scientist could know the laws of thermodynamics or of planetary motion. Marx was wrong, not right, in believing he could understand history the way a scientist understood nature.

The second error of Marxism, which was the error of Rousseau, was the philosophical or existential error of deducing from the fact, well known to any Jew or Christian, that there was something radically wrong with the world as it was, that what was wrong was that man was oppressed, deprived of his true identity, home, and existence by a force alien to him, a force that needed to be identified and destroyed. The Marxist error was to declare this force to be wholly outside an originally innocent humanity, and not inside all of us, as Jewish and Christian theology declared. This error had all the consequences noted by Havel, and many others as well. In combination with the first error, that you could construct a science of history, it meant that Marxists arrogantly believed they could identify the alien force as the "class enemy." Next, it meant that, given that this force was evil and inhuman, they had the moral as well as scientific right to eradicate it. Finally, it meant that they believed that once they had extirpated the evil, then innocent humanity would come into its own without possibility of future error or mistake. If errors and mistakes persisted, it must be because remnants of evil were still infecting a sound body, and such infection then required radical cure in the shape of mass genocides, prison camps, deliberate murder by starvation of dozens of millions of potential class enemies, wars of aggression, and the like.

False science and a gnostic, nihilistic error in locating the source of evil in the world were the errors of Marxism. It was simplistic to identify these errors with the scientific, rational, and capitalist West.

Havel's misidentification of the problem then led him to a fateful conclusion about democracy:

> Many of the traditional mechanisms of democracy created and developed and conserved in the modern era are so linked to the cult of objectivity and statistical average that they can annul human individuality.[21]

Liberal democracy in the West in the 1990s doubtless suffered from many distortions and imperfections, measured by its own highest standards, but a "cult of objectivity" was surely not one of them. Rather the contrary. Western politics since the 1960s was dominated not so much by a cult of objectivity as cult of emotion, rhetoric, misrepresentation, and a finely honed ability among all parties to conceal interest-group struggle as conflicts of principle.

Havel had special reasons for misdirecting his attack, but the misidentification of the target of discontent was common in the 1990s, both on the left, where one would expect it, and on the right, where one would not. The people who attacked rationalism, technocracy, and modernity as inhuman, imperialistic, environmentally destructive, or, more cosmically, a "betrayal of mankind" typically found the source of the error in the Enlightenment. A similar error was that of the English political philosopher John Gray, known in the 1980s as a free-market liberal, who turned against what he called the Enlightenment and its universalism in the 1990s in terms similar to Havel's, and with arguments vitiated by the same flaws, to which he added the further flaw of misidentifying the causes, nature, and consequences of the environmental crisis supposedly engulfing the world. But what Havel and Gray called the Enlightenment was, once again, only its radical and moralistic wing, as embodied in the late twentieth century in the American liberalism of rights, and not the sceptical Enlightenment of David Hume, who knew that "reason is the slave of the passions," and whose adherents sought the historical and social bases of liberty and prosperity, and not abstract principles.

Gray's observations of some of the problems of modernity were on the mark. It was when it came to stating the causes of the problems and therefore their solutions that he veered onto what, for supporters of a rational, prosperous, and free West, was dangerous ground.

Gray's anti-Enlightenment turn surprised some who had not read his earlier essays. In fact Gray had never been an uncritical admirer of the radical Enlightenment. Gray was a conservative, and as such opposed to philosophies of human nature that saw man as an abstract creature equipped with rights but not with duties or the unchosen obligations to family, country, faith, personal honor, or institutions that come with every life that is seriously lived in the world. Accepting such unchosen obligations and making them your own was what Virgil and the Romans called *pietas*. It was the moral glue of the social bond, and to violate it subverted not just one's personal commitments but order itself. In the words of another conservative thinker:

> Impiety is the refusal to recognize as legitimate a demand that does not arise
> from consent or choice. . . . the social bond . . . is transcendent: it contains oblig-
> ations and allegiances which cannot be seen as the result of contractual choice.[22]

Piety was common but not collective. You could not deny your obligations, but you could shirk them. Gray's objection to the Enlightenment, from his conservative perspective, had always been that it ignored piety in favor of individual abstract rights. The ideology of rights artificially reduced people to individuals defined as bearers of rights, ignoring their communal and historically given identities and ignoring the many different reasons different people had for claiming particular rights.

Gray's turn in the 1990s was both against the Enlightenment and against the market liberalism of the British and American governments in the 1980s. This liberalism had, he now concluded, gone too far. It undermined the social bond, tore people from their communities, threatened them with economic and social insecurity, and generally made a civilized life in the continuity of generations and with respect for piety impossible.

> The Westernizing project of Enlightenment humanism has desolated traditional cultures in every part of the globe and visited devastation on their natural environments. The Soviet experience, in which an Enlightenment ideology wrecked the cultures of the Russian and many other peoples and a western Promethean conception of human relations with the earth wrought irreversible damage to the environment on a vast scale, will likely go down . . . as merely a particularly dramatic episode in the world revolution of Westernization.[23]

To the middle part of this statement applied the objection to Havel's impassioned list of grievances: it was directed against the wrong party. It was not because they were enlightened or were followers of Locke, Montesquieu, Kant, Adam Smith, or Jefferson that Lenin, Stalin, and their followers found it necessary to kill scores of millions of their own people or wreck the natural environment of their country. It was because they were followers of Marx and believed in his two errors, the error about science and the error about why the world was not perfect.

The first and third part of Gray's indictment were no less misdirected. He provided no examples in this passage of "traditional cultures" or their environments devastated by Enlightenment humanism, so assertion must stand against assertion. Gray appeared to believe that the last four centuries of world history could be reduced to a drama with two main characters: the West and the Rest. The West was mobile, productive, aggressive, rationalist, and unable to sit still and let others live. The Rest lived a placid life in traditional communities, respecting gods and ancestors, and protected by piety and culture from upsetting the balance between society and its natural environment.

Against this rather eighteenth-century vision of rustic idyll and noble savages faced with civilized aggression, certain facts could easily be adduced. Life among the Rest, before the Europeans came, was undoubtedly in many cases governed by piety and tradition, as indeed it was in the West for most people until well into the New West. But the notion that the Rest, unlike the West, lived in harmony with nature and that Westernization devastated an aboriginal purity was pure obscurantist myth. It was not the Rest that brought cures for endemic plague, cholera, malaria, smallpox, hookworm, tuberculosis, or sleeping sickness, but Western science. It was not the Rest that discouraged the use of human fertilizer on fields, a practice that guaranteed widespread tapeworm infestations where it was common and to which scholars plausibly attributed part of China's failure to achieve economic growth and thereby solve its persistent problems of famine and mass misery. And to take a commonly cited but not therefore trivial example, it was not the Rest that abolished the trade in human slaves, a practice virtually universal in human history until the Enlightenment, but the West.

Gray agreed with Nietzsche that liberalism inevitably ended in nihilism. Yet he rejected any culturally conservative response, such as a restoration of order, as an impossible "cultural fundamentalism." Rather, he asserted, "the post-modern condition of plural and provisional perspectives, lacking any rational or transcendental ground or unifying world-view, is our own."[24] Although liberalism was defunct, Gray still insisted that it should survive as a cover for a tolerant multiculturalism, for he was unwilling to grant to Western societies the right he claimed for others, namely, the right to assert and defend a cultural identity.

Gray's attack on Western "devastation" of the environment was a commonplace on both left and right since the later 1960s. It repeated, in better English, the simpleminded clichés made famous by an American politician and later vice president, Albert Gore Jr., who claimed in a best-selling book published in 1992 that "modern industrial civilization, as presently organized, is colliding violently with our planet's ecological system." Gore went further than Gray, however, in denouncing those who disagreed with him as the moral equivalents of Hitler and the Nazis. The American politician demonstrated, more clearly than the English philosopher, the inveterate tendency of the heirs of the radical and moralistic Enlightenment, and of the progressive mindset, to demonize their adversaries, to assume that anyone who did not submit to their version of reality was not merely in error but a knowing enemy of truth and justice. In fact, the environmentalist argument that the West was uniquely destructive, though it had a long and respectable pedigree, was wrong. "Without important exception," environmentalist arguments about increasing pollution, energy shortages, species extinction, global warming, or impending crashes of the world economy due to ecological limits, "have turned out to be without merit, and many of them have been revealed as not simply a function of ignorance but of fraud." Those were the words of a genuine optimist, the economist Julian Simon, denounced by Greens and global warming advocates as a "terrorist" and a "criminal," and who reappears in the final chapter.[25]

The four teams of contenders over the empty mantle of Western identity were found in both America and Europe, though the battle in America in the 1990s appeared harsher and less tolerant than east of the Atlantic. This struggle within America and the West over democracy, capitalism, and science had many names and definitions. One definition, common in the 1990s, was that of a culture war, or wars. The culture war was a verbal and sometimes violent struggle to define the right answers to a variety of social, political, and educational issues, for example: abortion, homosexuality, affirmative action, multiculturalism, the curricula of schools and universities, the legal and moral limits of permissible speech and opinion, or even the legitimacy of American and Western civilization itself. "Western civilization is at stake," was one participant's definition, and it was not uncommon.[26] At issue in the culture war was not only the right definition of America, its constitution, schools, and social policies, but the political and legal power to impose a definition as binding on others, especially one's enemies in the war. As a perceptive analyst of the culture war put it, "*cultural conflict is ultimately about the struggle for domination* . . . a struggle to achieve or maintain the power to define reality."[27] Participants were convinced that they stood for truth against error, justice against injustice, and hence summoned the energy to write, demonstrate, litigate, blacklist job candidates, argue, and insult, "not because they are quarrelsome by nature but rather because their prior moral commitments—to what they personally believe is true, just, good, and in the public interest—have compelled them to become involved."[28] In that struggle, old alignments, especially the alignment that had divided religious from agnostic or atheistic Americans, shifted. What was at bottom a struggle to enforce, or condemn, the legacy of the radical Enlightenment became in 1980s and 1990s America a fight within moral and religious traditions. The culture war was preeminently a moral struggle in which each side defended what it saw as truth against the error of the opposition, and since each side also considered that the truth was obvious and simple to understand, the opposition's error could be due only to malice or corruption. The culture war proved once again that moral disagreements were the most vicious and intolerant. In the words, again, of James Davison Hunter:

> Because this is a culture war, the nub of political disagreement today on the range of issues debated—whether abortion, child care, funding for the arts, affirmative action and quotas, gay rights, values in public education, or multiculturalism—can be traced ultimately and finally to the matter of moral authority. By moral authority I mean the basis by which people determine whether something is good or bad, right or wrong, acceptable or unacceptable, and so on. Of course, people often have very different ideas about what criteria to use in making moral judgments, but this is just the point. It is the commitment to different and opposing bases of moral authority and the world views that derive from them that creates the deep cleavages between antagonists in the contemporary culture war. . . . this cleavage is so deep that it cuts *across* the old lines of conflict, making the distinctions that long divided Americans—those between Protestants, Catholics, and Jews—virtually irrelevant.[29]

The culture war pitted what Hunter defined as "the orthodox" against "the progressives." The orthodox were those, of whatever religion or moral tradition, who believed that "moral authority comes from above and for all time" and who wanted to rest social and cultural norms on "commitment . . . to an external, definable, and transcendent authority." Progressives, on the other hand, identified with the radical Enlightenment's peculiar combination of rationalism and subjectivism, or individualism. "Truth" to progressives, whether modernist or postmodernist, "tends to be viewed as a process, as a reality that is ever unfolding." Progressive ideals and demands "share in common the tendency to resymbolize historic faiths according to the prevailing assumptions of contemporary life," without questioning too deeply where those assumptions came from.[30] Agnostics and secularists found themselves split along an analogous dimension, with some, the social conservatives, arguing for a natural law that society ought to respect, and others, the late-twentieth-century American liberals, arguing for subjectivism. But in all groups, religious and secular, the culture war split progressives in all moral and religious traditions from orthodox in all traditions in "a conflict over 'the means of cultural production'" and "the power to define the meaning of America."[31]

Because the positions in the culture war derived from prior moral convictions, no reasonable compromise was possible. This was one reason that the communitarian proposal to put the culture war aside and agree on a minimal consensus about social norms and values was unlikely to gain much support among serious participants in the culture war. The communitarian idea was that reason would yield some basic principles of order to which all could subscribe. But it was precisely a feature of the culture war that it illustrated David Hume's dictum that "reason is the slave of the passions." Reason was not a sovereign arbiter, but a tool of argument and political struggle. Human beings had always been clever at inventing rational grounds for their beliefs or actions, and the culture war was no exception; on the contrary, the very intensity of the conflict stimulated participants to construct ingenious, elaborate, and often highly rational justifications for their beliefs. As Hunter wrote:

> The moral arguments on either side of these disputes appeal with equal facility to the evidence of science (as, for example, in discussions about human biology), the precedents (or lack of precedents) from social history, and the legitimations of theology and biblical textual analysis. At least from a lay person's point of view, the logic of the competing claims is equally rigorous. But in the end, whether concerned with abortion, homosexuality, women's rights, day care, or any other major moral or political issue of the day, the tools of logic and the evidence from science, history, and theology can do nothing to alter the opinions of their opposition. Because each side interprets them differently, logic, science, history, and theology can only serve to enhance and legitimate particular ideological interests. The willingness or unwillingness of opposing groups to have a "dialogue" about their differences is largely irrelevant. Even a spirit of compromise maintained by either side would be irrelevant. In the final analysis, each side of the cultural divide can only talk past the other.[32]

Hunter concluded his general analysis of the culture war by emphasizing that it split political and religious traditions that had formerly been united, and that while putting an end to old conflicts among Catholics, Protestants, Jews, and agnostics, it constituted in itself a new conflict between the orthodox in all four groups and the progressives. This new conflict, the culture war, was therefore not a struggle to define and enforce the right kind of Christianity, or for or against accepting Jews and agnostics, but a struggle over the Enlightenment. But like that of many other analysts, Hunter's Enlightenment was only its radical wing, that of "Rousseau, Voltaire, Diderot, and Condorcet, and especially their philosophical heirs (including Nietzsche and [Richard] Rorty)."³³ This radical Enlightenment and its descendant, what Hunter defined as the progressive side in the culture war, was only one part of the Enlightenment, its ideological, moralistic, and revolutionary aspect. The other aspect was the Enlightenment of Montesquieu and Hume, which sought not to moralize but to understand, and specifically to understand the conditions of emergence of the modern West and hence the conditions of its survival. In the legacy of this sceptical Enlightenment, reason was less the slave of the passions than the tool to understand history, including the history and role of passions.

There was a false note about the vehement Western anti-Westernism in the 1990s. It was more popular than the radical pessimism of the 1930s, but it was also less serious. Georges Bataille hated bourgeois society and lived a life on the limits of bourgeois security, health, and normality; the 1990s despisers of the West preferred to exercise their contempt in the smoke-free security of academia. The denunciations of liberalism, capitalism, and modernity coexisted, in America at least, with a cult of health, security, blandness, and safety that precisely matched Nietzsche's famous prognosis of the "last men" who considered themselves the pinnacle of enlightened sophistication but wanted life risk-free, simple, and inoffensive. Were such timid folk really a threat to the vigorous, optimistic, technological, and capitalist West?³⁴

No and yes. The critics of the West within the West were not about to mount a frontal attack on the political, economic West of the year 2000. No movements comparable to that of Hitler or to the communist parties of Western Europe in the 1920s through 1950s could be detected even on the farthest horizon, alarmist fears to the contrary notwithstanding. Those who claimed, for instance, to see in the anti-immigrant political parties or gangs of Britain, France, or Germany, or in the American militia groups, anything remotely similar to the antidemocratic forces of earlier decades were either deluding themselves or using sensationalism for their own political purposes. Faced with a real storm trooper or Red Front street fighter, the average National Front voter or rioting skinhead of Birmingham, Rostock, or Marseilles would have cowered in terror. The American militiamen proved in Oklahoma City that they were able and willing to kill innocent civilians in their war against the American regime, but they had no electoral support and could only dream of the 44 percent of the vote won by the National Socialists in Germany in 1933.

In a different sense, though, the "last men" who attacked the West while reaping its rewards presented, if not a mortal danger to, then at least a substantial problem for, the upbeat story of the West as eternal prosperity, progress, and democracy. They attacked the central premise of modernity by attacking science and the idea of objective knowledge, on which the idea of progress depended, for without knowledge how could you determine or direct progress? Environmentalism, multiculturalism, feminism, and the notions of postmodernity, or of the end of history, were examples of this kind of Western anti-Westernism, even though their proponents often argued that they wished not to subvert the West but to improve it—the criterion of improvement being provided in each case by the ideology. The reason these beliefs were a problem for the ideology of the West as progress, liberty, and prosperity lay in their political and pedagogical consequences. As teachers, journalists, advisers, commentators, and makers of both policy and opinion, Western anti-Westerners were able to sabotage the confidence of the capitalist, progressive, rational West in the 1990s, using two tools that they had acquired and learned to use since the late 1960s: humanitarian rhetoric, that is, the ability to convince listeners that you held the moral high ground and should therefore be obeyed; and indoctrination—the will, power, and ability to teach their own story of the West as a flawed experiment that therefore needed cure by an enlightened elite, that is, by themselves. They gained ground precisely because they were faced not with people confident in their historical and sociological understanding of the West, but with weak defenders whose West was a thin, moralistic West vulnerable to moralistic assault.

The multiculturalists who attacked the modern, capitalist West in the culture war argued that the United States was not or no longer part of this West, but should seek a new, non-Western identity beyond such European legacies as Judeo-Christianity, liberalism, and scientific curiosity. Meanwhile, elsewhere in the world, and not only in Europe, critics of the West saw in America the heartland of the West, but an immoral, uncivilized, exploitative West. In a mirror image of the American anti-Western case, European cultural critics from Arnold Toynbee on argued that Europe should liberate itself from American dominance and from a West that elided transatlantic differences and obscured European cultural specificity.

Such critics saw the Cold War West as an American device to impose American economic and cultural hegemony. This criticism came in a left-wing and a right-wing version. The left-wing version, familiar since the 1960s, denounced the West as capitalist oppression that had its heart and source in the United States. Abolish America and you would abolish the West and emancipate humanity. In the 1990s, this formerly neo-Marxist tradition moved close to the Toynbeean line of thought that saw in America the heartland of a spiritless, secularist, money-grubbing, and therefore capitalist West, which by its commercialism, exploitation, and greed undermined religion and cultural stability. So, for example, the Italian Catholic philosopher and anticommunist Augusto Del Noce concluded late in his life that one must distinguish "Westernism," centered in America, from the "religious spirit" that Christians needed to recover in opposition to this godless, American "West." For most of the twentieth century, he argued, Christians had been seduced by their own humanitarian impulses to concede the moral high ground to communism, or at least to the antifascist mentality. Emmanuel Mounier and his group in France illustrated this tendency, as did large parts of the Christian Democratic party in Italy, and certainly, though Del Noce was unaware of it, the political theology of post-1960s official American Catholicism as represented by the United States Catholic Conference. The failure of communism was, he hoped and predicted, forcing a return journey of such Christians, as well as of ex-communists, to transcendent faith. In his view, which he expressed as early as the 1960s, when communism, in both its Soviet and its Western European versions, seemed on the side of history, the West was going to prevail over communism because it was better than communism at being secular, that is, at producing economic growth and consumerism. The technocratic consumer society embodied in the ideological construct of the Cold War West, dominated by America, was a Westernism destined for global victory, because it appealed to the material or animal interests of secularized, materialist humanity.[35] Del Noce's defense of a revised Christendom version of the West against American "Westernism" formed a paradoxical counterpart to the American culture war, in which multiculturalists, who represented fairly accurately what Del Noce denounced as "Westernism," saw themselves as anti-Western. Thus what one group demanded in the name of liberation from an oppressive West could appear to others as the very expression and essence of an oppressive West. Del Noce denounced a West devoid of history, culture, religion, or tradition; precisely what the American anti-Westerners wanted. Their West, by contrast, which they rejected, was what people like Del Noce wanted to keep, namely, the common transatlantic culture of Christianity, democracy, liberal philosophy, science, and the common literary and political tradition—the West, in short, of the sceptical Enlightenment that did not reject religion but included it in the liberal triad.

Outside the United States, then, the attack on the West in the 1990s took the form of anti-Americanism; in America, of anti-Eurocentrism. One party's target of attack was the other's favored goal. The anti-Americanists claimed to want to restore cultural traditions that, in America, were called Western and attacked or defended accordingly. The American anti-Westerners wanted a rootless, contentless culture that was precisely what people like Del Noce decried as empty "Westernism." The students who shouted "Hey hey, ho ho, Western culture's gotta go!" at Stanford University in 1986 would have been surprised to learn that, according to the anti-Americans, they were not rejecting the West, but representing its worst aspects.

One way of resolving this paradox of a West hated in America for being European and hated in Europe for being American was to see it not as two entirely distinct concepts but as two sides of the same Janus-faced complex of institutions and cultural traits. What the American anti-Westerners despised was the combination of scientific reason and cultural tradition; what the European anti-American anti-Westerners feared was American consumer culture and secular liberalism. Yet scientific reason, tradition, consumer culture, and secular liberalism were not necessarily parts of opposing wholes, but were all parts of a single thing—the New West of capitalism, democracy, and rationality.

While some non-Americans criticized America for being too Western in a bad sense, others criticized America for no longer being Western, that is to say, they regarded the campaign to de-Westernize America as represented, for example, by the Stanford students, as having largely succeeded. The Syrian-born scholar Bassam Tibi, who worked in Germany from 1973 and who was often in the United States, confessed to being critical of America but for the same reason pro-Western. "Although I vehemently defend Western modernity, I reject the American model. . . . The unmistakable signs of decay in the West have little to do with cultural modernity. They are signs of age of Western civilization. As someone who knows both 'old' Europe and 'young' America I know that the signs of decay are much greater in American society than on the old continent."[36] America, on this reading, was departing from a Western consensus that it had done much to shape but now, apparently, no longer wanted. Such a reading was not an attack on the West for being either too Americanized or too Eurocentric, but a lament that the West had lost its

American heartland. Tibi's sense that America had ceased to be Western was a defense of modernity against an America that, in his view, was rejecting it. It was in their stand on modernity, as threat or as promise, that the Western elites divided in the 1990s.

Western elites in the 1990s often appeared to want nihilism without the consequences; that is, they wished to denounce rationalism and what they considered displeasing aspects of the modern West without surrendering any of its material, economic, medical, or cultural advantages. The question was how long such genteel consorting with the enemy could continue before the advantages began to disappear.

CHAPTER TWELVE

The Failure of Universalism and the Future of Western Identity

It is closing time in the gardens of the West
—Cyril Connolly

Oh, East is East, and West is West, and never the twain shall meet
Till Earth and Sky stand presently at God's great Judgement Seat.
But there is neither East nor West, Border, Breed nor Birth,
When two strong men stand face to face, though they come from
    the ends of the Earth
—Rudyard Kipling

Universalism was the world view of choice across the American policy landscape in the late 1990s. In foreign policy, it meant humanitarian diplomacy; in social and educational policy, it meant multiculturalism; in economic policy, it meant free trade. Although multiculturalism might seem to contradict universalism, the two were compatible;

indeed, multiculturalism was simply universalism applied to cultural politics—the idea that no culture was better than any other, and that no culture should enjoy the preferential support of American public opinion or American government.[1]

In the real world, universalism was less viable. As a doctrine of late modern liberalism, a liberalism browbeaten by the movements that began in the 1960s, and yet buoyed by the worldwide advance of democracy and capitalism, universalism never solved its fundamental dilemma of being both a Western idea—the idea that Westernization was global and irresistible—and an anti-Western idea—the idea that Western identity had fortunately come to an end and been superseded by a lowest common denominator of communications technology, capital markets, free trade, and doses of American entertainment.

The dilemma of universalism derived from the ambiguities of the New West itself: was it a new civilization, defined by its departure from its own and all other pasts, or was it the fruit of a historic identity? If the New West was free of its past, then its fate was to become global and, in so doing, to lose its remaining identity. If the New West, on the other hand, was viable only as a descendant of the Old West, then universalism denied Western identity by threatening to dissolve it in a global culture. The dilemma posed the question of Western identity for the third millennium. Was this identity to be bland and universal, or rich and specific? This question cannot be answered without first placing the logic of Western identity in the framework of a macrohistory that makes clear, in global terms, the relation of the New West to the Old. Only when that relation is clarified can we determine what Western identity will plausibly be in the third millennium.

It will be helpful first to examine Ernest Gellner's account of the rise of civil society and liberty in the West—two preconditions of universalism—for it was an account full of premonitions of the macrohistorical vision, but without some key elements that completed the vision, namely, an understanding of the role of economics and a view of human nature grounded in social reality. After examining Gellner, I look at some of the important responses to universalism and Westernization—neohumanists, Catholics, environmentalists, Islamists, and the so-called Singapore school. These, again, were responses to ideas and images, not judgments about macrohistorical reality. Therefore, after looking at them, we return to the macrohistorical vision, stressing its analysis of the short twentieth century of totalitarianism and ideological conflict. Finally, with these arguments and analyses in place, I offer a concluding vision of a viable Western identity.

Gellner directly addressed the question whether it was possible to de-Westernize, to annul the New West of rationalism and science. In his last years, he thought much about this question and arrived at a resounding no! The synthesis of reason, prosperity, and liberty, what he called "civil society," could not be dismantled, whatever the antics of certain elites. The synthesis was not as fragile as Weber assumed and as much of the twentieth century seemed to demonstrate. The reasons for Gellner's confidence were worth rehearsing for themselves and as preparation for assessing the macrohistorical vision, which he foreshadowed without quite formulating his own version of it.

Modern Western civilization, Gellner held, was a gamble that ordinary men were capable of disinterested reason. Their autonomy and freedom from coercion required that they refrain from coercing others in the name of morality or belief. Their prosperity rested on inventive use of specific, instrumental links to others who were their equals, not on bribery, extortion, or being the client of a boss or chieftain who rewarded subservience with scraps of loot. Both their freedom and their prosperity depended on virtues of dependability, reciprocity, and performance—virtues reinforced neither by ritual nor by revelation, but by the interest each member of society had in the disinterested performance of obligations by himself and others. Gellner held, as had Weber before him, that this mutual respect of freedom and performance was an unlikely thing to arrive and spread in any society, but he also held, unlike Weber, that once it arrived its advantages were such that it became indestructible.

The type of society that arose where such rational, diligent, autonomous, endlessly innovative, honest, and reliable folk were the norm rather than the exception was that of Western democratic capitalism, of the classical liberal synthesis explained and recommended by the sceptical Enlightenment. Of all its unusual features, perhaps the oddest was that power in this society, whether political, economic, or ideological, was fragmented. This fragmentation of social power was, as Montesquieu noted, a precondition of liberty and autonomy. Not because diffusion of power in itself yielded freedom; in most of human history, it yielded anarchy, followed in short order by despotism. Rather because, for a variety of implausible reasons, diffusion of power in the West caused or allowed people not to band together in sects or conspiracies, but to form, autonomously, sets of associations and institutions that were "strong enough to prevent tyranny, but which are, none the less, entered and left freely, rather than imposed by birth or sustained by awesome ritual."[2]

These associations, and the desire and tendency to form them, were the essence of "civil society," defined by the freeing of economic activity from political control. Thus, one definition of civil society was a place where "production becomes a better path to wealth than domination," so that "the best way to make money is to make money," as opposed to places where the way to make money was to capture political power and exploit the populace. Another was that "a real Civil Society is one which does not rechristen all its railway stations and boulevards and issue a new city plan each time the government changes." The first definition contrasted civil society to traditional society; the second contrasted it to totalitarianism. Gellner praised precisely the features of the modern West that Václav Havel criticized—the rationality, the use of science, the ideas of objective rules and justice. Modernity was Janus-faced; what to some were its wonders and promise was to others its oppressive uniformity, its inhumanity, its mindless dynamism.

Civil society required that its members actively desire and cultivate responsibility, autonomy, and disinterested competence. This was where Gellner's optimistic account met the reality of the culture war. In America, many parents, schools, universities, media, and cultural figures in the 1990s taught incompetence, passivity, and short-term gratification. The cultural dumbing down of America threatened civil society with death by triviality. Meanwhile, rapid economic changes threatened it with death by inanition, because overworked and anxious citizens had neither the energy nor the time to nourish it.

Gellner considered these threats unimportant. One reason was that he found civil society so obviously attractive that he could not accept that substantial social and economic forces within the West might tend, deliberately or not, to undermine it. "Some of us actually like it," he wrote, explaining how "one of the main glories" of civil society was its separation of social roles, so that, for example, not everyone needed to be a warrior to enjoy the blessings of peace. Thus, "Civil Society bestows liberty even on the non-vigilant," and, he continued:

> Only the brave deserve the fair, says the poet. But may we not aspire to a social order in which even those of us who are timid can enjoy feminine beauty? Such has always been my pious hope. Civil Society is an order in which liberty, not to mention female pulchritude, is available even to the timorous, non-vigilant and absent-minded.[3]

Another reason that Gellner focused on the benefits and the glories of civil society rather than on the dangers facing it within the West was his point of departure. Not only was he himself by birth a Central European; he was, in his last years, a founding member of the Central European University in Prague, where he directed the Centre for the Study of Nationalism. Nationalism and civil society were intimately related, not only historically but in the specific context of anticommunist resistance and of the collapse of communist tyranny in Central Europe.

Gellner noted the rediscovery of the term "civil society" in the thought and writings of Czech and Polish dissidents of the 1970s and 1980s, such as Leszek Kolakowski, Milan Kundera, Adam Michnik, and Václav Havel.[4] Starting in Central Europe and moving west, civil society reappeared as a practical aspiration for the victims of communism, and for Westerners as a description of what was most valuable, and why, in their own society. Why then, and why there? Because, said Gellner, "the crisis which has led to the re-emergence of the idea of Civil Society as a standard and as an ideal is one in which the fear of atomization was for once exceedingly realistic." In other words, civil society re-emerged where it had been most effectively crushed, namely, under Marxist ideocracy.

The fear of atomization was felt not only by Central Europeans under communism. In Gellner's usage, atomization was what Marxism did, indeed must do, to societies under its control. Its ideology prescribed a unitary society ruled by an elite of managers, interpreters, and enforcers, what Gellner, borrowing a phrase from Islam, dubbed an *Umma*, "an overall community based on the shared faith and the implementation of the law." That the faith was secular only made it harsher. "Social control worked by deliberately implicating virtually everyone in moral and economic dirt," because "with everyone guilty and contaminated both morally and legally, the likelihood of dissent inspired by moral indignation was diminished."[5]

Both the original evolution of civil society in Europe and its reemergence from under Marxist domination were examples of Gellner's Law of Implausible Development: the fundamental social breakthroughs from prehistory to the present were all, given what we know of human nature and human society, counterintuitive and implausible.[6] Once each breakthrough had taken place, however, the resulting advantages were such that it was quickly copied more or less widely, with the result that each seemed, in retrospect, inevitable. The list of these breakthroughs was not long: it included agriculture, the state, the alphabet, science, nationalism, the market, and civil society. As for the latter's revival, it "is of course intimately connected with the *Krach* of the Marxist system," and "this collapse . . . has taught us how better to understand the logic of our situation, the nature of our previously half-felt, half-understood values."[7]

Fundamental to Gellner's macrohistorical view was that civil society stood in contrast to two other social forms that, until recently, were the only ones on offer. The first such form, which was the original form of all society, he called "segmentary": these were "cousin-ridden and ritual-ridden" societies characterized by "stifling communalism."[8] In such societies, found everywhere from the early Neolithic villages through the Greek city-state to the near-contemporary Far East, individual status was internalized, given by birth or acquired by ritual. It was not voluntary, and it was certainly not pluralistic.

The second traditional form of society, which evolved later and usually wound up encompassing the former, was command-administrative authoritarianism; this was the form of the traditional empires of human history, from the Assyrians to the Chinese. These despotisms added power to segmentation and were thus able to dominate large numbers of people across large areas. They did this not only by brute force, but more effectively by developing sophisticated systems of command and administration based on literacy, accounting, and mobilization. Marxist socialism, in this perspective, was "the command-administrative manner of running an industrial society." And a command-administrative system, Gellner repeated, was not unusual, it was "the normal condition of humanity."[9]

Literate, urban culture began appearing in Europe in the Middle Ages. By the eighteenth century, the lineaments of civil society were in place in northwest Europe: diffusion of social power, separation of production from domination, the decline of the warrior ethos, religious toleration.

But why did Christian Europe not develop a modern *Umma* that would do the expected thing and quash civil society in its cradle? The answer to this last and most important of the breakthroughs, according to the law of implausible development, was that Europe did produce an incipient *Umma*, for so Gellner labeled the Calvinist and Puritan communities that Max Weber identified as the forerunners of capitalism and rationality. But whereas in Islam the puritan, rationalist *Umma* held the social high ground in the urban centers, in the West, the puritan *Umma* took control only sporadically, in marginal places like Scotland, Geneva, and New England. Its power was great enough to nourish the seeds of civil society by developing the famous Protestant ethic of work, accumulation, and deferred gratification, but not great enough to suppress the resulting secularism, liberalism, and belief in human autonomy. As David Hume wrote, "superstition is an enemy to civil liberty, and enthusiasm a friend to it."[10]

What, finally, about the prospects for the classical liberal synthesis in the West? Gellner was sanguine mainly because he marveled at civil society's rebirth in the East, and because he himself liked it. The only reason civil society might fail, in his view, was if economic growth stopped permanently, because then "anyone's gain is balanced by someone else's loss," and society might "revert to the condition that has characterized most societies, and complex ones most of all—a hierarchical system in which status is deeply internalized."[11]

Gellner thought that the anti-Western Westerners were no serious threat to the continued vigor of the Weberian synthesis. Their achievements in education, academia, the media, and politics, touted under the banner of multiculturalism or postmodernism, rested on the idea that the Western way of doing things was no better than any other, indeed, that one could not determine whether any way of knowledge, morality, government, or justice was superior to any other or even existed. This was the late-twentieth-century form of relativism, changed beyond recognition from its Spenglerian and Nietzschean roots. In Spengler, relativism took the form of showing that the West was not the only culture in the world and that it was not the continuation of classical antiquity. Relativism meant that the art, philosophy, customs, laws, beliefs, and creative imagination of the West were not the only or the highest versions of these things. In its second incarnation, in the post-1960s West, relativism reappeared as the idea that there was no such thing as sure knowledge outside any given culture. The anti-Western Westerners gave this notion the added twist that the West had in the past, imperialistically and mistakenly, tried to impose the idea of an absolute knowledge on the world, but that this attempt, already undermined by liberation movements and other forms of cultural reaction, now had to stop.

Gellner's view was clear: relativism was a cultural luxury, not a genuine philosophical choice, and moreover, it would not work as a belief about knowledge. He illustrated this with examples from his own field of anthropology, where questions of Western identity and dominance had been hotly debated since the 1960s. The starting point was both political and epistemological: political opposition to Western dominance that pretended to be based on objective knowledge but was in fact the result of superior power. Politics and epistemology came together in the attack on the supposedly imperialistic notion of positivism:

Positivism would appear to mean a belief in the existence and availability of objective facts, and above all in the possibility of explaining the said facts by means of an objective and testable theory, not itself linked to any one culture, observer or mood. . . . Positivism is a form of imperialism, or perhaps the other way round, or both. Lucidly presented and (putatively) independent facts were the tool and expression of colonial domination; by contrast, subjectivism signifies intercultural equality and respect. The world as it truly is (if

indeed it may ever truly be said to be anything) is made up of tremulous sub-
jectivities; objective facts and generalizations are the expressions and the tools
of domination. . . . the whole idea of objectivity and clarity is simply a cunning trick of dominators.[12]

Late-twentieth-century Western relativism and postmodernism discarded
objectivity because it was culture-bound and because of its alleged political
history. Epistemology, the philosophical investigation of knowledge and of
whether knowledge was certain, fell under the same judgment. It was merely
an historical event. It appeared in seventeenth-century Europe and went
along, in some fashion, with the rise of Western science, imperialism, and
capitalism. But if you got rid of epistemology along with the idea of objectivity and knowledge, you had some problems, at least if you were consistent (although consistency could also be got round as a Western prejudice).
Critics of objectivity, rationality, and epistemology got themselves tied in
some tangled knots, because by their own standards they could, of course,
make no truth claims of any kind, but for political reasons they wanted very
much to make certain truth claims, namely, the claim that there was no
such thing as objective knowledge and that the very idea of such knowledge
was a Western plot.

The problem for the relativists and postmodernists was that they wanted
to deny both a morality and a knowledge beyond culture, while keeping their
own anti-Western morality immune from that denial. But, according to
Gellner, although no one could be sure

> whether indeed we possess morality beyond culture . . . we do indeed possess
> knowledge beyond both culture and morality. This, as it happens, is both our
> fortune and our disaster. The fact that we do so *is the central and by far the*
> *most important point about our shared social condition*: any system which de-
> nies it, such as "interpretive anthropology," is an appalling travesty of our real
> situation. The existence of trans-cultural and amoral knowledge is *the* fact of
> our lives. I am not saying that it is *good*; but I am absolutely certain that it is
> a fact. It must be the starting point of any remotely adequate anthropology
> or social thought.

The transcultural and amoral knowledge was the "really comprehensive,
powerful, cumulative understanding of nature" called science. Science differed from both religion and relativism; from the former in denying privilege to any particular source; there was no revelation, only experiment and
testability. And from relativism in distinguishing morality and truth. In the

world of science, morality might be culture-bound or it might not; all questions of that kind were, in Gellner's metaphor, like the wallpaper or the other decorations of a house that could be changed at the relativist whim of the occupant without affecting or being able to affect the foundations or the plumbing.

The liberal synthesis held because its three legs were not equal; the most important element in it was rationality, the use of reason, and the absolute validity of the scientific method, whatever its uses, good or bad.

> This is the world we live in, for better or for worse. We have absolutely no choice in this matter. The problems we face flow precisely from these features of our world, and we cannot evade them. To pretend that we are somehow or other living in a pre-scientific . . . world, in which all meanings-systems are equal, in order to provide titillation for Middle America, and to indulge in a rite of expiation for a vanishing hegemony, is simply absurd. The sooner this nonsense stops the better.[13]

Relativism, Gellner concluded, was "an affectation, specially attractive amongst the more naïve provincials in privileged cultures," by which he meant American academics. It was popular among those who could afford it, who derived some moralistic and masochistic satisfaction from it, and who mistakenly believed that they were doing the rest of the world a favor by adopting it. But they were not; the poor countries did not want Western postmodernism but Western science and technology, and in particular the methods by which science and technology became prosperity. "Precariously modernizing societies, with an uncertain grip on the new benefits, are perhaps a little less likely to indulge in an orgy of science-bashing. . . . But a really rich industrial country," like the United States, "can and does afford the luxury of denouncing and renouncing it all." It was therefore in America, where the liberal synthesis had worked best of all and was therefore taken for granted, that relativism found the most fertile ground.

If relativism and postmodernism were really just the pastimes of academics or part of an obligatory ritual required in certain fields to get tenure in American universities, one would conclude with Gellner and Fukuyama that such fashions did not seriously threaten the Weberian synthesis or, in Fukuyama's image, the ability of the wagon of culture to follow the road to the prosperous, if soulless, end of history. Yet the relativists and postmodernists taught their pupils that knowledge was culture-bound and perpetuated the confusion between knowledge and morality, so that many emerged from what passed for higher education with the idea that because morality was culture-bound, then so was knowledge. But if, as Fukuyama and many before him pointed out, the scientific method, whether in physics and chemistry or in economics, social policy, and strategy, was one of the premises of future peace and prosperity, what would it mean for peace and prosperity worldwide as well as in the West if substantial parts of the Western elite no longer believed in it?

Among those responding to aggressive universalism at the end of the twentieth century, three categories stood out. The first was those who focused on its humanitarian aspects—the demand for human rights and dignity—and interpreted them in spiritual terms. In this sense, universalism could be either a denial of religion in favor of a pure humanism or a radical revision of it, a religious humanism that combined the best of Judeo-Christianity with the best of the Enlightenment. The second was that of the environmentalists, for whom universalism was simply Western technology gone mad, a destructive force that needed to be put down if the planet was to survive. The third was that of the non-Westerners, the Islamists and Singaporeans.

Universalism as a spiritual impulse could be understood in two ways. The first yielded a prospect based on philosophical speculation and moral principles. This prospect, as described by the French political philosopher Luc Ferry, suggested that the end of the Cold War revealed the true dilemma of the West as the search for the meaning of life. This search was the Western version of the universal search for identity defined by Samuel P. Huntington as the universal trait of post–Cold War politics across the globe: "the question, 'Which side are you on?' has been replaced by the much more fundamental one, 'Who are you?'"[14] According to Ferry, what happened during the twentieth century and especially since the democratic and humanistic turn of Catholic teaching that came into full force at the Second Vatican Council in the early 1960s was a double and convergent process: the humanization, in religious imagination, of the divine, and the divinization, in social and political values, of the human. Driving both processes was the rise of individualism since the Enlightenment; of the political individualism of vigorous civic virtue first adumbrated by Locke and Montesquieu, but also of the sentimental individualism of Rousseau. The Swiss philosopher appeared in Ferry's story because he represented and dramatized the modern discovery of the autonomous self. This discovery occurred in part for concrete, physical, biological reasons. In the eighteenth century, for the first time, life expectancy began to grow consistently and infant mortality to decline. Longer life expectancy enabled people to conceive of themselves as autonomous, as having their own lives. The revolution in sentiment that this represented was overwhelming. The nuclear family based on the loving couple appeared as a sentimental and social ideal. Its children became objects of affection, rather than hostages to fortune; as Rousseau so eloquently argued, children were no longer imperfect and sinful little creatures who had to be socialized into tradition and order, but innocent representatives of man's original and perfectible state, and, as such, the potential builders and citizens of the just republic of the future. As such precious beings, children demanded the best care; hence Rousseau became also the father of modern child-centered pedagogy and psychology.

Ferry claimed that this sentimental individualism had produced great horrors in the Jacobin and totalitarian regimes that tried to enforce virtue and turn the postulate of perfectibility into fact. But he also claimed that people in the West had learned from these errors. Sentimental and political individualism were converging after the Cold War. The sacred self of the Marquis de Sade, represented by Don Giovanni in Mozart's opera of that name, had disgraced itself by its hedonistic nihilism, but also by falling for totalitarian ideologies. Now, the sacralization of the self was moving into a new phase, which Ferry saw as analogous in both its language and its political implications to the humanistic turn of Catholic teaching. Nihilistic materialism had proved to be not humanistic but antihumanistic, because it denied what was true in the insights of sentimental individualism in favor of the errors and had disregarded the lives of real men, women, and children in favor of an idealized humanity. What was left, Ferry said, was a "transcendental humanism" that saw man as part of nature and yet more than nature, that is, more than determined by biology, habit, or force. "The mystery at the heart of the human being is its capacity to free itself from the mechanism that rules absolutely in the non-human world and permits science to predict and to know it completely."[15] Liberty, in short, was a "mystery" analogous to the mystery of truth propounded by Christianity. Therefore, "the cardinal opposition is not, as was long believed, between a dogmatic religion on the one hand, and on the other, a deterministic materialism, between priests and anticlericals." No, "the true cleavage passes through the heart of modern humanism itself, between its materialist interpretation and its spiritualist aspect." And the second, which Ferry was advocating, was poised to inherit the social and cultural mantle of religion, creating not a revived Christendom version of the West, and not a deification of humanity, but a quasi-religion of the highest aspirations and self-sacrifice of which man was capable. The political ideologies had deified humanity and put real people in concentration camps; transcendental humanism identified man's highest aspirations and capacity for self-sacrifice as something beyond nature. Thus, "attachment to values that radically transcend the world of simple objects, because these values are of another order, implies opposition to materialism and an aspiration to a *spirituality* which will, at last, be authentic. At last, because today it is on a human foundation that this spirituality places the religious category of That Which is Beyond human life. Downstream from our conscious awareness and no longer upstream, as the principles of moral theology would have it."[16]

Transcendental humanism was a comprehensive effort to integrate the divided legacies of the Enlightenment. The true humanism of the future, he argued, was prefigured in the heroic resistance of dissidents in communist regimes, in international humanitarian movements on behalf of the Vietnamese "boat people," the Afghan freedom fighters, and the victims of genocide in Uganda and Rwanda, and in the selfless work of groups such as the French Doctors without Borders. Ferry distinguished transcendental humanism from the humanistic turn in Catholicism over the question of where truth came from. To him, it was to be found "downstream from conscious awareness," in the reasoned insight, drawn from history, psychology, and reflection, that man was more than a material being. Realizing this truth was the source of freedom.

The pope's answer was different. The humanistic turn in Catholicism had, so its proponents argued, led not to a humanization of truth but to a fuller understanding of how divine truth was revealed in human and social behavior; in civilization, in fact. The beginnings of that turn went back to the early years of the twentieth century, to the worker priest movement in France, and to the social theology of Leo XIII. The church had condemned liberalism and democracy as wrong and dangerous, because they placed autonomous reason above revelation. But equally wrong, and for the same reason, was liberal capitalism with its materialism and greed, which exploited the worker and enriched the factory owner for no other purpose than money itself. Thus, in 1891, Leo XIII launched, in the encyclical *Rerum novarum*, modern Catholic social teaching by condemning capitalism as the cult of money and insisting that the worker, as a human being, was entitled to the means of basic dignity. In the brief interval between World War I and the Fascist takeover in Italy, a Sicilian priest, Don Luigi Sturzo, formed a political party, the Partito Popolare, which earned him censure from the Vatican but which represented the first organized attempt to break out of the self-imposed barrier of the *Syllabus of Errors*. What Sturzo did was intended to show that democracy need not conflict with Catholicism and was compatible with it on condition that Catholics not reject or despise democracy, but make it work according to Christian principles of justice, as stated, for example, in Leo XIII's encyclical. When Mussolini forbade all political parties and movements other than the Fascists, Sturzo emigrated to America, where he encountered a Catholicism deeply loyal to Rome, but also pervaded by the sceptical Enlightenment ethos of American capitalism and democracy. Although America remained profoundly Protestant in political culture and suspicious of Catholicism as a movement owing allegiance to a foreign power, Americans were, by and large, much less anticlerical than liberal Europeans. In America, Sturzo met a modernity that saw itself as the heir to Christendom and not its enemy. With this new intellectual and political baggage on board, he returned to Italy at the end of World War II and helped to found the Christian Democratic party. The political fate of that party was bound up with special interests, corruption, and the inertia of ancient social and cultural cleavages in Italy, but its creation in 1944–45 demonstrated that the message of the *Syllabus* was defunct: Catholics had an obligation to participate in the democratic conversation, and democracy was not intrinsically and irremediably contrary to Christian truth.

The Second Vatican Council confirmed this recent history, thanks in part to the work of the American Jesuit John Courtney Murray, who brought to Rome the argument that the American experiment was compatible with Catholic teaching. Murray's teaching, which echoed in the social encyclicals of the 1980s and 1990s, was that democracy was the best political regime because of all regimes it was the most in accordance with true human nature; or, conversely, that democracy and liberal political culture were the best means in an imperfect world of encouraging people to act according to their better natures. Democracy was therefore both just and right. On the centenary of *Rerum novarum*, John Paul II confirmed this trajectory of Catholic theology in *Centesimus annus*. It was theology from the bottom up, where the *Syllabus* had preached from the top down. "Man is the way of the Church," the pope wrote, explaining that the church's "sole purpose has been *care and responsibility* for man, who has been entrusted to her by Christ himself: for *this human being*, whom, as the Second Vatican Council recalls, is the only creature on earth which God willed for its own sake, and for which God has his plan, that is, a share in eternal salvation. We are not dealing here with man in the 'abstract,' but with the real, 'concrete,' 'historical' man. We are dealing with *each individual*." This was humanism in the sense that the doctrine took its cue from individual existence in society. It was Catholic in the sense that it looked to concrete existence for clues to divine intention and for traces of divine action. It was also anti-collectivist and anticommunist, acknowledging more forthrightly than many church documents of the 1960s and 1970s that "communist totalitarianism" meant that "many peoples lost the ability to control their own destiny and were enclosed within the suffocating boundaries of an empire in which efforts were made to destroy their historical memory and the centuries-old roots of their culture." World War II, fought to secure freedom and national self-determination, "ended without having attained these goals. Indeed, in a way, for many peoples, especially those which had suffered the most during the war, it openly contradicted those goals."[17] Most of all, one could say, for the pope's native Poland, whose invasion provoked the war, which lost more than ten percent of her population, and which ended the war still conquered, divided, and exploited.

The papal answer to the question of the West after the Cold War was, then, that democracy and liberty were inherently good, but that their true significance emerged only in the light of Christian revelation, which demonstrated that the truth about human nature embodied in democratic principles and in the desire for political liberty was not something that came from within history but from God. Democracy and liberty were valuable because they embodied divine truths. The pope was a defender of modernity in an age of postmodernism, since he asserted the claim of the Enlightenment that reason, liberty, and prosperity were natural and good tendencies of human effort.

Tocqueville and those who followed him implied that the New West was the natural emergence from the Old of certain authentic expressions of human nature, namely, democracy, reason as applied in science, and economic development. For a long time, the Catholic Church regarded such a claim with deep suspicion. By the 1980s, the church had come full circle and stood as the major institution arguing unequivocally that the advocates of democracy as the natural human regime had been right: it accorded with just human desires.

The neohumanist and Catholic responses to the universalism of the late modern West identified it as a generous impulse compatible either with Enlightenment or Christian anthropology. The large and varied army of the environmentalists, by contrasts, stigmatized universalism as the latest ugly face of the technocratic West.

The story of Western environmentalism since the 1960s illustrated Tocqueville's law that a problem did not cause concern among elites until it was being solved; then, the smaller the residual problem, the greater the excitement and panic. It also illustrated the perennial need for a secular faith of progressive Western elites who, even in the 1960s, could not as a rule stomach communism. Anti-Americanism worked in the Vietnam era, and was then reformulated as anti-Westernism, that is, opposition to the bad effects of the West: capitalism, consumerism, and pollution. After the fall of communism, environmentalism came into its own both as belief system and as institutionalized interest-group politics—the new collectivism of the West, the psychological replacement of the progressive mindset that gripped so many Western intellectuals and policymakers from the 1940s through the 1980s. As such, environmentalism had no logical end point. There were always new emergencies, new crises, new obstacles to environmental harmony and stability. The only fully logical end point to this secular religion was the collective mass suicide of the human race, which was indeed advocated by some of the more consistent green thinkers in the West.

Worry that human activity was damaging the natural environment began as an aesthetic response to mass tourism in the early twentieth century. By the 1950s, a few people were becoming concerned that pesticides and other chemicals were entering the food stream and changing the natural balance of rivers and lakes. The first major environmental publication was *Silent Spring*, by the biologist Rachel Carson, who claimed in 1962 that DDT, a pesticide used primarily to destroy mosquitoes carrying malaria in poor countries, was absorbed by birds from fish they ate and made their eggshells thin. The book became the Old Testament of the environmentalist movement, with what to many was its shocking claim that careless human use of chemicals was threatening a "silent spring" by destroying bird life across the world. Carson's book had serious effects. Governments discouraged and then banned DDT. As a consequence, India, which had reduced its number of malaria cases from 75 million in 1951 to 50,000 in 1961, was back to "at least 30 million" by the 1980s.[18]

In the late 1960s, attention shifted from chemical pollution to resource scarcity. Two hugely influential books, *Blueprint for Survival*, published in 1970, and *Limits to Growth*, published in 1972, together constituted the New Testament of the fast-growing green mentality in the West. *Limits to Growth* was presented as a report by a group of four scientists to the Club of Rome, an association of business leaders and other distinguished public figures from various countries founded by an Italian industrialist, Aurelio Peccei, which had invited reports from scientists worldwide on "the human predicament." *Limits*, the first and more successful of these, had several qualities that ensured broad appeal. It was cast in scientific language, with graphs and computer-generated extrapolations of trends for population, energy, raw materials, and food. The four authors claimed to show that if these trends continued, the world would experience major shortages, pollution, famine, poverty, and social collapse by the early twenty-first century. To avoid these crises, people needed to respect the "limits to growth" and reduce consumption, energy use, and the number of children.

Critics responded that the projections were worthless because they were based on a simplistic model of the earth and assumed that resources were irreplaceable, that new sources would never be found, and that resource use would never become more efficient. The Club of Rome itself disavowed *Limits* four years after it appeared and began speaking positively of economic growth. Twenty years later, in 1992, the authors of *Limits* revisited the problems, admitting that none of the trends had turned out to match reality, but that people should still worry. Meanwhile, the original study sold four million copies and produced a generation's mindset that said that resources were limited, energy should be saved, there were too many people in the world, and that scarcities were inevitable.

In 1980, pessimistic environmentalism became official in the United States when the government commissioned *The Global 2000 Report to the President*, which reinforced the message of limits, scarcity, energy saving, and fear of population growth. One of the most insistent activists on behalf of this message was the biologist Paul Ehrlich, who from the late 1960s on spoke, published, and agitated for zero population growth and for government intervention against energy use and for resource conservation. In 1980, he accepted a bet from the economist Julian Simon that certain scarce metals would become even scarcer by 1990, as measured by their price. Simon had stated publicly that he would bet up to $10,000 "on my belief that mineral resources (or food or other commodities) will not rise in price in future years, adjusted for inflation." Ehrlich could not believe his eyes and decided to "accept Simon's astonishing offer before other greedy people jump in."[19] In 1990, the prices of the raw materials in question had fallen, as indeed they had done ever since data became available. Ehrlich paid up, but refused to admit error. Throughout the 1990s, he was still insisting that scarcities were inevitable, that prices of resources would rise, and that Simon was a "flat-earther" and as stupid as a "cranberry." However, he also refused to make another bet that raw materials would become more expensive.

The end of the Soviet Union provided the environmentalists with more public and political influence than ever. These new opportunities coincided with a third wave of fear, after pesticides and scarcities.[20] The new fear was that energy use was changing the climate of the earth through a mechanism known as global warming. The basic physics and chemistry of the process were uncontroversial. The trace amounts of carbon dioxide in the earth's atmosphere helped the atmosphere retain more solar heat than it reflected into space. This so-called greenhouse effect was essential for life on earth, for without it the average temperature would be well below freezing. The question raised by the new scare of the 1990s was whether carbon dioxide resulting from human activities was going to increase the amount in the atmosphere so much that it would reinforce the greenhouse effect, causing a man-made rise in average global temperatures—global warming. The United Nations, supported by public opinion in many Western countries, established an Intergovernmental Panel on Climate Change, representing several thousand atmospheric scientists, who recommended political action to reduce carbon dioxide emissions. Otherwise, temperatures by the end of the twenty-first century might be several degrees centigrade above their 1990s values, leading to desertification, rising sea levels, flooding of heavily inhabited, low-lying countries, and large-scale disruptions of health, food supplies, and mobility.

Green and greenish politicians, riding the global warming consensus, influenced government policy in a number of rich countries, notably in the European Union and in the United States. Many of them took their cue from the German philosopher Martin Heidegger, who argued in the 1950s that technology alienated man from his true being. Technology, in turn, was the material manifestation of a flawed metaphysic first proposed by Plato, which read man as an acting, creative being rather than as contemplative, and which moreover stated that the fundamental reality of the world was that things came into being and passed away into nothing. According to Heidegger, Platonic metaphysics encouraged discovery and hence science and technology, which increasingly divorced man from his authentic essence. By the twentieth century, these wrong steps had taken Western civilization to the edge of an abyss, a horror of technical manipulation of people and things and a life of utter inhumanity.

In addition to Heidegger, another source of what became known as deep ecology was the British scientist James Lovelock's "Gaia hypothesis," the idea that the earth and its biosphere were a sort of conscious superorganism. If threatened with imbalance, the earth "may shake off the human species so as to gain for itself another lease on life."[21] Gaia proved widely popular with the Western public, perhaps because the hypothesis seemed to combine science and mysticism—an attractive symbiosis to many, and one anticipated by writers in the 1960s and 1970s who sought to derive a sort of mysticism from the most advanced frontiers of quantum physics. One who was strongly influenced by the Gaia hypothesis, as well as by the Ehrlich ideology of inevitable scarcity and the global warming hypothesis, was Al Gore. In *Earth in the Balance,* the senator and vice presidential candidate for 1992 argued that Western civilization had been on the wrong track for centuries, destroying the environment and its own quality of life in an orgy of irresponsible waste. As an American and someone who wanted to recruit capitalists to his cause, Gore was unclear about who was the original criminal responsible for environmental devastation, but he finally settled on René Descartes and Francis Bacon, two pioneers of the autonomy of reason in science and philosophy, and on the scientific revolution in general. Neither indictment made much sense. To accuse liberalism and capitalism of environmental destruction overlooked the fact that the more liberal and capitalist a society, the less pollution it produced. To accuse the scientific revolution overlooked the fact that environmentalism as a movement depended on science to define and measure pollution and on technology to cure it. Gore's prescriptions for a nonpolluting society yielded the vision of a Stone Age Soviet Union run by moralistic enforcers who had a monopoly of the means of coercion and propaganda; the very denial of liberalism and economic development, the only historically tested and reliable means to a cleaner environment.

The global warming scare became the official basis of energy and tax policy in many countries in the late 1990s, even as the IPCC revised its estimates of warming downward, from originally five degrees to two degrees, plus or minus one. People unfamiliar with how big science operated tended to take the IPCC's claim that it spoke for the vast majority of climatologists at face value. But the world of climatology was a small one, and it did not require a great deal of consensus management by a few leading experts in the 1980s to create a bandwagon that few dared reject. Once global warming was on the political agenda, a great deal of funding, not to mention prestige and political influence, became available for climatology and atmospheric research. Was anyone going to say that these funds were not needed? It was more likely for the average scientist to support the joint declarations. Matt Ridley, a British scientist, aptly named the IPCC "the quango-cum-travel-agency for those whose salaries depend on keeping the world worried about global warming." And he added a more general point:

> When you tell environmentalists and scientists they have vested interests, too, they get cross. But they do. Imagine that you have been toiling away at atmos-

pheric physics for thirty years in impoverished obscurity, and suddenly along comes global warming. Next thing you know the United Nations is paying you hundreds of pounds a day to sit in Madrid sampling the room service and appearing on *Newsnight*. Would you admit that the whole thing was nothing to worry about?[22]

Scientists who dissented from the IPCC consensus speculated that any warming would be more than swamped by the natural variation in temperatures and pointed out that if man-made carbon dioxide increases resulted in global warming, the effect should already have been noticeable. Temperatures had indeed been rising, but faster in the first half of the twentieth century than after 1940. In fact, in the 1970s, the big climate scare was not warming but cooling. An atmospheric scientist, Stephen Schneider, warned in 1976 that "a cooling trend has set in—perhaps one akin to the Little Ice Age," a period in European history from the fourteenth to the eighteenth centuries when average temperatures were about two degrees centigrade lower than in the twentieth century, producing shorter growing seasons, more ice winters, and wetter summers. "Climatic variability," Schneider continued, "can be expected to increase along with the cooling."[23]

From the late 1980s on, the same Schneider was among the most eager activists on behalf of the global warming hypothesis. Without alluding to his earlier arguments for cooling, he explained that to gain public and political attention for environmental problems, it was necessary, and indeed ethically required, to stretch the truth:

> On the one hand, as scientists we are ethically bound to the scientific method, in effect promising to tell the truth, the whole truth, and nothing but— which means that we must include all the doubts, the caveats, the ifs, ands, and buts. On the other hand, we are not just scientists but human beings as well. And like most people we'd like to see the world a better place, which in this context translates into our working to reduce the risk of potentially disastrous climatic change. To do this we need to get some broad-based support, to capture the public's imagination. That, of course, entails getting loads of media coverage. So we have to offer up scary scenarios, make simplified, dramatic statements, and make little mention of any doubts we might have. This "double ethical bind" we frequently find ourselves in cannot be solved by any formula. Each of us has to decide what the right balance is between being effective and being honest.[24]

Schneider did not say whether he thought his "scary scenarios" of global warming were any more or less "honest" than his earlier scenarios of cooling. Either might be true; the balance of temperature variation in the 1980s and 1990s was, if anything, in support of Schneider (1976) and against Schneider (1989); that is, the global trend showed a mild cooling compared with the first half of the century.

The direction of technology in democratic societies, however, was in any event not toward ever more pollution or environmental devastation, but toward better health, less pollution, and more efficient use of resources. The environmentalists, left and right, missed the fundamental point about technology when they asserted that it harmed the environment. The level of pollution in a society depended not on how much technology, how many cars, how many factories, but on the political and economic system. And here the record was unambiguous. Since at least the early 1970s, Western capitalist economies produced more, using fewer resources, and with less pollution, than the collectivized economies of the communist world. The more state control of the economy, the dirtier the air, water, and food; the more it cost to produce anything; and the poorer, therefore, the inhabitants:

> In the 1970s and 1980s, an amazing divergence took place in the trends in resource use and pollution within the developed industrial world. This divergence between Western market economies and the socialist economies of the USSR and Eastern Europe went virtually unnoticed. Yet, it may have signified the most important reversal in economic and environmental history since the Industrial Revolution.[25]

The pollution of the Soviet Union was not the automatic result of what John Gray called "a Western Promethean conception of human relations with the environment," but of communism.[26] Gray assumed a radical divide, not just between the West and the innocent Rest, but between man and nature. But there never was such a divide. Human beings were part of nature; every human act since Adam delved and Eve span marked interference in nature. Every much-loved garden, every antibiotic, every cat and dog changed the natural "order." The point of any sensible environmental policy could not be a blanket condemnation of an alleged "Promethean" and exploitative view of nature, but how to maintain and increase prosperity by the most efficient use of resources.

The issue was not merely whether a few Western academics were willing to give up their cars, though actually few found themselves ready for what, in their world view, was surely a moral obligation. The issue was whether misunderstanding the environmental question and the sources of growth risked not just undermining prosperity in the West but depriving the rest of the world of any chance of it, all in the name of pseudoscientific superstitions.

Even if pesticides, resource scarcities, global warming, acid rain, ozone depletion, and the other scares were groundless, this had no impact on the environmental lobbies, who continued to press for, and obtain, policies in support of their beliefs with substantial impact on people worldwide. One example among many: forbidding chlorofluorocarbon (CFC) refrigerants in the 1990s made refrigeration slightly less efficient in rich countries—a form of unnecessary masochism, but not a major disaster. In poor, tropical countries, however, banning the most efficient refrigerant was a more serious matter. Poor people might not be able to afford the less efficient replacements, and the replacements, since they were less efficient, might not keep vital foods and medicines cold enough. Many medicines for tropical diseases deteriorated if not kept cold. But no one proposed a study to measure the cost in suffering and death among poor people of the rich countries' decision—on the basis of flimsy scare science—to ban CFCs.[27]

In addition to all these alleged problems, one major and undeniable fact remained to be adduced by the environmentalist lobbies—population. No one could deny that the world population was growing. No one could deny that everyone, all over the world, preferred to increase consumption. And—not everyone, but many people—assumed a conflict between the growing numbers and their growing demands. A hypothetical conflict that descended directly from Thomas Malthus, an English clergyman who predicted in 1798 that the number of people would always increase faster than the food supply, causing periodic famines that would bring the numbers back into balance with the carrying capacity of the earth.

Malthus was disproved in his own lifetime, but in the 1990s he had more followers than ever before. A broad consensus maintained in the 1980s and 1990s that consumption in the West, plus population in the Third World, were growing too fast—whatever that meant—and that this growth condemned most people to misery. At the very least, the population explosion required of the West that it reduce its own consumption and transfer much of its wealth to the poor of the Third World.

The socialist historian Perry Anderson, for example, wrote in 1992:

The style of life enjoyed by the majority of citizens of the rich capitalist nations today is what [Roy] Harrod called oligarchic wealth, and [Fred] Hirsch subsequently termed a positional good, whose existence—like a site of natural beauty—depends on its restriction to a minority. If all the peoples of the earth possessed the same number of refrigerators and automobiles as those of North America and Western Europe, the planet would become uninhabitable. In the global ecology of capital today, the privilege of the few requires the misery of the many. . . . If all human beings simply had an equal share of food . . . the globe could not support its present population. . . . But even with such staggering inequality, the ozone layer is being rapidly depleted, temperatures are rising sharply, nuclear waste is accumulating, forests are being decimated, myriad species wiped out.[28]

The defeatism of this passage was surprising, coming from a socialist who was supposed to look to the future as the source of hope and the target of aspiration. The reason for the defeatism became clear in a later passage where Anderson explained that the population and resource crisis he had just described—invented, rather—required an end to capitalism and a redistribution of wealth from the West. Unless the crisis could be asserted in the direst terms, the socialist could not plausibly justify his anticapitalism, now that it was no longer, after communism, possible to justify it as leading to more prosperity. In times past, Marxists claimed that socialism was superior because it was more efficient; under it, people would be better off as well as more equal. Then, as people began to notice how poor communist societies were, socialists retreated to egalitarianism alone: socialism might not make people better off, but it did make them more equal. Finally, after communism revealed its hierarchical nature and the rigid social divisions between ruling class and subjects, socialism seemed driven back to its final bastion, a simplistic moralism that stated without justification that even though no socialist society was actually equal, equality was still better than inequality. Then, environmentalism arrived to the rescue, yielding a political, theoretical, and strategic alliance of great power and one likely to contest control in the twenty-first century with the forces of the liberal West and the sceptical Enlightenment.

Even assuming Anderson proposed redistribution because he believed it necessary to reduce the West's environmental damage, that would neither make the West more moral, nor the poor better off, nor the planet cleaner. Mikhail Bernstam pointed out in his analysis of resource use and pollution that the driving force of economic development was "the race between population growth and resource productivity."[29] Population growth was not something that would be stopped by redistribution but by economic growth reducing the incentives in poor countries to have many children. To achieve growth, poor countries would have to win the race between population and resource productivity, and this could be done only by using the same liberal methods and the same "Promethean conception" of the relation between man and nature that had lifted the West out of poverty over the previous five centuries. And unless they were distracted by ideologues and special interests, the poor countries would not need five centuries to become rich, for the West had blazed the trail, and the transcription of established methods of modernity to new settings was infinitely easier than discovering them by trial and error.

Anderson's claim that everyone in the world could not live like people in the West was a green myth. His main argument in its support was that the world could not produce enough food, and that equipping all the world's families with cars and refrigerators would ruin the global environment. Food production in the later twentieth century outstripped population growth except in places and times where political ideology interfered. In the half-century between 1945 and 1995, world population doubled, but food production more than kept pace, while the amount of land under cultivation rose only 6 percent. Real prices fell over that period—food became cheaper, in other words—and the long-term trend of food prices remained downward. Economists estimated that the earth could support something like twice its population of the 1990s at substantially higher prosperity for most; and most demographic experts in the late 1990s were predicting that the maximum world population would likely never exceed ten billion, the dire alarmism of the Malthusians notwithstanding.[30]

Anderson listed a number of problems supposedly caused by the existing consumption of the West and that would be made worse if affluence spread. Had Anderson investigated the scientific evidence available by 1992 on each of the points he raised, he would have discovered either that the problem did not exist or was easily soluble by means far short of, indeed radically opposed to, universal collectivism, which throughout history had made pollution only worse, not better.

The environmentalist legend of inevitable scarcity, pollution, and unavoidable Malthusian clashes was a legend invented by people to serve authoritarian agendas and adopted by others who did not know better because it made them feel virtuous. The West became cleaner and more resource-efficient the richer it became; sabotaging growth by imposing taxes and regulations in the supposed interests of the environment would, in the situation prevailing in much of the West at the year 2000, be counterproductive. At the most, it would spur a demand for new regulators and bureaucrats.

On this topic, where positions were often held with the fervor of intolerant sects, a reasonable summary was that of the former activist and subsequent sceptic, Wallace Kaufman:

> We have unleashed dangerous forces in the world. We created them and we understand them a lot better than primitive people understood the weather or the waxing and waning of the animal populations they hunted. We are in no worse position than humans ever were. We have lost some things and gained much. We may regret the loss of Glen Canyon or the forests of Manhattan Island or the clouds of passenger pigeons that once darkened midwestern [*sic*] skies. But we don't regret the passing of yellow fever, malaria, or bubonic plague. Few people really want a simpler life. We may turn down the thermostat a few degrees, but we won't take out the heat pump. We all want more, for ourselves and for the rest of the world, because that is the way to peace. And we know it is possible.[31]

The green superstition was the heir to both Marxism and the 1968 generation's ideology of liberation in the Western world. It promised moral status, a sense of solidarity, a feeling of virtue, of being part of a great and good movement, and it even, for those who wanted it, could be made compatible with a measure of trust in reason and science, for example, in the computer models of the *Limits to Growth* group and in Gore's vision of a high-tech environmentalism. But it was a strictly limited trust, which quickly flipped into its opposite, suspicion, when science failed to justify the politically necessary doomsday scenarios. Thus, for example, Gore's "Senate office was involved in an effort to discredit S. Fred Singer, a prominent sceptic about the greenhouse effect, after Singer published an article co-signed by Roger Revelle— the father of global-warming theory and an inspiration to Gore—suggesting that there wasn't evidence to justify radical actions to prevent global warming."[32] Rather than change one's mind as required by traditional precepts of rationality, the green believer either ignored the science or invoked junk science or ideological suspicion to provide the required underpinnings of belief. When, for another example, the British science writer Nigel Calder reported new research in a book published in 1997 that suggested that solar particles and not man-made greenhouse gas emissions probably determined climate change, this interesting discovery was wrongly denounced as funded by the oil and gas industry.[33] And so, on the basis of belief and junk science, well-meaning or less-well-meaning politicians introduced and enforced policies that were at best environmentally irrelevant and at worst caused actual harm to both nature and man.

The ecological mindset permeated the political thinking across the political spectrum. It was the most substantial internal Western manifestation of the antiscientific, self-doubting mood after the Cold War. It was matched, in a different dimension, by the non-Western responses to universalism.

Outside the West, the two main alternatives, after the Cold War put an end to Marxism as a practical project of domination, were Islam and China. The two most powerful non-Western cultures posed two challenges to the West. Islamic revivalists insisted that the liberal triad of science, democracy, and economic development was part of Western imperialism and should be resisted or transformed into Islamic terms before being allowed to shape the culture and society of Muslim nations. They accused the West of spiritual emptiness and political imperialism. They stood the Western dilemma, as Gellner described it, on its head.

This dilemma, according to him, was that Western modernity produced a universal epistemology, a way of knowledge, namely, reason and the scientific method, an epistemology that quite simply could not be denied and had to be used if one wanted to know, make, or do. For example, an airplane did not fly because its pilot was Christian, Muslim, Confucian, or of any other faith, but because of the science of aerodynamics. The universal epistemology invalidated all other modes of knowledge. It did not, however, necessarily invalidate cultures, that is, habits, beliefs, and ethics, which remained local. In Islamic revivalism, on the other hand, knowledge was culture-bound but morality, that is, the morality of Islam, its Holy Book, and its practices, was universal. Islam was the final revelation, but it was also the truth in every religion and faith; to the extent that non-Muslims unconsciously followed the law of Islam, they were Muslims, since Islam was the universal religion.

Islamic universalism of faith and ethics was, in it own sphere, as absolute and uncompromising as the universality of the scientific method. Its argument with the West was that Westerners had not yet admitted the truth of Islam while imposing on Muslims an alien epistemology that, to them, seemed often no more than a philosophical cover for economic and political exploitation. From the Islamic point of view, the problem with the scientific method was that accepting it entailed, in practice, accepting Western influence in a range of other areas. The universality of the scientific method seemed to Muslims to be analogous to the universalism of Western political and cultural ideas, such as human rights and democracy. "What is universalism to the West is imperialism to the rest," noted Samuel P. Huntington.[34]

Calling the Islamic revival fundamentalist was problematic, because fundamentalism properly referred to a movement within American evangelical Protestantism of the twentieth century based on a literal interpretation of the Bible. The designation "fundamentalist" made sense only in a context where the analysis of nonliteral meanings of holy texts had been going on for centuries, so that being "fundamentalist" was unusual.[35] In Islam, no analysis of texts in the Christian or Jewish sense had ever been possible, for the Holy Book of Islam was not the word of God passed through fallible and sinful men and therefore a text that had to be properly understood to get past the fallible writer to the divine message. The Holy Book of Islam was the literal Word of God, dictated to the last and final of God's messengers, the Seal of the Prophets, *khâtim al-anbiyâ'*, Muhammad, who was removed from mundane reality to a state of divine infallibility when he spoke and wrote down the words, so that every single word of the Book was God's own, with no possibility of error. Therefore, the question of fundamentalism versus critical analysis had never arisen in Islam; all Muslims were, by definition and unavoidably, fundamentalist. No Muslim had ever felt himself entitled to read the Koran in any way other than the literal, so there was no question of liberal versus fundamentalist approaches to the Holy Book of Islam.[36]

In America, fundamentalism was a movement of churches and groups in smaller cities, in the South and West, and among social groups far from the centers of cultural, political, and intellectual power. The Islamic revival, by contrast, was a movement of the center, not the periphery. Why this was so explained both the power of the movement and its claim to represent a culture-bound yet superior form of knowledge.

In premodern Islam, the *Umma* was the community of literate believers, which consisted of the urban elites of the Middle East with their puritan, legalistic, Koran-based "High" Islam. Urban elites formed a literate society that was similar from town to town, characterized by shared values and expectations and by proximity to political and economic power. The religion of an urban elite, whether Muslim, Christian, Hindu, or Buddhist, was likely to be universalistic, ethical, theologically abstract, opposed to the mumbo-jumbo of clerical hierarchies, and somewhat contemptuous of the superstitions, myths, and intermediaries between the divine and the human so typical of the faith of the vast majority of premodern people.

Such an urban religion, in short, was likely to resemble Protestantism, which began as the religion of commercial and bureaucratic urban elites in Germany. Now the peculiar history of Islam, as opposed to that of Christianity, was that, to use a Western analogy, it was born Protestant. Islam began not as a religion of peasants, but as one of traders and townsmen.[37] From the beginning, the proper and classical form of Islamic religion was therefore that of an urban, elite faith; scripturalist, literate, lacking hierarchy and ritual, and based on the radical distinction of man and God and therefore on prohibiting mediators between the two, such as mystics, saints, relics, rituals, and holy places. The laws, codes of conduct, and rules of commerce, government, and public morality in High Islam were based on elaborate interpretation by trained experts of the Koran and of the various other authorized sources of law: the traditions of the Prophet and the habits and decisions of the first four "rightly guided" caliphs of Islam.

Within its own epistemological framework of Holy Book and sacred law, High Islam was rationalist; the right rule of action in each case was arrived at by deduction from an original source or by induction from similar approved examples of right conduct. From the beginning, the urban centers of Islamic civilization sheltered and nourished this literate, rationalizing, puritanical tendency, which throughout the centuries until the modern age was in constant struggle with popular traditions, laden with mystics, legends, saints' tales, relics, and the other apparatus of mediation between man and God outlawed by High Islam but constantly reappearing through the back door of popular devotion. The Islam of peasants, the "Folk Islam" of segmentary, rural society, was characterized by such local cults, rituals, propitiation, mysticism, and ascribed status. To use again a Western analogy, Folk Islam was Islam's Catholic tendency; comforting to the many at the expense of some doctrinal purity and consistency; promising mediators to bridge the awful gulf in Islam between the human creature and his Creator, and providing an informal ladder of approach to the divine through a hierarchy of holy men and women and communities of prayer, ecstatic dancing, and mystical rapture, and, socially most important, of mutual economic and psychological aid and support for their members.

With population growth, urbanization, and social mobility, the mutual-aid societies, hierarchical structures, and mediating rituals of Folk Islam lost meaning. What happened to Catholicism under the onslaught of humanism, Bible criticism, and economic ambition on the part of North European princes and preachers in the sixteenth century happened to Folk Islam in the twentieth. The difference was that whereas in Europe the Catholic Church rode out the storm by adopting much of the rationalism, intellectualism, and puritanism of its opponents and thus modernizing itself, Folk Islam lost credibility at the centers of Islamic culture. Unlike Catholicism, Folk Islam had never been the religion of the center but of the periphery. When political and economic modernization undermined rural society and reinforced the prestige and power of the center, it also reinforced the prestige of High Islam, which had always been the religion of the center, but formerly in competition with the popular pull of the mediating cults and beliefs. "Urbanization, political centralization, incorporation in a wider market, labour migration, have all impelled populations in the direction of the formally (theologically) more 'correct' Islam."[38]

So, Islamic societies modernized in a setting where a scripturalist, orthodox *Umma* held the cultural and social high ground in the cities, whereas the West modernized in a setting where a scripturalist, puritan elite controlled only bits of the periphery, such as England in the 1640s or New England in the 1600s and 1700s. This was part of the reason that High Islam was not swept away by modernization, but, on the contrary, strengthened its hold. In the nineteenth and twentieth centuries, a series of religious and cultural philosophers rethought the modes of expression and the interpretation of High Islam and reformulated it for a changing society, so that from the early twentieth century it was more appropriate to speak of Reformed Islam.

Reformed Islam survived and strengthened its hold because it was eminently suited as a religion to uprooted, newly urbanized, often unemployed or underemployed masses, anxious for education and for upward mobility. Reformed Islam also "played a role very similar to that played by nationalism elsewhere." Because it was a rationalist religion based on texts and interpretation, it served social and psychological needs similar to those served by nationalism in Europe, which was also a movement providing a binding force among literate but rootless masses torn from their age-old rural roots by the call of jobs, prospects, and the chance of a better life in the towns.

Many of the new urban masses adopted strict practices unknown to their rural, Folk-Islamic ancestors, to show their membership in Reformed Islam, to show their commitment to the one social force that bound them together, to show, in fact, that in terms of their society they were modern and had aspirations to the sort of cultural and social prestige that High Islam had always implied in their world:

> The typical Muslim woman in a Muslim city doesn't wear the veil because her grandmother did so, but because her grandmother did *not*: her grandmother in her village was far too busy in the fields, and she frequented the shrine without a veil, and left the veil to her betters. The granddaughter is celebrating the fact that she has joined her grandmother's betters, rather than her loyalty to her grandmother. Islam also continues to perform its old role of a kind

of eternal entrenched constitution, by means of which the now rather expanded bourgeoisie can criticize, and perhaps on occasion check, the technocratic mamluks at the top. When the mamluks become persuaded to introduce genuine elections (by the desire to implement internationally respected norms of political practice, say), they are liable to find themselves replaced at the voting booths not by populists, but by fundamentalists.[39]

The fundamentalists, or revivalists, represented the third stage after the victory of High Islam and its transformation into Reformed Islam; this third stage was Reformist, or "fundamentalist," Islam. During the twentieth century, in response both to Western power and influence and to the perceived corruption and inadequacies of the rulers of Islamic countries, Muslim thinkers and activists refined and reshaped Reformed High Islam to serve the political needs of the age: radical change at home, power abroad in order to outface and, if possible, defeat the infidel West. In the words of the single most influential thinker of Reformist Islam, Sayyid Qutb:

> The leadership of western man in the human world is coming to an end, not because western civilization is materially bankrupt or has lost its economic or military strength, but because the western order has played its part, and no longer possesses that stock of "values" which gave it its predominance. . . . The scientific revolution has finished its role, as have "nationalism" and the territorially limited communities which grew up in its wake. . . . The turn of Islam has come.[40]

These were not the words of a defeatist or of someone ashamed of his primitive faith in an era of atomic bombs and antibiotics. It was the voice of someone fully confident that the rehoned sword of Islam was eminently able to defeat the enemies of the faith and conquer new lands. The Nasser regime in Egypt executed Qutb in 1966, but his influence in the 1990s was greater than ever. Reformist Islam won support because it offered religion without superstition and a social solidarity that was not part of an alien doctrine, like Marxism.

> A man who turns to Reformist Islam does not . . . thereby convey his contempt for his own ancestors and tradition. On the contrary, he re-affirms what he considers the best elements in the local culture, and which were genuinely present. And a man who turns to Reformist Islam is also close to "the people". . . without at the same time committing himself to any implausible, far-fetched idealization of peasant or shepherd life as such. At the same time, whilst it is truly local, and genuinely resonates throughout the

whole of society, this reformist ideal is also severely demanding, and unambiguously condemns and reprobates that folk culture which can, with some show of plausibility, be blamed for "backwardness," and for the humiliation imposed by the West. High Islam had always opposed the ecstatic, undisciplined, personality-oriented variant of Islam. Now it could oppose it and be reinforced with some new arguments: it was *this* that had held us back![41]

And that was how it came about that, at the end of the twentieth century, the West faced in Islam a critic, a rival, and on occasion an enemy that was both modern and religious, possessed of a way of knowledge it considered its own, revealed in its Holy Book, and formulated for personal and political use by elaborate textual interpretation by experts using sophisticated techniques. Reformist Islam and its adherents were, in their own terms, rationalist. They also, in their own opinion, had access to religious truth and therefore to spiritual wealth unavailable to the West. The discipline gave them pride, the doctrine gave them tradition and hope, the fact that this Islam was obviously both ancient, universal, and ever new gave them the secure sense that there was no necessary split between power in the technological era and belief in a revealed religion.

Reformist Islam was the pervasive belief and the social and political doctrine not only of those the West called fundamentalists in a strict sense, the activists who blew up American soldiers, but also of the broad consensus of educated people and intellectuals in the Arab world, if not necessarily of those large parts of Islam outside the Middle East.

Islamic revivalists of this stripe wanted what Bassam Tibi called the "dream of half-modernity." They rejected what they called "modernism," by which they meant the attempt by Islamic scholars and statesmen such as Muhammad Iqbal and Fazlur Rahman to develop an Islamic social and political thought open to liberal ideas and universal reason, to the modern triad, in fact. Rahman in particular sought an interpretation of the Koran that would be "true to the spirit of Islam but provide for the needs of modern life" by distinguishing the literal words of scripture from their modern implications.[42] What Rahman proposed was analogous to what liberal Christian theologians since the late eighteenth century had tried to do: distinguish the form of the Word of God from its message and extract the universal meaning from the ancient words. But this was exactly what Reformist Islam could never accept. The form and the meaning could not be distinguished; that was a Western and infidel heresy.

The revivalists emphatically rejected "modernism" as applied to Islam, but for the same reasons they welcomed postmodernism in a particular sense. Islamic revivalists wanted Western postmodernism if it weakened the West, made Westerners feel insecure and guilty, and made it easier to enforce claims for political and economic concessions on the West. They absolutely did not want postmodernism if it meant that they themselves should question their own morality, their own Grand Narratives, and their own forms of knowledge. Postmodernism was fine, in their view, if it helped to undermine a Western culture that was anyway, in their opinion, immoral and heretical; as a general attitude of scepticism and epistemological doubt applied to any system of universal belief and morals, it was not.

In Islamic revivalism, to be postmodern was accordingly to reject liberal modernism and to accept the integralism of Sayyid Qutb and other revivalists. It was not to be a relativist or to believe that there was no such thing as knowledge beyond culture. It was, however, to dispute the universalism of Western rationality and political doctrines that Islamic revivalism welcomed and agreed with Western postmodernism, because both despised and rejected the West in both its major incarnations—as Christendom and as classical liberalism. Reformist Islam welcomed a fashion such as postmodernism, which weakened Western universalism but remained committed to its own dogmatic universalist belief that all knowledge came from the Koran. "In most works published in Arabic by Islamic fundamentalists, the relations between 'the West' and the 'world of Islam' are defined in terms of the incompatible and rival concepts of knowledge as a conflict between civilizations."[43]

Such authors accepted only the Muslim definition of knowledge; Islam was superior to the West because Islam offered more perfect knowledge of the world. The conflict of civilizations, from their perspective, took the form of constant, open, and surreptitious Western attempts to subvert Islam by introducing its inferior forms of knowledge and attacking Islamic knowledge. The favored interpretation of this conflict from the revivalist perspective was as a constant and never-ceasing Western "conspiracy," for only a conspiracy could explain how it was that a plainly inferior form of knowledge, the Western, could so insistently attack a superior form without being destroyed in the process. "From this perspective the conspiracy of Western penetration of the *Dar-al-Islam*/House of Islam becomes a *ghazu al-fikri*/intellectual invasion." The protection and spread of true knowledge thus became "the prevalent cultural current throughout Islamic civilization."[44]

Western postmodernists and Islamic revivalists agreed that modern rationalism and the Weberian West's claim to have discovered a universal method of investigation of the world were wrong and evil. They differed in what con-

sequences to draw. The Western postmodernist remained a relativist and refused to recognize any knowledge beyond culture. The Islamic revivalist insisted that the West be relativist but that his own religious knowledge remain
exempt from the postmodern deconstruction: Islam provided the true knowledge beyond culture that the West mistakenly and temporarily thought it had
discovered. His ambitious project for the twenty-first century was not to beat
the West at its own game, but to de-Westernize knowledge, to unmask the
idea of universal science as a tool of defunct Western domination, and to introduce a new, higher form of knowledge. Where would this higher knowledge find its base, as science had its base in rationality, method, experiment,
testability, and result? On scripture: "The holy Koran is the complete and definitive revelation . . . and there is no other knowledge that can guide and save
man, other than the knowledge that rests on that source."[45]

The Islamic answer to the West was that it was without spirit and truth,
and that the idea of objective knowledge beyond culture, first formulated effectively in the West, was an imperialist conspiracy to be superseded by a truer
form of knowledge beyond culture, because this superior knowledge would
rest not on any particular society but on divine revelation. The spiritless and
decadent West would be in no position either politically or morally to object
to this superior knowledge. Indeed, eventually the West would abandon both
its areligious hedonism and its Judeo-Christian heresies and submit to Islam,
where fullness of truth was uniquely and universally available.

China was an alternative path of human development not in its guise as
the last great Marxist regime but as Chinese civilization manifested in
family values, entrepreneurship, work ethic, a serious attitude to education,
competence, and learning, respect for parents, superiors, and social hierarchy,
and a strong communitarianism—all these things propagated under the labels of Confucianism, Asian values, or, as some put it, the revenge of the East
over the debilitated, ex-colonial West.

In particular, proponents of the so-called Singapore school pointed to
Singapore and other East Asian societies as evidence that the liberal triad
could function quite well on only two of its legs—capitalism and rationality—while discarding the third leg, liberty. Some Singapore school spokesmen asserted that the triad functioned better as a simple duality of reason
and economic development, and shorn of the excesses of Western freedom,
which, so they argued, had reached a point where they subverted prosperity
and rationality. Kishore Mahbubani, the head of the Singapore civil service,

argued in 1995 that America and Europe were "breaking down and falling apart" because of "an excess of democracy and an overdose of freedom. An obsession with individual fulfilment has led to the breakdown of the family. An over-vigorous press has destroyed respect for institutions."[46] Western rationality and the scientific and economic methods of knowledge and development were indeed excellent and all the claims made for their universality and validity beyond cultures were correct. Unfortunately, the West had forgotten what it had itself discovered. It had become not so much immoral and infidel as incompetent. Proponents of Asian values coined a sharp-edged redefinition of the abbreviation NDC, which in international relations and development parlance meant "newly developing countries." No longer, said the Asian values people; NDC applied not to places like Thailand, Taiwan, or Singapore, but to the West, and it stood for "newly decaying countries."

The causes of Western incompetence were variously defined by various authors, but one useful way of explaining the idea was to see it as a crisis of Western individualism. Western political, economic, and cultural success rested at bottom on a Western notion of the individual as autonomous and self-reliant but at the same time moderate, respectful of tradition, civic-minded, and culturally literate—the individual of the vigorous virtues and their corresponding obligations. Western incompetence, whether manifested in sloth and decline of technological prowess or in social anarchy was what happened when the ideal Western individual discarded the vigorous virtues in favor of other values such as self-realization, consumerism, and the need for self-esteem rather than the desire for knowledge, and began to prefer emotional satisfaction to hard-earned skill.

The Asian argument began with the premise that economic growth and prosperity was the only reasonable goal of policy. Given this goal, what social and political arrangements would best promote it? In the West, capital accumulation began in the later Middle Ages in the shelter of property rights, and accelerated in northwest Europe after the Reformation in the guise, at first irrational and later highly rational, of the Calvinist and Puritan work ethic. The Weberian argument held that this work ethic yielded both early capitalism and a certain dispassionate view of the world, divorced from superstition, that in turn led to science and the scientific principles of investigation.

The Enlightenment in the West added political liberty and personal autonomy of belief to this mixture of reason and science. Thus arose the classical liberal synthesis of capitalism, science, and democracy that shaped Western debate, whether liberal, socialist, or conservative, over the two centuries since the American and French Revolutions. By the mid-twentieth century, Americans were convinced that prosperity and economic growth required political liberty as well as scientific rationality. The Grand Narrative supported this belief, but ignored the difficult and often contradictory history of how liberty, rationality, and economic development had emerged in favor of an idealized schema that looked clear and simple but in fact rested on dangerously weak foundations.

The Singapore school denied that rationality and economic development required political liberty. The long-time prime minister of Singapore, Lee Kuan Yew, expressed its view when he stated that "I don't accept the simplistic idea that a free market in order to develop needs a liberal democracy."[47] Singapore and other Far Eastern economic centers, until the late 1990s, had achieved growth rates beyond anything seen in the West since the 1960s. Slowing Western growth rates correlated with worsening social pathologies and a proliferation of rights liberalism. The Singapore school claimed that Singapore and other Far Eastern economic cities and regions enjoyed growth and social stability because they did not have to deal with the growth-inhibiting effects of social anarchy, litigiousness, declining performance standards, petty crime, affirmative action, and other cultural traits of the United States. Singapore was a challenge to the remaining Westernists in America, people who were deeply committed to the idea that democracy went along with prosperity and who wanted more of both.

Both the Singapore school and Western liberals who wanted to keep freedom central ignored one crucial fact about East Asian economic development: it copied the West. The question was not whether economic development required liberty in general, but whether economic development required liberty to get started in the first place. That authoritarian states were able to copy economic development after it had already been invented in the West neither proved nor disproved that liberty was necessary for the first economic development anywhere to get going. It proved only that it was possible to repeat economic development using authoritarian methods.

The city-state of Singapore was a unique case. Its people achieved, in the three decades after 1960, outstanding economic success. Lee Kuan Yew, who was prime minister from 1959 to 1990, knew that one of the reasons was stable government: "If we had mistaken our priorities, if we had put democratic forms ahead of economic substance, we would never have attained this level of development. . . . They accuse me of having interfered too much in the private life of the citizens. They are right, but if I hadn't done it, we wouldn't be where we are today."[48] In 1960, Singapore was a semicolonial town where the port and its business provided most of the employment in the form of unskilled labor at low wages. From the mid-1960s on, the Lee government invited foreign businesses on favorable terms; by the early 1990s, over three thousand had established production on the fewer than 400 square miles of the island of Singapore. Average annual income had risen from a few hundred dollars to $13,000. The population had changed from low-skilled Malays, Indians, and South Chinese to one of specialized workers ranging from engineers to managers, high-tech workers, and professionals.

The single-party government of Lee Kuan Yew and his successors displayed features that placed it in no camp familiar to Western observers, not liberal, socialist, or right-wing authoritarian. The regime encouraged complete freedom and security of investment. It managed to solve to an amazing extent a constant problem of large-scale capitalism, namely, that whereas innovation and growth depended on people taking risks and reaping unexpected rewards, large businesses and investors did not want risk but long-term security. Lee gave them that. He also provided something else that was unusual. It was a standard rule of economic development that economic inequalities grew fastest during the early phases of takeoff, creating, in many countries, political and social tensions, producing in the West, among other things, the novels of Charles Dickens and the ideology of Karl Marx. In Singapore, economic inequality did not increase during the 1960s and 1970s, a factor of intangible value but that certainly supported Lee's claims that his government was acting in the common interests of all Singaporeans.

At the same time, his regime in the 1960s and 1970s expropriated land at one-tenth of market value when it needed it to offer businesses or for government housing. Lee's transport policy was likewise draconian: the government did not allow the number of privately owned cars to grow at a faster rate than the road capacity. Since road building was not a priority of the regime, that meant that the number of cars also could only grow slowly. How to restrain demand? By high taxes, four to five times the value of the vehicle, and by an ingenious system of driving permits auctioned off in a limited number once a month, and, once obtained, good for the lifetime of the holder.

As good Aristotelians and Weberians, the Lee government likewise in its legislation and through its economic incentives encouraged its citizens to act with a degree of foresight, competence, and self-sacrifice worthy of a Calvinist. Government required that workers save a third of income for retirement, the policy being that welfare was the responsibility of families and not of the state. For the same reason the government offered cheap housing to persons with a college degree, the rent being lower the larger the applicant's family.

Demographics was one area where the Lee government seemed to have failed to provide the right incentives. Until 1983, the policy was to restrain births by any reasonable means, given the scarcity of land. From 1983 and for some years after, the government changed tack and said that it was important that the most educated people have more children, because of the feared dysgenic effects of larger and faster generations among the unskilled Malays and Indians than among the more highly skilled Chinese. The policy appeared to have failed, and the most educated in Singapore, as elsewhere in the world, were also those with the lowest fertility.

The Singapore school presented these and many other accomplishments of the regime and argued that they were possible only because of the soft authoritarianism of the government. Certainly they were not due to some effect of Confucian culture. There was very little of that in Singapore until the 1970s, when economic growth was already well under way. Before that, the Chinese population of Singapore was, in the majority, unskilled and illiterate and native to parts of China in the extreme south where Confucianism had never held sway.

The school's defenders argued that human rights advocates criticizing Singapore were not in good faith, that they wanted to impose Western-style democracy on Singapore knowing that Singaporean firms were competing with American firms, and that such firms would be helped if the costs of doing business in Singapore grew, as they invariably would if Singapore became more like America; that they were hypocritical, given the West's own expensive social pathologies; and that the West did not criticize other authoritarians, so why pick on Singapore? One representative of the school asked if there were not

> reason to suspect that Western attitudes reflect, not hubris, but a demoralization so deep that few dare acknowledge its existence. Many in the West have not yet adjusted psychologically to the post–Cold War world. They are disheartened by the loss of economic competitiveness and seemingly intractably social and political problems. Rather than adapt, their instinct is to insist that others adopt their own problems. They have lost the confidence to believe that their own life is worth living without seeing it as obligatory for the entire human race.[49]

Western critics of the supposed Singapore model were arguing from a parochial perspective. No one in Singapore was claiming that science, knowledge, or the rational methods of investigation and experiment were not valid; on the contrary, they were claiming that they were indeed, as the Enlightenment West had always held, universally valid. What seemed to offend some Western critics was that the Singapore experiment could also be taken to demonstrate that there was a morality beyond culture, which it was advisable to adopt if you wished to guarantee continued prosperity and stability in your society, and that this cross-cultural morality resembled that of early modern Puritans more than that of late-twentieth-century American "last men."

The Singapore experiment was unique and unrepeatable. The country was both tiny and exposed, both factors that gave Lee Kuan Yew and his aides powerful arguments to coerce local grandees and local workers to maintain an iron social discipline. For example, the Lee government succeeded almost alone in the Third World in virtually destroying government corruption in the 1960s, apparently mostly by pointing out that if Singapore could not quickly attract foreign investment, the country would be occupied either by Malaysia or by Indonesia. And to get foreign investment, you had to minimize corruption.

Observers in the mid-1990s included those who believed, like Eric Jones, that once Singapore acquired a substantial middle class, then democratization could not be indefinitely delayed. "A middle class," he wrote, "transforms society." The middle class would want freedoms, and before many decades had passed, the demand for political change would become a "Juggernaut. . . . Unless one-party ideology becomes once again more suffocating than it currently seems, political entrepreneurs will arise to supply the demand and, no doubt, to pretend that they have invented the fresh, nonmaterial commodities they will put on offer."[50]

The other position was that there was no sign whatever that Singaporeans wanted to start acting like Americans. They had, from the 1970s to the 1990s, transformed their city-state from a "rugged society" to a "gracious society," fully equipped with a sophisticated and demanding middle class, which nevertheless, to the evident irritation of unimaginative and parochial Americans, was not demanding a Bill of Rights. One observer concluded in 1996 that

> the contrast between the theoretical expectations of liberty and the persistence of an enlightened autocracy in a developed society such as Singapore (but also in other Asiatic situations) leads one to suppose that the relation between culture and freedom may be somewhat more complex than Western liberals imagine. The necessitating link between culture and freedom rises from an anthropological vision which, on the basis of Western experience, posits individual freedom as a universal need of human nature.[51]

At an economic summit meeting with Western political leaders in 1996, the prime minister of Malaysia, Mahathir Mohamad, told his guests: "Asian values are universal values. European values are European values."[52] Since Mahathir

Mohamad was a Muslim, his "Asian values" were clearly some amalgam, some refined joint essence of Islam and Confucianism, being presented as "universal" with the same confidence that Montesquieu and Voltaire assumed that the West was "civilization" pure and simple, a universal standard.

In such a statement, Islam and Confucianism moved from being alternatives to being replacements for the West, better models of human development and spiritual fulfillment. Indeed, advocates of the alternatives in the 1990s were moving from proclaiming alternatives to proclaiming replacements, and the amalgamation of Islam and China in a common set of "Asian values" was a new development. It was noteworthy, however, that the behavior that followed from "Asian values" was largely the same as the behavior that followed from the liberal triad in the West, that is to say, diligence, responsibility, study and hard work, foresight, and respect for law. It was also noteworthy that proponents of Asian values did not insist, in public at least, that Asian values excluded democracy and equality before the law; on the contrary, such proponents usually claimed that their governments were democratic and liberal, just like the West, only without the excesses. But if Asian values simply repeated those of the political West, but short of expressive individualism, what was Asian about them? They might rather be said to resemble those of America in the 1950s, when, as many Americans would certainly argue, America was more truly Western than in the 1990s.

While the postmodernists, the moralists, the universalists, and others were busy denying or ignoring that there was such a thing as historical reality, a quiet revolution had been taking place in social science and history; not the petty social science that tied itself in knots studying the contemporary landscape, and certainly not the postmodern history that dominated American universities, but the macrosociological and macrohistorical study of human social evolution on the largest scale, from the Paleolithic on. This revolution had yet to percolate into the higher reaches of American academia, which remained in thrall to the fashionable antipositivism of the 1960s. But viewed from outside, this antipositivism was starting by the late 1990s to appear increasingly antiquated and unsuited to understanding and assessing the true significance of the global transformations of the age. Postmodernism was not, as its adherents continued to claim, some kind of daring and adventurous exploration of the new. It was the boring and repetitive recital of ancient irritations and secondhand resentments, with as little purchase on an exploding reality as the political manipulations of the king of France in the last days of the old regime.

The macrohistorical revolution of the 1980s and 1990s offered what Arnold Toynbee had never delivered: a vision of human history that made sense of the largest-scale facts: of civilizations, wars, poverty, and prosperity. It was unfortunate that Toynbee had been discredited, for the antipositivists used his example to show that it was not possible to say anything about the big questions that was not mainly a reflection of personal prejudices. The macrohistorical revolution confounded this scepticism. The human race did have an intelligible history, and in the late twentieth century, this intelligible history moved into a higher gear and a broader framework. It was from the results of this revolution that we would learn the true prospects of the West. But it was not until the global transformation approached critical mass in the 1970s that a number of disparate observations and insights began to come together in the work of people such as David S. Landes, Ernest Gellner, Eric Jones, Jean Baechler, Richard O'Connell, and, in different and mutually opposed senses, Francis Fukuyama and Samuel P. Huntington. They were the spearhead of the macrohistorical revolution, and it was on their work that a reconstruction of the past and an assessment of the future of the West must henceforth rest: an assessment not of universalist ideology, but of the real conditions of human social evolution, of stratification, war, culture, and economic development in the long term. This assessment revealed the extraordinary nature of the global transformations in all these areas, which were changing irrevocably from patterns going back a hundred centuries.

The macrohistorians argued that the West and the rest of the world were entering upon the most important transition in human history in the later twentieth century. They also argued that one could not understand the transition without understanding the logic of human history in the very long term.

It was a tenet of the macrohistorians that human history had a ternary structure. The first was an indefinite era in which small human groups lived a hunter-gathering existence without social stratification, war, or inner tension. In this early stage, all humans were able to live the lives that they were able to devise for themselves; they lived in accordance with their nature and desires. Second, a period of ten thousand years from the beginnings of agriculture to the rise of modernity, in which human social life was characterized by variation, evolution, and change, but also by stratification, war, and social conflict.

Neolithic society introduced stratification and conflict by creating, for the first time, a distinction between those humans who got to realize their ambitions and those, the majority, who did not, and who lived and toiled to serve the first group. It was the insight of an American scholar, Richard

O'Connell, that provided the missing piece for the ternary analysis of history and allowed it to be presented as a coherent and universal interpretation. As Jean Baechler summarized the macrohistorical insight, "the Neolithic mutation, which began around ten thousand years ago" was

> a totality of phenomena, of which the earliest symptoms are detectable in the Middle East around the eighth millennium before the current era. They express a radical transformation of the human condition, which can be caricatured as follows. Before it, humanity lived by hunting and gathering, taking from the interest of a capital freely offered by nature; it was organized in tiny bands of some tens or hundreds of individuals, each of which exploited its own territory of some thousands of square kilometers and, for the most part, in ignorance of each other. After it, people drew their nourishment from agriculture and pasturage; they develop the craft of weaving, pottery, and mining; they practice long-distance trade; they fix themselves in villages and towns and form societies of thousands, hundreds of thousands, and even millions of individuals; these societies organized in polities wage war more or less incessantly on one another.[53]

The Neolithic mutation was slow and gradual, but as it began to occur across the globe, it transformed human life. Paleolithic societies were more or less the same everywhere, and "prudent inferences on the basis of contemporary ethnographic facts" permitted the conclusion that "cultural diversity was minimal." After the Neolithic mutation took hold in a given region, everything changed. Cultures became huge in extent and few in number: the geopolitical civilizations known to history began to appear—Europe, China, India, western Asia, North America, South America. Each region was defined, above local variation, by a particular way of thinking, doing, sensing, or imagining the conditions of life and supernatural reality. Within each of these geopolitical spaces, a succession of large states or empires emerged, each seeking dominance within its space, and each governed by what Gellner called command-administrative methods. Each civilization evolved religions with universal, but widely differing, claims. Also in each, social stratification became necessary to order and discipline the new masses of people and to extract from them the surplus to feed the religious and administrative elites. Thus, the benefits of civilization were limited to 20 percent or less of the population. "Neolithization implied an immense increase in the field of possible variations for humanity, for culture, and for the social elites." Thus, the one great result of the Neolithic mutation was "a great leap forward for human diversity."

And for war. The macrohistorical theory of war joined and completed the macrohistorical theory of the leap of diversity, of stratification, and of geopolitical variation by arguing that the Neolithic mutation to agriculture necessarily produced war, because it multiplied human numbers while at the same time making human life increasingly dependent on exploiting agriculture. Competition for resources, both spiritual and material, a type of competition unheard of in the Paleolithic, was the fundamental cause of war.

The chain of logic was as follows. Over centuries and millennia, certain hunter-gatherers in certain places, starting in the upper Euphrates valley, began to domesticate and grow crops. In the process of domestication, the plants would themselves mutate into versions offering higher yields, but more vulnerable to parasites and weeds. This entailed more hard work for the early farmers, but also greater rewards, as yields grew. But as yields grew, so did the population. "It is a stark commentary on the system," wrote Richard O'Connell, "that the modifications in cereal plants brought about by domestication . . . would be balanced by changes in the opposite direction among humans subject to an agroeconomy—decrease in stature, earlier reproduction, greater number of offspring, and less parental investment. . . . It was as if we had been lured aboard an ecological teeter-totter, the dynamics of which increased the well-being of a select group of plants at the expense of our own, at least on an individual basis—a veritable plant trap."[54]

But agriculture in itself and the plant trap did not fully explain war. For war to arise, other elements had to appear in the matrix of growing possibilities offered by Neolithization. The most important element was pastoralism. As some people domesticated plants and suffered the perverse effects, while toiling to supply the emerging strata of chieftains and priests secreted by cultural development, others domesticated animals. These others became, in the course of time, the nomads of history, the denizens of the great steppe of Eurasia, those living on or beyond the margins of the sown lands. But pastoralism was a marginal existence, and even more than agriculture, was a constant race between the food the animals could yield and the needs of growing populations. Since it was not possible to increase animal yields fast enough by endogenous means, the solution often chosen was either to steal the animals of other tribes or to invade and pillage the towns of the sown land. "Subsistence strategies robust enough to support large populations (either human or ruminant, depending on the context) were a necessary prerequisite for the emergence and perpetuation of true warfare in our species."[55]

But war was not yet endemic, as the archaeological record showed. Indeed, in the 1960s and after a popular focus of feminist scholarship was to argue that the Neolithic mutation, so far from introducing strife and conflict to humanity, in fact inaugurated the peaceful rule of feminine values, since tilling the soil was an activity that corresponded to those values: repetitive, seasonal, tied to the earth, disturbed by violence and demanding peace and tranquillity. A good friend of Joseph Campbell's, the Lithuanian feminist prehistorian Marija Gimbutas, came over her career to be convinced by this model and argued that the early millennia of Neolithic agriculture in the Old World was an era if not of matriarchy then at least of female divinities and feminine, peaceful patterns of social structure, individual ethics, and behavior. All this was ruined in the fourth millennium B.C. when tribesmen worshipping male, warlike gods invaded Europe and South Asia from the central steppes, demolishing the world of the goddesses and imposing the masculinist world of the gods that dominated ever after, or at least until the rise of Western feminism in the 1960s and after.

The archaeological record indicated, to the contrary, that war became endemic in the Old World at the time signaled by Gimbutas as the heyday of maternal values. But the macrohistorical approach identified endogenous reasons that war became endemic, rather than asserting a dichotomy between peaceful, protofeminist farmers and warlike, protomale chauvinist warriors from the steppes. The key was that agrarian societies were, by necessity, densely populated and hard-working. Drudgery and proximity "imposed on our consciousness the general structure of public and private, and . . . ambivalence and suspicion among neighbors." People hemmed in by ceaseless toil and in narrow spaces became prone to despair and anger. Few if any could escape, for there was no life outside the community for people specialized to till the soil and produce the items needed by an agrarian society. "Psychologically, this is the stuff out of which armies and wars arise, especially when combined with the need for territory. For agriculture demanded that we protect not only our homes and possessions but the land necessary to grow food. And, as the world suitable for agriculture filled up with people and farms, the proclivity to wander would come to be increasingly frustrated by a patchwork of exclusivity. Meanwhile, within such societies the need for stability amid growing disparities of wealth would lead to the formalization of social stratification and its enforcement through coercion." Feminist or not, the early agrarian societies knew about discipline, exploitation, and ruling classes. And "so it was that the human spirit would be progressively enmeshed in a web of institutions, obligations, and objective conditions that would create a profound discordance between daily life and our intuitive expectations of what life should be."[56]

What life should be was the Paleolithic balance when everybody was much the same everywhere, and everyone fulfilled his or her desires. The price, which no one realized, was that human groups were few and their members short-lived. The Neolithic mutation increased numbers, wealth, diversity, and possibilities, but for most it made physical life worse—shorter, poorer, and more desperate. The one chance of escape was to leave the sown land and join the pastoralists. Some did so, and pastoralists became more numerous. The nomads were free and mobile and to some extent succeeded in recapturing the Paleolithic harmony. But this harmony was deceptive. Pastoralism rested on fragile ecological foundations. Nomads were not hunter-gatherers but lived off their flocks. And "since their basic possessions, animals, were highly removable, they probably stole from and raided each other virtually from the beginning. But the brunt of pastoralist aggression likely would have been directed elsewhere. For the dynamics of their existence argue that they would come to view the agriculturalists as prey and targets of opportunity. In the eyes of nomads, the tillers of the soil were lesser beings, and would be treated accordingly."[57]

The macrohistorical vision of the engine of human history was thus a vision that conformed to an ancient realism about the human condition, namely, that progress had a price, and that human nature had a dark as well as a light side. Rousseau's vision of how evil entered into history was that one man fenced a field and called it his. The macrohistorical vision did not distinguish between the fencer and his fellows; it did not matter who was first; the Neolithic mutation, whose origins were lost in time, was a logical expression of the human need to diversify and produce, but that expression entailed hierarchy, density, suffering, and exploitation. Agricultural society engendered war by itself; the fact that war first became endemic because nomads invaded the sown land was simply the sequence of history, but nomads by themselves were too few and scattered to make war into the universal practice that it soon became. Agrarian societies secreted cities, states, and empires; empires dominated and exploited, provoking imitators and dissidents; these raised armies to destroy the empires, sometimes in coalition with nomads; they erected new empires that in turn provoked internal or external disruption, and so it went.

Until modernity. The macrohistorical vision asserted two fundamental transitions in history, the one that started social evolution as well as war, and the one that launched modernization and thereby the prospective Universal History of the species. The second transition seemed on the way to producing a peaceful, productive, pluralistic world when the short twentieth century intervened. After the Cold War, so the macrohistorians held, the universal trajectory would resume. But in the most developed versions of the vision, this trajectory would be economic, not political. Therefore, war would remain a possibility, but a decreasing one, for if the macrohistorical insight into its origins held true, the reasons for war—the plant trap, despair, rivalry for empire, and nomadic predation—had disappeared. As Benjamin Constant foresaw in 1814, the energies of war would be turned to commerce, for the same talents that formerly found outlets in military grandeur found greater and more lucrative outlets in business, entrepreneurship, and a different kind of empire building.

Baechler defined "modernity" as the triad of democracy, corresponding to the human drive to liberty; economic growth, which provided the incentives for individual action; and scientific method and its technical fruits, corresponding to the use of reason. Democracy was in essence a political regime of "calculated obedience." The democratic citizen obeyed not by force or constraint, but because he calculated that he could best achieve his ends, which he defined for himself, by temporarily submitting to the direction of someone else. Power in a democracy was rooted in "those who obey from calculated [common] interest."[58] Democratic citizens obeyed the government because they judged it competent to lead them toward a commonly agreed objective, and because they judged the costs of cheating to outweigh the benefits of participation. Democracy also enjoyed legitimacy because it distinguished between public and private, leaving social space open for particular interests, such as economic and religious interests.

Majority rule and natural rights were not intrinsic to democracy, Baechler said; what was intrinsic was the "calculus of consent" whereby citizens gave power to the leadership to promote their common and joint interests, while expecting the same leadership to leave them free to pursue their particular and individual interests. Democracy was the most natural but not therefore the inevitable regime of humankind. It was susceptible to corruption, deformation, and death. Human history contained two other forms of regime: autocracy, the rule of a few, but leaving a broad space for individual freedom so long as that freedom did not threaten the regime; and hierocracy, the rule of someone claiming to represent a higher power, such as the caliphs of medieval Islam or, at certain periods, the popes of Rome. The history of the short twentieth century, according to Baechler, revealed a third and hitherto unheard-of form of nondemocratic regime: ideocracy, or rule by the leaders of a totalitarian movement based not on claims to represent a higher power and not on mere force but on ideology, on a vision of history and of the road to a human society purified of negative elements.

The history of the twentieth century was the history of how a series of accidents produced a "monstrous deformation" of the antidemocratic options, and how examples of such deformation took power in Russia, Germany, and China and almost succeeded in dominating the world. They failed to do so mainly because the United States "succeeded in preserving its democratic regime and surviving the tempests of the twentieth century: the conditions of possibility of democracy are exceptionally well assembled there, the institutions are reasonably adequate, the polity is an abundantly peopled continent. Thanks to this fortunate concatenation of favorable factors by the United States, democracy survived the autocratic and ideocratic regimes that seemed on the verge of swallowing us all."[59]

From what one knew of human nature and of the potential worldwide expansion of the modern transcription of that human nature, one would predict, given the world situation in 1914, that the future of humanity would be one in which democracy, scientific rationality, and the principles of economic growth would be slowly spreading across the globe. This did not happen because World War I, the second fall of man, derailed this expected course of events; expected not so much in 1914 as expected in hindsight, given Baechler's macrosociological understanding of human nature and its conditions of activity.

Baechler considered the start of the war an event easily explainable within the terms of European great power politics and the dynamics of an oligopolar system, that is, one with a few powerful poles but organized in opposing alliances and therefore tending toward an unstable bipolar condition, with the Central Powers of Germany and Austria flanked on both sides by the members of the Triple Entente, Britain, France, and Russia. Baechler's theory of war and international relations stated that the structure of the international or "transpolitical" system was a determining cause of democratic liberties within the member states of the system; the beginnings of democratic and capitalist modernity in certain European countries was, in part, a function of the pluralist nature of that transpolitical system, the fact that Europe was not a single empire.

The end of the Roman Empire was the earliest beginning of the European transpolitical system, which evolved into its classic form in the thirteenth and fourteenth centuries. As Eric Jones suggested in 1981, the competition among states encouraged each member state to mobilize its resources most efficiently; those states with incipient local democracy and local liberties were also the most economically productive; this gave them an edge in the competition; the competition thus encouraged liberty and economic development. The transpolitical system had to have a certain number of members to be stable over the long term and therefore to be able to provide the competitive stimulus to democracy and capitalism. This number must be more than four and less than ten. A system with four or fewer members tended toward bipolarity, and bipolarity was inherently unstable because each side would be constantly on guard against the other or would be constantly seeking to destroy the other and establish a monopolar hegemony. Likewise, a system with more than ten members would be so complex that it would encourage free riding and cheating by members, which in turn was destabilizing and promoted conflict. Only a transpolitical system with five to ten members was stable, for in such a system cheaters would be easily identified and no single member would be able to plan for hegemony without provoking a balancing alliance.

The European system from the fifteenth to the early twentieth century was such a stable one. So why did World War I happen? The unexpected accident that produced the entire "tragic parenthesis" of war, ideocracy, and totalitarian rule of the short twentieth century was that the war did not stop, but continued after the first few weeks until it could not stop because neither side could or would accept that it could not win. What happened was that the war brought about the "military transcription" of modernity, of the technical, scientific, even democratic potential of modernity. Mass mobilization turned every citizen into a defender of his country on whom its fate depended; the fact that all the states of Europe enjoyed similar levels of technical and scientific skill meant that every military innovation was immediately matched by the other side. These two factors combined meant that the war became self-reinforcing. When it ended, it had discredited, by its very intensity, violence, and duration, the "modern transcription" of human nature: "democracy lost credibility; capitalism was condemned; rationality was despised. The result was either the belief that one needed to find salvation elsewhere, either in fascist anti-modernism or in communist hyper-modernism, or a weakness that meant that active defenders of democracy were few and those of capitalism fewer still." This was an accurate sociological account of the condition of the West, and especially of Europe, between the world wars; the condition of pessimism and desperation that led T.S. Eliot and Ernst Robert Curtius to seek salvation in the Roman and medieval past and led Carl Schmitt and others to

despair of parliamentary democracy and to hope for salvation in a restored
Holy Roman Empire.

The fall of communism in 1989–91 in Europe reinstated the trends broken in 1914 and permitted the liberal and peaceful modern transcription of
human nature to regain its supremacy as the standard model. Baechler was
announcing an end of history, but only in the sense that he saw the return to
a history interrupted in two senses: in the twentieth century, by the accidents
of 1914 and what followed, and since the Neolithic age, by the constraints
put by various hierocratic and autocratic regimes on the ability of "human
nature" to flourish under its appropriate conditions, those of democracy.

Human nature remained human and tempted by the advantages to be
gained by distorting democracy, so there was no guarantee that liberal
democracy, rationality, and economic growth would continue to form the
framework of history, whether in the West or worldwide. Baechler was no
determinist. His only prediction for the future was that ideocracy would not
be able to return, anywhere. After 1991, no one could any longer doubt that
the only way to economic prosperity was some form of capitalism. This
would therefore spread, since everyone would like to fulfill material ambitions, and most people wanted more goods than they had. As capitalism
spread, so would the people and institutions that made it work, the skilled
and professional middle classes. But that did not imply that democracy, too,
would be universal. Democracy was instrumental in starting capitalism in
the West, but it was not necessary, and might even be a hindrance, to starting
capitalism elsewhere. Capitalism, or economic development, was transcrib-
able outside its culture of origin as a set of legal and economic techniques
and did not require, to take root in alien soil, the same political circumstances that provoked its birth in Europe. Economic development was like
science. It needed certain circumstances to get started but, once started, became a universal patrimony to be mobilized anywhere and by anyone willing
to understand its rules of operation and to invest the necessary effort:

> Just as the discovery of capitalism in Europe and its continuation in the West
> was due, in the final instance, to the conditions of its possibility being assem-
> bled by, on the one hand, an oligopolar transpolitical system, and, on the
> other hand, democratic or mildly authoritarian regimes, so, similarly, the
> problem of its spread and adoption outside of Europe and the West appears as
> a dual political problem. The first question is about free trade. Is it conceiv-
> able that free trade should extend across the planet and that the entire planet

should become one global integrated economic market? The answer is clearly yes. This is not a matter of culture but of political calculation. More precisely, humanity is single in the sense of forming a distinct species, which enables all its representatives, individually or in groups, to undertake all forms of human interaction, including commercial exchanges. These exchanges have been real since the species made its appearance in the Paleolithic, a thin reality, perhaps, for tens of millennia, but that is not the question. The question is whether capitalism *can be* universalized: the answer is positive as to the possibility of a planetary market. We may even say that it is plausible and even that this market is an emerging reality.[60]

Democracy, on the other hand, had "almost no chance" of spreading beyond the West. Even there, it was hardly safe. The dangers to democracy within the West would be partly old and partly new. The old danger was now reduced to a single option: some form of autocracy, rule by a narrow elite permitting the majority some private freedoms but preventing those freedoms from threatening its rule. The new danger was that although democratic procedures always benefited more people in the long run, most people lived in the short run and some might be tempted to short-circuit democratic procedures to gain advantage for themselves. Thus, history in the future, Baechler concluded, would consist of oscillations between democratic and autocratic government. Democracy, for all its inherent virtues, was not destiny. Arguments against it would be easy to mobilize, for example, that democracy denied or ignored man's higher essence by reducing everything to numbers and to money; democracy failed to provide equal rights, equal esteem, or equal recognition; democracy was boring; democracy involved too much conflict, strife, and debate on trivial issues, ignoring people's true needs.

The macrohistorical vision thus denied that that History would be democratic. It would, however, be modern and capitalist. "The entire planet will be capitalist two or three generations from now, that is to say, by the end of the twenty-first century. It will be capitalist as to its economic organization, and this organization, producing everywhere roughly the same effects, will provide every polity, apart from local exceptions, with comparable levels of economic development."[61]

But it would not be a democratic and Western history, for, as Samuel Huntington pointed out, the effect of modernization, including economic development, was that it made those who experienced it richer and stronger, so that they were better able to resist Western political and ideological hegemony. Civilizations would not converge. "In fundamental ways," he noted, "the world is becoming more modern and less Western."[62]

The macrohistorical prediction was that universal economic development would be accompanied, in the political sphere, by a coalescence of states and communities around a limited number of centers. In order for this global transpolitical system to be stable in the long term as was its European predecessor, it needed at least five and not more than ten members; Baechler suggested the United States, China, Russia, India, Brazil, a major Islamic power, and perhaps Europe, if the European Union ever developed from a bureaucratic and legal regulation machine to an actual federation with political authority. The global system would be more peaceful the more it moved toward actual confederation with organizations and treaties binding the main actors, and more prone to war the more it resembled a large-scale version of the European system, which was characterized by being both very stable and prone to internal conflict. "An oligopolar system," Baechler wrote in 1993, "in order to cover the transpolitical space between the conditions of peace and war, a transpolitical legal order or international law. . . . The more the system approaches the confederal pole, the less the risks of war, the more the recurring conflicts can be negotiated peacefully and the more matters of collective interest can be dealt with in common. It is not too soon to predict that this is the pole toward which the planet is tending. . . . one can detect the symptoms of it in the rejuvenated role of the United Nations, in the assertion of a right of intervention, in the proliferation of public and private organizations pursuing transpolitical activities."[63] Samuel Huntington agreed, but with a note of warning that the elements of the system would identify with their civilizations, and that this identification could prove a greater source of conflict than the kind of rivalries familiar from the European transpolitical system, which consisted of states that all belonged to a single civilization.

The West was not, therefore, likely to suffer from an absence of history, for there would be history as least as long as there were many civilizations, and at the end of the second millennium, the macrohistorical evidence leaned in favor of many and against the notion of a universal civilization. The macrohistorical vision left open many questions, for it was not a futurology, only a sociology and therefore one that offered plausible predictions, not final schemes. Nor was the vision equally shared by all its contributors. Huntington argued that civilizational identity would shape political alignments; Baechler declared that "civilizations will not fight, for civilizations are not actors," but left open the possibility that "polities," that is, states or federations, the actors of the transpolitical system, "might fight in the name of civilizations, just as they formerly fought in the name of religions."[64] In his view, existing civilizations, including the West, Islam, China, India, and the others, would most likely all dissolve into their constituent religious, artistic, literary, popular, and political elements, and these elements would recombine in new and unheard-of patterns.

If a thin, New Western universalism—as the responses to it, as well as the macrohistorical analysis, suggested—was unrealistic, where did that leave Western identity in the third millennium? Extrapolating the macrohistory of the human race, one would conclude that the future held universal economic development, but continued threats to democracy, partly because democracy would remain confined to the West, to India, and to a few other places, and partly because democracy, even where it existed, engendered its own opposition. In the short twentieth century, this opposition had been that of the "innumerable children of the French Revolution" within the West, and of the Soviet Union from the margins of the West. In future it would be an opposition of fundamentalists and conservatives, anti-Western conservatives like Arnold Toynbee and Joseph Campbell, an opposition based on aesthetic and religious revulsion from manifestations of democratic populism and the culture of entertainment.

The history of the West is where understanding of Western identity and prospects must begin. Therefore, the radical Enlightenment and its legacy, which sought justice, fairness, equality, and the full protection of rights in future improvements, was not a pattern for the West, but an ideological illusion drawn from certain Western ideals and distorted into coercive patterns of political practice that always served, and would always serve, particular interests. The key to Western evolution and identity was the historical and sociological insights first developed in the sceptical Enlightenment by Montesquieu and Hume, carried on in the nineteenth century by Tocqueville, and restored in the late twentieth century by the macrohistorians, who were the true heirs of Montesquieu the sociologist, just as the brawling, imperfect, and productive American republic remained the real-life heir of Montesquieu the philosopher and of the American founders.

Universalism failed because, despite its appearance of optimism and boldness, it was merely the last in a long list of late liberal failures of nerve. It suggested that a set of minimal principles—democracy and capitalism—were becoming global, but was unwilling to declare this a victory of the West. Multiculturalists and macrohistorians agreed that Westernization was not the right word to describe the global political processes operating at the threshold of the third millennium. I propose to put universalism out of its misery by relieving it both of its claims and of its historical burden. The world is becoming modern, in the sense that market principles and freedom of communication are spreading to all cultures. But it is not becoming Western, and probably not even becoming especially democratic.

The historical burden of universalism is that it is both Western and anti-Western. Its proponents want to argue that Western principles are winning, but since they include both multiculturalists and Western liberals, they cannot agree on whether this means Westernization, or if Westernization is a good idea. Again, they need not worry. Universalism is not Westernization, and Westernization is not the dominant political or cultural trend of the twenty-first century.

Some version of the West will continue to play a part in the global balance of cultural and political power. The question for those interested in the West and its prospects is therefore what version that will be. I propose that the only viable West is the West whose identity has been traced in this book—a New West that is the loyal descendant and not the disobedient child of the Old.

The Old West was the synthesis of classical, Christian, and Germanic culture, enriched and added by the creative passion of those who developed it. But a narrative of the Old West that moves simply in the sphere of ideas is misleading. The Old West was not only a culture of pious people who married early, lived faithfully, prayed often, and worked hard. The Old West included looters as well as builders, bigots as well as scientists and discoverers open to what they saw. But unlike the vacuous openness of the late liberal New West, which prides itself on being ahistorical, the openness of the Old West derived from a strong identity.

That identity also included, for example, people like the Platter family of the sixteenth and seventeenth century.[65] Thomas Platter was the son of poor farmers and goatherds who lived in the upper Rhone valley of Switzerland. Orphaned at a young age, Thomas left his mountain valley at about eight years old. Having already learned his letters from older relatives, the boy crossed the Grimsel pass, descended through Lucerne and Zurich, continued on into Germany, and eventually found himself in Silesia. He survived, grew up, eventually prospered, and returned to Switzerland as a printer, boarding-house keeper, and proprietor of schools. At the age of thirty-six, he had been "shepherd, goatherd, cowherd, mountain peasant, pupil, beggar, nomad, student, singer, teacher of Latin, Greek, and Hebrew, ropemaker, printer, finally school director and manager-developer of rental properties." He married

Anna Dietschi and they had four children, three daughters, who died in the various plague epidemics that swept through Europe every ten years or so, and a son, Felix, who survived. Thomas was too old to pursue his own dream of becoming a doctor, but he sent Felix to the best medical college in Europe, at Montpellier in France. Felix became a doctor and, later, professor of medicine at Basel. Late in life, as a widower, Thomas married again, at age seventy-four, and had six more children, including another son, also called Thomas, who was raised by his uncle Felix and, like him, became a doctor at Basel in the early seventeenth century.

We know all this, and much more, because both the Thomases and Felix wrote journals, in the Swiss German dialect, which have been often studied and appreciated for the dramatic picture they provide of the sixteenth century, the pivotal age of the Old West. When Thomas was born, the Catholic Church reigned still, though she was losing the allegiance of the humanists and freethinkers. In his thirties and forties, Thomas the elder took a leading part in moving to the Swiss form of Protestantism. These were Old and New Westerners: living in the age of religious conflict, war, and sudden death, yet curious, sharp-witted, open to experience and change.

The gravamen of the radical attacks on the Grand Narrative and on centrist liberalism was that they were empty and inhuman. Similarly, the gravamen of criticism of the universalism of the 1990s was that it perpetrated a narrow, economic view of man, a twenty-first-century version of the bourgeois pathology. If there is a single point about the Old West and its enduring significance that needs to be drawn out, it is that this empty liberalism is a travesty of historical reality. Of course, a liberalism of pure acquisitiveness, a liberalism of hegemonic markets and of anemic, abstract rights demeans both the individual and the civilization. But a vigorous liberalism was always far more than that. If it can shed its three weaknesses—the illusion of newness, the economism of the bourgeois pathology, and its dangerous tendency to see liberty as empowerment rather than as something that grows with, and not against, power and necessity—it may have a future.

In the 1990s, the political scientist Seymour Martin Lipset conducted a broad survey of American society, politics, and culture. In it, he noted that the way out of social or cultural crisis for Americans had always been what he named "moral individualism," adding that "an emphasis on individual morality is an elemental component of the American polity." In America, surveys showed a "positive relationship between self-oriented values and placing importance on charitable activities. In other words, people who were the most individualistic were also the most likely to value doing things to help others."[66] This observation illustrated once again the fundamental intuition of the sceptical Enlightenment, that entrepreneurship, civic activism, and civil and political liberty were intimately connected. Charitable and civic-minded behavior was what one would expect from a person possessed of vigorous virtues or moral individualism, contrary to the leftist cliché that defined individuals in strongly capitalist societies, such as America, in terms of the bourgeois pathology, as necessarily shortsighted, selfish, and greedy. The contrary seemed to be the case, as a moment's reflection would suggest: the capitalist who was shortsighted, selfish, and greedy would soon find himself without customers, profits, or income.

The vigorous virtues were the qualities of character that made responsible self-assertion possible and thus ensured that recognition was deserved and that it would not lead to resentment, but to justified pride in achievement. Nothing society could do could make the vigorous virtues equally present in all citizens. Politicians, intellectuals, and other influential people could, however, by the policies they recommended, legislated, or approved make the vigorous virtues more or less worth seeking. Society could make the vigorous virtues more or less desirable, and whether they were desirable and therefore practiced by many in turn determined whether society stayed within the triad of reason, liberty, and prosperity.

All of which means that America remains, willy-nilly, the heartland of the West. First, America is indubitably the geopolitical and strategic center of the West as a political civilization. Second, America most faithfully represents the organic West as it grew out of the Old into the New West simultaneously diagnosed and represented by the sceptical Enlightenment. The essence of that diagnosis and representation lay in three features of the sceptical Enlightenment. First, that it did not disparage religion or the Christendom version, but acknowledged itself to be its child, continuator, and heir. Second, that it did not disparage economic development, but understood that democratic practices and capitalist production were mutually dependent, that economic activity leading to prosperity occurred most reliably not in despotic or anarchic regimes but in places "where several govern." Third, that it realized that both emerging self-government and economic development rested, in complex and often ironic ways, on the legacy of Christendom, on the divided authority of the ancient bargain of church and empire, and on the productive behavior inculcated by the early Protestant sects.

There are those who argue that even the shadow of the Old West will soon depart from our civilization, and many look forward to that prospect. Sociology and historical precedent do not support this prognosis. But even if they did, those who value the Western mix of ordered liberty, the constraint of duty and work, and the vigorous virtues have an interest in cherishing the legacy of the sceptical Enlightenment. In the future pattern of world civilizations, that legacy and those who represent it may be only minority voices, but they have their part to play in the global balance.

Capitalism rests on liberty, not the other way around. The economically rational individual is but one manifestation of Western identity. If that individual becomes a pure wealth maximizer, regarding economics as the end of life and not the tool of other ends, he displays the bourgeois pathology. Western identity does not consist in worshipping gain for its own sake, but in providing the liberty to pursue gain so that the greatest number of people acquire the means to pursue the good life. The universalism of democracy and capitalism ignores the historic dependence of economic growth on political freedom, and ignores the complex relation of political freedom to power. As I said at the outset of this book, liberty did not grow and become the core of Western identity because it contradicted the interests of power, but because, in the particular geopolitical and cultural conditions of the Old West, it served power.

The relationship of prosperity to liberty and power remains the chief feature of Western identity, and that is why history becomes more, not less, important in the supposed age of universal values. It is precisely because that relationship was not universal, but particular, that it needs to be constantly recalled and understood if Western identity is not to evaporate. In the multicivilizational world of the third millennium, the West will not long survive if it forgets its history or the dynamic that produced its particular voice and contribution to the chorus of humanity.

Universalists argue that the West needs to discard its historic identity to accommodate other cultures; in effect they argue that the fate of the West is to be multicultural. Nothing could be further from the truth. A multicultural West is a contradiction in terms; the only West that can be accommodating to other cultures is a West that knows itself and, on the strength of that understanding, encounters other cultures. An empty vessel, a historically illiterate people, cannot give to others the respect it does not give itself. Anticolonialists, feminists, and environmentalists say that what the West owes the world is to disappear. They are, of course, right that the West included many cruel and unjust people, much bigotry, many wars, and many examples of passion devoted to violence and oppression rather than to creativity and liberty. But so did all civilizations. The point of cultural interaction is not to apportion blame in a moralistic fashion, but to understand the conditions of liberty and human flourishing. A cultural interaction in which one side blames the other, and the other blames itself, is a dialogue of the deaf, for it deprives all parties of some portion of wisdom. Western civilization owes it to the world not to abandon its identity.

Virgil, who helped to create Western identity, praised the rural life rooted in place and soil, and then, in the *Aeneid*, sang of loss, journey, reconciliation, and empire. A Virgil of the third millennium will not lack for subjects in the history of the West. The theme must be, as it was for Virgil himself, passion—the passion that creates as it destroys. All civilizations display certain common features—urban life, philosophical arguments, an evolved religion, mass mobilization of resources, high skills in arts and crafts—but each has its own unmistakable tone, a set of features that it emphasizes over others. Western identity, it seems to me, emphasizes passion, focusing on the conflicts of the human heart that drive both creativity and destruction. The universalist caricature of the West is that it is rational. True, but not true enough. For the point of reason is, as Hume said, that it is the slave of the passions. It is therefore correct to note that Western culture developed rational methods of economic, technological, and philosophical activity. Equally if not more important, however, is how the resources set free by reason were used. The economically rational individual is a bloodless creature of calculated interest. Few real people are like that. The superstar of research, investment, sports, or medicine is driven not by calculation but by passion.

To point to passion is to remember that people, despite Rousseau and the modern secularists, are not born good but made evil by society. Despite Freud, they are not born twisted and neurotic, either.[67] They are born programmed with a genetic inheritance that, as evolutionary psychology teaches, may be extensive, diverse, and specific. Family, culture, and education are the triggers that evoke the program. The religion of the West, Christianity, with its Judaic and Hellenic legacies, suggests that people are reasoning beings, capable of great good, but also of great evil, and that, all things being equal, the temptation to evil—call it power, bourgeois pathology, self-seeking arrogance—will prevail. The only defense against that temptation is institutions that make it more attractive to follow one's better angels, and provide sure sanctions if one does not. History provides little evidence to contradict that wisdom, and much evidence that confirms it.

The epic of a twenty-first century Virgil might, therefore, deal with the tragic face of passion in the twentieth century, with the dark epic of Bolshevism from its origins in St. Petersburg in 1903, when Lenin and a few friends, with twelve revolvers among them, decided to conquer the world. It will describe how these men, with great heroism and dedication, established the most brutal tyranny in the history of the human race; how they exported this tyranny not just to other parts of the West but to China; how their enemies in fear and frustration abandoned democracy and liberty, believing them liabilities in the struggle. It will jump to Central Europe, where the most committed enemies of Bolshevism launched their own dark epic when they decided that the Jews were the enemy of the human race, responsible for Bolshevism and for all other evils. It will describe the monumental clash of these two rival perversions of power, and how one defeated and destroyed the other.

But then the scene will move to the democracies, rescued from destruction by the youngest and most peculiar of Western societies, America, where the New Western triad of liberty, science, and prosperity flourished free of the paralyzing neuroses and conflicts of the old world. The epic will tell how, even in this facsimile of the good society, temptation lurked: power concealed as freedom, decline camouflaged as progress. It will describe how the societies of liberty outlasted the societies of despotism. Finally, it will once again pose, as Virgil did, the endless journey and the homecoming to an alien land as the only destiny, in this world, of Western man.

I write these final lines as dusk falls on a late summer's day. The West, in metaphor as well as in geopolitical fact, has been the evening country. The idea of the West has been accompanied since Roman times by three conflicting connotations: of twilight, sunset, and therefore of decline; of movement, of westering, of the restless search for new horizons and new challenges; and of youth, of the call of new, younger lands to be found in the direction of the sunset, away from the old, mysterious, and dangerous lands of the East. But there is a fourth connotation that is not ancient but modern. The inhabitants of the countries and cultures we call the West did not, until the late nineteenth century, usually call themselves by that name. They were, if they thought of themselves collectively at all, Europeans, or Christians, or simply civilization. The idea of the West took shape in public discourse as the classic civilization of the Old West, that of medieval and early modern Christendom, dissolved under the blows of political democracy and economic change that put new groups up high and pulled old groups, such as priests, down low. Christianity first, and then all religion, lost collective power and became a private matter. The question whether the West as the posthumous version of Christendom without a public, binding faith could long survive as a secular civilization had been posed, but was, at the end of the twentieth century, not yet answered. Two conditions are necessary for a positive answer. The first is that religion not be expelled as a foreign body but kept as a secret or not so secret resource. The second is that the triad of reason, liberty, and prosperity, which remains the unavoidable and indeed valuable framework of the New West, not be distorted into rationalism, license, and self-gratification. Which is simply another way of saying that the sceptical Enlightenment needs to be protected against its radical, impatient, and moralistic counterpart. And in the age of illusory universalism, the way to restore that balance is to recover the Old West in its full color and passion, not as a caricature to be rejected, but as the source of one's social and cultural being.

Et iam summa procul villarum culmina fumant,
maioresque cadunt altis de montibus umbrae

[And now far off the cottage chimneys smoke,
From the high hills deep shades of evening fall]
—Virgil

FINIS

Notes

Author's note: Unless otherwise noted, translations are my own.

Introduction

1. A slight paraphrase to bring out the limitless voluntarism of the sentiment, *il est absurde que la volonté se donne des chaînes pour l'avenir.* From *The Social Contract* (1762) in *Œuvres complètes,* vol. 3 (Paris: Gallimard, 1964), 368, quoted in Holmes, *Passions and Constraints* (see note 2, below), 134. *The Social Contract* was the favorite book of Napoleon, who clearly absorbed the lesson. I owe this last bit of information to Thomas Gress-Wright.

2. The main sources of my interpretive schema of Western history are Jean Baechler, *Démocraties* (Paris: Calmann-Lévy, 1985) and id., *Le Capitalisme* (Paris: Gallimard, 1995); Alfred W. Crosby, *The Measure of Reality: Quantification and Western Society, 1250–1600* (New York: Cambridge University Press, 1997); Ernest Gellner, *Conditions of Liberty* (London: Allen Lane, 1994); Eric L. Jones, *The European Miracle* (New York: Cambridge University Press, 1981); David S. Landes, *The Unbound Prometheus: Technological Change and Industrial Development in Western Europe from 1750 to the Present* (Cambridge: Cambridge University Press, 1969); Alan Macfarlane, *The Origins of English Individualism* (Oxford: Blackwell, 1978); Alexander Murray, *Reason and Society in the Middle Ages* (Oxford: Oxford University Press, 1978); Douglass C. North and Robert P. Thomas, *The Rise of the Western World* (New York: Cambridge University Press, 1973); Paul A. Rahe, *Republics Ancient and Modern* (Chapel Hill: University of North Carolina Press, 1992), and id., "The Constitution of Liberty within Christendom," *Intercollegiate Review,* Fall 1997, 30–36; Susan Reynolds, *Kingdoms and Communities in Western Europe 900–1300* (Oxford University Press, 1984); Brian Tierney, *Religion, Law and the Growth of Constitutional Thought 1150–1650* (Cambridge: Cambridge University Press, 1982); Walter Ullmann, *Medieval Foundations of Renaissance Humanism* (London: Elek, 1977). David S. Landes, *The Wealth and Property of Nations: Why Some Are So Rich and Some So Poor* (New York: Norton, 1998), deserves special mention. Landes tells, in clean, clear, vigorous prose, the story of modern Western economic and political achievement and why that achievement was different from the experience of other cultures. Both the work and its bibliography are indispensable masterpieces. A nonacademic defense of the proposition that "it was the Middle Ages that nourished the institutions of free government, in contrast to the ideas and customs of the ancients" is M. Stanton Evans, *The Theme Is Freedom: Religion, Politics, and the American Tradition* (Washington, D.C.: Regnery, 1994). Few of these authors combine all three elements—power, religion, and liberty—though Gellner, Rahe, and Tierney come the closest. Jack Goody, *The East in the West* (Cambridge: Cambridge University Press, 1996), shows that economic rationality, scientific

method, individualism, and entrepreneurship were not Western prerogatives but found also in China and India, and emphasizes (226) "the common heritage of both parts of Eurasia from the urban revolution of the Bronze Age." That is valid but fails to explain the unique scope granted to them in the West and in Western identity. For a spirited argument that scientific method was known to the ancient Mesopotamians, see Jean Bottéro, *Mesopotamia* (Chicago: University of Chicago Press, 1992). Stephen Holmes, *Passions and Constraints: On the Theory of Liberal Democracy* (Chicago: University of Chicago Press, 1995), stresses (131) "the paradox that limited power is more powerful than unlimited power," which is part of the logic that supported the niches of liberty, although Holmes, a good modern American liberal, slights the role of Christianity as the classic and fundamental source of political pluralism in the West. Peter Berkowitz, *Virtue and the Origins of Modern Liberalism* (Princeton, N.J.: Princeton University Press, 1998) supports, in the spirit of Montesquieu, Adam Smith, and Tocqueville—the guardian angels of wisdom in these matters—the necessary effort of recovering the rich core of a tradition wrongly identified, in much late-twentieth-century writing, with secularism, individualism, and an anemic universalism. Having lived for over twenty years at the time of writing with the basic intuition that Christianity, the European or Western state system, democracy, and capitalism were mutually dependent on a very deep level, I am hard put to trace it to a particular moment or author. Perhaps it was John Salmon's graduate seminar on French political thought in the early modern period in the fall of 1975 at Bryn Mawr College that first set some of these ideas gelling, notably the idea that the early modern state arrived at religious toleration as a means of containing civil war and thus as a source of other liberties. Also, approaching these matters as a historian rather than a social scientist, I did not consciously adopt a particular model or theory; retroactively, I now see that I am an instinctive public-choice theorist as well as, apparently, a functionalist—a definition I owe to Uffe Østergård of Aarhus University after he read the final chapter.

3. Daniel Bell, *The End of Ideology* (Glencoe, Ill.: Free Press, 1960). Bell's argument was identical to that of Francis Fukuyama in the 1990s, the only difference being that Bell thought that ideological conflict might still continue outside the West, whereas Fukuyama's point was that the consensus was becoming global. Serious conflict over ends was no longer necessary or conceivable, since everyone now agreed on the basic goals of autonomy, equality, prosperity, rationality, and individual rights. The age of the end of ideology in the West was also the age of affluence, of annual growth rates of personal income never before achieved and never since rivaled.

4. New Brunswick, N.J.: Rutgers University Press. A second volume appeared in 1991. At least two more were promised, but had not appeared by 1998.

5. Kirkpatrick Sale, *The Conquest of Paradise* (New York: Knopf, 1990).

6. New York: Simon & Schuster.

7. New York: Random House.

8. This widespread undercurrent of response to Kennedy's book—the Schadenfreude or glee at the impending discomfort of America—was a common psychological syndrome of progressive opinion. One of the few people to devote serious attention to this syndrome was James Burnham in *Suicide of the West* (New York: Knopf, 1964), chapter 11, "The Guilt of the Liberal."

9. Francis Fukuyama, "The End of History," *National Interest* 15, Spring 1989; *The End of History and the Last Man* (New York: Free Press, 1992).

10. I use public opinion in the sense defined by Timur Kuran, *Private Truths, Public Lies* (Cambridge, Mass.: Harvard University Press, 1995), 55, namely, "the distribution of public

preferences." The point of this seminal study in sociology and social psychology is that public opinion is not the same thing as what most people think. Applied to our case, this insight may mean that the collapse of the Grand Narrative in public opinion does not necessarily mean that most Americans or Europeans have abandoned it in their personal understandings. All the more reason for this book, which defends the West while rejecting the Grand Narrative.

11. "Frozen Miracle: A Survey of East Asian Economies," *Economist,* March 7, 1998.

12. Arthur Herman, *The Idea of Decline in Western History* (New York: Free Press, 1997), 10.

13. Norman Davies, *Europe: A History* (New York: Oxford University Press, 1996), 22–25, 40.

14. Anthony Pagden, "The Children of Ham," *Times Literary Supplement*, May 2, 1997, and letter by Tom Hastie, ibid., May 16, 1997.

15. Jan Assmann, *Ägypten. Eine Sinngeschichte* (Munich: Hanser, 1996), 179. The Egyptian idea of an enduring space-time of result and duration is eerily reminiscent of a line from Richard Wagner's opera *Parsifal*. As the old grail knight Gurnemanz leads the innocent young fool, Parsifal, across the boundary separating the mundane world from the sacred space of the grail castle, Monsalvat, he says *zum Raum wird hier die Zeit*, "time here becomes space." Evidently, the idea of a sacred time having its own spatial and material quality of completion, and related in some way with an existence beyond the barriers delimiting an ordinary time of becoming and of change, is one of the deep recurring constructs—or perceptions—of the mind. The classic study of the two kinds of time and their implications for social and religious beliefs is Mircea Eliade, *The Myth of the Eternal Return* (Chicago: University of Chicago Press, 1962).

16. From a poem composed in 1856 by John Cameron of Ballachulish (at the lower end of Glencoe in the Western Highlands of Scotland), "Chi mi na morbheanna," "I see the Great Mountains." For the mythology, see Christa M. Löffler, *The Voyage to the Otherworld Island in Early Irish Literature*. Salzburg Studies in English Literature. Medieval and Renaissance Studies, no. 103 (University of Salzburg, 1983).

17. The Germano-Celto-Catholic mythology of the twentieth-century philologist and Anglo-Saxon scholar J.R.R.Tolkien used the idea of the West as the land of the immortals, and the desire for it as the temptation of mortals as a fundamental motivator of tragedy and history in his imagined universe. Some of his invented words echoed those of old myths; thus "Avalon" appeared as the haven of *Avallónë*, "a city white-shining on a distant shore . . . the first sight that the mariner beholds when at last he draws nigh to the Undying Lands over the leagues of the sea." *The Silmarillion* (Boston: Houghton Mifflin, 1977), 260, 262.

1. The Grand Narrative and Its Fate

1. There is a good case for replacing the iconic "1968" with 1965 as the year of symbolic and significant turning points in the twentieth-century political and cultural history of the West, and particularly of the United States. Much of the activism of 1968 began taking recognizable shape at mid-decade, which was also when U.S. deployments to Indochina reached their maximum, draft resistance began, and the first race riots took place. Both Lyndon Johnson's fall from grace with cultural liberals and the schism within American liberalism between the centrist (meritocratic, assimilationist, tolerant) and the radical (multiculturalist, white-guilt-ridden, ideological) wings became overt and, arguably, irreversible in 1965.

2. Denmark, where I began my university studies, required until 1971 that all entering undergraduates, whatever their subject of study, take a one-year introductory course in formal logic and the history of philosophy. But this was hardly even a shadow of the American Grand

Narrative, which was a history of political and social ideas as well as of philosophy, and which did not include formal logic. Furthermore, the Danish requirement was abolished at precisely the time that Danish universities became mass institutions. Before the late 1960s, less than five percent of a Danish cohort went to university. Thus, the Danish requirement was part of an elite system not designed for the average citizen, contrary to the American system, which was designed to assimilate and socialize average citizens by giving them a heavy dose of culture and history.

3. Martin L. Gross, *The End of Sanity: Social and Cultural Madness in America* (New York: Avon, 1997), 151.

4. William H. McNeill, "*The Rise of the West* after 25 Years," published as an introductory essay to the 1988 reprint of the book (Chicago: University of Chicago Press), xv.

5. My summary is not based on any specific text. It is constructed to emphasize the points most often attacked by revisionists and ideological critics.

2. The Battle over Hellas

1. A view restated with passion and verve by Victor Davis Hanson and John Heath, *Who Killed Homer? The Demise of Classical Education and the Recovery of Greek Wisdom* (New York: Free Press, 1998). This marvelous polemic against fashionable pedagogy and the self-corruption of higher education in America in the era of political correctness and the culture war is on the mark—except for its mistaken insistence that everything Western began in Greece. The Greeks absolutely have much to teach, but among those things is how they differ from both the Old and the New West. Still, Hanson and Heath are definitely on the side of the angels. We are arguing points among allies in the culture war here.

2. This was becoming the new orthodoxy, thanks to the pathbreaking work of Robert Drews in *The Coming of the Greeks: Indo-European Conquests in the Aegean and the Near East* (Princeton, N.J.: Princeton University Press, 1988) and *The End of the Bronze Age: Changes in Warfare and the Catastrophe ca. 1200 BC* (Princeton, N.J: Princeton University Press, 1993).

3. Scholars have argued for centuries whether the one ambiguous reference to writing in the epics, at *Iliad* 6.168–70, meant that Homer knew of writing, or whether the passage as we have it was a later addition.

4. How the stories came to be invented in dark age Greece no one knows. Heinrich Schliemann, an amateur nineteenth-century German archaeologist, read Homer as a poor country boy and dreamed of growing up and proving that the story had a basis in fact. After working hard and saving money for decades, Schliemann realized his dream and excavated a site at Hissarlik in northwestern Anatolia that he called Troy and that seemed to prove that the stories had some historical basis, because he found traces of burning. Later archaeologists decided that the destruction first spotted by Schliemann was due to an earthquake and not to violence. Part of the difficulty in interpreting the site at Hissarlik was that it contained a dozen different settlements, one on top of the other, and had at various times been abandoned and reoccupied. Schliemann determined, with the confidence of an amateur, that the most elaborate of the early settlements, later known as Troy VI, was the Troy of Homeric legend.

In the mid-1980s, a popular book and television series on the Trojan War revived Schliemann's identification of Troy VI, the elaborate early palace at Hissarlik, as the Troy of legend, and in the 1990s, scholars were coming round to the opinion that Troy VI may have been destroyed as part of the cataclysmic events that put an end to the Mycenaean palace culture around 1200 B.C. The new theory suggested that the destruction of Troy VI was the first of those events, that it was the first of the great palaces of the eastern Mediterranean to fall to the invaders with their new weapons and tactics. If this was correct, it meant that the Homeric stories had some basis, however remote, in fact. It also meant that the Greeks, or Achaeans, who sacked Troy were not representatives of Mycenaean culture, but were among those who destroyed that culture and precipitated the Greek dark ages.

5. Montesquieu, the founder of modern social science and the leading political analyst of the sceptical Enlightenment, observed that a monarchy or a despotism did not require probity in its subjects to survive, because laws or coercion would suffice. "But a popular government needs an additional principle of action, and that is virtue." *De l'Esprit des lois*, III.3.

6. From the entry on Plutarch by Donald A. Russell in the *Oxford Classical Dictionary*, 3rd ed. (New York: Oxford University Press, 1996).

7. Ernst Robert Curtius, *Kritische Essays zur europäischen Literatur* (Bern: Francke, 1950), 84.

8. Quoted by Wolfgang Schadewaldt in "Winckelmann und Homer," *Hellas und Hesperien*, 2d ed., vol. 2 (Zurich: Artemis, 1970), 64.

9. These and subsequent quotes from Johann Joachim Winckelmann, *Geschichte der Kunst des Altertums*, reprint of the 1764 edition (Darmstadt: Wissenschaftliche Buchgesellschaft, 1993).

10. Hugh Lloyd-Jones, "Goethe," in *Blood for the Ghosts* (London: Duckworth, 1982). This essay originally formed the introduction to a reprint of Humphry Trevelyan, *Goethe and the Greeks* (Cambridge: Cambridge University Press, 1981), a book first published in 1941.

11. Hugh Lloyd-Jones, "Greek in a Cold Climate," in *Greek in a Cold Climate* (London: Duckworth, 1993), 224.

12. Quoted in Wolfgang Schadewaldt, "Goethe und die Antike," in his *Goethestudien* (Zurich: Artemis, 1963), 62.

13. Quoted in Werner Dahlheim, *Die Antike* (Paderborn: Schöningh, 1993), 694–95.

14. Quoted in Arnaldo Momigliano, "Genesi e funzione del concetto di ellenismo," in his *Contributo alla storia del mondo classico* (Rome: Edizioni di Storia e Letteratura, 1955), 172.

15. "Brot und Wein," from stanzas 4 and 7.

16. "Patmos."

17. Aeschylus, *Persae* 402–5.

18. Michael Tanner, *Nietzsche* (Oxford University Press, 1994), 16.

19. "Burnt Norton," in T.S. Eliot, *Collected Poems 1909–1935* (New York: Harcourt Brace, 1936), 214.

20. Friedrich Nietzsche, *Die nachgelassenen Fragmente* (Stuttgart: Reclam, 1996), 280.

21. Lest anyone should suppose that Nietzsche was a relativist or a forerunner of Michel Foucault, I should stress that he never questioned that science, for example, might provide extraordinary discoveries about human nature and life. He did, however, wonder whether such perfect knowledge would not make "the highest forms of morality impossible," ibid., 83.

22. Ibid., 180–81, Nietzsche's emphasis.

23. "Burnt Norton," *Collected Poems*, 216.

24. Rainer Maria Rilke, *Duino Elegies*, trans. Stephen Mitchell. Quoted by Tanner, *Nietzsche*, 17.

25. Nietzsche, *Fragmente*, 169–70.

26. The information on Wilamowitz derives from the entry on him, by Robert L. Fowler, in Ward W. Briggs and William M. Calder III, eds., *Classical Scholarship: A Biographical Encyclopedia* (New York: Garland, 1990).

27. Wilamowitz coined this phrase in English; it is quoted by Albert Heinrichs, "Die Glaube der Hellenen," in William M. Calder III et al., eds., *Wilamowitz nach 50 Jahren* (Darmstadt: Wissenschaftliche Buchgesellschaft, 1985), 295.

28. E.M. Butler, *The Tyranny of Greece over Germany* (Cambridge: Cambridge University Press, 1935), was both a history of German philhellenism and a political attack on the German nationalist tradition derived from Fichte, which asserted that the Germans, like the Greeks, were a uniquely civilized and perfect nation and therefore—in the extreme version of the doctrine—called on to save the world. Although the National Socialist regime was not notably friendly to classical studies, some German academics transferred their Fichtean sense of national purpose to an allegiance to Hitlerite racism.

29. Homer, *Iliad*, 6.407–11 and 431–32, my translation.

30. The famous lines where Hector predicts the fall of Troy—"there will come a day when holy Troy shall perish, and also Priam and the people of Priam of the ashen spear"—were among the best known of Homer in antiquity. According to Plutarch, the Roman commander Scipio Aemilianus was heard quoting them after he leveled Carthage in 146 B.C. The message, that doom and destruction come to all, and that the proud should always remember that, was particularly apt at that moment of rising Roman power.

31. Ibid. 464–65.

32. Arthur Adkins, *Merit and Responsibility* (Oxford: Oxford University Press, 1960).

33. Homer, *Iliad*, 24.486–506.

34. Ibid., 525–26.

35. E. A. Judge, "The Quest for Mercy in Late Antiquity," in Patrick T. O'Brien and D. G. Peterson, eds., *God Who Is Rich in Mercy* (Sydney: Macquarie University Press, 1986), 107.

36. *Histories* 5.5.

37. Lawrence E. Stager, from an article in *Biblical Archaeology Review*, July-August 1991, quoted in Rodney Stark, *The Rise of Christianity* (Princeton, N.J.: Princeton University Press, 1996), 118.

38. Hugh Lloyd-Jones in his introduction to vol. 1 of his edition of Sophocles for the Loeb Classical Library (Cambridge, Mass.: Heinemann, 1994), 4.

39. *Histories* I.3 in the translation of the Loeb Classical Library (Cambridge, Mass.: Heinemann, 1938).

40. Act 4, scene 1, lines 37–38.

41. Hugh Lloyd-Jones, *The Justice of Zeus*, 2d ed. (Berkeley: University of California Press, 1983) is the classic statement of the view that early Greek religion turned on the notion of justice as the basic order of the universe, which the gods upheld. This basic order was not always made clear to mortals, who therefore transgressed. This was the opposite outlook to that of the Abrahamic religions, where God gave a clear command that man disobeyed, making his fall entirely his own fault.

42. This paraphrase and reflection on Agamemnon's story owes much to the brilliantly concise introduction by Denys Page to J. D. Denniston's edition of Aeschylus, *Agamemnon*, 2d ed. (Oxford: Clarendon Press, 1970).

43. Paraphrase of Theognis, lines 341–44, quoted in E. Lucchesi and H. D. Saffrey, eds., *Mémorial André-Jean Festugière*. Cahiers d'Orientalisme 10 (Geneva: Patrick Cramer, 1984), xiv. Theognis lived in the sixth century B.C., between the time of Homer and the golden age of Athens.

44. Learning how to write authentic, idiomatic classical Greek was a phenomenally demanding task, and all honor is due to those who achieved it. But it was pre-eminently a task of erudition, not of practical skill.

45. From volume 6 of the *History*, quoted in Guy MacLean Rogers, "Multiculturalism and the Foundations of Western Civilization," in Mary Lefkowitz and Guy MacLean Rogers, ed., *Black Athena Revisited* (Chapel Hill: University of North Carolina Press, 1996), 433.

46. Benjamin Constant, *Écrits politiques*, ed. Pierre Manent (Paris: Livre de Poche, 1984).

47. Arnaldo Momigliano, "Liberty and Peace in the Ancient World," in his *Nono contributo alla storia degli studi classici e del mondo antico* (Rome: Storia e Letteratura, 1992), 483. This text was first given as a lecture, in English, by Momigliano in 1940, soon after his arrival in Britain as an exile from Mussolini's Italy.

48. Thucydides 2.40.2, my translation, slightly altered relative to the version in chapter 1 to emphasize the point at issue.

49. I.F. Stone, *The Trial of Socrates* (New York: Doubleday, 1989), 63.

50. Ibid., 38.

51. *La Cité de l'homme* (Paris: Fayard, 1994).

3. The Burden of Rome

1. Or Roman Empire, even though the government at this time was still that of the republic. It is perfectly legitimate to refer to the territories ruled by the Senate and People of Rome in the time of Caesar, Cleopatra, and Mark Antony as the Roman Empire, since the Latin *imperium romanum* merely meant "territory beyond the boundaries of the city of Rome under Roman command" and could be applied at any time in Roman history. Some textbooks refer to the Roman-controlled world as the empire as early as the late second century B.C. But it is most usual to reserve the word *empire* to the period after the battle of Actium, when Octavian, known as Augustus, and his successors ruled as *imperatores*, or "emperors," even though they maintained the forms of republican government.

2. The Latin is both more colloquial and blunter: *Romam a principio reges habuere*, connoting that "kings had control" of Rome and implying that this control was rough and exploitative.

3. A fragment of the second-century B.C. historian Cassius Hemina, quoted in T.J. Cornell, *The Beginnings of Rome* (London: Routledge, 1995), 128.

4. "Horatius," stanzas 27–28, in Lord Macaulay, *Lays of Ancient Rome and Miscellaneous Essays and Poems* (London: J.M.Dent, 1968), 425.

5. My evidence that Macaulay's *Lays of Early Rome* were normal fare in American public schools is personal but to the point. Some time in the fall of 1968 I came back from my (Danish) school and informed my American stepfather that we had just started to read "Horatius" in class. My stepfather, who attended public schools in and around Seattle in the 1920s and 1930s, but who had never, to me, shown much interest in ancient civilization, said, "Horatius of the bridge! But he was no poet!" and went on to recount the story of the Sublician Bridge related in the text. Only after some confusion did we establish that I was speaking of the poet Horace, whose Latin name was Horatius.

6. Momigliano, "Liberty and Peace in the Ancient World," *Nono contributo alla storia degli studi classici e del mondo antico* (Rome: Storia e Letteratura, 1992), 493.

7. Ibid., 497.

8. Eric R. Dodds, *The Greeks and the Irrational* (Berkeley: University of California Press, 1954); ed., *The Bacchae* (Oxford: Oxford University Press, 1962); *Pagan and Christian in an Age of Anxiety* (Cambridge: Cambridge University Press, 1965).

9. Barker was confused about Rome in two ways: he was not sure of its value to the West and therefore not sure whether its fall was as much of a disaster as Edward Gibbon had thought in the 1770s. Gibbon, although partial to democratic government, shared the general belief of liberal thinkers of the Enlightenment that democracy was possible only in small and close-knit communities, such as the Swiss mountain cantons or self-governing medieval towns. The Roman Empire could never have been ruled by popular sovereignty; indeed, the fate of the republic showed what happened when one tried to rule a world empire by semipopular means. So, for Gibbon, the best possible government for the Roman Empire was enlightened despotism, such as prevailed, as he believed, in the second century A.D. Barker, writing a century and a half later, knew about representative government and shared the confident liberal and Whiggish faith that such government was not only possible but morally superior to any other and destined to spread across the globe. To him, enlightened despotism was not the best possible form of government, and Rome could never, in his eyes, live up to the absolute standard first set by Athenian democracy and later surpassed by the liberal regimes of Europe and North America in his own day. He was also confused in a different way, in the meaning of the terms *West* and *East*, and in his understanding of how the East-West division began in Roman times. Scholarship since the 1920s overturned former certainties on these matters.

10. Ibid., 496.

11. From his inaugural lecture as professor of Latin at Cambridge, in *Collected Poems and Selected Prose* (London: Penguin, 1988), 307.

12. S. C. Woodhouse, in the preface to his *English-Greek Dictionary*, 2d ed. (London: Routledge & Kegan Paul, 1932), v.

13. The case was described by Tacitus and paraphrased by Charles Freeman, *Egypt, Greece and Rome* (New York: Oxford University Press, 1996), 423.

14. Norman Davies, *Europe: A History* (New York: Oxford University Press, 1996). This is a spectacular and indispensable work, and the fact that, by writing this book, I am violating Professor Davies's strictures on the dangerous implications of the idea of "the West" is a risk I must take and that I hope he, as a friend and colleague, will forgive.

15. Friedrich Nietzsche, *Die nachgelassenen Fragmente* (Stuttgart: Reclam, 1996), 147.

16. The history of how the word *Europe* was used and the example from the *Historia Augusta* are analyzed by Santo Mazzarino, "Il nome e l'idea di Europa," in his *Antico, tardoantico ed èra costantiniana*, vol. 2 (Bari: Dedalo, 1980), 412–30. The article was first published in 1960.

4. Christianity and the Fall of Rome

1. Quoted in André-Jean Festugière, O.P., *Personal Religion among the Greeks* (University of California Press, 1954), 113–14.

2. Edward Gibbon, *The History of the Decline and Fall of the Roman Empire,* ed. David Womersley (New York: Penguin Classics, 1995), 1:110, from chapter 4.

3. Like Willie Stubbs, the bank robber who, asked why he robbed banks, replied "Because that's where the money is."

4. Alexander Demandt, *Der Fall Roms. Die Auflösung des römischen Reiches im Urteil der Nachwelt* (Munich: C.H. Beck, 1984), 314 n. 8.

5. Peter Brown, *Augustine of Hippo* (London: Faber & Faber, 1967); *The World of Late Antiquity: From Marcus Aurelius to Mohammad*, 2d ed. (London: Thames & Hudson, 1989, illustrated); *The Making of Late Antiquity* (Cambridge, Mass.: Harvard University Press, 1978); *The Cult of the Saints* (Chicago: University of Chicago Press, 1981); *The Body and Society: Men, Women, and Sexual Renunciation in Early Christianity* (New York: Columbia University Press, 1988); *Power and Persuasion in Late Antiquity: Towards a Christian Empire* (Madison: University of Wisconsin Press, 1992); *The Rise of Western Christendom* (Cambridge, Mass.: Blackwell, 1996). Brown, like his teacher Arnaldo Momigliano, is fundamental. Anyone with the least interest in the subject of this chapter, or in cultural change generally, should read him, in chronological order of publication. Let me add as a personal note that I did not much like Brown when I first read him in the 1970s. He, like his characters, can convert.

6. *Annals* 15.44.

7. Ibid., 13.32. The Latin *superstitio* is not quite the same as "superstition" in English. It connotes not so much irrationality as excessive devotion and exaggerated ritualism. Pomponia was being accused of religious fervor. See also Rodney Stark, *The Rise of Christianity* (Princeton, N.J.: Princeton University Press, 1996), 31.

8. Quoted ibid., 98.

9. Ibid., 111–15.

10. Ibid., 101–3.

11. Edward Gibbon, *The History of the Decline and Fall of the Roman Empire*, ed. David Womersley (London: Penguin Classics, 1995), 2:57–59 (from chapter 27).

12. Ibid., 3:1068 (from the concluding reflections in the final chapter).

13. Ibid., 2:1083 (note 136 to chapter 26).

14. Ibid., 1:56.

15. Their daughter was the playwright and philosopher Anne-Louise-Germaine Necker de Staël-Holstein, known as Madame de Staël, opponent of Napoleon, mistress for fifteen years of Benjamin Constant, to whom she bore a daughter, and author, among other works, of *De l'Allemagne* (1811), which introduced German romantic literature and philosophy to France.

16. Gibbon, *History*, 2:511 (from the "General Observations on the Fall of the Roman Empire in the West" appended to chapter 38).

17. André Piganiol, *L'Empire chrétien*, 2d ed. (Paris: PUF, 1972), 466.

18. Arnaldo Momigliano, *Quarto Contributo alla storia degli studi classici e del mondo antico* (Rome: Edizioni di Storia e Letteratura, 1969), 646.

19. Quoted in Demandt, *Fall Roms*, 182.

20. Paraphrased and quoted ibid., 268–69, 479. This volume is an exhaustive catalogue and interpretation of all the explanations ever given for the fall of Rome, presented with verve, unbelievable learning, and fine doses of erudite humor. It is a great pity that nothing like it exists in English.

21. Ibid, 547.

22. Quoted ibid., 528.

23. Quoted ibid., 589.

24. This model received its full formulation by the fifth-century writer Orosius, who posited a Christian vision of history against the pagans of his own time, who blamed Christianity for the disasters afflicting the Roman Empire. According to Orosius, world history had one path, which led humanity through four empires: Persian, Babylonian, Alexandrian, and Roman. Rome was not falling but would last until the end of time and the Second Coming of Christ. Orosius knew, of course, that the empire was divided, but he insisted that it was a common empire, divided for practical purposes only. Since his scheme posited the Roman Empire as the last and final empire, it could not accommodate a world without the Roman Empire. When Charlemagne in 800 and the German kings in the tenth century and after were crowned emperors in the West by the popes, they were accordingly known as emperors of the Christian, or Holy Roman, Empire, because that empire could never end as long as the world lasted. Nor could the Four Empires doctrine allow decline and renewal. The Three Ages idea, on the other hand, implied that the ancient world had declined and its learning was lost until the renewal of modern times. Both antiquity and modernity were, therefore, distinct from the unfortunate intervening period, the "middle age."

25. Alexander Demandt, *Die Spätantike* (Munich: C.H. Beck, 1989), 477.

26. Quoted in Brown, *Rise of Western Christendom*, 44.

27. From the *Life of Melania* by Gerontius, quoted in Averil Cameron, *The Mediterranean World in Late Antiquity, AD 395–600* (London: Routledge, 1993), 146; and Demandt, *Die Spätantike*, 285.

28. Quoted in Demandt, *Fall Roms*, 251.

29. *Études ou discours historiques sur la chute de l'Empire romain*, in his *Œuvres* (Paris: Gallimard, 1969).

30. Cameron, *Mediterranean World*, 6.

31. Brown, *World of Late Antiquity*, 118–19.

32. Michael Grant, *The Fall of the Roman Empire*.

33. Mazzarino, "Democratizzazione della cultura nel tardoantico," in his *Antico, tardoantico ed èra costantiniana,* vol. 2 (Bari: dedalo, 1980).

34. Ibid.

35. Cameron, *Mediterranean World*, 129.

36. Toynbee was not the first to do so; the idea that ancient civilization began its inevitable decline when the two leading cities of Greece went to war with each other derived from the liberal German historian Otto Seeck, writing in 1898.

37. Information about the Goths in this section is derived from Herwig Wolfram, *The Goths* (Berkeley: University of California Press, 1988), which I consulted in the original German, *Die Goten*, 3d ed. (Munich: C.H. Beck, 1990), 125–41.

38. Unfortunately the marvelous scene of the barbarian hordes crossing the frozen Rhine on New Year's Eve is fictitious. It was invented through fertile interpretation of sources by the historians E.A. Thompson and Henri-Irénée Marrou. See Demandt, *Die Spätantike*, 143.

39. Tacitus, *Germania*, 33.

40. Demandt, *Die Spätantike*, 487.

41. Niccolò Machiavelli, *Discourses on Livy*, trans. Harvey C. Mansfield and Nathan Tarcov (Chicago: University of Chicago Press, 1996), 2.10, 148.

42. Machiavelli, *The Prince*, chapter 13 (New York: Modern Library, 1940).

43. Arnaldo Momigliano, *Essays in Ancient and Modern Historiography* (New York: Oxford University Press, 1977), 127–40.

44. Robert A. Markus, *The End of Ancient Christianity* (Cambridge: Cambridge University Press, 1990), 219–20.

45. Charles Martindale, "Ruins of Rome: T.S. Eliot and the Presence of the Past," Arion, 3d series 2–3 (Fall 1995–Winter 1996): 102.

46. Quotations of Eliot's poems are from *Collected Poems 1909–1935* (New York: Harcourt, Brace & Co., 1936).

47. Jessie L. Weston, *From Ritual to Romance* (1920; reprinted New York: Doubleday, 1957), 187.

48. Ibid., 135.

5. Germanic Freedom and the Old Western Synthesis

1. Paradoxically, the ideal university envisaged by the Columbia and even more by the Chicago authors of the liberal story of the West was the German university, as they conceived it—a community of scholars each of whom was entirely free to teach what and how he wanted, but who were bound in a fellowship of shared culture and values. The hegemony of the German model of higher education—1920–1965—corresponded fairly exactly with the hegemony of the anti-German, hellenocentric liberal narrative.

2. The Oxford Latinist Arthur M. Duff, quoted in Alexander Demandt, *Der Fall Roms. Die Auflösung des römischen Reiches im Urteil der Nachwelt* (Munich: C.H. Beck, 1984), 383.

3. David Starr Jordan, *The Human Harvest: A Study of the Decay of Races through the Survival of the Unfit* (Boston: American Unitarian Association, 1907), 25, 42, 116.

4. Madison Grant, *The Passing of the Great Race, or the Racial Basis of European History*, 4th ed. (New York: Scribner's, 1926).

5. Adolf Hitler quoted in Demandt, *Fall Roms*, 268.

6. Herwig Wolfram, *Die Germanen*, 2d ed. (Munich: C.H. Beck, 1995), 21.

7. *De l'Esprit des lois*, XI.6.

8. Hugh Trevor-Roper, "Introduction" in Lord Macaulay, *The History of England* (London: Penguin Books, 1979), 9.

9. Adams and Jefferson quoted in Demandt, *Fall Roms*, 131–32.

10. For those who may want to visit, this is Sankt Olof's church (note the Swedish spelling), in the village of the same name in Scania (southernmost Sweden, formerly eastern Denmark), about two hours from Copenhagen.

11. Bruce Mitchell and Fred C. Robinson, *A Guide to Old English*, 5th ed. (Cambridge, Mass.: Blackwell, 1992), 283.

12. Theodor Schieffer, *Winfried-Bonifatius und die christliche Grundlegung Europas* (Freiburg: Herder, 1954).

13. Pierre Riché, *Éducation et culture dans l'Occident barbare* (Paris: Seuil, 1962), 548.

14. Ludwig Bieler, *Irland. Wegbereiter des Mittelalters* (Bern: Francke, 1961), English translation *Ireland: Harbinger of the Middle Ages* (New York: Oxford University Press, 1966).

15. Quoted in Christopher Hibbert, *Rome: Biography of a City* (London: Penguin Books, 1985), 78–79.

16. Oswald Spengler, *Der Untergang des Abendlandes* (Munich: C.H.Beck, 1968), 657.

17. The major work relating the *Song of Roland* to the Germanic warrior ethic and tracing how that ethic, joined with Christianity, produced a doctrine of holy war was that of the German scholar Carl Erdmann, discussed in the text below.

18. The edition quoted is *La Chanson de Roland*, Old French text and facing version in modern French (Paris: Union Générale d'Éditions 10/18, 1968).

19. Christopher Dawson, *Religion and the Rise of Western Culture* (1950, reprinted New York: Doubleday, 1991), 147.

20. Carl Erdmann, *Die Entstehung des Kreuzzugsgedankens* (1935; repr. Darmstadt: Wissenschaftliche Buchgesellschaft, 1974), 84.

21. H.P. Willmott, *The Great Crusade: A New Complete History of the Second World War* (London: Michael Joseph, 1989). MacArthur's Scottish descent, of which he was proud, opens another link to the Western past that might be worth exploring. At least one other famous American general, Ulysses S. Grant, was of Highland stock, and the Celtic element in American military history is both pronounced and distinguished. Few things can be more evocative than the call of Clan Arthur: *eisd o eisd*, "listen o listen."

22. Quoted in Ernst Robert Curtius, *Europäische Literatur und lateinisches Mittelalter*, 2d ed. (Bern: Francke, 1954), 391.

23. Klaus von See, "Der Germane als Barbar," in his *Barbar—Germane—Arier. Die Suche nach der Identität der Deutschen* (Heidelberg: Winter, 1994), 57.

24. "Vom 'edlen Wilden' zum 'Volk der Dichter und Denker'," ibid. 72.

6. Faith, Passion, and Conquest

1. Leo III did not himself explicitly refer to the Donation of Constantine, but the premise of that document, that the popes had the power to create imperial authority, was also the premise of his act in St. Peter's in December of 800.

2. Text of the Donation, quoted by Lorenzo Valla, *La Falsa Donazione di Costantino*, ed. Olga Pugliese, Latin text with Italian translation (Milan: Rizzoli, 1994), 138, 142, 180.

3. Oswald Spengler, *Der Untergang des Abendlandes* (Munich: C.H. Beck, 1968), 238.

4. But what if the very point of the West was that change was real and possible? If this were so, the spirit of conquest defined not a futile rebellion against fate, but a dynamic aspect of a civilization that believed in changing the world and itself. A century before Spengler, the liberal philosopher, political thinker, and author of the first free constitution of France, Benjamin Constant, coined the phrase "spirit of conquest" as that which motivated tyrants and dictators to use military power to force political change. In a broader sense, the spirit of conquest was that element in the West that drove scientific and technological change, but also the element that drove exploration, exploitation, and war. In classical liberalism, as formulated by Montesquieu and Constant, the fundamental principle of the West was that the original spirit of conquest was channeled from its violent to its creative, productive, and civilian purposes. Modern commerce in particular was the field where the spirit of conquest could exercise itself to beneficial purposes. Therefore, the purpose of political action was to make commerce more desirable and war less desirable, while maintaining the Faustian energies that made the West possible.

The difference between Spengler and the classical liberals was that, to Spengler, civilizations, including the West, were closed entities that could never change the conditions of their own life cycle. Montesquieu, Constant, and the American Founders, by contrast, believed that reason informed by historical understanding and tempered by modesty could, in fact, change the underlying conditions of civilization so that what was a seemingly inevitable fate could become instead the hope of continued progress. Classical liberalism, unlike its late modern descendants, implied no simple faith in progress. To Constant, history was a tragedy, which meant that accidents and disasters could always happen. Just because it was possible to reduce poverty, abate war, and turn the spirit of conquest to humane uses without weakening its energies did not mean that it would happen.

5. Carlrichard Brühl, *Deutschland-Frankreich. Die Geburt zweier Völker* (Cologne: Böhlau, 1990) demolished, leaving no stone standing, any argument that distinct German or French national identities existed before the eleventh century or that such identities predated the political structures of the East and West Frankish kingdoms. Nationalist historians in both France and Germany had claimed that national identity came first, then its political expression in a state. Brühl, by contrast, argued that it was the kingdoms that created national identity, not the other way round. Christian ethnicity, in these terms, was what resulted when groups of tribes living together developed distinct identities thanks to the mobilizing and unifying influence of Christian rulers who, in addition to being Germanic chieftains, drew on the consolidated legacy of the ancient Mediterranean—Rome and Christianity. To which one can add that the basic Christian understanding of kingship and national identity was, naturally, that of the Old Testament, so that one should perhaps speak of Judeo-Christian ethnicity.

6. By the late twentieth century, it had become a commonplace for historians to observe that the early European civilization I am here calling the Old West was marginal, rustic, and primitive compared with the contemporary, urban, and literate civilizations of Asia—Islam, India, and China. For much of the history of the Old West, it was a borrower of knowledge, skills, technology, and wisdom. Some concluded from this inferiority that the West was largely a derivative, rather than a creative, civilization; in more hostile terms, that it rudely looted the achievements of others. This argument, in its moralistic form, misunderstood the logic of cultural evolution, which is that marginal cultures have only two choices: to learn from their betters or to perish. Others concluded that the genius of the West lay precisely in how, starting from a marginal and inferior position, it managed to catch up and overtake its rivals. This argument understood the logic of cultural evolution, but overstated the barbarism of the early Old West. The creative potential of the synthesis of Greco-Roman, Christian, and Germanic elements was latent from the beginning, and when the Old West borrowed from others, it was to advance its own identity. This is an important point that relates to the general argument of this and the following chapter, namely, that the New West of democracy, capitalism, and science was not in itself a radical departure from the Old West, although the dominant variants of twentieth-century progressive liberalism, anxious to reject Greece, Rome, Christianity, and the Germanic legacy in favor of a bland universalism, argued that it was. According to this post-1960s multicultural liberalism, the identity of the New West was not to have any identity at all, but to be simultaneously liberal and universal.

7. Thus, those radicals in the English Civil War of the 1640s who called themselves Fifth Monarchy Men were being deliberately apocalyptic. They were proposing a social and political order beyond the repertory of the West, a utopian design for a new creation.

8. A process classically described by Michael T. Clanchy, *From Memory to Written Record: England 1066–1307*, 2d ed. (Cambridge, Mass.: Blackwell, 1993).

9. Christopher Dawson, *Religion and the Rise of Western Culture* (1950, reprinted New York: Doubleday, 1991), 137.

10. Paolo Delogu, "Federico II di Svevia imperatore," in the catalogue of the exhibition *Federico II e l'Italia* (Rome: Edizione de Luca, 1995), 14.

11. Then 575 years later, Napoleon Bonaparte, perhaps unwittingly, copied his predecessor, when he took the crown presented to him by a reluctant pope Pius VII and crowned himself emperor of the French on December 2, 1804.

12. "What is a Classic?" in *Selected Prose*, ed. Frank Kermode (New York: Harcourt Brace Jovanovich, 1975), 122.

13. Quoted in Mario Praz, "T.S. Eliot and Dante," in id., *The Flaming Heart* (New York: Norton, 1973), 350; the essay was first published in 1937.

14. Quoted ibid., 358.

15. Quoted in Anthony Pagden, *Lords of All the World: Ideologies of Empire in Spain, Britain and France c. 1500–c. 1800* (New Haven: Yale University Press, 1995), 16.

16. From the *Convito*, quoted in Frances A. Yates, *Astraea: The Imperial Theme in the Sixteenth Century* (London: Routledge, 1975), 9.

17. Denis de Rougemont, *L'Amour et l'Occident*, rev. ed. (Paris: Plon, 1972), 389. I quote from the paperback edition, 1979 and later, published by Union Générale d'Éditions with the same pagination. The standard U.S. edition is *Love in the Western World* (New York: Harper Torchbook, 1972).

18. Letter to Anna Lindsay, quoted in Peter Wivel, *Tvesind: En bog om Benjamin Constant* (Copenhagen: Gyldendal, 1996), 37. Once one accepts Rougemont's basic thesis, examples are literally everywhere. It is a rare popular novel that does not have a doomed passion at the core of its plot.

19. Rougemont, *L'Amour et l'Occident*, 53, Rougemont's emphasis.

20. Ibid., 77, Rougemont's emphasis.

21. Ibid., 121.

22. Quoted ibid., 130.

23. Quoted in the booklet accompanying the recording of Karol Szymanowski's "Song of the Night," a symphony based on Rumi's poem; Antal Dorati conducting the Detroit Symphony Orchestra, London CD 425 625–2.

24. J.P. Jacobsen, *Samlede Skrifter*, vol. 1, 10th ed. (Copenhagen: Gyldendal, 1928), 322–25.

25. Rougemont, *L'Amour et l'Occident*, 154, Rougemont's emphasis.

26. Passion derives via French from the Latin verb *pasci*, to suffer, the antonym of *agere*, to act. *Pasci*, like the English "suffer," does not necessarily imply pain but simply denotes the posture of him to whom something is done. "I suffer it to happen," does not mean it hurts me, but that I am *passive* (another derivative of *pasci*). In practice, in semantics, and in the myth, the jump from "passive" to "enduring pain" was a short one.

27. Rougemont, *L'Amour et l'Occident*, 264, Rougemont's emphasis. Paul Valéry, *Mélange* II, in his *Œuvres* 1 (Paris: Gallimard, 1975, first published 1957), 287.

28. One is reminded here that Richard Wagner at the end of his life planned an opera about the Buddha to be called *The Victors*, presumably using the term to mean victory in the Buddhist and dualist sense of going beyond the world into annihilation of self.

29. Johan Huizinga, *The Autumn of the Middle Ages*, trans. Rodney J. Payton and Ulrich Mammitzsch (Chicago: University of Chicago Press, 1996), 83. In this exceptional case, I used an

existing translation, because I had no access to the Dutch original. The passage, quoted in French by Rougemont, *L'Amour et l'Occident*, 272, seems less stilted there than in the translation, but without the original text I did not want to venture any improvements.

30. Ibid., 296, Rougemont's emphasis.

31. Ibid., 422–23, Rougemont's emphasis.

32. Victor D. Hanson, *The Western Way of War: Infantry Battle in Classical Greece* (New York: Knopf, 1989), 9.

33. Aeschylus, *Persae*, 403–5.

34. Edward Gibbon, *The History of the Decline and Fall of the Roman Empire*, ed. David Womersley (London: Penguin Classics, 1995), 3:149 (chapter 49), Gibbon's emphasis.

35. Walter Ullmann, *Medieval Foundations of Renaissance Humanism* (London: ELEK, 1978). The classic statement of the view that Renaissance humanism was unique and original is Myron P. Gilmore, *The World of Humanism* (New York: Harper, 1952). John Hale, *The Civilization of Europe in the Renaissance* (New York: Harper Collins, 1993), is a learned and lively presentation that stresses the later epochs—the sixteenth and early seventeenth century—rather than the fifteenth century and Italy.

36. Quotes from Pico and St. Augustine from the introduction by Carlo Carena to his Italian translation and edition of Giovanni Pico della Mirandola, *De hominis dignitate*, 2d ed. (Milan: Mondadori, 1995).

37. Chaim Wirszubski, *Pico della Mirandola's Encounter with Jewish Mysticism* (Cambridge, Mass.: Harvard University Press, 1989).

38. Alfred W. Crosby, *The Measure of Reality: Quantification and Western Society, 1250–1600* (New York: Cambridge University Press, 1997). Alexander Murray, *Reason and Society in the Middle Ages* (Oxford: Oxford University Press, 1978), a beautiful work of social and psychological history with wide ramifications, traced the calculating mentality deep into the earliest centuries of the Old Western synthesis.

39. Henri-Irénée Marrou, "Qu'est-ce que l'histoire," in Charles Samaran, ed., *L'Histoire et ses méthodes* (Paris: Gallimard/Encyclopédie de la Pléiade, 1961), 21.

40. Blandine Kriegel, *L'Histoire à l'âge classique*, vol. 2: *La Défaite de l'érudition* (Paris: Presses Universitaires de France, 1988), 40.

41. Ibid., 44.

42. Quoted ibid., 95.

43. Jean-Pierre Lallemant in 1708, quoted ibid., 261.

44. The Salic Law was not invented by Shakespeare. The original Salians were a Frankish tribe, and the Salic Law was a rule against female succession that applied, in general, to Germanic territories. The question in Act 1 of *Henry V* was whether the French monarchy, founded by the Germanic Franks, was, or ever had been, subject to it. Even in the twentieth century, in an age of constitutional monarchy, the Salic Law sometimes cropped up. For example, in 1972, Frederik IX, king of Denmark, died and, having no sons, was succeeded in Denmark by his eldest daughter Margrethe II. Frederik, however, was not only "by the grace of God king of Denmark" but titular "duke of Schleswig, Holstein, Stormarn, Ditmarsh, Lauenburg, and Oldenburg." All these hereditary titles, which had no practical significance whatever, were subject to the Salic Law, and so they could not pass to his daughter, whose titulature and coat of arms were therefore drastically simplified; she became merely "Denmark's queen."

45. *Sacra* untranslatably connotes "holy, supernatural, demonic, divine"—a hunger that seemed like an outside force, changing the personality and desires of its victim.

46. Alfred Kohler, ed., *Quellen zur Geschichte Karls V.* Ausgewählte Quellen zur deutschen Geschichte der Neuzeit, 15 (Darmstadt: Wissenschaftliche Buchgesellschaft, 1990), 47–49.

47. Ibid., 59.

48. Quoted, in the 1603 John Florio translation, by Hale, *Europe in the Renaissance*, 50.

49. Tzvetan Todorov, *La Conquête de l'Amérique* (Paris: Seuil, 1982), 63–64, 205.

50. Bernal Diaz, *The Conquest of New Spain*, trans. J.M. Cohen (London: Penguin Classics, 1963), 9.

51. Quoted in Todorov, *Conquête*, 179–81.

52. Ibid., 54.

53. Diaz, *Conquest of New Spain*, 111–13.

54. Todorov, *Conquête*, 185.

55. Quoted ibid., 207.

56. Quoted ibid., 237–38.

7. From Christendom to Civilization

1. Strobe Talbott, the deputy U.S. secretary of state, stated in 1996 that a democratic universal humanism was the desirable and inevitable political future of the world. "Democracy and the National Interest," *Foreign Affairs* 75:6 (November-December 1996): 47–63.

2. "In the *Chronicle of Nauclerus*, published in 1516, the coronation of Charlemagne is hailed as proof of the divinely ordained superiority of the German people; it marks the passing of the Roman Empire to the Germans. God has chosen the Germans to dominate the nations and to have sovereignty over the whole world. And he has chosen wisely, for are not the Germans the most sincerely noble, the most just, the most prolific, the strongest and most tenacious in war of all peoples?" Frances A. Yates, *Astraea: The Imperial Theme in the Sixteenth Century* (London: Routledge, 1975), 17. Since the Germans were the new Romans, the new imperial race, it was clearly insufferable that they should be financially and theologically subject to a church hierarchy run by Italians. This German version of Christian ethnicity paradoxically required that the Germans, as the new Romans, reject the domination of papal Rome, held to be a morally inferior authority, usurping the dignity of the true, imperial, and genuinely Christian Rome, now located in Germany.

3. Elizabeth L. Eisenstein, *The Printing Revolution in Early Modern Europe* (New York: Cambridge University Press, 1983).

4. Quoted in English by Felipe Fernández-Armesto and Derek Wilson, *Reformations: A Radical Interpretation of Christianity and the World, 1500–2000* (New York: Scribner, 1996), 18.

5. From Luther's autobiographical statement of 1545, quoted in Joseph Lortz, *Die Reformation in Deutschland* (1940; repr. Freiburg: Herder, 1962), 180–81. Lortz is the great Catholic text on Luther and the Protestant Reformation, issued by the leading Catholic publisher in Germany. When first published in 1940, its profoundly sympathetic view of Luther drew suspicion of heresy on its author. By the 1960s, this view had become general, at least in official Catholic circles. By the 1990s, traditional Catholics often seemed to have more in common with orthodox Lutherans than with their own liberal and progressive coreligionists.

6. Quoted in Robert Stupperich, *Die Reformation in Deutschland*, 3d ed. (Gütersloh:

Mohn, 1988), 178–79. Stupperich is a classic Lutheran text on the same subject, issued by Germany's leading Lutheran publisher.

7. In Bernd Roeck, ed., *Gegenreformation und Dreißigjähriger Krieg 1555–1648* (Stuttgart: Reclam, 1996), 40, 44.

8. Hadrian VI's confession of guilt published in Nuremberg 1523 by his legate Francesco Chieregati, quoted in Stupperich, *Reformation*, 182.

9. This is the theme of Germaine de Staël, *De l'Allemagne*, written in 1810. Anne-Louise-Germaine Necker de Staël-Holstein was Swiss, the daughter of the last man who tried to save the finances and the power of the French kings, the Genevan banker and millionaire Jacques Necker. For fifteen years she was Benjamin Constant's lover and closest friend. As he was creating modern liberalism, she was creating the modern Western blend of emotion and sensibility.

10. Douglass C. North and Robert Paul Thomas, *The Rise of the Western World: A New Economic History* (New York: Cambridge University Press, 1973), 1.

11. Ibid., 51–52.

12. Ibid., 97.

13. Ibid., 136.

14. The Tilbury speech of August 9, 1588, quoted in Brian MacArthur, ed., *The Penguin Book of Historic Speeches* (New York: Penguin, 1995), 40–41.

15. Colonel Rainborowe's speech of October 29, 1647, quoted ibid., 54–55.

16. Ireton quoted in Antonia Fraser, *Cromwell: Our Chief of Men* (London: Weidenfeld & Nicolson, 1973), 212–17.

17. Ernest Gellner, *Reason and Society* (Oxford: Blackwell, 1992), 45, summarizing this part of Weber's theory.

18. Ibid., 47.

19. David Hume, *Political Essays*, ed. Knud Haakonssen (Cambridge: Cambridge University Press, 1994), 48–49, Hume's emphasis.

20. Blandine Kriegel, *L'Histoire à l'âge classique,* vol. 1, *Jean Mabillon* (Paris: Presses Universitaires de France, 1988), 108–11.

21. From the pamphlet of 1683 supposedly written by the Protestant minister Daniel de Larroque and quoted by Chateaubriand in his *Vie de Rancé*, ed. Pierre Clarac (Paris: Imprimerie Nationale, 1977), 109.

22. Kriegel, *Mabillon*, 124–33.

23. Edward Whiting Fox, *History in Geographic Perspective: The Other France* (New York: Norton, 1971).

24. Eric L. Jones, *The European Miracle: Environments, Economies, and Geopolitics in the History of Europe and Asia* (Cambridge: Cambridge University Press, 1981), 84.

25. Ibid., 20, and Richard S. Schofield, quoted ibid., 16.

26. Quoted in Kriegel, *L'Histoire*, vol. 2, *La Défaite de l'érudition*, 293.

27. Quoted ibid., 296.

28. Quoted ibid., 298.

29. The name *Jacobin* was applied first to the radical political club located in the rue Saint-Jacques in Paris. Because the members of this particular club were particularly noteworthy, the name Jacobin came to be used of all the allied clubs throughout France and of their members, who included virtually all the leaders of the radical Revolution.

30. Jules Michelet, *Histoire de la Révolution française*, vol. 2 (Paris: Gallimard, 1952), 7.

31. Quoted in Conor Cruise O'Brien, *The Great Melody: A Thematic Biography of Edmund Burke* (Chicago: University of Chicago Press, 1992), 611.

32. Quoted in Marcel Gauchet, *La Révolution des pouvoirs* (Paris: Gallimard, 1995), 17.

33. Quoted in O'Brien, *The Great Melody*, 403, 443.

8. The High Tide of Liberalism

1. Max Gallo, *Napoléon*, vol. 1, *Le Chant du départ* (Paris: Robert Laffont, 1997), 127–28.

2. Emmanuel de Las Cases, comp., *Mémorial de Sainte-Hélène* (Paris: Seuil, 1968), 559, entry of November 11, 1816. The *Mémorial* consists of the notes taken, on Saint Helena, by his faithful servant, the count de Las Cases, of Napoleon's recollections on various subjects in 1815–16. As the novelist Walter Scott pointed out when they were published in the 1820s, it was not only the record of what Napoleon thought but of what he wanted the world to believe he thought.

3. The phrase "all the Russias" in the czar's titulature referred to the traditional division of Russian ethnicity into three parts: Great Russia, Little Russia (Ukraine), and White Russia, or Ruthenia. In Russian, the titulature ran *tsar i imperator vsyerossiyskiy*, "all-Russian czar and emperor." The word *imperator* was a direct transliteration from Latin; but so in a sense was *tsar*, since it was a contraction of *Caesar*, which, in honor of Julius Caesar, had become the personal name of all ancient Roman emperors and had also given rise to the German word for emperor, *Kaiser*.

4. Paul Schroeder, *The Transformation of European Politics 1763–1848* (New York: Oxford University Press, 1994), 579–80.

5. The French historical sociologist Jean Baechler pointed out that Aristotle distinguished between "economics," the science of household management for the purpose of securing the means of the good life, and "chrematistics," the pursuit of business and gain as a way of life and as the end of life. A chrematistical economy was one in which the inner rationality of economic activity, of "seeking to produce more with less in an endless race toward growth and development," became dominant, as first happened in the West, thanks to its niches of liberty. Once the Western economy had entered on the chrematistical path, it opened the gates to the bourgeois temptation of liberalism, which forgot capitalism's political roots in liberty and focused only on "individual and collective enrichment as the final end of the species and its members." Thus the fruit of liberty—economic development—tended to overshadow liberty itself, in two ways: through the bourgeois pathology, and through the anticapitalist ideologies, such as Marxism, that arose to judge and abolish capitalism seen only as an economic system of exploitation, and not as the economic counterpart of democracy. The bourgeois pathology was, however, also a reflection of the political impotence of liberalism in much of Europe. Jean Baechler, *Le Capitalisme* (Paris: Gallimard, 1995) 1:80, 90, on chrematistical economy, and 2:268–87 on the reasons and nature of anticapitalist ideology.

6. A bad conscience that twentieth-century American liberals salved by abandoning economism and reinterpreting liberalism as a social and political doctrine that emphasized rights, whether individual rights or, in the late twentieth century, group rights. This was the opposite error to that of the classical liberals who reduced their doctrine to economism. Both errors forgot the essence of liberalism, namely, the combined understanding of liberty—political and social—as the stimulus as well as the subsequent beneficiary of economic development.

7. The rise of the rational mentality spawned a huge literature from Max Weber on; much of this was recapitulated and interpreted by Alfred W. Crosby, *The Measure of Reality: Quantification and Western Society, 1250–1600* (New York: Cambridge University Press, 1997), and, for a more strictly Weberian account, Ernest Gellner, *Reason and Culture* (Cambridge, Mass.: Blackwell, 1992).

8. Régine Pernoud, *Histoire de la bourgeoisie en France*, vol. 2 (Paris: Seuil, 1962, repr. 1981), 401.

9. Edmund Burke, writing in 1790, expected the French Revolution to degenerate into the despotism of barbarous fanatics, a prediction confirmed by the Jacobin terror of 1792–94. But had he read Michelet's close analysis of how liberty and property supported and fed on each other in the first years of the revolution, he would have found his own diagnosis of the roots of ordered liberty confirmed. Michelet explained how the National Assembly, in 1789, abolished the feudal privileges of aristocrats and the church, of which the most important were immunity from tax and local jurisdiction, and replaced them with a uniform network of local government responsible for law, order, and taxes, in which rights and duties were equal for all. This network demanded over a million new officers and administrators. "This immense number created huge practical problems, but as the education of a people, as its initiation into public life, it was admirable." The four million property holders resulting from the abolition of privileges were not enough to fill the needs of local government. The assembly, therefore, decided to sell church and noble lands to those who worked the land, who were allowed to use the land itself as security. "It was necessary to create a new class of property-holders. The peasants on church and noble lands were now, as purchasers of the lands put up for sale, going to find themselves owners, electors, local magistrates, judges of the peace, etc., and, as such, were to become the most solid supporters of the Revolution." Jules Michelet, *Histoire de la Révolution française*, vol. 1 (Paris: Gallimard, 1952), 402.

10. Isaiah Berlin, *Four Essays on Liberty* (New York: Oxford University Press, 1969).

11. Two schools of thought on nationalism disputed the English-speaking scholarly terrain in the 1990s. One, headed by Ernest Gellner, saw it as a consequence of social modernization, of the rise of new social classes without local, religious, or political affiliation. For members of this school, the political, social, and economic revolutions of the eighteenth and early nineteenth centuries came first, and nationalism appeared as one of their effects, to compensate for the loss of old social bonds. Although this approach held the high ground at first, it began to seem increasingly implausible to those who looked at the written and pictorial evidence from much older periods of European history, and which strongly suggested to the unprejudiced observer that nationalism, or something very like it, had appeared repeatedly in both ancient and medieval Western civilization. It seemed to be much older than modernization, although modernization certainly strengthened it. The most productive of these critics of Gellner's thesis was Anthony Smith. He examined national identity, found it hard to distinguish from nationalism, and traced elements of both deep into the Old West. Ernest Gellner, *Nations and Nationalism* (Ithaca, N.Y.: Cornell University Press, 1983); Anthony Smith, *National Identity* (London: Penguin Books, 1991). A third line of argument, that of Jean Baechler, defined nationality as a stage in the normal evolution of a Western polity and nationalism as an exaggeration or pathology of that stage—rather in the sense that economism was the pathology of liberalism. Jean Baechler, "L'Universalité de la nation," *La Pensée politique*, ed. Marcel Gauchet, Pierre Manent, and Pierre Rosanvallon, vol. 3: *La Nation* (Paris: Seuil, 1995), 9–25. None of these approaches

to nationalism emphasized the link suggested by the phrase "Christian ethnicity," that is, that national identity and nationalism, as they evolved in Europe and the West, were results of the synthesis of Christianity with ancient and Germanic culture. Nationality was not a fruit of modernization but a fundamental aspect of the Western synthesis, and was not an alien latecomer to Western identity, but one of its essential building blocks. Adrian Hastings, *The Construction of Nationhood: Ethnicity, Religion and Nationalism* (Cambridge: Cambridge University Press, 1998) was one of the few scholars who specifically pointed to this nexus as crucial to an understanding of Western development.

12. Tocqueville was, let me note for the record, the most impressive. He predicted from observation in the 1830s what Nietzsche only surmised from psychological insight fifty years later. His greatness consists of two things: he was the most spectacularly successful futurologist of all time, and he did not let his predictions turn into defeatism. He retained, to the end, a guarded hope for democracy, because people were free and could, sometimes, defeat their fate. Yet the resources they needed to do so were precisely those undermined by modernity.

13. Classical liberalism claimed equal rights and liberties for all against coercion, which in Europe meant state and church; the peculiar American corollary to this was that the state must be mobilized to help achieve these rights. Hence the familiar paradox that European liberals in the 1980s and 1990s defended market economics, whereas American liberals defended state power. Both currents, however, believed in equality and rights. In the larger perspective, they were part of a common doctrine, a common psychology, and a common ambition.

14. Giacomo Leopardi, *Discorso sopra lo stato presente dei costumi degl' italiani*, intro. by Salvatore Veca, ed. Maurizio Moncagatta (Milan: Feltrinelli, 1991), 43–44. The reference to Horace is to the tag *leges sine moribus vanae*, which can be paraphrased: laws are pointless unless people have the *mores*, the habits, breeding, and civic virtue, to act responsibly.

15. *Pensieri* no. 11, ed. Dino Basili (Milan: Mondadori, 1993), 31.

16. *Discorso*, 95.

17. Ibid., 83.

18. Democracy in America, ed. Richard D. Hefner (New York: Mentor Books, 1956), 151–55.

19. From an unpublished passage of *Democracy in America*, quoted in English by Larry Siedentop, *Tocqueville* (New York: Oxford University Press, 1994), 102.

20. From book 1 of *Democracy in America*, quoted ibid., 52.

21. *Pensieri* no. 29, ed. Basili, 48.

22. Quoted in Siedentop, *Tocqueville*, 26; Royer-Collard's emphasis.

23. Quoted ibid., 93.

24. *The Eighteenth Brumaire of Louis Bonaparte*, in Karl Marx, *Selected Writings*, ed. David McLellan (New York: Oxford University Press, 1977), 300.

25. *The Communist Manifesto*, ibid., 221, 238, 246.

26. *The German Ideology*, ibid., 171.

27. Martin Malia, "The End of the Noble Dream," in *Times Literary Supplement*, November 7, 1997.

28. The phrase was Engels's definition of Marxist revolution; ibid.

29. *A Critique of Political Economy*, in *Selected Writings*, 390.

30. As happened in Russia, when Marxist revolution was actually tried. Ibid., 170.

31. *Capital*, ibid., 487.

32. *Critique of the Gotha Programme*, ibid., 569.

33. Pernoud, *Histoire de la bourgeoisie en France,* vol. 2, 414.

34. Denis Mack Smith, *Mazzini* (New Haven: Yale University Press, 1994), 40.

35. Ibid., 29.

36. Quoted ibid., 52.

37. Rino Cammilleri, *Elogio del sillabo* (Milan: Leonardo, 1994).

38. Quoted ibid., 48.

39. Quoted in Siedentop, *Tocqueville,* 103.

40. Friedrich Nietzsche, *Die nachgelassenen Fragmente* (Stuttgart: Reclam, 1996), 203–5, Nietzsche's emphasis.

41. Ibid., 149.

42. François Furet, *Le Passé d'une illusion,* paper ed. (Paris: Livre de Poche, 1996), 65.

43. Quoted in Norman Angell, *The Great Illusion* (London: Heinemann, 1912 reprint), 290.

44. Quoted in Furet, *Passé d'une illusion,* 67; from *De l'esprit de conquête et de l'usurpation,* ed. Marcel Gauchet (Paris: Pluriel, 1980), 118–19.

45. Quoted in Furet, *Passé d'une illusion,* 68.

46. Ibid., 64.

47. Oswald Spengler, *Der Untergang des Abendlandes* (Munich: C.H. Beck, 1968; unchanged reprint of the 1923 edition), 451.

48. Ibid., 576–77.

9. *The Totalitarian Trap*

1. Quoted in François Furet, *Le Passé d'une illusion* (Paris: Livre de Poche, 1996), 87.

2. Anyone who writes about ideology must decide whether the various anticommunist regimes of interwar Europe, of which those of Hitler and Mussolini were the most important, had enough in common to warrant a joint label, and if so, what that label should be. Marxist and Marxist-inspired social science sanctioned the label "fascist," borrowing the name of Mussolini's movement and extending it to a number of other regimes allegedly sharing the same basic features, being hostile to socialism, nationalistic, and protective of corporate capitalism. The objections to this label are, first, that since the Western left used it to smear all those it disliked—as the French said, *tout le monde est le fasciste de quelqu'un* (everybody is somebody's fascist)—it lost all substantive, historical, and sociological meaning. Second, the regimes of Mussolini, Hitler, Franco, Antonescu, Horthy, Salazar, and Metaxas did not share critical features, as the left believed, so that calling them all "fascist" obscured more than it enlightened. A second possible label is "right-wing," but what sense does it make to call, for instance, Hitler's regime right wing, since the German right included some of its bitterest enemies as well as enthusiastic supporters? A third candidate is "nationalist," and this makes some sense, since nationalism was clearly a feature of all the regimes mentioned. But many governments in history have been nationalist, so the label is too vague to specify something distinctive about these interwar states. Nor can one call them the "dictatorships," for this obscures the differences between the more traditional dictatorships, such as Franquist Spain, and Hitler's Germany. The same goes, unfortunately, for "anticommunist," for opposition to communism was arguably *the* single most significant common feature that aligned Hitler with Mussolini and the rest. But since the post-1945 liberal Western governments were also, by and large, anticommunist, that label risks granting the communist argument that liberal democracy and the

regimes of Hitler, Mussolini, and the rest were all bad in the same way because they all opposed communism. And again, anticommunism obscures what seem to be some critical differences among those regimes, for example, the Catholicism of Franco and Salazar compared with Hitler's hostility to Christianity and Mussolini's opportunism. Finally, none of these joint labels captures the most decisive difference among these regimes. What meaningful label can encompass the regime of Mussolini, which executed some twelve hundred political enemies in twenty-three years, and that of Hitler, which by a rough count got rid of some five to six million during a mere third of its short life of twelve years—not counting the victims of German military aggression?

2. Since the discussion in this chapter concerns only one of these regimes, namely, the most important, that of Adolf Hitler, I have decided to remain historically specific and refer to it by its own name, National Socialist. I generally avoid the short form, "Nazi," just as I avoid referring to communists as "commies." Both forms are derogatory acronyms that have no place in a scholarly discussion.

The label "totalitarian" came back in from the cold to which leftist social science had consigned it after the 1960s, and was being used in the 1990s again in its original sense, to describe the regimes of the Soviet Union and of National Socialist Germany in terms of their commonalities, which distinguished both not only from liberal democracies, but from the other nondemocratic regimes of their era. See Martin Malia, "The end of the noble dream," *Times Literary Supplement*, November 7, 1997.

3. Martin Malia, *The Soviet Tragedy: A History of Socialism in Russia, 1917–1991* (New York: Free Press, 1994), 93, 105.

4. Furet, *Passé d'une illusion*, 119.

5. Ibid., 134. For Russia as the weakest link in the capitalist order, see Malia, *Soviet Tragedy*, 51.

6. This analysis of communism draws eclectically on various thinkers; the ones that come to mind as I write, apart from Aleksandr Solzhenitsyn, are Leszek Kolakowski, Alain Besançon, and Martin Malia. Examples of their relevant writings are Kolakowski, *Main Currents of Marxism* (New York: Oxford University Press, 1978); Besançon, *Les Origines intellectuelles du léninisme* (Paris: Calmann-Lévy, 1977); Malia, *Penser la révolution russe* (Paris: Seuil, 1982) and *The Soviet Tragedy*. But similar notions can be found in such other experts on the matter as Robert Conquest, Konrad Löw, or Jose Guilherme Merquior. It is a temperament about what communism was rather than a sketch of ideological history I am recapitulating.

7. Quoted in Furet, *Passé d'une illusion*, 258.

8. Ibid., 503–4.

9. Quote from Solzhenitsyn's Templeton Speech given in London in 1983 and taken from Os Guinness, *The American Hour: A Time of Reckoning and the Once and Future Role of Faith* (New York: Free Press, 1993), 402.

10. Novalis, *Die Christenheit oder Europa* (Stuttgart: Reclam, 1984), 67–70.

11. T.S. Eliot, "What is a Classic?" in *Selected Prose*, ed. Frank Kermode (New York: Harcourt Brace Jovanovich, 1975), 128.

12. Charles Martindale, "Ruins of Rome: T.S. Eliot and the Presence of the Past," Arion, 3d series 2–3 (Fall 1995–Winter 1996): 107.

13. Theodor Haecker, "Betrachtungen über Vergil," in his *Essays* (Munich: Kösel, 1958), 455, emphasis his; Eliot quoted in Martindale, "Ruins of Rome," 106.

14. Oswald Spengler, *Der Untergang des Abendlandes* (Munich: C.H. Beck, 1968), 465, his emphasis.

15. Quoted in Theodore Ziolkowski, *Virgil and the Moderns* (Princeton, N.J.: Princeton University Press, 1993), 100.

16. Quoted by David L. Edwards in his introduction to T.S. Eliot, *The Idea of a Christian Society and Other Writings* (London: Faber and Faber, 1982), 39.

17. Ziolkowski, *Virgil and the Moderns*, 6, 56.

18. J.W. Mackail quoted in Martindale, "Ruins of Rome," 103.

19. Ziolkowski, *Virgil and the Moderns*, 26. Virgil's two thousandth birthday fell on October 15, 1930, and was celebrated in many countries.

20. Theodor Haecker, *Vergil, Vater des Abendlandes* (Munich: Kösel, 1947), 129–30.

21. Quoted ibid., 37.

22. Quoted in Ziolkowski, *Virgil and the Moderns*, 111.

23. Parthenope was a Greek name for Naples. It can still be encountered in Italian, where the adjective *partenopeo* means Neapolitan.

24. The title of the last volume of Leonard Woolf's autobiography (London: Hogarth Press, 1973).

25. Quoted in Ziolkowski, *Virgil and the Moderns*, 199.

26. Theodor Haecker, *Tag- und Nachtbücher 1939–1945* (Munich: Kösel, 1947), 93. The date of publication is noteworthy, since all books published then in the American zone of occupation of Germany needed a "U.S. Military Government Information Control License," so they had to be anti-Nazi and antimilitarist. Also, paper was scarce and devoting it to Haecker's books shows that they were in substantial demand after the war. Kösel was and remained a well-known Catholic publishing house, specializing in philosophy and literature.

27. Haecker, *Vergil*, 75–77, Haecker's emphasis.

28. Ibid., 120.

29. Quoted in Ziolkowski, *Virgil and the Moderns*, 23.

30. But Goethe, like Whitman, "contained multitudes" and cared not if he contradicted himself. On August 11, 1815, he said to Sulpice Boisserée, "Everything Roman attracts me. This great intelligence, this order in all things appeals to me; the Greeks not so much." Quoted in Ernst Robert Curtius, *Europäische Literatur und lateinisches Mittelalter*, 2d ed. (Bern: Francke, 1954), 20.

31. Ibid., 25.

32. Quoted in Gian Enrico Rusconi, *Resistenza e postfascismo* (Bologna: Il Mulino, 1995), 56.

33. Quotes from his 1932 book on *Deutscher Geist in Gefahr*, cited in Harald Weinrich, "Das Deutschlandbild eines großen Romanisten," in Walter Berschin and Arnold Rothe, eds., *Ernst Robert Curtius* (Heidelberg: Winter, 1989), 145.

34. The definition is that of Martindale in "Ruins of Rome," 113.

35. Curtius, *Europäische Literatur*, 363.

36. Quoted by Louis Menand in his positive review of Anthony Julius, *T.S. Eliot, Anti-Semitism and Literary Form* (Cambridge: Cambridge University Press, 1995), in *New York Review of Books*, June 6, 1996.

37. Ibid., 505.

38. Paul Piccone and Gary L. Ulmen, "Introduction to Carl Schmitt," *Telos* 72 (Spring 1987): 13.

39. Quoted in Andreas Koenen, *Der Fall Carl Schmitt. Sein Aufstieg zum "Kronjuristen des dritten Reiches"* (Darmstadt: Wissenschaftliche Buchgesellschaft, 1995), 623. The phrase quoted in the subtitle is Gurian's famous denunciation. Koenen's book revolutionized Schmitt studies.

40. People who knew him personally, whether German, Jewish, American, French, or any other background, almost invariably found him a generous host, courteous, possessed of the rare gift of using his own intellectual powers not to make guests intimidated but to make them feel more intelligent in his company.

41. The German word *Gerichtsherr* (court master) originally referred to the feudal lord who had full and unappealable jurisdiction over his tenants, hence, in modern usage, a person or body with power to determine jurisdiction, to tell courts what to do.

42. Quoted in Paul Noack, *Carl Schmitt* (Frankfurt: Ullstein, 1993), 196.

43. Quoted ibid., 193–94.

44. Quoted ibid., 204.

45. Ibid., 182–83.

46. Quoted in Koenen, *Der Fall Carl Schmitt*, 155.

47. A decree of July 10, 1939, ordered the media to stop using the phrase "Third Reich." The public had already been so warned on June 13 of the same year; ibid., 819.

48. Quoted in Noack, *Carl Schmitt*, 29.

49. Quoted ibid., 52.

50. *Souverän ist, wer über den Ausnahmezustand entscheidet*, the first sentence of Schmitt's *Politische Theologie I* (Berlin: Duncker & Humblot, 1985, first published 1922), is classic in its aesthetic form and semantic force. *Entscheiden über* can mean both "decide" when something begins and ends and "determine," that is, "control." The sovereign is therefore he who not only rules in an emergency, but decides when an emergency exists; he sets the conditions for his own exercise of power.

51. Quotes in this and previous paragraphs from Noack, *Carl Schmitt*, 60, 70–72. Juan Donoso Cortés, a descendant of Hernán Cortés, the conquistador, was a Spanish diplomat who, around 1850, wrote eloquent, original, and scathing denunciations of liberalism and democracy, defining them, in counterrevolutionary terms, as heresies and rebellions against the divine order. In his later years, Schmitt came to regard Donoso as a sort of alter ego.

52. Ibid., 75.

53. Quoted in Koenen, *Der Fall Carl Schmitt*, 589–91.

54. Quoted ibid., 48.

55. Quoted in Noack, *Carl Schmitt*, 230.

56. *New York Review of Books*, June 6, 1996.

57. Henri Massis, *Defence of the West* (New York: Harcourt, Brace, 1928). Emphasis in original.

58. Quoted in Jean Lacouture, *Les Jésuites*, vol. 2 (Paris: Seuil, 1992), 347.

59. Quotes and paraphrase in Furet, *Passé d'une illusion*, 340.

60. Quoted ibid., 512–13.

61. Jacques Maritain, *Man and the State* (Chicago: University of Chicago Press, 1951), 73–75.

62. Giovanni Filoramo, *Le Vie del sacro—modernità e religione* (Turin: Einaudi, 1994), 50, quoting, in part, the scholar of Iranian mysticism and gnostic thinker Henry Corbin.

63. Furet, *Passé d'une illusion*, 582.

64. Ibid., 585.

10. The Cold War West

1. Winston S. Churchill, *The Second World War*, vol. 1, *The Gathering Storm* (London: Cassell, 1948), 238.

2. François Furet, *Le Passé d'une illusion*, paper ed. (Paris: Livre de Poche, 1996), 632.

3. Quoted in Charles Maier, "The Two Post-war Eras," *American Historical Review* 86 (1981): 327. For an assessment of the causes and the costs of this belief to British society and the British economy, see Corelli Barnett, *The Audit of War* (London: Macmillan, 1986), and *The Lost Victory* (London: Macmillan, 1995).

4. Walter McDougall, *Promised Land, Crusader State: The American Encounter with the World since 1776* (Boston: Houghton Mifflin, 1997), 151–52.

5. Furet, *Passé d'une illusion*, 623–24.

6. Ibid., 673. Blum was doubtless one of the "innumerable children of the French Revolution." His change of heart about communism between 1936 and 1946 showed that not all these children became pro-communist after World War II. Blum was an emblematic figure among those who tried to combine loyalty to the revolutionary legacy with commitment to both socialism and liberty—a commitment that might seem absurd after 1989, but did not appear so to many during the Cold War. These issues and the personal and political struggles they provoked formed an essential part of the drama of Western identity in the twentieth century. Those struggles and their moral implications are investigated and interpreted by Tony Judt, *The Burden of Responsibility: Blum, Camus, Aron and the French Twentieth Century* (Chicago: University of Chicago Press, 1998).

7. Robert Gutman, *Wagner: The Man, His Mind and His Music* (London: Faber & Faber, 1968), launched a tradition of seeing Wagner's anti-Semitism as central and his music as deeply colored by anti-Semitic and nationalist ideology. Bryan Magee, *Aspects of Wagner* (London: Faber & Faber, 1968), launched a contrary tradition of understanding Wagner's attitude to Jews as a sociologically sophisticated reaction to assimilation, which led to an explosion of pent-up Jewish talent in science, the arts, the professions, and scholarship. The literature on Richard Wagner is as immense as that on Karl Marx and substantially more interesting for a history of Western identity. A survey of the issues raised both by the life and the music is Barry Millington, ed., *The Wagner Compendium: A Guide to Wagner's Life and Music* (London: Thames & Hudson, 1992).

8. André Tarbeuf in the sleeve notes to the recording of Ludwig van Beethoven, *Symphony No. 9 in d minor, op, 125, the "Choral"*, Wilhelm Furtwängler conducting the Bayreuth Festival Orchestra and Chorus on June 29, 1951, EMI CDC-7470812.

9. Recusants were English Catholics, so called because by holding on to their inherited faith, they were refusing to conform to the laws of Elizabeth I and her successors forbidding Catholic worship. In certain parts of England, recusant families survived throughout the period of the penal laws, maintaining Catholic practice until their religion was again permitted by the Catholic Emancipation Act of 1829.

10. Evelyn Waugh, *The Sword of Honour Trilogy* (London: Penguin Books, 1984, first published 1952–61), part 1, *Men at Arms*, 11, emphasis added.

11. Ibid., part 2, *Officers and Gentlemen*, 383.

12. Ibid., part 3, *Unconditional Surrender*, 568.

13. Quoted in Furet, *Passé d'une illusion*, 346; Mann's emphasis.

14. Quoted in my "Dangerous Liaisons," *The New Criterion*, January 1993, 63.

15. Quoted in my "Raymond Aron: Philosopher of Liberal Democracy," *The New Criterion*, June 1990, 25.

16. Ibid., 696.

17. Andreas Koenen, *Der Fall Carl Schmitt* (Darmstadt: Wissenschaftliche Buchgesellschaft, 1995), 160.

18. Ibid., 323–24.

19. Arnold Toynbee, *An Historian's Approach to Religion* (New York: Oxford University Press, 1956); quoted in Albert Mirgeler, *Revision der europäischen Geschichte* (Freiburg: Karl Alber, 1971), 260. Mirgeler's reference is to the German translation of Toynbee's work.

20. Ibid., 7.

21. William H. McNeill, *Arnold J. Toynbee: A Life* (New York: Oxford University Press, 1989), 246.

22. The classic study of the case and its context is Allen Weinstein, *Perjury: The Hiss-Chambers Case,* rev. ed. (New York: Random House, 1997). This book, first published in 1975, was written by a man who started out believing Hiss innocent, as did almost everyone on the American academic left, to which Weinstein belonged. What he found in his research convinced him that he had been wrong, and he changed his mind, an example of scholarly probity for which the academic left never forgave him. The revised edition includes evidence from Soviet sources unavailable in 1975. On Chambers see Sam Tanenhaus, *Whittaker Chambers: A Biography* (New York: Random House, 1997).

23. McNeill, *Toynbee*, 212.

24. Ibid., 211.

25. Ibid., 245.

26. José Ortega y Gasset, *La Rebelión de las masas,* 3d ed. (Madrid: Revista de Occidente, 1981), final chapter.

27. Denis de Rougemont, *L'Aventure occidentale de l'homme* (Paris: Albin Michel, 1957), 9–12, 78–79.

28. William H. McNeill, *The Rise of the West: A History of the Human Community* (Chicago: University of Chicago Press, 1963; 1988 reprint), xvi.

29. Ibid., 807.

30. Ibid., 806–7. McNeill pursued the history of disease and society in *Plagues and Peoples* (1976), and that of technology and social organization in *A History of Power, AD 1000–2000* (1982), both also published by the University of Chicago Press.

31. James Burnham, *Suicide of the West* (New York: Knopf, 1964), 278.

32. Quoted in Stephen and Robin Larsen, *A Fire in the Mind: The Life of Joseph Campbell* (New York: Doubleday, 1991), 329, emphasis added.

33. Quoted ibid., 414.

34. Richard D. Noll, *Jung: The Aryan Christ* (Princeton, N.J.: Princeton University Press, 1997), xiv–xvi.

35. Sonu Shamdasani, *Cult Fictions: C.G. Jung and the Founding of Analytical Psychology* (London: Routledge, 1998). Compare Noll, *Aryan Christ,* 153–60.

36. The text of the "Seven Sermons" is printed as an appendix to Jung's *Memories, Dreams, Reflections* (New York: Pantheon, 1962). Jung insisted that this book not be included in his *Collected Works* and he did not want it used as evidence of his own religious beliefs.

37. "Gegenwart und Zukunft," *Gesammelte Werke,* vol. 10 (Freiburg: Walter Verlag, 1974), 308.

38. Larsen and Larsen, *Fire in the Mind*, 508–9.

39. Ibid., 287–90.

40. Quoted in my "The Year That Changed Everything: 1968," *The New Criterion*, May 1989, 16.

11. Battle in the Heartland

1. Francis Fukuyama, *The End of History and the Last Man* (New York: Free Press, 1992), xi.

2. Ibid., xii.

3. Ibid., xiv. Fukuyama seemed not to have heard of postmodernism, which denied precisely what he claimed was "common consensus," namely, that science was cumulative and directional. Not at all, said the postmodernists; science was a social construction, and so was the illusion of cumulative directionality. If Fukuyama had been writing from within a university rather than from the State Department and the RAND Corporation, he could not have been so innocent.

4. Ibid., xv–xvii, Fukuyama's emphasis.

5. Ibid., 108, Fukuyama's emphasis.

6. Ibid., 130.

7. Ibid., 306.

8. David Lowenthal, *Possessed by the Past: The Heritage Crusade and the Spoils of History* (New York: Free Press, 1996), 168.

9. The phrase "the short twentieth century," used to describe the years from the outbreak of World War I in 1914 to the end of the Soviet Union in 1991, was first coined by the Hungarian economic historian Ivan Berend and applied by Eric Hobsbawm, as he described it in his essay "The Present as History," in his *On History* (New York: New Press, 1997). It quickly gained ground as a useful shorthand for the sense that many observers had that these years shared some decisive characteristics not found either before, in the long nineteenth century (1789–1914), or afterwards, in the new world order of the 1990s and 2000s. Those characteristics were conflict between advanced industrial states, either as war, as the threat of war, or as Cold War; antidemocratic ideologies, defined as theories about how the world should be ordered and strategies of how to gain power; pervasive fear or defeatism among liberals and democrats; a sense that world history was heading in an uncertain, dangerous, or even fatal direction. Jean Baechler, whose theories of world history are discussed in the next chapter, arrived at a similar diagnosis from a perspective opposed to that of the Marxist Hobsbawm; according to Baechler, the short twentieth century was a tragic interruption that temporarily derailed a global political and socioeconomic evolution toward more liberty, prosperity, variety, and interaction of cultures.

10. Charles Jencks, quoted in Richard Appignanesi and Chris Garratt, *Postmodernism for Beginners* (Cambridge: Icon Books, 1995), 102–3.

11. Ibid., 3.

12. Quoted in James Davison Hunter, *Culture Wars: The Struggle to Define America* (New York: Basic Books, 1991), 313.

13. Jean Baechler, *Le Capitalisme* (Paris: Gallimard, 1995), 1:40.

14. Alasdair MacIntyre, *After Virtue* (South Bend, Ind.: University of Notre Dame Press, 1981), 68–69, 263.

15. Quoted in Gerald Holton, *Science and Anti-Science* (Cambridge, Mass.: Harvard University Press, 1993), 170.

16. Etzioni, *The New Golden Rule*, 244, emphasis added.

17. Michael Walzer, *On Toleration* (New Haven: Yale University Press, 1997), 100, who refers to Robert Putnam, "Bowling Alone: America's Declining Social Capital," *Journal of Democracy* 6 (1995): 65–78.

18. Shirley Robin Letwin, *The Anatomy of Thatcherism* (London: Fontana, 1992), 33.

19. Agnes Heller, *The Grandeur and Twilight of Radical Universalism* (New Brunswick, N.J.: Transaction, 1991), from the Introduction.

20. Quotes from Martin Meyer, *Ernst Jünger* (Munich: Hanser, 1990), 395–99.

21. Havel's speech was excerpted in *New York Times*, March 1, 1992.

22. Roger Scruton, *The Meaning of Conservatism*, 2d ed. (London: Macmillan, 1984), 32, 171.

23. John Gray, *Enlightenment's Wake* (London: Routledge, 1995), 178.

24. Ibid., 153.

25. Julian L. Simon, *The Ultimate Resource 2* (Princeton, N.J.: Princeton University Press, 1996), 257, 611–12.

26. A Catholic educational activist quoted in Hunter, *Culture Wars*, 25.

27. Ibid., 52, Hunter's emphasis.

28. Ibid., 32.

29. Ibid., 42–43, Hunter's emphasis.

30. Ibid., 44–45, emphasis removed.

31. Ibid., 64.

32. Ibid., 130–31, emphasis removed.

33. Ibid., 132.

34. Fukuyama, *The End of History*, 312.

35. Marcello Veneziani, *L'Antinovecento* (Milan: Leonardo, 1996), 127–29.

36. Bassam Tibi, *Krieg der Zivilisationen* (Hamburg: Hoffmann & Campe, 1995), 277.

12. The Failure of Universalism and the Future of Western Identity

1. An old-fashioned liberal might protest that universalism was a doctrine about the equal and universal dignity of individuals, and that therefore universalism was not compatible with the collectivist, group identity approach of multiculturalism. But such old liberals were few on the ground and politically irrelevant by the 1990s. In practice, and indeed in ideology, the multiculturalist and universalist agendas strengthened each other.

2. Ernest Gellner, *Conditions of Liberty* (New York: Allen Lane, 1994), 103.

3. Ibid., 203, 80.

4. Gellner called this rediscovery surprising, for two reasons. First, Poland and Czechoslovakia were Marxist states, and according to Marxism, "Civil Society is a fraud." Civil society was a counterweight to the state; it rested on the diffusion of social power, on institutional pluralism. Marxism contended that no such counterweight was necessary under communism, and that, meanwhile, institutional pluralism was "a façade for a hidden and maleficent domination." And though they rejected Marxism and "real existing socialism," the Czech and Polish dissidents were not conservatives; why, then, would they turn to an eighteenth-century concept to explain their predicament and launch their appeal for freedom?

The second reason the Central European rediscovery of civil society was surprising, according to Gellner, was that it was not a concept widely used by Western scholars, journalists, or politicians—the people who otherwise provided many of the dissidents' ideas and to whom they, in turn, directed much of their appeal. "The phrase," Gellner says, "had no living resonance or evocativeness. Rather, it seemed distinctly covered with dust." It belonged to the history of political ideas of the Enlightenment and of German Idealism, not to the language of daily politics, much less of the East-West conflict.

5. Ibid., 26, 133–35.

6. Gellner, as I mentioned, did not so label his insights, which can be found in the following books: *Plough, Sword and Book* (Chicago: University of Chicago Press, 1989); *Nations and Nationalism* (Ithaca, N.Y.: Cornell University Press, 1983), and *Postmodernism, Reason and Religion* (London: Routledge, 1992).

7. Gellner, *Conditions of Liberty*, 210.

8. Ibid., 12.

9. Ibid., 165, 145. Noting that most of human social existence took place in segmentary societies or command-administrative empires and that modern civil society marked a wholly new and unexpected departure from this formerly universal pattern brought Gellner close to, but not quite over the frontier of, the new macrohistorical insight. Because however persuasive his theory was in explaining how traditional, that is, segmentary or command-administrative, societies functioned, his theory did not explain how they arose in the first place. The fact of the matter, as the new macrohistorians were trying to demonstrate, was that segmentary and command-administrative societies were indeed universal, until the rise of modernity. But they were not the original form of human society, and understanding why that was so also provided the key to understanding the transition to modernity, or civil society, or capitalism.

Gellner's aperçu of the rise and fall of Marxist socialism was brilliant: no one else ever so well explained, first, why it succeeded, and could only succeed, in backward countries, and second, why it failed as an ideology even among its beneficiaries. The answer to the first question was that it promised "the rectification of injustice and inequality," which in the leading case, that of Russia, meant both "the incorporation of Russia in a prosperously materialist West" and "a morally superior transcendence of the West." The answer to the second was that by sacralizing the economic and the profane, Marxism left no escape when enthusiasm waned and the economy stagnated. "When the *nomenklatura* switched from shooting each other to bribing each other, faith evaporated." And because that faith was secular, its failure in concrete reality was fatal. With the mobilizing unity of faith, truth, and order gone, the political and social elite of communist societies, their "secular *Umma*," fragmented into the nationalisms and the incipient civil societies that emerged as communism collapsed, for example in Havel's Czech Republic. Ibid., 36, 143–44.

10. See note 17 to chapter 7.

11. Gellner, *Conditions of Liberty*, 214.

12. Gellner, *Postmodernism*, 25–30.

13. Ibid., 54, 60, emphasis in Gellner.

14. Samuel P. Huntington, *The Clash of Civilizations and the Remaking of World Order* (New York: Simon & Schuster, 1996), 125.

15. Luc Ferry, *L'Homme-Dieu ou le sens de la vie* (Paris: Grasset, 1996), 233.

16. Ibid., 236–37.

17. John Paul II, *Encyclical Letter Centesimus Annus*, sections 18–19, 53.

18. J. Gordon Edwards, "DDT Effects on Bird Abundance and Reproduction," in Jay Lehr,

ed., *Rational Readings on Environmental Concerns* (New York: Van Nostrand, 1992). This book is a compendium of often surprising information about environmental problems.

19. Julian L. Simon, *The Ultimate Resource 2* (Princeton, N.J.: Princeton University Press, 1996), 35.

20. These had by no means disappeared as sources of fear, as shown, for example, by the Alar apple panic in America or the recurrent obsession of Western governments with restricting the use of so-called nonrenewable resources. Simon provided a useful list of scares, ibid., 260–65.

21. John Gray, *Enlightenment's Wake* (London: Routledge, 1995), 183.

22. Matt Ridley, *Down to Earth II* (London: Institute for Economic Affairs, 1996), 99.

23. Stephen Schneider, *The Genesis Strategy* (New York: Plenum Press, 1976), 90.

24. Quoted in Simon, *Ultimate Resource*, 574.

25. Mikhail S. Bernstam, *The Wealth of Nations and the Environment* (London: Institute of Economic Affairs, 1991), 15.

26. John Gray, *Enlightenment's Wake* (London: Routledge, 1995), 178, in a section headed by a quote by Heidegger.

27. According to Matt Ridley, "the ozone layer is getting thicker, not thinner, over temperate latitudes" in the 1990s. *Down to Earth II*, 104.

28. Perry Anderson, "The Ends of History," in his *A Zone of Engagement* (London: Verso, 1992), 353.

29. Bernstam, *Wealth of Nations*, 59.

30. *Economist*, December 16, 1996. Global demographic tendencies in the 1990s indicated a future rather different from that of the Malthusian scare scenarios. Starting in the late 1960s, the birthrate in most poor countries fell far more rapidly than observers expected. In the 1990s, some forecasts estimated a maximum world population by the mid-twenty-first century of fewer than eight billion, to be followed by a slow, continuous decline—a decline that began in western Europe in the 1970s but that would affect all societies, not just the most prosperous ones, by the year 2030. If these projections turned out to be reliable, the challenge of the future was not going to be a population *explosion* but a population *implosion*, a startling and wholly unprecedented prospect that had barely begun to receive the analysis it deserved. Nicholas Eberstadt, "World Population Implosion?" *Public Interest* 129 (Fall 1997) was one of the first experts to put this new perspective on the agenda.

31. Wallace Kaufman, *No Turning Back: Dismantling the Fantasies of Environmental Thinking* (New York: Basic Books, 1994), 181.

32. Rich Lowry in *National Review*, October 14, 1996, 69.

33. The book was Nigel Calder, *The Manic Sun* (London: Pilkington Press, 1997).

34. Hedley Bull, "The Revolt against the West," in id. and Alan Watson, eds., *The Expansion of European Society* (New York: Oxford University Press, 1988). Huntington, *Clash of Civilizations*, 184. In *The Challenge of Fundamentalism* (Berkeley: University of California Press, 1997), Bassam Tibi argued for a democratic Islam opposed to both universalism and imperialism.

35. Semiotic and structural analysis of scripture was usually held to have begun with Friedrich Schleiermacher around 1800, but the idea that text and meaning might differ was as old as Christianity, whose founder often said "You know that it is written—but I tell you," and so on. In the Middle Ages, theologians distinguished four senses of scripture according to the charming couplet *littera gesta docet, quid credas allegoria,/ moralis quid agas, quo tendas anagogia*, meaning in paraphrase, "the letter teaches what happened; allegorical interpretation

teaches you what to believe; the moral lesson of the text tells you how to act; the anagogical sense tells you where you are going." The anagogical sense of a passage was its significance as a pointer to eternal destiny. Obviously, some passages of scripture were richer in some senses than in others, but it was a tenet of medieval interpretation that all four senses were found throughout the Bible.

36. The word *fundamentalist*, applied to Islam, therefore referred not to an unusual or especially traditional way of reading the Koran, for only one way was possible, but rather to a set of social and political attitudes defining a primarily political movement to bring back the Holy Law and to restructure Islamic societies in accordance with the traditions handed down from the earliest decades and centuries of the faith, from the customs or "way" (*sunna*) of Muhammad himself and from the traditions about him.

This was the opposite of what American fundamentalists wanted in their society; they wanted to have their biblical interpretation in peace, but had no ambitions to restructure all of American society according to the precepts of the Bible.

37. Patricia Crone, *Meccan Trade and the Rise of Islam* (Cambridge: Cambridge University Press, 1987).

38. Gellner, *Postmodernism*, 15.

39. Ibid., 16.

40. Quoted in Albert Hourani, *A History of the Arab Peoples* (Cambridge, Mass.: Harvard University Press, 1991), 445–46.

41. Gellner, *Postmodernism*, 20–21.

42. Hourani, *History of the Arab Peoples*, 447.

43. Bassam Tibi, *Krieg der Zivilisationen* (Hamburg: Hoffmann & Campe, 1995), 248.

44. Ibid., 249.

45. Sayed al-Attas, quoted ibid., 261.

46. Quotes and paraphrase in *Economist*, April 22, 1995.

47. Quoted in Giovanni Bonazzi, *Lettera da Singapore* (Bologna: Il Mulino, 1996), 103, from an interview on the prospects for Hong Kong under Chinese communist rule.

48. Quoted ibid., 115.

49. Bilahara Kausikan, letter in response to Eric Jones (see next note), *National Interest* 36 (Summer 1994), 108.

50. Eric Jones, "Asia's Fate: A Response to the Singapore School," *National Interest* 35 (Spring 1994), 28.

51. Bonazzi, *Lettera da Singapore*, 167–68.

52. *Economist*, March 9, 1996.

53. Jean Baechler, *Le Capitalisme* (Paris: Gallimard, 1995), 2:405.

54. Richard O'Connell, *Ride of the Second Horseman: The Birth and Death of War* (New York: Oxford University Press, 1995), 57–58.

55. Ibid., 64.

56. Ibid., 66–67.

57. Ibid., 68.

58. Gellner, *Postmodernism*, 23, and see Jean Baechler, *Démocraties* (Paris: Calmann-Lévy, 1985).

59. Ibid., 67.

60. Baechler, *Le Capitalisme*, 2:310–11.

61. Ibid., 2:402.

62. Huntington, *Clash of Civilizations*, 78.

63. Jean Baechler, "Vers un nouvel ordre planétaire," in his *Contrepoints et commentaires* (Paris: Calmann-Lévy, 1995), 460.

64. Baechler, *Le Capitalisme*, 2:422.

65. Emmanuel Le Roy Ladurie, *Le Siècle des Platter 1499–1628*, vol. 1: *Le Mendiant et le professeur* (Paris: Fayard, 1996).

66. Seymour Martin Lipset, *American Exceptionalism: A Double-Edged Sword* (New York: Norton, 1996), 275, 277.

67. Richard Webster, *Why Freud Was Wrong: Sin, Science and Psychoanalysis*, 2d ed. (New York: Basic Books, 1996), demolished Freud's claim to be a scientist and relieved the modern West of the therapeutic temptation. But Webster's fine work was marred by his belief that Freudianism was the last in a long line of patriarchal, rationalist Western doctrines, of which Christianity was the original and most sinister. To Webster, the West would not be free until it shucked off this patriarchal, rationalist mantle and became feminist and multiculturalist. Two things can be said in response to this. One is that patriarchy and rationalism were hardly dominant features of the late-twentieth-century West. Webster, in calling for their abolition, was flogging a dead horse. In any event, rolling Freud into a long history of misguided rationalism and mind-body dualism and rejecting the lot was a little too facile. In taking such a posture and claiming himself to be unaffected by it, Webster came close to saying that Western culture did not deserve to be understood on its own terms—an approach he would not, presumably, apply to multiculturalist or feminist world views. The other is that the Western temptation was never, as Webster says, excessive rationalism but the perversion of rationalism. To abandon rationalism because it has been abused is like abandoning medicine because some doctors overprescribe antibiotics. Reason may be the slave of the passions, but it's the best tool we have for understanding the world and ourselves.

Index